"2016年度西北民族大学校级规划教材"资助项目。
"2014年度西北民族大学教育教学改革研究项目"（项目编号：2014JG-2670030626）阶段性成果。

A New Course of the English Literary History

新编英国文学史教程

水彩琴 主 编
王谋清 康维华 副主编

中国社会科学出版社

图书在版编目(CIP)数据

新编英国文学史教程/水彩琴主编. —北京：中国社会科学出版社，2017.1
ISBN 978 – 7 – 5203 – 0195 – 4

Ⅰ.①新… Ⅱ.①水… Ⅲ.①英语—高等学校—教材②文学史—英国 Ⅳ.①H319.4：I

中国版本图书馆 CIP 数据核字(2017)第 067876 号

出 版 人	赵剑英
责任编辑	陈肖静
责任校对	牛　玺
责任印制	戴　宽

出　　版	中国社会科学出版社
社　　址	北京鼓楼西大街甲 158 号
邮　　编	100720
网　　址	http：//www.csspw.cn
发 行 部	010 – 84083685
门 市 部	010 – 84029450
经　　销	新华书店及其他书店
印刷装订	北京君升印刷有限公司
版　　次	2017 年 1 月第 1 版
印　　次	2017 年 1 月第 1 次印刷
开　　本	880×1230　1/16
印　　张	29.75
插　　页	2
字　　数	751 千字
定　　价	138.00 元

凡购买中国社会科学出版社图书，如有质量问题请与本社营销中心联系调换
电话：010 – 84083683
版权所有　侵权必究

Contents

Preface ··· (1)

Part One   The Anglo-Saxon Period ··· (1)
  Chapter 1   The Early Invasions of the British Isles ··· (1)
  Chapter 2   Anglo-Saxon Literature ··· (2)
    2.1   Poetry ··· (2)
    2.2   Prose ·· (4)

Part Two   The Medieval Age ··· (7)
  Chapter 3   Anglo-Norman Literature ·· (7)
    3.1   Norman Conquest ··· (7)
    3.2   Literature ·· (7)
  Chapter 4   Literature in the Age of Chaucer ·· (9)
    4.1   William Langland ··· (10)
    4.2   Geoffrey Chaucer ··· (10)
  Chapter 5   Literature in the 15th Century ··· (13)
    5.1   Popular Ballads ·· (13)
    5.2   Sir Thomas Malory ··· (14)

Part Three   The Renaissance Period ··· (18)
  Chapter 6   English Renaissance ··· (18)
    6.1   Background ··· (18)
    6.2   Renaissance ··· (18)
  Chapter 7   Poetry in the Renaissance Period ··· (20)
    7.1   Sir Thomas Wyatt ·· (20)
    7.2   Henry Howard, Earl of Surrey ·· (21)
    7.3   Sir Philip Sidney ·· (21)
    7.4   Edmund Spenser ·· (23)
  Chapter 8   Prose in the Renaissance Period ·· (26)

8.1	Sir Thomas More	(26)
8.2	John Lyly	(27)
8.3	Thomas Nashe	(28)
8.4	Francis Bacon	(30)

Chapter 9　Drama in the Renaissance Period .... (31)

9.1	English Drama	(31)
9.2	Thomas Kyd	(32)
9.3	Christopher Marlowe	(33)
9.4	William Shakespeare	(36)
9.5	Ben Jonson	(46)

Part Four　The Period of Revolution and Restoration .... (55)

Chapter 10　Historical Context .... (55)

Chapter 11　Literature in the Period of Revolution .... (56)

11.1	Literary Characteristics	(56)
11.2	Metaphysical Poets	(56)
11.3	Cavalier Poets	(61)
11.4	John Milton	(62)

Chapter 12　Literature in the Period of Restoration .... (65)

12.1	Literary Characteristics	(65)
12.2	John Bunyan	(66)
12.3	John Dryden	(68)
12.4	The Restoration Theater	(72)

Part Five　The Age of Enlightenment .... (78)

Chapter 13　Introduction .... (78)

13.1	Background	(78)
13.2	Enlightenment	(79)
13.3	Literature	(80)

Chapter 14　Neoclassical School .... (81)

14.1	Alexander Pope	(82)
14.2	Joseph Addison and Sir Richard Steele	(86)
14.3	Samuel Johnson	(87)
14.4	James Boswell	(89)

Chapter 15　Fiction of Realistic Tradition .... (89)

15.1	Daniel Defoe	(90)
15.2	Jonathan Swift	(93)

15.3	Henry Fielding	(96)
15.4	Tobias George Smollett	(101)
Chapter 16	Sentimentalist Novels	(104)
16.1	Samuel Richardson	(104)
16.2	Laurence Sterne	(108)
16.3	Oliver Goldsmith	(111)
Chapter 17	Poetry of Pre-Romanticism and Sentimentalism	(114)
17.1	Pre-Romanticism	(114)
17.2	Sentimentalism	(115)
17.3	Representative Poets	(115)
Chapter 18	Drama in the 18th Century	(125)

Part Six The Romantic Period ······ (136)

Chapter 19	English Romanticism	(136)
19.1	Background	(136)
19.2	Romanticism	(136)
19.3	Literature	(137)
Chapter 20	Romantic Poetry	(138)
20.1	Representative Poets of the First Generation	(138)
20.2	Representative Poets of the Second Generation	(148)
Chapter 21	Fiction in the Romantic Age	(162)
21.1	Sir Walter Scott	(162)
21.2	Jane Austen	(168)
Chapter 22	Essays in the Romantic Age	(170)
22.1	Charles Lamb	(170)
22.2	William Hazlitt	(172)
22.3	James Henry Leigh Hunt	(174)
22.4	Thomas Penson De Quincey	(174)

Part Seven The Period of Realism ······ (182)

Chapter 23	Critical Realism	(182)
23.1	Background	(182)
23.2	Realism	(183)
23.3	Literary Currents	(183)
Chapter 24	Critical Realist Novels	(184)
24.1	Charles Dickens	(185)
24.2	William Makepeace Thackeray	(191)

24.3 George Eliot ……………………………………………………………………… (193)

24.4 The Bronte Sisters …………………………………………………………… (198)

24.5 Elizabeth Gaskell ……………………………………………………………… (202)

24.6 George Meredith ……………………………………………………………… (203)

24.7 Samuel Butler ………………………………………………………………… (205)

24.8 Thomas Hardy ………………………………………………………………… (207)

Chapter 25　Victorian Poetry ……………………………………………………………… (212)

25.1 Alfred, Lord Tennyson ……………………………………………………… (212)

25.2 The Brownings ………………………………………………………………… (215)

25.3 Matthew Arnold ……………………………………………………………… (219)

Chapter 26　Victorian Essays ……………………………………………………………… (221)

26.1 Thomas Carlyle ……………………………………………………………… (221)

26.2 John Stuart Mill ……………………………………………………………… (223)

26.3 John Ruskin …………………………………………………………………… (224)

Chapter 27　Literary Trends at the End of the 19th Century ………………………… (225)

27.1 Naturalistic Trend …………………………………………………………… (225)

27.2 New Romanticism …………………………………………………………… (227)

27.3 Aestheticism and Decadence ……………………………………………… (228)

Part Eight　The Early Twentieth Century ……………………………………………… (238)

Chapter 28　Introduction …………………………………………………………………… (238)

28.1 Background …………………………………………………………………… (238)

28.2 Literature ……………………………………………………………………… (239)

Chapter 29　Drama in the Early 20th Century ………………………………………… (239)

Chapter 30　The Edwardians ……………………………………………………………… (243)

30.1 Arnold Bennett ……………………………………………………………… (244)

30.2 Rudyard Kipling ……………………………………………………………… (246)

30.3 John Galsworthy ……………………………………………………………… (247)

30.4 H. G. Wells …………………………………………………………………… (249)

30.5 Joseph Conrad ………………………………………………………………… (250)

30.6 E. M. Forster ………………………………………………………………… (252)

30.7 Katherine Mansfield ………………………………………………………… (253)

Chapter 31　The Georgians and the War Poets ………………………………………… (254)

31.1 W. H. Davies ………………………………………………………………… (254)

31.2 Walter de la Mare …………………………………………………………… (255)

31.3 Philip Edward Thomas ……………………………………………………… (255)

31.4 John Drinkwater ……………………………………………………………… (256)

31.5 Rupert Brooke ... (257)
31.6 Wilfred Owen ... (257)
31.7 David Jones ... (259)
31.8 Robert von Ranke Graves ... (259)
31.9 Edmund Blunden ... (260)
Chapter 32 The 1920s' Literature ... (261)
32.1 Novel ... (262)
32.2 Poetry ... (274)
Chapter 33 The 1930s' Literature ... (277)
33.1 Poetry ... (277)
33.2 Fiction ... (286)

Part Nine The Postwar Period ... (303)
Chapter 34 Postwar Poetry ... (303)
34.1 The Movement Poetry ... (303)
34.2 Poetry since the 1960s and 1970s ... (308)
34.3 Younger Poets of the Later Period ... (312)
Chapter 35 Postwar Fiction ... (317)
35.1 "Angry Young Men" ... (317)
35.2 Other Writers on the Postwar Literary Scene ... (325)
Chapter 36 Postwar Drama ... (343)
36.1 Samuel Barclay Beckett ... (344)
36.2 Harold Pinter ... (348)
36.3 Sir Tom Stoppard ... (350)
36.4 John James Osborne ... (353)
36.5 Sir Arnold Wesker ... (355)

Glossary ... (363)

Key to Exercises ... (418)

Appendix I List of Nobel Laureates in Literature ... (431)

Appendix II List of Poets Laureate of the UK ... (442)

Appendix III List of Recipients of the Golden PEN Award in English Literature ... (444)

Appendix IV List of Winners of the Booker Prize for Fiction ·· (445)

Appendix V Periods in British History ·· (448)

References ·· (460)

Preface

A New Course of the English Literary History is a diachronic study of the literature of the United Kingdom of Great Britain and Northern Island, covering its whole range from the Anglo-Saxon Period all the way down to the Postwar Period. It aims to offer a basic framework of the English literary history. The general layout of the book follows the different literary periods chronologically, with every part typically discussing a new period. Accordingly, the whole book consists of nine parts, which are subdivided into 36 chapters. Each part gives a brief account of the historical background against which the literary works emerged, the major literary trend(s) and current(s) of thought that dominated the literary scene in the given period, and the representative literary figures and their literary achievements that attract the critical attention.

The book begins with the Old English Literature or the Anglo-Saxon Period, which stretched out to six centuries from the mid-5th century to the mid-11th century marked by the Norman Conquest in 1066. Part One, composed of two chapters, focuses on *Beowulf*, England's national epic and the oldest surviving epic in the English language. The second part deals with the Medieval Literature, which covers the years from the mid-11th to the 15th century. The three chapters in this part discuss the Anglo-Norman period, the Age of Chaucer and the 15th century respectively, into which the Medieval Period is further divided. The romance, represented by *Sir Gawain and the Green Knight*, was the prevailing form of the Anglo-Norman literature. The Age of Chaucer roughly refers to the second half of the 14th century, when Geoffrey Chaucer lived and produced *The Canterbury Tales*, the peak of the medieval English literature. The 15th century witnessed the popularity of popular ballads, the most important of the English popular literature. The only important writer was Thomas Malory, whose *Mort d'Arthur*, based on Arthurian mythology, is the first major work of English prose.

Part Three gives a sketch of the English literature during the Renaissance Period, which, according to some critics, lasted about one and a half centuries from 1476 or 1485 till 1625, and whose culmination came between 1578 and 1603. William Shakespeare was the most important literary figure in this period. He was so influential that the period is also called the "Age of Shakespeare." Along with Shakespeare, there emerged not only a host of playwrights, including the other giant figures like Christopher Marlowe and Ben Jonson, but also some outstanding poets like Philip Sidney, Edmund Spenser, and others. Meanwhile, Thomas More, John Lyly and Francis Bacon made great contributions to the prose-writing. Hence this part is composed of four chapters. After a general introduction to the English Renaissance in the first chapter, the following three chapters handle drama, poetry and prose separately. Part Four, consisting of three chapters, is devoted to the Period of Revolution and Restoration (roughly the 17th century), which naturally falls into two phases—the Revolution and the Restoration—with the year 1660 as a dividing point. The 17th century is also called the age of "Four Johns" in the English literary history, as the notable writers of the century include John Donne, John Milton, John Bunyan and John Dryden. The "Four Johns" are therefore the primary interests here, among whom Donne and Milton are categorized under the heading of the Revolutionary Period, and Bunyan and Dryden under the Restoration Period. The years before 1660 is usually called the "Age of Milton" as Milton was the greatest writer of the years or even in the whole 17th century, while the years after 1660 is sometimes called the "Age of Dryden" as Dryden was the greatest poet between Milton and Pope and the most notable representative of English Classicism in the Restoration Period. The Age of Enlightenment, which roughly covers the 18th century, witnessed the emergence of several literary trends in English literature like Neoclassicism represented by Alexander Pope and Pre-Romanticism represented by William Blake and Robert Burns in poetry, and realism represented by Daniel Defoe, Jonathan Swift and Henry Fielding and Sentimentalism represented by Samuel Richardson and Oliver Goldsmith in prose writing. Moreover, in the second half of the 18th century there appeared two great playwrights, Oliver Goldsmith and Richard Brinsley Sheridan, who brought English drama to life. Accordingly, the fifth part, dealing with the 18th-century English literature, is made up of six chapters, centering on the reign of Classicism, the emergence of Sentimentalism and Pre-romanticism, the spread of realism as well as the rise of modern novel.

Part Six is about the Age of Romanticism, which began with the publication of *Lyrical Ballads* in 1798 and ended with the death of Walter Scott in 1832. This age was emphatically an age of poetry. The glory of the age is seen in the poetry of William Wordsworth, Samuel Taylor Coleridge, Robert Southey, Lord Byron, John Keats and Percy Bysshe Shelley. The first three are usually accepted as the first generation of Romanticists or the Passive Romantic poets, the second three as the second generation of Romanticists or the Revolutionary Romantic poets. In essays there appeared Charles Lamb and William Hazlitt; and in fiction Walter Scott and Jane Austen are two important figures. The Romantic period is arranged in four chapters according to the literary achievements in such different genres as poetry, fiction and essay-writing. After Romanticism there came the Age of Realism in the English literary history, which is also called the Victorian Age, covering the years between 1832 and 1902 or between 1837 and 1901. The major contribution made by the English Critical Realists was their perfection of the novel. Hence much space of the seventh part is devoted to the prominent novelists like Charles Dickens, William Makepeace Thackeray, the Bronte sisters, George Eliot and Thomas Hardy as well. Additionally, one chapter is opened to handle the great poets like Alfred Tennyson, Robert Browning and Matthew Arnold, one chapter to discuss the essay-writing with Thomas Carlyle as the focus, and another chapter is offered to the literary trends at the end of the 19th century, including the Naturalistic trend, New Romanticism, and Aestheticism and Decadence.

The English literature in the 20th century contains two periods—the early 20th century and the postwar period—with the Second World War as a dividing point. Part Eight outlines the early 20th-century literature in six chapters, which, except for drama that is exclusively introduced in one chapter, is chronologically grouped into the 1900s' (i.e., the Edwardians), the 1910s' (i.e., the Georgians and the war poets), the 1920s' and the 1930s'. In drama, the early 20th century produced two important realist writers—William Butler Yeats and Bernard Shaw. The former dealt realistically with the daily life of the Irish country people in his plays, while the latter's plays like *Mrs. Warren's Profession* and *Widower's Houses* explore a range of social themes, including middle-class British society, militarism, education, and the situation of women. The greatest poets in this period are William Butler Yeats, who is better known as a poet than as a dramatist, and T. S. Eliot, who was also a great critic and a fine playwright. T. S. Eliot was the chief leader among writers during the first half of the 20th century. His *The Waste Land* expressed the temper of his age, the spiritual disease of the 20th century. He is accepted as the experimentalist of Modernist poetry in English language. Novelists of the early 20th century can be roughly divided into two groups, the realists (i. e., the Edwardians represented by Arnold Bennett, H. G. Wells and John Galsworthy) and the Modernists. The most remarkable one among the first group should be John Galsworthy, who has been noted for portraying the history of English bourgeois life in his famous trilogies, especially in his first trilogy *The Forsyte Saga*. The representative writers of the second group mainly include D. H. Lawrence, James Joyce and Virginia Woolf. What they shared in their novels was that all of them turned their interest to describe what is happening in the minds of their characters. They insisted that fiction should explore the depths and recesses of personality, revealing an unending stream of impression, feelings and thoughts. In this sense, Lawrence was somewhat exceptional. He looked inward, not to show us a stream of impressions as Virginia Woolf did, but to explore those mysterious areas of feeling. Among these outstanding writers of the period four were awarded the Nobel Prize for literature. They are Rudyard Kipling, William Butler Yeats, George Bernard Shaw and John Galsworthy.

The Postwar Period produced even more Nobel Prize winners for literature—T. S. Eliot, Bertrand Russell, Winston Churchill, Samuel Beckett, Elias Canetti, William Golding, Seamus Heaney, V. S. Naipaul, Harold Pinter and Doris Lessing. Centering on these Nobel Prize winners and other great literary figures, Part Nine, the last part of the book, sketches the English literature in the postwar context, which is sorted out in three chapters according to the literary genres like drama, poetry and fiction. The postwar poetic scene was a colorful one. On the one hand, such poets of the previous decades as Robert Graves, William Empson and Dylan Thomas were still highly visible. On the other hand, a new generation was emerging. While the Movement poets like Philip Larkin and Donald Davie became popular and attractive in the 1950s, in the following decades there appeared the outstanding contemporary poets like Ted Hughes, whose harsh, post-apocalyptic poetry celebrated simple survival, and Seamus Heaney, an Irish poet who was hailed for his exquisite style. In actuality different groups existed and tried to exhibit their own identities on the postwar poetic stage. In fiction the young writers of the 1950s created characters that represented their radical, parochial attitudes and became known as the "Angry Young Men." These include Kingsley Amis' Jim Dixon in his *Lucky Jim*, William Cooper's Joe Lunn in his *Scenes from Provincial Life*, John Gerald Braine's Joe Lampton in his *Room at the Top*, Alan Sillitoe's Arthur Seaton in his novel *Saturday Night and Sunday Morning*, and others. The glory of the postwar fiction is also seen in works by Lawrence Durrell, William Golding, Doris Lessing, Iris Murdoch and Muriel Spark. In addition, those writers like Anthony Powell, C. P. Snow and Joyce Cary became really established in the postwar years, although they made their presence already felt in the 1930s. The 1950s and the first part of the 1960s was the period in which the drama of the absurd prospered as a fashion. Samuel Beckett, a monumental figure, was instrumental in revitalizing the fine dramatic traditions by bringing in an existentialist and absurdist element, and ushering in the era of the drama of the absurd in recent literary history. His most famous play *Waiting for Godot* is thematically concerned with man's salvation through God's grace. Then there were John Osborne, whose play *Look Back in Anger* gave manifest expression to the disaffection of the postwar generation, and Harold Pinter and Tom Stoppard, who were to pick up where the older dramatists left off and make headway in their unique fashion.

* * *

The book is based on my years of teaching and research experience in English literature. To some extent, it is an expansion of my reading and lecture notes and a kind of sorting of the related materials in the literature. It is thus applicable to undergraduates, graduates and all those who tend to get acquainted with the literature, and is intended to serve both as a textbook and a reference book. The book distinguishes itself from the common kindred textbooks for this course. First, it is characterized by wide coverage. To satisfy its readers with a wide range of options, the book tries to contain the influential writers and their representative works as comprehensively as possible. Then, centering on the literary survey, each part of the book is complete with related exercises, objective and subjective, so that readers will get impressed. Another highlight of the book is the "Glossary" appended to the survey (the main body of the book). It picks out all the terms mentioned in the book, which might be unfamiliar to some readers, and explains and/or defines each of them. This benefits not simply learners of English literature but also learners of other Western literatures, especially those of American literature. Lastly, the five appendices at the end also add value to the book. They not just list the Nobel Laureates in literature, the Poets Laureate of the UK, the recipients of the Golden PEN Award in English literature, and the winners of the Booker Prize for fiction, but provides some basic information about the different periods in English history as well. All these facilitate those who take interest in English literature.

* * *

A New Course of the English Literary History is my collaborative work with Professor Wang Mouqing and Miss Kang Weihua. In practice, around half of the book is attributed to the two co-authors, that is, 250,000 words to Wang Mouqing (王谋清) and 140,000 words to Kang Weihua (康维华). My (Shui Caiqin's [水彩琴]) contribution to the book is the other half, which totals up to 361,000 words.

Shui Caiqin

Part One　The Anglo-Saxon Period

(mid-5th c. -1066)

Chapter 1　The Early Invasions of the British Isles

　　The British Isles have experienced a long history of migration from across Europe. The ancient migrations have mainly come via two routes: along the Atlantic coast and from Germany-Scandinavia. The main settlement came in the Paleolithic and Mesolithic periods. But the arrival in Britain of cultural traits identified as Celtic is usually considered to be from about the 6th century BC. The Celts were probably the first inhabitants of the British Isles in recorded history. One of their tribes, the Britons, came over in the 5th century BC and stayed for some five hundred years. From the Britons the island got its name "Britain," which means "the land of the Britons." The Celts, those powerfully built and fair-haired people, were tenacious and loved war. They left behind a rich oral tradition of myths and legends, of which the Arthurian legends are an important part. In 55 BC, Celtic Britain was in turn invaded by the Romans under Julius Caesar (100 BC - 44 BC). The Roman soldiers came to stay for five centuries and transplanted their civilization to the land. Britain was a province of the Roman Empire from 43 to 410 AD.

　　As the Roman Empire declined at the beginning of the 5th century, its hold on Britain loosened. By 410 AD, Roman forces had been withdrawn, and small, isolated bands of migrating Germans began to invade Britain. There seems to have been no large invasion with a combined army or fleet, but the Germanic tribes named Teutons (mainly including Anglos, Saxons and Jutes) quickly established control over modern-day England and settled down there in around 450 AD. The cultural heritage of the Celts and the Romans was therefore destroyed by the invading Anglo-Saxons. Those, now called the "Anglo-Saxons," largely came from Scandinavia and northern Germany, first landing in Eastern Britain. They drove the Celts to the north and the west, and slowly developed their own language (Anglo-Saxon) and culture. Anglo-Saxon became Old English, and the place they occupied became England, which was derived from the word "Angle-land" meaning "the land of the Angles." Thus began the Anglo-Saxon period in English history.

　　The period was generally one of wars between the petty kingdoms in the land. Of the seven main kingdoms Mercia and then Northumberland in the north flourished particularly in wealth and culture in the 7th and 8th centuries, while Wessex in the south became a more important center of military and political power and assumed supremacy in culture and learning in the 9th and 10th centuries. Beginning from the late 8th century the Danes came to invade England and for more than a century they made intermittent raids on the eastern coast of Britain and occupied for fairly long periods of time large areas of northeastern England. In the late 9th century King Alfred the Great of the Kingdom of Wessex successfully led the English people in a protracted war against the invading Danes. The invaders were repulsed and gradually all the kingdoms in England were united into one. It was King Alfred the Great who decided that literature should be written in the vernacular, or Old English.

In the early 11th century the Danes again came to invade England and under Canute (c. 995 – 1035) they conquered and ruled over all England for a quarter of a century (1017 – 1042). Then, following the expulsion of the Danes the Normans from Normandy in northern France came to invade England in 1066, and under the leadership of William the Conqueror (c. 1028 – 1087), Duke of Normandy, who claimed the succession to the English throne, they succeeded in defeating the English troops and conquering the whole of England. The Norman Conquest marked the end of the Anglo-Saxon period.

The Anglo-Saxons were heathen upon their first arrival in England. In 597 AD the first missionaries led by St. Augustine (first third of the 6th century – 604) came to England from Rome and within a century all England was Christianized. Churches were built and the heathen mythology was gradually replaced by the Christian religion. The coming of Christianity meant not simply a new life and leader for England; it also meant the wealth of a new language (i.e., Latin). The scops were now replaced by the literary monks, who were among the most learned in the country. The monks had behind them all the culture and literary resources of the Latin language. The effect was seen instantly in the early English prose and poetry. However, the heathen concepts of nature and the supernatural persisted for a considerable period of time and were often curiously mixed with Christian views and expressions. This phenomenon also found its expressions frequently in the literary works of the Anglo-Saxon period.

Chapter 2 Anglo-Saxon Literature

The Anglo-Saxon period was basically barren in literary creations. What have been left through the ravages of time are mostly fragments. The Anglo-Saxon literature is almost exclusively a verse literature in oral form. It was passed down by word of mouth from generation to generation and was not given a written form until long after its composition. Its creators are, for the most part, unknown.

2.1 Poetry

The poetry of this period falls into two groups—the pagan/secular poetry like *The Song of Beowulf* and the Christian/religious poetry. The former refers to the poetry which the Anglo-Saxons probably brought with them in the form of oral sagas—the crude material out of which literature was slowly developed on the English soil. The latter contains the poetry which, chiefly based on the Biblical stories, dealt with Christian teachings, themes or references. Caedmon and Cynewulf were among the great religious poets. Caedmon, living in the latter half of the 7th century, was the first known religious poet of England and is accepted as the "father of English song." Some of his poems survive in a Wessex dialect. These include the paraphrases of Genesis, Exodus, Daniel and Judith, and a poem about Christ and Satan as well. He was a transitional poet from the pagan to the religious way of writing and was at his best writing about fighting, seafaring, and passions of strong men. Cynewulf, living a century later, was the first poet ever to sign his compositions. He knew Latin and religious literature. He was famous for his poetical works like *Christ*, *Juliana*, *The Fates of the Appostles* and *Elene*, among which the first one, happy in mood and alive with the poet's creative talent, consists of three parts—the Virgin Birth, the Ascension of Christ and the Day of Judgment. Except the unknown composer of *Beowulf*, he is regarded as the greatest Anglo-Saxon poet.

The Song of Beowulf, England's national epic, is an Old English poem consisting of 3,182 alliterative long lines. It is probably the oldest surviving epic in the English language and is commonly cited as the greatest work of the Anglo-Saxon literature. The story was possibly brought over to England at the time of the Anglo-Saxon conquest, and was handed down by word of mouth from generation to generation until it was anonymously recorded in Anglo-Saxon/Old English, in the 8th century. The full poem survives in the manuscript dated the 10th century and known as the Nowell Codex, which is currently located in the British Library. It has no title in the original manuscript, but has become known by the name of the protagonist. The poem tells the story of Beowulf, a 6th-century hero of the Geats. The story takes place in Scandinavia, and there is no mention of England at all. It is basically a two-part narrative—Beowulf's fight with the sea-monsters (Grendel and his mother) in the first part, and his killing a fiery dragon and his death in the second—with an interpolation between.

The first part centers on Beowulf's deeds in Denmark. Hrothgar, the present king of the Danes, is in great trouble. His great hall Heorot has been for twelve years harassed by a sea-monster Grendel, who comes to grab and devour the king's people as he pleases, and no one seems to be his match. The king of Sweden sends over his nephew Beowulf with some retainers to help out. After a feast of welcome, at nightfall Beowulf and his men wait in the hall for the monster to show up. As is expected, Grendel appears. He seizes and devours one of Beowulf's men. His next target is Beowulf. Beowulf, who has the strength of 30 men in his grip, grapples with him single-handed as the monster is vulnerable to no weapons of steel, tears off one of his arms, and sends him howling away to his death in his haunted pool. The overjoyed king celebrates the victory, but little expects that a greater danger is to appear and play havoc with his peace. That very night Grendel's mother, furious over her son's death, storms in to avenge him and kills several of the king's retainers. Beowulf follows her to her lair, dives in, fights with the she-monster, almost loses to her, but manages to kill her in the end with the help of a magic sword. He returns to the great hall with the heads of the two monsters and receives gifts from the grateful king at another celebration.

In the second part of the poem, Beowulf goes back to Geatland in Sweden, and succeeds his uncle and his cousin as king of the Geats and rules the country well for half a century. The last adventure he has in his old age is his fight with a fiery dragon. One day, the fire-spitting monster comes and threatens to devastate the country. Beowulf goes with a servant to kill it, which he does, but not before he is fatally wounded. He dies for his people as an ideal king. After his death, his attendants bury him in a tumulus, a burial mound, in Geatland. The poem ends with his funeral.

In theme, *Beowulf* has little new to offer as another adventure story about a hero killing monsters to make the world safe for people, but the story is unique as a hybrid of fact with legend. It also serves to add testimony to a universal tradition that humans always manage to get a sense of control over life with the help of their imaginative powers. What's more, the epic is essentially pagan in spirit and matter, and has a great social significance. It presents readers an all-round picture of the tribal society and faithfully records the social conditions and customs of the time.

In terms of poetical form, the epic is characterized first by the use of alliteration. The use of the strong stress and the predominance of consonants are very notable here. A line, containing an indefinite number of words or syllables, generally has four stresses, with a pause, between the second and the third stresses, breaking the line into two parts. Alliteration invariably falls upon the stressed syllables, but not all four of the stresses in a line alliterate, and usually two or three of them do, with at least one from each half-line. Another peculiar feature is the frequent use of compound-words to serve as indirect metaphors that are sometimes picturesque. For instance, "treasure-keepers" refer to chieftains; the "whale-path," the "swan-road" and the "seal-bath" are used to refer to the sea; the "shield-bearer," the "battle-hero" and the "spear-fighter" are used as substitutes for the soldier. In addition, the use of understatements such as "not troublesome" for very welcome and "need not praise" for a right to condemn gives an impression of reserve and at time a tinge of ironical humor.

2.2 Prose

In the 8th century, Anglo-Saxon prose appeared. The famous prose writers of that period were Venerable Bede and Alfred the Great. Venerable Bede (672/673 – 735), also referred to as Saint Bede, was the first scholar in English literature and has been regarded as the Father of English learning. He was also the man who first described Caedman's legendary life story. His works, over forty in number, written exclusively in Latin, cover the whole field of human knowledge of his day. The most important of his works is *The Ecclesiastical History of England*, which gained him the title the "Father of English History." Bede wrote scientific, historical and theological works, featuring the range of his writings from music and metrics to exegetical Scripture commentaries. His Latin is generally clear, but his Biblical commentaries are more technical. They employ the allegorical method of interpretation and his history includes accounts of miracles, which to modern historians has seemed at odds with his critical approach to the materials in his history. Although Bede is mainly studied as a historian now, in his time his works on grammar, chronology and biblical studies were as important as his historical works. The non-historical works contributed greatly to the Carolingian renaissance.

Alfred the Great (849 – 899) was king of Wessex kingdom from 871 to 899. He successfully defended his kingdom against the Viking attempt at conquest, and by the time of his death he had become the dominant ruler in England. He was the first King of the West Saxons to style himself "King of the Anglo-Saxons" and is the only English monarch to be accorded the epithet "the Great." Alfred had a reputation as a learned and merciful man of a gracious and level-headed nature. He encouraged education and improved his kingdom's legal system, military structure and his people's quality of life. Conscious of the decay of Latin literacy in his realm, Alfred proposed that primary education be taught in English, with those wishing to advance to holy orders to continue their studies in Latin. He tried every means to improve the state of education. He was a well-known translator and translated some important Latin works into English. His most important work is *Anglo-Saxon Chronicles*, which is regarded as the best monument of the Old English prose.

Part One The Anglo-Saxon Period

Exercises

I. Multiple choices

1. _____ were probably the first inhabitants of the British Isles in recorded history.
   A. Anglo-Saxons
   B. Jutes
   C. Teutons
   D. Celts

2. The cultural heritage of the Celts and the Romans was destroyed by the invading _____ in the 5th century.
   A. Anglo-Saxons
   B. Normans
   C. Britons
   D. Greeks

3. It was King Alfred the Great who decided that literature should be written in the vernacular or _____.
   A. Modern English
   B. Old English
   C. Middle English
   D. London Dialect

4. In 597 A. D. the first missionaries led by St. Augustine came to England from Rome and within a century all England was _____.
   A. destroyed
   B. united
   C. Christianized
   D. divided

5. The Anglo-Saxon literature is almost exclusively a verse literature in _____ form.
   A. oral
   B. written
   C. religious
   D. pagan

6. _____ is the first known religious poet of England and accepted as the "father of English song."
   A. Alfred the Great
   B. Cynewulf
   C. Venerable Bede
   D. Caedmon

7. Except the unknown composer of *The Song of Beowulf*, _____ is regarded as the greatest Anglo-Saxon poet.
   A. Alfred the Great
   B. Cynewulf
   C. Venerable Bede
   D. Caedmon

II. Blank-filling

1. _____ was a well-known translator and translated some important Latin works into English. His most important work is *Anglo-Saxon Chronicles*, which is regarded as the best monument of the Old English prose.

2. The "_____" marked the end of the Anglo-Saxon period.

3. The Old English poetry can be divided into two groups: the pagan/secular poetry and the _____ poetry.

4. _____, England's national epic, is the oldest poem in the English language and the most important specimen of Anglo-Saxon literature.

III. Term definition

1. Alliteration
2. Assonance
3. Consonance
4. Prose
5. Understatement
6. Metaphor

7. Epic
8. Motif
9. Theme

IV. Essay questions

Give a comprehensive introduction to *The Song of Beowulf*.

Part Two   The Medieval Age

(Mid-11th c. – 15th c.)

Chapter 3   Anglo-Norman Literature

3.1   Norman Conquest

The Normans were originally a hardy race of sea rovers inhabiting Scandinavia. In the 10th century they conquered a part of northern France, which is still called Normandy, and rapidly adopted French civilization and the French language. William the Great, Duke of Normandy, was an able general and statesman. In 1066 he led the Norman army to invade England. The two armies met at Hasting. Finally the Anglo-Saxons were defeated, and William became the King of England. The conquest, later known as Norman Conquest, marked the beginning of the Middle English or Anglo-Norman period (1066 – 1350).

After the conquest, feudal system was established in English society. The new king ruled England with a high hand. He made a thorough job of taking over the country, and had everything inventoried. William saw himself as the owner of the country and bestowed large patches of land on his Norman barons. The feudal social structure was just like the pyramid in Egypt, which secured King William's authority over his noblemen such as barons and knights. Thus the former loose union of Saxon tribes was replaced by a strong centralized government.

That the conquest ensured the Normans' supremacy over the Anglo-Saxons was strikingly reflected in the language and the literature. The courtiers and feudal lords spoke French while the lower-class people spoke English. There was almost no written literature in English for a time. Chronicles and religious poems were in Latin, whereas romances were at first all in French. Another chief effect of the conquest was the bringing of Roman civilization (i. e., chivalry) to England.

3.2   Literature

With the import of chivalry as well as romantic tales of love and adventure, romances became a prevailing form of literature in the three centuries after Norman Conquest. Romances are long compositions, sometimes in verse, sometimes in prose, describing the life and adventures of a noble hero. They have in common essential features like lacking general resemblance to truth or reality, containing perilous adventures more or less remote from the ordinary life, exaggerating the vices of human nature and idealizing the virtues, laying emphasis on supreme devotion to a fair lady, choosing knights, men of noble birth skilled in the use of weapons, as the central characters, and having nothing to do with the common people as they were written for the noble class.

These romances falls mainly into three cycles or three groups—"matters of Britain," "matters of France" and "matters of Rome and Greece." The first group mainly focuses on the exploits of King Arthur and his Knights of the Round Table. The second group mainly centers on the exploits of Charlemagne. The famous work of this group is *Chanson de Roland* (composed 1040 – 1115). The last group is an endless series of fabulous tales of Alexander the Great (356 BC – 323 BC) and about the Trojan War as well. Among them the Arthurian Legends are more noteworthy.

The legends of King Arthur and his knights had existed as an oral tradition since the time of the Celts. It was not put down on paper until 1147 when Geoffrey of Monmouth (c. 1100 – 1154), a 12th-century Welsh priest came out with his Latin *Historia Regum Britanniae*. He might have been collecting the legends about the king, and he certainly had a very rich imagination. With Monmouth's effort, the Arthurian Legends, which has become in time one of the vitalizing sources of inspiration for English writers, came into being. Then the legends were enriched by a good number of later writers. One of these was Wace of Jersey (c. 1110 – 1174) whose *Roman de Brut* (c. 1150 – 1155) made the story a romance of chivalry. Then in 1205, a priest named Layamon wrote his vast verse work of 32,341 lines *Brut* (also known as *The Chronicle of Britain*) in English; this event has been seen ever since as the beginning of the revival of English as a literary medium. "Brut" means "chronicle," and the book is in the main an English rendition of a French version of King Arthur's legends. It was here that the Arthur story first appeared in English. The latter part of the 12th century saw a sudden growth of the legend. New additions emerged either in the form of the writers' inventions or incorporations from other sources. Such stories include those of the Holy Grail, Merlin, Sir Lancelot, Quest for the Holy Grail, and the death of the king. These romances were compiled by Robert de Borron, a French poet of the late 12th and early 13th centuries, and Walter Mapes (1140 – c. 1208). Then in the 13th and 14th centuries, the legend flourished first in verse and then in prose, and the Celtic King Arthur became a national hero for the English nation. In 1470 Sir Thomas Malory, a Welsh Knight, compiled his *Morte d'Arthur* from certain French sources after a good deal of revision. This has become the source book of the Arthur Saga for later generations.

Sir Gawain and the Green Knight is the culmination of the Arthurian romances. It is a late 14th-century (about 1375) Middle English chivalric romance of a type known as the "beheading game." The Green Knight is interpreted by some as a representation of the Green Man of folklore and by others as an allusion to Christ. Written in stanzas of alliterative verse, it draws on Welsh, Irish and English stories, as well as the French chivalric tradition. Little is known about its author except that he was a contemporary of Chaucer and probably a Christian priest.

The poem was composed as an evident effort to extol Sir Gawain and his knightly virtues of loyalty, valor, rectitude and integrity. It describes how Sir Gawain, a knight of King Arthur's Round Table, accepts a challenge from a mysterious Green Knight. In his struggles to keep his bargain Gawain demonstrates chivalry and loyalty until his honor is called into question by a test involving the lady of the Green Knight's castle.

Sir Gawain is upright and ever ready to uphold the ideals of King Arthur's court. On New Year's day, while King Arthur and his knights are holding a feast, a knight all in green appears at court and challenges the bravest knight present to cut off his head on the condition that the knight abides a blow in return a year later at the Green

Chapel. Sir Gawain accepts the challenge and beheads the visitor. Then the Green Knight takes up his head, warns Gawain to keep his word and leaves. When the appointed time comes, Sir Gawain sets off to meet the Green Knight. He comes to a castle and is well received by its lord and lady. The lord invites Sir Gawain to go hunting with him, but Gawain prefers to stay at home. The two agree to share in the evening whatever they may have attained during the day. This goes on for three days. On the first day, while the lord of the castle hunts for a deer, the lady tries in vain to induce Gawain to make love to her, and ends by giving him a kiss. In the evening the lord gives the game he has killed to Sir Gawain and Gawain returns the kiss. The second day also ends with the lord giving his game to Gawain for another brief kiss. On the third day, when the lord returns and offers his game, Gawain returns the kiss but says nothing of the girdle that the lady has forced on him for his safety. Then the day comes to meet the Green Knight at the Green Chapel. Sir Gawain shrinks a little but soon recovers his valor to face the blow. Twice the Green Knight's ax swings harmlessly; the third time it falls on Gawain's shoulder and wounds him. Whereupon Gawain jumps for his armor, draws sword, and warns the Green Knight that the compact calls for only one blow, and that, if another is offered, he will defend himself. Then the Green Knight tells Gawain that he is the lord of the castle, and explains to him that the first two swings of ax were harmless because Gawain has been true to his compact and twice returned the kiss and that the last blow would not have wounded him had he shared the girdle with him in honesty. Full of shame, Gawain throws back the girdle and is ready to atone for his deception; but the Green Knight thinks he has already atoned, and presents the girdle as a free gift. They become good friends. Gawain returns to Arthur's court and tells the whole story frankly. Ever after that, the Knights of the Round Table wear a green girdle in Gawain's honor.

Sir Gawain and the Green Knight is a 4-part/canto verse-romance of 2,530 lines in 101 sections. The first canto deals with the beheading; the second canto tells of the long and arduous trip Gawain makes to the castle; the third relates the three days Gawain spends in a bargain with the lord; and the last wraps up Gawain's trip with his final encounter with the Green Knight and the anti-climatic revelation of the moral of the story. In terms of form, the narrative is well conceived and neatly knit into an organic unity. The different parts and sections interlock and the threads are pulled together to offer a sense of finality. In line structure and the use of devices such as alliteration, the poem is notably similar to the Old English poems like *Beowulf*. It is written in an elaborate stanza combining meter and alliteration. At the end of each stanza there is a rimed refrain. There is also a fine psychological element that enriches the plot and adds to the characterization. The portrait of Sir Gawain is vivid and fully rounded. There is in him a strange medley of conflicting qualities that makes him perfectly human. He is just a little short of an ideal hero. In addition, the poem is written in the north Midland dialect, so it is less approachable than Chaucer's London dialect.

Chapter 4   Literature in the Age of Chaucer

Geoffrey Chaucer lived in the 14th century. As a scholar, traveler, businessman and courtier, he shared all the stirring life of his age and reflected it in his works. He was the representative writer of the century. Hence the "Age of Chaucer" is used to refer to the 14th century in English literature, especially the second half of the century, which produced five major writers. These include John Wycliffe (c. 1331 – 1384), the greatest of the English religious reformers and the first translator of the *Bible* into English, John Gower (c. 1330 – 1408), a scholar and a literary man who criticized the social life in his works, John Mandeville, a traveler writing about the wonders he had seen abroad, William Langland and Chaucer. Among them the later two are more important and better remembered.

4.1　William Langland (c. 1332 – c. 1386)

Langland was a reformer. He wrote about social discontent in his works and preached the equality of men and dignity of labor. He was the conjectured author of the 14th-century 7,000-line poem **Vision of Piers the Plowman**. *Vision of Piers the Plowman* describes a series of wonderful dreams the author dreamed. Through these dreams, Langland showed us a picture of the life in the feudal England and attacked evil in both church and state. It is a great work of medieval preaching, a Christian poem dealing with salvation. The book is very difficult with its ambiguous language and imagery. It survives in about 50 manuscripts, in three widely varying versions known as the A-text (in 9 books), the B-text (in 21 books) and the C-text (in 28 texts), of which the B-text is the best-known. This text can be divided into two parts, with the first part covering the first 7 books and the second part the rest of the poem. The first part touches on the physical aspect of human life such as the procurement of necessities and the reform of society. The second part deals with the spiritual aspect of life, the winning of salvation. Basically, the book consists of a series of dreams of a vagrant with whom the poet identifies himself. Langland wrote in Middle English with the mastery not really inferior to Chaucer's, though he was not as easily approachable.

Vision of Piers the Plowman is considered by many critics to be among the greatest works of the English literature of the Middle Ages, along with *Sir Gawain and the Green Knight* and Chaucer's *The Canterbury Tales*. The poem was very popular throughout the 14th and 15th centuries. It praises the poor peasants, and condemns and exposes the sins of the oppressors. Therefore it played an important part in arousing the revolutionary sentiment on the eve of the Rising of 1381.

Vision of Piers the Plowman is a Middle English allegorical narrative poem written in unrhymed alliterative verse. It is written in the form of a dream vision. The author tells his story under the guise of having dreamt it. The poem, as an allegory, relates truth through symbolism. Meanwhile, the poet used indignant satire in his description of social abuses caused by the corruption prevailing among the ruling classes, ecclesiastical and secular.

4.2　Geoffrey Chaucer (c. 1343 – 1400)

Chaucer, known as the "father of English poetry," the "father of English fiction" and even the "father of English literature," is widely considered the greatest English poet of the Middle Ages. He was the first poet buried in Poets' Corner of Westminster Abbey. Although he maintained an active career in the civil service as a bureaucrat, courtier and diplomat, Chaucer achieved fame during his lifetime as an author, philosopher, alchemist and astronomer, and is best remembered for his literary works, among which the major ones include *The Book of the Duchess*, *The House of Fame*, *The Legend of Good Women*, *Troilus and Criseyde* and *The Canterbury Tales*. It was in *The Canterbury Tales* that he focused on English subjects, with bawdy jokes and respected figures often being undercut with humor that cemented his reputation.

Chaucer's writing career can be divided into three periods. The first period, stretching till 1370, is a period of French influence. His main works in this period are translations from French, the most important of which is *Romance of the Rose*. The second period, which covers the following fifteen years, is a period of Italian influence, the influence from *Decameron* (1353) by Boccaccio (1313 – 1375) in particular. Chaucer produced works adapted from Italian writers. His chief work during this period is *Troilus and Criseyde*. The third period (i. e., Chaucer's last fifteen years) is generally known as the English period. Chaucer's masterpiece *The Canterbury Tales* was completed during this period.

Chaucer's first major work *The Book of the Duchess* is an elegy for Blanche of Lancaster, who died in September 1368. It is possible that this work was commissioned by her husband John of Gaunt. Most sources put the date of composition after the death of Blanche of Lancaster, with many recent studies privileging a date as early as the end of 1368. Chaucer's two other early works are *Anelida and Arcite* and *The House of Fame*. The former is a 357-line English poem. It tells the story of Anelida, queen of Armenia, and her wooing by false Arcite from Thebes, Greece. The latter, probably written between 1379 and 1380, is over 2,000 lines long in three books and takes the form of a dream vision composed in octosyllabic couplets. Chaucer wrote many of his major works in a prolific period when he held the job of customs comptroller for London from 1374 to 1386. He is believed to start work on *The Canterbury Tales* in the early 1380s. His *Parlement of Foules*, *The Legend of Good Women* and *Troilus and Criseyde* all date from this time. *Parlement of Foules*, made up of approximately 700 lines, is also in the form of a dream vision in rhyme-royal stanza and is the first reference to the idea that St. Valentine's Day was a special day for lovers. *The Legend of Good Women*, another poem in the form of a dream vision, is the third longest of Chaucer's works after *The Canterbury Tales* and *Troilus and Criseyde*, and is possibly the first significant work in English to use the iambic pentameter or decasyllabic couplets, which Chaucer later used throughout *The Canterbury Tales*. *Troilus and Criseyde*, with its reliance on the forms of Italian poetry, was little known in England at the time. It retells in Middle English the tragic story of the lovers Troilus and Criseyde, set against a backdrop of war during the Siege of Troy. It was composed in rhyme royal and probably completed during the mid 1380s. Its use of the classical subject and its elaborate, courtly language set it apart as one of Chaucer's most complete and well-formed works. Many Chaucer scholars regard it as his finest work, in which the author drew heavily on his source Boccaccio and on the early 6th-century Latin philosopher Boethius (c. 480 – 524 AD). As a finished long poem, *Troilus and Criseyde* is more self-contained than the better known but ultimately uncompleted *The Canterbury Tales*. This poem is often considered the source of the phrase: "all good things must come to an end."

Chaucer translated such important works as Boethius' *Consolation of Philosophy* and *The Romance of the Rose* by Guillaume de Lorris (c. 1200 – c. 1240). What needs pointing out is that, while many scholars maintain that Chaucer did translate part of the text of *The Romance of the Rose*, others claim that this has been effectively disproved. One other significant work by Chaucer is his *Treatise on the Astrolabe*, possibly for his own son, which describes the form and use of that instrument in detail and is sometimes cited as the first example of technical writing in the English language. Although much of the text may have come from other sources, the treatise indicates that Chaucer was versed in science in addition to his literary talents. Another scientific work discovered in 1952, *Equa-

torie of the Planetis, has similar language and handwriting, compared to some considered to be Chaucer's, and it continues many of the ideas from the Astrolabe. Furthermore, it contains an example of early European encryption. The attribution of this work to Chaucer is still uncertain.

The Canterbury Tales is a collection of stories told by fictional pilgrims on the road to the cathedral at Canterbury. It consists of a prologue (i. e., the General Prologue) and twenty-four tales. In the General Prologue, the author revealed his plan for writing this work and also vividly described the teller of each tale. Chaucer told us that one spring day, he came to the Tabard Inn in Southwark at the south end of London Bridge. Here he met some thirty pilgrims, who were going to Canterbury. Then he joined this company. At supper, the inn-keeper suggested that, in order to enliven the journey, each of the pilgrims was to tell two stories on their way to Canterbury and two more on their way back. The best storyteller would be treated with a fine supper at general expense when they came back. The inn-keeper was to be the judge of the contest. According to the number of the persons in the company, thirty-two, the author evidently planned to produce an immense work of one hundred and twenty-eight tales, exceeding that of Boccaccio's *Decameron*. Actually only twenty-four tales were written, twenty-two in verse form and two in prose form. These tales would help to shape English literature, dealing with all aspects of medieval literature: romances of knights and ladies, folk tales, animal fables, stories of travels and adventures, legends, allegories and so on. They came from different sources like the French sources, the Italian, the biblical, the Asian, and others.

The General Prologue is usually regarded as the greatest portrait gallery in English literature. It comprises a group of vivid sketches of typical medieval figures. All classes of the English feudal society, except the royalty and the poorest peasant, are represented by these pilgrims. They range from the knight, the squire and the prioress, through the landed proprietor and the wealthy tradesman, down to the drunken cook and the humble plowman. There are also a doctor and a lawyer, monks of different orders and nuns and priests, and a summoner, a sailor, a miller, a carpenter, a yeoman (a small independent farmer), and an Oxford scholar. In the center of the group is the Wife of Barth, the owner of a large cloth-factory. The pilgrims are people from various parts of England. They serve as the representatives of various sides of life and social groups, and are a microcosm of the 14th-century English society. That is why Chaucer was praised by Gorky as the "founder of English realism."

The purpose of the General Prologue is not only to present a vivid collection of character sketches, but also to reveal the author's intention in bringing together a great variety of people and narrative materials to unite the diversity of the tales by allotting them to a diversity of tellers engaged in a common endeavor, to make clear the plan for the tales, to motivate the telling of tales, to introduce the pilgrims and the time and occasion of the pilgrimage, and to set the tone for the story-telling—one of jollity which accords with the tone of the whole work: that of grateful acceptance of life. There is also an intimate connection between the tales and the Prologue, both complementing each other. The Prologue provides a framework for the tales.

The Canterbury Tales gives us a true-to-life picture of the society of Chaucer's time. The work is characterized by the realism of its narrative, the variety of stories the pilgrims tell, and the varied characters who are engaged in the pilgrimage. Many of the stories narrated by the pilgrims seem to fit their individual characters and social standing, although some of the stories seem ill-fitting to their narrators, perhaps as a result of the incomplete state of the work. Chaucer drew on real life for his cast of pilgrims: the innkeeper shares the name of a contemporary keeper of an inn in Southwark, and real-life identities for the Wife of Bath, the Merchant, and the Man of Law have been suggested. The many jobs that Chaucer held in medieval society—page, soldier, messenger, valet, bureaucrat, foreman and administrator—probably exposed him to many of the types of people he depicted in the *Tales*. He was able to shape their speech and expose and satirize the evils of his time and attack the degeneration of the noble, the heartlessness of the judge, and the corruption of the church. Chaucer was a great satirist, but he was almost never bitter when he poked fun at the foibles and weaknesses of people. Taking the stand of the uprising bourgeoisie, the author also affirmed men and praised men's energy, intellect, quick wit and love of life in the work. It is in this sense that Chaucer is known as a forerunner of humanism.

Chaucer's contribution to the English poetry lies chiefly in the fact that he introduced from France the rhymed couplet of iambic pentameter ("heroic couplet") to English poetry. Moreover, Chaucer was a crucial figure in developing the legitimacy of the vernacular, Middle English, at a time when the dominant literary languages in England were French and Latin. He was the first great poet who wrote in the current English language—he wrote in the dialect of London. His poetry is full of swiftness and vividness. Chaucer's style in *The Canterbury Tales* is remarkably flexible. His prose, like his vocabulary, is easy and informal.

Chapter 5 Literature in the 15th Century

The 15th century was a period of general unrest. It marked the definite decline of feudalism and the rapid growth of capitalist relations in trade and industry. The ascension of Henry VII (1457 – 1509, king 1485 – 1509) in 1485 began the period of Tudor monarchy with strong central authority, which was dependent upon merchants and other elements of the bourgeoisie for cooperation and support. People's attention was absorbed in Wars—the Hundred Years' War (1337 – 1453) and the Wars of the Roses (1455 – 1485)—and many nobles who had been patrons of arts were killed. The continuous wars greatly affected the development of literature. So the 15th century has traditionally been described as the barren age and a period of transition from the medieval to the Renaissance world in English literature.

Yet in this barren age, popular literature became very prosperous, which covered ballads, lyrics, popular dramas, and the like. The most important of English popular literature was popular ballads. So the 15th century became the especial spring tide of English ballads. Meanwhile, the century produced its only important writer Thomas Malory.

5.1 Popular Ballads

Ballads are anonymous narrative songs that have been preserved by oral transmission. In the 15th century, songs and ballads were widespread among the populace of England and Scotland; they were effectually created and preserved by the people. Therefore, in full justice, they are termed "popular Ballads."

Popular ballads were originally dance songs. They were little stories in verse form and could be sung or recited by the common people. The origin of the English and Scottish ballads was obscure. They were simple and crude in story, and highly condensed and dramatic in presentation. In the 15th century, there were several kinds of ballads:

historical, legendary, fantastical, lyrical and humorous. Many of them were devoted to historical events. In the numerous "border ballads" the age-long struggle between the Scots and the English is reflected.

Of paramount importance are the beautiful ballads in which Robin Hood's feats are celebrated. **Robin Hood** is a collection of the 15th-century medieval ballads about the title hero, who is a partly historical and partly legendary character, and the hero of the poor and the enemy of the rich and the powerful. The ballads reveal the cruel reality of the medieval life with its gross injustice and its underlying discontent as well as the aspirations of the poor.

Robin Hood, according to legend, has been a well-to-do farmer, who is also a highly skilled archer and swordsman. He is evicted from his property when he kills some knights to save a poor serf. Thus outlawed, he takes to greenwood life. Traditionally depicted as being dressed in Lincoln green, he and his band of Merry Men, the group of outlaws who follow him, vow to be just and harm no good people. They give to the poor what they take from the rich and win the love of the people. Robin Hood thus becomes a popular folk figure in the late-medieval period and continues to be widely represented in modern literature, films and television.

The ballads are many in number, complex and intriguing in plot, and each and all self-sustaining. They all possess the basic features of folk ballads such as repetition of words, uniform in mood, and dramatic in plot or character portrayal. All have gone through changes over time, but the major stories are still intact with their medieval theme. These include "Robin Hood and the Monk," "Robin Hood and Guy of Gisborne," "Robin Hood and the Porter" and the *Lytell Geste of Robin Hood*.

English ballads also include a great number of humorous ballads which were in general very popular in Great Britain. They reveal the unbounded optimism, ingenuity and resourcefulness of common people. "Get Up and Bar the Door" is a good example.

5.2 Sir Thomas Malory (c. 1395 – 1471)

Thomas Malory was the only important English prose writer in the 15th century. He wrote in prison *Morte d'Arthur* (*Death of Arthur*), the only monumental work of prose in the 15th-century English literature. The work was completed in 1470 and published first by William Caxton (c. 1422 – c. 1491) in 1485.

Morte d'Arthur begins with the mysterious birth of Arthur and ends with his equally mysterious death. The central concern is with the adventures of Arthur and his famous Knights of the Round Table. The knights fight many battles and win glory, all of which is a credit to the name of King Arthur. Near the end of the story, however, the tide of good fortune turns. Launcelot, one of Arthur's knights, falls in love with Arthur's queen Guinever and the lady returns his love. One by one, the other knights become discontented, selfish or disillusioned. Thus weakened, the kingdom is attacked by force under Sir Mordred, Arthur's treacherous nephew, and ultimately it goes down in defeat. Arthur is borne away on a barge by three mysterious ladies of the Lake.

Morte d'Arthur is a kind of final summing-up of the Arthurian legend built up from the 12th to the 15th century, though it does not contain all the stories about King Arthur and all his knights. In the 21 books that make up the romance, Malory linked up the various threads of the legend centering round the birth, the exploits and the death of Arthur, including the stories about Merlin, about Arthur's queen, about his Knights of the Round Table, and about the quest for the Sangrael (i. e., the Holy Gail). Alongside the wars and tournaments and all sorts of knightly adventures, there are long passages on love intrigues and descriptions of deeds of treachery. The book was written in a time of transition. The feudal order was dying. By the time Malory began writing his story, soldiers were fighting with gunpowder, a middle class of tradesmen was arising, and the practices of chivalry were being superseded by a new aristocratic code. Malory, in a desire to escape the disorder and uneasiness of his day, tried to recapture the lost ideals of the romantic past as recounted in his tale of noble kings, adventurous knights and damsels in distress. He meant his romance to be a sort of an elegy mourning the passing of the age of feudal knighthood and chivalry. However, the objective effect of this realistic rather than idealized presentation of the Arthurian legend is an unmistakable though unintended expose not only of the barbarism, hypocrisy, treachery and immorality of the supposedly brave and heroic knights and their beautiful ladies, but also of the thoroughly unreal and fantastic pictures of feudal grandees in meeting with all sorts of strange superstitious situations and performing ridiculous and unbelievable deeds.

Morte d'Arthur is an important landmark in the development of English prose from the Middle English to the early Modern English. It has the distinction of being written in a lucid and simple style. Both the Arthurian legendary material it contains and its facile prose style had their wide and lasting influence upon the English literature of later centuries.

Exercises

I. Multiple choices

1. In 1066 _____ led the Norman army to invade England.

    A. William the Great   B. Alfred the Great

    C. William Langland   D. Venerable Bede

2. With _____ 's effort, the Arthurian Legends, which has become in time one of the vitalizing sources of inspiration for English writers, came into being.

    A. William Langland   B. Geoffrey Chaucer

    C. Geoffrey of Monmouth   D. Caedmon

3. In 1470 _____ compiled his *Morte d'Arthur* from certain French sources after a good deal of revision. This has become the source book of the Arthur Saga for later generations.

    A. Wace of Jersey   B. Thomas Malory

    C. Robert de Borron   D. Walter Mapes

4. *Sir Gawain and the Green Knight* is written in the north Midland dialect, so it is _____ than Geoffrey Chaucer's London dialect.

    A. more interesting   B. less approachable

    C. simpler   D. easier

5. _____ was the greatest of the English religious reformers and the first translator of the *Bible* into English.

    A. William Langland   B. Alfred the Great

    C. Venerable Bede   D. John Wycliffe

6. Geoffrey Chaucer is the _____ and one of the greatest narrative poets of England.
   A. father of English poetry   B. greatest playwright of his age
   C. father of English prose   D. father of English drama

7. Songs and ballads were widespread among the populace of England and Scotland in the 15th century. They were created and preserved by the people. Therefore, they are, in full justice, termed _____.
   A. "Popular Ballads"   B. historical ballads
   C. lyrical ballads   D. humorous ballads

8. *The Canterbury Tales* consists of a prologue and _____ tales.
   A. 32   B. 128
   C. 64   D. 24

9. The 15th century has traditionally been described as the barren age and a period of transition from the medieval to the _____ world in English literature.
   A. Realist   B. Renaissance
   C. Romantic   D. modern

10. "Get Up and Bar the Door" is a good example of _____.
    A. legendary ballads   B. historical ballads
    C. lyrical ballads   D. humorous ballads

11. Thomas Malory is the only important prose writer in the _____ century.
    A. 14th   B. 12th
    C. 15th   D. 13th

12. Geoffrey Chaucer's narrative poem _____ is based on Boccaccio's poem "Filostrato."
    A. *Troilus and Criseyde*   B. *Vision of Piers the Plowman*
    C. *Sir Gawain and the Green Knight*   D. *Morte d'Arthur*

13. Heroic Couplet is a rhymed couplet of iambic pentameter. It is first introduced from France into English poetry by _____.
    A. William Shakespeare   B. John Milton
    C. Geoffrey Chaucer   D. Alexander Pope

14. The three greatest English poets in the Middle Ages are the author of *Sir Gawain and the Green Knight*, Geoffrey Chaucer and _____.
    A. William Langland   B. Thomas Malory
    C. Geoffrey of Monmouth   D. John Gower

15. The work that presented, for the first time in English literature, a comprehensive realistic picture of the medieval English society and created a whole gallery of vivid characters from all walks of life is most likely _____.
    A. *Sir Gawain and the Green Knight*   B. *Vision of Piers the Plowman*
    C. *The Canterbury Tales*   D. *Morte d'Arthur*

II. Blank-filling

1. The _____ marked the beginning of the Middle English or Anglo-Norman period (1066 – 1400).

Part Two The Medieval Age

2. The _____ are the prevailing form of literature in the Middle Ages. They are long compositions, sometimes in verse, sometimes in prose, describing the life and adventures of _____.

3. *Robin Hood* is a collection of the 15th-century medieval ballads about Robin Hood, the hero of _____, and the enemy of _____.

4. Geoffrey Chaucer's masterpiece _____ is one of the most famous works in all literature.

5. The central concern of *Morte d'Arthur* is with the adventures of _____ and his famous Knights of the Round Table.

6. Geoffrey Chaucer's literary career is generally divided into three periods: the _____ period, the French period and the _____ period.

7. Geoffrey chancer was the first great poet who wrote in the current English language, that is, in _____.

8. In his works, Chaucer affirmed man's right to _____ and opposed _____; he praised man's energy, intellect, quick wit and love of life; he exposed and satirized the social vices, including religious abuses. It can thus be said that though essentially still a medieval writer, Chaucer bore marks of _____ and anticipated a new era to come.

9. The folk ballad is a popular literary form; it comes from _____ rather than from _____ or _____.

III. Term definition

1. Romance
2. Legend
3. Arthurian legend
4. Stanza
5. Couplet
6. "Heroic Couplet"
7. Foot
8. Meter
9. Canto
10. Rhyme
11. Ballad

IV. Short-answer questions

1. What are the essential features of Romances?
2. What are the artistic Features of *Vision of Piers the Plowman*?
3. What are the salient features in Chaucer's writings?
4. What are the stylistic features of ballads?

V. Essay questions

1. Give a brief introduction to *Sir Gawain and the Green Knight*.
2. Recount the function of the General Prologue to *The Canterbury Tales*.

Part Three   The Renaissance Period

(1476/1485 – 1625)

Chapter 6   English Renaissance

6.1   Background

The War of the Roses was a cataclysm for the whole noble class in England. The King, being always threatened with the violence and lawlessness of the noble lords, now assumed greater power. Henry VII took the advantage of this situation and founded the Tudor Dynasty (1485 – 1603), a centralized monarchy of a totally new type. Then started the English Reformation, which was in essence more a political movement than a theological dispute. Henry VIII (1491 – 1547, king 1509 – 1547) broke off with the Pope and proclaimed himself head of the Church of England, and thus consolidated secular and ecclesiastical power under the king and furthered the strengthening of the English monarchy. The political centralization and consolidation of monarchy met the needs of the rapid growth of trade and the formation of the national market and won the support of the rising bourgeoisie. Absolute monarchy reached its summit during the reign of Queen Elizabeth (1533 – 1603) from 1558 to 1603. She secured a 30-year period of peace for England so that the country slowly and steadily crawled to the zenith of wealth and power.

The political and religious turmoils of the age were but the reflection of the changes in the national economy of England. From the 15th century onward manufactories were developing and the wool trade was rapidly growing in bulk in England. This stimulated the greed of the moneyed classes to seize more and more land out of the hands of the peasants in order to turn the arable land into pasture, which was satisfied in the heartless Enclosure Movement. While the helpless, dispossessed peasants flocked to the cities, became hired laborers and added to the proletariat there, the merchants and the master artisans in cities grew in wealth and power and became the bourgeoisie. Although there emerged the aggravation of the contradiction between the wealth of the ruling class and the poverty of the people, the foundations of capitalism were firmly established.

Intellectually, materialistic philosophy and scientific thought gradually replaced the church dogmas and religious mysticism of the Middle Ages. The interest in God and in the life after death was transformed into the exaltation of man and absorption in earthly life. A totally new culture, exploring the infinite capabilities of man, rose out of the revival of the old culture of ancient Greece and Rome.

6.2   Renaissance

The Renaissance was a cultural movement that profoundly affected European intellectual life. It had its origin in north Italy in the 14th century and spread northward to other European countries like France, Germany, the Low Countries and lastly to England. Its influence was felt in literature, philosophy, art, music, politics, science, religion and other aspects of intellectual inquiry. The term Renaissance originally indicated a revival of classical (Greek and Roman) arts and sciences after the dark ages of medieval obscurantism. It encompassed innovative flowering of Latin and vernacular literatures. The study and propagation of classical learning and art were carried on by the progressive thinkers of the humanists, who emphasized the capacities of the human mind and the achievements of human culture. In other words, humanists held their chief interest not in ecclesiastical knowledge, but in man, his environment and doings, and bravely fought for the emancipation of man from the tyranny of the church and religious dogmas. In politics, the Renaissance contributed to the development of the conventions of diplomacy, and in science an increased reliance on observation. Therefore humanism became the keynote of the Renaissance.

The English Renaissance dated from the late 15th to the early 17th century. Like most of northern Europe, England saw little of these developments until more than a century later. The beginning of the English Renaissance is often taken, as a convenience, either to be 1476, when William Caxton introduced a printing press into England, or to be 1485, when the Battle of Bosworth Field ended the Wars of the Roses and inaugurated the Tudor Dynasty. The Renaissance style and ideas, however, were slow to penetrate England, and the Elizabethan era in the second half of the 16th century is usually regarded as the height of the English Renaissance. The dominant art forms of the English Renaissance were literature and music. Visual arts in the English Renaissance were much less significant than in the Italian Renaissance.

England had a strong tradition of literature in the English vernacular, which gradually increased as the English use of the printing press became common by the mid-16th century. The Elizabethan era saw a great flourishing of literature, especially in the fields of poetry and drama. The works of such playwrights as William Shakespeare and Christopher Marlowe and of the poets like Philip Sidney and Edmund Spenser circulated in manuscript form for some time before they were published, and comparatively the plays were the outstanding legacy of the period.

The English Renaissance in literature can be roughly divided into three periods. The first period stretched from 1476 or 1485 to 1558. The important writers include Thomas More in prose, who gave a profound and truthful picture of the people's sufferings and put forward his ideal of a future happy society in his masterpiece *Utopia*, and Thomas Wyatt and Henry Howard, Earl of Surrey in poetry. It was Wyatt who first introduced sonnets into English literature and Surrey who gave the English form to sonnets. The latter also introduced blank verse into English literature. The second period, which is also named the Elizabethan era or the Age of Shakespeare, covers the years between 1558 and 1603. The important writers are Edmund Spenser with his *The Faerie Queene*, Philip Sydney, who wrote some of his best sonnets in *Astrophel and Stella*, William Shakespeare with his 154 sonnets, and the Metaphysical poet John Donne in poetry; the University Wits (John Lyly, Robert Greene, Thomas Kyd, Christopher Marlowe, and others) and Shakespeare, who produced his early tragedies and comedies, in drama; and Lyly and Thomas Nashe in prose. The third period spans over some two decades (1603 – 1625). The important writers include Shakespeare, who completed his great tragedies and produced some great tragi-comedies, and Ben Jonson in drama, some imitators of Spenser in poetry, and Francis Bacon in prose.

Chapter 7 Poetry in the Renaissance Period

The vigor of the new age found better expression in the sphere of poetry. This was partly attributed to Queen Elizabeth, who herself was a product of Renaissance humanism and wrote occasional poems such as "On Monsieur's Departure" at critical moments of her life. The Renaissance poetry was characterized by the flourishing of lyrics in particular. In the first half of the 16th century there appeared lyrical poets like Thomas Wyatt, Henry Howard, Earl of Surrey and others who initiated new poetical forms like the sonnet and blank verse, borrowing freely from English popular songs and Italian and French poetry. The second half of the century witnessed the great contributions of the outstanding poets like Philip Sidney, Edmund Spenser and William Shakespeare. As a matter of fact, poetry was so popular in Renaissance England that reading and writing it became part of the education of a gentleman and that numerous poetic anthologies appeared in print, among which the most famous is Tottel's Miscellany, *Songs and Sonnets* (1557).

7.1 Sir Thomas Wyatt (1503 – 1542)

Thomas Wyatt was a 16th-century English ambassador and lyrical poet. He is credited with introducing the sonnet into English literature. None of Wyatt's poems were published during his lifetime. Fifteen years after his death, the printer Richard Tottel (died 1594) included 97 poems attributed to Wyatt among the 271 poems in Tottel's Miscellany, *Songs and Sonnets*.

Wyatt's professed object was to experiment with the English tongue, to civilize it, and to raise its powers to those of its neighbors. A significant amount of his literary output consists of translations and imitations of sonnets by the Italian poet Petrarch (1304 – 1374); he also wrote sonnets of his own. He took subject matter from Petrarch's sonnets, but his rhyme schemes make a significant departure. Petrarch's sonnets consist of an octave, rhyming *abba abba*, followed, after a turn (volta) in the sense, by a sestet with various rhyme schemes. Wyatt employed the Petrarchan octave, but his most common sestet scheme is *cddc ee*. This marked the beginnings of an exclusively "English" contribution to sonnet structure—three quatrains and a closing couplet. Wyatt also experimented in stanza forms including epigrams, terza rima, ottava rima, satires, and others. He is acknowledged a master of the iambic tetrameter.

Wyatt is generally accepted as the most interesting lyric poet of the first half of the 16th century. His verse is full of dramatic energy and personal expressiveness. His lyrics show tenderness of feeling and purity of diction. Most love poetry of the early Renaissance was concerned with a single basic situation: a lover has been rejected by a beautiful but cold and disdainful woman, and he pours out his longing and frustration in a series of comparisons or images. Wyatt took over this situation from Petrarch and the Italian poets, but his handling was often distinctively fresh, and sometimes witty and ironic.

While many of Wyatt's poems deal with the trials of romantic love and the devotion of the suitor to the unavailable mistress, some others are scathing, satirical indictments of the hypocrisies and flat-out pandering, required of courtiers ambitious to advance at the Tudor court.

7.2　Henry Howard, Earl of Surrey (c. 1517 – 1547)

Surrey was an English aristocrat and one of the founders of English Renaissance poetry. He was a first cousin of Catherine Howard, the fifth wife of King Henry VIII. Most of his poems are love poems addressed to a girl whom he once loved. Surrey's poems are more graceful, more sensitive and more given to the love of nature than Wyatt's. Forty of his poems were printed in Tottel's Miscellany, *Songs and Sonnets*.

Surrey's metrical innovations are very important in English poetry. He was the first to give the sonnet its English form, the rhyming meter and the division into quatrains, which was used by Shakespeare later and therefore is usually called Shakespearean Sonnet. Surrey and Wyatt, due to their excellent translations of Petrarch's sonnets, are together known as "Fathers of the English Sonnet."

Another important contribution of Surrey to English literature is his introduction of blank verse into English poetry around 1540 in his translations of Book II and Book IV of the *Aeneid* (written 29 – 19 BC) by Virgil (70 BC – 19 BC). Surrey's blank verse is merely decasyllabic line without rhyme. Thanks to Surrey, English prosody has gained a magnificent instrument, which was used by many writers, such as Marlowe, Shakespeare, Milton, Byron and Shelley.

7.3　Sir Philip Sidney (1554 – 1586)

Philip Sidney was an English poet, courtier, scholar and soldier, who is remembered as one of the most prominent figures of the Elizabethan era. He is well-known as poet and critic of poetry. His three principal works include *Astrophel and Stella* (1591), *The Defence of Poesy* (1595) (also known as *The Defence of Poetry* or *An Apology for Poetry*), and *The Countess of Pembroke's Arcadia* (1593).

Like other poets of the time, Sidney went to classical and Italian writers for his models. The experimental French poets and the classic beauties of such poets as Petrarch and the overriding Renaissance freshness all proved conducive to his imagination. Sidney drew on classical traditions, imbibed the Renaissance spirit, tried with different rhymes, meters and stanzas, and strove untiringly for excellence in versification. Sidney's experimental daring was amazing. There was nothing in verse that he did not regard as his legitimate province of experiment: rhyme, meter, line, stanza, and overall form. His verse reveals his stunning accomplishments in poetic techniques, the variety and diversity of which alone are enough to dazzle the readers. He left behind a good number of sonnets, lyrics and pastoral poems all notable for their formal virtuosity. Sidney was, along with Spenser, one of the two most important poets to break through the dullness of English poetry of the time and paved the way for the success of other subsequent literary careers that made the Elizabethan era flourish into one of the most distinguished periods in the English literary history.

Astrophel and Stella is Sidney's sonnet cycle and best poetic compositions of 108 sonnets and 11 songs. The first of the famous English sonnet sequences, it was probably composed in the early 1580s. The sonnets were well-circulated in manuscript before the first (apparently pirated) edition was printed in 1591; only in 1598 did an authorized edition reach the press. The sequence was a watershed in English Renaissance poetry. Sidney partly nativized the key features of his Italian model Petrarch, including an ongoing but partly obscure narrative, the philosophical trappings of the poet in relation to love and desire, and musings on the art of poetic creation. He also adopted the Petrarchan rhyme scheme, though he used it with such freedom that fifteen variants were employed.

As a sonnet sequence, *Astrophel and Stella* was probably the first of its kind ever to appear in the English literary history. While Astrophel derives from the two Greek words, "aster" (star) and "phil" (lover), the Latin word "stella" means star. Thus Astrophel is the star-lover, and Stella is his star. The sonnets tell a love story between Astrophel and Stella, but they do not offer a sequential plot; they reveal Astrophel's mind. Astrophel falls in love with Stella, secretly admires her, feels happy at intimations of her returning his love, but also torn between passion and reason. Nothing happens in the end, and the lovers part company. Most of the time it is Astrophel talking, living through the stages of his love odyssey, and Stella does not show up though she is heard in the dialogues of some of the songs.

Some have suggested that the love represented within the sequence may be a literal one as Sidney evidently connected Astrophel to himself and Stella to Lady Penelope Devereux, afterward Lady Rich. Sidney and Lady Penelope had been betrothed when the latter was a child. For some reason the match was broken off, and Lady Penelope married Lord Rich, with whom she lived for a while most unhappily. The sonnets came, as Sidney claimed, straight from his heart. In these poems, the poet poured out his bitter sorrow for lost happiness, the unconquerable longing to possess his love, the despair when he found his lady was cold to him, and the dawning hope when she confessed her love to him.

The Countess of Pembroke's Arcadia, also known simply as the *Arcadia*, is a long pastoral prose-verse romance written towards the end of the 16th century. It is Sidney's most ambitious literary work and as significant in its own way as his sonnets.

Arcadia exists in two significantly different versions. Having finished one version of his text, Sidney later significantly expanded and revised his work. Scholars today often refer to these two major versions as the *Old Arcadia* and the *New Arcadia*. The early version is narrated in a straightforward, sequential manner. Later, Sidney began to revise it on a more ambitious plan, with much more back-story about the princes, and a much more complicated storyline, with many more characters. He completed most of the first three books, but the project was unfinished at the time of his death—the third book breaks off in the middle of a swordfight. There were several early editions of the work. Fulke Greville (1554 - 1628) published the revised version alone in 1590. The Countess of Pembroke, Sidney's sister, published a version in 1593, which pasted the last two books of the first version onto the first three books of the revision. In the 1621 version, Sir William Alexander (c. 1567 - 1640) provided a bridge to bring the two stories back into agreement. It was known in this cobbled-together fashion until the discovery, in the early 20th century, of the earlier version.

Arcadia was written for the entertainment of the poet's sister. The narrative follows the Greek model: stories are nested within each other, and different storylines are intertwined. The scene of the romance is laid in Arcadia, a beautiful place in Greece. The King of Arcadia retires into the countryside, where he brings up his two daughters, who become shepherdesses after growing up. They live a happy and peaceful life there. Unfortunately, their peaceful and quiet life is broken by wars. Two shipwrecked princes are brought to the country. They fall in love with the two beautiful princesses. In this romance, the poet sings of the delights of rural life and the love of the young people.

The romance enjoyed great popularity for more than a century after its publication and was imitated by many later poets. William Shakespeare borrowed from it for the Gloucester subplot of *King Lear*; parts of it were also dramatized by John Day (1574 – c. 1638) and James Shirley (1596 – 1666). According to a widely-told story, King Charles I (1600 – 1649, king 1625 – 1649) quoted lines from the book as he mounted the scaffold to be executed; Samuel Richardson named the heroine of his first novel after Sidney's Pamela.

An Apology for Poetry was written in approximately 1579 and published in 1595 after Sidney's death. It is one of the earliest English literary essays and one of the most important contributions to literary theory written in English during the Renaissance. It was written to answer a pamphlet by Stephen Gosson (1554 – 1624) called "The School of Abuse," which expresses an emerging antipathy to poetry and in essence an attack on imaginative literature. Sidney defended the noble nature of poetry and its moral value against Puritan criticism and elevated poetry as the supreme form of art that helps enrich and make nature. The significance of the nobility of poetry is its power to move readers to virtuous action. True poets must teach and delight.

Sidney dwelt on the variety of poetry like the pastoral, elegiac, satiric, comic, tragic, lyric and heroic, and discussed both ancient and modern versification. Sidney touched on the nature of the poet and poetry, compared poetry with both philosophy and history, and held that poetry enjoyed superiority over philosophy and history. The philosopher is concerned with the abstract and general, the historian is concerned with what is and not with what should be, while the poet can better the function of both. For Sidney, the poet could create through images what is only a matter of speculation to the philosopher, and through his gift of vision bring readers to contemplate the ideal, not merely the actual. That is to say, poetry, by combining the liveliness of history with the ethical focus of philosophy, is more effective than either history or philosophy in rousing its readers to virtue. These views on poetry represent the spirit of literary criticism of the Renaissance. The work also offers important comments on Edmund Spenser and the Elizabethan stage.

In an era of antipathy to poetry and puritanical belief in the corruption engendered by literature, Sidney's defense was a significant contribution to the genre of literary criticism. Here Sidney advocated a place for poetry within the framework of an aristocratic state, while showing concern for both literary and national identity. *An Apology for Poetry* was England's first philosophical defense which describes the ancient and indispensable place of poetry in society, its mimetic nature and its ethical function. Sidney, as a traditionalist, however, gave attention to drama in contradistinction to poetry. For Sidney, drama was "observing neither rules of honest civility nor of skillful poetry" and thus could not do justice to this genre.

Sidney wrote *An Apology for Poetry* in the form of a judicial oration for the defense, and thus it is like a trial in structure. Crucial to his defense is the descriptive discourse and the idea that poetry creates a separate reality. Sidney employed forensic rhetoric as a tool to make the argument that poetry not only conveys a separate reality, but also has a long and venerable history, and does not lie. It is defensible in its own right as a means to move readers to virtuous action.

7.4 Edmund Spenser (c. 1552 – 1599)

Spenser is generally acknowledged as "the poet's poet," the greatest non-dramatic poet of the Elizabethan era, one of the premier craftsmen of Modern English verse in its infancy, and one of the greatest poets in the English language. His fame in English literature is chiefly based upon his masterpiece *The Faerie Queene* and his special verse form named the Spenserian stanza. He has been the model for many poets of different generations. Shakespeare's plays reveal traces of acquaintance with Spenser's poems. Milton called him his "poetical father." Dryden and Pope were both indebted to him. And so were Wordsworth, Byron, Shelley, Keats, Tennyson, and others.

Spenser's poetry possesses the following qualities: a perfect melody, a rare sense of beauty, a splendid imagination, a lofty moral purity and seriousness, and a delicate realism. It is his idealism, his love of beauty and his exquisite melody that make him known as "the poet's poet." Spenser's major works include *The Shepherd's Calendar* (1579), *The Faerie Queene* (1590, 1596), *Colin Clouts Come Home Againe* (1595), two odes to Marriage—*Epithalamion* (1595) and *Prothalamion* (1596)—and *Amoretti* (1595), a collection of 89 sonnets, which were addressed to Spenser's second wife Elizabeth.

Almost all of Spenser's numerous relatively short poems are concerned with love or sorrow. *Complaints* (1591), a collection of poems, expresses complaints in mournful or mocking tones. *Amoretti* commemorates Spenser's courtship of Elizabeth Boyle. Spenser used subtle humor and parody while praising his beloved, reworking Petrarchism in his treatment of longing for a woman. *Epithalamion*, similar to *Amoretti*, deals in part with the unease in the development of a romantic and sexual relationship, and celebrates the poet's own wedding. The poem consists of 365 long lines, corresponding to the days of the year; 68 short lines, claimed to represent the sum of the 52 weeks, 12 months, and 4 seasons of the annual cycle; and 24 stanzas, corresponding to the diurnal and sidereal hours. Some have speculated that the attention to disquiet in general reflects Spenser's personal anxieties at the time, as he was unable to complete his most significant work *The Faerie Queene*. *Prothalamion* is a wedding song written for the daughters of a duke, allegedly in hopes to gain favor in the court.

The Faerie Queene is a grand epic poem and fantastical allegory celebrating the Tudor Dynasty and Elizabeth I, and one of the longest poems in the English language. The work was originally planned in twelve books, of which Spenser finished only six and a fragment of the seventh. The first three books of *The Faerie Queene* were published in 1590, and a second set of three books were published in 1596. Fusing adroitly the strands of legend, fable, and praise of Elizabeth I's England in itself, the whole poem is suffused with genuine devotion to the queen and the country, and can be read, as Spenser presumably intended, on several levels of allegory. In a completely allegorical context, the poem follows several knights in an examination of several virtues. In his "A Letter of the Authors," Spenser stated that the entire epic poem was "cloudily enwrapped in allegorical devises," and that the aim behind *The Faerie Queene* was to "fashion a gentleman or noble person in virtuous and gentle discipline."

The plan of the whole poem is like this: The faerie Queene, who represents Queen Elizabeth, holds a feast of twelve days, and on each day a stranger in distress appears telling a woeful story of dragons and enchantresses and asking the Queen to send a knight to right the wrong and let the oppressed go free. Then a knight is assigned to each guest, and the twelve books are to describe the twelve adventures. Moreover, each knight represents a virtue—Holiness, Temperance, Chastity, Friendship, Justice, or Courtesy. The knights as a whole symbolize England, and the evil figures stand for her enemies, as King Philip of Spain, Mary Queen of Scots or the Church of

Rome. The Faerie Queene would eventually marry King Arthur—the paragon of supreme virtue. The dominating thoughts of the poem are nationalism (as shown in its celebration of Queen Elizabeth), humanism (as shown in its strong opposition to Roman Catholicism) and Puritanism (as shown in its moral teaching), all typical of the poet's age. However, these new ideas are expressed under the guise of medieval knighthood. Actually, modernism and medievalism are blended in the poem, but they are at the same time harmonized by the beauty of sound and color in the Spenserian poetry.

The stories of the six finished books go as follows: Book I recounts the adventures of a knight called Redcross, who stands for Holiness. Redcross helps a lady slay a dragon, which is besieging her father's castle. Book II tells the adventurers of a knight representing Temperance. He captures an enchantress and destroys her bower of Bliss. Book III describes the adventures of a woman knight standing for Chastity, who saves a lady from a magician's hands. Book IV is the legend of two knights, who stand for Friendship. The story symbolizes the eternal friendship and love. Book V recounts the story of a knight standing for Justice, and Book VI tells the adventures of a knight representing Courtesy.

The Faerie Queene is notable for its sweet melody and the musical lines. It is the origin of a verse form that came to be known as Spenserian stanza, a special verse form Spenser invented for the poem. Each stanza has nine lines, each of the first eight lines is in iambic pentameter form, and the ninth line is an iambic hexameter line. The rhyme scheme is abab bcbc c. Because of its rare beauty, this verse form was much used by nearly all the later poets, especially imitated by the romantic poets of the 19th century. Elizabeth I liked the poem so much that Spenser was granted a pension for life amounting to £ 50 a year, though there is no evidence that Elizabeth I read any of the poem. This royal patronage helped the poem along to such a level of success that it became Spenser's defining work.

The Shepherd's Calendar is Spenser's first major poem and the one only next to his masterpiece. In emulation of Virgil's first work, the *Eclogues*, Spenser wrote this series of pastorals to begin his career. The poem consists of twelve pastoral eclogues, which are assigned to the twelve months of a year. Each eclogue is named after a different month, which represents the turning of seasons. An eclogue is a short pastoral poem that is in the form of a dialogue or soliloquy. This is why, while the months come together to form a whole year, each month can also stand alone as a separate poem. The months are all written in a different form. For example, Aprill has a lyrical "laye" which honors the Queen. Maye gives off characterization and greater description. As the reader passes through each month and gets closer to the end of the year, the wording becomes less beautifully lyrical and more straightforward, closing together the poem the way the month of December closes up the year. Spenser used rhyme differently in each month. There is a very cyclical pattern that shows off the kind of style that Spenser was going for, making readers feel as though they were going through the cycle of each year just as the narrator does. The months all have repetition of elements and arguments. The style of the poem is also influenced by writers such as Chaucer and John Skelton (c. 1460 – 1529). Its text is full of archaic or "Chaucerian" words, which Spenser meant as an echo to Chaucer and also an attempt to bring into relief a rustic effect. The eclogues in the *Calendar* fall into three groups—the plaintive, the recreative and the moral. They deal with different themes such as love, religion and poetry. The poem introduces Colin Clout, a folk character originated by John Skelton, and depicts his life as a shepherd through the twelve months of the year. The work, encompassing considerable formal innovations, anticipates the even more virtuosic *Arcadia* (the old version), the classic pastoral romance by Philip Sidney, with whom Spenser was acquainted. It is also remarkable for the extensive commentary included with the work in its first publication.

The Shepherd's Calendar was a success; between 1579 and 1597 five editions were published. It was crucial to the naturalization of the English Language and the introduction of vocabulary along with literary techniques. What separates the poem from others of its time is Spenser's use of allegory and his dependence on the idea of antiquity. It laid the groundwork for *The Faerie Queen*.

Chapter 8   Prose in the Renaissance Period

The epoch of Renaissance witnessed the emergence of prose writings. At the beginning of the 16th century stood out Thomas More with his *Utopia*, which gave a profound and truthful picture of the people's sufferings and put forward the author's ideal of a happy future society. The later 16th century, to some extent, was characterized by the publication of romances, including John Lyly's *Euphues*, which gave rise to the term "euphuism" and designated an affected style of court speech, and Thomas Nashe's *The Unfortunate Traveler*, whose language is more natural and stands in direct opposition to the artificiality of euphuism. The greatest achievement in Renaissance prose lies in Francis Bacon and his philosophical and literary essays, which are noted for clearness, brevity and force of expression.

8.1   Sir Thomas More (c. 1477 – 1535)

Thomas More was an English lawyer, social philosopher, author and statesman. He opposed the Protestant Reformation and the King's separation from the Catholic Church. Tried for treason, he was convicted and beheaded. Since 1980, the Church of England has remembered More liturgically as a Reformation martyr.

More was first and foremost a humanist at heart. He witnessed the evils of the world and sought to help mend things. His masterpiece *Utopia* takes a look forward to the future of man and offers an ideal which has inspired generations of serious social thinkers, political scientists, writers as well as humankind as a whole ever since its publication.

Utopia, first written in Latin in 1516, is More's most controversial work. The word "Utopia" came from two Greek words meaning "no place." In the work, it was used to name More's ideal society. The book became very popular after its publication, though it was not translated into English and published in his native land until 1551 (long after More's execution). The 1684 translation is the most commonly cited. *Utopia* was written in the form of a conversation between More (also a character in the book) and the narrator and returned sailor Raphael Hythlodaeus. More and Hythlodaeus discuss modern ills in contemporary England and describe the political arrangements of the imaginary island country of Utopia.

The whole work is divided into two books. Book I is a picture of contemporary England. The author severely criticized English society and exposed social evils. He pointed out that the enclosure of land and the ensuing expulsion of peasants was the source of social evils, and the whole system of society around him seemed to him "nothing but a conspiracy of the rich against the poor." He condemned the rich and the ruling class for bringing miseries to the poor peasants. Generally speaking, Book I is a forcible exposure of the evil things of English society. Book II, consisting of nine sections, offers us a good picture of an ideal society in some unknown ocean. In this society property is held in common and there is no private property. All citizens in Utopia are politically equal. Everybody takes part in labor. The products of the society are distributed according to the needs of the citizens. More emphasized the importance of labor for every member of the society, and insisted upon working six hours a day. After work the citizens spend their time in studying literature, science and art. All religions in this ideal society are authorized and tolerance is the law. Life there is pleasant. People enjoy cleanliness, comfort and well-being.

Utopia is regarded as one of the earliest work of Utopian socialism. Karl Marx (1818 – 1883) highly commented this work and mentioned it in his great work *The Capital* (1867 – 1894). More was honored by the Soviet Union, due to the Communistic attitude regarding property in the work. *Utopia* outlines the ideal set of basics governing human institutions and regulating human life. It is amazing how More figured out the nuts and bolts of the best government and lifestyle for man. Utopia is an imaginary country where democracy replaces tyranny, commonwealth replaces private property, the work ethic is valued and idleness frowned upon, there is no distinction between the rich and the poor, education is free for all, money is abolished and gold and silver depreciated, religious tolerance is enforced and bigotry outlawed, and there is peace and abundance for all. On the whole the Utopian system represents a substantial improvement over the existing system of England.

However, the picture of Utopia shows up some problems in clear outline. One of these is its strict adherence to conformity, which would result in the curbing of individual rights and freedom and would in the long run encompass the collapse of the visionary system. The emphasis on uniformity in dress, behavior and lifestyle would deprive life of its intrinsic diversity and complexity and reduce human existence to simplicity and monotony totally incompatible with the human nature. There is also the slave system, which allows some humans to be superior and rule over their fellow creatures. This is the obvious injustice which goes against individual dignity and self-worth. Furthermore, in the discussion of wars, there is a hint of possible superpower politics at work, however faint it may be. Then there is patriarchy. The Utopian society is clearly male-dominated: there is no mention of gender equality, no equal opportunity for administrative and religious jobs, no clear recognition of the females and their rights, but a very clear indication that the women folk have to submit to their men folk. All these weaknesses reveal the force of the temporal and spatial constraints out of which even a man of genius like More cannot break with complete success. Despite all these, Utopia is unique in more than one way and forms a direct, positive contrast to England and Europe of the time.

Utopia gave rise to a literary genre, Utopian and dystopian fiction, which features ideal societies or perfect cities, or their opposite. Early works influenced by *Utopia* include *New Atlantis* (1627) by Francis Bacon, *Erewhon* by Samuel Butler and *Candide* (1759) by Voltaire (1694 – 1778). Although Utopianism combined classical concepts of perfect societies (Plato's and Aristotle's) with Roman rhetorical finesse, the Renaissance genre continued into the Age of Enlightenment and survives in modern science fiction.

8.2 John Lyly (c. 1553 – 1606)

Lyly was an English poet, playwright, politician and, above all, prose writer. He is best remembered for his prose romance *Euphues* and its peculiar mannered literary style known as "Euphuism." Its principal characteristic is the excessive use of antithesis, which is pursued regardless of sense and emphasized by balanced sentences and words alliterating, riming or identical. Besides, Lyly decorated his prose with odd similes and comparisons drawn from natural history, history and geography.

Euphues, derived from Greek meaning "graceful, witty," contains two parts. The first part *Euphues: The Anatomy of Wit* was published in 1578 while the second part *Euphues and His England* came out in 1580. The plot of each is very slender and little but a peg on which to hang discourses, conversations and letters, mainly on the subject love. The story is based on the author's own experiences. The hero, a young Athenian named Euphues visits Naples, where he makes the acquaintance of an Italian man called Philautus. They become friends. Then Philautus introduces his fiancée to Euphues, and Euphues falls in love with the girl. For this reason the two friends break off with each other. Later on, they get reconciled again because the girl whom they both love has married a third man. This is the story of the first part. In the second part, Euphues and Philautus travel to England, where their adventures are even less entertaining than at Naples. They are largely concerned with the love affairs on which Philautus embarks, in spite of the advice of Euphues to use circumspection in his dealings with English ladies; and much space is occupied by a discussion on such questions as "whether in love be more required secrecie or constancie." Finally Euphues returns to Greece. From Athens he writes a letter to the ladies of Italy. In this letter, he criticizes England through describing its institutions, its ladies, its gentlemen and its queen. A final letter of advice from Euphues to Philautus completes the work. This part is, on the whole, a satire on England.

Lyly was one of the University Wits. Although *Euphues* was his most popular and influential work in the Elizabethan period, his plays are now admired for their flexible use of dramatic prose and the elegant patterning of their construction. Lyly's major plays include those collected in *Six Court Comedies* (the first printed collection of his plays)—*Campaspe* (1584), *Sapho and Phao* (1584), *Endymion* (1591), *Gallathea* (1592), *Midas* (1592), and *Mother Bombie* (1594)—and the others like *The Woman in the Moon* (1597) and *Love's Metamorphosis* (1601). Of these, all but *The Woman in the Moon* are in prose.

8.3 Thomas Nashe (1567 – c. 1601)

Nashe is considered the greatest of the English Elizabethan pamphleteers. He was also a playwright, poet and satirist.

Nashe's first publication was a preface to Robert Greene's *Menaphon* (1589), surveying the follies of contemporary literature. Nashe expanded this theme in *The Anatomie of Absurditie* later in the same year. In 1592 he avenged the attack of Gabriel Harvey (c. 1552/3 – 1631) on Greene with *Strange News*. A florid religious meditation *Christ Tears over Jerusalem* came out in 1593. Despite the apparently devotional nature the pamphlet contains satirical material which gave offence to the London civic authorities and Nashe was briefly imprisoned in Newgate. Nashe attempted to apologize in the preface to the pamphlet, but the appearance of Gabriel Harvey's *Pierce's Supererogation* (1953) shortly after offended him anew. He replied with *Have with You to Saffron-Walden* (1596), his final shot in his four-year literary feud with Harvey. Alongside this running dispute, Nashe produced his more famous works. In October 1592 he wrote an entertainment called *Summer's Last Will and Testament*, a "show" with some resemblance to a masque, which is notable for breaking new ground in the development of English Renaissance drama. The play was performed in 1592 and published in 1600. In brief, the plot describes the death of Summer, who, feeling himself to be dying, reviews the performance of his former servants and eventually passes the crown on to Autumn. Nashe is widely remembered for three short poems, all drawn from this play and frequently reprinted in anthologies of Elizabethan verse: "Adieu, farewell, earth's bliss," "Fair summer droops" and "Autumn hath all the summer's fruitful treasure." Nashe may also have contributed to *Henry VI, Part I*, the play later published under Shakespeare's name as the first part of the *Henry VI* trilogy. Many scholars believe that Shakespeare himself, who was just starting out as a writer, only contributed some scenes to the play. Nashe subsequently promoted the play in his pamphlet *Pierce Penniless, His Supplication to the Divell* (1592), a tall tale or a prose satire, which was among the most popular of the Elizabethan pamphlets. The pamphlet was reprinted in 1593 and 1595, and was translated into French in 1594, when Nashe's well-known picaresque novel *The Unfortunate Traveler* came out.

The Unfortunate Traveler: *Or the Life of Jack Wilton* (1594) is a medley of picaresque narrative, literary parody and mock-historical fantasy. It was set during the reign of Henry VIII of England. In this rollicking and stylistically daring work of prose fiction, Nashe's protagonist Jack Wilton adventures through the European Continent and finds himself swept up in the currents of 16th-century history. Episodic in nature, the narrative jumps from place to place and danger to danger. Jack begins his tale among fellow Englishmen at a military encampment, where he swindles his superiors out of alcohol and money, framing others as traitors. Commenting by the way on the grotesque "sweating sickness," Jack arrives in Munster, Germany, to observe the massacre of John Leyden's Anabaptist faction by the Emperor and the Duke of Saxony; this brutal episode enabled Nashe to reflect on religious hypocrisy, a theme to which he frequently returned.

Following the massacre of the Anabaptists at Munster, Jack Wilton has a number of personal encounters with historical figures of the 16th century, many of them important for their literary contributions. Henry Howard, Earl of Surrey functions as a sustained travel partner for Jack, and the two journey to Italy to fulfill the Earl's pledge to defend the honor of his beloved Geraldine in a tournament. They pass through Rotterdam, a city in the Netherlands where they meet both Erasmus and Thomas More. After this episode, the two reach the university city of Wittenberg, Germany, which enabled Nashe to mock the customs of Renaissance academia, especially its convoluted orations and bizarre gestures and body language. Passing into Italy, the land where the remainder of the narrative unfolds, Jack and Surrey exchange identities as a security measure. The two engage in acts of deceit and trickery with pimps, prostitutes and counterfeiters. While imprisoned for fraud, Surrey and Jack meet Diamante, who has been falsely accused of adultery and cast out by her husband; Jack takes her up as his romantic companion and financier. All three characters are freed soon enough thanks to an English connection to the famous satirist Pietro Aretino.

Departing from Venice, Surrey and Jack arrive in Florence, the city where Geraldine was born. Surrey is overcome with poetry and speaks a sonnet in honor of her fair room. Here Nashe slyly mocked the overbearing, lovesick verse of contemporary imitators of Petrarch. The copia of Surrey's verse then gives way to a tournament in which the Earl competes for his beloved's fair name, and Nashe offered gratuitous descriptions of the competitors' armor and horses in a manner that recalls printed accounts of early modern masques and other festive spectacles. The most worthy competitor Surrey emerges from the tournament victorious, but is suddenly called back into England for business matters.

Jack and Diamante then travel to Rome, which Jack admires for its classical ruins. Jack stumbles into one of the most memorable episodes of the narrative. Esdras of Granado and his lackey Bartol the Italian break into the house where he and Diamante are lodging, and Esdras rapes the virtuous matron Heraclide, who commits suicide after an eloquent oration. Heraclide's husband accuses Jack of the rape, but another English character known as the Banished Earl stays Jack's execution. This comes at a slight cost, however; banned from his beloved home country, the Earl rattles off a catalogue of reasons to avoid travel at all costs. In spite of the Banished English Earl's suggestions, Jack remains in Italy.

The final episode returns to the character of Esdras, who figures now as a victim. At Bologna, Jack and Diamante observe the public execution of Cutwolf, Bartol's brother. Standing before the crowd, Cutwolf delivers a speech recounting his vile actions. Seeking vengeance for his brother's murder, Cutwolf tracked down the villain Esdras, confronted him and forced him to blaspheme against God and against salvation before discharging a pistol into his mouth, thereby damning his soul eternally in death. Self-righteously, he declares in his own defense before the crowd that "This is the fault that hath called me hither. No true Italian but will honor me for it. Revenge is the glory of arms and the highest performance of valor." In spite of such an oration, Cutwolf joins the ranks of the narrative's brutally-executed characters, and Jack and his newly-wed Diamante flee back toward the English encampment in France, where the story first began.

8.4　Francis Bacon (1561 – 1626)

Bacon was an English philosopher, statesman, scientist, jurist, orator and essayist. He served both as Attorney General and Lord Chancellor of England. After his death, he remained extremely influential through his works, especially as philosophical advocate and practitioner of the scientific method during the scientific revolution. Bacon was the one who first put forward the saying that "knowledge is strength." If the imaginative powers of literary creations of English Renaissance found their expression in the poetry of Spenser and the drama of Shakespeare, the intellectual energy of this age showed itself in the achievement of Francis Bacon. Bacon is acknowledged as a key figure in the transition from the intellectual world of the late Medieval Ages to that of modern Europe, a prophet of a new century, and a scholar in several fields including science, literature and philosophy.

As a philosopher, Bacon was greatly concerned with human beings' understanding of themselves and the world they live in. He is generally acknowledged as the founder of the English materialist philosophy. As a scientist, Bacon is accepted as the founder of modern science in England. His major contribution to modern science is his promotion of the inductive method of reasoning, often called the Baconian method, or simply the scientific method, which, exactly contrary to the deductive method used by medieval scholars, formulated generalizations only after close observation of facts. Bacon has been called the father of empiricism. His works established and popularized inductive methodologies for scientific inquiry. His demand for a planned procedure of investigating all things natural marked a new turn in the rhetorical and theoretical framework for science, much of which still surrounds conceptions of proper methodology today. In literature, Bacon was the first English essayist. He is famous for his *Essays*, a collection of his essays, whose first edition in 1597 contained ten pieces, as notes of his observations. The collection was reissued and enlarged in 1612 and again in 1625.

Bacon's works consist of three groups: the philosophical, the literary and the professional. *Maxims of the Law* (1596) and *The Learned Reading of Sir Francis Bacon upon the Statute of Uses* are his professional works. Bacon's major philosophical works include *The Advancement of Learning* (1605), a survey of the accomplishments of science up to his time and an examination of the reasons why it has not achieved more, and *The New Instrument* (1620), a statement of what is called the Inductive Method of reasoning. Bacon also wrote a long treatise on Medicine, *History of Life and Death* (1623), with natural and experimental observations for the prolongation of life.

Bacon's literary works are chiefly his essays, which are noted for their style and striking observations about life. They are the first true English prose classic. The final edition of the *Essays* published in 1625 contains 58 pieces. These essays cover a wide variety of subjects, such as love, truth, friendship, parents and children, beauty, studies, riches, youth and age, garden, death and many others. Among these essays the famous pieces are "Of Studies," "Of Travel" and "Of Wisdom." Bacon's essays have a literary style peculiar to their own. They are noted for their clearness, brevity and force of expression. His chief concern is to express his thought with clearness and in as few words as possible. His sentences are short, pointed, incisive and often of balanced structure. Many of them have become wise old sayings. Generally speaking, Bacon's literary style has three prominent qualities—directness, terseness and forcefulness.

Besides, Bacon wrote a novel or romance titled *The New Atlantis* (1627), in which his vision for a utopian New World in North America is laid out, a vision of the future of human discovery and knowledge, expressing his aspirations and ideals for humankind. The novel depicts the creation of a utopian land where "generosity and enlightenment, dignity and splendor, piety and public spirit" are the commonly held qualities of the inhabitants of the mythical Bensalem. The plan and organization of his ideal college Salomon's House envisioned the modern research university in both applied and pure sciences. It is a matter of debate whether the novel may have actually influenced later ideas, such as women's rights, abolition of slavery, elimination of debtors' prisons, separation of church and state, and freedom of political expression. There is no reference to any of these reforms in *The New Atlantis* itself.

Chapter 9 Drama in the Renaissance Period

9.1 English Drama

By the Elizabethan era, English drama had gone through several types like the mystery, the miracle, the morality, the interlude and the classical drama. The **mysteries** were religious or sacred dramas which the church found one most effective way to instill Christian teachings in the hearts of people. They dramatized the biblical mysteries, both from the Old and New Testaments, such as the Creation, the stories of Adam and Eve, the murder of Abel, and the last judgment, and the like. The plays were staged on the religious holidays like Easter and Christmas with the holy clerics acting out the parts. Oftentimes they were performed together in cycles which could last for days. The **miracles** are barely distinguishable from the mysteries; yet there is some hair-splitting between the two. The phase of the miracles began when the lives and the legends of the saints were acted out along with the mysteries. This introduced a change, which was substantial in nature and became more and more noticeable as the human element was represented along with the divine and the stage productions grew more secular and less religious. The most famous miracle play was probably *The Harrowing of the Hell* (c. 1250). The mysteries and the miracles were first brought in by the Normans at the beginning of the 12th century. They flourished in the 13th, became a huge business in the 14th, and reached their full potential in the 15th and the 16th before they gave way to the newer kinds of productions, among which were the interlude and the morality play. The **interlude** and the **morality** play are also somewhat indistinguishable. The only difference probably lies in the fact that the interludes came earlier, were generally shorter in length and simpler in plot, and required fewer characters. Generally speaking, the interludes and the morality plays were allegorical, dealing with moral subjects relating to the real facts of life like virtues and vices, and concerned with teaching people to be good and virtuous. These were peopled with one-dimensional characters personifying human qualities, with characters as abstractions bearing quaint names like Good Deeds, Knowledge, Beauty and Death. Whereas the most famous interlude is *The Four P's* in which all the names of the four characters begin with a P—Palmer, Pardoner, Pothecary and Peddler, the best-known morality play is *Everyman* (c. 1509 – 19), which, probably a Buddhist work in origin, presents a parable about one aspect of life, i. e. the judgment day that all have to face.

The **classical drama/true drama** appeared in the middle of the 16th century. English playwrights came into contact with Greco-Roman drama through the revival of classical literature, from which they learned all the important rules in structure and style, the more exact conceptions of comedy and tragedy, and the orderly division into five acts. The true drama swept all the other categories off the stage with its representation of real life as lived by real people. Characters, with real names with no abstract personifications, were involved in real events that were culled from reality, and replicated human behavior in their daily existence. Plots evolved around intriguing true-to-life stories in some conceivable order, which were normally sequential at first in well-arranged acts and scenes. The first true drama was probably *Ralph Roister Doister* (1552/1566), a comedy by Nicholas Udall (1504 – 1556). The first wholly English comedy was a domestic drama entitled *Gammer Gurton's Needle* (1566/1575), while *Gorboduc* (1561) by Thomas Sackville (1536 – 1608) in collaboration with Thomas Norton (1532 – 1584) was the first tragedy in English literature.

These early plays did much in training actors and keeping alive the English dramatic tradition, and paved the way for the flourishing of drama during the Elizabethan era. The English theatre scene, which performed both for the court and nobility in private performances, was the most crowded in Europe, with a host of other playwrights as well as the giant figures of Christopher Marlowe, William Shakespeare and Ben Jonson.

9.2 Thomas Kyd (1558 – 1594)

Kyd was an English playwright and one of the most important figures in the development of Elizabethan drama. Although well known in his own time, Kyd fell into obscurity until 1773 when Thomas Hawkins (an early editor of *The Spanish Tragedy*) discovered that Kyd was named as the author of *The Spanish Tragedy* by Thomas Heywood

(1570s – 1641) in his *Apologie for Actors* (1612). A hundred years later, scholars in Germany and England began to shed light on his life and work, including the controversial finding that he may have been the author of a *Hamlet* play pre-dating Shakespeare's, which may have been one of Shakespeare's primary sources for *Hamlet*. Kyd's is now known as the *Ur-Hamlet* (1589). The success of Kyd's plays extended to Europe. Versions of *The Spanish Tragedy* and his *Hamlet* were popular in Germany and the Netherlands for generations. The influence of these plays on European drama was largely the reason for the interest in Kyd among German scholars in the 19th century.

Kyd wrote **The Spanish Tragedy** probably in the mid to late 1580s. The earliest surviving edition was printed in 1592. Highly popular and influential in its time, the play established a new genre in English theatre, the revenge play or revenge tragedy. Its plot contains several violent murders and has as one of its characters a personification of Revenge. The play was often referred to or parodied in works written by other Elizabethan playwrights, including William Shakespeare, Ben Jonson and Christopher Marlowe. Many elements of *The Spanish Tragedy*, such as the play-within-a-play used to trap a murderer and a ghost intent on vengeance, appear in Shakespeare's *Hamlet*.

The Spanish Tragedy was influenced by many writers, notably Seneca (c. 4 BC – AD 65) and those from the medieval tradition. The play is ostensibly Senecan with its bloody tragedy, rhetoric of the horrible, the character of the Ghost and typical revenge themes. The characters of the Ghost of Andrea and Revenge form a chorus similar to that of Tantalus and Fury in Seneca's *Thyestes*. The Ghost describes his journey into the underworld and calls for punishment at the end of the play. The use of onomastic rhetoric is also Senecan, with characters playing upon their names. However, the play subverts typically Senecan qualities, especially the use of a ghost character. In Kyd the Ghost is part of the chorus, unlike in *Thyestes* where the Ghost leaves after the prologue. Also, the Ghost is not a functioning prologue as he does not give the audience information about the major action on stage nor its conclusion. The Ghost is similar to those in metrical (meaning in meter form) medieval plays who return from the dead to talk about their downfall and offer commentary on the action.

Other plays attributed in whole or in part to Kyd include *Soliman and Perseda* (1588), *King Leir* (1605), *Arden of Feversham* (1592) and *Edward III* (1596). Kyd also completed translations like *The Householder's Philosophy* (1588) and some poems. He is the presumed author of a pamphlet in prose entitled *The Murder of John Brewen* (1592), a grisly report on murder in a family, in which a goldsmith is murdered by his wife. It is noting that most of Kyd's works seem to be lost or unidentified.

9.3 Christopher Marlowe (1564 – 1593)

Marlowe was an English playwright, poet and translator of the Elizabethan era. He was the foremost Elizabethan tragedian of his day and the most gifted of the University Wits. As the greatest playwright before Shakespeare, Marlowe greatly influenced William Shakespeare and is the only dramatist of the time who ever touched Shakespeare in power and beauty. His plays paved the way for Shakespeare whose achievements were the monument of the English Renaissance.

Marlowe produced six plays and several poems in his lifetime. His best plays include *Tamburlaine the Great* (1587), *The Jew of Malta* (1592) and *The Tragical History of Doctor Faustus* (1594), for which Marlowe is chiefly remembered today. His other plays include *Dido, Queen of Carthage* (c. 1586), possibly co-written with

Thomas Nashe and believed to be Marlowe's first, *Edward II* (c. 1592), one of the earliest English history plays, and *The Massacre at Paris* (c. 1593). Marlowe also wrote the poem *Hero and Leander* (1598) and the popular lyric "The Passionate Shepherd to His Love," and did some translations.

Tamburlaine the Great, published in 1590, is Marlowe's first play performed on the regular stage in London. It pushed the young playwright instantly to prominence. The play is a dream vision in blank verse and, along with Thomas Kyd's *The Spanish Tragedy*, is generally considered the beginning of the mature phase of the Elizabethan theatre. It marked a turning away from the clumsy language and loose plotting of the earlier Tudor dramatists, and a new interest in fresh and vivid language, memorable action and intellectual complexity. The play is loosely based on the life of Tamburlaine or Timur the Lame, the terrible 14th-century Mongol conqueror, who is said to be a descendant of Genghis Khan (1162 - 1227) and rose from shepherd to war-lord, and whose irresistible troops played havoc with vast areas of the world from Turkestan through Siberia to Persia and India. Marlowe based his work on a translation of the biography by a Spanish scholar. The play is divided into two parts. The first part traces the legendary conqueror's rise from humble and his conquest of the Turkish Empire, and the second deals with his continued victories in Babylon where he makes the defeated kings draw his chariot. There is also a love interest in the form of Zenocrate, an Egyptian princess, whom Tamburlaine captures and spares out of love. The tragedy ends with the death of both of them.

Tamburlaine is portrayed as a man of superman ambition and energy with his exuberant aggressive spirit and high sense of accomplishment. His tragic flaw is his insatiability that drives him to his never-ending endeavor for acquisition. The influence of *Tamburlaine* on the drama of the 1590s cannot be overstated. The play exemplified, and in some cases created, many of the typical features of high Elizabethan drama: grandiloquent and often beautiful imagery, hyperbolic expression, and strong characters consumed by overwhelming passions.

The Jew of Malta was probably written in 1589 or 1590 and was first performed in 1592. It was a success and remained popular for the next fifty years. The play was entered in the Stationers' Register on 17 May 1594, but the earliest surviving printed edition is from 1633. Its plot is an original story of religious conflict, intrigue and revenge, set against a backdrop of the struggle for supremacy between Spain and the Ottoman Empire in the Mediterranean that takes place on the island of Malta. The hero Barabas is a rich merchant and a Tamburlaine in the narrow sphere of finance. He, like Tamburlaine, is greedy of sovereignty, but for him it lies not in kingship but in riches. He, the rich Jew of Malta, refuses to pay as the governor demands and is stripped of all his wealth as well as his house. He avenges himself by scheming to poison the Governor's daughter and her lover. He becomes a traitor when Malta is under Turkish siege and is made governor in return for his service. Now he begins to plot the destruction of the Turkish troops by means of a collapsible floor, beneath which he places a boiling cauldron for the victims. He is betrayed and thrown into the cauldron himself. His tragic flaws are his lust and greed and his capacity for anger, foul play and evil when he deems it necessary to achieve his ends. *The Jew of Malta* is considered to have been a major influence on Shakespeare's *The Merchant of Venice*.

The Tragical History of the Life and Death of Doctor Faustus, commonly shortened as *Doctor Faustus*, was based on the German Faust legend, in which the hero sells his soul to the devil for power, experience, pleasure and knowledge. *Doctor Faustus* was first published in 1604, eleven years after Marlowe's death and at least ten years after the first performance of the play. It is the most controversial Elizabethan play outside of Shakespeare, with few critics coming to any agreement as to the date or the nature of the text.

Doctor Faustus was a collaborative work, consisting of 13 scenes. It was staged in Germany and led to the popularity of the Faust legend and Faust drama, and also to the interest of Goethe (1749 – 1832) two centuries later, whose drama *Faust* came out in two parts in 1808 and 1832 respectively. Marlowe's tragedy places emphasis on the cosmic nature of Faustus' quest for knowledge and power. The first part of the play tells of Faustus' dissatisfaction with earthly knowledge and of his pact with the devil Mephistophilis, the bond that he signs in blood, for selling his soul in return for 24 years of supreme power and joy. The second part tells of Faustus' satisfaction with his newly acquired knowledge and power with which, among other things, he plays tricks on the Pope, conjures up, from the dead, Alexander the Great and his beautiful paramour at a palace feast, causes a pair of horns to grow on the head of an irritating knight, and offers a duchess ripe southern grapes in the middle of winter. The third part concludes with Faustus' soul being dragged down to the Hell as the pact requires. While versions of "The Devil's Pact" can be traced back to the 4th century, Marlowe deviated significantly by having his hero unable to "burn his books" or repent to a merciful God in order to have his contract annulled at the end of the play.

Doctor Faustus is a textual problem for scholars as two versions of the play exist: the 1604 version, also known as the A text, and the 1616 version or B text. Both were published after Marlowe's death. Scholars have disagreed which text is more representative of Marlowe's original, and some editions are based on a combination of the two. The latest scholarly consensus (as of the late 20th century) holds that the A text is more representative because it contains irregular character names and idiosyncratic spelling, which are believed to reflect a text based on the author's handwritten manuscript. The B text, in comparison, was highly edited, censored because of shifting theatre laws regarding religious words onstage, and contains several additional scenes which scholars believe to be the additions of other playwrights.

Thematically, the image of Faustus is historically significant as a "photo" record of the new man, the modern man, the Renaissance humanist, who steps into modern light with all the glitter of Reformation and Renaissance. Faustus, the medieval man, has already had nearly everything including knowledge and power to make him happy, but he is not happy. Insatiability is his name. He sees the world as one of infinite power and profit and wants all that moves between the two poles to be at his command. He wants to be a superman, a virtual god figure, and he becomes one, though he has to pay an exorbitant price. Thus Faustus represents the archetypal Renaissance humanist of the 16th century and a supreme specimen of Everyman for all time. Marlowe's tragedy marked a new phase in human epistemology, the one in which man emerges from his initial total submission to external forces and awakens to his own importance and power and begins to assert himself. As he is human, his potential is circumscribed and he often ends up overreaching himself, but the striving endows his life with meaning and purpose and makes it worth living.

Formally, the play uses some dramatic devices like the choruses and the accompanying quarrels between the good angels and the evil ones. The three choruses in the play all serve to help guide the readers to keep track of the whereabouts of the man and his thought process. The constant verbal fights between the opposing angels serve at least two purposes, one of which is the indication they furnish for the readers that Faustus lives still in part in the traditional religious shadow. The other purpose is that they help externalize the continual inner struggle that goes on in Faustus' mind, or his incessant interior dialogue. It is obvious that Faustus debates within himself all the while whether it is worthwhile doing what he is doing.

Marlowe was a daring Renaissance humanist. His plays show, in various ways, the spirit of the rising bourgeoisie, its eager curiosity for knowledge, its towering pride, and its insatiable appetite for power whether that be won by military might, knowledge or gold. This is well expressed in Marlowe's overreaching protagonists including the three tragic heroes in his major plays, who, cosmic in appetite and behavior, defy all limitations and crave for the best of all in the universe. These heroes are generally distinguished by a resolute character, a scorn of orthodox-creeds and an overpowering passion; in Tamburlaine, it is ambition; in Doctor Faustus, desire for knowledge; in the Jew of Malta, greed for wealth. All these were typical of the Elizabethan era, an era of the primitive accumulation of capital.

Through these impressive protagonists Marlowe evidently praised individuality freed from the restraints of medieval dogmas and law, and the conviction of the boundless possibility of human efforts in conquering the universe. There is a combination of the soaring aspiration after power and knowledge and beauty in their ideal forms, and the bold, critical, analytic spirit which leads to the questioning of all old traditions and standards of conduct. Man's reason and power is everything. This is the progressive side of the young bourgeois ideal. However, the heroes in Marlowe's plays are merely individualists. Their individualistic ambition often brings ruin to the world and to themselves.

Marlowe was the greatest of the pioneers of English drama. He reformed the English drama and perfected the language and verse of dramatic works. It was Marlowe who first made blank verse the principal instrument of English drama. His blank verse is a living thing; it is vigorous, fluid and precise. It translates thoughts and emotions into rhythmical speech with happy exactness, thus interpreting the restlessly moving and questing spirit of the Renaissance. His blank verse has been described as "titanic" and compared to a swollen river sweeping down on its dried-up channel, filling its broad banks and moving on majestically.

Marlowe's dramatic achievement lies chiefly in his epical, and at time lyrical, verse. He rarely supplied a model in dramatic technicalities. In his plays there is a lack of variety in characterization and construction. But he was famous for his mighty and plastic line.

9.4 William Shakespeare (1564 – 1616)

Shakespeare, an English poet, playwright and actor, has been universally acknowledged as the summit of the English renaissance, the greatest writer in the English language and the world's preeminent dramatist. He is often called England's national poet and the "Bard of Avon." His extant works consist of about 38 plays including two collaborations, 154 sonnets, two long narrative poems, and a few other verses, of which the authorship of some is uncertain. His plays have been translated into every major living language and are performed more often than those of any other playwright.

Shakespeare's literary career may be roughly divided into three periods. The earliest period (1590/1588 – 1600) is generally accepted as the period of his apprenticeship in play-writing, during which he made experiments in a number of dramatic forms like historical plays, varieties of comedy, and the romantic tragedy. The works produced in this period are generally happy and cheerful. They include nine of his ten historical plays (except *Henry VIII*), two of his well-known early tragedies (*Romeo and Juliet*, 1594 and *Julius Caesar*, 1599), and all his "romantic" comedies, among which are his four mature, "romantic" comedies—*The Merchant of Venice* (1596), *Much Ado about Nothing* (1598), *As You Like It* (1599) and *Twelfth Night* (1600). The nine historical plays are *Henry IV* (Parts I and II, 1597), *Henry V* (1598), *Henry VI* (Parts I, 1591; Parts II and III, 1590), *Richard II* (1595), *Richard III* (1592) and *King John* (1596). During this period he also wrote two narrative poems, *Venus and Adonis* (1593) and *The Rape of Lucrece* (1594). The first period showed a general tendency of the gradual diminishing and disappearance of rhyme as the principal impediment in Shakespeare's dramatic composition. With the influence of Marlowe, Shakespeare began to use blank verse as the primary form of poetry in his play-writing. Under his hands, blank verse developed into a happy vehicle to express all kinds of thought and emotion freely.

The second period (1601 - 1608) is the most important period in Shakespeare's literary career, mainly a period of "great tragedies" and "dark comedies." He produced his great tragedies like *Othello* (1604), *King Lear* (1605), *Hamlet* (1601), *Macbeth* (1605), *Troilus and Cressida* (1602), *Timon of Athens* (1607), and others, and two comedies—*All's Well That Ends Well* (1603) and *Measure for Measure* (1604). Besides, Shakespeare wrote some of his tragicomedies. In the plays of this period, the tragic note was aggravated. The sunshine and laughter of the early period turned into clouds and storms. The cause of such a change should be sought from Shakespeare's change of moods as influenced by the social upheavals at the turn of the century as well as his personal tragedy, including the death of his only son. It was amid the atmosphere of general unrest that Shakespeare wrote his great tragedies and "dark comedies," in which complicated social contradictions were mercilessly exposed. Whereas the tragedies are full of scenes of murder, lust, treachery, ingratitude and crime, the comedies give somber pictures of the world.

The third period, stretching from 1609 to 1612/1613, witnessed Shakespeare's production of four romances or "reconciliation plays" including *Cymbeline* (1609), *The Winter's Tale* (1610), *The Tempest* (1611) as well as the collaboration *Pericles, Prince of Tyre* (1609) and his last historical play *Henry VIII* (1612). Here Shakespeare turned to "a great peacefulness of light" and a harmony of earth and heaven from the storm, the gloom and the whirlwind of the previous period. The tone of calm and reconciliation of this period might not only have something to do with the change of life and mood in the later years of Shakespeare but also the decline of the stage during the reign of James I (1566 - 1625, king 1603 - 1625). So the scenes of reunion of husband and wife, the love of fathers for their daughters, and their watchful care over their children's destiny may reflect his renewed life with his wife and his loving care of his own daughters. Shakespeare placed his hopes and aspirations with the future of mankind.

In his comedies Shakespeare portrayed numerous young people who had just freed themselves from the feudal fetters. He sang of their youth, their love and ideal of happiness. The heroes and heroines are sons and daughters of the Renaissance. They trust not in God or King but in themselves. Usually there are two groups of characters in Shakespeare's comedies. The first group is composed of characters of young men and young women. They live in the world of youth and dreams and laughter, and fight for their happiness. The second group consists of simple and shrewd clowns and other common people. These characters make the play full of humor and laughter. The success of Shakespeare's comedies owes much to the appearance of clowns, without whom the plays would have become dull and humorless.

Shakespeare put women characters at a prominent place in his comedies. He showed great respect for the dignity, honesty, wit, courage, determination and resourcefulness of women. The young heroines in his comedies are independent in character and very frank. They are no longer controlled by their parents or husbands. They are a new type. They are happy and make others happy. They carry their destinies in their hands. In speaking, thinking and feeling they are equal or even superior to men. Shakespeare's comedies are imbued with bourgeois ideas and show progressive significance.

Shakespeare produced 16 comedies altogether. His main comedies are *A Midsummer Night's Dream* (1595), *The Merchant of Venice*, *Much Ado about Nothing*, *As You Like It*, *Twelfth Night* and *The Winter's Tale*. *The Winter's Tale* was originally published in the First Folio, which is used by modern scholars to refer to the 1623 collection of Shakespeare's plays titled *Mr. William Shakespeare's Comedies, Histories, & Tragedies*. Although it was grouped among the comedies, the play has been relabeled by some modern editors as one of Shakespeare's late romances. It is also considered to be one of Shakespeare's "problem plays" because the first three acts are filled with intense psychological drama while the last two acts are comedic and supply a happy ending.

A Midsummer Night's Dream is a beautiful fairy-tale combined with the story of the struggle for happiness of two pairs of lovers—Hermia and Lysander, and Helena and Demetrius. The play is full of delightful fancy and fun and ends with happy nuptials. It is the most lyrical of all Shakespeare's plays, in which elements of Greek mythology are fancifully combined with those of British folklore. The play is one of Shakespeare's most popular works for the stage and is widely performed across the world.

Much Ado about Nothing is generally considered one of Shakespeare's best comedies, because it combines elements of robust hilarity with more serious meditations on honor, shame and court politics. Although interspersed with darker concerns, the play is a joyful comedy that ends with multiple marriages and no deaths. By means of "noting," which, in Shakespeare's day, sounded the same as "nothing," and which is gossip, rumor and overhearing, Benedick and Beatrice are tricked into confessing their love for each other, and Claudio is tricked into rejecting Hero at the altar on the erroneous belief that she has been unfaithful. At the end, Benedick and Beatrice join forces to set things right, and the others join in a dance celebrating the marriages of the two couples.

Twelfth Night centers on the twins Viola and Sebastian, who are separated in a shipwreck. Viola, who is disguised as a boy, falls in love with Duke Orsino, who in turn is in love with the Countess Olivia. Upon meeting Viola, Countess Olivia falls in love with her thinking she is a man. The play expands on the musical interludes and riotous disorder expected of the occasion, with plot elements drawn from the short story "Of Apollonius and Silla" by Barnabe Rich (c. 1540 – 1617). The play was not published until its inclusion in the First Folio.

The Merchant of Venice, though classified as a comedy in the First Folio and sharing certain aspects with Shakespeare's other romantic comedies, is perhaps most remembered for its dramatic scenes and is best known for Shylock and the famous "Hath Not a Jew eyes?" speech. Also notable is Portia's speech about "the quality of mercy." Bassanio is considered as the central hero of the story, and his dearest friend Antonio, the title character, mainly described as the kindest man in this world.

The story is of Italian origin. Young Bassanio, who needs money to win the hand of the rich young heiress Portia, comes to Antonio for help. Antonia, with no ready cash, goes to Shylock, the Jewish usurer, who has been at odds with Antonio because of the competition and racial discrimination he has suffered. The Jew decides to loan the money but asks Antonio to sign a bond which demands a pound of flesh from him in case he fails to pay in time. With the money Bassanio wins Portia, but Antonio is in trouble. His ships wreck, leaving him in a great quandary: he is unable to meet the deadline for the payment. Now Shylock insists on having his pound of flesh to have his revenge on Antonio and his friends. At a critical moment at court when the Jew is about to have his way, Portia arrives in disguise as a young lawyer and points out that, as the bond mentions nothing of blood, the flesh should be exactly one pound cut without bloodshed, and that any blood or difference in weight will be an offense to the law for which Shylock will receive severe punishment. Shylock's scheme is thus foiled. Nor is this all for him. He is then accused of conspiring against a Venetian, and, as a consequence, loses all his wealth, half to the state and half to Antonio. Antonio gives up his share on condition that Shylock embraces the Christian faith and gives the money to Jessica, Shylock's runaway daughter. Jessica becomes a Christian and her husband inherits half of Shylock's property.

The Merchant of Venice was staged at a time when a high anti-Semitic mood prevailed in England, so its happy ending of triumph of the Christian over the Jewish faith pleased the Elizabethan in general. Shylock, an archetype of vice, is created to body forth the sum total of social and human evil and is eventually brought to justice. His ending functions well as the effective proof of the moral nature of the universe. The audiences of successive generations have tended to come away with the impressions of the Jew's vengeance, his cruelty and his malice, along with the sense of gratification of the good guys winning over the bad.

Many modern readers and theatergoers have read the play as a plea for tolerance, noting that Shylock is a sympathetic character. They cite as evidence that Shylock's "trial" at the end of the play is a mockery of justice, with Portia acting as a judge when she has no right to do so. The characters who berated Shylock for dishonesty resort to trickery in order to win. It is difficult to know whether the sympathetic reading of Shylock is entirely due to changing sensibilities among readers, or whether Shakespeare, a writer who created complex, multi-faceted characters, deliberately intended this reading. One of the reasons for this interpretation is that Shylock's painful status in Venetian society is emphasized. To some critics, Shylock's celebrated "Hath Not a Jew eyes?" speech redeems him and even makes him into something of a tragic figure; in the speech, Shylock argues that he is no different from the Christian characters. Shylock ends the speech with a tone of revenge: "if you wrong us, shall we not revenge?" Those who see the speech as sympathetic point out that Shylock says he learned the desire for revenge from the Christian characters.

As You Like It was first published in the First Folio. Adapted from the prose romance *Rosalynd* (1590) by Thomas Lodge (c. 1558 – 1625), the play is romantic and pastoral. It is one of the most charming comedies of Shakespeare and embraces almost all of the important characteristics of a comedy. There are two main characters—Orlando and Rosalind. The story centers on the love affair between them. The scene is laid in one of the provinces in France. The duke of that place has been driven out of his throne by his brother and lives in banishment. The usurper Frederick now becomes the new king of the kingdom. The banished duke has a daughter called Rosalind, who has not gone with her father and still lives in the court, for she cannot tear herself away from her cousin Celia because they have been intimate friends since their infancy. One day, there is a wrestling match in the court, to which young Orlando, an orphan, comes. Rosalind goes to watch it. Orlando's wicked elder brother Oliver has instigated a wrestler to kill Orlando, but is killed by Orlando. Rosalind and Orlando meet and fall in love with each other at first sight. Then Frederick banishes Rosalind from the court. She dresses herself as a boy and goes to the forest with her good friend Celia. Orlando follows them and joins the exiled Duke. The young lovers meet in the forest. Oliver, coming to kill Orlando, is saved by Orlando from a hungry lioness, so repents and is accepted by Celia. At the nuptial of Celia and Oliver in the presence of the old Duke, Rosalind appears in her wedding frock, to the happy surprise of all. The usurper Frederick, converted by "an old religious man," gives up the dukedom to Rosalind's father.

Historically, critical response has varied, with some critics finding the work of lesser quality than other Shakespearean works and some finding the play a work of great merit. The play features one of Shakespeare's most famous and oft-quoted speeches, "All the world's a stage." The play remains a favorite among audiences and has been adapted for radio, film and musical theatre.

Shakespeare's most famous plays are his tragedies, especially the four great tragedies—*Hamlet*, *Othello*, *King Lear* and *Macbeth*. He completed 12 tragedies in total. His great tragedies are associated with a period of gloom and sorrow in his life. They express a profound dissatisfaction with life and show the struggle and conflicts between good and evil, and between justice and injustice. The dark and evil society of the time is condemned in these plays.

The Tragedy of Hamlet, Prince of Denmark (often shortened to *Hamlet*) is Shakespeare's longest play and among the most powerful and influential tragedies in English literature, with a story capable of "seemingly endless retelling and adaptation by others." (Thompson, 2006: 74) The play seems to have been one of Shakespeare's most popular works during his lifetime and still ranks among his most-performed, topping the performance list of the Royal Shakespeare Company and its predecessors in Stratford-upon-Avon since 1879. It has inspired writers from Goethe and Dickens to Joyce and Murdoch, and has been described as "the world's most filmed story after *Cinderella*." (Thompson, 2006: 17)

The story of *Hamlet* is from an old Danish legend and is fairly simple in outline. The play dramatizes the revenge Hamlet, the young prince of Denmark, is instructed to enact on his uncle Claudius. Hamlet learns through his father's ghost the truth about his uncle Claudius' fratricide and usurpation of the throne, and feels furious over this and his mother's hasty marriage to the new king. In order to make sure that the spirit is really the ghost of his father rather than an evil spirit posing as his father, he stages in the palace a play, the plot of which resembles his uncle's act of murder. When watching it, Claudius is shaken, and Hamlet knows instantly that the man is the culprit. Then he kills Polonius, mistaking him for Claudius. He is sent to England to be executed, but manages to escape and return home. In a duel with Laertes, Polonius' son, arranged by Claudius, he is fatally wounded but does not die before he kills his rival and his uncle. Altogether six lives are lost in the confusion. An interesting subplot concerns the love between Hamlet and Ophelia, Polonius' daughter. Because of the tension Hamlet feels against her father, the girl gets caught in between the two important men of her life, loses her mind and dies in misery.

The secret of Shakespeare's success in *Hamlet* lies chiefly in the fact that he injected the thrilling renaissance spirit into the story. Specifically, Shakespeare expressed his own humanist ideas through the portrayal of Hamlet, a multifaceted Renaissance idealist and the representative of humanism, made to face a world of debilitating evil and having to learn to deal with it before he is ready. All of his "antic-disposition," his feigning insanity and his momentary but true madness, and his impulsive action stem from the thinking mind of a Renaissance humanist as he picks up wisdom and fast matures to act properly. The other characters are similarly deftly transformed from the stock characters of the other versions of the story into complex individuals of this play, so that they all serve to rivet attention on Hamlet and enrich his personality. As a result, Shakespeare' Hamlet is no longer the mere agent of revenge and violence. Although his first priority is to avenge his father's death, this Hamlet has now a much larger and more worthy ideal, i. e. the Renaissance humanist ideal, which he knows sadly is lost to him and would probably never again be retrieved. He would still assert man's power—his noble reason and infinite faculties; he would still help mend the social ills and save a society that is "out of joint"; but he knows that he is fighting a losing battle. He keenly feels that he is not born at the right time, and that reality is so sinister and overwhelming that it is probably not worthwhile fighting it out any more. Viewed in this way, the theme of the story assumes a much graver magnitude than one of mere blood and violence. The corrupt and criminal ancient Danish court versus Prince Hamlet becomes, in the hands of Shakespeare, a metaphor for—or a mirror reflection of—the real world of Shakespeare's England in confrontation with Renaissance humanism. Shakespeare showed his great creative abilities in writing this play, which is usually regarded as the summit of the author's art.

It is very likely that Shakespeare borrowed something from Thomas Kyd's *The Spanish Tragedy* and *Ur-Hamlet*, though some scholars believe Shakespeare himself wrote the *Ur-Hamlet*, later revising it to create the version of *Hamlet* we now have. Three different early versions of the play are extant—the First Quarto (Q1, 1603), the Second Quarto (Q2, 1604) and the First Folio (F1, 1623). Each version includes lines and even entire scenes, missing from the others. The play's structure and depth of characterization have inspired much critical scrutiny. One such example is the centuries-old debate about Hamlet's hesitation to kill his uncle, which some see as merely a plot device to prolong the action, but which others argue is a dramatization of the complex philosophical and ethical issues that surround cold-blooded murder, calculated revenge and thwarted desire. More recently, psychoanalytic critics have examined Hamlet's unconscious desires, and feminist critics have re-evaluated and rehabilitated the often maligned characters of Ophelia and Gertrude.

The Tragedy of Othello, the Moor of Venice is a tightly-constructed work revolving around four central characters—Othello, a Moorish general in the Venetian army, his beloved wife Desdemona, his loyal lieutenant Cassio and his trusted but unfaithful ensign Iago. Because of its varied and current themes of racism, love, jealousy, betrayal, revenge and repentance, *Othello* is still often performed in professional and community theaters alike and has been the basis for numerous operatic, film and literary adaptations.

The story of *Othello* takes place in Venice and Cyprus. The hero Othello is a splendid general. In Venice he falls in love with a senator's beautiful daughter called Desdemona. In spite of the senator's objection they get married. Then Othello and Desdemona go to Cyprus and live happily together. Iago, who envies Othello's fame and happiness, wants to wreck Othello's happy life. He thinks out an evil plan. One day he tells Othello that his wife has betrayed him and fallen in love with his lieutenant Cassio. In order to prove what he said is true, Iago steals a handkerchief from the lady's chamber and secretly puts it into Cassio's hands. Thus Othello's suspicion is aroused. He becomes so suspicious that one night he strangles his wife. After that the truth comes to light. Othello becomes so remorseful that he kills himself at last. Shakespeare's principal innovation consists in the developing of the character of Iago the villain, who represents the dark power which crushes everything that is great and noble, and is also an artistic generalization of envy, selfishness, utter depravity and hypocrisy, concealed by good manners and a show of noble intentions.

Othello is a tragedy of humanism. The title character is a new man of the Renaissance and an incarnation of moral beauty. He loves Desdemona, who is young, beautiful, sincere and lofty-minded, and is rewarded with the love of his ideal wife. They live happily but they are too noble-minded to belong to the present world. Their tragedy shows that noble-minded people may be led astray by evil forces in an evil society and commit heinous mistakes if they cannot distinguish falsehood from truth, and evil from good.

King Lear is a well-constructed story of an old king's relationship with his daughters, which, taken from *Holinshed's Chronicles* (also known as *Holinshed's Chronicles of England, Scotland, and Ireland*, a collaborative work published in several volumes and two editions, the first in 1577, and the second in 1587), was based on the legend of Leir of Britain, a mythological pre-Roman Celtic king. King Lear has three daughters—Goneril, Regan and Cordelia. In his old age, he divides his kingdom and gives the shares away according to the protestations of love the girls cook up for him. Deceived by the flattery of Goneril and Regan, the king disposes of his estate between the two, leaving nothing to Cordelia who is unwilling to lie to her father. Then the indignant father marries Cordelia off to the King of France. But when they have got what they wanted, the two elder daughters mistreat their father and finally drive him out in storm. He goes insane. The King of France comes with an army to his rescue but suffers defeat, Cordelia is hanged, and Lear dies in agony. A parallel subplot runs on the loyalty of Kent, Gloucester, and Gloucester's estranged son Edgar, reinforcing the theme of the major plot.

Thematically, the play focuses on the protagonist's transformation from a self-willed despot through a humble discard to a compassionate old man with spiritual sublimity. Banished by his daughters, Lear wanders all night amidst storm and rain over a lonely heath; Great changes are wrought in his soul. He begins to have compassion for what he calls "houseless poverty," and eventually utters a protest against social inequality. The miseries of Lear disclose the essence of a corrupt society, in which each is ready to destroy the other. No images are more frequently met with in the play than the images of animals and beasts like the lion, the bear, the wolf, the fox, the dog, the monkey and the rat. This is a reflection of the jungle law of the age of primitive accumulation, symbolically presented with poignancy and power in the famous storm scene. The play also presents Shakespeare's affirmation of national unity and royal responsibility. The root of Lear's tragedy lies in his irresponsibly dividing up his kingdom. Here Shakespeare seems to point out that the king should be responsible for the people at any time. If, in one way or another, he betrays the people's trust, he is sure to be punished.

Of all Shakespeare's tragedies, *King Lear* is the most complex in plot and also the most painful. It is a sublime poem but an unstageable play. It has the exalted poetic dialogues, the frequent references to the lower animals and the comparison of man to animals. After the Restoration, the play was often revised with a happy ending for audiences who disliked its dark and depressing tone, but since the 19th century Shakespeare's original version has been regarded as one of his supreme achievements. The tragedy is particularly noted for its probing observations on the nature of human suffering and kinship. Some literary critics hold that *King Lear* is Shakespeare's greatest achievement. George Bernard Shaw once wrote, "No man will ever write a better tragedy than *Lear*." (qtd. in Wilson, 1961: 111) The play has been widely adapted for the stage and motion pictures, with the title role coveted by many of the world's most accomplished actors.

The Tragedy of Macbeth, Shakespeare's shortest and most compressed tragedy, is considered one of his darkest and most powerful works. It was most likely written during the reign of James I, who had been James VI of Scotland before he succeeded to the English throne in 1603. James was a patron of Shakespeare's acting company, and of all the plays Shakespeare wrote during James' reign, *Macbeth* most clearly reflects the playwright's relationship with the sovereign. The play was first published in the First Folio.

The story of *Macbeth* was borrowed from the account of Macbeth, King of Scotland, in *Holinshed's Chronicles*, which is a large, comprehensive description of the British history familiar to Shakespeare and his contemporaries; yet the events in the play differ extensively from the history of the real Macbeth. In recent scholarship, the events of the tragedy are usually associated more closely with the execution of Henry Garnett (1555 – 1606) for complicity in the Gunpowder Plot of 1605.

The play tells the story of a brave Scottish general named Macbeth who receives a prophecy from a trio of witches that one day he will become King of Scotland. Consumed by ambition and spurred to action by his wife, Macbeth murders King Duncan and takes the throne for himself. He is then wracked with guilt and paranoia, and soon becomes a tyrannical ruler as he is forced to commit more and more murders to protect himself from enmity and suspicion. The bloodbath and consequent civil war swiftly take Macbeth and Lady Macbeth into the realms of arrogance, madness and death. He is killed by the son of the murdered king. Set in Scotland, the play dramatizes the corrosive psychological and political effects produced when evil is chosen as a way to fulfill the ambition for power. Here Shakespeare condemned ambition. Macbeth's fate is that of all the ambitious rulers, who are doomed to be defeated in the end though they are strong in appearance.

The play is swift in action and simple in outline. The poetry is simple and intense. The language is violent and terrible. Over the course of many centuries, the play has attracted some of the most renowned actors to the roles of Macbeth and Lady Macbeth. It has been adapted to film, television, opera, novels, comic books, and other media.

Shakespeare is also noted for his historical plays. They are political plays, whose principal idea is the necessity for national unity under one sovereign. This idea was anti-feudal in nature and summed up the general opinion of the rising bourgeoisie in Shakespeare's day. Nine of Shakespeare's ten historical plays (except *King John*) cover the historical events of two centuries from Richard II (1367 – c. 1400, king 1377 – 1399) to Henry VIII. They show the horrors of civil war, the necessity for national unity, the responsibilities of an efficient ruler, and the importance of legitimate succession to the throne.

Like the majority of humanists of his time, Shakespeare believed in a wise and humane King who would live to serve his country. But, in the historical plays, Shakespeare's treatment of real English kings is extremely critical.

Richard II is condemned for his vanity, political blindness and inability to subdue the feudal lords. Richard III (1452 – 1485, king 1483 – 1485) is represented as a king strong-willed and vicious, who came to power through a series of horrible crimes and turned his country into a dungeon. Henry IV (1367 – 1413, king 1399 – 1413), though glorified for his suppression of the rebellion of feudal lords, is criticized for his participation in the murder of Richard II and his treacherous arrest of the rebels after the truce. Shakespeare created in these historical plays only one ideal king Henry V (1386 – 1422, king 1413 – 1422), though his real prototype differs little from the other kings. Thanks to Shakespeare's portrayal, Henry V, for English patriots of that time, was associated with the military victories of England in the Hundred Years' War and became a symbol of English glory in the eyes of the well-to-do citizens of England.

Among Shakespeare's historical plays, *Henry IV* and *Henry V* are two remarkable plays. *Henry V* is the continuation of *Henry IV*. The two plays deal with the events of the 15th century and give the picture of a troubled reign.

Henry IV includes two plays—*Henry IV, Part I* and *Henry IV, Part II*—in Shakespeare's tetralogy dealing with the successive reigns of Richard II, Henry IV and Henry V. Henry IV takes the crown from Richard II, but he never feels easy on the throne. His rebellious noblemen league against him and give him no rest. It's Henry's young son Prince Hal, the future Henry V, who leads the army to victory over the rebels. Shakespeare's primary source for *Henry IV*, as for most of his chronicle histories, was *Holinshed's Chronicles*. But he added life to the subject matter. Like the Elizabethan bourgeoisie, he stood for monarchy and unity. The subject of *Part I* is the rebellion of the Percy family and its defeat. This part is a mixture of the richest Shakespearian comedy with the finest Shakespearian history. It gives us the full blast of Shakespeare's genius in his maturity. The play features three groups of characters that interact slightly at first, and then come together in the Battle of Shrewsbury, where the success of the rebellion will be decided. First there is King Henry himself and his immediate council. He is the engine of the play, but usually in the background. Next there is the group of rebels, energetically embodied in Henry Percy and his father, the Earl of Northumberland, and led by his uncle Thomas Percy, Earl of Worcester. The Scottish Earl of Douglas, Edmund Mortimer and the Welshman Owen Glendower also join. Finally, at the center of the play are the young Prince Hal and his companions Falstaff, Poins, Bardolph and Peto. Streetwise and pound-foolish, these rogues manage to paint over this grim history in the colors of comedy. *Part II* is often seen as an extension of aspects of *Part I* rather than a straightforward continuation of the historical narrative, placing more emphasis on the highly popular character of Falstaff and introducing other comic figures as part of his entourage, including Ancient Pistol, Doll Tearsheet and Justice Robert Shallow. Several scenes specifically parallel episodes in *Part I*, but the mood in this part is grimmer, humor is less gay, and laughter dies.

Henry V tells the story of King Henry V of England, focusing on events immediately before and after the Battle of Agincourt (1415) during the Hundred Years' War. The play is the final part of the tetralogy, preceded by *Richard II*, *Henry IV, Part I* and *Henry IV, Part II*. The audiences would thus have already been familiar with the hero, who was depicted in the *Henry IV* plays as a wild, undisciplined lad known as "Prince Harry" and nicknamed "Hal" by his friend Falstaff. In *Henry V*, the young prince has become a mature man and embarks on a successful conquest of France. He represents the upsurging patriotism of the time. In depicting Henry V as a prince and as a man, Shakespeare looked deep into the personality of his hero and showed a profound understanding of politics and social life of the time. In a sense, Henry V represents Shakespeare's ideal of a good king and his aspiration for the national unity of England under a powerful and efficient monarchy.

Taken as a whole, Shakespeare's dramatic works share a lot both in content and form. First, all Shakespeare's plays, either histories or comedies and tragedies, are mirrors of his age. Shakespeare was a realist. He was one of the first founders of realism and a master at realistic portrayal of human characters and relations in English literature. Living in the transitional period from feudalism to capitalism, Shakespeare faithfully and vividly reflected the major contradictions of his time. His historical plays describe the decaying of the old feudal nobility and the rising of the new bourgeois spirit. His comedies reflect the life and love of the young men and women who just freed themselves from the fetters of feudalism and were striving for individual emancipation. The comedies lay emphasis on emancipation of women in particular. In his tragedies, Shakespeare depicted the life-and-death struggle between the humanists—the newly emerging forces—and the corrupted king and his feudal followers—the dark power of that time, and also the contradictions between the rich and the poor.

Second, the stories of Shakespeare's plays often took place in other countries or in the past rather than in England of his own age. He borrowed his plots either from Greek legends and Roman history, or from Italian stories and English chronicles. Sometimes he rewrote old plays by certain inferior writers. Whatever he touched sparkled with a peculiar beauty of its own. Old stories were thus turned into superb dramatic works. Although Shakespeare's characters are often clothed in old, foreign dresses, their thought and feelings and their attitudes toward life belong to the age of Shakespeare. These characters are, as a whole, representatives of the people of Renaissance England. And each of the main characters is a representative of a group of peaple. They are typical characters in typical situations. Their fundamental traits are revealed in their conflicts with their surroundings, in their relations with their fellowmen. These full-blooded characters, bearing manifold qualities, represent the complexities and implications of real life.

Next, Shakespeare's drama is elastic. His dramatic form fits the content of his plays very well. His plays are not controlled by the rules of the classical unities of time, place and action. The action develops freely from place to place and covers either several days, or several weeks, or even many years. A single play may contain more than one theme, and the main plot always exists side by side with the subplot(s). In order to reproduce the manifold images of real life, Shakespeare used peculiar combination in his drama—combination of the majestic and the funny, of the poetic and the prosaic, and of the tragic and the comic. Shakespeare was especially at home with the dramatic blank verse, which is the principal form of his drama. In his hand, blank verse became a most flexible means of expression to utter all the possible thoughts and feelings of his characters. Shakespeare was also skilled in such poetic forms as the sonnet and the couplet.

Another salient feature concerning Shakespeare's plays is his great mastery of the English language. The language of each of his characters fits his position in society and reveals the peculiarities of his character. Many of his coinages and turns of expression have become everyday usage in English life. Shakespeare and *King James Bible* (1611) are the two great reservoirs of Modern English.

Finally, Shakespeare's character-portrayal features his emphasis on the psychological make-up of each of his major characters. The character's inner world is well reflected through the exquisite soliloquy.

Shakespeare's poetical works include two long narrative poems—*Venus and Adonis*, *The Rape of Lucrece*—and 154 sonnets written in the 1590s. The sonnets were first published as a collection in 1609. They may be divided into three groups: the first 126 seem to be addressed to a young man, the last two read like free translations of a Greek poem of the 5th century, and the rest seem to be concerned with a "dark lady" who played the poet false. In the first group the first 17 urge the young man to marry to reproduce his beauty and numbers 18 to 126 form a sequence of 109 sonnets, a number close to Sidney's sequence *Astrophel and Stella*. In the sequence, the poet enjoys his friendship and is full of admiration, promising to bestow immortality on the young man by the poems he writes in his honor. The climax of the series comes when the young man seduces the poet's mistress. But eventually the poet reconciles himself to the situation and realizes that his love for his friend is greater than his desire to keep the woman. Soon after the publication, the sonnets drew instant attention and were ranked among the most excellent of Elizabethan poetry for their mastery of diction, grace in form, depth in thought and vivacity in tone. They are peerless in freshness, poetical beauty and human interest. Each of Shakespeare's sonnets or Shakespearean sonnet is made up of three quatrains with different rhymes, followed by a couplet. Each line is in iambic pentameter. The rhyme scheme is abab cdcd efef gg.

9.5 Ben Jonson (c. 1572 – 1637)

Jonson was an English playwright, poet and literary critic of the 17th century, whose artistry exerted a lasting impact upon English poetry and stage comedy. He popularized the comedy of humors and is generally accepted as the founder of comedies of manners in English literature. He was the last great Elizabethan playwright and the first literary dictator in English history. Of the many contemporaries and successors of Shakespeare, the best known was Ben Jonson. His stature as a poet is no less imposing. His reputation as a playwright was established by the success of his first comedy *Every Man in His Humor* (1598).

Jonson was a classically educated, well-read and cultured man of the English Renaissance with an appetite for controversy (personal and political, artistic and intellectual) whose cultural influence was of unparalleled breadth upon the playwrights and the poets of the Jacobean era (1603 – 1625) and of the Caroline era (1625 – 1642). He is remembered today chiefly as a satirical playwright. Of his 18 plays, the best include *Every Man in His Humor*, *Volpone, or The Fox* (1605), *The Alchemist* (1610), *Bartholomew Fayre: A Comedy* (1614) and *The Sad Shepherd, or A Tale of Robin Hood* (1641). As a poet, Jonson is known for his lyric poetry.

Every Man in His Humor is Jonson's first play and a key to all his plays. The word "humor" in the title is used in the sense of "essential temperament" to denote that everyone has a basic character trait in his personality. To his leading characters Jonson gave some prominent humor and exaggerated it that all other qualities are lost sight of. The special aim of the play was to ridicule the humors of the city, lash the variously-exaggerated caprices of persons and disclose the vanity of society. In the play many human foibles—jealousy, undue worry, credulity and boasting—are satirized.

The main character Kitely is a merchant and jealous husband, fearing that his young wife is cuckolding him with some of the riotous but harmless gallants brought to his home by his brother-in-law Wellbred. One of these young men Edward Knowell, whose father's "humor" is excessive concern for his son's morals, is not indifferent to young Bridget, Kitely's sister. Bodadill, one of Jonson's greatest creations and Kitely's friend, is a "Paul's man" and a boastful cowardly soldier with an immense capacity for mischief. Dame Kitely, when put on the spot, can be vigilant and credulous. The villain is Knowell's servant, the cunning Brainworm, who plans, through the devices and disguises in which Babodill gets involved, for the Kitelys to meet at a house where, when face to face, they each suspect the other of having some ulterior designs. Eventually, Babodill is exposed and beaten; Knowell marries Bridget. The misunderstandings are cleared up by the shrewd and kindly Justice Clement. In a word, the play tells the story of a jealous husband, a credulous young wife and a boasting coward soldier, and gives readers an excellent study of the "humor" (i. e., temperaments or dispositions) of various characters and the contemporary manners. It is basically an effort to amuse and entertain. Besides, Jonson added a prologue, which gives an exposition of his dramatic theory.

The details of the plot, are, however, less important than the style of the play. The play follows out the implicit rejection of the romantic comedy of his peers. It sticks quite carefully to the Aristotelian unities; the plot is a tightly woven mesh of act and reaction; the scenes a genial collection of depictions of everyday life in a large Renaissance city.

Volpone, or The Fox is the most excellent satirical comedy written by Jonson. Drawing on elements of city comedy and beast fable, the play is a merciless satire of greed and lust, and remains Jonson's most-performed play. It is ranked among the finest comedies of the Jacobean Era. The hero Volpone is a rich Venetian without children but a miser greedy of money for its own sake. His method of increasing his wealth is to play upon the avarice of men. He feigns that he is dying, in order to draw gifts from his would-be heirs. His "suitors" endeavor hypocritically to sweeten his last moments. But Volpone, wishing to enjoy a general disappointment to the full, draws up a will, in which he bequeaths all his property to his servant Mosca. The latter, also a cunning fellow, avails himself of the will, proclaims his master dead, and, as his heir, claims possession of Volpone's wealth. But in the end both knaves are exposed and receive due punishment. Volpone is imprisoned and his property confiscated while Mosca is condemned to penal servitude in the galleys.

This comedy is a keen and merciless analysis of a man governed by an overwhelming love of money. Jonson wrote this play to attack cupidity, to show to what infamous depth avarice will lead the greedy and cunning men. The satirical edge of the play is obvious: Jonson was a ruthless satirist as he set out to help people recognize their faults and improve their nature. The names of the play are highly suggestive of the predatory nature of human life: Volpone means "fox," Mosca "fly," Voltore "vulture," and Corvino "raven," all out to harm others for selfish ends. In formal terms the play observes the theory of the unities, with a single plot occurring in one day in the same place Venice.

The Alchemist is generally considered Jonson's best and most characteristic comedy. Its clever fulfillment of the classical unities and vivid depiction of human folly have made it one of the few Renaissance plays (except the works of Shakespeare) with a continuing life on stage (except for a period of neglect during the Victorian era). In the play, with the aid of two rascals, a servant who is left in charge of a big house sets himself up as an alchemist and cheats a number of persons by promising them the philosopher's stone. This story is an exposure of dupers and the duped. It satirizes those people who let themselves cheated by the hope of sudden riches.

Jonson's plays are in strong contrast with those of Shakespeare and the later Elizabethan dramatists. He fought with the romantic tendency of the age and to restore the classic standards. The whole action of his drama usually covers only a few hours or a single day. He tried through his writings to bring the classic form of the three unities back to the stage. He insisted on an adherence to the unities of time, place and action. His plays are carefully and logically constructed.

Jonson was a realistic writer. His comedies are worth careful reading because they are intensely realistic and present men and women of the time exactly as they are. His plays may not approach those by Shakespeare and Marlowe in the depth of thought and the poetic quality of language, but they are the best as leverages of satire on reality. For Jonson, a play should be realistic, showing "an image of the times." Characters should be selected to illustrate particular "humors." Comedies should portray manners and follies, and thus could expose, ridicule and censure life. In this way, Jonson attempted to stop the theater from going downhill to immorality and evil. He rejected the admixture of comedy and tragedy, and thought romantic comedy and chronicle history full of absurdities.

If Jonson's reputation as a playwright has traditionally been linked to Shakespeare, his reputation as a poet has, since the early 20th century, been linked to that of John Donne. In this comparison, Jonson represented the cavalier strain of poetry, emphasizing grace and clarity of expression; Donne, by contrast, epitomized the Metaphysical school of poetry, with its reliance on strained, baroque metaphors and often vague phrasing. Since the critics who made this comparison were, to varying extents, rediscovering Donne, this comparison often worked to the detriment of Jonson's reputation.

In his time Jonson was at least as influential as Donne. He was once named the best and most polished English poet in the Jacobean era. Jonson was described as the "father" of cavalier poets. Even those poets whose accomplishments in verse are generally regarded as superior to Jonson's took inspiration from his revival of classical forms and themes, his subtle melodies and his disciplined use of wit. In these respects Jonson may be regarded as among the most important figures in the prehistory of English Neoclassicism. Jonson largely avoided the debates about rhyme and meter that had consumed Elizabethan classicists. Accepting both rhyme and stress, Jonson used them to mimic the classical qualities of simplicity, restraint and precision.

The best of Jonson's lyrics have remained current since his time. For the general reader, Jonson's reputation rests on a few lyrics—"On My First Sonne," "To Celia," "To Penshurst" and the epitaph on boy player Solomon Pavy—that, though brief, are surpassed for grace and precision by very few Renaissance poems.

Exercises

I. Multiple choices

1. The epoch of Renaissance witnessed a particular development of _____.

    A. English novel   B. English drama

    C. English essay   D. English novel and poetry

2. In the history of English literature the "Age of Shakespeare" roughly refers to the age of _____.

    A. Enlightenment   B. Renaissance

    C. Romanticism   D. Critical Realism

Part Three The Renaissance Period

3. The keynote of Renaissance is _____.

   A. reason
   B. individuality
   C. humanism
   D. truth

4. The Renaissance originated in north _____ in the 14th century.

   A. England
   B. Germany
   C. Denmark
   D. Italy

5. _____ is generally accepted as the most interesting lyric poet of the first half of the 16th century.

   A. Thomas Wyatt
   B. Philip Sydney
   C. William Shakespeare
   D. Edmund Spenser

6. Thomas Wyatt frequently translated and imitated the sonnets of the great 14th-century Italian poet Petrarch and was usually credited with introducing the _____ into English.

   A. heroic couplet
   B. Spenserian stanza
   C. blank verse
   D. sonnet

7. One of Surrey's important contributions to English literature is his introduction of _____ into English poetry in his translations of Book II and Book IV of Virgil's *Aeneid*.

   A. heroic couplet
   B. Spenserian stanza
   C. blank verse
   D. sonnet

8. _____, due to their excellent translations of Petrarch's sonnets, are together known as "Fathers of the English Sonnet."

   A. Surrey and Wyatt
   B. Wyatt and Shakespeare
   C. Surrey and Sidney
   D. Sidney and Spenser

9. In English poetry, a four-line stanza is called a _____.

   A. heroic couplet
   B. quatrain
   C. Spenserian stanza
   D. terza rima

10. _____ is one of the earliest English literary essays.

    A. *An Apology for Poetry*
    B. *Morte d'Arthur*
    C. *Arcadia*
    D. *Astrophel and Stella*

11. _____, Philip Sidney's most ambitious literary work, exists in two significantly different versions.

    A. *An Apology for Poetry*
    B. *Morte d'Arthur*
    C. *Arcadia*
    D. *Astrophel and Stella*

12. _____ was England's first philosophical defense which describes the ancient and indispensable place of poetry in society, its mimetic nature and its ethical function.

    A. *An Apology for Poetry*
    B. *Morte d'Arthur*
    C. *Arcadia*
    D. *Astrophel and Stella*

13. _____ is a grand epic poem and fantastical allegory celebrating the Tudor Dynasty and Elizabeth I and one of the longest poems in the English language.

    A. *Prothalamion*
    B. *The Faerie Queene*

  C. *Amoretti*   D. *The Shepherd's Calendar*

14. _____ is the origin of a verse form that came to be known as Spenserian stanza.

  A. *Prothalamion*   B. *The Faerie Queene*

  C. *Amoretti*   D. *The Shepherd's Calendar*

15. In addition to his well-known plays, Shakespeare also wrote a large number of _____ and remembered as a great poet.

  A. odes   B. sonnets

  C. elegies   D. epics

16. Karl Marx once regarded Aeschylus and _____ as "the two greatest dramatic geniuses the world has ever known."

  A. William Shakespeare   B. R. B. Sheridan

  C. Bernard Shaw   D. Henry Fielding

17. _____ is considered the summit of Shakespeare's art and is the profoundest expression of the author's humanism and his criticism of contemporary life.

  A. *Hamlet*   B. *Twelfth Night*

  C. *King Lear*   D. *Macbeth*

18. William Shakespeare's four great tragedies are *Hamlet*, *Othello*, _____ and _____.

  A. *King Lear*, *Romeo and Juliet*   B. *King Lear*, *Macbeth*

  C. *King John*, *Julius Caesar*   D. *King John*, *The Merchant of Venice*

19. _____ (first written in Latin in 1516) is Thomas More's masterpiece, written in the form of a conversation between More and a returned sailor.

  A. *The Faerie Queene*   B. *Utopia*

  C. *Arcadia*   D. *Astrophel and Stella*

20. *The Unfortunate Traveler* by _____ is a medley of picaresque narrative, literary parody and mock-historical fantasy.

  A. Thomas Nashe   B. John Lyly

  C. William Shakespeare   D. Thomas More

21. Among Francis Bacon's essays, the famous pieces are _____, "Of Travel" and "Of Wisdom."

  A. *The Faerie Queene*   B. *Utopia*

  C. "Of Studies"   D. *Julius Caesar*

22. *The Spanish Tragedy* by _____ was often referred to or parodied in works written by other Elizabethan playwrights.

  A. Christopher Marlowe   B. Ben Jonson

  C. William Shakespeare   D. Thomas Kyd

23. _____ is accepted as the greatest playwright before William Shakespeare and the most gifted of the University Wits in English literature.

  A. Christopher Marlowe   B. John Lyly

C. Ben Jonson D. Thomas More

24. _____ was the only dramatist of the Renaissance period who ever touched William Shakespeare in power and beauty in English literature.

A. Ben Jonson B. Thomas More
C. Christopher Marlowe D. John Lyly

25. *Tamburlaine the Great*, a dream vision in blank verse, pushed _____ instantly to prominence.

A. William Shakespeare B. Ben Jonson
C. Christopher Marlowe D. John Lyly

26. _____ is NOT among Christopher Marlowe's best plays.

A. *Tamburlaine the Great* B. *The Jew of Malta*
C. *The Tragical History of Doctor Faustus* D. *As You Like It*

27. It is _____ who first made blank verse the principal instrument of English drama.

A. William Shakespeare B. Thomas More
C. Christopher Marlowe D. John Lyly

28. William Shakespeare's main comedies include *The Merchant of Venice*, *A Midsummer Night's Dream*, *Much Ado about Nothing*, *As You Like It*, _____ and *The Twelfth Night*.

A. *Venus and Adonis* B. *The Winter's Tale*
C. *The Rape of Lucrece* D. *The Jew of Malta*

29. *King Lear* is a well-constructed story of an old king's relationship with his _____.

A. subjects B. daughters
C. chancellors D. sons

30. In _____, William Shakespeare condemned ambition. The hero's fate is that of all the ambitious rulers, who are doomed to be defeated in the end though they are strong in appearance.

A. *The Merchant of Venice* B. *Hamlet*
C. *Macbeth* D. *King Lear*

31. The principal idea of William Shakespeare's historical plays is the necessity for national unity under one sovereign, which summed up the general opinion of the _____ in Shakespeare's own day.

A. aristocracy B. working class
C. proletariat D. rising bourgeoisie

32. Ben Jonson, the last great Elizabethan playwright and the first literary dictator in English history, popularized the _____.

A. comedy of humors B. tragicomedy
C. romantic comedy D. English drama

33. Of Ben Jonson's 18 plays, the best include _____, *Volpone* and *The Sad Shepherd*.

A. *Every Man in His Humor* B. *The Jew of Malta*
C. *Julius Caesar* D. *Tamburlaine the Great*

34. The names of the play *Volpone* are highly suggestive of the predatory nature of human life: Volpone means

"_____," Mosca "_____," Voltore "vulture," and Corvino "raven," all out to harm others for selfish ends.

  A. fox; fly   B. wolf; fly

  C. fly; penguin   D. fox; penguin

II. Blank-filling

1. Surrey's metrical innovations are very important in English poetry. He was the first to give the _____ its English form, which was used by William Shakespeare later.

2. _____ is accepted as the "poet's poet" and the greatest non-dramatic poet of the Elizabethan era.

3. Edmund Spenser's fame in English literature is chiefly based upon his masterpiece _____, a long poem planned in twelve books, of which he finished only six.

4. In *The Faerie Queene*, the knights as a whole symbolize _____, and the evil figures stand for her enemies.

5. The dominating thoughts of *The Faerie Queene* are nationalism (as shown in its celebration of Queen Elizabeth), _____ (as shown in its strong opposition to Roman Catholicism) and Puritanism (as shown in its moral teaching).

6. It is Edmund Spenser's idealism, his love of beauty and his exquisite melody that make him known as the "_____."

7. Edmund Spenser's best-known poem *The Shepherd's Calendar* consists of 12 _____ poems or eclogues, which are assigned to the twelve months of a year.

8. Edmund Spenser's *Amoretti* is a series of about 90 _____ in which he linked each quatrain to the next by a continuing rhyme: abab bcbc cdcd ee. This form is usually called _____.

9. "Utopia," used by Thomas More to name his ideal society, comes from two Greek words meaning "_____."

10. John Lyly wrote poetry, court comedies and _____.

11. As a prose writer, John Lyly was famous for his prose romance _____.

12. Generally speaking, the development of the early English drama experienced three periods: religious period, moral period and _____ period.

13. The story of *Hamlet* comes from an old _____ legend.

14. _____ is usually regarded as the summit of Shakespeare's art.

15. In *The Tragical History of Doctor Faustus*, the image of Faustus is historically significant as a "photo" record of the new man, the modern man, the Renaissance _____, who steps into modern light with all the glitter of Reformation and Renaissance.

16. Christopher Marlowe's plays show, in various ways, the spirit of the _____, its eager curiosity for knowledge, its towering pride, and its insatiable appetite for power whether that be won by military might, knowledge, or gold.

17. The theme of Christopher Marlowe's plays is the praise of _____ freed from the restraints of medieval dogmas and law, and the conviction of the boundless possibility of human efforts in conquering the universe.

18. The heroes in Christopher Marlowe's plays are merely _____. Their individualistic ambition often

brings ruin to the world and to themselves.

19. _____ is the essence of the Renaissance. But in the medieval society, people as individuals were largely subordinated to the feudalist rule without any _____ and _____; and in medieval theology, people's relationships to the world were largely reduced to a problem of adapting to or avoiding the circumstances of _____ in an effort to prepare their souls for a _____.

20. The early stage of the English Renaissance was one of _____ and _____.

21. _____, the first important English essayist, is best known for his essays which greatly influenced the development of this literary form.

22. Apart from Humanism, another important part of Renaissance movement was the _____, which was initiated by _____ (1483 – 1546), a German Protestant.

23. _____, in its totality, is the real mainstream of the English Renaissance.

24. As the most gifted of the University Wits, _____ wrote six plays within his short lifetime.

25. William Shakespeare's major characters are neither merely _____ nor _____; they are individuals representing certain types. Each character has his/her own personalities; meanwhile, they may share features with others. By employing a _____ approach, Shakespeare succeeded in exploring the characters' inner mind.

26. William Shakespeare's 154 sonnets seem to fall into three groups: the first 126 seem to be addressed to a young man, the last two read like free translations of a Greek poem of the fifth century, and the rest seem to be concerned with a "_____" who played the poet false.

27. Edmund Spenser's most ambitious poetic achievement is _____, set in the mythical world of King Arthur and his knights.

28. William Caxton is important to the development of English literature in that he introduced _____ into England.

29. _____ is a play based on the German legend of a magician aspiring for knowledge and finally meeting his tragic end as a result of selling his soul to the Devil.

30. _____ is Ben Jonson's first play and a key to all his plays.

III. Term definition

1. Renaissance
2. Humanism
3. Sonnet
4. Shakespearean Sonnet
5. Blank verse
6. Spenserian Stanza
7. Soliloquy
8. Eclogue
9. Dirge
10. Farce
11. Comedy
12. Tragedy
13. Tragicomedy
14. Miracle plays
15. Morality plays
16. Interludes
17. Revenge tragedy
18. Genre
19. Three unities
20. Euphuism
21. Prose romance

IV. Short-answer questions

1. What is *An Apology for Poetry* about?
2. What are the writing features of *The Faerie Queene*?
3. What are the characteristics of Edmund Spenser's poetry?
4. What is the writing style of Francis Bacon's essays?
5. What is Christopher Marlowe's chief literary achievement?
6. What are the features of William Shakespeare's dramatic works?
7. What are the features of Ben Jonson's dramatic works?

V. Essay questions

1. Give a brief introduction to Thomas More's *Utopia*.
2. Comment on *The Tragical History of Doctor Faustus* from the thematic and formal perspectives.
3. Analyze the theme of *The Merchant of Venice*.

Part Four The Period of Revolution and Restoration

(Roughly the 17th c.)

Chapter 10 Historical Context

With the end of the Tudor Dynasty and the beginning of the Stuart Dynasty (1603 – 1688), England changed from a united state to a divided one.

Socially, the 17th century was one of the most tempestuous periods in English history. It was a period when absolute monarchy impeded the further development of capitalism in England and the bourgeoisie could no longer bear the sway of landed nobility. With Charles I coming to the throne in 1625, the contradictions between feudalism and capitalism became sharper and sharper and eventually resulted in a revolutionary outburst, a political struggle between the King and the Cavaliers and the Parliamentary forces/bourgeoisie.

The political struggle went hand in hand with the religious struggle between the Anglican church, which supported and was supported by the royalists and emphasized the divine right of kings, and the dissidents or the Puritans, who were supported by the parliamentary forces and emphasized the divine right of the individual conscience, renouncing a life of joy in this world in hope of an eternal joy in the world to come. There were religious division and confusion. Therefore this period is also named the Puritan Age.

Politically, with Charles I beheaded in 1649, England was declared a commonwealth by Oliver Cromwell (1599 – 1658), leader of the parliament. In 1653 Oliver Cromwell imposed a military dictatorship on the country; after his death monarchy was again restored by Charles II (1630 – 85, king 1660 – 85) in 1660. Thus began the period of Restoration. Another crisis came in the revolution of 1688, when James II (1633 – 1701, king 1685 – 1688), another son of Charles I, attempted to establish despotism in church and state and the parliament invited Prince William of Orange (1650 – 1702, king 1689 – 1702), James II's son-in-law, to the throne. The new king and his wife Mary (1662 – 1694, queen 1689 – 1694), James II's daughter, became the joint ruler of England. This was known as "the Glorious Revolution," which meant three things—the supremacy of parliament, the beginning of modern England, and the final triumph of the principle of political liberty for which the Puritans had fought and suffered hardship for a hundred years.

The political and religious conflicts in the 17th-century England found their expression in the divided camps of the Cavaliers and the Puritan writers in the poetry and prose of the period. In poetry, there appeared different groups like the Cavalier poets including Thomas Carew (1594/5 – 1640), John Suckling (1609 – 1642), Richard

Lovelace (1618 – 1658) and Robert Herrick (1591 – 1674); the Metaphysical school represented by John Donne, George Herbert, Andrew Marvell, Richard Crashaw (c. 1613 – 1649) and Henry Vaughan (1621 – 1695); the Puritan poets like John Milton and George Wither (1588 – 1667); the Anti-Puritan poet Samuel Butler and the outstanding poet and dramatist and prose-writer John Dryden. In prose, before the Restoration there was John Milton, who was famous for a series of pamphlets and after the Restoration were John Bunyan and John Dryden. England's theaters were closed in 1642. The Restoration drama was chiefly for the court and the aristocracy, though it also had some appeal for the bourgeoisie of the time.

In a word, the literature of the Puritan Age was one of confusion, due to the breaking-up of old ideals and the absence of any fixed standard of literary criticism. The literature of the Restoration Period was a sudden breaking-away from old standards and followed the French style.

Chapter 11   Literature in the Period of Revolution

11.1   Literary Characteristics

The main literary form of the Revolutionary Period was poetry. John Milton was the greatest poet in this period and one of the most important poets in English literature as well. In his work the indomitable revolutionary spirit found its noblest expression. For this reason, this period is also called the Age of Milton. Besides the Puritan poetry represented by Milton, there were two other groups—the Metaphysical poetry and the Cavalier poetry. All in all, the literature of this period was, as a whole, one of confusion. It witnessed a conflict between the two antagonistic camps in politics, and carried several differences from the Elizabethan literature. First of all, the Elizabethan literature had a marked unity and the feeling of patriotism and devotion to the Queen, but in the Period of Revolution, all this was changed, the King became the open enemy of the people, and the country was divided by the struggle for political and religious liberty. So literature was as divided in spirit as were the struggling parties. Next, the Elizabethan literature was generally inspiring. It throbbed with youth and hope and vitality. Literature in the Puritan Age expressed age and sadness. Even its brightest hours were followed by gloom and pessimism. For, in this transitional, chaotic and perplexing period, the old value system was on its way out, new values were taking shape, and the conflict generated an acute sense of loss. Hence the literary works were enveloped in the prevalent mood—decadence, frivolity and despondency. Finally, the Elizabethan literature was intensely romantic. The romantic spirit sprang from the heart of youth. People believed all things, even the impossible. But in literature of the Puritan Period, we cannot find any romantic ardor.

11.2   Metaphysical Poets

The Metaphysical poets appeared in England at about the beginning of the 17th century. Although these poets were not formally affiliated and most of them did not even know one another or read one another's works, John Donne is generally acknowledged as the father of the school and George Herbert "the saint of the Metaphysical school."

The term was coined by Samuel Johnson, the literary dictator of the second half of the 18th century, to describe a loose group of English lyric poets of the 17th century, whose works were characterized by mysticism in content and fantasticality in form, and by speculation about topics such as love or religion. The 17th-century poet and critic John Dryden anticipated Johnson when he complained that Donne loved to play with metaphysics both in his satirical and love poetry, so that his love poems revealed the subtleties of metaphysics instead of focusing on love. Johnson elaborated Dryden's concept when he criticized Donne and his group for showing off their knowledge rather than describing natural human sentiment in their love poetry. Johnson did admit that these poets would not have been able to write this kind of poetry had they not read much and thought hard. His views later found echoes from such 19th-century critics as William Hazlitt. Thus "Metaphysical" became derogatory, and Metaphysical poetry lay in silence and obscurity for the long period of the 18th and 19th centuries. It managed to recover from this eclipse only in the early years of the 20th century, first anthologized by a well-known scholar Herbert J. C. Grierson (1866 – 1960) and then brought back to light especially by T. S. Eliot, another literary dictator so to speak, who took interest in it. Today the school is so well known that no one ignores it without good reason. Now the nomenclature "Metaphysical" has long lost its pejorative denotation and come to mean simply the poems by Donne and his group.

The style of the Metaphysical poetry was specified by wit and Metaphysical conceits. "Wit" here means being clever at "yok[ing]" the most heterogeneous ideas together by violence so as to impress people (to paraphrase Johnson's statement on the subject), and "conceit" denotes a fantastic fancy or way of thinking in the form of peculiar, ingenious, knotty, many-sided similes or metaphors, such as in Andrew Marvell's comparison of the soul with a drop of dew. These were employed along with far-fetched, difficult imagery. Also, in an expanded epigram format, the poets of this school used simple verse forms, octosyllabic couplets, quatrains or stanzas in which length of line and rhyme scheme enforce the sense. There is good reason to believe that the poets tried to conquer by sheer unconventionality rather than follow the normal channel of communication. They went out of their way to find a way of expression which demanded the readers to stretch their perspective and imaginative powers to the farthest limit possible to make sense of it. Hence the prophecy of Ben Jonson that this kind of poetry was too difficult for people to catch on in history. So it has remained unprecedented with virtually no successful followers, and it is often an exacting exercise of the mental powers for those who read it. The reward, however, hard-won often after a battle of wit and intellect, is often a combination of grateful pleasure, gratification and fun.

The Metaphysical poetry diverged from the style of their times, containing neither images of nature nor allusions to classical mythology, as were common. Several Metaphysical poets, especially John Donne, were influenced by Neo-Platonism. One of the primary Platonic concepts found in Metaphysical poetry is the idea that the perfection of beauty in the beloved acted as a remembrance of perfect beauty in the eternal realm. The Metaphysical poets as a group include John Donne, George Herbert, Richard Crashaw, Henry Vaughan, Robert Herrick, Thomas Carew, Abraham Cowley (1618 – 1667) and Andrew Marvell.

11.2.1 John Donne (1572 – 1631)

Donne was an English poet and a cleric in the Church of England. He is considered the preeminent representative and the founder of the Metaphysical school. Donne was gifted and ambitious; his works are noted for their strong, sensual style and include sonnets, love poems, religious poems, Latin translations, epigrams, elegies, songs, satires and sermons. His poetry is noted for its vibrancy of language and inventiveness of metaphor, especially compared to that of his contemporaries. Donne's style is characterized by abrupt openings and various paradoxes, ironies and dislocations. These features, along with his frequent dramatic or everyday speech rhythms, his tense syntax and his tough eloquence, were both a reaction against the smoothness of conventional Elizabethan poetry and an adaptation into English of European baroque and mannerist techniques. His early career was marked by poetry that bore immense knowledge of English society and he met that knowledge with sharp criticism. Another important theme in Donne's poetry is the idea of true religion, something that he spent much time considering and about which he often theorized. He wrote secular poems as well as erotic and love poems. He is particularly famous for his mastery of Metaphysical conceits.

Donne's works can be divided into two categories—the youthful love lyrics published in the collection *Songs and Sonnets* in 1633 and the later sacred pieces, which also came out in a collection titled *Devotions upon Emergent Occasions* early in 1624. His holy sonnets, dwelling on the themes of humility before God and the horror of the last judgment, made him a St. Augustine figure of his time, as both led a depraved lifestyle early in life but embraced religion later. Donne's love poetry features its dexterous interweaving of passion with reason. His famous works include such poems as "The Flea," "A Valediction: Forbidden Morning," "Song," "The Canonization," "Death Be not Proud" and "Better my Heart, Three-personed God, for You," and his prose work, the 23-section *Devotions*, which contains his *Meditations*.

Donne's early career was notable for his erotic or love poetry, especially his elegies, in which he employed unconventional metaphors. His conceits touch upon diverse fields of knowledge, and his comparisons tend to be amazingly grotesque. These manage to fuse lively thought and strong passion well in the white heat of the metaphysical imagination, and exert their impact not so much by virtue of their depiction of physical beauty and tender feelings, as by the compelling force of their "strong lines," masculine, dramatic and colloquial. **The Flea** (1633), for instance, is disconcertingly fantastic in equating "the flea" with "love." This is a three-stanza work, the scenario of which is a lover proposing to his beloved. The man first draws the lady's attention to the fact that the flea has bitten him and is now sucking her and that their two bloods are mingled in it. So he feels, according to a prevailing conception of marriage in the 17th century, that the two of them are already married. Then he tells the woman, now apparently bringing her hand down upon the flea, to stop and desist from killing it because she would have committed murder, self-murder and sacrilege. The last stanza shows that the lover feels angry, sad and sorry that the woman has killed the flea, and calls her cruel and false for her rejection of him. The poem gives people a clear sense of how ridiculous, outrageous and impossible Metaphysical conceits can be. The flea is the most sordid, disgusting and hateful parasite in the world while love is the sweetest, noblest and purest human emotion in life. No one else would have ever thought of the flea as the "marriage bed" and "marriage temple" and as embodying the consummation of love. Donne's uniqueness lies in this sudden jump from the conventional to the unconventional and metaphysical, and in making the jump appear rational and acceptable. Thus when the one is used to represent the other, the sense of unpleasant yet funny incongruity becomes so strong and revolting that it has better chances of engraving itself upon the mind than a stereotyped expression does. Anyone who ever reads the poem will surely find it hard to brush its impression off his memory. Here lies its permanent and immortal power. "To His Mistress Going to Bed" (1654) is another example, in which the poet-speaker poetically undresses his mistress and compares the act of fondling to the exploration of America.

Donne's numerous illnesses, financial strain and the deaths of his friends all contributed to the development of a more somber and pious tone in his later poems. The change can be clearly seen in "An Anatomy of the World" (1611), a poem that Donne wrote in memory of Elizabeth Drury, daughter of his patron, Sir Robert Drury of Hawstead, Suffolk. This poem treats Elizabeth's demise with extreme gloominess, using it as a symbol for the Fall of Man and the destruction of the universe. The poem "A Nocturnal upon S. Lucy's Day, Being the Shortest Day" concerns the poet's despair at the death of a loved one. In it Donne expressed a feeling of utter negation and hopelessness, saying that "I am every dead thing... re-begot/Of absence, darkness, death." This famous work was probably written in 1627 when both Donne's friend Lucy, Countess of Bedford, and his daughter Lucy Donne died. Three years later, in 1630, Donne wrote his will on Saint Lucy's day (13 December), the date the poem describes as "Both the year's, and the day's deep midnight."

The increasing gloominess of Donne's tone may also be observed in the religious works that he began writing during the same period. His early belief in the value of skepticism now gave way to a firm faith in the traditional teachings of the *Bible*. Having converted to the Anglican Church, Donne focused his literary career on religious literature. He quickly became noted for his sermons and religious poems. The lines of these sermons and devotional works would come to influence future works like *For Whom the Bell Tolls* (1940) by Ernest Hemingway (1899 – 1961), which took its title from a passage in "Meditation XVII" of *Devotions upon Emergent Occasions*.

Towards the end of his life Donne wrote works that challenged death and the fear that it inspired in many men on the grounds of his belief that those who die are sent to Heaven to live eternally. One example of this challenge is his Holy Sonnet X, "Death Be Not Proud" (1633), from which come the famous lines "Death, be not proud, though some have called thee/Mighty and dreadful, for thou art not so." Even as he lay dying during Lent in 1631, he rose from his sickbed and delivered the sermon titled "Death's Duel," which, later described as his own funeral sermon, portrays life as a steady descent to suffering and death, yet sees hope in salvation and immortality through an embrace of God, Christ and the Resurrection.

John Donne, as a representative of the Metaphysical School, was original and great. In all of his poems there is a mystery. His poems possess a highly idiosyncratic quality that reveals a peculiar, brilliant imagination at work, with an unconventional mood of perception and thinking, and the power of a mind, at once voluptuous and meditative, and capable of leaving an enduring imprint on readers. They are uneven, startling and fantastic. He threw style and all literary standards to the winds. However, most of his poetry purports to deal with life, descriptively and experimentally, and the first thing to strike the reader is Donne's extraordinary frankness and penetrating realism. The next is the cynicism which marks certain of the lighter poems and which represents a conscious reaction from the extreme idealization of woman encouraged by the Petrarchan tradition.

11.2.2 George Herbert (1593 – 1633)

Herbert was a Welsh-born English poet, orator and Anglican priest. His poetry is associated with the writings of the Metaphysical poets, and he is recognized as "the saint of the Metaphysical School" and "a pivotal figure: enormously popular, deeply and broadly influential, and arguably the most skillful and important British devotional lyricist."

Herbert wrote poetry in English, Latin and Greek. In 1633 all of his English poems were published in *The Temple: Sacred Poems and Private Ejaculations*, which includes his 160 short poems. The book went through eight editions by 1690. The poems imitate the architectural style of churches through both the meaning of the words and their visual layout. Herbert used the very format of the poems to reinforce the theme he was trying to portray. The themes of God and love are treated by Herbert as psychological forces as much as metaphysical phenomena. Herbert thought that a poet should sing the glory of God. He described his joys, fears and doubts in a symbolic way. Many of his poems are overloaded with far-fetched conceits, too obscure to be appreciated.

All of Herbert's surviving English poems are religious, characterized by precise language, metrical versatility and the ingenious use of imagery or conceits. Charles Cotton (1630 – 1687) described him as a "soul composed of harmonies." Some of Herbert's religious poems have been used as hymns, including "King of Glory, King of Peace," "Let All the World in Every Corner Sing" and "Teach me, my God and King." They are characterized by directness of expression and some conceits which can appear quaint. Many of the poems have intricate rhyme schemes and variations of lines within stanzas. "The Altar" is a pattern poem in which the words form a shape on the page suggesting an altar. The altar is used as his conceit or metaphor for how the individual offers himself as a sacrifice to the Lord. Herbert also made allusions to the *Bible*, where it states that the Lord requires the sacrifice of a broken heart and a contrite spirit. In "The Windows," another example of Herbert's religious pieces, the poet compared a righteous man to a glass window, through which God's light shines.

Herbert's only prose work, *A Priest to the Temple* (usually known as *The Country Parson*), offers practical advice to the rural clergy. In it, he advised that "things of ordinary use" such as ploughs, leaven, or dances, should be made to "serve for lights even of Heavenly Truths." It was first published in 1652 as part of *Herbert's Remains, or Sundry Pieces of That Sweet Singer, Mr. George Herbert*, edited by Barnabas Oley (1602 – 1686). Like many of his literary contemporaries, Herbert was a collector of proverbs. His *Outlandish Proverbs* (1640) listed over 1,000 aphorisms in English, which were gathered from many countries ("outlandish" meaning foreign). The collection includes many sayings repeated to this day, such as "His bark is worse than his bite" and "Who is so deaf, as he that will not hear."

11.2.3 Andrew Marvell (1621 – 1678)

Marvell was an English Metaphysical poet and Parliamentarian. He is associated with John Donne and George Herbert. He was a colleague and friend of John Milton. Marvell became well known in the early 20th century along with the revival of "Metaphysical poetry."

Although his works reveal some "Metaphysical" features, Marvell had his own unique style, which is a subtle amalgam of "Metaphysical" with Elizabethan features: he was sensitive to the influences of Edmund Spenser and Philip Sidney. And the couplet, which he was fond of using, helped pave the way for its perfection in the hands of John Dryden and Alexander pope. That is why his place in the English literary history is not altogether negligible. Some of his works like "To His Coy Mistress," "The Garden" and "An Horatian Ode upon Cromwell's Return from Ireland," and the country house poem "Upon Appleton House" belong among the best and most permanent of English poetry.

"**To His Coy Mistress**" is the most famous of the carpe diem poems coming out of the 17th century. Although the date of its composition is not known, it may have been written in the early 1650s. It is written in iambic tetrameter and rhymes in couplets. The speaker of the poem addresses a woman who has been slow to respond to his sexual advances. In the first stanza he describes how he would love her if he were to be unencumbered by the constraints of a normal lifespan. He could spend centuries admiring each part of her body and her resistance to his advances (i. e., coyness) would not discourage him. In the second stanza, he laments how short human life is. Once life is over, the speaker contends, the opportunity to enjoy each other is gone, as no one embraces in death. In the last stanza, the speaker urges the woman to requite his efforts and argues that in loving each other with passion they will both make the most of the brief time they have to live.

"**The Garden**" exhibits the profundity which the poet's thought is capable of touching as he tried to explore the dichotomous nature of the world. The poem has been regarded as an account either of mystical ecstasy by some commentators or of Horatian Epicureanism by others; some find in it an anti-libertine version of the poetry of rural retirement, while others interpret it in terms of "the politics of landscape." What seems indisputable is its congruence with the vision of reality proposed by the "Horatian Ode" and "Upon Appleton House": a virtually unbridgeable chasm is seen between contented withdrawal into contemplation and the actual life of man in the world. Ostensibly a celebration of the contemplative garden hints equally at the Garden of Eden and the enclosed garden of the Song of Songs and the garden of the mind of classical philosophy. "The Garden" subverts the solemnity of the meditative theme by engulfing it in irony.

Marvell was a pioneer in the kind of political verse satire that would be perfected by his younger contemporary John Dryden and in the next generation by Alexander Pope (both writing for the other side)—even as his satirical prose anticipated the achievement of Jonathan Swift in that vein. Marvell's satires won him a reputation in his own day and preserved his memory beyond the 18th century as a patriotic political writer—a clever and courageous enemy of court corruption and a defender of religious and political liberty and the rights of Parliament. It was only in the 19th century that his lyrical poems began to attract serious attention, and it was not until the 20th century that Marvell attained recognition as one of the major lyric poets of his age.

11.3 Cavalier Poets

The Cavalier poetry was another school of poetry prevailing in this period. Most of the poets were courtiers and soldiers. They sided with the King (particularly Charles I) and spoke outwardly against the Roundheads who supported the rebellion of Parliament against the crown. The intent of their works was often to promote the crown. Most Cavalier works had allegorical and/or classical references. They drew upon the knowledge of Horace (65 BC – 8 BC), Cicero (106 BC – 43 BC) and Ovid (43 BC – AD 17/18). By using these resources they were able to produce poetry that impressed King Charles I. The Cavalier Poets strove to create poetry where both pleasure and virtue thrived. Commonly held traits certainly exist in Cavalier poetry in that most poems "celebrate beauty, love, nature, sensuality, drinking, good fellowship, honor, and social life." (2006: 790) In many ways, this poetry embodies an attitude that mirrors "carpe diem." Cavalier poets wrote in a way that promoted seizing the day and the opportunities presented to them and their kinsmen. They wanted to revel in society and come to be the best that they possibly could within the bounds of that society. This endorsement of living life to the fullest, for Cavalier writers, often included gaining material wealth and having sex with women. These themes contributed to the triumphant and boisterous tone and attitude of the poetry. Cavalier poets mostly wrote short songs on the flitting joys of the day, but underneath their lightheartedness lay some forbidding and impending doom. Their poetry expresses the spirit of pessimism. Platonic Love is also another characteristic of Cavalier poetry, where the man would show his divine love to a woman, where she would be worshipped as a creature of perfection. As such it was common to hear praise of womanly virtues as though they were divine.

Closely linked to the Royalist cause in that its main intent was to glorify the crown, Cavalier poetry is often grouped in a political category. While most of the poetry does advocate the cause of the monarchy in some way, not all of the writers we now consider Cavalier poets knew that they fell under this categorization during their lifetime. Cavalier poetry was recognized as its own genre during the English Civil War in 1642 when men began to write in defense of the crown. However, the poets like Thomas Carew and Sir John Suckling, who had died before the war began, are still classified as Cavalier poets for the political nature of their poetry. Once the conflict began between the monarchy and the rebellious parliament, the content of the poetry became much more specifically aimed at upholding Royalist ideals. These men were considered by many to write in a nostalgic tone in that their works promoted the principles and practices of the monarchy that was under philosophical and, eventually, literal attack. The other representatives of this school are Ben Jonson, Richard Lovelace and Robert Herrick.

Between the Metaphysical poets and the Cavaliers there is a similar awareness of morality, which is expressed as an intense melancholy by the former, and by the latter as a bitter consciousness of the transitoriness of human glory and joy. Also, like the Metaphysical poetry, the works by the Cavaliers are characterized by metaphor and fantasy.

11.4 John Milton (1608 – 1674)

Milton is accepted as the third greatest English poet after Chaucer and Shakespeare, the greatest writer of the 17th century and one of the giants in English literature. He towered over his age as Shakespeare towered over the Elizabethan era and Chaucer over the Medieval Period. He wrote at a time of religious flux and political upheaval and is best known for *Paradise Lost*. Milton's poetry and prose reflect deep personal convictions, a passion for freedom and self-determination, and the urgent issues and political turbulence of his day. Writing in English, Latin, Greek and Italian, he achieved international renown within his lifetime.

Milton's literary career can be roughly divided into three periods. The first period, stretching from 1629 to 1638, was his Cambridge days and Horton period. Milton did a lot of reading and wrote his early lyrics. The main works produced during this period include *On the Morning of Christ's Nativity* (1629), *Comus* (a masque, 1637), *Lycidas* (1638) and the companion pieces—*L'Allegro* (the cheerful man, 1632) and *Il Penseroso* (the meditative man, 1632). The years between 1639 and 1660 was Milton's middle period, a period of service in the Puritan Revolution and pamphleteering for it. He wrote pamphlets falling into three major groups—the religious tracts, the four divorce tracts and the six political tracts. The major political tracts include *Of Education* (1644), *Eikonoclastes* (1649), *Defense for the English People* (1650) and *Areopagitica: A Speech of Mr. John Milton for the Liberty of Unlicenc'd Printing, to the Parliament of England* (1644), which, written in condemnation of pre-publication licensing and censorship, is regarded as one of the most influential, the most impassioned and the most eloquent defences of free speech and press freedom ever written because many of its expressed principles form the basis for modern justifications of that right. The last period (1660 – 1674) was Milton's greatest. He completed his three major poetical works—*Paradise Lost*, finished in 1665 and published in 1667; *Paradise Regained*, published in 1671; and *Samson Agonistes*, a tragedy in verse published in 1671.

Paradise Lost, Milton's masterpiece, is an epic poem in blank verse and is accepted as the greatest in English literature. The work helped to solidify Milton's reputation as one of the greatest English poets of his time. It was composed by the blind and impoverished Milton from 1658 to 1664. *Paradise Lost* was originally published in 1667 in ten books, with a total of over ten thousand individual lines of verse. A second edition followed in 1674, changed into twelve books (in the manner of the division of Virgil's *Aeneid*) with minor revisions throughout and a note on the versification. As a blind poet, Milton dictated his verse to a series of aides in his employ. It has been argued that the poem reflects his personal despair at the failure of the Revolution, yet affirms an ultimate optimism in human potential. Some literary critics have argued that Milton encoded many references to his unyielding support for the "Good Old Cause," a retrospective name given by the soldiers of the New Model Army for the complex of reasons for which they fought on behalf of the Parliament of England.

The stories were taken from *Genesis*, the biblical story of creation in the Old Testament, which covers the creation of the earth and of Adam and Eve, Satan and his fellow-angels' rebellion in Heaven, their defeat and expulsion from Heaven, the fallen angels in hell plotting against God, Satan's temptation of Eve, and the departure of Adam and Eve from Eden. Book I records the downfall of Lucifer (Satan) into the burning lake of Hell. There he and his fellow rebels lie for nine days before they recover and decide to foil God's plan by guile. In Book II the evil cohorts discuss about the best course of action for them. They decide to take over the control of Earth and turn the human beings against their creator. Book III gives an account of Satan flying over to Earth to get some first-hand information for himself, and Book IV shows God knowing everything and observing Satan on earth trying to learn about Adam and Eve and the Tree of Knowledge. The angels, Uriel and Gabriel, try to protect the abode of Adam and Eve, but Satan acts more promptly. Assuming the form of a toad, he has already influenced Eve's dreams. Book V relates how Eve tells Adam about her dream in which she tastes the fruit of the tree. Raphael is sent to warn the couple against disobeying God, tells them about Satan's rebellion and the creation of the world, and alerts Adam against becoming too curious about God's scheme. Adam recounts God's warning about the Tree and His creating Eve out of his rib to keep him company. Book VI records the eating of the Tree of Knowledge. Satan takes the form of a serpent and tempts Eve to eat the fruit of the tree. Eve does it and takes a fruit to Adam. Though horrified, Adam eats it out of love for his woman. Book VII tells about the result of the taste: both humans learn about shame. The angels go back to report to God, who says that the occurrence has been inevitable. Book VIII records the punishment of the sinners: Satan is to become a snake, for ever the hated enemy of mankind; Eve is to bear children and suffer pain; and Adam is to toil and sweat for his bread. In Book IX Satan's daughter Sin and his son Death come down to join their father on Earth. Back in Hell, Satan finds himself and his hosts all turned into snakes. Book X shows an angry God bringing about changes to earth: the seasons are established instead of the eternal spring, and all manners of violence and suffering are introduced. The humans are to suffer the violence of the elements, and are to prey upon one another. Book XI notes how God expels Adam and Eve from Eden, how His angel Michael reveals the future history of mankind, the flood, Noah, bloodshed, violence and humans' return to evil, and the coming of Christ as their redeemer. The last book relates Adam and Eve coming down hand in hand to the plains below.

The main idea of the poem is the heroic revolt against God's authority. Satan is the real hero of the poem, and represents the spirit of rebellion against an unjust authority. Adam and Eve embody Milton's belief in the powers of man. Their craving for knowledge adds a particular significance to their character. It is this longing for knowledge that opens before mankind a wide road to an intelligent and active life. The picture of God surrounded by his angels resembles the court of an absolute monarchy, while Satan and his followers bear resemblance to a republican parliament. This alone is sufficient to prove that Milton's revolutionary feelings made him forget religious orthodoxy.

Milton followed up *Paradise Lost* with its sequel *Paradise Regained*, published alongside the tragedy *Samson Agonistes* in 1671. *Paradise Regained* shares similar theological themes with *Paradise Lost*; indeed, its title, its use of blank verse and its progression through Christian history recall the earlier work. However, the later work deals primarily with the temptation of Christ as recounted in the Gospel of Luke. It also resonates with Milton's post-Restoration political situation.

Samson Agonistes is a poetical drama modeled on the Greek tragedies. The story was taken from the Old Testament. Samson was an athlete of the Israelites. He stood as their champion fighting for the freedom of his country. But he was betrayed by his wife and blinded by his enemies, the Philistines. One day he was summoned to provide amusement for his enemies by feats of strength in a temple. There he wreaked his vengeance upon his enemies by pulling down the temple upon them and upon himself in a common ruin.

In this poetical drama, Milton told us his own story. Like Samson, he was betrayed by his wife. He suffered from blindness and was scorned by his enemies, and yet he struggled heroically against his enemies. Samson's miserable blind servitude among his enemies, his agonizing longing for sight and freedom, and the last terrible triumph are all allusions to the poet's own story. So the whole poem strongly suggests Milton's passionate longing that he too could bring destruction down upon the enemy at the cost of his own life. Samson is Milton.

Milton was an outstanding political pamphleteer of the Period of Revolution and the greatest revolutionary poet of the 17th century. His poetry is characterized by his own political stand, which exerted a great influence on the later progressive English poets. In his political writing, Milton addressed particular themes at different periods. The years from 1641 to 1642 was dedicated to church politics and the struggle against episcopacy. After his divorce writings, *Areopagitica* and a gap, he wrote in 1649 – 54 in the aftermath of the execution of Charles I and in polemic justification of the regicide and the existing Parliamentarian regime. Then in 1659 – 60 he foresaw the Restoration and wrote to head it off. Milton's own beliefs were in some cases both unpopular and dangerous, and this was true particularly to his commitment to republicanism. In coming centuries, Milton would be claimed as an early apostle of liberalism.

Milton was a great master of blank verse. He was the glorious pioneer to introduce blank verse into non-dramatic poetry. He used it as the main tool in his masterpiece *Paradise Lost*. His blank verse is rich in every poetic quality and never monotonous. At the time, poetic blank verse was considered distinct from its use in verse drama, and *Paradise Lost* was taken as a unique exemplar. Isaac Watts (1674 – 1748) said in 1734, "Mr. Milton is esteemed the parent and author of blank verse among us." (Watts, 1810: 619) Milton's use of blank verse, in addition to his stylistic innovations, influenced later poets. "Miltonic verse" might be synonymous for a century with blank verse as poetry, a new poetic terrain independent from both the drama and the heroic couplet. It was a reaction against conservative values entrenched within the rigid heroic couplet. Within a dominant culture that stressed elegance and finish, Milton granted primacy to freedom, breadth and imaginative suggestiveness, eventually developed into the romantic vision of sublime terror. Milton himself considered the rhymeless quality of *Paradise Lost* to be an extension of his own personal liberty. Milton's blank verse was also characterized by the use of unconventional rhythm.

Milton was a great stylist. He is famous for his grand style, which is attributed to his lifelong study of the literary classics and the *Bible*. His poetry is noted for sublimity of thought, majesty of expression, and peculiar diction and phraseology. Milton liked to use Latinisms and proper names of resonance and color to create an elevated and dignified effect. To read and appreciate Milton in the original, it is necessary to know the English language thoroughly and with a close intimacy, as his works include some of the greatest poems of the world.

Chapter 12 Literature in the Period of Restoration

12.1 Literary Characteristics

The Restoration literature was characterized by a cliquish culture centering on the court and deeply influenced by the French Classical taste. English writers began to imitate the strict order and regularity of the French Classicism. In such a world, the range of literary experiment was not wide. Apart from some of Dryden's poems and his masterful prose, the greatest Restoration works are the worldly, witty comedies of William Congreve, William Wycherley, and others. On the whole, the writing of the age reflected the general mood of forced cleverness and anxious currying of favor at court.

The Restoration literature witnessed two marked tendencies. One was the tendency to realism. The early Restoration writers sought to paint realistic pictures of a corrupt society. They emphasized vices rather than virtues. They produced coarse, low plays without interest or moral significance. Later, this tendency to realism became more wholesome. Another tendency in literature of this age was toward directness and simplicity of expression, which was featured by John Bunyan and his works in particular. The Restoration writers emphasized close reasoning rather than romantic fancy and tended to use short and clean cut sentences without an unnecessary word. English literature is greatly indebted to this tendency, which the writers brought back from France.

The adoption of the heroic couplet was another salient feature of the Restoration literature. Edmund Waller (1606 – 1687), the most noted poet of the age, began to use it in 1623. Hence he is regarded by some critics as the father of the heroic couplet. Waller and his pupil Dryden made the couplet the prevailing literary fashion. It was dominant in England for a full century and was used by the later writers such as Pope, Goldsmith and Byron.

The Restoration literature may be thus summarized in four things—the tendency to vulgar realism in the drama, a general formalism, the development of a simpler and more direct prose style, and the prevalence of the heroic couplet in poetry. They were all exemplified in the works of John Dryden. Therefore, the Restoration period was traditionally called the "Age of Dryden."

12.2 John Bunyan (1628 – 1688)

Bunyan was an English writer and preacher, and occupied the most important place in the field of prose writing of the age. Unlike Milton, who was the child of the Renaissance and inherited all its culture, Bunyan inherited nothing from the Renaissance but received an excess of that spiritual independence from the reformation, which had caused the Puritan struggle for liberty. He and Milton represented the extremes of the English life in the 17th century and wrote two works that stand today for the mighty Puritan spirit, i. e., Milton's *Paradise Lost*, the only epic since *Beowulf*, and Bunyan's *The Pilgrim's Progress*, the only great allegory, for which the author is best remembered. Bunyan exerted influence on those writers like Nathaniel Hawthorne (1804 – 1864), Herman Melville (1819 – 1891), Charles Dickens, Louisa May Alcott (1832 – 1888) and George Bernard Shaw.

Bunyan and his writing were greatly influenced by both religion and his marriage. The religious ferment of the age left a tremendous impression on Bunyan's sensitive imagination. He occasionally went to church, only to find himself wrapped in terrors and torments by some fiery itinerant preachers. Visions of hell and the demons swarmed in his brain. Then he got married to a good woman, whose only dowry was two old threadbare books—*The Plain Man's Pathway to Heaven* and *The Practice of Piety*. Reading the books instantly gave fire to Bunyan's imagination. He saw new visions and dreamed terrible new dreams of lost souls; his attendance at church grew exemplary; he began reading the *Bible* for himself. The real reformation in his life began. Bunyan became an open-air preacher. All this was instrumental in his production of *The Pilgrim's Progress*. In addition to *The Pilgrim's Progress*, Bunyan wrote nearly sixty titles, many of them expanded sermons. Bunyan's other main allegorical works include *Grace Abounding to the Chief of Sinners* (1666), a spiritual autobiography written while Bunyan was serving a twelve-year prison sentence in Bedford gaol for preaching without a license, *The Life and Death of Mr. Badman* (1680), a satire against the evil practices of the upper classes, which was designed as a companion to *The Pilgrim's Progress*, and *The Holy War* (1682), a novel written in the form of an allegory, telling the story of the town Mansoul (Man's soul).

The Pilgrim's Progress, Bunyan's masterpiece, consists of two parts, the first part coming out in 1678 and the second part in 1684. After its publication, the work immediately became the most popular and is said to be second only to the *Bible*. It was one of the most published books in the English language and 1,300 editions had been printed by 1938 (250 years after the author's death).

The book is written in the old-fashioned, medieval form of allegory and dream. It reads like a medieval miracle play with vivid and lively personifications of virtues and vices and all the human qualities in between. General concepts such as sin, despair and faith are represented as people or as aspects of the natural world. The images Bunyan used in *The Pilgrim's Progress* are reflections of images from his own world: the strait gate is a version of the wicket gate at Elstow Abbey church; the Slough of Despond is a reflection of Squitch Fen, a wet and mossy area near his cottage in Harrowden; the Delectable Mountains are the image of the Chiltern Hills surrounding Bedfordshire. Even his characters, like the Evangelist influenced by John Gifford, are reflections of real people.

The basis of the allegorical narrative is the idea of a pilgrimage. The pilgrim and protagonist's name is Christian, and he represents every Christian in the human world. The figures and places Christian encounters on his journey stand for the various experiences every Christian must go through in the quest for salvation. Part One, generally acknowledged as the better part, mainly describes the protagonist's pilgrimage through the Slough of Despond, Vanity Fair, Doubting Castle, the Valley of Humiliation and the Valley of the Shadow of Death. It contains ten stages of the pilgrim's progress. In stage one, the narrator begins by saying that he dreams of Christian with a book in his hand and a great burden on his back, who keeps crying out, "What shall I do?" The story is about his effort to find faith and salvation by making his pilgrimage to the Celestial Kingdom. In stage two Christian meets Goodwill who shows him a narrow way to the House of the Interpreter (i. e. Holy Spirit). From the Interpreter Christian learns about salvation and judgment. In stage three Christian, freed of his burden, with sin forgiven, is clothed in a new garment and given a roll to read, feeling happy and ready to help his fellow humans. He keeps on going up a hill, experiences some doubt and recovers his faith, and goes on to reach a stately palace where he stays for a few days. The fourth stage is one in which Christian kills the monster Apollyon in the Valley of Humiliation and labors through the two parts of the Valley of the Shadow of Death. In stage five Christian and Faithful meet, get rid of the irritable company of Talkative and go on their way together. In the sixth stage Christian and Faithful come to the Town of Vanity in which Vanity Fair is located. As their presence causes a commotion, they are thrown in prison and then tried. Faithful is found guilty and put to a cruel death, but Christian manages to escape with the help of the Lord and resumes his journey to Mt. Zion. In stage seven Christian, joined by Hopeful, reaches the river of God and rests to refresh himself for a few days. Then they are trapped in the Doubting Castle of Giant Despair who throws them into its dungeon, but finally escape with the help of the key, Promise, and get once more on the King's high way. The eighth stage witnesses Christian and Hopeful meeting the shepherds—Knowledge, Experience, Watchful and Sincere—on the Delectable Mountains, who take them to the Hill of Error and the Hill of Caution, give them more instructions and warn them to beware of Flatterer and the Enchanted Ground. They meet the two and Atheist in the ninth stage and reach the borders of heaven in the last stage. Eventually, Christian and Hopeful are welcomed and transfigured into a city of gold and enjoy eternal bliss. Just at that time, the dreaming narrator awakes. Part Two deals with the pilgrimage of Christiana, Christian's wife, and her children, accompanied by her neighbor Mercy and escorted by Greatheart. Social satire in the second part is much weaker, however.

For us today, the rich variety of concrete situations, living characters and vital experiences, presented in the rapid narrative, is no less than a faithful reflection of Bunyan's age. Christian's encounters are actually a vivid picture of England in the 17th century, the Restoration Period in particular. More importantly, the book features the satires centered upon the ruling class. Especially well-known are the descriptions of Vanity Fair and of the experience of Christian and Faithful in it, for here Bunyan not only gave us a symbolic picture of London at the time of the Restoration but of feudal-bourgeois society in general where all things were bought and sold and where cheating and roguery, murders and adultery were normal. Meanwhile, the book is highly religious with its earnest appeal to the human soul to have faith and hope for the bliss of the Kingdom of God.

Additionally, the book is written in prose, which is simple, familiar, lucid and forceful. It is a nice amalgam of the basic features of the language of the *Bible* and popular speech. This style helped upgrade English prose and paved the way for the rise of the modern English novel in the 18th century. Moreover, the household words and picturesque similes abound in the book, which enriched the English language.

To sum up, Bunyan seemed to make efforts to preach his religious views in his writing. His works were all of a religious character. Bunyan drew realistic portraits of persons of his day and realistic pictures of his society. In his works were his thoroughgoing expose and satire on his contemporary world. He voiced the thoughts and feelings of the common people. Meanwhile, Bunyan used a simple, unaffected language of the common people. He used everyday idiomatic expressions naturally. His prose, modeled on that of the *Authorized Bible*, is clear enough to be followed by any reader. His way of relating stories and revealing ideas is always direct and straightforward. This, together with his details taken from ordinary circumstances of ordinary life, is largely responsible for the modernness of his prose. *The Pilgrim's Progress* is in any sense Bunyan's representative work.

During the 18th century Bunyan's unpolished style fell out of favor, but his popularity returned with Romanticism. Bunyan's reputation was further enhanced by the Evangelical revival and he became a favorite author of the Victorians. Although popular interest in Bunyan waned during the second half of the 20th century, academic interest in the writer has increased and Oxford University Press brought out a new edition of his works, beginning in 1976. *The Pilgrim's Progress* has reached a wider audience through stage productions, film, TV and radio. An opera based on the work was first performed at the Royal Opera House in 1951 as part of the Festival of Britain and revived in 2012 by the English National Opera.

12.3 John Dryden (1631 – 1700)

Dryden was an English poet, literary critic, playwright and translator. He received education from Cambridge University and was regarded as the most learned person of his time. He was the greatest poet between Milton and Pope and was awarded England's Poet Laureate in 1668. The most notable representative of English Classicism in the Restoration Period, Dryden is acknowledged as "the father of English criticism." He dominated the literary life of the Restoration England to such a point that the period came to be known in literary circles as the "Age of Dryden."

Dryden was a versatile and prolific writer. His works consist of poems, plays and critical essays. In poetry, Dryden set an enduring style with his neat "heroic couplets." His finest works were his long poems in heroic couplets on political, religious and literary themes. He was a poet of intellect, not of emotion. He had superb gifts in verse satire. His greatest achievements were in satiric verse. As he himself wrote, the great art of the satirist was to do his job elegantly rather than crudely. His controversial and satirical poems were on a higher plane. The best-known and a masterpiece of this kind is *Absalom and Achitophel* (1681), an allegory that uses the story of the rebellion of Absalom against King David as the basis for discussion of the background to the Monmouth Rebellion (1685), the Popish Plot (1678) and the Exclusion Crisis (1679 – 1681). Religion also occupied an important position in Dryden's poetry. Among his poems dealing with religious subjects, the representative one is the allegory *The Hind and the Panther* (1687), the longest of Dryden's poems, translations excepted, and perhaps the most controversial. In this poem, Dryden celebrated his conversion to Roman Catholicism and defended the Roman Catholic Church against the Anglican Church. Besides, Dryden wrote some odes, of which the notable ones are

Alexander's Feast (1697), whose main body describes the feast given by Alexander the Great at the Persian capital Persepolis, after his defeat of Darius, and *Annus Mirabilis* (1667), a lengthy historical poem celebrating the sea fights against the Dutch and dealing with the great fire of London in 1666. *Annus Mirabilis* is a modern epic in pentameter quatrains that established Dryden as the preeminent poet of his generation, and was crucial in his attaining the posts of Poet Laureate and historiographer royal (1670).

What Dryden achieved in his poetry was neither the emotional excitement of the early 19th-century romantics nor the intellectual complexities of the Metaphysicals. His subject matter was often factual, and he aimed at expressing his thoughts in the most precise and concentrated manner. Although he used formal structures such as heroic couplets, he tried to recreate the natural rhythm of speech; he knew that different subjects needed different kinds of verse. In his preface to *Religio Laici* (1682), a poem published as a premise to his subsequent *The Hind and the Panther*, Dryden said that "the expressions of a poem designed purely for instruction ought to be plain and natural, yet majestic," that "the florid, elevated and figurative way is for the passions; for [these] are begotten in the soul by showing the objects out of their true proportion," and that "a man is to be cheated into passion, but to be reasoned into truth."

In prose, Dryden established the Neoclassical standards of order, balance and harmony, and had a marked influence on English literature in shortening his sentence and especially in writing naturally. He tried to state his thought clearly and concisely. With his prose, he rapidly developed his critical ability and became the foremost critic of his age. His greatest work of literary criticism *An Essay of Dramatic Poesy* (1668), in which appears his famous appreciation of Shakespeare, established his position as the leading critic of the day.

With the reopening of the theaters after the Puritan ban, Dryden wrote plays. His first play *The Wild Gallant* appeared in 1663 and was not successful but was still promising, and from 1668 on he was contracted to produce three plays a year for the King's Company in which he became a shareholder. During the 1660s and 1670s, theatrical writing was his main source of income. Dryden was never a great playwright, even though he produced 27 plays in his literary career. His plots were often impossible, his dialogues absurd, and his themes infused with court ideas and sentiments. Of the plays he wrote for the Restoration theater, only one, *All for Love* (1678), an adaptation of Shakespeare's *Antony and Cleopatra* written in blank verse, is anything worth mentioning.

Dryden translated works by Horace, Juvenal (late 1st century – early 2nd century AD), Ovid, Lucretius (c. 99 BC – c. 55 BC) and Theocritus (c. 310 BC – c. 250 BC), and found translating far more satisfying than writing for the stage. In 1694 he began working on what would be his most ambitious and defining work as translator, *The Works of Virgil* (1697), which was published by subscription. The publication of the translation of Virgil was a national event and brought Dryden a good sum of money. His final translations appeared in the volume *Fables Ancient and Modern* (1700), a series of episodes from Homer, Ovid and Boccaccio, as well as modernized adaptations from Geoffrey Chaucer interspersed with Dryden's own poems. As a translator, Dryden made great literary works in the older languages available to readers of English.

Absalom and Achitophel is a powerful political satire used by Dryden to ridicule and attack the Whigs, and to revenge himself upon his enemies. It is still well read today not so much because of its thematic concern as for its striking formal features. The poem is based on a biblical story concerning the power struggle between King David and his son Absalom. Absalom harbors the ambition to replace his father as king of Israel and starts a rebellion with the support of one of the king's advisers, Achitophel. When the conspiracy fails, Absalom meets his doom. Dryden's poem was written as a spearhead against the ambitions of Charles II's bastard son, Duke of Monmouth, and his fellow conspirator Earl of Shaftsbury who, out of the interest of his political group, supported the Duke's bid for succession. The 17th-century scenario was amazingly similar to that in the *Bible*. The poet, taking the side of Charles II, felt obligated to write this to show his support for the throne. The historic significance of the work has to do with its stylistic aspect. Dryden, making the best of the heroic couplet as a satirical instrument and exhibiting its potential power, molded a style at once effective and pungent, revealed himself as a master of satire and a dexterous manipulator of language, and won a place of preeminence which few have ever touched.

In ***An Essay of Dramatic Poesy***, Dryden took up the subject that Philip Sidney had set forth in his *Defence of Poesie* and attempted to justify drama as a legitimate form of "poetry" comparable to the epic, and thus defend the English drama against that of the ancient and the French.

The treatise is a dialogue between four speakers—Eugenius, Crites, Lisideius and Neander. The speakers represented, respectively, Sir William Davenant (1606 – 1668), Dryden's "ingenious" collaborator on their revision of *The Tempest* (1667), Sir Robert Howard (1626 – 1698), playwright and Dryden's brother-in-law, Roger Boyle, 1st Earl of Orrery (1621 – 1679), who is the author of the first heroic play in rhymed couplets, and Dryden himself. Neander means "new man" and implies that Dryden, as a respected member of the gentry class, is entitled to join in this dialogue on an equal footing with the three older men who are his social superiors. The four friends discuss about the advances made by modern civilization. They agree to measure progress by comparing the ancient arts with the modern, focusing specifically on the art of drama or "dramatic poesy." They debate a series of three topics—the relative merit of the Classical drama upheld by Crites versus the modern drama championed by Eugenius, whether the French drama, as Lisideius maintains, is better than the English drama supported by Neander, who famously calls Shakespeare "the greatest soul, ancient or modern," and whether plays in rhyme are an improvement upon blank verse drama—a proposition that Neander, despite having defended the Elizabethans, now advances against the skeptical Crites, who also switches from his original position and defends the blank verse tradition of the Elizabethan drama. Invoking the so-called unities from *Poetics* (c. 335 BC) of Aristotle (384 – 322 BC) as interpreted by the Italian scholars and refined by the French scholars over the last century, the four speakers discuss what makes a play "a just and lively imitation" of human nature in action. This definition of a play, supplied by Lisideius, whose rhymed plays have dazzled the court and are a model for the new drama, gives the debaters a versatile and richly ambiguous touchstone. To Crites' argument that the plots of the Classical drama are more "just," Eugenius can retort that modern plots are more "lively" thanks to their variety. Lisideius shows that the French plots carefully preserve Aristotle's unities of action, place and time; Neander replies that English dramatists like Ben Jonson also kept the unities when they wanted to, but that they preferred to develop character and motive. Even Neander's final argument with Crites over whether rhyme is suitable in drama depends on Aristotle's *Poetics*: Neander says that Aristotle demands a verbally artful ("lively") imitation of nature, while Crites thinks that dramatic imitation ceases to be "just" when it departs from the ordinary speech (i. e. prose or blank verse). A year later, the two brothers-in-law quarreled publicly over this third topic. In "Defense of an Essay of Dramatic Poesy"

(1669), Dryden tried to persuade the rather literal-minded Howard that audiences expect a play to be an imitation of nature instead of a surrogate for nature itself.

Dryden is chiefly remembered for the two great contributions he made to English literature. One was his successful effort to prune the Elizabethan language of its formless exuberance and turn it into a cool, lucid, plain and natural medium for English writing. Musical, precise and dignified, Dryden's language received reinforcements from Alexander Pope and the other Neoclassic writers, and stretched its impact well into the 19th century. Even the Romantic movement of the early 19th century, which was in fact a strenuous reaction to the excesses of Popian Classicism, showed decent respect for Dryden's legacy. The fact was that the enthusiasm, which had characterized the romantic outburst of the Elizabethan era, had brought forth at once a colorful variety in theme and diction, and an obvious lack of form and discipline with it. It was like a sprawling botanical garden that needed proper trimming. Dryden saw the need for rectification and introduced the classic elements and heralded the beginning of Neoclassicism that was to become a tyrannical vogue in the next century. He was, in this sense, the first Neoclassic writer in the English literary history. It was he who made the heroic couplet almost the only poetic medium acceptable for poetry and thus paved the way for the rise of Alexander Pope.

The other, more significant in nature, is his contribution to the English literary criticism. Dryden was basically good at literary criticism. His insight and perspicacity of observation are well demonstrated in his critical works such as *An Essay of Dramatic Poesy* and the number of prefaces he wrote for his various works, the most famous of which is the one for *Fables Ancient and Modern*. He was a highly influential literary dictator of his time as Ben Jonson before him. His critical writings helped establish the canons of taste and principles of the English literary criticism. These include, among other things, a catholic taste and a balanced approach, the critical emphasis on textual analysis rather than on juggling with theoretical abstraction, emphasis on erudition, deep thought and comparative analysis, the critical focus on the major points of interest rather than attempting a systematic exposition, and the use of a succinct yet lucid essay form. These Drydenian features have been visible in the English literary criticism ever since. Some of Dryden's comments on certain authors like Chaucer and Shakespeare are still held in high esteem today. Thus Dryden has been seen as "the father of English criticism."

Dryden was the dominant literary figure and influence of his age and the forerunner of the English Classical school of literature in the next century. Following the standards of classicism, he clarified English prose and developed a direct, concise and flexible prose style, and developed the art of literary criticism in his essays and in the numerous prefaces to his poems and raised English literary criticism to a new level. What's more important, Dryden established the heroic couplet as the fashion for satiric, didactic and descriptive poetry, and a standard form of the English poetry by writing successful satires, religious pieces, fables, epigrams, compliments, prologues, and plays with it; he also introduced the Alexandrine and triplet into the form. In his poems, translations and criticism, he established a poetic diction appropriate to the heroic couplet that was a model for his contemporaries. Dryden's heroic couplet became the dominant poetic form of the 18th century. Alexander Pope was heavily influenced by Dryden and often borrowed from him; other writers were equally influenced by Dryden and Pope. Samuel Johnson summed up the general attitude with his remark that "the veneration with which his name is pronounced by every cultivator of English literature, is paid to him as he refined the language, improved the sentiments, and tuned the numbers of English poetry." In the 19th century, such Romantics like Lord Byron and Walter Scott were still keen admirers of Dryden. Scott edited Dryden's works and once called him "Glorious John." John Keats admired the "Fables" and imitated them in his poem *Lamia*. William Wordsworth also admired many of Dryden's poems, and his famous "Intimations of Immortality" ode owes something stylistically to Dryden's "Alexander's Feast," even though one of the first attacks on Dryden's reputation came from Wordsworth, who complained that Dryden's descriptions of natural objects in his translations from Virgil were much inferior to the originals. The next major poet to take interest in Dryden was T. S. Eliot (1932: 305-306), who wrote that he was "the ancestor of nearly all that is best in the poetry of the eighteenth century," and that "we cannot fully enjoy or rightly estimate a hundred years of English poetry unless we fully enjoy Dryden." However, in the same essay, Eliot accused Dryden of having a "commonplace mind." Critical interest in Dryden has increased recently, but, as a relatively straightforward writer his work has not occasioned as much interest as Andrew Marvell's or John Donne's or Alexander Pope's.

12.4 The Restoration Theater

After the closing of the theaters in London in 1642 by the order of the Puritan parliament, the English drama was practically at a standstill for 18 years. The only theatrical activities that took place during the days of the Commonwealth and the Protectorate were those engineered by Sir William d'Avenant (1606-1668), especially with his so-called "Entertainments" like *The Siege of Rhodes* (1656) which were really somewhat like operas. Then, three months after the Restoration in 1660, Charles II gave patents for the opening of two theaters with two dramatic companies.

In addition to the distinctive genre of the heroic play and the dominating figure of John Dryden who wrote comedies and tragedies as well as heroic plays, the English drama of the Restoration consisted chiefly of a great number of comedies of manners representing the "manners" of the King and his court and the nobles, and of a few tragedies by Natheniel Lee (c. 1653-1692) and Thomas Otway (1652-1685). Translations of the French tragedies by the Neoclassicists Corneille (1606-1684) and Racine (1639-1699) had their influence upon the English stage in the first years after the Restoration. Nathaniel Lee (c. 1653-1692) and Thomas Otway (1652-1685) were very much under the influence of the French Neoclassical drama and both wrote their tragedies mostly in blank verse. Lee was chiefly known for his *Sophonisba, or Hannibal's Overthrow* (1676), a tragedy written in rhymed heroic couplets in imitation of Dryden, and a blank verse tragedy *The Rival Queens, or the Death of Alexander the Great* (1677), which deals with the jealousy of Alexander's first wife Roxana for his second wife Statira. The latter was a favorite on the English stage right up to the days of Edmund Kean (1787-1833), who was celebrated Shakespearean stage actor. Otway was a more important dramatist. Besides his few comedies and adaptations of plays by Racine and Moliere (1622-1673), he wrote chiefly three tragedies *Don Carlos, Prince of Spain* (1676), *The Orphan, or The Unhappy Marriage* (1680) and *Venice Preserv'd, or A Plot Discover'd* (1682), of which the first two are simply domestic tragedies while the last, known as Otway's masterpiece and the most significant tragedy of the English stage in the 1680s, has an essentially political theme, with a love story attached to it.

Whereas the serious drama of the Restoration was largely artificial, the comedies of manners were in a sense more realistic reflections of the immoral existence led by the aristocracy at the court of the Stuart kings. Most writers of these comedies of manners were either themselves the nobility or themselves led dissolute lives of the aristocrats so that they were simply recording faithfully in their comedies what they knew and saw, without any conscious attempt to expose the social vices or to laugh them out of existence. The comedies of manners reached maturity in the works of the three eminent dramatists of the period—George Etherege (c. 1636 – c. 1692), whose only three comedies—*The Comical Revenge or, Love in a Tub* (1664), *She Would if She Could* (1668) and *The Man of Mode, or Sir Fopling Flutter* (1676)—were all quite well known at the time, William Wycherley (c. 1641 – 1715), who was best known for the plays *The Country Wife* (1675), which reflects an aristocratic and anti-Puritan ideology, and was controversial for its sexual explicitness even in its own time, and *The Plain Dealer*, which is based on Moliere's *The Misanthrope* (1666), and William Congreve (1670 – c. 1728), who is generally acknowledged as the greatest dramatist of the Restoration comedy of manners. Always with a high moral purpose topmost in his mind, **William Congreve** is well noted for his comic genius and his witty and exquisite dialogues. He wrote a number of brilliant comedies such as *The Old Bachelor* (1693), *The Double Dealer* (1694), *The Way of the World* (1700) and *Love for Love* (1695), a comical farce enlivened by its witty dialogue and its humorous characters, and perhaps more successful in its day than *The Way of the World*. Congreve also wrote a tragedy titled *The Mourning Bride* (1697), which centers on Zara, a queen held captive by Manuel, King of Granada, and a web of love and deception which results in the mistaken murder of Manuel who is in disguise, and Zara's also mistaken suicide in response. **The Way of the World** has been seen as Congreve's best work. Whereas it is about the moral concerns regarding the relationship between the two sexes, the play reveals the author's stance clearly, i. e. exalting true love and fidelity between husband and wife and censuring anything immoral and selfish in marriage. The genuine love and marriage of Mirabell to Millamant is made to contrast with the marriage of the lecherous, prudish old widow Lady Wishfort and the greedy and hypocritical dandy Mr. Fainall. The bargaining scene and the scene in which Lady Wishfort falls into a trap prove to be among the most entertaining of the whole performance.

Exercises

I. Multiple choices

1. With the end of the Tudor Dynasty and the beginning of the Stuart Dynasty, England changed from a _____ state to a _____ one.

    A. Christian, secular   B. united, divided

    C. weak, strong   D. small, large

2. The term "Metaphysical" came first from the 17th-century poet-critic _____.

    A. Samuel Johnson   B. William Hazlitt

    C. George Herbert   D. John Dryden

3. John Donne's _____ sonnets, which dwell on the themes of humility before God and the horror of the last judgment, made him a St. Augustine figure of his time, as both led a depraved lifestyle early in life but embraced religion later.

    A. love   B. holy

    C. lyric   D. satirical

4. John Donne's love poetry is characterized by its dexterous interweaving of _____.

    A. passion with reason   B. humility with horror

    C. calmness with violence   D. satire with humor

5. One of John Donne's most famous poems, "The Flea," is disconcertingly fantastic in equating "the flea" with "_____."

    A. love   B. horror

    C. trouble   D. harassment

6. _____'s chief work is a collection called *The Temple*, which includes his 160 short poems.

    A. John Milton   B. John Donne

    C. George Herbert   D. John Dryden

7. "The Altar," a religious poem by _____, is a pattern poem in which the words form a shape on the page suggesting an altar.

    A. John Milton   B. John Donne

    C. George Herbert   D. John Dryden

8. Although his work reveals some "Metaphysical" features, _____ has his own unique style, which is a subtle amalgam of "Metaphysical" with Elizabethan features.

    A. John Dryden   B. John Donne

    C. George Herbert   D. Andrew Marvell

9. The following poems were all written by Andrew Marvell EXCEPT _____.

    A. "To His Coy Mistress"   B. "The Garden"

    C. "Horatian Ode"   D. "The Flea"

10. Closely linked to the Royalist cause in that its main intent was to glorify the crown, _____ is often grouped in a political category of poetry.

    A. Cavalier poetry   B. romantic poetry

    C. Metaphysical poetry   D. Classical poetry

11. _____ is Milton's masterpiece and the greatest English epic. It consists of 12 books and is done in blank verse.

    A. *Don Juan*   B. *The Song of Beowulf*

    C. *Paradise Lost*   D. *Prometheus Unbound*

12. _____ towered over his age as Shakespeare towered over the Elizabethan era, and as Chaucer towered over the Medieval Period.

    A. Andrew Marvell   B. John Milton

    C. John Bunyan   D. George Herbert

13. *The Pilgrim's Progress* is _____'s most important work. It is written in the old-fashioned, medieval form of allegory and dream.

    A. Joseph Addison   B. William Blake

    C. John Bunyan   D. John Donne

Part Four The Period of Revolution and Restoration

14. _____ occupied the most important place in the field of prose writing of the 17th century.
    A. Andrew Marvell   B. John Bunyan
    C. John Milton   D. George Herbert

15. _____ was the child of the Renaissance and inherited all its culture. He was the greatest writer of the 17th century and one of the giants in English literature. He gave us the only epic since *Beowulf*.
    A. John Bunyan   B. Francis Bacon
    C. John Milton   D. John Donne

16. After he went blind, Milton wrote and finished his three great works—*Paradise Lost, Paradise Regained* and *Samson Agonistes*, among which _____ is (are) regarded as the poet's masterpiece(s).
    A. *Paradise Lost*   B. *Paradise Regained*
    C. *Paradise Regained* and *Samson Agonistes*   D. *Samson Agonistes*

17. _____, the most noted poet of the Restoration Period, began to use the heroic couplet in 1623.
    A. John Dryden   B. John Donne
    C. John Milton   D. Edmund Waller

18. _____ was the greatest poet between John Milton and Alexander Pope and was appointed the Poet Laureate in 1668.
    A. John Bunyan   B. John Donne
    C. Andrew Marvell   D. John Dryden

19. _____, most notable representative of English Classicism in the Restoration Period, is accepted as the "father of English criticism."
    A. John Dryden   B. John Donne
    C. John Milton   D. John Bunyan

20. John Dryden's greatest work of literary criticism is _____, in which appears his famous appreciation of Shakespeare.
    A. *Devotion upon Emergent Occasions*   B. *An Essay of Dramatic Poesy*
    C. *Defense for the English People*   D. *Poetics*

21. In English literature, the Restoration Period is traditionally called the "_____."
    A. Age of Chaucer   B. Age of Shakespeare
    C. Age of Milton   D. Age of Dryden

22. The best known and a masterpiece of John Dryden's satirical poems is _____.
    A. *The Hind and the Panther*   B. "Annus Mirabilis"
    C. *Absalom and Achitophel*   D. "Alexander's Feast"

23. The English drama of the Restoration consisted chiefly of a great number of _____, and of a few tragedies.
    A. heroic plays   B. tragic-comedies
    C. historical plays   D. comedies of manners

24. The best dramatist of the Restoration comedy of manners was probably _____.

A. John Dryden B. William Congreve
C. George Etherege D. William Wycherley

25. _____, the best work of William Congreve reveals the author's stance clearly, i. e., exalting true love and fidelity between man and wife and censuring anything immoral and selfish in marriage.

A. *The Way of the World* B. *The Old Bachelor*
C. *The Double Dealer* D. *The Mourning Bride*

II. Blank-filling

1. The Metaphysical poets appeared in England at about the beginning of the _____ century.

2. The works of the Metaphysical poets are characterized by _____ in content and fantasticality in form.

3. John Donne is the father of the _____.

4. _____ is "the saint of the Metaphysical School."

5. The basic feature of the "Metaphysical" poetry is its "_____" or "conceit."

6. *Songs and Sonnets* is a collection of John Donne's _____ poems while *Devotion upon Emergent Occasions* consists of his _____ pieces.

7. During the second period of his literary career, Milton produced numerous well-known pamphlets, which could be classified into three major groups: _____ tracts, _____ tracts and _____ tracts.

8. Although isolated and embittered, John Milton fulfilled the tasks he had set for himself and completed the three great poems—*Paradise Lost*, _____ and _____.

9. *Samson Agonistes* is a poetical drama modeled on the _____ tragedies.

10. John Bunyan and John Milton represented the extremes of English life in the 17th century and wrote two works that stand today for the mighty Puritan spirit, i. e., Milton's _____, the only epic since *Beowulf*, and Bunyan's _____, the only great allegory.

11. The Restoration literature was characterized by a cliquish culture centering on the _____ and deeply influenced by the French Classical taste.

12. The Restoration literature witnessed two marked tendencies. One is the tendency to _____ and the other is the tendency toward _____.

13. The main characteristics of the Restoration literature include the tendency to vulgar realism in drama, a general formalism, the development of a simpler and more direct prose style, and the prevalence of the _____ in poetry.

14. John Dryden's works consist of _____, _____ and critical essays.

15. John Dryden's finest works were his long poems in heroic couplets on _____, _____ and literary themes.

16. In prose, John Dryden established the Neoclassical standards of order, _____ and harmony.

17. Dryden was a poet of _____, not of emotion.

III. Term definition

1. Metaphysical poetry 2. Conceit
3. Pamphlet 4. Allegory

Part Four The Period of Revolution and Restoration

5. Dream vision
6. Literary criticism
7. Carpe diem
8. Pastoral
9. Prose
10. Prose poem
11. Epithalamion
12. Masques
13. Style

IV. Short-answer questions

1. What are the literary characteristics in the Period of Revolution?
2. What are the features of John Donne's poetic writings?
3. How much do you know about John Milton's *Paradise Lost*?
4. What are the major features of John Milton's poetry?
5. What are the writing features of John Bunyan's works?

V. Essay questions

1. Analyze the character of Satan in *Paradise Lost*.
2. Give a brief introduction to *The Pilgrim's Progress*.
3. Comment on John Dryden's contributions to English literature.

Part Five The Age of Enlightenment

(Roughly the 18th c.)

Chapter 13 Introduction

13.1 Background

In terms of social context, the 18th century in England can be divided into two halves. The first half was a comparatively peaceful period. Due to the Revolution of 1688 (i. e., the glorious revolution), the new century witnessed the end of the long struggle for political freedom and the beginning of the constitutional monarchy in England. Politically, the people in control of the government split into two parties—the liberal Whigs and the conservative Tories. The two main parties were so well balanced that power shifted easily from one to the other. The balance was a kind of compromise between the aristocracy and the bourgeoisie, which placed in the hands of the Whigs for the next century, except for short intervals, the control of the central state apparatus, while the Tory Squirearchy had the control of the local government in the country districts, and thus a kind of dualism was created round which much of the political conflict of the 18th century turned. Economically, England became increasingly affluent, the factory system began to develop, trade flourished, and there was an outburst of productivity. A mercantile system came into being to meet the needs of trade and productivity. People's living standards greatly improved and this made for a superficial optimism. A feeling of prosperity was up in the air. Thanks to the economic prosperity as well as the political dualism, England became the first powerful capitalist country.

But troubles began to appear in the second half of the century. Technology and science jumped, and inventions and the protection for patents facilitated change and growth. The discovery of the steam power, the advent of the steam engine, the adoption of the steam-driven machines in factories, the steam ships, the subsequent expansion of the merchant fleet, the use of chemicals, the mechanization of farming, and the further pillaging of the colonies—all these brought about huge changes in the basic eco-social scene of the country. The Industrial Revolution was now in full swing. The second half of the century was a period of growing fortune for the middle class, but one of intensified debasement for the working class. With factories making life ever more dirty, ugly and unhealthy, the workers suffered nondescript degradation. Hence there occurred widespread social upheavals. The farmers went bankrupt and swarmed to the cities where, along with the city poor, they struggled for survival. The proletariat came into being and there came the long drawn-out conflict between capital and labor. With the growing discontent and disaffection among the poor, cries of rebellion began to rumble. The French Revolution was in the making and so was the American War of Independence. Sensing imminent danger from these quarters, the British ruling class lost no time intensifying their repressive rule. This was roughly the backdrop against which the age of reason began to take a backseat.

Meanwhile, there was a significant change in religion. People did not believe in formal religion with its tenets of revelation and supernatural elements, though they still believed in God. With the 1687 publication of Newton's *Philosophiae Naturalis Principia Mathematica* ("Mathematical Principles of Natural Philosophy") in which his laws of motion and the ideas of universal gravitation were embodied, the universe became, in the minds of thinking people, something mechanical, like a clock, subject not to the close supervision of God but to certain physical and mechanical laws. This gave rise to a whole set of new ideas and philosophies, predominant among which were deism. The deists held that God indeed was the creator of the universe, "the maker of the clock," but He had left it to operate according to natural law. Thus the best way to worship God is to study his handiwork, namely, the natural world and the human world, and to do good things to mankind. There was no doubt that people were good believers. But religion was now considered private and personal, and it was bad taste to bring it out in public and let it interfere with public affairs.

Within such a context, the concept of John Locke (1632 – 1704) on human understanding as well as on civil government became active and influential. In *An Essay Concerning Human Understanding* (1690), Locke argued that people had to learn through their senses, through their experience of feeling, seeing, touching, measuring and weighing, that reason was of the primary importance in learning to understand the world. In his *Two Treatises of Government* (1689), he stated that men were born equal with no innate prejudices and capable of reason, that all the people had the right to pursue their happiness, that reason led to cooperation and general welfare, that people came together in a civil contract for mutual defense of their rights, property and labor, and that the pursuit of one's self-interest was a way to serve society. These ideas prompted human rights and justified the growth of capitalism and the middle-class control in parliament. Consequently, in England, as in other European countries, there sprang into life a public movement known as the Enlightenment.

13.2 Enlightenment

The Enlightenment was a progressive intellectual movement throughout Western Europe in the 18th century. It was an expression of struggle of the bourgeoisie against feudalism. The enlighteners fought against class inequality, stagnation, prejudices and other survivals of feudalism. They thought that the chief means for bettering the society was "enlightenment" or "education" for people. In other words, they believed in the power of reason, and that's why the 18th century in the history of Europe has often been called "the Age of Reason."

As a movement, the Enlightenment developed many ramifications. In their attempt to rationalize the government and the law, the Enlightenment thinkers regarded government as the political expression of law. And law itself was defined as the "necessary relationships which derive from the nature of things." According to them, the law of all lands was valid only when it conformed to the law which reason perceived in nature. As regards religion, the Enlightenment was completely secular in outlook. The tendency was rather toward deism, which held that the universe was set in motion by God as a self-regulating mechanism, and that everything operated according to natural laws, which could be understood by the human mind. In art and literature, what coincided with the Age of Reason was a period called Neoclassicism represented by John Dryden and Alexander Pope in England. These people were on the whole traditionalists and they had a great respect for the classical artists and authors, and for their rules of art. They thought that reason and judgment were the most admirable faculties and that decorum was essential.

The English enlighteners were bourgeois democratic thinkers. Most of the English writers were enlighteners. They fell into two groups—the moderate group including Alexander Pope, Joseph Addison, Richard Steele, Daniel Defoe and Samuel Richardson, who supported the principles of the existing social order and considered that partial reform would be sufficient, and the radical group including Jonathan Swift, Henry Fielding, Tobias George Smollett, Oliver Goldsmith and Richard Brinsley Sheridan, who struggled for more resolute democratization in the management of the government and defended the interests of the exploited masses, the peasants and the working people in the cities.

13.3 Literature

In literature, there existed also a balance between the respect for the old and the emergence of new forms, and between reason and emotion. The English literature was of reason, common sense, and repudiation of enthusiasm and sentiment in the early 18th century in particular. Classical rules were prized and enforced, especially in Alexander Pope's works. Hence the nomenclature of the period as "the classic age." The Popian Neoclassicism was furthered by such writers as Joseph Addison, Richard Steele and Samuel Johnson. Although the Neoclassical tastes dominated the better part of the 18th century, reason was not strong enough to totally stamp out the sparks of emotion. There was, almost from the very outset, an undercurrent that moved in a different direction, the current that eventually led to a fresh outburst of romantic feeling. This was well illustrated by the advent of the Pre-romantic poets Robert Burns and William Blake in the later century.

However, the main literary stream of the 18th century was realism. Writers took a closer look at the social problems. What they described in their works were social realities. The main characters were usually common men. Most of the writers concentrated their attention on daily life. This naturally resulted in the popularity of prose in literary writing. The 18th century was an age of prose. There appeared a group of excellent prose writers such as Joseph Addison, Richard Steele and Jonathan Swift. With the improvement of literacy and with leisure now available in life, the demand for literature increased, which generated new forms of literary writings, on top of which appeared novel. The new genre differed from the traditional romances, which dealt with fantasy and far-away things, in telling stories about ordinary life as was lived. The main characters in the novels were no longer kings and nobles but the common people. Those representative novelists include Daniel Defoe, Henry Fielding, Tobias George Smollett, Samuel Richardson and Laurence Sterne.

Meanwhile, satire was much used in writings in this age. Since there was fierce strife of the political parties in society, nearly every writer of the century was employed and rewarded by the Whigs or the Tories for satirizing their enemies. The English literature of this age produced some excellent satirists such as Alexander Pope, Jonathan Swift and Henry Fielding.

The 18th-century English literature went through three stages/periods. The first or early period, stretching roughly from the "Glorious Revolution" to the end of the 1730s, was characterized by the so-called Neoclassicism in poetry, of which the representative poet was Alexander Pope. Meanwhile a new prose literature appeared in the essays of Addison and Steele and in the first realistic fiction of Defoe and Swift. The second or mature period, lasting from the 1740s to the 1750s, produced the more important works, chiefly the novels of Richardson, Fielding and Smollett. In their novels Fielding and Smollett made rather fierce attacks on the existing social conditions. The third or last period, covering the last decades of the 18th century, witnessed the emergence of the new literary tendencies of Sentimentalism and Pre-romanticism, both of which served as protests against the social injustices of the day. Sentimentalism did find its representative writers like Edward Young and Thomas Gray in the field of poetry, but it manifested itself chiefly in the novels of Lawrence Sterne and Oliver Goldsmith. Pre-romanticism found its expression chiefly in poetry. Most of the poets who followed this tradition were minor ones; the more important ones were William Blake and Robert Burns. They struggled against the poetic tradition of Neoclassicism. The chief dramatist of the century Richard Brinsley Sheridan also wrote his plays in this period.

Generally speaking, the literature of the 18th century was complex. We may simply classify it under the general heads: the reign of Classicism, the emergence of Sentimentalism and Pre-romanticism, the spread of realism and the rise of modern novel.

Chapter 14 Neoclassical School

Neoclassicism was a reaction against the intricacy and occasional obscurity, the boldness and the extravagance of the European literature of the late Renaissance, as seen, for instance, in the works of the Metaphysical, in favor of simplicity, clarity, restraint regularity and good sense. The general tendency of Neoclassical literature was to look at social and political life critically, to emphasize intellect rather than imagination. Writers intended to repress much of their personal emotion and enthusiasm, and to use precise and elegant methods of expression.

Neoclassicism in Britain was initiated by John Dryden in the 17th century. Thenceforth, it made a rapid growth in the hands of such writers as Joseph Addison, Richard Steele and Alexander Pope, and reached its culmination in Pope in the early 18th century. In the middle decades of the century, Samuel Johnson became the leader of the Classical school. English Neoclassicism thus prevailed for the better part of the 18th century.

The writers, considered Neoclassic, modeled themselves on classical Greek and Latin authors in order to achieve perfect form in literature. They tried to make English literature conform to rules and principles established by the great Roman and Greek classical writers. In general, the Neoclassical works were characterized by frequent allusions and references to the Greek and Roman mythology and to the ancient writers and historians, predilection for abstractions and excessive use of personifications, respect for and promotion of order and reason with emphasis on clarity of thought and orderly structure, focus on formal perfection like metric regularity, aversion to verbosity and love of graceful language, and a conspicuous want of feeling and sentiment. The dominant Neoclassic form was the heroic couplet. Specifically, they thought that poetry should follow the ancient divisions, falling into lyric, epic, didactic, satiric or dramatic, and that each group should be guided by some peculiar principles to produce the effect of an artificially trimmed beauty. In writing plays they used rimed couplet instead of blank verse and observed the three unities, while the Neoclassical prose was always precise, direct and flexible.

14.1 Alexander Pope (1688 – 1744)

Pope was an English poet best known for his satirical verse as well as his translation of Homer. In the field of satiric and didactic verse, he was the undisputed master. His influence completely dominated the poetry of his age. Many foreign writers and the majority of English poets looked to him as their model. His poetry clearly reflected the spirit of the age in which he lived. He was the representative writer of the Neoclassical school and weeded feeling and emotion successfully out of poetry. It is always an enjoyable experience to read him for knowledge, and for his rhythms, rhymes and the musical ring of his words. One of his major functions, as his poetry well illustrates, seemed to help readers remember things. His fame as a poet was established rather early in life and his influence upon other poets was very great both during his time and after his death.

Pope was a master of the heroic couplet, which became a perfect poetic medium in his hands, so powerful and fascinating in his time that the rest of the works could not but write in the same manner. The heroic couplet, since it was introduced by Geoffrey Chaucer in the Middle Ages, had been constantly used by those writers like Edmund Spenser and Christopher Marlowe in the Renaissance Period except being superseded for some time by blank verse. In the 17th century it resurfaced especially in the works of John Dryden. But it was Pope's painstaking effort that helped the heroic couplet reach its perfection. Famous for his use of the heroic couplet, Pope is the second most frequently-quoted writer in *The Oxford Dictionary of Quotations*, after William Shakespeare.

Pope's well-known works chronologically include his translation of Homer, *Essay on Criticism* (1711), *The Rape of the Lock* (1712), *Essay on Man* (1733), *An Epistle to Dr. Arbuthnot* (1735) and *The Dunciad* (1743).

Essay on Criticism, a verse essay written in heroic couplet, is primarily concerned with how writers and critics behave in the new literary commerce of Pope's contemporary age. The poem is accepted as a manifesto of the English Neoclassicism as Pope put forward his aesthetic theories in it. It is an attempt to identify and refine his own positions as a poet and critic. The poem is said to be a response to an ongoing debate on the question of whether poetry should be natural or written according to predetermined artificial rules inherited from the classical past. It covers a range of good criticism and advice, and represents many of the chief literary ideals of Pope's age.

The poem consists of 744 lines and is divided into three parts. The first part expresses the poet's sorrow over the scarcity of true taste in critics and points out the need to turn to nature as the best guide for critical judgment. The second part praises the ancient writers, particularly Homer and Virgil, and their rules in writing. It also names the dangers that may beset the critics and lead them into faulty criticism. Part Three offers the rules to be followed by the critics and traces the history of literary criticism from Aristotle down to Boileau (1636 – 1711), pointing out that critics serve an important function in aiding poets with their works, as opposed to the practice of attacking them.

Essay on Criticism is a comprehensive study of theories of literary criticism and has been regarded as one of the important works in English literary criticism. The work is famous chiefly not for what its author said, but for the way he said it. He wrote to introduce the accepted canons of tastes in memorable, beautiful language and help people remember them. Some of the critical theories that he discussed so well in his own words and style were actually gleaned from such previous works as *Poetics* by Aristotle, *Ars Poetica* ("The Art of Poetry," c. 19 BC) by Horace, *De Arte Poetica* ("On the Art of Poetry," 1527) by Vida (1485? – 1566) and *L'Art poetitique* (1674) by Boileau. In addition, he also drew from the works of the Roman rhetorician Quintilian (c. 35 – c. 100 AD), Ben Jonson's *Timber, or Discoveries* (1640), and the prefaces of John Dryden.

The Rape of the Lock, Pope's most famous poem, came out in three versions. The first version in two cantos (334 lines), published anonymously in *Miscellaneous Poems and Translations* in 1712, was a great success. Then it was revised, expanded and reissued in 1714. This was a five-canto version, consisting of 794 lines accompanied by six engravings. Pope brought in the mythological and supernatural elements and their epic behaviors. He boasted that the poem sold more than 3,000 copies in its first four days. The final version was available in 1717. It added a good deal of humor to the poem but little substance to the satire.

The Rape of the Lock is a mock-heroic narrative poem about "a Homeric struggle of the teacups." It was based on an actual epistle of little or no significance, which led to the discord of two noble families. Lord Petre, a fop of court, playfully cut a lock of hair from the head of Arabella Fermor, a lady he adored, and there ensued a bitter quarrel between the Fermors and the Petres. Pope was requested to write a poem so as to reveal the trivial nature of the row and help pacify the two houses, and the result was the humorous poem, in which he satirized the triviality and silliness of high society with a delicate wit. Pope revealed, in a mild satirical tone, the idle and silly high-society life of cards, parties, tea, lap dogs, lovers, toilets, the vanity of women and the foolishness of fawning men. He also touched, though only in a tangential manner, on the position of women in a man-oriented social setting. In addition to his perfect heroic couplets, Pope showed his poetic virtuosity in his adroit use of detail, his eloquent mastery of the epic conventions, and his ingenuity to turn a trifle into one of the most popular, the finest, satiric poems in his country's history.

Essay on Man, a poem written in heroic couplet, indicates the poet's political and philosophical viewpoint. It deals with man's relation to the universe, to society, to himself, and to happiness. Pope assumed an optimistic view, denying the existence of any contradictions in human life. This poem tells us that Pope approved of and upheld the existing aristocratic-bourgeois society of England of that age.

Essay on Man is probably the most important of all Pope's works, and certainly the best known and most often quoted. As an authentic record of the views and values of the 18th century, this "ethic work" (as Pope called it), Pope's philosophical poem, is significant in the cultural and intellectual history of his country as well. As his survey of man and society, the essay presents a lucid synthesis of Pope's deliberations on the cosmos, the theology and the ethics of his time following his conversations with his philosopher friend Lord Bolingbroke (1678 – 1751). In addition, the poet also picked up many clues for his ideas from Plato (428/427/424/423 – 348/347 BC), Aristotle and some Enlightenment philosophers like the German philosopher G. W. Leibnitz (1646 – 1716). The poem is an attempt to "vindicate the ways of God to Man," a variation on Milton's attempt in *Paradise Lost* to "justify the ways of God to Man." All through the work, Pope kept praising God as the source of goodness and telling people not to judge Him and His creation but accept and obey His plan for universal good and happiness. The essay is a cogent justification of the gradation or multitier hierarchy of God's creation and also of the 18th-century emphasis on order and harmony. It is not solely Christian; however, it makes an assumption that man has fallen and must seek his own salvation.

In *Essay on Man*, Pope presented an idea on his view on the Universe; he said that no matter how imperfect, complex, inscrutable and disturbing the Universe appeared to be, it functioned in a rational fashion according to the natural laws. The natural laws consider the Universe as a whole a perfect work of God. To humans it appears to be evil and imperfect in many ways; however, Pope pointed out that this was due to our limited mindset and limited intellectual capacity. Pope got the message across that humans must accept their position in the "Great Chain of Being," which is at a middle stage between the angels and the beasts of the world. If we were able to accomplish this then we potentially could lead happy and virtuous lives.

The essay consists of four epistles addressed to Lord Bolingbroke. Epistle one is a brilliant summary of the basic concepts of wide currency in England and Europe at the time. It offers the optimistic 18th-century view of the world created by God. God is the ultimate source of all creation in His carefully ordered system of gradation. In God's grand scheme of things, man who has reason stands in the middle, between the lower creatures at one end and angels and God at the other. Thus placed in the "Great Chain of Being," man has limited knowledge and perceptive powers, his judgment of the cosmos (seeing it as imperfect) is faulty, and his errors such as his pride and aspirations tend to disrupt God's plan. Man can be happy if he is ignorant and knows only to hope for a better future. Evil exists to make for good. Pope affirms the goodness of all that exists and proves himself to be a supporter of the existing system. Pope was not a social critic as was Jonathan Swift. He was very conservative in his opinions. Epistle two discusses human nature and the human condition. In his middle position between God and beast, man possesses both virtue and vice. His self-love motivates him to action, and his reason controls him so as to do good. When the two work together, nothing can go wrong. Passions are modes of self-love. The ruling passion in man determines his basic personality. Human weaknesses contribute to mutual dependence. Man should know his place and stay content with it. Epistle three talks about man's role in society. All is interrelated in the chain of being: all is allotted his share of happiness and should love itself and others. With regard to the species below him, man is given power as well as responsibility. In society there exist self-love and social love, the two linking with each other to work toward harmony and happiness for all. True religion and government are united in love; superstition and tyranny disrupt nature's order. Epistle four relates to man's happiness. God intends all in His chain to be equally happy. Man's happiness depends on health, peace and competence. Virtue's reward is not earthly and external. It is not his possessions and gifts of fortune, but his virtuous personality that matters to man. Virtue and love of God and man lead to the happiness of one and all. Self-love is a blessing when it transcends its limits and devotes itself to social and divine love.

On its publication, *Essay on Man* received great admiration throughout Europe. More than any other work, it popularized optimistic philosophy throughout England and the rest of Europe. Voltaire (2003: 147) called it "the most beautiful, the most useful, the most sublime didactic poem ever written in any language." In 1756 Rousseau (1712 – 1778) wrote to Voltaire admiring the poem and saying that it "softens my ills and brings me patience." (qtd. in Solomon, 1993) Immanuel Kant (1724 – 1804) was fond of the poem and would recite long passages from it to his students. Later, however, Voltaire renounced his admiration for the optimism of Pope and Leibniz (1646 – 1716) and even wrote a novel *Candide* as a satire on their philosophy of ethics. Rousseau also critiqued the work, questioning "Pope's uncritical assumption that there must be an unbroken chain of being all the way from inanimate matter up to God." (qtd. in Damrosch, 2005)

An Epistle to Dr. Arbuthnot, one of Pope's best poems, was composed in 1734, when Pope learned that Dr. Arbuthnot (1667 – 1735), the physician of Queen Anne (1665 – 1714), was dying. Pope described it as a memorial of their friendship. It has been called Pope's "most directly autobiographical work," in which he defended his practice in the genre of satire and attacked those who had been his opponents and rivals throughout his career. Arbuthnot was a friend of such literary celebrities as Pope and Jonathan Swift and a celebrity of the time in his own way. He wrote on his sick bed a letter to Pope, advising him to be kind when writing satires. Pope wrote the poem in response, trying to convince the doctor that his satires had been all self-defenses and never meant to be vituperative. Thus the work was intended to be his "apologia" justifying his life, work and personality. It is necessary to read it to get to know about the man and his mentality. As he said in the epistle, Pope was not happy, and he bitterly complained about a joyless existence. He was dutiful and loving to his parents, willing to learn and write, and proud of his independence. He hated people picking on his deformity and detested sleights of hand against him. His enemies include cohorts of people ranging from the friends and confidants of the queen to powerful politician-men of letters such as Joseph Addison. Pope could be cruel and mean in his satire, but he exercised tact as well. For Addison, for instance, he left room for making friends with the man in the future.

The Dunciad is Pope's famous satirical poem and a landmark literary satire. It is full of bitter personal attacks on the poet's personal enemies, and it also gives a broad satirical picture of the whole literary life in the early 18th-century England. It shows the poet's struggle against ignorance and barbarism as well as "dullness" and "emptiness" all around him. The work was published in three different versions at different times. The first version—the three-book *Dunciad*—was published in 1728 anonymously. The second version, the *Dunciad Variorum*, was published anonymously in 1729. The *New Dunciad*, in a new fourth book conceived as a sequel to the previous three, appeared in 1742, and *The Dunciad in Four Books*, a revised version of the original three books and a slightly revised version of the fourth book with revised commentary, was published in 1743 with a new character Bays replacing Tibbald as the hero. The poem celebrates the goddess Dulness and the progress of her chosen agents as they bring decay, imbecility and tastelessness to the Kingdom of Great Britain.

The poem was first composed as part of a controversy on Pope's edition of Shakespeare and a comment on the literary climate of the time. But as the poet proceeded with the writing, it became a leverage of revenge for his long pent-up bitterness against some of his literary rivals. The truth was that some of Pope's works might have suffered some slight, and that he might have had quarrels with some literary men and have been subject to humiliation on account of his deformity. Thus in his ruthless blows at his enemies, Pope occasionally descended very low so that his effort boomeranged somehow as it showed him to be narrow-minded and lacking in catholic taste. The good part about the work is, however, its revelation of the dreadful widespread dullness to his age and its brilliant satire on the vices of the literary world then. Though it is couched in humorous mock-epic form, Pope was dead serious with his warning to his country of the real danger coming from ignorance and the triumph of dullness.

Pope was known as a great poet in his day. He brought the heroic couplet to its perfection and exerted much influence upon the other writers of the age. He popularized the Neoclassical literary tradition. He was one of the early representatives of the Enlightenment, who introduced into English culture the spirit of rationalism and greater interest in the human world. He was a great satirist and a literary critic. He occupied a prominent place in the literary world of his time. The early period of the 18th century has often been named after him the "Age of Pope." His influence on Byron was great and strong, so Byron thought highly of him and defended him while he was criticized by some critics in the 19th century.

14.2 Joseph Addison (1672 – 1719) and Sir Richard Steele (1672 – 1729)

Addison was an English essayist, poet, playwright and politician. He was the greatest literary man of his time and is acknowledged as one of the greatest English essayists of all time. His name is usually remembered alongside that of his long-standing friend Richard Steele because of their joint literary work. The two literary periodicals—*The Tatler* and *The Spectator*—are Addison and Steele's chief contribution to English literature.

Addison began writing essays quite casually when he wrote to *The Tatler*, the first journal of his childhood friend Richard Steele. Addison contributed 42 essays to the periodical. Steele once remarked on Addison's help that "when I had once called him in, I could not subsist without dependence on him." (Montgomery, 1865: 148) Addison and Steele founded *The Spectator* collaboratively two months after *The Tatler* was discontinued. In *The Spectator*, Addison soon became the leading partner. He contributed 274 essays among a total of 555; Steele wrote 236 for this periodical. Besides, Addison wrote an essay *Dialogues on Medals* and left incomplete a work *Of the Christian Religion*.

The Spectator was a daily paper, beginning on 1 March 1711 and continuing until 6 December 1712. It achieved great popularity and exercised a great deal of influence on the reading public of the time. It made fun of all that was wrong and foolish in society and praised all that was good. It told odd stories about imaginary characters and the most striking features of the paper are the character sketches of Mr. Spectator and the members of his club, and these sketches become the forerunner of the modern novel. Each "paper" or "number" was approximately 2,500 words long, and the original run consisted of 555 numbers, which were collected into seven volumes. The paper was revived without the involvement of Steele in 1714, appearing thrice weekly for six months, and these papers when collected formed the eighth volume.

Richard Steele was an Irish writer and politician. His first published work *The Christian Hero* (1701) attempted to point out the differences between perceived and actual masculinity. Written while Steele served in the army, it expressed his idea of a pamphlet of moral instruction. *The Christian Hero* was ultimately ridiculed for what some thought was hypocrisy because Steele did not necessarily follow his own preaching. He was criticized for publishing a booklet about morals when he himself enjoyed drinking, occasional dueling, and debauchery around town. Steele's first comedy *The Funeral* (1701) was a wide success. Performed at Drury Lane, the play brought its author to the attention of the King and the Whig party. Steele's next play *The Lying Lover* was one of the first sentimental comedies but a failure on stage. In 1705, Steele wrote *The Tender Husband* with contributions from Addison's, and later that year he wrote the prologue to *The Mistake* by John Vanbrugh (1664 – 1726), an important member of the Whig Kit-Kat Club along with Addison and Steele.

The Tatler first came out on 12 April 1709 and appeared three times a week: on Tuesdays, Thursdays and

Saturdays. It was published for two years. It was started by Steele, who used the pseudonym Isaac Bickerstaff and gave Bickerstaff an entire, fully developed personality. He described his motive in writing *The Tatler* as "to expose the false arts of life, to pull off the disguises of cunning, vanity, and affectation, and to recommend a general simplicity in our dress, our discourse, and our behavior." Steele wrote the majority of the essays, though he and Addison collaborated, and Addison was a better writer than him and made *The Tatler* a great success. Of the 271 essays published in *The Tatler*, Joseph Addison wrote 42, Richard Steele wrote roughly 188, and the rest were collaborations between the two writers. So, although Addison contributed to *The Tatler*, it is widely regarded as Steele's work. *The Tatler* was closed down to avoid the complications of running a Whig publication that had come under Tory attack. Addison and Steele then founded *The Spectator* and also the *Guardian*, a short-lived newspaper published in London from 12 March to 1 October 1713.

Steele and Addison wrote in different styles. Steele took very little pains with his language. He wrote as he pleased, right from his heart. His style is intimate, easy-going and careless. But Addison was a careful writer and great stylist. He created a perfect style, which is lucid, colloquial, full of individuality and yet refined by that choice of words which he had cultivated in writing Latin verse. It could win the approval of the scholars by virtue of its correctness and at the same time could be well understood by the middle-class readers and even by people of little culture owing to its simplicity. Addison's Spectator essays were looked upon as the model of English composition by the British authors all through the 18th century. Samuel Johnson thus praised Addison's style: "Whoever wishes to attain an English style, familiar but not coarse, and eloquent but not ostentatious, must give his days and nights to the study of Addison."

The Spectator and *The Tatler* are the first important recognitions by literature of the special interests of women readers, notwithstanding they were by no means limited to the doings of the women. The periodicals brought literature down to everyday life and kept it clean and wholesome. There was no trace of malice in Addison's genial humor, no spitefulness and no coarseness. The many journals which followed *The Spectator* maintained its tone of courtesy and good breeding. Its influence, indeed, extended beyond the essays of the 18th century to all the periodical literature which has continued to multiply with such rapidity. Addison's prose remained for over a century the model for those writers like Oliver Goldsmith, Benjamin Franklin (1706 – 1790) and Washington Irving (1783 – 1859).

Addison and Steele's writings in *The Tatler* and *The Spectator* provided a new code of social morality for the rising bourgeoisie. They gave a true picture of the social life of England in the 18th century. In their hands, the English essay completely established itself as a literary genre. Using it as a form of character-sketching and story-telling, they ushered in the dawn of the modern novel.

14.3 Samuel Johnson (1709 – 1784)

Samuel Johnson, often referred to as Dr Johnson, was an English writer who made lasting contributions to English literature as a poet, essayist, dramatist, prose romancer, moralist, literary critic, biographer, editor and lexicographer. Johnson was a devout Anglican and committed Tory, and has been described as "arguably the most distinguished man of letters in English history." He is also the subject of James Boswell's *Life of Samuel Johnson*, "the most famous single work of biographical art in the whole of literature." (Bate, 1977: xix)

Johnson was a voluminous and versatile writer. His early works include *Life of Mr Richard Savage* (1744), an affectionate biography of a literary friend with whom he had shared extreme poverty, *Irene* (1749), his only play (tragedy) in which Johnson observed the Classical rules, and the two satirical poems *London* (1738) and *The Vanity of Human Wishes* (1749). Both of the two poems were written in heroic couplet and with much consciousness and polish in the true Classical style. In *London* Johnson gave satirical descriptions of the degeneracy in the aristocratic-bourgeois society in London, including the sufferings of the poor and the arrogance of the wealth. In *The Vanity of Human Wishes*, Johnson tried to point out how utterly vain all human ambitions and endeavors were. Then in 1755 Johnson published *A Dictionary of the English Language*, which had a far-reaching effect on Modern English and has been described as "one of the greatest single achievements of scholarship." (Bate, 1977: 240) Johnson's later works include his essays, an influential annotated edition of *The Plays of William Shakespeare* (1765), the widely-read tale *The History of Rasselas, Prince of Abissinia* (1759), a didactic romance which has been praised highly by some critics for being a full expression of Johnson's rationalism and great wisdom but was hurriedly finished when Johnson's mother died and he could not afford to bury her, his travel narrative *A Journey to the Western Islands of Scotland* (1775), in which Johnson described his 83-day journey through Scotland with James Boswell, and his massive and influential work *Lives of the Most Eminent English Poets* (1779 - 1781). Johnson's essays were published in the two periodicals—*The Rambler* (1750 - 1752) and *The Idler* (1758 - 1760). They dealt with all sorts of subjects, including character-sketches, allegories, Oriental tales, critical essays and moral essays. Among all Johnson's works, the best-known are *A Dictionary of the English Language* and *Lives of the Most Eminent English Poets*.

A Dictionary of the English Language, sometimes published as **Johnson's Dictionary**, is among the most influential dictionaries in the history of the English language. There was dissatisfaction with the dictionaries of the period, so in June 1746 a group of London booksellers contracted Johnson to write a dictionary. Johnson took nearly nine years to complete the work, although he had claimed he could finish it in three. Remarkably, he did so single-handedly, with only clerical assistance to copy out the illustrative quotations that he had marked in books. Johnson produced several revised editions during his life.

Until the completion of the *Oxford English Dictionary* 173 years later in 1928, Johnson's was viewed as the preeminent English dictionary. According to Walter Jackson Bate (1918 - 1999), the *Dictionary* "easily ranks as one of the greatest single achievements of scholarship, and probably the greatest ever performed by one individual who labored under anything like the disadvantages in a comparable length of time." (Bate, 1977: 240) This enormous work brought Johnson popularity and success. It is remarkable for the definitions of the meaning of words and for the quotations in illustration of their use. It became the foundation of all the subsequent English dictionaries and marked an epoch in the study of the English language and the end of English writers' reliance on the patronage of noblemen for support.

Lives of the Most Eminent English Poets is a collection of short biographies and critical appraisals of 52 poets, most of whom lived during the 18th century. It is arranged, approximately, by date of death, and affords some of the best-known pictures of the early English poets. When Johnson was seventy years old, he was asked to write the prefaces to a new edition of the English poets. The result was his *Lives of the Poets*. Six of the lives have been singled out as the most important, including John Milton, John Dryden, Alexander Pope, Joseph Addison, Jonathan Swift and Thomas Gray. One of the lives, Richard Savage, was previously printed as *Life of Mr Richard Savage* in 1744.

Lives of the Poets and the preface and comments of individual plays in Johnson's edition of Shakespeare are accepted as the two most important of all his literary works and pass judgment on a century of English poetry. Johnson was a Classicist. His essays of literary criticism were written according to the rules of Classicism, sometimes moderated with the author's sober common sense, which was especially shown in his estimation of Shakespeare.

14.4　James Boswell (1740 – 1795)

Boswell, a Scottish lawyer, diarist and author, is best known for the biography he wrote of Samuel Johnson entitled *The Life of Samuel Johnson LL. D.* (1791). While Boswell's personal acquaintance with his subject only began in 1763, when Johnson was 54 years old, Boswell covered the entirety of Johnson's life by means of additional research. Boswell's surname has passed into the English language as a term (Boswell, Boswellian, Boswellism) for a constant companion and observer, especially one who records those observations in print. Boswell was a member in Johnson's club.

The Life of Samuel Johnson LL. D. offers us a vivid and detailed portrait of Johnson. From it we can see all the man's vanity as well as his greatness, his prejudices, superstitions, and even the details of his personal appearance. It is also a record of the 18th-century England. Owing to this successful work, Boswell has been called the best biographer in English literature. The work is regarded as an important stage in the development of the modern genre of biography.

When it was published, the work at once commanded the admiration that Boswell had sought for so long, and it has since suffered no diminution. Its style was unique in that, unlike other biographies of that era, it directly incorporated conversations that Boswell had noted down at the time for his journals. He also included far more personal and human details than those to which contemporary readers were accustomed. Instead of writing a respectful and dry record of Johnson's public life in the style of the time, he painted a vivid portrait of the complete man, brought to life through a "dramatic" style of dialogue. The biography takes many critical liberties with Johnson's life, as Boswell made various changes to Johnson's quotations and even censored many comments. It has often been described as the greatest biography ever written in the English language.

Chapter 15　Fiction of Realistic Tradition

The 18th century produced the first English novelists who followed two traditions in writing and thus fell into two groups—the Sentimentalist novelists and the realist novelists. The rise and growth of the realistic novel was the most prominent achievement in the 18th-century English literature. The novelists of this group told the reader in their novels, not about knights or kings but about the ordinary people, about their thoughts, feelings and struggles. The major realist novelists of this century are Daniel Defoe, Jonathan Swift, Henry Fielding and Tobias George

Smollett.

15.1 Daniel Defoe (c. 1660 – 1731)

Defoe was an English journalist, pamphleteer, poet, and, above all, novelist. He is now famous for his novel *Robinson Crusoe*. A prolific and versatile writer, he wrote more than five hundred books, pamphlets and journals on various topics including politics, crime, religion, marriage, psychology and the supernatural. He was also a pioneer of economic journalism. Defoe's chief contribution to English literature lies in his novels. He is notable for being one of the earliest proponents of the novel, as he helped to popularize the form in Britain. He is among the founders of the English novel and has been regarded as the discoverer of the modern novel by some critics. His strong creative spirit in novel writing even won him the title "Father of English and European Novels."

Defoe's first notable publication was *An Essay upon Projects*, a series of proposals for social and economic improvement, published in 1697. His well-known pamphlets include *The True-born Englishman* (1701) and *The Shortest Way with the Dissenters, Or Proposals for the Establishment of the Church* (1702). The former exposes the aristocracy and the tyranny of the church, satirizes the English claim to racial purity, attacking the prejudice against the king of foreign birth, and won its author the favor of King William III (1650 – 1702, king 1689 – 1702). The latter ironically demands the total suppression of the dissenters, who were supported by the Tories. Thus Defoe enraged the government which was controlled by the Tories; he was arrested and put into prison. In prison he continued his struggle against the ruling class. To defend himself and satirize his persecutors, he wrote a poem *Hymn to the Pillory* (1703), which was printed by his friends for street distribution upon his first appearance at the pillory. His courage and the humor of his verse won him the immediate sympathy of many people. According to legend, his audience at the pillory threw flowers instead of the customary harmful and noxious objects, and drank to his health. The truth of this story is questioned by most scholars, although John Robert Moore (1890 – 1973) later said that "no man in England but Defoe ever stood in the pillory and later rose to eminence among his fellow men." (qtd. in Richetti, 2005)

Within a week of his release from prison, Defoe witnessed the Great Storm of 1703, which caused severe damage to London and Bristol, uprooted millions of trees and killed over 8,000 people, mostly at sea. The event became the subject of Defoe's *The Storm* (1704), a pioneering work of journalism and science reporting, which includes a collection of witness accounts of the tempest. It is the first detailed account of a hurricane in Britain and is regarded as one of the world's first examples of modern journalism. In the same year he set up his periodical *A Review of the Affairs of France* which chronicled the events of the War of the Spanish Succession (1702 – 1714). The *Review* ran three times a week without interruption until 1713.

Not all of Defoe's pamphlet writing was political. One pamphlet entitled *A True Relation of the Apparition of One Mrs. Veal the Next Day after her Death to One Mrs. Bargrave at Canterbury the 8th of September, 1705* (1706), originally published anonymously, is a vivid report of a current ghost story. It deals with interaction between the spiritual realm and the physical realm. It describes Mrs. Bargrave's encounter with an old friend Mrs. Veal after the latter's death. It is clear from this piece and other writings, that, while the political portion of Defoe's life was fairly dominant, it was by no means the only aspect.

When he was nearly 60 years old, Defoe turned to writing novels. His first novel *The Life and Strange Surprising Adventures of Robinson Crusoe* (1719) was a great success. It made Defoe a well-known writer all over Europe. The second book *The Farther Adventures of Robinson Crusoe* (1719) has generally been considered as much inferior to the first. Another book *The Serious Reflections during the Life and Surprising Adventures of Robinson Crusoe* (1720) has never been reprinted and is no longer read.

At the head of Defoe's works stands his most important work and masterpiece *The Life and Strange Surprising Adventures of Robinson Crusoe*, or **Robinson Crusoe** briefly. It has held its popularity for more than two centuries. The first edition credited the fictional protagonist Robinson Crusoe as its author, leading many readers to believe he was a real person and the book a travelogue of true incidents. Epistolary, confessional, and didactic in form, the book is a fictional autobiography of the title character, a castaway who spends years on a remote tropical island near Trinidad, encountering cannibals, captives and mutineers before being rescued.

Robinson Crusoe, a strong individual, does not feel happy with the easy comforts that his father has provided him with. He heads out to sea and becomes a planter in South America, but he is insatiable. He ventures further out, experiences a shipwreck, and is left all by himself on an island without any trace of civilized life. He soon overcomes his despair and sets about building a life for himself. With the things he salvages from the ship, he builds a shelter and then a house, finds food, raises goats, plants crops, makes clothing, builds boats, and beats back savages from other islands. He saves a savage Friday as he names him, and makes him his servant. Later on he saves Friday's father and a Spaniard and becomes the master on the island. He begins to enjoy some comfort little by little and stays there for some 28 years. When an English ship goes by later, he saves its captain from mutiny, and helps the captain to recover the ship. Grateful for Robinson's assistance, the captain takes him back to England. The last pages of the novel deal with the hero's adventures after leaving the island. After his departure from the island, he sails to Lisbon and then to Brazil. He sells the plantation there to his partner. With much money he returns to England and gets married.

The story is widely perceived to have been influenced by the life of Alexander Selkirk, a Scottish castaway who lived for four years on a desert island off the coast of Chile, which was renamed Robinson Crusoe Island in 1966. Other possible sources for the primary narrative have also been suggested. It is told in the first person singular as if it were told by some sailor-adventurer himself.

The novel is first and foremost a middle-class book, offering justifications for the forthcoming rise of the middle class to predominance in national life. Defoe created the image of a true-builder, colonizer and foreign trader, who has the courage and will to face hardships, and who has determination to preserve himself and improve his livelihood by struggling against nature. Crusoe represents the English bourgeoisie at the earlier stage of its development. Being a bourgeois writer, Defoe glorified the hero and defended the policy of colonialism of British government.

The book also tells a typical Puritan tale. Robinson is characterized by Puritan individualism: he is eager for self-discovery, detests comforts, opts for adventure, and rebels in youth. He never surrenders to any difficulty but always feels confident about creating a life for himself. He sets a good example of the Puritan spirit of self-reliance and self-sustaining. He is a veritable picture of the self-made, hardworking Puritan, believing in diligence and the work ethic, laboring from sunrise to sundown, and resourceful and creative with a thinking mind and a skilful pair of hands. He discovers God for himself, and affirms his faith with which he begins his effort to civilize the island on the cultural and moral pattern that he has inherited but has left behind. However, when taken out of his temporal and spatial context, free from his middle-class background and his religion, Robinson could be simply seen as a true-to-life specimen of the ordinary humankind, bodying forth the sum total of the perseverance and indomitableness of the human spirit.

Despite its simple narrative style, *Robinson Crusoe* is well received in the literary world and is often credited as marking the beginning of realistic fiction as a literary genre. Before the end of 1719, the book had already run through four editions, and it has gone on to become one of the most widely published books in history, spawning numerous sequels and adaptations for stage, film and television.

Among Defoe's other novels, the most interesting are *Captain Singleton* (1720), *Moll Flanders* (1722) and *Colonel Jacque* (1722). **Captain Singleton** is believed to have been partly inspired by the exploits of the English pirate Henry Every. The narrative describes the life of an Englishman Singleton, stolen from a well-to-do family as a child and raised by Gypsies and eventually making his way to sea. The work, with the title character as its narrator, is a novel of adventure. The first half of the book concerns Singleton's crossing of Africa and the second half concerns his life as a pirate. Singleton takes part in a mutiny. Then he reaches Africa and crosses the continent from east to west. He meets with a lot of adventures and obtains much gold. Then he returns to England. But he goes to sea again later and becomes a pirate, carrying on his piracies in the Indian Ocean and China Sea. He becomes very rich at last. Defoe's description of piracy focuses for the most part on matters of economics and logistics, making it an intriguing if not particularly gripping read. The pirate Singleton behaves more like a merchant adventurer, which is perhaps Defoe's comment on the mercantilism of his day.

Colonel Jacque is another novel of adventure. In common with many of Defoe's other works, the novel prominently tackles the subjects of money and crime. The hero Jacque is abandoned by his parents and becomes a pickpocket. But gradually he begins to dislike the profession. He enlists in the army but deserts from it soon. Then he is kidnapped and sent to Virginia to be sold to a planter. After his master dies, he becomes a planter himself and acquires much wealth. Later he returns to England and experiences a series of adventures in his married life. The picaresque novel can be considered as a crime fiction, along with some of Defoe's other works such as *Moll Flanders* and *Roxana: The Fortunate Mistress* (1724). It shares many plot elements and themes with *Moll Flanders*, the novels being published only eleven months apart.

The Fortunes and Misfortunes of the Famous Moll Flanders, commonly shortened as **Moll Flanders**, is written in the form of biography. By 1721 Defoe had become a recognized novelist with the success of *Robinson Crusoe* in 1719. His political work was tapering off at this point, due to the fall of both Whig and Tory party leaders with whom he had been associated; Robert Walpole was beginning his rise, but Defoe was never fully at home with the Walpole group. Within this context, Defoe wrote *Moll Flanders*, which evidently expresses his Whig views. The novel is a true account of the life of a woman called Moll, whose mother was sent to Virginia after her birth. The novel details Moll's exploits from birth until old age, including her adventures. Moll is brought up by a stranger. When she grows up, she becomes a whore for 12 years, a wife for 5 times and a thief for 12 years. Finally she becomes rich and dies a penitent.

Realism and moral aesthetic are the salient features of Defoe's fiction. Defoe, as a moralist, wrote with the conviction that his works could be educational and help people behave. He extolled reason, love, liberty and equality, and infused these into his narratives to enrich them in a manner unobtrusive to the realism and artistic nature of the works. The central idea of his novels is that man is good and noble by nature but may succumb to an evil social environment. The writer wanted to make it clear that society was the source of various crimes and vices.

Defoe's novels are true records of facts, based on true events as part of history, or as historical narratives of living persons' life experiences. He made it clear that any story failing to deal with the human experience was pure fiction and a lie. He focused his narrative on the representation of life as being lived. Defoe's intention was that readers should regard his novels as real realities. His novels all take the form of memoirs or pretended historical narratives, everything in them gives the impression of reality. Thus his protagonists are common people with real common names and speak as "I," telling their own stories in the first-person narrative, addressing the readers directly without any mediation, just so as to increase the realistic effect of immediacy and involvement. Although this had to do with the theory of "literature imitating nature," Defoe's "nature" was not the Neoclassic kind of human nature in general; it was the portrayal of the individual character that caught his attention. All these were the initial efforts in the history of the English novel to leave the traditional notions of romances, fables, legends and myths behind and blaze a new trail for the genre.

15.2　Jonathan Swift (1667 – 1745)

Swift was an Anglo-Irish satirist, essayist, political pamphleteer (first for the Whigs, then for the Tories), poet and cleric who became Dean of St Patrick's Cathedral, Dublin. The 18th century in English literature was an age of prose, not because the poetry was very bad but because the prose was very good. Swift was the supreme master in the first part of the century. He has been seen by some people as the literary king of his day. He wrote a lot of powerful satirical essays and books, relentless and biting when dealing with the injustice and corruption of the rich and the upper classes. He is remembered for such works as *Gulliver's Travels* (1726), *A Modest Proposal* (1729), *A Journal to Stella* (1766), consisting of 65 letters to his friend Esther Johnson, whom he called Stella and may have secretly married, *The Drapier's Letters* (1724), *An Argument against Abolishing Christianity* (1708), *A Tale of a Tub* (1704), and *The Battle of the Books* (1704), a short satire which depicts a literal battle between books in the King's Library, as ideas and authors struggle for supremacy. Because of the satire, "The Battle of the Books" has become a term for the Quarrel of the Ancients and the Moderns. *An Argument against Abolishing Christianity* is an essay defending Christianity and in particular Anglicanism against contemporary assaults by its various opponents, including freethinkers, deists, Antitrinitarians, atheists, Socinians, and other so-called "Dissenters." As was common at the time, it was distributed widely as a pamphlet. The essay is well known for its sophisticated, multi-layered irony, and is widely regarded as one of the prime examples of political satire. In fact, Swift's major works are all satires. *The Tale of a Tub* and *Gulliver's Travels* are accepted as the greatest satires in the English language. Among the pamphlets he wrote about Ireland, the best known are *The Drapier's Letters* and *A Modest Proposal*. Swift's pamphlets were then the most powerful political weapons. He is regarded by the *Encyclopædia Britannica* as the foremost prose satirist in the English language. He is less known for his poetry. Swift originally published all of his works anonymously or under pseudonyms such as Lemuel Gulliver, Isaac Bickerstaff and MB Drapier. He is also known for being a master of two styles of satire—the Horatian and Juvenalian styles.

A Modest Proposal for Preventing the Children of Poor People from Being a Burthen to Their Parents or Country, and for Making Them Beneficial to the Publick, commonly referred to as ***A Modest Proposal***, is a Juvenalian satirical essay written and published anonymously. It is one of the most caustic satires ever written in literary history. Swift suggested that the impoverished Irish might ease their economic troubles by selling their children as food for rich gentlemen and ladies. The intensity of the attack on the English oppressions enraged the English government beyond measure. It was written in face of the utmost wretchedness of the Irish people suffering from the ruthless rule of both the British and the Irish governments. In order to address the problem of overpopulation in Ireland that was discussed then, Swift made a "modest" proposal that Irish babies should be reared and cut and sold as food for the British rich to help earn money and alleviate the misery of their poor parents. The author wrote it in such a grave manner that the readers tended to think that the man was serious all the way until they suddenly realized that he was proposing in fact that the English ate Irish babies and relished their food, while the Irish got their money, and that the problem of overpopulation would be happily resolved for all. The explosive power of the essay is self-evident. In English writing, the phrase "a modest proposal" is now conventionally an allusion to this style of straight-faced satire.

In the period when he was closely linked with the Irish people and firmly supported their struggle for independence and freedom, Swift wrote his best-known full-length work and a classic of English literature, ***Travels into Several Remote Nations of the World by Lemuel Gulliver, First a Surgeon, and Then a Captain of Several Ships***, commonly known as ***Gulliver's Travels***. The work became popular as soon as it was published, and has never been out of print. John Gay (1685 – 1732) wrote in a 1726 letter to Swift that "[i]t is universally read, from the cabinet council to the nursery." (Gay, 1995: 21)

Gulliver's Travels is a savage satire on human nature in the form of a fabulous travelogue. It appears as the personal narrative of a Captain Lemuel Gulliver, who is said to have traveled for some eleven years to distant places unknown to his contemporaries. The book was able to pass as a real travelogue of a real person (while both were fictional) because the people of the 18th century knew there existed some parts of the world they had not been to, and the editor's note concerning the book helped a good deal to make it sound like a true story.

The book contains four parts, each of which deals with one particular voyage of the hero and his extraordinary adventures on some remote island. The first part, dealing with Gulliver's travel on the island of Lilliput, is full of references to current politics. Lilliput is the miniature of England. Swift's satire was directed against the English ruling class, the two political parties and the religious disputes. In the second part, Gulliver comes to the land of Brobdingnagians. Here the writer censured the evils of the English (the social system and the aggressive wars) through the mouth of the king of Brobdingnagians. The third part, the least interesting part, is about Gulliver's adventures in several places like the floating island of Laputa and the island of Sorcerers. It contains Swift's sharp satire against all kinds of English social institutions. While condemning the English ruling class, Swift praised the English people, thinking they were honest, brave, and had true love for freedom. In the fourth part, the best part, Gulliver travels to the country of Houyhnhnms. The satire in this part is the sharpest and bitterest. Swift expressed a strong dislike for those people who brought evils and inhuman life modes to human society and cherished a great love for the common people.

A Tale of a Tub was Swift's first major work. It is arguably his most difficult satire, and perhaps his most masterly. It is a prose parody which is divided into sections of "digression" and a "tale" of three brothers, each representing one of the main branches of western Christianity.

The work was long regarded as a satire on religion itself, and has famously been attacked for that, starting with William Wotton (1666 – 1727). The tale presents a consistent satire of religious excess, while the digressions are a series of parodies of contemporary writing in literature, politics, theology, Biblical exegesis, and medicine. The overarching parody is of enthusiasm, pride and credulity. At the time it was written, politics and religion were still linked very closely in England, and the religious and political aspects of the satire can often hardly be separated. "The work made Swift notorious, and was widely misunderstood, especially by Queen Anne herself who mistook its purpose for profanity." "It effectively disbarred its author from proper preferment within the church." (Ousby, 1993) However, it is considered one of Swift's best allegories, even by himself. It was enormously popular, but Swift believed it damaged his prospect of advancement in the Church of England.

The Drapier's Letters is the collective name for a series of seven pamphlets written to arouse public opinion in Ireland against the imposition of a privately minted copper coinage that Swift believed to be of inferior quality. William Wood (1671 – 1730) was granted letters patent to mint the coin, and Swift saw the licensing of the patent as corrupt. In response, Swift represented Ireland as constitutionally and financially independent of Britain in *The Drapier's Letters*. Since the subject was politically sensitive, Swift wrote under the pseudonym M. B. Drapier to hide from retaliation.

Although the letters were condemned by the Irish government, with prompting from the British government, they were still able to inspire popular sentiment against Wood and his patent. The popular sentiment turned into a nationwide boycott, which forced the patent to be withdrawn; Swift was later honored for this service to the people of Ireland. Many Irish people recognized him as a hero for his defiance of the British control over the Irish nation. Beyond being a hero, many critics have seen Swift, through the persona of the Drapier, as the first to organize a "more universal Irish community," although it is disputed as to who constitutes that community. (Moore, 2005: 84)

The first complete collection of *The Drapier's Letters* appeared in the 1734 George Faulkner (c. 1703 – 1775) edition of the *Works* of Jonathan Swift along with an allegorical frontispiece offering praise and thanks from the Irish people. Today, the book is an important part of Swift's political writings, along with *Gulliver's Travels*, *A Tale of a Tub* and *A Modest Proposal*.

Swift was one of the realists. His realism was quite different from Defoe's. Defoe's stories were based upon the reality of human life, while all of Swift's plots came from imagination, which was the chief means he used in his satires. He not only criticized the evils of the English bourgeoisie but those of other bourgeois countries as well. Swift expressed democratic ideas in his works. This exerted strong influence on later writers like Sheridan, Fielding, Byron and even Bernard Shaw. Swift was a master satirist. His irony was deadly. But his satire was masked by an outward gravity, and an apparent calmness concealed his bitter irony, which made his satire all the more powerful as shown in *A Modest Proposal*. Meanwhile, Swift was one of the greatest masters of the English prose. His language is simple, clear and vigorous. There are no ornaments in his writings. He seemed to have no difficulty in finding words to express exactly the impression which he wished to convey. In simple, direct and precise prose, Swift is almost unsurpassed in English literature.

15.3 Henry Fielding (1707 – 1754)

Fielding is the greatest novelist of the 18th century and the founder of English realistic novels. He set up the theory of realism in literary creation. He is one of the most artistic that English literature has produced. He wrote not only as a novelist, but as a dramatist, an essayist and a political pamphleteer as well, and was known for his rich earthy humor and satirical prowess. Aside from his literary achievements, he has a significant place in the history of law-enforcement, having founded (with his half-brother John) what some have called London's first police force, the Bow Street Runners, using his authority as a magistrate.

Fielding began his literary career as a dramatist. His most important contributions to the English drama were his politico-satiric plays, which won great success on the stage. From 1729 to 1737, he produced 26 plays, including regular comedies, farces, burlesques and dramatic satires. Among them, burlesques and dramatic satires are his best works. His brilliant play is *The Historical Register for the Year 1736* (1737), which is a denunciation of contemporary society and politics. In this play Fielding gave a critical survey of English manners and morals, satirized some influential figures of the London theatre of its time, and exposed the corruption of the English government headed by the Prime Minister Robert Walpole (1676 – 1745, in office 1721 – 1742). The satire here was fiercer than Walpole's government would tolerate. Hence the Licensing Act of 1737, which put drama under the direct control of the Lord Chamberlain (a law which was not changed until 1968). This censorship has been blamed for the decline of drama in the 18th century. It also brought Fielding's career in the theater to an end. Nevertheless, Fielding's experience of play-writing paved the way for writing his great novels.

Fielding never stopped writing political satire and satires of current arts and letters. During the late 1730s and the early 1740s Fielding continued to air his liberal and anti-Jacobite views in satirical articles and newspapers. Almost by accident, in anger at the success of Samuel Richardson's *Pamela, or Virtue Rewarded*, Fielding took to writing novels in 1741. As a matter of fact, he began his novel writing by attacking Richardson. His first major success was *An Apology for the Life of Mrs. Shamela Andrews*, or simply *Shamela* (1741), an anonymous parody of and a direct attack on *Pamela*. Composed, like *Pamela*, in epistolary form, the satirical burlesque follows the model of the early famous Tory satirists like Jonathan Swift and John Gay. Fielding never admitted to writing the novella, but it is widely considered to be his. Fielding's great novels include *The History of the Adventures of Joseph Andrews and of His Friend Mr. Abraham Adams* (1742), *The Life and Death of Jonathan Wild the Great* (1743), *The History of Tom Jones, a Foundling* (1749) and *Amelia* (1751). In his novels, Fielding continued to expose and fight against social evils of his time.

The History of the Adventures of Joseph Andrews and of His Friend Mr. Abraham Adams, or simply **Joseph Andrews**, begun as a parody, developed into an accomplished novel in its own right and is considered to mark Fielding's debut as a serious novelist. He wrote this novel with the intention of ridiculing Richardson's novel *Pamela. He chose Joseph Andrews, Pamela's brother, to be the hero of the novel.

Joseph, a very handsome young man, is a man-servant in Lady Booby's house. Lady Booby, attracted by Joseph's charms, pursues him, but Joseph repels her temptation. Lady Booby is quite angry with him and drives him out of her house. Joseph goes to his sweetheart, a country girl named Fanny. On the way, he is knocked down and stripped by robbers, and is carried to an inn, where he is found by Parson Adams who becomes his good friend. Then the two men travel together and meet with many ridiculous adventures. In fact, the main portion of the novel is occupied with the two's adventures. After overcoming a lot of difficulties, Joseph and Fanny get married and live together happily.

The most outstanding character in the novel is Parson Adams, a poor, old honest man. He is high-minded, simple-hearted and ardently devoted to ideals, and is always ready to help the weak and the oppressed. He is, to some extent, like Don Quixote. He meets with a lot of strange experiences in the course of his wonderings and is often placed in ridiculous situations. He is jeered at and fooled by the vulgar and the sophisticated. However, he is a man of extraordinary learning, familiar with many languages and has a masterly knowledge of the Greek and Latin classics. In fact, he is so completely absorbed in the bygone world of the classical books that he is ignorant of the real world. Meanwhile, he is extremely absent-minded and is always taken up with his own thoughts and with meditating upon what he has read, so he is constantly forgetting or mislaying things. Despite all these weaknesses, Parson Adams is a good man. He loves the poor and humble. Even in humiliating situations, Adams himself is not humiliated. He always has his dignity. It is this truthfulness and uprightness that give the character a peculiar beauty.

The moral nature of the story is self-evident. The world, despite its various forms of evil and imperfection, is still one which God presides over and regulates. The eventful career of the two major characters—Joseph and Parson Adams—through life, with all its misery and agony, concludes happily for the good and the kind. The novel's satiric edge is sharp and cutting. Although the story lauds the triumph of good over evil and showcases the goodness of human nature, it can be relentless to expose human foibles, one obvious manifestation of which is human hypocrisy, vanity and affectation. The novel's eternal fascination also stems from its good number of deftly placed farces and events of a melodramatic nature.

The Life and Death of Jonathan Wild the Great, or simply **Jonathan Wild the Great**, published in the *Miscellanies* (1743), is sometimes considered Fielding's first because he almost certainly began composing it before he wrote *Shamela* and *Joseph Andrews*. It is a satirical novel, in which Fielding exposed the English bourgeois-aristocratic society and mocked at its political system as well as the exploiting and oppressing class. The protagonist Jonathan Wild is a figure taken from actual life. He was a notorious English gang leader and highwayman, hanged in London in 1721. The novel relates his career, from his birth to death.

Jonathan Wild has a disposition to steal in his childhood. When he grows up, he becomes a pickpocket. Gradually he becomes the chief of a gang of robbers. He guides their activities in the background and takes the largest share of the spoils. His attempt is to ruin the fortune and domestic happiness of his old school fellow, Mr. Heartfree. He robs the gentleman and makes him bankrupt. Moreover, he induces his wife to leave England, and then accuses Heartfree of having deserted her. He nearly brings the gentleman within an inch of execution. But his trickery is finally exposed and Jonathan Wild meets his end on the gallows.

In this novel, Fielding satirized the English high-ranking officials. The thieves represent the corrupt politicians and the chief of the gang represents the English Prime Minister Walpole. Fielding implicitly compared the Whig party in Parliament with a gang of thieves being run by Walpole, whose constant desire to be a "Great Man" (a common epithet for Walpole) should culminate only in the antithesis of greatness—being hanged. Wild's band is divided into two conflicting parties: one suggests the Tories and the other represents the Whigs. They often quarrel about little things. Fielding satirized the struggle between the two political parties. *Jonathan Wild the Great* is one of the best exposures of the corruption of the bourgeois society.

Fielding's masterpiece **The History of Tom Jones, a Foundling**, or simply **Tom Jones**, is a meticulously constructed picaresque novel telling the convoluted and hilarious tale of how a foundling comes into a fortune. The main plot of the novel centers on the conflicts between Tom and Blifil, the two half-brothers, who stand in sharp contrast. Tom is described as an upright, frank, kind-hearted young man who is always ready to help others and never once tries to harm anyone for his own benefit. He is praised by Fielding as the embodiment of the simple folk. Blifil, on the contrary, always thinks up tricks and practices them upon the other people, in order to get what he wants by lying and cheating, and is condemned by Fielding as the embodiment of the social evils of his day. The half-brothers, along with Tom's lover Sophia, make up the outstanding characters of the novel. The lovers are rebels of the society. Sophia represents the young women of the day with sufficient courage and independence to defy the bad world. From this novel we can see the novelist's strong hatred for all the hypocrisy and treachery in the society of his age and his sympathy for the courageous young rebels in their righteous struggle.

The novel consists of 18 books falling in three parts and the structure is well balanced and symmetrical: the first six are set in the Allworthy estate, the middle six relate events on the road to London, and the last six, the climax, are set in London. Each book begins with a long chapter of detailed discussions of the characters' motives, so that the chapters, if culled and put together, would make a good volume on the art of fiction.

The kindly and wealthy Squire Allworthy and his sister Bridget live in their wealthy estate in Somerset. One day, when he returns from London after an extended business trip, Allworthy finds an abandoned baby sleeping in his bed. People suspect Jenny Jones, a former maid in Schoolmaster Partridge's house, of being the mother, and Partridge being the father. Partridge has to leave the country as a result of the scandal. The foundling is named Jones after his supposed mother Jenny Jones and brought up by the squire. Bridget marries Captain Blifil and gives birth to a son Master Blifil, who becomes the squire's heir. Tom grows into a vigorous and lusty, yet honest and kind-hearted, youth so that Mr. Allworthy likes him.

Tom has been close to the Westerns: Mr. Western likes the lad for his hunting skills, and his daughter Sophia is in love with him. Once rescuing Sophia from danger when her horse runs away, Tom is wounded and is taken care of in the Western house. The two young people fall in love with each other and confess mutual love. Due to Tom's status as a bastard, both Sophia's father and Mr. Allworthy oppose their love.

Then Allworthy gets very ill and disposes of his fortune, giving Tom a generous share. As Mr. Allworthy is kind to Tom, Blifil feels jealous. So when Tom gets drunk as he happily celebrates the Squire's recovery, and has a quarrel with Master Blifil, Blifil slanders Tom before Allworthy for getting drunk on the day he is very ill. Allworthy becomes furious and drives Tom out. At the same time, Sophia's father is intent on marrying her to the hypocritical Master Blifil. To escape from the marriage, Sophia runs away from home with her maid. Then Tom is involved in an inn brawl and gets wounded. The man who treats him turns out to be Mr. Partridge. The two become good friends and travel together. Tom rescues a Mrs. Waters from a rape, and the latter invites him to dine with her. Sophia comes to the same inn with her maid and learns that Tom and Mrs. Waters have been sleeping together. Disappointed, she leaves a muff of hers on his bed and goes to London. Tom follows her there and meets her and assures her of his attachment. But Sophia's father and Allworthy come and find them. They insist on marrying Sophia to Blifil. Desperate and penniless, Tom gets in a fight and is sent to jail for murder.

Partridge meets Mrs. Waters who is in fact Jenny Jones. Mrs. Waters then reveals the real identity of Tom as the son of Bridget who slept with a student. Bridget paid Jenny for her to play the scapegoat. Bridget also wrote a letter before her death telling the truth to her brother, but the letter was stolen and destroyed by Blifil. Eventually the secret of Tom's birth is revealed. He turns out to be Blifil's half-brother and Allworthy's nephew. Now Tom is cleared of the murder charge, and survives Blifil's plan to have him hanged. Allworthy disowns Blifil and makes Tom his heir. Tom marries Sophia and moves to the Western house after this revelation of his true parentage, as Squire Western no longer harbors any misgivings over Tom marrying his daughter. Sophia bears Tom a son and a daughter and the couple live on happily with the blessings of Squire Western and Squire Allworthy.

The book is well planned on Fielding's own literary theory. Its plot moves in a sequential order, from Tom's childhood vantage through his fall from his benefactor's favor to his worming his way into the old man's graces. Tom stays in the center of the narrative, receiving most of the attention while his opposing forces are given enough coverage to form a sizeable contrast so that he stands out in strong relief. The moral theme of the book is self-evident. Fielding saw the novel as a vehicle for moral teachings. His is a typical 18th-century universe in which the moral verities still function well. The good gets rewarded while the evil receives its due punishment, and the characters all act out their lives within God's grand scheme of things.

Moreover, the book is characterized by realism. It is a truthful portrayal of the life and manners of the 18th-century England. It touches upon all kinds of people and social problems, and shows the author's great sympathy for the poor and the oppressed, and his dislike for the wicked and deceitful persons and their bad and terrible actions. The author's own experience with life and people ensures the effect of verisimilitude that his novel produces. In a sense, Fielding can be seen as a social historian of his time as he tried his best to reflect the tenor and temper of his period.

Fielding's last novel **Amelia** (1751) is a sentimental novel. It was printed in only one edition while the author was alive, although 5,000 copies were published of the first edition. *Amelia* follows the life of Amelia and Captain William Booth after they get married. It contains many allusions to classical literature and focuses on the theme of marriage and feminine intelligence, but Fielding's stance on gender issues cannot be determined because of the lack of authorial commentary discussing the matter. In spite of the praise from many writers and critics, the novel received much criticism from Fielding's competition, possibly resulting from the "paper war" in which the author was involved.

Fielding was called the father of English novel by Sir Walter Scott. He was certainly the one to usher English fiction into its modern phase. His ideas cover a wide range of subjects relating to fiction. These include the definition of the novel as a genre, the truthfulness of its descriptions of life, its formal features, and the qualifications of a novelist. His was the first attempt ever to define the novel as a prose epic that is not inferior to an epic poem. For Fielding, a novel is comic but not grotesque with its lively and funny plot, its vulgar and crude common characters, and its humorous mood. It is a representation of real life. Concerning the fictional nature of the novel, Fielding saw the novel as a vehicle for moral inculcation, a mirror and an imitation of nature and life. All the characters and events should come from the author's observations and experience. Truthfulness includes probability and invariability in representing the reality of human nature and the inner world of man. Fielding's emphasis on psychic reality has contributed well to the growth of psychological realism. Within the frame of probability, Fielding encouraged the depiction of the extraordinary and disapproved of total copying, thus making a distinction between artistic reality and real life. Though imitating life, art is, to him, not life.

With regard to the formal features of the novel, Fielding emphasized sequential movement, priority and probability. The author-narrator is like a God figure, planning, creating, and manipulating as he pleases, and the story as an organic whole moves sequentially from the beginning through the middle to the end. Priority should be given to important scenes and events, and plots must be made probable by the coherent actions and personalities of the characters. Regarding characterization, Fielding saw it as important for portraying real people and true human nature which is a mixture of good and evil, and for describing types or archetypes to reveal universal human characteristics. He touched upon the possible differences that exist between individuals and insisted on their individuality. In addition, he attached importance to the use of contrasts between good and evil, between plots, characters and settings, which would add to the exquisite symmetry of the story and bring the types into relief.

On the qualification of a novelist, Fielding deemed it necessary for a writer to have four qualities—native gift, adequate learning, rich experience with life, and a kind heart. Native gift or endowment refers to the capacity to observe and judge, which learning activates and increases. Social experience makes it possible for authors to represent people and life authentically, while sympathy and compassion endows a work with the power to touch the readers. Fielding found value in constantly communicating with his readers both in his prefaces and the beginning chapters of his book and through plot development and various insinuations in the stories. In his critical commentaries, he explained the objectives of his stories, guided the readers through their reading, advised them to observe and judge well, and told them about educational value of the novel. Within the stories, he left room for the imagination of the readers by means of suspense, foreshadowing and omission, and helped them conjecture about the plot, the formal devices and the author's structural considerations. Fielding's theories impacted novel-writing not only of his own age but of all time.

Fielding was a realistic novelist. The exact observation and study of the real life was the basis of his work. He made a close and constant study of real men and women in real life. He gave us genuine pictures of men and women of his own age. Fielding's novel is a story told directly by the author. This enables the author to develop his narrative in the fullest, freest, clearest and most straightforward manner, and also affords him opportunities of giving, at suitable places, personal explanations. Meanwhile, humor and satire abound everywhere in Fielding's works. Whereas the former is instructive and corrective, and is employed to get rid of the follies of the general public, the latter is severe, scathing and relentless, and is used to lash the cardinal evils of the corrupt ruling classes.

Another salient feature of Fielding's novel is its educational function. Fielding shared the Enlighteners' view that the purpose of the novel is not only to amuse but also to instruct. The object of his novel is to present a faithful picture of life with sound teaching woven into the very texture. Fielding was a master of style. His style is easy, unlabored and familiar, but extremely vivid and vigorous. His sentences are always distinguished by logic and musical rhythm.

15.4　Tobias George Smollett (1721 – 1771)

Smollett, a Scottish poet and novelist, was one of the most original writers of his time. He was best known for his picaresque novels, such as *The Adventures of Roderick Random* (1748) and *The Adventures of Peregrine Pickle* (1751), which influenced later novelists such as Charles Dickens and George Orwell, who admired Smollett very much. Of the eight novels that Dickens loved most in his youth as he said in his autobiography, three were by Smollett: *The Adventures of Roderick Random*, *The Adventures of Peregrine Pickle* and *The Expedition of Humphrey Clinker* (1771). Dickens learned from him a good number of things such as his manner of linking adventures in a loose way, putting a hero through a series of archetypal contemporary scenes, his comic devices with his comic breadth and buoyancy, his fearless censure of social evil, and his caricaturist manner of characterization. Smollett is now read chiefly for his wit and satire.

Smollett's first published work was a poem about the Battle of Culloden entitled "The Tears of Scotland." His poetry was described as "delicate, sweet and murmurs as a stream." But it was *The Adventures of Roderick Random* that made his name. A year later in 1749 he got his tragedy *The Regicide* published, though it was never performed. In 1750 Smollett took his MD degree in Aberdeen and travelled to France, where he obtained material for his second novel *The Adventures of Peregrine Pickle*, another great success. With the publication of *The Adventures of Ferdinand Count Fathom* in 1753, Smollett was recognized as a leading literary figure, and associated with the figures like David Garrick (1717 – 1779), Laurence Sterne, Oliver Goldsmith and Samuel Johnson, whom he famously nicknamed "that Great Cham of literature." In 1755 he published a translation of *Don Quixote* (the first part in 1605; the second part in 1615) by the Spanish writer Miguel de Cervantes (1547 – 1616), which he revised in 1761. In 1756, he became editor of *The Critical Review*.

Smollett then began what he regarded as his major work *A Complete History of England* and got it published in four volumes in 1757 – 1758. During this period he served a short prison sentence for libel, and produced another novel *The Life and Adventures of Sir Launcelot Greaves* (1760). Having suffered the loss of a daughter, Smollett went abroad with his wife and the result was *Travels through France and Italy* (1766). He also wrote *The History and Adventures of an Atom* (1769), which gave his view of British politics during the Seven Years' War—the war was fought between 1755 and 1764, the main conflict occurring in the seven-year period from 1756 to 1763—under the guise of a tale from ancient Japan. Smollett's last visit to Scotland helped inspire his last novel *The Expedition of Humphry Clinker*, published in the year of his death.

The Adventures of Roderick Random, Smollett's first work, is an immediate success. It is a typical 18th-century picaresque novel, which is in part autobiographical as it is partially based on Smollett's experience as a naval-surgeon's mate in the British Navy. In the preface, Smollett acknowledged the connections of his novel to the two satirical picaresque works he translated into English: *Don Quixote*, and *Gil Blas* (1715 – 47) by the French writer Alain-René Lesage (1668 – 1735).

The novel is set in the 1730s and the 1740s and tells the life story (in the first person) of Roderick Random, who was born to a Scottish gentleman and a lower-class woman and is thus shunned by his father's family. His mother dies at his birth and his father, disinherited, has left him penniless with a neglectful grandfather. The boy suffers in school as well as at home and gets nothing when his grandfather dies. His maternal uncle Tom Bowling sends him to a university, but the man has to leave the country as the result of a duel. The naive Random then drops out of school and embarks on a series of adventures and misadventures. The story is thus told in these episodes through the mouth of the hero.

After a brief apprenticeship to a surgeon, the innocent Roderick, accompanied by an old schoolfellow Strap, travels to London, where he encounters various rogues. Eventually, after struggling against assault, deception and other tribulations, he qualifies as a surgeon's mate. He is then pressed as a common sailor aboard a man-of-war, where he becomes mate to the ebullient Welsh surgeon Morgan, but is abused by his superiors. Roderick is present at the siege of Cartagena and, after much suffering and maltreatment, he returns to England. He becomes footman to a rich spinster and falls in love with her niece Narcissa. Unfortunately, he is once again kidnapped, this time by smugglers, who bear him off to France where he meets his uncle Tom Bowling and joins the French army. He again encounters his generous friend Strap, who arranges his release from the army and undertakes to serve Roderick as his valet. The two return to England, where Roderick intends to marry a lady of fortune. Again in London, he becomes embroiled in a riotous life, amatory adventures and fiery debates on a great range of subjects. He courts, among others, Miss Melinda Goosetrap, but does not succeed in deceiving her mother; other matrimonial enterprises are no more successful. He meets Narcissa agian, but he is shortly in prison for debt. On his release, he sinks into despair as he cannot find her. He is rescued by Tom Bowling and embarks as surgeon on a ship to Guinea Coast. In Brazil he meets Don Roderigo, who turns out to be his long-lost father, now a wealthy merchant. Reunited with his father and inheriting some funds immediately, he goes back to England and finds Narcissa. He drives her suitors away and eventually wins her hand. The novel ends happily when Random and Narcissa go to live on their ancestral Scotland estate.

Roderick Random is a picaresque hero of both virtue and vice, being forced to face a world of vice and making shift for survival. He is combative, often violent, but capable of great affection and generosity. He is basically a good person with a kind nature. A boy thrown in adversity, he has no choice but brave the world of evil and learn to live on. On quite a few occasions he is on the verge of losing his virtues. However, he picks up wisdom, learns to improve himself and remains essentially good. So he earns his reward—his financial rehabilitation and emotional gratification. He is best rewarded with Narcissa, his beloved.

The world of *The Adventures of Roderick Random* is a stage on which all types of people live and act out their dramas. The book deliberately reveals human nature in its variegated forms. There are the rich and the poor, the ill-natured relatives and the faithful friends, the effete lords, the kind-hearted whore, and the lecherous and greedy priests. It is a stage on which good and evil are entrenched in battle, good nature faces the challenge of sinful behavior, and wins out in the end. Smollett's is a moral world, where good gets its reward. In addition to the experience of Roderick, Hugh Strap's life is a telling example as well. He comes to the rescue of Roderick and is well assured of a good life in return. Roderick's story serves to disseminate the values of the age—temperance, virtue, fortitude and honesty, and urge people to love virtue and hate vice. Smollett is committed to his world as a satirist.

Formally, the book has little structure, but it enriches and endears itself to the readers with a series of engaging descriptions of the incidents. These occurrences seem disconnected but skillfully integrate themselves into a coherent whole, and are rendered enormously entertaining with a variety of humorous devices. The novel is episodic and full of disguises. With Roderick venturing out, the author saw the opportunity to observe, record with minute detail, and satirize ruthlessly the ills of his crude and violent age. Here Smollett depicted the seamy side of life in a frank way.

The Adventures of Peregrine Pickle is the story of the fortunes and misfortunes of the egotistical dandy Peregrine Pickle. The novel provides a comic and caustic portrayal of the 18th-century European society. The central satire is directed at the upper class of England. Unlike *Roderick Random*, it is told by an omniscient narrator, and its principal target appears to be Pride, in all its manifestations. The novel begins with the description of the hero's childhood, and then describes his adventures in some European countries. Finally, the hero enters the higher society as a pleasure-seeker and woman's corrupter. Through the vivid portraiture of the hero, the writer gave an excellent exposure of a representative bourgeois adventurer.

At the beginning of the novel Peregrine is a young country gentleman. Rejected by his cruel mother, ignored by his indifferent father, and hated by his degenerate brother, he is raised by Commodore Hawser Trunnion who is greatly attached to the boy. Peregrine's upbringing, education at Oxford, journey to France, debauchery, bankruptcy, jailing at the Fleet, unexpectedly succeeding to the fortune of his father, final repentance and marriage to his beloved Emilia—all provide scope for Smollett's satire on human cruelty, stupidity and greed. The novel is written as a series of adventures, with every chapter typically describing a new adventure. There is also a lengthy independent story, "The Memoirs of a Lady of Quality," inside the novel.

Peregrine Pickle features several amusing characters, most notably Commodore Hawser Trunnion, a retired naval officer and misogynist. Commodore Trunnion thinks, talks and behaves wholly in terms of his profession, and lives on shore as though he were still on his ship. His house is a garrison, watches are kept, guns fired to welcome guests, and women are not allowed on the premises after dark. The Commodore is a misogynist, but he is finally pursued and harassed into marriage by Peregrine's aunt and is henpecked ever after. Trunnion's lifestyle may have inspired Dickens to create Wemmick of *Great Expectations*. Another interesting character is Peregrine's friend Cadwallader Crabtree, an old misanthrope who amuses himself by playing ingenious jokes on naive and gullible human creatures.

The Expedition of Humphrey Clinker is written in the form of letters and has been regarded as the best, the mellowest and the most laughable work by Smollett. The letters are written by six characters: a Welsh Squire Matthew Bramble, his spinster sister Tabitha, their niece and nephew Jeremy and Lydia Melford, Tabitha's maid Winifred Jenkins and Lydia's suitor Wilson. The novel deals with the travels and adventures of the Welsh family through England and Scotland. Matthew Bramble, the master of the family, leads a group of people, including his sister, his niece and nephew to travel. On the way they pick up a foundling named Humphrey, who is found later to be no other but Mr. Bramble's natural child. Humphrey's miseries and sufferings arouse the gentleman's anger against the English law and his sympathy for the poor.

Much of the comedy arises from the differences in describing the same events by the participants. Attributions of motives and descriptions of behavior show wild variation and reveal much about the character of the teller. The setting, amidst the high-society spa towns and seaside resorts of the 18th century, provides the characters with many opportunities for satirical observations on English life and manners. The author's travels in Scotland, France and Italy helped provide inspiration for the plot. This work has been considered by some critics to be Smollett's highest achievement in prose fiction, chiefly on account of the vivid portraits of the major characters, the subtle humor that runs through the work, and the many-sided observations and reflections of the same scenes and persons and events from different viewpoints of different writers of the letters. Together with *Tom Jones* and *Clarissa*, it remains among the greatest masterpieces of English fiction.

Smollett's are picaresque novels, which are, in a great degree, recollections of his own adventures. His characters are drawn from personages with whom he became acquainted in his own career of life: acquaintances he made in Glasgow University, in the country apothecary's shop, in the gunroom of the man-of-war where he served as a surgeon, and in the hard life on shore where he struggled for a living. Smollett's picaresque novel was followed by some later novelists such as Dickens. Dickens was a great reader of Smollett, whose influence can be seen in *The Posthumous Papers of the Pickwick Club*. Besides, humor is characteristic of Smollett's novels. This is better shown in *Humphrey Clinker* than anywhere else. Thackeray wrote, "[t]he novel of *Humphrey Clinker* is the most laughable story that has ever been written since the goodly art of novel-writing began."

Chapter 16 Sentimentalist Novels

In the field of prose fiction of the 18th century, Sentimentalism had its most outstanding expression. There were three novelists who followed this tradition in novel writing. They are Samuel Richardson, Oliver Goldsmith and Laurence Sterne.

16.1 Samuel Richardson (1689 – 1761)

Richardson is generally accepted as the founder of the English domestic novel and was the first novelist of Sentimentalist tradition. He is famous for his epistolary novels. Richardson was also an established printer and publisher for most of his life and printed almost 500 different works, including journals and magazines. He had little education and chanced to begin his writing career as a novelist when he was over fifty years old. His first novel *Pamela, or Virtue Rewarded* (1740 – 1741), was an immediate popular success so that he became famous almost overnight next to Defoe. Encouraged and inspired, he went on to write another two novels in the same epistolary style. These are *Clarissa Howe* (1748 – 1749) and *Sir Charles Grandison* (7 volumes, 1753 – 1754). Of the three works the second one is generally considered as his major work, though *Pamela* has been the object of much critical attention over the centuries. Richardson won admiration of such famous writers as Henry Fielding, Diderot (1713 – 1784), Balzac (1799 – 1850) and George Sand (1804 – 1876).

Pamela, or Virtue Rewarded, written in the epistolary form, marked the beginning of this controversial manner of narration. The novel became immediately popular and was translated into foreign languages. It relates a love story between a maid and her master. Pamela Andrews, a servant girl, often writes long letters home to tell her folks about her life at her mistress' household. After the mistress' death, her son Mr. B. asks Pamela to stay on, but harasses her, kissing her one day by surprise, intercepting her letters and hiding himself in her closet at night. When the virtuous girl's responses annoy the man, he separates her from her friends and dispatches her to his remote house, leaving her there a prisoner. In her confinement, Pamela continues to send letters home with the help of Mr. Williams, the village minister. The young minister proposes to her and, though rejected, tries to help her to escape but fails. The insistent Pamela drops herself from one window to get away from Mr. B. 's clutches, but once again meets with failure. Mr. B. arrives from London and tries to ravish her, but she conveniently suffers from seizures of fits. Then both Mr. B. and Pamela begin to be aware of their faults and of the genuine nature of their affection. Mr. B. repents and offers Pamela an honorable marriage. Pamela overcomes her pride and caution, decides to trust Mr. B. and accepts his offer. They get married in the presence of her father. Now Mr. B. 's relatives behave rudely toward her, but Pamela's virtue wins over both the man's sister and his uncle. Mr. B. confesses to having had a previous affair with a woman who gave birth to a little girl, but Pamela forgives him and asks to bring up the girl. Then Mr. B has another affair with a countess. Pamela, giving birth to a son, controls her anger, and Mr. B. repents and stays faithful to her.

The novel bears some prominent characteristics. First, it manages to focus on one episode—love—rather than on many as was the case with the episodic novels of his contemporaries like Henry Fielding's *Tom Jones*. The one-episodic narrative has since become a tradition for later novelists to carry forward. Moreover, *Pamela* is realistic in its descriptions of the vicissitudes of the love process like the complex emotional responses, the clever tricks of hiding pens and ink and letters in the probable places on the human body, and the efforts to ward off harmful attention. Next, there is palpable growth in Pamela's character from an ideal—almost allegorical—to a real human figure. Her virtue is put to test and proved to be no mere myth. The impeccable perfection of Pamela as a woman is punctured by a couple of things she is revealed to be capable of, such as her womanly feeling of jealousy and pain and anger, and her redeeming self-awareness and self-censure of such foibles as her long-windedness and her weakness for praises and flattery. Finally, *Pamela* is the first English psycho-analytical novel. Here lies Richardson's chief contribution to the development of the English fiction, i. e., the penetrating psychological study of the heroine. There are the psychological excavations into the human inner world where the events are frequently digested and ruminated upon. In the novel the author describes not only the sayings and doings of the heroine and the other characters but also their secret thoughts and feelings. Richardson has been seen as the beginning point for psychological realism in the history of the English novel.

Meanwhile, in this novel Richardson gave a detailed description for the first time of the English family in the middle of the 18th century. He discarded the "improbable and marvelous" accomplishments of the former heroic romances, and pictured the life and love of ordinary people. Besides, the novel criticizes the bourgeois moral standards and moral hypocrisy. Its intention is to afford not merely entertainment but also moral instruction. Actually, the novel was undertaken with a clear moral purpose topmost in the author's mind.

Clarissa Howe, Richardson's masterpiece, is another epistolary novel published in eight volumes. About one-third of the work consists of the letters of Clarissa and Lovelace, mainly written to Anna Howe and John Belford respectively, but there are over 20 correspondents in all, displaying many points of view and variations in style. It tells a tragedy of the heroine Clarissa, a young lady, who is the daughter of a rich middle class family. Clarissa is distinguished for her virtue, beauty and intelligence, and is attracted to a young man called Robert Lovelace who is heartless and corruptive in nature. But her tyrannical family forces her to marry a man whom she does not love. In order to rebel against her tyrannical family and the venal marriage, she runs away from home with the help of Lovelace. Lovelace takes her to a sort of brothel, and there he employs every means and finally resorts to drugs to rape her. She suffers terribly later and pines to death with grief and shame. One of her cousins witnessing her tragic death challenges Lovelace in a duel and kills him.

Here the writer created an image of a young woman who is weak and helpless but who dares to rebel against tyranny. The theme of *Clarissa*—female virtue pursued by masculine viciousness—is much the same as that of *Pamela*; but the theme is raised to a higher level and treated on the tragic plane. The heroine's indomitable spirit makes the novel a powerful book and brings it widespread influence and admiration. The book was not only popular in England but had its far-reaching influence on the European Continent as well. In France it was highly praised by the great French Enlighteners Diderot and Rousseau. In Germany, it made a strong influence upon Goethe, particularly upon his early work *The Sorrows of Young Werther* (1774). In England the novel had its effect upon Jane Austen of the early 19th century.

The History of Sir Charles Grandison, commonly called *Sir Charles Grandison*, was a response to Henry Fielding's *Tom Jones*, which parodied the morals presented in Richardson's previous novels. The novel has generally been regarded as the last important of Richardson's three novels. In this novel Richardson took a man as the hero and tried to make him a model of virtuous gentlemen. The hero Sir Charles Grandison is not only depicted as morally perfect, but seems to stand for the benignant force in society capable of counteracting against social evils. *Grandison* is overloaded with morality and lacks the villainous intent that is manifested by Lovelace or Mr. B (characters of *Clarissa* and *Pamela* respectively). Richardson was motivated to create such a male figure because of the prompting of his many female friends who wanted a counterpart to the virtues exhibited by his female characters.

Sir Charles Grandison begins with Harriet Byron leaving the house of her uncle George Selby to visit Mr. and Mrs. Reeves, her cousins, in London. Byron is an orphan who was educated by her grandparents, and, though she lacks parents, she is an heiress to a fortune of fifteen thousand pounds, which attracts many suitors to her. In London, she is pursued by three suitors, Mr. Greville, Mr. Fenwick and Mr. Orme. This courtship is followed by more suitors: Mr. Fowler, Sir Rowland Meredith and Sir Hargrave Pollexfen. Pollexfen pursues Byron vigorously. He is unwilling to be without her. So he decides to kidnap her while she attends a masquerade at the Haymarket. Byron is then imprisoned at Lisson Grove. She attempts to escape from the house, but fails. To prevent her from trying to escape again, Pollexfen transports Byron to his home at Windsor. However, he is stopped at Hounslow Heath, where Charles Grandison hears Byron's pleas for help and attacks Pollexfen. Byron is rescued; Grandison takes her to Colnebrook, the home of his brother-in-law, the "Earl of L."

After the rescue, Pollexfen sets out to duel Grandison. However, Grandison refuses on the grounds that dueling is harmful to society. By explaining why obedience to God and society is important, Grandison wins Pollexfen over, who apologizes to Byron for his actions. Byron accepts Pollexfen's apology, which is followed by his proposal to her. She declines it because she, as she admits, is in love with Grandison. However, a new suitor, the Earl of D, appears, and it emerges that Grandison promised himself to an Italian woman, Signorina Clementina della Porretta. Thus with Grandison's appearance, the novel turns to focus on his history and life, and Grandison becomes its central figure. Grandison, as he himself explains, was in Italy years ago and rescued the Barone della Porretta and a relationship developed between himself and Clementina, the baron's only daughter. However, Grandison could not marry her, as she demanded that he, an Anglican Protestant, become a Catholic, and he was unwilling to do so. After he left, she grew ill out of despair, and the Porrettas were willing to accept his religion if he could come back to Clementina and make her happy once more. Grandison, feeling obligated to do what he can to restore Clementina's happiness, then goes back to Italy; however, Clementina resolutely refuses to marry a "heretic." After Grandison returns to England again, Harriet Byron accepts him and gets married to him.

The epistolary form unites *Sir Charles Grandison* with the previous novels *Pamela* and *Clarissa*, but in the previous novels, the letters operate to express internal feelings and describe the private lives of characters while the letters in *Grandison* serve a public function. The letters are not kept to individuals, but forwarded to others to inform a larger community of the action. *Grandison* stresses characters acting in the socially accepted ways instead of following their emotional impulses. The psychological realism of Richardson's earlier works gives way to the expression of exemplars. In essence, *Grandison* promises "spiritual health and happiness to all who follow the good man's exemplary pattern." (Flynn, 1982: 47) The protagonist is a static, passive character, who, in all situations, obeys the dictates of society and religion, fulfilling obligations rather than expressing personality. Although a character like Harriet is able to express herself fully, it is possible that Grandison is prohibited from doing likewise because of his epistolary audience, the public.

Richardson was a pioneer in the history of the novel. He claimed that he was a creator of fiction rather than an imitator of life and that art differed from life. Richardson placed emphasis on the harmony between structure and theme and between the different aspects of the novel. He endeavored to offer a sense of coherence and totality in the narrative effect. The three novels—*Pamela*, *Clarissa* and *Grandison*—introduced elements that are still standard in full-length fiction. Each book has a unified central plot, rather than a loosely connected series of episodes. The characters maintain a consistent point of view, without interference from the author. Richardson avoided authorial intrusion in the narrative and dramatized the life of the moment.

In characterization he consciously avoided one-dimensional portrayal and tried to endow individuals with their multi-faceted nature. His main achievement as a novelist lies in his technique to show characters as personalities, thinking and feeling for themselves with the author himself absent from the stage, refusing to intervene in the action. The characters thus show up and speak for themselves and reveal their inner world to the readers in a direct way. These all exhibit a degree of modernity in Richardson's artistic awareness, original and rare for his time. His influence could be traced in the works of such later novelists as Henry James (1843 – 1916), James Joyce and Virginia Woolf. And the detailed descriptions of real people in common situations has formed the basis of most literature ever since.

All of Richardson's novels are written in the form of letters, a style Richardson himself invented and remained popular through the early 19th Century. Richardson was the master of writing epistolary novels, which granted him "the tools, the space, and the freedom to develop distinctly different characters speaking directly to the reader." (Flynn, 1982: 235) He had a faith in the act of letter writing, and believed that letters could be used to accurately portray character traits. The characters of *Pamela*, *Clarissa* and *Grandison* are revealed in a personal way, with the first two using the epistolary form for "dramatic" purposes, and the last for "celebratory" purposes. (Flynn, 1982: 236) In *Pamela*, the author explored the various complexities of the title character's life, and the letters allow the reader to witness her development and progress over time. The novel was an experiment, but it allowed Richardson to create a complex heroine through a series of her letters. When Richardson wrote *Clarissa*, he had more experience in the form and expanded the letter writing to four different correspondents, which created a complex system of characters encouraging each other to grow and develop over time. However, the villain of the story, Lovelace, is also involved in the letter writing, and this leads to tragedy. Leo Braudy (1974: 203) described the benefits of the epistolary form of *Clarissa* as, "Language can work: letters can be ways to communicate and justify." By the time Richardson wrote *Grandison*, he had transformed the letter writing from telling personal insights and explaining feelings into a means for people to communicate their thoughts on the actions of others and for the public to celebrate virtue. The letters are no longer written for a few people, but are passed along in order for all to see.

Richardson's novels have a moral purpose. His chief object in most of his works is to inculcate virtue and good deportment. He had much sympathy for women in their inferior social status and entered into a detailed psychological study of female characters. He not only showed the conflict between the helpless woman and the social evils around her, but also laid bare the moral hypocrisy of the aristocratic-bourgeois society of his day. However, the priggish morality Richardson's books express was mocked in their own time, especially by Henry Fielding, who parodied *Pamela* with his novels *Shamela* and *Joseph Andrews*.

Richardson's books are too long and verbose to be much read today, though their vast influence has assured Richardson of lasting importance as a writer. *Clarissa Howe*, regarded as his masterpiece, totals over a million words, for instance. It is not popular now because its length, among other things, tends to test the patience of the modern readers.

16.2 Laurence Sterne (1713 – 1768)

Sterne was an Anglo-Irish novelist and an Anglican clergyman. As a novelist, he was conscious and original, and contributed a good deal toward perfecting the art of the genre in its early phase. He was an iconoclast, an innovator, a trail-blazer, and an eternal presence in the English literary history, and is remembered for his originality and his daring to break new ground. One of the 18th-century writers whom Charles Dickens admired and learned from, Sterne managed to leave an enduring imprint on later writers. Dickens felt deeply impressed by the major features in his fiction such as their themes of grotesque goodness, sweet humility, sensitive humanity, their boisterous humor, and idiosyncratic discursiveness.

Sterne's early works were letters; he also had two ordinary sermons published (in 1747 and 1750) and tried his hand at satire. He was involved in, and wrote about, local politics in 1742. His major publication prior to *Tristram Shandy* was the satire *A Political Romance* (1759), aimed at conflicts of interest within York Minster. A posthumously published piece on the art of preaching, *A Fragment in the Manner of Rabelais*, appeared to have been written in 1759. Sterne did not begin work on *Tristram Shandy* until he was 46 years old.

Sterne's fame now rests chiefly on the two books, *The Life and Opinions of Tristram Shandy, Gentleman* (1760 – 1767) and *A Sentimental Journey through France and Italy by Mr. Yorick* (1768), especially the former. Two volumes of Sterne's *Sermons* were published during his lifetime; more copies of his *Sermons* were sold in his lifetime than copies of *Tristram Shandy*, and for a while he was better known in some circles as a preacher than as a novelist. The sermons, though, are conventional in both style and substance. Several volumes of letters were published after his death, one of which was *Journal to Eliza* (1904), a more Sentimental than humorous love letter to a woman Sterne was courting during the final years of his life. Compared to many 18th-century authors', Sterne's body of work is quite small.

The Life and Opinions of Tristram Shandy, Gentleman (or, more briefly, **Tristram Shandy**), Sterne's masterpiece and most enduring work, is a humorous novel published in nine volumes, the first two appearing in 1759, and seven others following over the next seven years (vols. 3 and 4, 1761; vols. 5 and 6, 1762; vols. 7 and 8, 1765; vol. 9, 1767). The first two books describe how the family anticipates the hero's birth and how the hero is born. In the four middle books (from the 3rd to the 6th) the excitement over the birth of the hero is described, and the unfortunate misnaming of the baby at the christening is followed by the discussions on the possibility of changing the name. His father consults with his mother and a scholar whether to put the growing boy into breeches and what kind of breeches to be made for the son. The 7th book deals with the author's own experience in his journey through the different parts of France. The 8th and the 9th books have to do almost entirely with Uncle Toby's amours and a married woman.

Although the novel purports to be a biography of the title character, its style is marked by digression and amplification. The novel has no regular plot. Despite the title, the book gives readers very little of the life, and nothing of the opinions, of the hero. It is full of digressions and episodes, which make it almost formless, and ends abruptly. The novel is totally different from the novels by Defoe, Fielding and Smollett. It does not pretend to be an objective narration of the life and adventures of any hero. Emphasis is laid upon the subjective consciousness of the characters rather than upon their external actions. Just like Richardson's novels, it gives a detailed psychological analysis of the characters. It seemed that Sterne tried to catch the actual flow of human mind and sentiment in ordinary life, in the manner of a modern stream-of-consciousness novelist. It arouses the readers' interest and curiosity by creating suspense and sometimes providing for them significant passages. *Tristram Shandy* is thus made one of the most original works in English literature. It is sometimes called a "fantasy."

The novel is also characterized by an unusual and queer artistic form. Sterne consciously played all sorts of tricks in his style of writing. Incidents are not arranged in their normal chronological order. The preface and dedication do not appear at the beginning of the novel but are placed in the middle of things. One episode would be cut short unexpectedly only for another episode to be introduced. A sentence would be written and called a chapter. Occasionally an entire chapter would be a blank, left to the imagination of the reader to fill in, and then sometimes the blank would be unexpectedly filled in by the author himself. Punctuation marks are frequently juggled with, and picture curves and fantastic drawings sometimes appear on the pages instead of words. Whimsicality dominates the form of the novel as well as its contents, and in the place of logic there is haphazardness and irrationalism. Underneath all this we may discern the author's humor and his apparent desire to supplant reason with sentiment. The novel is rich in characters and humor, and the influences of Rabelais (between 1483 and 1494 – 1553) and Cervantes are present throughout. The novel ends after nine volumes, published over a decade, but without anything that might be considered a traditional conclusion. Sterne inserted sermons, essays and legal documents into the pages of his novel; and he explored the limits of typography and print design by including marbled pages and, most famously, an entirely blank page within the narrative. Many of the innovations that Sterne introduced, adaptations in form that should be understood as an exploration of what constitutes the novel, were highly influential to Modernist writers like James Joyce and Virginia Woolf, and more contemporary writers such as Thomas Pynchon (1937 –) and David Foster Wallace (1962 – 2008).

Sterne had read widely, which is reflected in *Tristram Shandy*. Many of his similes, for instance, are reminiscent of the works of the Metaphysical poets of the 17th century, and the novel as a whole, with its focus on the problems of language, has constant reference to John Locke's theories in *An Essay Concerning Human Understanding*. The publication of *Tristram Shandy* made Sterne famous in London and on the Continent. Almost immediately the work was translated into all the major European languages. Sterne influenced European writers as diverse as Diderot and the German Romanticists.

A Sentimental Journey through France and Italy by Mr. Yorick is a less influential book, although it was better received by English critics of the day. The book has many stylistic parallels with *Tristram Shandy*, and indeed, the narrator is one of the minor characters from the earlier novel. Although the story is more straightforward, *A Sentimental Journey* can be understood to be part of the same artistic project to which *Tristram Shandy* belongs. It can be read as an epilogue to *Tristram Shandy*, and also as an answer to Tobias Smollett's decidedly unsentimental *Travels through France and Italy* (1766).

A Sentimental Journey recounts the title character's various adventures, usually of the amorous type, in a series of self-contained episodes. The narrator is Mr. Yorick himself, who is slyly represented to guileless readers as Sterne's barely disguised alter ego. The novel shows how the narrator makes himself at home with all sorts of French people, including the flower girls of the shops, the servants of his hotel, the coachman who drove him from town to town, and the peasant maidens dancing in the fields. It gives readers many pleasant pictures full of joy, merriment and sunshine, with occasionally a jest or a tear by way of variety.

Compared with *Tristram Shandy*, *A Sentimental Journey* is a shorter and minor work. Less eccentric and more elegant in style than the former, it is not so much a travelogue as an outlet for the author's self-expression. Unlike prior travel accounts which stress classical learning and objective non-personal points of view, *A Sentimental Journey* emphasizes the subjective discussions of personal taste and sentiments, of manners and morals over classical learning. It best illustrates Sterne as a novelist. An account of the author's own experiences of travels through different parts of France, the novel overflows with emotionalism, humor and romantic enthusiasm. The emotions permeating its pages are basically love, compassion and other sentiments. Like *Tristram Shandy*, it is another curious blending of humanism and sentimentalism. Sterne would like to help bring warmth and sentiments of love into life so that people would love their world and their fellow creatures more. All the episodes in the book show the writer's unlimited sympathy for all the miserable people he met and his overmuch sentiment toward everybody and everything, which is usually accepted as the major shortcoming of Sterne as a true Sentimentalist: he seemed to show his sympathy and love for everyone everywhere, regardless of the distinction between the oppressed and the oppressor or between the exploited and the exploiter. So in *A Sentimental Journey*, more even than in *Tristrum Shandy*, is revealed very clearly the blending of both the strength and the weakness of Sterne as an author of the tradition both of the Enlightenment and of Sentimentalism in the 18th-century England.

However, the novel was extremely popular and influential and helped establish travel writing as the dominant genre of the second half of the 18th century. Throughout the 1770s female travel writers began publishing significant numbers of Sentimental travel accounts. Sentiment also became a favorite style among those expressing non-mainstream views including political radicalism.

Sterne was the representative of Sentimentalism in the 18th century. To him sentiment was more important than reason. He gave detailed descriptions of the characters' inner thoughts and feelings. His deep psychological analysis was a good example for later writers. His characters are ordinary persons. Sterne described the unimportant interest of the characters ironically and humorously. There is a unique artistic effect that stems from the dexterous amalgam of a huge amount of humor, comedy and laughter with occurrences that touch and move the human heart, which is instrumental in portraying his characters as vivid and real persons with faults and merits.

16.3　Oliver Goldsmith (1728 – 1774)

Goldsmith was the most versatile and lovable genius of the 18th century. He was one of the important poets among the romantic school of his age. His pastoral poem *The Deserted Village* (1770) is one of the most familiar poems in the English language. He was an excellent essayist. His essays have sympathy for human life. He was a playwright. One of his comedies *She Stoops to Conquer* (1771, first performed in 1773) has never lost its popularity. But greater than the poet and essayist and dramatist was Goldsmith the novelist. His masterpiece *The Vicar of Wakefield* (1766) is one of the most enduring works in English fiction. In his manner, especially in his poetry, Goldsmith was much influenced by his friend Dr. Johnson and the Classicist; but in his matter, in his sympathy for nature and human life, he belonged to the school of romanticism and Sentimentalism.

An Enquiry into the Present State of Polite Learning in Europe (1759) was Goldsmith's first original book. In it the author made a survey of the cultural state of the countries of Europe, from ancient times through the middle ages to the 18th century in France, Holland, Italy, Germany and England.

The Vicar of Wakefield, subtitled *A Tale, Supposed to be written by Himself*, was written from 1761 to 1762 and published in 1766. It was one of the most popular and widely read 18th-century novels in the Victorian era. The book is Goldsmith's masterpiece and only novel which definitely established his fame as a writer. It is a romantic novel told in the first person singular by the central character Dr. Primrose, the vicar, kindly, charitable, devoid of worldly wisdom and not without some literary vanity. Dr. Primrose lives a happy and idyllic life with his wife Deborah and six children in a country parish. His son George is to marry Arabella, a neighbor's daughter, but the change in the family fortune makes it impossible: Primrose's broker runs away with all his money. With the neighbor canceling the wedding, George goes off to London. In the meantime the Primroses move to the estate of Thornhill. A fellow traveler, Mr. Burchell, happens to rescue from drowning one of the Primrose daughters, Sophia, who is instantly attracted to him. However, Sophia's ambitious mother does not encourage her feelings. The young squire of Thornhill comes to visit the family regularly. While Olivia, another daughter of the family, is captivated by his hollow charm, he also encourages the social ambitions of Mrs. Primrose to a ludicrous degree. The father does not favor Burchell who has lost his fortune. Later the two sisters are thrilled at the prospect of going to the city as companions to two noble ladies, but fail to go because Burchell writes slanderous letters about them to the ladies. The angry father orders him to leave the house. Although Olivia believes that the squire of Thornhill is in love with her, she is convinced by her father to marry a young farmer. She disappears, however, a few days before the wedding. Informed by the squire that it is Burchell's doing, the father sets out to find her. He meets Arabella who asks about the whereabouts of George, but he has nothing to tell her about him. Then George comes back, as poor as ever, and receives the squire's help to join the army. Arabella, whom the young squire is courting, vows to wait for George to return. The vicar finally finds Olivia in an inn and learns that the villain has been the squire, who has ravished and deserted her. Father and daughter come home only to find that their house has been burnt down. The young squire, while he intends to marry Arabella, is also trying to find a house for Olivia so as to keep her close to him. The vicar feels furious and drives the squire from his house. But the villain asks him to pay the rent and sends him to a debtor's prison when he fails to do so. There the father meets his son George who, having attacked the squire for his villainy, is waiting to be hanged. Then, to add to his despair, the vicar hears of the kidnapping of Sophia. But then Mr. Burchell arrives and solves all problems. He turns out to be the worthy Sir William Thornhill, the squire's uncle, who travels through the country in disguise. He rescues Sophia, exposes the squire's evil plans, and restores the Primroses to their happiness. The story ends up happily: Burchell marries Sophia; George marries Arabella; Olivia's disgrace is cleared; Mr. Wakefield eventually gets back the money that his broker has stolen from him.

The Vicar of Wakefield is a Sentimental work based on the moral vision of man as innocent and kind. It appeals to human sentiment as a means of achieving happiness and social justice. There is goodness, nobility and fidelity in life, and old values and verities still function well. In addition, there is such to consider as Goldsmith's wit, humor, his craft of planting ballads and tales within tales, and his philosophical depth, which all make for the fascination it holds for its readers, modern as well as ancient. By depicting the joys and sorrows of the simple, poor family who represent the oppressed people, Goldsmith showed sympathy for the family and condemned Squire Thornhill, who stands for the cruelty, hypocrisy and moral degradation of the wicked feudal landlord and of the city bourgeoisie. But the solution for the righting of the social wrongs is not satisfactory, for the happy denouement at the end hints the existence of a good and benevolent landlord in the person of Sir William Thornhill whose righteous intervention alone can check the villainy of Squire Thornhill and restore the vicar's family to happiness.

Goldsmith's two poems—*The Traveler* and *The Deserted Village*—are both written in the heroic couplet, which is the ruling poetic form in the 18th century. *The Traveler* (1764) is based on Goldsmith's personal observations during his European wanderings. Its plan is simple and striking. An English traveler sitting on an Alpine height, below which three countries (i. e. France, Switzerland and Italy) extend into the distance, views the scenes, thinks of his personal lot and philosophizes on the general conditions of various countries, coming to the conclusion that human happiness depends less on political institution than on our own minds.

The Deserted Village, Goldsmith's best poem, is a work of social commentary, which condemns rural depopulation and the pursuit of excessive wealth, and protests against the large scale enclosures of common land for the rich landlords and capitalists. Goldsmith expressed his fear that the destruction of villages and the conversion of land from productive agriculture to ornamental landscape gardens would ruin the peasantry. The location of the "deserted village" is unknown, but the description may have been influenced by Goldsmith's memory of his childhood in rural Ireland, and his travels around England.

The poem begins with Goldsmith's happy reminiscences of his home village, which are followed by his lament over the decline of the happy village life. Goldsmith put the blame on the Enclosure Movement. He described how the peasants became homeless and landless, how the poor men became beggars and the poor women became prostitutes. The poem, to a large extent, reflects the poet's conservative stand, looking backward with nostalgia at the deserted village which merely illustrated the replacement of the feudal countryside by capitalist agriculture. Whereas the attack on the encroaching forces is genuine and forceful, the idealizing of the village life is no less apparent. In fact, the rural life was never that happy and beautiful and country people had always suffered, though differently, in the old days. Therefore, when the poem came out in 1770, it enraged George Crabbe, who knew rural poverty and its degrading effects from personal experience and observations at close quarters, and, as a reply to *The Deserted Village*, wrote *The Village*, in which Crabbe appeared to make similar efforts to idealize village life but presented the suffering of the peasants who toil from sunrise to sundown for their bread. Anyhow, Goldsmith's sentiments of grief and nostalgia are genuine and convincing.

Goldsmith's comedies include *The Good-Natured Man* (1768) and *She Stoops to Conquer*. The former, a comedy of character, was written as a counterblast of the "weeping comedy," i. e. the comedy full of sentimental moralizing. It was a middling success for Goldsmith, and the printed version of the play became popular with the reading public.

She Stoops to Conquer, initially titled *The Mistakes of a Night*, is Goldsmith's best comedy. It is a classic in the world theater, ranking among the best English comedies of the 18th century and second only to Sheridan's *The School for Scandal*. The play has always been successful when staged. It is one of the few plays from the 18th century to have an enduring appeal and is still regularly performed today. It has been adapted into a film several times, including in 1914 and 1923.

She Stoops to Conquer is a funny boisterous comedy of melodramatic misunderstandings. The wealthy countryman Mr. Hardcastle would like to marry his daughter Kate to Marlow, son of his old friend Sir Charles, and Mrs. Hardcastle is busy arranging a match between Tony, her son from her previous marriage, and Constance, her ward. Tony, who does not like Constance, plays a trick on the two visitors to his stepfather's house—Marlow and his friend Hastings, the latter being in love with Constance. He directs Marlow and Hastings to the house but tells them that it is an inn and that they have to stop there as they are lost. The two young men mistake Mr. Hardcastle as the inn keeper and Marlow takes Kate for a serving girl. Marlow really loves the "serving girl" and Kate finds him a fine gentleman. Her father is convinced of her truth when he hears the still hoodwinked Marlow confessing his love to her before she reveals her identity. The story ends well for all—the two pairs of young people get married, and Tony is able to wrestle himself free from his mother's control.

The play has been regarded as one of the most beloved comedies of all time. The humor and humanity of the characters, of Kate and Tony in particular, add a touch of immortal power to it. As a satire on the artificial and pretentious behavior of the day, the play exalts the quality of truth and honest feelings. Kate is not dressed in her Sunday best when she wins her man's love, and Marlow loves her for what she is and not as a respectable young lady of standing and expectations. The play also brings out in full relief the notion of individual choice and the right to choose one's own happiness. Tony can be scheming, but he is good-natured essentially, not self-serving and inflicting hurt on others. Goldsmith was generous and tolerant of human foibles and follies; he did not censure or punish any of his characters, but took pains to see to it that everyone got fair treatment in the end. The way, in which the characters interact in their cultured and well-intentioned manner, makes for geniality and interpersonal cordiality, and helps civilize public behavior and decrease its violent and crude elements. The salutary influence the play exerted on the 18th century is said to be considerable. In addition, Goldsmith's dialogues are vivacious and immensely humorous, and the whole performance impresses the audience with its vitality and joyful mood.

The Citizen of the World is Goldsmith's collection of familiar essays. Inspired by the earlier essay series *Persian Letters* (1721) by the French writer and philosopher Montesquieu (1689 – 1755), Goldsmith began to publish a series of letters in the *Public Ledger* under the title *The Citizen of the World* in 1760. The book contains 98 essays originally contributed to the magazine. These essays are supposed to be letters written by a Chinese residing in London to his friends in the east. In these letters Goldsmith described and criticized the strange customs of the country or countries where he lived or traveled. Goldsmith voiced through the Chinese traveler his satirical comments on the English society of his day. He showed how the English talked so much about political liberty but did not really understand its meaning, how in England money might buy reputation and even a fine monument or an imposing-looking tomb in the Westminster Abbey, how religious worship in English churches was simply a sham and most worshipers went to churches to see the spectacle and listen to music and then dose off during the sermon, how ridiculous the legal processes were and how long-drawn-out lawsuits profited only the lawyers, and how hypocrisy existed everywhere in human relationship. The language used by Goldsmith in these essays is quite effective, lightfully racy and is almost always full of humor and subtle wit. These essays are certainly among the outstanding specimens of English prose of the period.

Today the Anglo-Irish writer Goldsmith is chiefly remembered for four books: *The Vicar of Wakefield*, *The Deserted Village*, *She Stoops to Conquer* and *The Citizen of the World*.

Chapter 17   Poetry of Pre-Romanticism and Sentimentalism

17.1   Pre-Romanticism

During the middle decades of the 18th century, there emerged the Romantic Revival in the European literature. It was characterized by a strong protest against the bondage of Classicism, by the recognition of the claims of passion and emotion, and by a reviewed interest in medieval literature. In England, this movement showed itself in the trend of Pre-romanticism in poetry, which was ushered in by Percy, Macpherson and Chatterton, and represented by Blake and Burns, and its inspiration came from Spenser, Shakespeare and Milton. We can hardly read a poem of the early Romanticists without finding a suggestion of the influence of one of these great leaders.

The Pre-romantic poets returned to nature and to plain humanity for their material. They tended to shake off the established rules and express the individual genius. They looked backward with nostalgia at the medieval age in which the stern realities of life were forgotten and the ideals of youth were established as the only permanent realities. In their writings, the sympathy for the poor and the cry against oppression grew stronger and stronger. In consequence, the literature of Romanticism was as varied as the characters and moods of the different writers.

17.2 Sentimentalism

Sentimentalism was another literary tradition followed by some poets and novelists of the 18th century. It indulged in emotion and sentiment, which were used as a sort of relief for the grief and heartaches felt toward the world's wrongs, and as a kind of mild protest against the social injustice. The writers who followed this tradition criticized the cruelty of the capitalist relations and the gross social injustices brought about by the bourgeois revolutions and the Industrial Revolution. They yearned for the return of the patriarchal times. They thought that the bourgeois society was founded on the principle of reason, so they began to react against anything rational and to advocate that sentiment should take the place of reason.

In English poetry of the 18th century, Sentimentalism first found its full expression in the forties and the fifties in Edward Young's *Night Thoughts* and Thomas Gray's *Elegy Written in a Country Church-yard*. In the later decades of the century, it was found in a number of the poems by William Cowper. The appearance and development of Sentimentalist poetry marked the midway in the transition from Classicism to its opposite, Romanticism, in English poetry.

17.3 Representative Poets

17.3.1 Edward Young (1683 – 1756)

Young was an English playwright, essayist and, above all, poet. He is chiefly remembered for his *The Complaint, or Night Thoughts on Life, Death, and Immortality* (1742), which is a didactic poem of about 10,000 lines of blank verse in nine books. Book I describes the poet's reflections of life, death and immortality at night. The next seven books form a soliloquy, addressed to a young man called Lorenzo, telling him to stop being an infidel and to turn to faith and virtue. The ninth book contains a vision of the last day of the world and eternity, a survey of the wonders of the firmament at night, a final exhortation to Lorenzo and an invocation to God. Although it is long and disconnected, the poem abounds in brilliant isolated passages.

The success of *Night Thoughts* was enormous. It enjoyed a whole century of great popularity after its publication, both in England and on the European Continent. It was translated into French, German, Italian, Spanish, Portuguese, Swedish, Welsh and Magyar. In France it became a classic of the romantic school. The poem shows the poet's strong dislike for the wealthy sinners and his belief in the natural virtue and nobility of man. It is a poetic treatment of sublimity and had a profound influence on the young Edmund Burke (1729 – 1797), whose philosophic investigations and writings on the Sublime and the Beautiful were a pivotal turn in the 18th-century aesthetic theory.

The mood of the poem is gloom, and the tone is definitely morbid, as the poet found happiness in the constant thought of death and hailed midnight as signaling the light of eternity. If Young did not invent "melancholy and moonlight" in literature, he did much to spread the fashionable taste for them. Today the poem is of value chiefly as a brilliant example of the graveyard poetry to which it belongs.

The work is of some historic significance: it radically deviated from the Neoclassical vogue of its time and was therefore instrumental in moving poetry forward toward the age of Romanticism. In form, it was written in blank verse, a verse form more amenable to the expression of feelings. Samuel Johnson pronounced *Night Thoughts* to be one of "the few poems" in which blank verse could not be changed for rhyme but with disadvantage. In content, the poem is an adequate expression of emotions, a restoring of the legitimate thematic concern to poetry at a time when Pope and Johnson had between them successfully banished feeling from poetic expression. It is also noted for its psychological probing and its mixing of personal sentiments with religious deliberations. It sees man and his life in a negative manner, and finds solace only in faith and religion.

17.3.2 James Thomson (1700 – 1748)

Thomson was a Scottish poet and playwright, who is generally accepted as the forerunner of the Romantic Movement. He wrote a miscellany of plays and poems, but is remembered now mostly for his poem *The Seasons* (1746). He found inspiration in Milton's blank verse and wrote about the country life. His last work, *The Castle of Indolence* (1748), with its medieval allegorical kind of story, is also read occasionally. Thomson is important in literary history first because he did not go with the flow of his day or write in the tyrannical heroic couplet: *The Seasons* was composed in blank verse while *The Castle of Indolence* in the Spenserian stanza. Besides, his choice of subjects decides the texture of his works.

The Seasons, with its theme of nature and the use of blank verse, has often been considered as epoch-making. It is the first significant poem written in the tradition of Pre-romanticism when Neoclassicism was still in predominance under the leadership of Alexander Pope. The poem of over 5,500 lines consists of the four seasons and a final "Hymn." It is devoted to the vivid description of nature and to the effect of natural phenomena upon man. Each of the four seasons begins with a prose preface introducing the verse that follows, and the preface to "Winter" (1726) can be read as a general introduction to the whole poem. Following "Winter" came "Summer" in 1727, with "Spring" out in 1728 and "Autumn" in 1730. The whole work first came out in print in 1730, and the revised and final edition in 1746. In "Spring" the poet realistically described spring ploughing, praised rural labor and condemned those living "in luxury and ease, in pomp and pride." In "Summer" the poet presented some interesting scenes of hay-making and sheep-shearing, singing of the joy of labor. "Autumn" describes the reaping of the fruits of the earth, the coming of fogs, the migration of birds and the mirth of the country-folks after the harvest is gathered in. "Winter" contains vivid pictures of the effects of the coming of cold wind and snow upon man. The poet's sympathy for the poor and the miserable is shown in this part. The poem is concluded by a hymn to the God of Seasons, who is omnipresent in the "rolling year."

Thomson borrowed Milton's Latin-influenced vocabulary and inverted word order. He extended Milton's narrative use of blank verse to describe the landscape and to give a meditative feeling. The lengthy blank verse poem, reflecting on the landscape of the countryside, was highly influential and much liked for at least a century after its writing.

17.3.3 Thomas Gray (1716 – 1771)

Gray was an English letter-writer, Classical scholar and, above all, poet of transition from the Neoclassic to the Romantic period. He was a minor forerunner of the Romantic Movement both in subjects and simple language. He is widely known for his *Elegy Written in a Country Churchyard*, whose publication in 1751 was an immediate success.

Gray began writing his **Elegy Written in a Country Churchyard** in 1742. Its origins are unknown, but it was partly inspired by Gray's thoughts following the death of the poet Richard West (1716 – 1742). Originally titled *Stanzas Written in a Country Church-Yard*, the poem was completed in 1750 when Gray lived near St Giles' parish church at Stoke Poges, England. It was sent to his friend Horace Walpole (1717 – 1797), who popularized the poem among London literary circles. Gray was eventually forced to publish the work on 15 February 1751, to pre-empt a magazine publisher from printing an unlicensed copy of the poem. Towering above most of Gray's other poems and also many works by other poets of the period, *Elegy* quickly became popular. It was printed many times and in a variety of formats, translated into many languages, and praised by critics even after Gray's other poetry had fallen out of favor.

Elegy was claimed as "probably still today the best-known and best-loved poem in English." (Griffin, 2002: 149) It established its author as about the best poet of his day and made him a desirable candidate for the position of the poet laureate in 1757, but he declined the offer. The poem started the tradition of graveyard poetry in English and American literatures. It follows a classical form, but the vivid descriptions of nature and the spirit of melancholy indicate clearly the influence of Sentimentalism and Romanticism. It is full of the gentle melancholy, which marked all the early romantic poetry. The most valuable thing of the work is seen in the democratic sentiments of the poet that reveal themselves so prominently in so many places in the poem, where the poet took a melancholy view of life. The "Country Churchyard" is the resting-place for the poor and the lowly, and the wealthy; naturally the poet compared the common folk with the great ones. He showed his sympathy for the poor and condemned the great ones who despise the poor and bring sufferings to the common people. The general mode is melancholy and meditative.

Elegy consists of 128 lines in 32 iambic pentametric quatrains, which can be roughly divided into seven broad sections. Section one (ll. 1 – 12) sets the scene for the poet's visit to the churchyard. It is enveloped in gloom and grief, which is archetypal of graveyard poets' fascination with night, graves and death. The tone is echoed by the sixth section (ll. 93 – 116). Section two (ll. 13 – 28) deals with the people entombed there and recalls their life experiences. The tone is one of melancholy and regret for the dead. Section three (ll. 29 – 44) warns the rich and powerful not to despise the poor since all are equal in face of death and the grave levels off all distinction. Section four (ll. 45 – 72) expresses, on the one hand, the poet's regret that their life was not congenial to the growth and full play of the poor farmers' native gifts and talents and, on the other, his feeling of "a blessing in disguise" for the farmers in the sense that, because they did not take up positions of power and get the opportunity to do evil, they did not commit any crimes to humankind nor have to play the obsequious social climber against one's integrity. Section five (ll. 73 – 92) asserts the notion that, even though they lived a less eventful life, there is no reason to forget these farmers.

Section six portrays the scenario that the poet envisions would happen after his own death. A villager would say of him: he got up early to go uphill to the lawn and lay there meditating under the tree until noon. He would wander in the wood, smiling at one moment, muttering to himself at the next, sad and pale, like one "in hopeless love." Then for a couple of days he did not show up, and on the third day he was buried in the churchyard. This is where the graveyard school of poetry exhibits its salient thematic feature: the indulgence in meditation on and obsession with death and solitude. Section seven (ll. 117 – 128), "The Epigraph," which picks up where the last section leaves off, is engraved on the poet's own tombstone. There he calls himself a youth, learned and melancholy, with a generous, loving soul, and equally loved by Heaven. As he showed sympathy for the poor, he gained the friendship of man and God. He asked the passers-by not to get to know any more about his merits and weaknesses as he waited in his grave for God's judgment.

The poem is an elegy in name but not in form; it employs a style similar to that of contemporary odes, but it embodies a meditation on death, and remembrance after death. It argues that the remembrance can be good and bad, and the narrator finds comfort in pondering the lives of the obscure rustics buried in the churchyard. With its discussion of, and focus on, the obscure and the known, the poem has possible political ramifications, but it does not make any definite claims on politics to be more universal in its approach to life and death.

Elegy is famous for its clarity in thought and its neatness in structure. Its style is graceful, effortless, spontaneous, and with no trace of laboring. Its diction is at once succinct and laded, fluent and tight-knit, and lucid with room for imagination. The work is also renowned for its regularity in meter and rhyme. Its sound, harmonious yet not monotonous, helps achieve its theme wonderfully well. With the use of long vowels in most lines, the mood of grief and lamentation stands out in bold relief. But there is evident variety that forestalls tedium. Alternating with the long vowels, the poem deftly employs short vowels in some lines and quatrains either to express a mood of utter helplessness, or irritation, or some dramatic effect. Even within the same line, long and short vowels intertwine at intervals for various effects. In addition, the colors, light and shade, flora and fauna, scenes culled from life, and symbols and figures that combine to make up the woof and warp of the poem—all these are well chosen, juxtaposed or superimposed so that the poem stands unique in history.

17.3.4 William Collins (1721 – 1759)

Collins, second in influence only to Thomas Gray, was an important English poet of the middle decades of the 18th century and is chiefly remembered for a series of odes. His lyrical odes mark a turn away from the Augustan poetry of Alexander Pope's generation and towards the Romantic era which would soon follow. Collins' well-known odes include "Ode to Evening," "Ode on the Poetical Character" and "Ode on the Popular Superstitions of the Highlands of Scotland," among which "Ode to Evening" is his best. The poem shows the poet's great zest for the beauty of nature and is a sort of protest against the poetic tradition of Neoclassicism. Collins displayed his gift in both the short lyrical expressions and long attempts at melodious verse. He paid special attention to the choice of words in his verse, so that there is a generally high level of artistic excellence in his more mature work.

17.3.5 Thomas Percy (1729 – 1811)

Percy was Bishop of Dromore, County Down, Ireland. His greatest contribution to English literature is considered to be his *Reliques of Ancient English Poetry* (1765), whose most valuable part is the remarkable collection of the old English and Scottish ballads. The work, published in three volumes, is the first of the great ballad collections and was the one most responsible for the ballad revival in English poetry that was a significant part of the Romantic Movement. This collection of ballads was an epoch-making book not only in connection with the development of ballad literature and folk literature in England but also as a new expression of medievalism, which was a revolt against the Neoclassicism of the day. Because the old ballads were folk literature of the late Middle Ages, the revival of interest in these old ballads led to greater interest in the themes and literary forms of folk literature and medieval literature. Even the simplicity of style of the old ballads became exalted and was imitated as a result of the popularization of these ballads.

17.3.6 William Cowper (1731 – 1800)

Cowper was an English poet and hymnodist. One of the most popular poets of his time, he changed the direction of the 18th-century nature poetry by writing of everyday life and scenes of the English countryside. In many ways, he was one of the forerunners of Romantic poetry. He also wrote a number of anti-slavery poems, among which is "The Negro's Complaint" (1788). This poem was often quoted by Martin Luther King, Jr. (1929 – 1968) during the 20th-century Civil Rights Movement.

Cowper's blank verse proved to be the best of his time; and his criticism, disapproving of the Neoclassic form and urging a return to nature and God, happened to signal the change of values and taste in anticipation of the coming of the Romantic outburst in the early 19th century. He was instrumental in a way in the transition to a more natural and simple style, and contributed in his way to the movement away from Pope and Johnson's classical influence. His subjects are basically personal, with an intense interest in rural and domestic settings, and his primary mood is lyrical and melancholy, expressing the sense of human limitations. In his poems Cowper gave us a truthful and charming picture of the country life. He satirized social ills and showed sympathy for the lower strata of society. His major works include the *Onley Hymns* (1779), a collaborative work with John Newton (1725 – 1807), and *The Task* (1785), whose success made its author the most popular poet of his time.

Cowper is today remembered for **The Task**, which is usually seen as his supreme achievement. The poem is a long meditative work of 5,000 lines, covering a wide range of topics such as country sights and sounds, village life, garden, parlor, occasional condemnation of cities and worldliness, war and slavery, luxury and corruption, freedom and tyranny. It, on the whole, shows Cowper's great love for nature and liberty and for England and a great hatred for slavery and oppression and for the life of debauchery and extravagance in the cities. Its tone is muted, its language is lucid and simple, and the diction throughout is, for an 18th-century poem, unusually conversational and unartificial. It was the first time Cowper ever wrote in blank verse instead of the heroic couplet.

The Task contains six parts, which are entitled "The Sofa," "The Timepiece," "The Garden," "The Winter Evening," "The Winter Morning Walk" and "The Winter Walk at Noon" respectively. The last three parts put together constitute a composite picture of the winter scene. Beginning with a mock-heroic account of the evolution of the sofa, the poem digresses to description, reflection and opinion. It stresses the delights of a retired life, describes the poet's own search for peace, and evokes the pleasures of gardening, winter evenings by the fire, etc. The moral passages condemn slavery, blood sports, fashionable frivolity, lukewarm clergy and French despotism among other things. The poet manifests tenderness not only for his pet bare, but even for worms and snails. Cowper's subjects are those that occur to him naturally in the course of his reflections rather than being suggested by poetic convention, and the discussions alternate with descriptions.

The six parts deal with various matters. The first part begins with describing the sofa, and then a morning walk in the country to express his love for nature, and then a comparative comment is made on the town life and country life. Here the writer praised life in the countryside and censured the dissipation in the big cities. He talked about the vanity of man's indulgence in comforts and the poem's intention to justify God's ways to man. The second part is a satire on the political situations of the day. It shows the poet's patriotic feelings for England, but he seemed to have erroneous view that there was true liberty and no slavery in England. The third part covers those subjects like nature, family life, compassion, condemnation of wars, praise of simple rural life, and renunciation of the city. It contains the poet's account of his own miseries in connection with his mental depressions and madness. He eulogized the domestic happiness in the countryside and the pleasures of gardening and criticized gambling and other bad ways in the cities. The fourth part is a continuation of the dichotomy between country and city. It opens with the comments on the news of the world. Then, satisfied with his happy home in a winter evening, the poet felt sympathy for the sufferings of the poor and condemned the debaucheries of the wealthy in the public-house as well as the bad influence of city life upon the countryside. The fifth part is the most significant part of the poem. It sees in winter a hope for immortality and attacks tyrants and slavery. Here the poet made his penetrating comments on the more important social and political problems of his day. It begins with a description of a winter morning walk, and then the poet pointed out wars as amusements of monarchs, and, in commenting on liberty, he attacked severely the Bastille in France and forecast its downfall. The sixth part begins with the description of a winter walk at noon, and then the poet devoted much space to a strong attack against cruelty to animals. Here the poet elevated rural harmony and anticipated spring.

17.3.7 James Macpherson (1736 – 1796)

Macpherson was a Scottish poet, literary collector and politician. He won immediate fame by a series of literary forgeries. He pretended to have discovered some ancient Gaelic poems, which were supposed to have been written by an ancient fictitious Gaelic bard named Ossian, and was hence known as the "translator" of the Ossian cycle of poems, which he published in 1765 in a collection called *Works of Ossian*. These poems in prose translation have a great and lasting success both in England and abroad. They were translated not only into German and French, but also into Italian and Spanish. They had great influence upon Herder (1744 – 1803) and Goethe in Germany and Chateaubriand (1768 – 1848) and Lamartine (1790 – 1869) in France and Pushkin (1799 – 1837) in Russia. In Germany Ossian was ranked together with Shakespeare and Homer. Macpherson was the first Scottish poet to gain an international reputation.

The Ossian poems were reflections of the popular tendency in the second half of the 18th century toward primitivism and medievalism, which was also an expression of Sentimentalism and romanticism. Scholarship and investigations in the 19th and 20th centuries have proved that they are mere inventions of Macpherson, but that does not lessen the great influence they have had since their appearance. As a matter of fact, Macpherson used these poems as a basis to write an epic entitled *Fingal* (1762), most of whose details were invented by the poet's imagination. The epic tells of the exploits of Finn, a hero of ancient Scotland, who rights wrongs and defends the oppressed. Here Macpherson succeeded in giving a primeval grandeur to his heroes. The work is marked by its magnificent imagery and romantic spirit. Its publication produced a literary storm. It exerted a widespread influence on both the English poets of the age like Blake, Burns and many others, and the poets on the Continent.

17.3.8 Thomas Chatterton (1752 – 1770)

Chatterton was an English poet and forger of pseudo-medieval poetry. He was fascinated by the old manuscripts which had been preserved in the old church of St. Mary Redcliffe for 300 years. He read those documents and later, based on these old materials, he began to write poems. In order to make these poems interesting, he invented a monk called Rowley to be the writer. Hence the title *Rowley Poems* when they were published in 1777 after Chatterton died. In these poems, the poet employed a variety of verse forms, including Spenserian stanzas, rhyme royal and the ballad. Chatterson showed his great sympathy for the poor and the miserable and also his hatred for the moneyed class.

17.3.9 George Crabbe (1754 – 1832)

Crabbe was an English poet, surgeon and clergyman. He is said to be the last great Neoclassic poet. Living through two ages—the Neoclassic and the Romantic, he showed a visible movement in his works toward concern with social life. His poetry is often Neoclassic in form (he used the heroic couplet) but emotional in theme. His humanity breaks through the bard crust of the surface and makes its voice well heard. In his small way Crabbe helped with the Neoclassic transition to the next phase of literary evolution. He is also remembered for his early use of the realistic narrative form and his descriptions of the middle-and working-class life and people. The three major poems on which Crabbe's fame rests are *The Village* (1783), *The Parish Register* (1807) and *The Borough* (1810).

The Village is a narrative poem, written in response to Goldsmith's poetic reflection of country life in *The Deserted Village*. It contrasts the traditional representation of the rural idyll in Augustan poetry with the realities of village life. The poem contains two books. At the beginning of the first book Crabbe declared that the aim of the poem was to give "the real picture of the poor" and he laid bare the untruthfulness of the idyllic scenes in pastoral poetry since the time of Virgil. Then the poet drew a realistic picture of the village and the life of the inhabitants there. He painted realistically the village workhouse and the miseries of the laboring people. Book two begins with the description of a scene of the repose and pleasure of a summer Sabbath. Then the poet compared the poor with the great, pointed out that the great had the same vice and distress as the poor, and asked the poor, not to envy the great. In this poem, we find realistic pictures of utter poverty in the English countryside at the end of the 18th century. We also see the poet's deep sympathy for the poor laboring people. The poem keeps a niche for Crabbe in English literary history.

The Parish Register, developing the form of *The Village*, first reveals Crabbe's gift for narrative and reaffirms his determination to present the truth, however sordid. It is based on the poet's own experience as country parson and is supposed to be the record of a parson's reminiscences of the births and marriages and deaths of his parishioners. Here again we find pictures of poverty and misery. The writer also condemned the wicked person and the society for bringing sufferings to the poor.

The Borough is the longest and the most ambitious work by Crabbe. It is a collection of poems written in heroic couplets. The poems are arranged as a series of 24 letters, covering various aspects of borough life, detailing the stories of certain inhabitants' lives, and giving a real comprehensive picture of a certain borough which is actually no other than the poet's own native place, Aldeburgh. The work was begun in 1804, three years before the publication of *The Parish Register*, and demonstrates a clear development in Crabbe's writing between the pastoral concerns shown in *The Village*, and the concentration on the life stories of individuals as seen in his collections of poetry like *Tales* (1812) and *Tales of the Hall* (1819).

The Borough is more important than *The Village* or *The Parish Register*, not only because it is a much longer poem and gives a broader picture of the bourgeois English society but also because it contains more penetrating satire on the political and social conditions through more realistic descriptions of the different institutions of the borough and through a series of more detailed artistic portraits of the men and women in that environment.

17.3.10 William Blake (1757 – 1827)

Blake was an English poet, painter and printmaker. Of all the Romantic poets of the 18th century, Blake was the most independent and the most original. In his early writings, he seemed to go back to the Elizabethan song writers for his models; but gradually he grew into the poet of inspiration alone. Largely unrecognized during his lifetime, Blake has been held in high regard by later critics for his expressiveness and creativity, and for the philosophical and mystical undercurrents within his works. His paintings and poetry have been characterized as part of the Romantic Movement and as "Pre-Romantic." Blake is now considered a seminal figure in the history of poetry and visual arts of the Romantic Age. In 2002, he was placed at number 38 in the BBC's poll of the 100 Greatest Britons.

Blake is famous for his short lyrics. They are remarkable and highly individual. His imagination is so little controlled by fact or logic that his works at times seem to lose contact with ordinary human experience. He looked toward an anarchistic society, and a religious mysticism seems to be the source of his inspiration. The two major thematic strands that make up the basic fabric of his poetry include his concern with social events and his mysticism. His poetry strikes us with its childish vision and simplicity.

Blake's poetry has generally been divided into two groups—his early lyrical poems including the three volumes of *Poetical Sketches* (1783), *Songs of Innocence* (1789) and *Songs of Experience* (1794), and his later "Prophetic Books" that contain all his other poems from "Tiriel" (1789) and "The book of Thel" (1789) to "Milton" (1808) and "Jerusalem" (1818) and "The Ghost of Abel" (1822). So far, Blake has been known chiefly as a great lyrical poet and his fame has rested mainly on *Songs of Innocence* and *Songs of Experience*. His numerous "Prophetic Books" have generally been consigned to oblivion.

Songs of Innocence was originally a complete work first printed in 1789. It is a conceptual collection of 19 poems, engraved with artwork. Poems in the collection express the poet's love for the beauty of the world through the mouths of the little children. Each poem here is the expression of love and tender feeling and of belief in the goodness of nature. Using the language of small babies, Blake expressed his delight in the sun, the hills, the streams, the insects and the flowers. The best-known poem in the collection is "The Lamb." The whole collection is pervaded with the breadth of simplicity and fancy. The sweetest poems are those cradlesongs. The melody is simple, artless, and yet exquisite.

Songs of Experience is a collection of 26 poems, published in 1794. Some of the poems, such as "The Little Girl Lost" and "The Little Girl Found" were moved by Blake to *Songs of Innocence*, and were frequently moved between the two books. *Songs of Experience* is the counterpart of *Songs of Innocence*. It is a much maturer and the most important work by Blake. The poems in this collection show that the poet's eyes are opened to the evils and vices of the world. Through symbolic devices, Blake expressed his progressive democratic ideas. The best-known poems in this collection are "The Tiger," "The Fly," "London" and "The Chimney Sweeper."

The contrast between *Songs of Innocence* and *Songs of Experience* is of great significance. It marked a progress in the poet's outlook on life. In the earlier collection there seem to be no shadows. In the poet's eyes, the world was a picture of light, harmony, peace and love. But in the later years, experience brought a fuller sense of the power of evil, and of the great misery and pain of the people's life. The poet had to set himself against the current of the capitalist world. It is enlightening to see the way the poems in the two volumes are well paired off and throw the contrast of their subjects in bold relief. Blake did this on the strength of his growing belief in the notion of contraries. Without contrast and contraries, he said that, in one context, there was no progression. Therefore the poems from *Songs of Innocence* like "Infant Joy," "The Blossom," "The Lamb" and "The Divine Image" stand respectively in direct opposition to the poems in *Songs of Experience*—"Infant Sorrow," "The Sick Rose," "The Tiger" and "The Human Abstract." There are also the two poems both entitled "The Chimney Sweeper," the two both entitled "A Little Lost Boy," and the other similar instances in which the mood and the tone change from happy to gloomy.

The Marriage of Heaven and Hell is Blake's most important prose work. It is a series of texts written in imitation of biblical prophecy but expressing Blake's own intensely personal Romantic and revolutionary beliefs. Like his other books, it was published as printed sheets from etched plates containing prose, poetry and illustrations. The plates were then colored by Blake and his wife.

The work was composed between 1790 and 1793, in the period of radical foment and political conflict immediately after the French Revolution. The poet expressed his revolt against the social oppression, exposed and attacked all civil, moral and religious codes. The central idea of this work is the poet's denial of the authority of injustice. The title is an ironic reference to the theological work *Heaven and Hell* (1758) by Emanuel Swedenborg (1688 – 1772). Swedenborg was directly cited and criticized by Blake in several places in the *Marriage*. Though Blake was influenced by his grand and mystical cosmic conception, Swedenborg's conventional moral structures and his Manichaean view of good and evil led Blake to express a deliberately depolarized and unified vision of the cosmos in which the material world and physical desire were equally part of the divine order; hence, a marriage of heaven and hell. The book is written in prose, except for the opening "Argument" and the "Song of Liberty." The book describes the poet's visit to Hell, a device adopted by Blake from *The Divine Comedy* (c. 1308 – 1321) by Dante (c. 1265 – 1321) and Milton's *Paradise Lost*.

The whole temper of Blake's genius was essentially opposed to the Classical tradition of that age. He identified Classicism with formalism. His lyric poetry displays the characteristics of the romantic spirit, according to which natural sentiment and individual originality are essential to literary creation. He paved the way for the Romantic Movement of the 19th century. It is in this sense that he is called a Pre-romantic or a forerunner of the English Romantic poetry.

Blake's revolutionary passion came near to that of Shelley. There is strong likeness between Shelley and Blake; the imagery and symbolism as well as the underlying spirit of Shelley's revolutionary epics, such as *The Revolt of Islam* and *Prometheus Unbound*, find their nearest parallel in Blake's prophetic books.

17.3.11　Robert Burns (1759 – 1796)

Burns is widely regarded as the national poet of Scotland. He is the best known of the poets who have written in the Scots language, although much of his writing is also in English and a light Scots dialect, accessible to an audience beyond Scotland. The publication of his *Poems, Chiefly in Scottish Dialect* (1786) marked an epoch in the history of English literature, like the publication of Spenser's *Shepherd's Calendar*. Burns also wrote in standard English, and in these writings his political or civil commentary is often at its bluntest. He is regarded as a pioneer of the Romantic Movement, and after his death he became a great source of inspiration to the founders of both liberalism and socialism, and a cultural icon in Scotland and among the Scottish diaspora around the world. Celebration of his life and work became almost a national charismatic cult during the 19th and 20th centuries, and his influence has long been strong on Scottish literature. In 2009 he was chosen as the greatest Scot by the Scottish public in a vote run by Scottish television channel STV.

Burns' poetry can be divided into three groups according to the subject matter: lyrical, political and satirical, among which his lyrics enjoyed a great popularity. Most of Burns' poems are lyrics on love and friendship, which are very musical and can be sung. These poems describe the poet's own emotions with such vividness and simplicity that they appeal directly to the reader's heart. Meanwhile, they carry with themselves a new spirit of romanticism, which would prevail as the main trend of English literature in the early 19th century. Burns' best known lyrics are "John Anderson, My Jo" (1789), "A Red, Red Rose" (1794) and "Auld Long Syne" (1788). "Auld Long Syne," set to the tune of a traditional folk song, is well known in many countries, especially in the English-speaking world, its traditional use being to bid farewell to the old year at the stroke of midnight. By extension, it is also sung at funerals, graduations and as a farewell or ending to other occasions.

Burns wrote some poems to express his hatred for the oppression of the ruling class and his love for freedom. The best-known one is "A Man's A Man for A'That" (1795), famous for its expression of egalitarian ideas of society, which may be seen as expressing the ideas of liberalism that arose in the 18th century. Burns was an outspoken supporter of the French Revolution, under the influence of which he wrote a number of poems on the theme of revolution, such as "The Tree of Liberty" and "A Revolutionary Lyric." In these poems Burns called on the people to rise in arms for a happy life in future. Some patriotic poems are written to express Burns' deep love for his motherland. "My Heart's in the Highland" is one of them.

Burns achieved success in the field of satire. The sting of his satire was often directed at the hypocrisy of the church leaders and the parasitism of the lackeys of the ruling classes. "The Toadeater" is a piece of bitter satire.

But his poems like "The Jolly Beggars" are characterized by humor and lightheartedness. They bespeak another aspect of the poet's character, i. e. optimism in spite of poverty and misery in life.

Burns also wrote some verse-tales which he based on old Scottish legends. In these poems, he sang of the heroic spirit of the Scottish people in their struggle against their oppressors. The best example is "John Barleycorn." John Barleycorn is a legendary Scottish peasant hero. He rose up and led the peasants in a rebellion. He became a symbol of the indestructible strength and indomitable courage of the people.

Burns' poetry is bone of the bone and flesh of the flesh of the Scottish common people. This was the main factor of his great success. For one thing, Burns had a deep knowledge and an excellent mastery of the old Scotch song tradition. He drew his inspiration from the treasury of Scottish folklore and his poems, most of which were written in Scotch dialect, became in their turn the people's property. For another, Burns was the people's poet. As a plowman, he came from the people and wrote for the people. He was a poet of peasants and is entirely in his element in the rural theme. In his poems he glorified a natural man—a healthy, joyous and clever Scotch peasant—contrasting him to cruel squires, greedy merchants, bigots and hypocrites. Burns was supremely human. His heart was full of love, compassion and warmth. He knew human nature well and knew how to express it well in ways appealing to his fellow creatures. He was critical of Calvinism and its hypocrisy and rigid morality. He valued human freedom and equality and was eloquent in defending the lower social strata. Human life and human feelings always remained topmost in his mind when he wrote poetry. Thus even his nature poetry offered not so much an aid to enjoying nature as a natural backdrop against which life was enacted.

Burns lived in a period of transition from the 18th-century Neoclassicism to Romanticism. His poems showed the strength of both Neoclassicism and Romanticism and adroitly avoided their weaknesses like extremes and excesses. They revealed a great virtuosity and competence in handling diverse stanza forms and styles.

Chapter 18 Drama in the 18th Century

The 18th-century drama was extensive but very little of it had permanent literary value. Though it continued to be active in appearance, it lost originality and talent, for the genius of the century appeared to more excel in novel.

In the first two decades of the century, the Italian opera and the English pantomime were active on the English stage and vied with the regular comedies and tragedies in their popularity with the audience of the time. In 1728 John Gay produced his famous opera *The Beggar's Opera*, which achieved one of the most conspicuous stage triumphs in English dramatic history and led to the production of *Polly*, a sequel, in 1729. Gay's contributions to the English drama in the 18th century lie chiefly in his introduction of political and social satire to dramatic literature, in his use of the theme of the robbers and highwaymen, in his employment of the excellent ballad opera medium as the vehicle for such satire, and in his writing numerous charming lyrics on serious subjects. His influence upon Henry Fielding, especially upon his satirical dramas and upon his novel *Jonathan Wild*, is very great.

The 1730s' English drama witnessed two highlights—the comedies (especially the political and social satires) of Henry Fielding and the introduction of bourgeois tragedy by George Lillo (1691 – 1739). Lillo's contribution to English drama is his famous play *The London Merchant, or The History of George Barnwell* (1731). This play had its great and far-reaching influence. In England it got the approval of even a Neo-classicist like Alexander Pope who attended the first performance. It was admired by Richardson and by Fielding as well. It was translated into French, German and Dutch and had its great influence on the European Continent. Fielding wrote a number of comedies before he found his true vocation as a novelist, but none of them brought him the same reputation as his novels did.

The second half of the 18th century produced two great playwrights—Oliver Goldsmith and Richard Brinsley Sheridan. Their plays are of high literary quality and still retain their interest upon the stage. Goldsmith's contribution to English drama lies chiefly in the two comedies—*The Good-natured Man* and *She Stoops to Conquer*.

Richard Brinsley Sheridan (1751 – 1816) was an Irish playwright and poet, buried at Poets' Corner in Westminster Abbey. He is generally acknowledged as the greatest playwright of the century. His dramatic writings marked the highlight of the 18th-century English drama. He inherited the tradition of realism in drama writing. In his plays, he attacked the hypocrisy of the Sentimentalists. His characters are remarkable for their dramatic qualities. He excelled at epigram, and no author was wittier. Sheridan mainly wrote comedies. In his dramatic works, the artificial comedy reached its climax, and the anti-Sentimental movement reached its culmination. He brought the comedy of manners to the highest perfection. His plays have amusing scenes, clever situations, epigrammatic wit, satiric character drawing, deep insight, and more sophisticated dramatic irony and satire.

Sheridan's plays, especially *The Rivals* and *The School for Scandal* were the best in his time and have since become world famous classics. As a matter of fact, *The Rivals* and *The School for Scandal* are in historical perspective two of the three best comedies of the 18th century, the other being Goldsmith's *She Stoops to Conquer*.

The Rivals (1775), Sheridan's first comedy, is a prose comedy of manners in five acts dealing with two stories. The main plot has to do with the love affair between a young man of a rich aristocratic family Captain Absolute and a romantically-and-sentimentally-inclined girl called Lydia. Lydia is a young lady full of romantic fancies. She is very interested in reading romantic and Sentimental novels of the day like Sterne's *A Sentimental Journey* and popular picaresque novels like Smollett's *Peregrine Pickle*. So she dreams all the time of the excitement of eloping with some romantic poor youth. But this meets with strong opposition from her aunt and guardian Mrs. Malaprop, who insists on her niece marrying Captain Absolute. If her niece does not listen to her, she will make her lose half of her fortune. In order to capture the young lady's heart, Captain Absolute pretends to be a poor, low-ranked army officer by the name of Ensign Beverley, and goes to woo the young lady, who accepts him as her lover. Finally when Absolute has to reveal his identity to her, she refuses to have anything more to do with him. Only after much ado does she agree to give up her romantic dream of elopement and to be married to the rich young man Captain Absolute. The secondary plot deals with a pair of sentimental lovers, Lydia's friend Julia and her jealous and mistrustful lover Faulkland. There appear a series of petty quarrels and conflicts between them. After much torture at the game of love, they get married.

The Rivals is a clever satire on the sentimental and pseudo-romantic fancies of many upper-class young women of the day, who were all victims to the Sentimental novels and to the illusion represented in those novels of harmony between romantic dreams and the real bourgeois world of practical money concerns.

The School for Scandal (1777), Sheridan's masterpiece, is one of the best English comedies of all times. It made Sheridan famous and rich, and ultimately entitled him to a place in the Poets' Corner of Westminster Abbey. The play is a five-act comedy of manners for its brilliant wit and satire. It gives a brilliant portrayal and a biting satire of English high society. Here two plotlines run parallel: Lady Teazle's loss of innocence and growth and Sir Oliver Surface's selection of an heir. There exists a sharp contrast between two brothers, Joseph Surface and Charles Surface. Joseph is a hypocrite, a backbiter, who always declares noble feelings and utters moral speeches while Charles is a reckless prodigal and a gambler but he is frank, honest and good-natured.

Charles is in love with Maria, the ward of Sir Peter Teazle, and his love is returned; Joseph is courting the same girl for her fortune and dallying with Lady Teazle at the same time. Sir Peter, an old man who has married his young wife six months previously, is made wretched by her frivolity and the fashionable society she inhabits. Members of this society include Sir Benjamin Backbite, Crabtree, Lady Sneerwell and Mrs Candour, who talk behind people and chatter with malicious brilliance whenever they meet, and thus make life troublesome for all people. Sir Oliver Surface, the rich uncle of Joseph and Charles, returns unexpectedly from India and decides to test the characters of his nephews before revealing his identity. He visits Charles in the guise of a moneylender, Mr. Premium, and Charles, always hard up, cheerfully sells him the family portraits, but refuses to sell his uncle's. Thus he unwittingly wins the old man's heart. Meanwhile Joseph receives a visit from Lady Teazle and attempts to seduce her. The sudden arrival of Sir Peter obliges Lady Teazle to hide behind a screen, where she is filled with shame and remorse as she listens to proof of Sir Peter's generosity to her, even though he suspects an attachment between her and Charles. Then Charles arrives unexpectedly, which sends Sir Peter in turn to hide. Sir Peter detects the presence of a woman behind the screen but is told by Joseph that it is a little French milliner, so he takes refuge in a cupboard instead. The conversation between Charles and Joseph proves to Sir Peter that his suspicions of Charles were unfounded. On Joseph's leaving the room, Sir Peter emerges and together he and Charles agree to reveal the little French milliner. When Charles flings down the screen he reveals Lady Teazle. Lady Teazle begs Sir Peter's forgiveness and Joseph returns, to be upbraided by both. Sir Oliver then comes to Joseph in the character of a needy relative, begging for assistance. However, he not only gets no penny from his nephew but also hears Joseph's complaint about his miserly uncle (Sir Oliver himself). Joseph's character now stands fully revealed. Sir Oliver forms his opinion of the two nephews. He makes Charles his heir and marries him to Maria; Sir Peter and Lady Teazle get happily reconciled.

In this play, Sheridan satirically criticized English high society for its vanity, greed, hypocrisy, depravity and corruption, and pointed out that self-serving and the human inclination to suspicion were the major root causes of all evil. These stay at the core of the parasitic existence of the upper class, which Sheridan saw as their breeding ground. Sheridan was perceptive and courageous enough to penetrate into the polite life in London and by extension in English society, and bring it under the close scrutiny of his minute analysis. The negative side of human nature in its variegated manifestations is examined and castigated, and the upper class suddenly finds itself somewhat stripped naked before the eyes of the world. The audiences tend to split their sides in full appreciation of the humor and the laughter at the expense of others' weaknesses and foibles, but often come away with a better awareness of their own behavior as humans. This is where the universal applicability of the work lies. This play has been a great success on the stage and regarded as the best English comedy since Shakespeare. Though written two centuries ago, it still remains a favorite with the English audience.

One of the salient features of *The School for Scandal* is Sheridan's character portrayal. It begins with the names of the characters. There are Teazle, Surface and Snake, along with the names referred to in the play like Flirt, Prim, Tattle, Candour, and more. Some names are concocted by yoking words together such as Sneerwell, Boastall, and Backbite. The names say a lot about the personalities of the people so named. This seems to be a borrowing of some medieval morality trick, but Sheridan went well beyond moralities in his dramatic endeavor. He fleshed out his main characters well with cogent details so that they are no mere skeletons for moral abstractions. Furthermore, Sheridan showed his consummate craftsman in leaving loose threads here and there but never failing to pull them together in some climatic scene, where the two plotlines nicely intersect with each other and converge and run to their final resolution. Such a scene appears when all the major people come together and square things out in Joseph's study. The ensuing hide and seek and the suspense it causes along with the fun ensure the all-time success of the work as a comedy. In addition, Sheridan's language is lucid and humorous and presents little of no paradoxes. His theatrical performances have always been famous for the boisterous laughter they bring to their audiences.

Exercises

I. Multiple choices

1. _____ marked the end of the long struggle for political freedom and the beginning of the constitutional monarchy in England.
   A. The Hundred Years' War   B. The Glorious Revolution
   C. The Wars of the Roses   D. The Norman Conquest

2. Alexander Pope was the representative writer of the _____ school in English literature.
   A. Metaphysical   B. Sentimental
   C. Neoclassical   D. Pre-romantic

3. _____ was a master in satire and heroic couplet in English literature.
   A. William Shakespeare   B. Alexander Pope
   C. John Bunyan   D. Henry Fielding

4. _____, probably the most important of all Alexander Pope's works, and certainly the best known and most often quoted, indicates the poet's political and philosophical viewpoint.
   A. *The Songs of Experience*   B. *Essay on Man*
   C. *Lives of the Poets*   D. *London*

5. In the middle decades of the 18th century, _____ became the leader of the Classical school.
   A. Joseph Addison   B. Richard Steele
   C. Alexander Pope   D. Samuel Johnson

6. _____, written in heroic couplet, consisting of 744 lines and divided into three parts, was a manifesto of English Neoclassicism as Alexander Pope put forward his aesthetic theories in it.
   A. *The Rape of the Lock*   B. *Essay on Criticism*
   C. *Essay on Man*   D. *The Dunciad*

Part Five The Age of Enlightenment

7. In _____ the poet described how a quarrel between two aristocratic families arose and satirized the triviality and silliness of high society with a delicate wit.

    A. *The Rape of the Lock*   B. *Essay on Criticism*

    C. *Essay on Man*   D. *The Dunciad*

8. The early period of the 18th century has often been named after the poet as the "_____."

    A. Age of Dryden   B. Age of Shakespeare

    C. Age of Pope   D. Age of Milton

9. _____ thus praised Joseph Addison's style: "Whoever wishes to attain an English style, familiar but not coarse, and eloquent but not ostentatious, must give his days and nights to the study of Addison."

    A. Richard Steele   B. Alexander Pope

    C. John Dryden   D. Samuel Johnson

10. Samuel Johnson was a voluminous writer. Among his works, the best-known are *A Dictionary of the English Language* and _____.

    A. *Jonathan Wild*   B. *The Temple*

    C. *Poetics*   D. *Lives of the Poets*

11. In _____, Samuel Johnson tried to point out how utterly vain all human ambitions and endeavors were.

    A. *London*   B. *The Vanity of Human Wishes*

    C. *The Rambler*   D. *Rasselas*

12. _____ has been known for his biography of Samuel Johnson entitled *The Life of Samuel Johnson, LL. D*, which offers us a vivid and detailed portrait of Johnson.

    A. Jonathan Swift   B. John Dryden

    C. James Boswell   D. Richard Steele

13. The major realist novelists of the 18th century are Daniel Defoe, Jonathan Swift, Henry Fielding and _____.

    A. Tobias George Smollett   B. Samuel Richardson

    C. Oliver Goldsmith   D. Laurence Sterne

14. The rise and growth of the _____ is the most prominent achievement in the 18th-century English literature.

    A. revolutionary essay   B. realistic novel

    C. modern drama   D. romantic poetry

15. At the head of _____'s works stands his most important work *Robinson Crusoe*, the story of which is based on the experience of a real Scotch sailor called Alexander Selkirk, who had marooned on a desert island off the coast of Chile and lived there in solitude for four or five years.

    A. Daniel Defoe   B. R. B. Sheridan

    C. Thomas Gray   D. Jonathan Swift

16. To defend himself and satirize his persecutors, Daniel Defoe wrote a poem _____, which was printed

by his friends for street distribution upon his first appearance at the pillory.

    A. *The Shortest Way with the Dissenters*   B. *Robinson Crusoe*

    C. *Moll Flanders*   D. *Hymn to the Pillory*

17. Daniel Defoe's _____ ironically demanded the total suppression of the dissenters, who were supported by the Tories, and thus enraged the government which was controlled by the Tories.

    A. *The Shortest Way with the Dissenters*   B. *Robinson Crusoe*

    C. *Moll Flanders*   D. *Hymn to the Pillory*

18. Daniel Defoe's novels include *Robinson Crusoe*, _____, *Moll Flanders* and *Colonel Jacque*.

    A. *The Shortest Way with the Dissenters*   B. *Captain Singleton*

    C. *The True-born Englishman*   D. *Hymn to the Pillory*

19. The 18th century in English literature is an age of prose, and the supreme master in the first part of the century is _____, who has been seen by some people as the literary king of his day.

    A. John Bunyan   B. Henry Fielding

    C. Jonathan Swift   D. Oliver Goldsmith

20. Among the pamphlets Jonathan Swift wrote about Ireland, the best known pieces are *The Drapier's Letters* and _____.

    A. *The Rape of the Lock*   B. *The Vanity of Human Wishes*

    C. *Hymn to the Pillory*   D. *A Modest Proposal*

21. *Gulliver's Travels* is _____'s masterpiece. The book contains four parts, each of which deals with one particular voyage of the hero and his extraordinary adventures on some remote island.

    A. John Bunyan   B. Geoffrey Chaucer

    C. Jonathan Swift   D. Daniel Defoe

22. _____ is accepted as the greatest novelist of the 18th century in English literature.

    A. Charles Dickens   B. T. S. Eliot

    C. Jane Austen   D. Henry Fielding

23. _____'s famous comedy *The School for Scandal* is considered the author's masterpiece. This play presents a brilliant portrayal of England's high society and a biting satire on the morals and manners of the age.

    A. William Shakespeare   B. R. B. Sheridan

    C. Bernard Shaw   D. Henry Fielding

24. Henry Fielding began his literary career as a dramatist. His brilliant play is _____.

    A. *The Historical Register for the Year 1736*   B. *The Life of Mr. Jonathan Wild the Great*

    C. *Amelia*   D. *The History of Tom Jones, a Foundling*

25. The main plot of Henry Fielding's novel _____, centering on the conflicts between Tom and Blifil, gives us a vivid and truthful panoramic picture of the 18th-century England.

    A. *The Life of Mr. Jonathan Wild the Great*   B. *Amelia*

    C. *The History of Tom Jones, a Foundling*   D. *The Historical Register for the Year 1736*

26. Henry Fielding wrote _____ with the intention of ridiculing Samuel Richardson's novel *Pamela*.

Part Five The Age of Enlightenment

    A. *The Life of Mr. Jonathan Wild the Great*   B. *Joseph Andrews*

    C. *Amelia*   D. *The History of Tom Jones, a Foundling*

27. _____ is a satirical novel, in which Henry Fielding exposed the English bourgeois-aristocratic society and mocked at its political system.

    A. *The Life of Mr. Jonathan Wild the Great*   B. *Joseph Andrews*

    C. *Amelia*   D. *The History of Tom Jones, a Foundling*

28. *The Expedition of Humphrey Clinker* is an epistolary novel and has been regarded as the best and most laughable work by _____.

    A. Henry Fielding   B. Tobias George Smollett

    C. Jonathan Swift   D. Daniel Defoe

29. With the advent of the 18th century, in England, as in other European countries, there sprang into life a public movement known as the _____, which on the whole was an expression of struggle of the then progressive class of bourgeoisie against feudalism.

    A. Enlightenment   B. Renaissance

    C. Romanticism   D. Critical Realism

30. The 18th century, as a whole, is an age of _____ rather than of poetry, and in this respect it differs from all preceding ages of English literature.

    A. drama and poetry   B. drama

    C. prose   D. novel and poetry

31. To Daniel Defoe is often given the credit for the discovery of _____; but whether or not he deserves that honor is an open question.

    A. English drama   B. English literature

    C. the modern poetry   D. the modern novel

32. _____ is often called the founder of the English domestic novel and chiefly remembered for his epistolary novels.

    A. Oliver Goldsmith   B. Tobias George Smollett

    C. Samuel Richardson   D. Laurence Sterne

33. _____, written in the epistolary form, marked the beginning of this controversial manner of narration.

    A. *Pamela*   B. *The Life and Opinions of Tristram Shandy*

    C. *Clarissa Howe*   D. *Sir Charles Grandison*

34. _____, Richardson's masterpiece, consists of eight volumes and tells us a tragedy of a young lady.

    A. *Pamela*   B. *The Life and Opinions of Tristram Shandy*

    C. *Clarissa Howe*   D. *Sir Charles Grandison*

35. Oliver Goldsmith's only novel _____, which definitely established his fame as a writer, tells a romantic story, which is told in the first person singular by the central character Dr. Primrose.

    A. *The Deserted Village*   B. *She Stoops to Conquer*

    C. *The Citizen of the World*   D. *The Vicar of Wakefield*

36. _____, written in heroic couplet, is Oliver Goldsmith's best poem.

 A. *The Deserted Village*   B. *She Stoops to Conquer*

 C. *The Citizen of the World*   D. *The Vicar of Wakefield*

37. _____, Oliver Goldsmith's best comedy, is a classic in world theater and ranks among the best English comedies of the 18th century—second only to R. B. Sheridan's *The School for Scandal*.

 A. *The Deserted Village*   B. *She Stoops to Conquer*

 C. *The Citizen of the World*   D. *The Vicar of Wakefield*

38. James Thomson's _____ consists of four parts, which are devoted to the vivid description of nature and to the effect of natural phenomena upon man.

 A. *Elegy Written in a Country Churchyard*   B. *The Task*

 C. *The Seasons*   D. *Night Thoughts*

39. Today Edward Young is chiefly remembered for his _____, which is a didactic poem of about ten thousand lines of blank verse in nine books.

 A. *Elegy Written in a Country Churchyard*   B. *The Task*

 C. *The Seasons*   D. *Night Thoughts*

40. Bishop Thomas Percy's great contribution to English literature is _____, which made strong influence on the whole Romantic Movement.

 A. *Works of Ossian*   B. *Reliques of Ancient English Poetry*

 C. *Rowley Poems*   D. *The Task*

41. _____ has been known chiefly as a great lyrical poet and his fame has rested mainly on *The Songs of Innocence* and *The Songs of Experience*.

 A. William Blake   B. Robert Burns

 C. George Crabbe   D. Edward Young

42. In addition to Richard Brinsley Sheridan, some other writers also made contributions to the English drama in the 18th century. Among them were John Gay, _____ and George Lillo.

 A. Henry Fielding   B. Tobias George Smollett

 C. Jonathan Swift   D. Daniel Defoe

43. It was _____ who brought the comedy of manners to the highest perfection.

 A. John Gay   B. George Lillo

 C. Richard Brinsley Sheridan   D. Tobias George Smollett

44. R. B. Sheridan's first play _____ is a clever satire on the sentimental and pseudo-romantic fancies of many young women of the upper classes of the day.

 A. *The School for Scandal*   B. *She Stoops to Conquer*

 C. *The Historical Register for the Year 1736*   D. *The Rivals*

II. Blank-filling

1. In the 18th-century England, the people in control of the government divided into two parties—the liberal _____ and the conservative _____, which were so well balanced that power shifted easily from one to the

Part Five   The Age of Enlightenment

other.

2. Most of the English writers were enlighteners. They fell into two groups—the _____ and the _____.

3. Daniel Defoe has been regarded as the discoverer of the modern novel. His strong creative spirit in novel writing won him the title _____.

4. The _____ period, which covered the time roughly from 1660 to 1798, was one of political and military unrest.

5. In writing plays the Neoclassicists used _____ instead of blank verse.

6. The Neoclassicists observed the three unities—the unities of _____, _____ and action.

7. The Neoclassicists thought that poetry should follow the ancient divisions, falling into _____, _____, didactic, satiric or dramatic, and that each group should be guided by some peculiar principles.

8. _____ made his name as a great poet with the publication of *Essay on Criticism* in 1711. The poem, written in _____, outlines critical tastes and standards based on Neoclassical doctrines.

9. *The Dunciad*, Alexander Pope's famous satirical poem, shows the poet's struggle against _____ and barbarism as well as "dullness" and "emptiness" all around him.

10. *An Epistle to Dr. Arbuthnot* was intended to be Alexander Pope's "_____" justifying his life, work and personality. It is necessary to read it to get to know about the author and his mentality.

11. The two literary periodicals—_____ and _____—are Joseph Addison and Richard Steele's contribution to English literature.

12. _____ took Samuel Johnson nearly eight years and is remarkable for the definitions of the meaning of words and for the quotations in illustration of their use.

13. _____ was the last great Neoclassicist enlightener in the second half of the 18th century.

14. The realist novelists told the reader in their novels, not about knights or kings but about the ordinary people, about their _____, _____ and struggles.

15. Among Henry Fielding's novels, the best known is _____, which established his reputation as a founder of the English novel.

16. Henry Fielding, founder of English _____ novels, set up the theory of _____ in literary creation. The exact observation and study of the _____ was the basis of his work.

17. The _____ period was also an age of Enlightenment, which was conventionally seen as a European intellectual movement exalting reason and the scientific method.

18. Of the eight novels that Charles Dickens loved most in his youth as he said in his autobiography, three were by _____: *The Adventures of Roderick Random*, *The Adventures of Peregrine Pickle*, and *The Expedition of Humphrey Clinker*.

19. In the field of prose fiction of the 18th century, _____ had its most outstanding expression. The novelists who followed this tradition in novel writing are Samuel Richardson, Oliver Goldsmith and Laurence Sterne.

20. Laurence Sterne's fame now rests chiefly on the two books, _____ and *A Sentimental Journey through France and Italy by Mr. Yorick*, especially the former.

21. As a versatile writer, today Oliver Goldsmith is chiefly remembered for four books: _____ (a poem),

_____ (a comedy), _____ (a collection of familiar essays) and _____ (his masterpiece and one of the most enduring works in English fiction).

22. Romanticism returned to nature and to plain humanity for its material, and it is in marked contrast to _____, which had confined itself largely to the clubs and drawing-rooms, and to the social and political life of London.

23. The _____ Movement was marked, and is always marked, by a strong reaction and protest against the bondage of rule and custom, which, in science and theology, as well as in literature, generally tend to fetter the free human spirit.

24. The Romantic Movement was the expression of _____ genius rather than of established rules.

25. James Thomson found inspiration in John Milton's blank verse and wrote about the country life. His chief fame rest upon the poem called _____.

26. Edward Young's _____ is noted for its psychological probing and its mixing of personal sentiments with religious deliberations.

27. William Collins' best-known ode is _____, which shows the poet's great zest for the beauty of nature and is a sort of protest against the poetic tradition of Neoclassicism.

28. The three major poems on which George Crabbe's fame rests are _____, *The Parish Register* and *The Borough*.

29. The publication of Robert Burns' *Poems Chiefly in Scottish Dialect* marked an epoch in the history of English literature, like the publication of Edmund Spenser's _____.

30. Robert Burns' poetry can be divided into three groups according to the subject matter: lyrical, political and satirical, among which his _____ enjoyed a great popularity.

31. In 1789 William Blake published his _____, followed with _____ in 1794.

III. Term definition

1. Enlightenment
2. Deism
3. Elegy
4. Burlesque
5. Picaresque novel
6. Epistolary novel
7. Melodrama
8. Sentimentalism
9. Graveyard poet
10. Pantomime
11. Comedy of manners
12. Irony

IV. Short-answer questions

1. What are the chief characteristics of the 18th-century literature in England?
2. What are Fielding's writing features?
3. What are the three stages of the English literature during the Enlightenment?
4. How much do you know about Alexander Pope's position in English literature?
5. What is the significance of the two periodicals—*The Tatler* and *The Spectator*?
6. What is Joseph Addison and Richard Steele's contribution to English literature?
7. What are the features of Daniel Defoe's novels?

Part Five The Age of Enlightenment

8. What are Jonathan Swift's writing features?

9. What are Tobias George Smollett's writing features?

10. In what way does *Pamela* attract the interest of the literary world today?

11. What are the features of Robert Burns' poetry?

V. Essay questions

1. Give a brief introduction to Alexander Pope's *Essay on Man*.

2. Give a brief introduction to Daniel Defoe's masterpiece.

3. Give a brief introduction to Jonathan Swift's *Gulliver's Travels*.

4. Give a brief introduction to Henry Fielding's masterpiece.

5. Give an account of Fielding's contribution to the craft of English fiction.

6. Give a brief introduction to Tobias George Smollett's *The Adventures of Roderick Random*.

7. Give an account of Samuel Richardson's literary theory.

8. Summarize the features of Samuel Richardson's novels.

9. Summarize the features of Laurence Sterne's novels.

10. Comment on Oliver Goldsmith's major works.

11. Comment on Thomas Gray's *Elegy Written in a Country Churchyard*.

12. Give a brief introduction to William Cowper's *The Task*.

Part Six   The Romantic Period

(1798 – 1832)

Chapter 19   English Romanticism

19.1   Background

If the 18th century in the social and political history of Britain and Europe was centripetal, influenced by the Enlightenment values like balance, reason, deism and moderation, the Romantic period was centrifugal, with all the forces falling apart and flying out from the center. It was one of exploration in many directions, a little like the Elizabethan period. The commonly accepted concepts of the period had to do with words such as "enthusiasm," "intuition," "inspiration" and the pronoun "I," all of which Alexander Pope might find odd and hard to accept. All the upheavals of the time testified to the fact that the British and European reliance on what Edmund Wilson (1895 – 1972) termed "Divine Authority" was weakened and that a new value system based on the personal and individual values was coming in as a replacement. The emphasis on the individual became a dominant feature of the new or Romantic era.

The outburst of Romantic feeling in England was triggered off by the specific events of historic significance, i. e., the Industrial Revolution and the French Revolution. On the one hand, the Industrial Revolution, made possible by technological advances such as the Watt steam engine patented by James Watt (1736 – 1819) in 1781, brought unforeseen changes to each individual and society as a whole. It pushed the bourgeoisie to the dominant position in the country, the ruling class, and brought great sufferings to a new class, proletariat. Thus the bourgeoisie got richer and richer while the laborers became poorer and poorer. Hence there emerged the extreme of poverty and wealth. Writers reacted by wanting to return to the simpler life of the Middle Ages or trying to find consolation in Nature, or doing both at the same time. On the other hand, the French Revolution established bourgeois democracy with its slogans of liberty, equality and universal brotherhood. Individualism prevailed. Writers and artists sought to express man's inner feelings freely. At the same time, national liberation movements spread, calling forth national literatures in their wake.

19.2   Romanticism

Romanticism was a movement in literature, philosophy, music and art which developed in Europe in the late 18th and early 19th centuries. In most areas it was at its peak in the approximate period from 1800 to 1850. Starting from the ideas of Rousseau in France and from the Storm and Stress movement (from the late 1760s to the early 1780s) in Germany, it held that Classicism, dominant since the 16th century, failed to express man's emotional nature and overlooked his profound inner forces. Romanticism stressed intense emotion as an authentic source of aesthetic experience and valued spontaneity. It assigned a high value to the achievements of "heroic" individualists and artists, and emphasized individual values and aspirations above those of society. It also promoted the individual imagination as a critical authority allowed of freedom from Classical notions of form in art.

Romanticism, as a reaction to the Industrial Revolution, the aristocratic social and political norms of the Age of Enlightenment, and the scientific rationalization of nature, looked to the Middle Ages and to direct contact with nature for inspiration. It had a significant and complex effect on politics, and while for much of the Romantic period it was associated with liberalism and radicalism, its long-term effect on the growth of nationalism was perhaps more significant. It gave impetus to the national liberation movement in the 19th-century Europe.

Romanticism as a literary movement came into being in England early in the latter half of the 18th century. It first made its appearance in England as a renewed interest in medieval literature. With the publication of William Wordsworth's *Lyrical Ballads* (1798) in collaboration with S. T. Coleridge, Romanticism began to bloom and found a firm place in the history of English literature. In fact, the first half of the 19th century recorded the triumph of Romanticism. The death of the last Romantic writer Walter Scott in 1832 marked the end of the Romantic Age in England.

The Romantic Age in England, resembling the Elizabethan era, was an age of poetry. Many young enthusiastic writers turned to poetry as a happy man to singing. The glory of the age is seen in the poetry of Wordsworth, Coleridge, Byron, Shelley and Keats.

19.3 Literature

The Romantic period has been considered the second great period in English literature, only next to the Elizabethan period. The general taste was decidedly set in the poetic direction. Poetry was the highest achievement of the English Romantic literature and seemed to have been most in harmony with the noblest powers of the English genius. A huge amount of energy was exhibited in the poets of this troubled period. The Romantics all revealed their singular talents and achieved a remarkable degree of success in their literary endeavors. Some of them like Wordsworth and Coleridge developed nature mysticism. Others such as Shelley and Keats embraced a sensual kind of aestheticism, while Byron bodied forth the new concept in action, the Byronic heroism. These poets were all part of the overall emotional and intellectual response to the sense of newness that came in the aftermath of the French Revolution.

The Romantic era also achieved great success in English novel-writing. For one thing, women novelists, with Mrs. Anne Radcliff (1764 – 1823) and Jane Austen as representatives, appeared in this age. It was during this period that women assumed, for the first time, an important place in English literature. While Radcliff was one of the most successful writers of the school of exaggerated romance, Austen offered us her charming descriptions of everyday life in her enduring works. For another, the greatest historical novelist Walter Scott appeared in this period. His historical novels combine a romantic atmosphere with a realistic description of historical background and common people's life. Scott marked the transition from Romanticism to the period of Realism which followed it.

Romantic essays were represented by Charles Lamb, William Hazlitt and De Quincey, among whom Lamb was the best. Lamb was famous for his familiar essays. His essays on Shakespeare are still a must on the reading list of Shakespearean scholars and his Shakespearean tales did a lot toward increasing Shakespeare's popularity.

Chapter 20 Romantic Poetry

The Romantic period witnessed English poetical revival. The Romantic poets split into two groups—the escapist/passive Romantics (or the first/elder generation of Romantics) and the active/revolutionary Romantics (or the second/younger generation of Romantics)—due to their different attitudes toward the capitalist society. The former include Wordsworth, Coleridge and Southey, who stood on the side of the feudal forces ruined by the bourgeoisie, turned to the feudal past and idealized the life of the Middle Ages to protest against capitalist development. The latter include Byron, Shelley and Keats, who expressed the aspiration of the laboring class and held out an ideal of a future society free from oppression and exploitation. They were the firm supporters of the French Revolution.

Romantic poetry expressed the ideology and sentiment of those classes and social strata that were discontent with and opposed to the development of capitalism. The general feature of the works of the Romantic poets is dissatisfaction with the bourgeois society, which finds expression in a revolt against or an escape from the prosaic, sordid daily life, the "prison of the actual" under capitalism. The Romantics paid great attention to the spiritual and emotional life of man. Nature, often personified, also plays an important role in their works. The passions of man and the beauties of nature appealed strongly to the imagination of the Romantic poets, and the glory of lakes and mountains, the little joys or sorrows of children, the weal and woe of ordinary, uncultured peasants, the wonder of the fairy world, and the splendor of the Greek art all became the fountain-heads of the poets' inspiration.

20.1 Representative Poets of the First Generation

20.1.1 William Wordsworth (1770 – 1850)

Wordsworth was a major English Romantic poet who, with Samuel Taylor Coleridge, helped to launch the Romantic Age in English literature with their joint publication *Lyrical Ballads* (1798). He was the representative of the first generation of the Romantic poets, who expressed the deepest aspirations of English Romanticism. He saw nature and man with new eyes. His whole work is an attempt to communicate that new vision. Wordsworth's masterpiece is generally considered to be *The Prelude* (1805 – 1806), a semi-autobiographical poem of his early years. Wordsworth was Britain's Poet Laureate from 1843 until his death in 1850.

Wordsworth's first publication of poems came out in 1793 in the collections *An Evening Walk* and *Descriptive Sketches*. Two years later, he met Samuel Taylor Coleridge in Somerset and the two poets quickly developed a close friendship. Together they, with insights from Wordsworth's sister Dorothy, produced *Lyrical Ballads*. Between 1795 and 1797 Wordsworth wrote his only play, *The Borderers*, a verse tragedy set during the reign of King Henry III (1207 – 1272, king 1216 – 1272), when Englishmen in the North Country came into conflict with Scottish rovers. He attempted to get the play staged in November 1797, but it was rejected by Thomas Harris, the manager of the

Covent Garden Theatre, who proclaimed it was "impossible that the play should succeed in the representation." The rebuff was not received lightly by Wordsworth and the play was not published until 1842, after substantial revision.

Wordsworth had for years been making plans to write a long philosophical poem in three parts, which he intended to call *The Recluse*. In 1798 he started an autobiographical poem, the "poem to Coleridge," which he planned would serve as an appendix to the larger work, *The Recluse*. Shortly afterwards, he decided to make it a prologue instead of an appendix and began expanding the autobiographical work in 1804. He completed this work, now generally referred to as the first version of *The Prelude*, in 1805, but refused to publish such a personal work until he had completed the whole of *The Recluse*. The death of his brother John, also in 1805, affected him strongly and might have influenced his decisions about these works.

In 1807 Wordsworth published *Poems in Two Volumes*, including "Ode: Intimations of Immortality from Recollections of Early Childhood." Up to this point Wordsworth was known only for *Lyrical Ballads*, and he hoped that this new collection would cement his reputation. Its reception was lukewarm, however. In 1810 Wordsworth and Coleridge were estranged over the latter's opium addiction—the two were fully reconciled by 1828, when they toured the Rhineland together. In 1814 Wordsworth published *The Excursion* as the second part of the three-part work *The Recluse*, even though he had not completed the first part or the third part, and never did. He did, however, write a poetic "Prospectus" to *The Recluse* in which he laid out the structure and intention of the whole work. The prospectus contains some of Wordsworth's most famous lines on the relation between the human mind and nature.

Nearly all of Wordsworth's good poetry was written during the first decade of his literary career (1798 – 1807). Some modern critics suggest that there was a decline in his work, beginning around the mid-1810s, perhaps because most of the concerns that characterized his early poems (loss, death, endurance, separation and abandonment) have been resolved in his writings and his life. By 1820 he was enjoying considerable success accompanying a reversal in the contemporary critical opinion of his earlier works.

Wordsworth's poetry is distinguished by the simplicity and purity of his language. It is his theory that the language spoken by the peasants, when purified from its defects, is the best of all. His theory and practice in poetical creation started from a dissatisfaction with the social reality under capitalism, and hinted at the thought of "back to nature" and "back to the patriarchal system of the old time."

As contrasted with the Classicists who made reason, order and the old, Classical traditions the criteria in their poetical creations, Wordsworth appealed directly to individual sensations like pleasure, excitement and enjoyment as the foundation in the creation and appreciation of poetry. His theory about the sources of poetry is quite different from that of the 18th century. According to Wordsworth, poetry comes from emotions, not from reason; it deals with feelings and attitudes instead of understanding or common sense; it is "the spontaneous overflow of powerful feeling" "recollected in tranquility" by men of deep feeling and much thought. The key words here are "emotion," "feeling," and "deep thought" which is another way of saying "meditation." A real poet is one who thinks a good deal, knows and learns about humanity and his times, has very deep feelings, and is able to recollect these powerful emotions and writes. Wordsworth was himself a masterhand in searching and revealing the feelings of the common people. The good illustrations include such poems as "I Wandered Lonely as a Cloud" and "The Solitary Reaper," and many other ones.

Wordsworth held that the subject of poetry should come from the "incidents and situations from common life" and that poetic diction and the coloring of the imagination should enable people to see the incidents in a new light, enable them to see the primary laws of human nature, and show them how to see, understand and enjoy their lives and judge them. Low and rustic life may be used to better represent the essential passions of the heart and the elemental feelings of men. People who come from the middle or lower classes of society, like peasants, children, outcasts, criminals and idiot boys, can be used as serious subjects of poetic or even tragic concern. The themes of many of his poems were therefore drawn from rural life and his characters belong to the lower classes in the English countryside. Deep-rooted in his native soil, Wordsworth succeeded in drawing pathetic pictures of the laboring people (e. g. in "The Solitary Reaper"), in depicting the naivety of simple peasant children (e. g. in "We Are Seven") and in delineating with deep sympathy the sufferings of the poor, humble peasants (e. g. in "Michael," "The Ruined Cottage," "Simon Lee" and "The Old Cumberland Beggar").

Wordsworth elevated the status of the poet. He viewed the poet in a new light as well. He felt that the poet should understand life better than other people did. The function of poetry was not simply entertaining readers or helping them remember things. He saw the poet as a "seer" of a kind as well, although he probably did not go as far as Ralph Waldo Emerson (1803 – 1882) or Walt Whitman (1819 – 1892).

Lyrical Ballads is generally considered to have marked the beginning of the Romantic Movement in England. The immediate effect on critics was modest, but it became and remains a landmark, changing the course of English literature and poetry. The majority of the poems in the collection were written by Wordsworth. Coleridge's contribution was only his five supernatural poems like his masterpiece "The Rime of the Ancient Mariner." The best-known poems contributed by Wordsworth include "The Last of the Flock," "Lucy Gray," "She Dwelt among the Untrodden Ways," "Lines Composed a Few Miles above Tintern Abbey," and "Lines Written in Early Spring."

The poems are characterized by the sympathy with the poor, simple peasants, a passionate love for nature and the simplicity and purity of the language. Wordsworth and Coleridge set out to overturn what they considered the priggish, learned and highly sculpted forms of the 18th-century English poetry and brought poetry within the reach of the average person by writing the verses using normal, everyday language. They placed an emphasis on the vitality of the living voice that the poor used to express their reality. Using this language also helps assert the universality of human emotions. Even the title of the collection recalls rustic forms of art—the word "lyrical" links the poems with the ancient rustic bards and lends an air of spontaneity, while "ballads" are an oral mode of storytelling used by the common people.

In the preface to the second edition in 1800, Wordsworth set forth his principles of poetry: poetry is "the spontaneous overflow of powerful emotion" "recollected in tranquility" by men of deep feeling and much thought; the purest poetry was written in the simplest words. He took the speech of the country people for his model. The preface hence has become the manifesto of the English Romantic poetry. In the 1802 edition, Wordsworth added an appendix titled *Poetic Diction* in which he expanded the ideas set forth in the preface. A fourth and final edition of *Lyrical Ballads* came out in 1805.

Wordsworth was at his best in descriptions of mountains and rivers, flowers and birds, children and peasants, and reminiscences of his childhood and youth. He, as a great poet of nature, was the first to find words for the most elementary sensations of man face to face with natural phenomena. The most famous poems in this group are "To the Cuckoo," "Lucy Poems," "I Wondered Lonely as a Cloud" and "The Solitary Reaper." The miscellaneous sonnets, written at different periods of his life, are also Wordsworth's principle poems. *The Prelude*, *The Excursion* and "Lines Composed a Few Miles above Tintern Abbey" are of course among the poet's best works.

Wordsworth's theory of nature and its importance to human life is well demonstrated in his famous "**Lines Composed a Few Miles above Tintern Abbey**, on revisiting the banks of the Wye during a tour, July 13, 1798." The title is often abbreviated simply to "Tintern Abbey," although that building does not appear within the poem at all. The poem was composed after Wordsworth touring with his sister in this section of the Welsh Borders. The description of the poet's encounters with the countryside on the banks of the River Wye grows into an outline of his general philosophy. The poem is written in the style of description and meditation that Wordsworth picked up from Coleridge's *Frost at Midnight*. As it best exemplifies the basic elements of the poet's theory of nature and, by extension, of poetry, it functions to Wordsworth's notion of nature poetry like a wire-puller to loose threads. The poem and the meditation it contains were prompted by the poet's revisiting the Wye valley that he had passed five years earlier during his tour of the country in 1793. It is a scene to which the poetic mind returns with its recollection. Thus it illustrates the poet's idea of poetry as "the powerful overflow of feeling" "recollected in tranquility."

The first stanza (ll. 1 – 22) describes the quiet pastoral beauty of the valley. Deep in nature, the poetic mind begins to meditate. The second stanza (ll. 23 – 48) focuses on the importance of nature in "[t]hese beauteous forms" when remembered at this moment of tranquility. The third stanza (ll. 49 – 57) reiterates the notion that nature offers a counterpoint against the world, with its joyless daylight, its unprofitable activity and its fever, all weighing heavily on the mind. The stanza ends with the self-reproach and by extension the complaint about people in general for having not cared about nature. The fourth stanza (ll. 58 – 111) emphasizes the three stages of progression of the poet's mind slowly learning about nature. The last and fifth stanza (ll. 112 – 159) is the poet's advice to his sister, and for that matter, to people like her or all his readers, as to what to do with nature.

The Prelude, or Growth of a Poet's Mind, Wordsworth's autobiographical conversation poem in blank verse, is composed of 14 books written at various periods and sometimes with another purpose. Intended as the introduction to the more philosophical *The Recluse*, which Wordsworth never finished, the poem is an extremely personal and revealing work on the details of Wordsworth's life. Wordsworth planned to write *The Recluse* together with Coleridge, their joint intent being to surpass John Milton's *Paradise Lost*. Had it been completed, *The Recluse* would have been approximately three times longer than *Paradise Lost* (33,000 lines versus 10,500); often, in his letters, Wordsworth commented that he was plagued with agony because he failed to finish the work. In the 1850 introduction, Wordsworth explained that the original idea, inspired by his "dear friend" Coleridge, was "to compose a philosophical Poem, containing views of Man, Nature, and Society, and to be entitled *The Recluse*; as having for its principal subject, the sensations and opinions of a poet living in retirement."

Wordsworth began *The Prelude* in 1798 at the age of 28 and a complete draft in 13 books was finished in 1805. The poet continued to work on it throughout his life. The poem was several times remodeled and published posthumously in its final version in 1850, with its present title, suggested by Mary Wordsworth. In the first book Wordsworth described his search for a conventional epic theme, and moved from this to an evocation of his own childhood which led him less by logic than by imagination. Although profoundly autobiographical, the poem does not proceed in terms of strict chronology; it is a spiritual account of the poet's mind, honestly recording his own intimate mental experiences which covers his infancy, his school days, his years at Cambridge, his walking tour through Alps, his political awakening in France and his reaction to these various experiences, and showing the development of his own thought and sentiment. The tone is simply flexible and variable; conversational and informal in some passages, narrative and naturalistic in others, it rises at points to an impassioned loftiness. A constant theme throughout is an overriding duty to his poetic vocation. Apart from its poetic quality, the work is remarkable for its psychological insight into the significance of childhood experience, a theme dear to Romanticism, but rarely treated with such power and precision.

The Excursion was intended to be the second part of *The Recluse*, the projected three-part poem "on man, on nature and on human life." The exact dates of its composition are unknown, but the first manuscript is generally dated as either September 1806 or December 1809. *The Excursion* is arranged into nine books: "The Wanderer," "The Solitary," "Despondency," "Despondency Corrected," "The Pastor," "The Churchyard among the Mountains," "The Churchyard among the Mountains, continued," "The Parsonage" and "Discourse of the Wanderer." There are four major characters: the Poet (the narrator of the poem), the Wanderer, the Solitary, who, plagued by the death of his wife and children, as well as by his disenchantment with the French Revolution, has chosen to live alone, wanting no more connection with the social world that has brought him so much pain, and the Pastor.

The first and second books introduce the characters of the Wanderer and the Solitary respectively. The third and fourth books consist of a conversation/debate between the Wanderer and the Solitary regarding the truth of Religion and the virtue of Mankind. The fifth, sixth, seventh and eighth books introduce the character of the Pastor and consist largely of the Pastor explaining the life stories of many of the townspeople who lie buried in the country-churchyard. In the final two books, all of the aforementioned characters travel to the Parsonage, are introduced to the family of the Pastor, and eventually part ways.

The story is very slight. The poet, traveling with the Wanderer, a philosophic pedlar, meets with the pedlar's friend, the sad and pessimistic Solitary. The source of the Solitary's despondency is found in his want of religious faith and of confidence in the virtue of man, and he is reproved with gentle and persuasive argument. The Pastor is then introduced, who illustrates the harmonizing effects of virtue and religion through narratives of people interred in his churchyard. They visit the Pastor's house, and the Wanderer draws his general and philosophic conclusions from the discussions that have passed. The last two books deal in particular with the industrial expansion of the early part of the century, and the degradation that followed in its train. The poem ends with the Pastor's prayer that man may be given grace to conquer guilt and sin, and with praise for the beauty of the world about them.

20.1.2 Samuel Taylor Coleridge (1772 – 1834)

An English poet, literary critic and philosopher, Coleridge was a rare genius in the history of English literature. Along with Wordsworth, he was a founder of the Romantic Movement in England and a member of the Lake

Poets. Coleridge is chiefly remembered for the poems "The Rime of the Ancient Mariner" and "Kubla Khan," as well as the major prose work *Biographia Literaria*. His critical work, especially on Shakespeare, was highly influential, and he helped introduce German idealist philosophy to English-speaking culture. He was a major influence on Emerson and American Transcendentalism. Just like Wordsworth, Coleridge became conservative in thinking in his later years. His works naturally divide themselves into three classes: the poetic, the critical and the philosophical, corresponding to the early, the middle and the later periods of his career.

Coleridge is better known for his poetry. He is one of the most important figures in English poetry. His poems directly and deeply influenced all the major poets of the age. He was known to his contemporaries as a meticulous craftsman who was more rigorous in his careful reworking of his poems than any other poet. Southey and Wordsworth were dependent on his professional advice. His influence on Wordsworth is particularly important because many critics have credited Coleridge with the very idea of "Conversational Poetry." The idea of utilizing common, everyday language to express profound poetic images and ideas, for which Wordsworth became so famous, may have originated almost entirely in Coleridge's mind. It is difficult to imagine Wordsworth's great poems, *The Excursion* or *The Prelude*, ever having been written without the direct influence of Coleridge's originality.

Coleridge the great poet was a medievalist, fond of the unusual and supernatural things. His imaginative power was intense and his language melodious. His early poetry showed the influence of Gray and Blake, especially of the latter. In his later poems his imagination was bridled by thought and study. His main poems include "The Rime of the Ancient Mariner," "Kubla Khan," "Dejection: An Ode" and "Christabel."

"The Rime of the Ancient Mariner," Coleridge's masterpiece and longest major poem, was written in 1797 – 98 and first published in the 1798 edition of *Lyrical Ballads*. Along with other poems in *Lyrical Ballads*, it was a signal shift to modern poetry and the beginning of English Romantic literature. It is one of the masterpieces of the Romantic poetry and an artistic rarity in world poetry. It tells a strange story in the four-line ballad stanza form, with the striking musical rhythms, the sounds of the words used, and the salient images, not the least of which relates to the vivid description of the colors. The atmosphere and the beauty of music and imagery make the poem stand alone of its kind.

"The Rime of the Ancient Mariner" relates the experiences of an ancient mariner who has returned from a long sea voyage. Three guests are on their way to a wedding party, but one of them is detained by the mariner, who tells him of his adventures on the sea. When the mariner's ship sails towards the South Pole, an albatross comes through the snow-fog and alights on the rigging. The mariner is thoughtless enough to shoot it. Then misfortunes fall on the ship. The whole crew except the mariner die of thirst as a punishment for the act of inhospitality shown to the bird by the old mariner. The spell breaks only when the mariner repents his cruelty. Despite his repeated repentance, the curse for his wanton killing returns at intervals, and he has to retell his tale of woe over and over in order to expiate his sin and feel better. He is like a wandering Jew or Cain, for ever on the move, roaming the wide world and catechizing people with his story of sin and confession. So the poem begins with him grabbing and stopping the wedding guest and forcing him to listen to his story, and ends with turning the listener into a different person, one like a prophet. The wedding guest's reaction turns from bemusement to impatience to fear to fascination as the mariner's story progresses, as can be seen in the language style: Coleridge used narrative techniques such as personification and repetition to create a sense of danger, the supernatural, or serenity, depending on the mood in different parts of the poem.

The story is simple enough, but possesses a wealth of meanings worth exploring. It is basically a Christian story, which also plants doubts in the readers' mind as to whether faith serves any purpose in life at all. It can be read as a Christian poem as repentance and love bring redemption. There is, however, a kind of skepticism imbedded in the texture of the poem. According to the Christian faith, after one sins, one confesses and repents once for it, and it should be enough to receive the absolution. But the old man in the poem has to repent over and again and there seems to be no end of repentance. The implication could be that God does not hear his confession and prayers. This strain of skepticism that Coleridge felt and put in the poem was prophetic of the impending crisis of faith in his century.

Coleridge spoke ahead of his time. For one thing, he saw nature differently from Wordsworth and his contemporaries. Nature in the poem behaves in a way which is at best apathetic. The old sailor's world is an amoral world, indifferent, naturalistic and basically Godless, in which man is utterly thrown upon himself for survival. As we know, this concept of the amoral universe did not take clear shape until the latter part of the 19th century. For another, the ancient mariner is seen all alone on a wide, wide sea, presenting a vivid, pathetic picture of an existentialist, trying to make sense of his world over which he has not the slightest control, and generating a frame of reference for himself. The matter of fact is that Sartre's existentialism became definable as a philosophy only in the 1940s.

The poem also demonstrates Coleridge's belief in the existence of the supernatural and an invisible higher plane of life. Although the story is anchored in the solid physical setting of the phenomenal human world, there is an extra dimension of existence that men need to learn about: the supernatural. Thus the tale here is not meant to be a Gothic story; it is a poetic expression of the poet's idealism. The glosses that Coleridge offered serve to make the point beyond doubt.

Coleridge is probably best known for "The Rime of the Ancient Mariner." Even those who have never read the poem have come under its influence: its words have given the English language the metaphor of an albatross around one's neck, the quotation of "water, water everywhere, nor any drop to drink" (almost always rendered as "but not a drop to drink"), and the phrase "a sadder and a wiser man" (again, usually rendered as "a sadder but wiser man"). The phrase "all creatures great and small" may have been inspired by the poem: "He prayeth best, who loveth best;/All things both great and small;/For the dear God who loveth us;/He made and loveth all."

"Kubla Khan; or, A Vision in a Dream: A Fragment" is a dream-poem, completed in 1797 and published in 1816. Although shorter, the poem is also widely known. During an illness in 1797 Coleridge retired to a lonely farmhouse. One day he fell asleep as he was reading a passage about Kubla Khan, the Mongol conqueror, from a book entitled "Purchas' Pilgrimages." According to Coleridge's Preface to the poem, while in sleep he composed a long poem about two or three hundred lines. Upon waking, he set about writing down the lines. But he was interrupted after 54 lines were written. The poem could not be completed according to its original 200 - 300 line plan as the interruption caused him to forget the lines. He left it unpublished and kept it for private readings for his friends until 1816 when, at the prompting of Lord Byron, it was published.

Some of Coleridge's contemporaries denounced the poem and questioned his story of its origin. It was not until years later that critics began to openly admire the poem. Most modern critics now view "Kubla Khan" as one of Coleridge's three great poems, along with "The Rime of the Ancient Mariner" and "Christabel." The poem is considered one of the most famous examples of Romanticism in English poetry.

Actually, the poem is not about the Mongolian Khan at all. It is really about the mystery of poetic creation. The king that Coleridge had in mind is not the Khan but the perfect poet, and the beautiful garden, the grand palace, which the Khan decrees to build, is in fact the poet's ideas of a perfect poem.

The poem is composed of three sections of different lengths. The first section, consisting of 11 lines, touches upon a few things which are essential to the understanding of the poem. The second section, of 19 lines, is probably the most difficult of all for the readers. It puts together a lot of images that do not seem to connect with one another well. The third section, of 24 lines, begins with the poet's vision of the perfect poem, the symbol of which is the Khan's dome (ll. 31 – 36). It connects well with the second section because the vision is possible only after the poet tastes of the chaos of the unconscious. Here Coleridge anticipated Sigmund Freud (1856 – 1939) in drawing attention to the importance of the subconscious. He spoke even well ahead of modern criticism concerning the concept of Dionysus as the emblem of the unconscious in modern poetry. In this sense, "Kubla Khan" is a highly symbolic poem, and Coleridge is a highly symbolic poet.

"**Dejection: An Ode**" (1802), a reply to William Wordsworth's "Resolution and Independence," is connected to Wordsworth's "Immortality Ode" in theme and structure. It is the work of a lonely and meditative mind. Its subject is the poet's sad awareness that he was losing his creative powers. The poem expresses his feelings of dejection and inability to write poetry or to enjoy nature. Wordsworth is introduced into the poem as a counter to Coleridge, because Wordsworth is able to turn such a mood into a benefit and is able to be comforted. However, Coleridge could not find anything positive in his problems, and he expressed how he felt paralyzed by his emotions. The poem also captures some feelings in Coleridge's previous works, especially in analyzing a problematic childhood and an exploration of religion. Partly, these feelings were fueled by his inability to accept his opium addiction and other problems.

The 8-stanza poem is thematically more significant in more than one way. In the first stanza the moaning of the wind mirrors the moaning of the poet's agonizing soul. The dreadful description of a relief-less grief in the first part of the second stanza expresses not only the pain the poet felt alone, but also proves to be an authentic picture of the kind of spiritual poverty which the intellectually sensitive minds of the time had already begun to feel. Moreover, this acute sense of grief would soon assail the masses in a few decades after the evolutionary theory of Charles Darwin (1809 – 1882) shook the Christian faith. If Mathew Arnold's "Dover Beach" is a faithful record of how people felt in the mid-19th century, Coleridge anticipated him by a whole period of 50 years. Also the second stanza talks about nature in a way drastically different from Wordsworth's. For Wordsworth, nature is all good and, even if it occasionally exhibits any threat of any kind, it is meant for man's good. Coleridge, in his dull pain, felt no comfort and no inspiration from his observation of a beautiful nature. He did not sound totally negative about nature, but the notion he expressed in his "The Rime of the Ancient Mariner," that nature may not be kind and may be apathetic and capable of evil, is subtly hinted here. In stanza three the poet lamented over the alienation of man's consciousness from the universe and the failure of nature to energize and vitalize his imagination. Stanza four puts forward a well-known Romantic notion that has prevailed ever since. Here Coleridge assigned a very seminal role to the human mind: the imagination helps give life to the external world. To Coleridge, nature is alive because the human mind sees it that way or endows it with life. The imagination is a shaping force. Thus if the world is faithless, loveless and joyless, it is the job of the poetic imagination to create all those things that make life tolerable. This is Coleridge's notion of the function of the poet and poetry. Then stanza five presents naturally the poet's thirst for that sense of joy and harmony which stems from overcoming the alienation between the soul and nature. Stanza six is the poet's woeful way of saying goodbye to health and happiness, with the sad awareness that his physical afflictions were "suspending" the shaping spirit of his imagination and "stealing" all the natural man from his nature and that he had to put up with his drug addiction in order to survive. Stanza seven begins with a sorrowful self-analysis and a description of the howling wind and the desolate scene outside, which is an externalization of the poet's total inner bleakness. The stanza ends with a scenario which reminds the reader of that of Wordsworth's "Lucy Gray," with the difference that Coleridge's picture is one of an existentialist nature: a person is all alone on a lonesome wilderness, his soul weeping and craving for help that is not forthcoming from any quarters. The last stanza is a wish for Sara Hutchinson, the "Lady" of the poem, for whom the poet had cherished deep love and to whom the poem was addressed. The poet wished all the best for her, good sleep, good spirits, divine guidance and protection, and harmony between her and nature. These also indicate the depth of despair that the poet felt for himself. In retrospect, it has been recognized that the poet's personal dejection was emblematic of the spirit of his own and the decades to come, a happy coincidence which ensures his greatness and permanence.

"**Christabel**" is a fragment, which is known for its musical rhythm, language and its Gothic tale. It is a long narrative poem in two parts. The first part was reputedly written in 1797, and the second in 1800. Coleridge planned three additional parts, but these were never completed. Coleridge prepared for the first two parts to be published in the 1800 edition of *Lyrical Ballads*, but on the advice of William Wordsworth it was left out; the exclusion of the poem, coupled with his inability to finish it, left Coleridge in doubt about his poetical power. It was published in a pamphlet in 1816, alongside "Kubla Khan" and "The Pains of Sleep."

The poem tells the story of a sorcerer who casts a spell over the title character, a pure young girl. Christabel goes into the woods to pray by the large oak tree, where she hears a strange noise. Upon looking behind the tree, she finds Geraldine who says that she was abducted from her home by a band of rough men on horseback. Christabel pities her and takes her home with her; the supernatural signs like a dog barking and a mysterious flame on a dead fire seem to indicate that all is not well. They spend the night together, but while Geraldine undresses, she shows a terrible but undefined mark on the bosom. Christabel's father Sir Leoline becomes enchanted with Geraldine, ordering a grand procession to announce her rescue. The unfinished poem ends here. The mysterious atmosphere and the supernatural terror may "freeze our blood." On this account it is not wholesome reading.

Coleridge was the first critic of the Romantic school. His philosophy of poetry, which he developed over many years, has been deeply influential in the field of literary criticism. He was good at giving lectures. His critical works chiefly include his lectures on Shakespeare, Milton and others, and his most important prose work *Biographia Literaria*. Among his lectures those on Shakespeare stand out as the most significant. Between 1808 and 1815 he delivered a series of lectures on Shakespeare, which were later collected in his *Notes and Lectures on Shakespeare*.

Biographia Literaria, or Biographical Sketches of My Literary Life and Opinions (1817) is a philosophic autobiography and a classic source to which modern criticism is directly traceable. It is long and seemingly loosely structured. In spite of the autobiographical elements, the work is not a straightforward or linear autobiography. Instead, it is meditative.

The work consists of twenty-three chapters in two parts. It was originally intended as a mere preface to a collected volume of Coleridge's poems, explaining and justifying his own style and practice in poetry. Nevertheless, it grew to a work of philosophic autobiography and Romantic literary criticism, including, together with many facts concerning Coleridge's education and studies and his early literary adventures, an extended criticism of William Wordsworth's theory of poetry as given in the preface to the *Lyrical Ballads*, and a statement of the author's own philosophical views.

The first part is about Coleridge's growth as a poet and the evolution of his philosophic creed. At first an adherent of the associational psychology of David Hartley (1705 – 1757), he came to discard this mechanical system for the belief that the mind is not a passive but an active agency in the apprehension of reality. The author believed in the "self-sufficing power of absolute Genius" and distinguished between genius and talent as between "an egg and an egg-shell." The discussion involves his definition of the imagination or "esemplastic power," the faculty by which the soul perceives the spiritual unity of the universe, as distinguished from the fancy or merely associative function. The second part deals with the nature of poetry and analyzes Wordsworth's poetic diction. While maintaining a general agreement with Wordsworth's point of view, Coleridge elaborately refuted his principle that the language of poetry should be one taken with due exceptions from the mouths of men in real life, and that there could be no essential difference between the language of prose and of metrical composition. A critique on the qualities of Wordsworth's poetry concludes the part.

The work offers the new Romantic poetry a new principle of criticism, whose task is not to judge but to appreciate and interpret. According to Coleridge, the poet was a creator and the critic was an assistant in the work of creation. The poet, as a man endowed with imaginative genius and fine perception, must be allowed to present the truth in his own without regard to rules or models. And the critic must enter into the poet's purpose and art, and interpret ideas and beauty for the benefit of the reader. This idea was taken up by I. A. Richards (1893 – 1979) in the 1920s as support for his New Critical thesis that a poem can be rationally analyzed, its textural structure is more important than its "period" background or the author's biographical information, and critcal focus should be placed on the text of the work. As a result, Coleridge was looked up to as an authority for the New Critics, and his *Biographia Literaria* was reprinted and exercised a far-reaching influence on the literary criticism of the time and a long time afterward.

20.1.3 Robert Southey (1774 – 1843)

Southey, together with Wordsworth and Coleridge, was a so-called "Lake Poet." Although his fame has long been eclipsed by that of his contemporaries and friends Wordsworth and Coleridge, Southey's verse, especially his prose work *The Life of Horatio, Lord Viscount Nelson* (1813) still enjoys some popularity.

Southey was a radical poet when he was young. He warmly acclaimed French Revolution. Later on he had a great change in thinking and became one of the defenders of the reactionary forces. In 1813 Southey was awarded the title of the Poet Laureate, which lasted thirty years till his death in 1843. Being a poet, Southey was not so important as Wordsworth and Coleridge. He held his place in this group more by personal association than by his literary gifts. He labored at literature for more than fifty years. He considered himself seriously as one of the greatest writers of the day. He set himself to the task of writing something every working day. The results of his industry were 109 volumes. But most of them are utterly forgotten. His poems, although containing some excellent passages, are on the whole too exaggerated and unread. His prose work is far better than his poetry.

Southey was also a historian and biographer. His biographies include the life and works of John Bunyan, John Wesley (1703 – 1791), William Cowper, Oliver Cromwell and Horatio Nelson (1758 – 1805). The last is still read and has rarely been out of print since its publication in 1813 and was adapted for the screen in the 1926 British film *Nelson*. He was also a renowned scholar of Portuguese and Spanish literatures and histories, translating a number of works from those two languages into English and writing *History of Brazil* (3 vols.) (1810 – 1819), which is part of his planned but never completed *History of Portugal*, and *History of the Peninsular War, 1807 – 1814* (3 vols.) (1823 – 1832). Perhaps his most enduring contribution to literary history is the children's classic "The Story of the Three Bears" (1837), first published in Southey's prose collection *The Doctor* (7 vols.) (1834 – 1847).

20.2 Representative Poets of the Second Generation

20.2.1 George Gordon, Lord Byron (1788 – 1824)

Byron was one of the most excellent representatives of English Romanticism and one of the most influential poets of his time. In the mid-19th century, he surpassed all his Romantic contemporaries as the leading poet not only in his own country but also in Europe. He exercised a marked influence on the continental literature and art, and is widely thought to be the greatest poet in the world. Byron's reputation as a poet is higher in many European countries than in Britain or America, although not as high as in his time. He is considered to be the first modern-style celebrity and is still remembered today among the Greeks as their national hero. The re-founding of the Byron Society in 1971 reflected the fascination that many people had for Byron and his work. This Society became very active, publishing an annual journal. 36 Byron Societies function throughout the world, and an International Conference takes place annually.

Byron's literary career was closely linked with the struggle and progressive movements of his age. He praised the people's revolutionary struggle in his works. He opposed oppression and slavery, and had an ardent love for liberty. Byron fought all his life for the liberty of the individual and the nation as well. His poems are favorites of the British workers and the laboring people of the other countries.

Byron created a hero of his own type, the Byronic hero, handsome, chivalrous, energetic, pathetic, lonely, remorseful over a sin, gloomy and misanthropic, sexually free, and capable of generous acts and magnanimity. The figure of the Byronic hero pervades much of his work. The protagonists in his major works like *Childe Harold* and *Don Juan* are all archetypes of the Byronic hero. Generally, the hero has disrespect for certain figures of authority and is doomed to be an exile or an outcast; he presents an idealized but flawed character. On the one hand, the hero has a rather high level of intelligence and perception, and is able to easily adapt to new situations and use cunning to his own gain. He is well-educated and by extension is rather sophisticated in his style. Hence he is charming and attractive. On the other hand, the hero struggles with his integrity, being prone to mood swings. He has a tendency to be arrogant and cynical, indulging in self-destructive behavior which leads to the need to seduce women. Although his sexual attraction through being mysterious is rather helpful, it often gets the hero into trouble. Byron himself is considered to epitomize many of the characteristics of this literary figure, which have since become ubiquitous in literature and politics. Scholars have traced the literary history of the Byronic hero from John Milton, and many authors and artists of the Romantic Movement showed Byron's influence during the 19th century and beyond, including Charlotte and Emily Brontë.

Byron is noted for the spontaneity, exuberance and humor in his poetry. His poems show energy and vigor, romantic daring and powerful passion. He said what he felt in a charming manner. Byron is a highly inspired poet. He had a direct, forthright and forceful voice. No one could ignore the enchanting beauty, the bewitching power and the sweeping fascination that radiate from his works. His theme of quest for freedom and against tyranny and his romantic spirit have made their imprint upon the life and the literature of the world. Byron had stronger ties to the 18th-century writers than any of his contemporaries. He was a great admirer of Dryden and Pope, but he lacked Pope's care for artistic finish; many of his lines are harsh, rugged and unrhythmical.

As a student, Byron published his first collection of poems *Hours of Idleness* (1807), an immature little book, dealing with childish recollections and early friendship, and showing the influence of the 18th-century traditions. His first important poem *English Bards and Scotch Reviewers* (1809) is noted for its biting satire, which caused great shock in the upper classes. Byron is chiefly remembered for his two long poems—*Childe Harold's Pilgrimage* (1812-1818) and *Don Juan* (1819-1824).

Childe Harold's Pilgrimage is a lengthy narrative poem in four cantos written in Spenserian stanza. The title comes from the term "childe," a medieval title for a young man who was a candidate for knighthood. The poem provides the first example of the Byronic hero. It describes the travels, experiences and reflections of a self-styled and self-exiled pilgrim Childe Harold, who, disillusioned with a life of pleasure and revelry, looks for distraction in foreign lands. The pilgrim's wanderings in some of the European countries correspond in many ways to Byron's own. Childe Harold is a young man from an English aristocratic family, who hates the English high society and loves freedom. Besides Harold's impressions of the countries he visits, the poem is interspersed with lyrical outbursts which reveal Byron's own philosophical and political ideas. In a wider sense, the poem is an expression of the melancholy and disillusionment felt by a generation weary of the wars of the post-Revolutionary and Napoleonic eras.

The first two cantos describe how Childe Harold, sated with his past life of sin and pleasure, finds distraction by travel: he journeys through Portugal, Spain, the Ionian Islands, and Albania. Here the wanderer salutes Albania and its wild, martial and exotically garbed people, and then once more laments the lost liberty of Greece. In Canto III, written six years later, the pilgrim still "wrung with the wounds that heal not," travels to Belgium, the Rhine, the Alps, and Jura. Byron turned to the political struggles of the day. He glorified the French Revolution which had shaken the old world and condemned the reaction that set in Europe after the downfall of Napoleon (1769-1821). Byron believed that, although the Revolution failed and the kings were restored to their thrones, the people would see better days again. The canto also deals with the poet's almost Wordsworthian love for nature. Some consider this canto the best of the poem in further fleshing out the features of the Byronic hero and in emotional substance and intensity. The fourth canto sings of Italy and the Italian people who have given the world great writers and thinkers like Petrarch, Dante, Boccaccio, Tasso (1544 – 1595) and Galileo (1564 – 1642). Byron exposed the reactionary rulers of Europe, especially the Holy Alliance. His ardent love for liberty and his firm belief in the people's final triumph find expression in the lyrical outbursts. Again the poet expressed his appreciation of the beauty of nature. The poem ends where it started, with the Byronic hero feeling weary, exhausted and wasted. To some extent, the reason for the everlasting power of *Childe Harold's Pilgrimage* is that the Byronic hero is depicted in full-fledged form: Childe Harold is gifted, capricious, human, anti-conventional, and misunderstood and hurt.

Don Juan, Byron's masterpiece, is a satiric poem, based on the legend of Don Juan, which Byron reversed, portraying Juan not as a womaniser but as someone easily seduced by women. It is a mock-epic, a variation on the epic form, and possibly the only great long epic poem in English. Byron himself called it an "Epic Satire." The satire has the whole of Europe as its backdrop, revealing as it does the poet's keen observation of life and his satirical depth and sweep. *Don Juan* is a fragment of 16 cantos (16,000 lines) in ottava rima, each stanza containing eight iambic pentameter lines rhymed abababcc. Byron left an unfinished 17th canto before his death in 1824.

The story takes place in the latter half of the 18th century. Don Juan is a Spanish youth of aristocratic birth. This long poem describes Don Juan's adventures in many countries. The hero is made to participate in different historical events. Thus we can get a broad panorama of the social life of the time. The poem begins with descriptions of the hero's childhood. Then it describes his love affairs with a married woman. When the love affair is discovered, he is sent abroad. The ship is wrecked. His fellow travelers die; he survives and swims to a Greek island where he is saved by a girl. They fall in love. But their love affair is broken when the girl's father returns to the island. Subsequently, Don Juan is sold as a slave. In the capital of Turkey, Constantinople, he is bought by the Sultana (sister of the king) who has taken a fancy to him. Don Juan lives there with the girl in the guise of a woman. After going through many adventures, he runs away to the camp of the Russian army that is besieging the Turkish fortress and is sent to St. Petersburg. Afterwards, Empress Catherine sends him to England on a political mission. The last cantos of the poem give a satirical description of English ruling classes and social conditions. The hero shows his disgust at the vanity and hypocrisy of English society. Byron meant to make the hero take part in the French Revolution and die a heroic death; yet he did not finish the poem. In *Don Juan* Byron displayed his genius as a romanticist and a realist simultaneously.

The effect of ottava rima in English is often comic, due to its few rhymed endings. Byron's choice of ottava rima automatically brings *Don Juan* a similar comic effect. The protagonist has a rather complex personality, or at least a show of it. He can be innocent and morally inhibited at times, but he can also, at other moments, be the opposite of all these, and behave as an imprudent worldly cynic. Any possible serious intention can be turned into a comic cynicism when he reveals these traits at moments inappropriate to the scenarios in which he is involved. The appearance of various speakers is also instrumental in the comic effect. Those speakers sometimes take over from the narrator and pop in with some comments so inapt to the situation that they would turn any serious potential into a comic water-down. In terms of structure, the poem seems to be loose. The different episodes appear to be separate beads. What is worth pointing out here is that, although Byron claimed that he had no plan when writing this work, the episodes somehow coalesce into an organic whole and are well strung together.

Byron also wrote a lot of beautiful lyrical poems, which deal with nature, love or the poet's political aspiration. The best-known pieces are "She Walks in Beauty," "When We Two Parted," "Hebrew Melodies" and "Sonnet on Chillon."

20.2.2 Percy Bysshe Shelley (1792 – 1822)

Shelley was one of the major English Romantic poets and is regarded by some as among the finest lyric, as well as epic, poets in the English language. He loved the people and hated their oppressors and exploiters. He called on the people to overthrow the rule of tyranny and injustice and prophesied a happy and free life for mankind. Shelley stood for this social and political ideal all his life. His advanced political and social thought impacted the Chartist and other movements in England, and reaches down to the present day. His theories of economics and morality, for example, had a profound influence on Karl Marx; his early—perhaps first—writings on nonviolent resistance influenced both Leo Tolstoy (1828 – 1910) and Mahatma Gandhi (1869 – 1948). Shelley and Byron are justifiably regarded as the two great poets of revolutionary Romanticism in England. A radical in his poetry as well as his political and social views, Shelley did not achieve fame during his lifetime, but recognition for his poetry grew steadily following his death. He was admired by Oscar Wilde, Thomas Hardy, George Bernard Shaw, Bertrand Russell (1872 – 1970), W. B. Yeats, and others. "Civil Disobedience" (1849) by the American writer Henry David Thoreau (1817 – 1862) was apparently influenced by Shelley's non-violence in protest and political action. Shelley's popularity and influence has continued to grow and his poetic achievements are widely recognized today.

Shelley is an idealistic and prophetic Romantic. He was a key member of a close circle of visionary poets and writers including Lord Byron, Leigh Hunt, Thomas Love Peacock (1785 – 1866), and his own second wife Mary Shelley (1797 – 1851), the author of the Gothic novel *Frankenstein: or, The Modern Prometheus* (1818). In his works he refused to accept life as it was and tried to envision life as devoid of oppression, injustice, tyranny and corruption current in the social life of his day. He visualized the birth of an ideal social order based on the regeneration of man and the virtue of love. He tended to create the ideal man despising authority and fighting tyranny with his indomitable spirit and saw this spirit as the most valuable human asset with which man can build a new, ideal life.

In addition to his themes of protest against tyranny and quest for freedom and an ideal social order, Shelley wrote a good number of lyrics, among which his love poems are the most impressive. Shelley is one of the best English lyrical poets. He is famous for the wild flights of his imagination, his dextrous use of colors, sounds, images and the touching beauty of his rhymes and music.

Shelley's major works include the long, visionary poems such as *Queen Mab*, *Alastor*, *The Revolt of Islam*, and *Adonaïs*, the visionary verse dramas like *The Cenci* and *Prometheus Unbound*, the lyrics on nature and love, the political lyrics, the famous sonnet "Ozymandias" and the prose work "A Defence of Poetry."

Queen Mab: *A Philosophical Poem* (1813) is Shelley's first long poem of importance. After substantial reworking, a revised edition of a portion of the text was published in 1816 under the title *The Daemon of the World*. The poem is in nine cantos with seventeen remarkable prose Notes attached as Appendices, using "didactic and descriptive" blank verse greatly indebted to Milton and Southey. It is furious and polemical in style, with occasional passages of grandiloquent beauty. Despite a vision of the woeful past in the first two cantos and a celebration of an ideal future of Republicanism, Free Love, Atheism and Vegetarianism in the last two cantos, the poem largely consists of fierce attacks on Monarchy, War, Commerce and Religion.

The poem is written in the form of a fairy tale that presents a future vision of a utopia on earth. Queen Mab, a fairy, descends in a chariot to a dwelling where Ianthe is sleeping on a couch. Queen Mab detaches Ianthe's spirit or soul from her sleeping body and transports it on a celestial tour to Queen Mab's palace at the edge of the universe. Queen Mab interprets, analyzes and explains Ianthe's dreams. She shows her visions of the past, the present and the future. The past and the present are characterized by oppression, injustice, misery, and suffering caused by monarchies, commerce and religion. In the future, however, the condition of man will be improved and a utopia will emerge. Humanity and nature can be reconciled and work in unison and harmony, not against each other.

Queen Mab is loved by the English working class. It is a revolutionary poem condemning tyranny and exploitation and the unjust war waged by the rich to plunder wealth, and expressing all the poet's major political ideas. However, Shelley in this poem was merely a Utopian-socialist in views, looking forward to a happy future for mankind but rejecting the path of revolution by violence. The theme of the work is the perfectibility of man by moral means.

Alastor, or *The Spirit of Solitude* (1816) is an introspective poem of 720 lines written in the form of allegory in 1815. An idealistic youth is fascinated by the contemplation of the universe and is deeply impressed by the grandeur and beauty of the external world. While he is aspiring for the eternal, he is joyful and calm, but he begins to wish for intercourse with the living essence of his vision and creates its image in his imagination. In this image are merged all the ideal traits, but in reality nothing answers to the imagined image. Disillusioned, the hero goes prematurely to his death. In the poem, Shelley tried to show that the chief defect of the dreamy youth was his not knowing life and his detachment from the society. However, the poet still placed the hero above those who lived vain, self-loving lives and were satisfied with their own miserable existence.

The Revolt of Islam (1818) is an epic political poem and a symbolic parable on liberation and revolutionary idealism following the disillusionment of the French Revolution. The poem is transposed to an Oriental setting and composed in Spenserian stanza (too ornate for effective narrative), forming twelve cantos. It was originally published under the title *Laon and Cythna; or, The Revolution of the Golden City: A Vision of the Nineteenth Century* in 1817. It tells of the insurrection of the people of Islam. The revolt is organized by a brother and a sister, Laon and Cythna. In spite that they experience temporary success, the tyrants recover power and Islam is subject to plague and famine. Brother and sister are burnt at the stake. Shelley pointed out at the close the "transient nature of error" and "the eternity of genius and virtue." In the poem Shelley called on the people to carry on their struggle for liberty, but he did not realize the importance and the necessity of armed struggle for a better society. Heroic struggle for the liberation of mankind and union with a sister-comrade are inseparable elements of Shelley's ideal, and the love between Laon and Cythna was but the symbol of their common devotion to a lofty cause. Besides the theme of revolution, the poem shows Shelley's attitude towards the position of woman in society. Cythna the woman warrior seeks the intellectual liberation of her sex.

Adonaïs: *An Elegy on the Death of John Keats, Author of Endymion, Hyperion, etc.* (1821), also spelled *Adonaies*, is written for John Keats and widely regarded as one of Shelley's best and most well-known works. The poem, consisting of 495 lines in 55 Spenserian stanzas, was composed in the spring of 1821 immediately after April 11, when Shelley heard of Keats' death seven weeks earlier. It is a pastoral elegy in the English tradition of John Milton's *Lycidas*. Shelley had studied and translated classical elegies. The title of the poem is likely a merging of the Greek "Adonis," the god of fertility, and the Hebrew "Adonai" (meaning "Lord"). Most critics suggest that Shelley used Virgil's tenth Eclogue as a model. Keats is lamented under the name of Adonaïs, together with other poets who had died young, such as Chatterton, Sidney and Lucan (39 AD – 65 AD). His deathbed is attended by various figures, both allegorical and contemporary, including Byron. Shelley, the atheist, accepted the physical facts of death, but insisted on some form of Neo-platonic resurrection in the eternal Beauty of the universe. The style is deliberately grand and marmoreal and lacks intimacy. Yet Shelley strongly identified himself with Keats' suffering.

The Cenci (1819, 1821) is a verse tragedy in five acts. The melodramatic plot is taken from the true story of Beatrice Cenci, who was tried and executed for the murder of her father Count Francesco Cenci in Rome in 1599. Shelley was attracted by the themes of incest and atheism in the original story and well expressed his views on freedom in his poetic drama. The father is the head of one of the oldest, noblest and richest families and a family tyrant and an immoral person. Wicked and debauching, he even shows his hatred against his children and entertains incestuous passion for his daughter Beatrice. His crimes become unbearable to the entire family and Beatrice plots with her brother Bernado and her stepmother Lucretia for the murder of the despot. They hire two killers to commit the murder, but the plot arouses suspicion and all the family members are arrested and tried. Although Beatrice courageously endures the tortures, she eventually admits the crime and is convicted and sentenced to death.

The play was not considered performable in its day due to its themes of incest and parricide, and was not performed in public in England until 1922 when it was staged in London. In 1886 the Shelley Society sponsored a private production at the Grand Theatre before the audience that included Oscar Wilde, Robert Browning and George Bernard Shaw. Though there has been much debate over its stageability, the play has been produced in many countries including France, Germany, Italy, Russia, Czechoslovakia and the United States. It was included in the Harvard Classics as one of the most important and representative works of the western canon.

Prometheus Unbound (1820), Shelley's masterpiece, is a lyrical drama in four acts. The story was taken from Greek mythology. The theme of this poetical drama is borrowed from the play *Prometheus Bound* by the Greek tragedian Aeschylus (c. 525/524 BC – c. 456/455 BC). But the two plays are quite different in ending. Aeschylus made Prometheus finally reconcile with Zeus, but, in order to express his faith in the ultimate victory of the people, Shelley made Prometheus the representative of mankind, who has four noble qualities, man's shaping intellect, his heroic endurance, his defiance against tyranny and his love for mankind. There is no reconciliation between Prometheus and Jupiter (Zeus) in Shelley's play. Though chained to the rock, Prometheus has "great allies" in the world. Mother Earth supports him by giving him strength to endure all sufferings and sending the spirits of heroes and martyrs to cheer him. Lovely shapes of Faith and Hope hover around him. His bride Asia, the spirit of love and goodness, awaits him in the distance. With a firm confidence in the final triumph of his just cause, Prometheus is perfectly calm in his sufferings. He knows the reign of Jupiter, the symbol of reaction, is but a passing period in the life of the universe, so to the last he refuses to yield to the tyrants in Heaven. Finally Jupiter is overthrown by Demogorgon, the symbol of change and revolution, and driven into the eternal abyss. Prometheus is set free by Hercules, the most valiant hero in Greek mythology. As Prometheus throws off his fetters, the whole world joins in a chorus to celebrate his liberation. The figure of Prometheus has been symbolic of those noble-hearted revolutionaries, who devote themselves to the just cause of the people and suffer great pains at the hands of tyrants. Prometheus' triumph symbolizes the victory of mankind over tyranny and oppression.

Thematically, Shelley's version is different from Aeschylus', due to the contrary ending: Prometheus is set free, and the vision of a better world for man concludes the play. Whereas confrontation and hate dominate the emotions of the two sides in the classic work, the note of love is heard almost from the outset in Shelley's drama, which throws the notion of universal love in relief, and proffers it as the cure for the ills of human life. The suffering Prometheus withdraws even his curse upon Jupiter because the Titan has learned positively from his ordeal and wishes no pain to any living being including Jupiter. This represents the poet's response to the troubled life of his time. The drama is a good exposition of Shelley's philosophy.

Technically, Shelley's play is a closet drama, which is designed for reading instead of performance; yet it is filled with suspense, mystery and other dramatic effects that make it, in theory, performable. Meanwhile, *Prometheus Unbound* is remarkable for the sheer force of its vital, fresh and varied lyric energy. Here Shelley revealed his lyric genius by the amazing variety of lyric forms he employed in the work. Not only did he create and perfect his own lyric patterns, he also successfully adapted other forms like the Pindaric ode, the Spenserian stanza, and the couplets, to serve his own lyrical outburst. Some critics even claim that, had Shelley not written anything else, his lyric passages alone here would have earned him a distinct place as one of the greatest English poets.

Shelley's short poems on nature and love form an important part of his literary output. To him nature exists as an unseen life of the universe and his love for nature is almost boundless. Shelley's love is not limited to mankind, but extended to every living creature. Flowers, trees, the sea, mountains and clouds are not only personified but also inspired or spiritualized. He held passionate communion with the universe. "Ode to the West Wind," "To a Skylark" (1820) and "The Cloud" (1820) are among his best short lyrics on nature. His love lyrics, which are also beautifully written, include such well-known poems as "Love's Philosophy" (1820) and "One Word Is Too Often Profound."

"Ode to the West Wind" (1820), written in iambic pentameter, is made up of five stanzas, each taking the form of a sonnet, which consists of four tercet sub-stanzas and one couplet sub-stanza, with the rhyme scheme aba bcb cdc ded ee. The sub-stanzas, along with the run-on lines, suit well the depiction of the unruly wind and the onrush of emotion. The emotional turmoil, long pent-up in the bottom of the poet, bursts out with its utmost force. It is reinforced with the use of appropriate imagery and impeccable rhyme and rhythm, though colored at times with a sentimentality that may detract a little (but never much) from the power of the eruption. Shelley's minute observations of wind, water, wood, cloud and sky combine imagery which is simultaneously scientific, mythical and even biblical. The total effect is one of transcendent hope and energy, achieved through suffering and despair.

The poem can be divided in two parts, with the first three stanzas as one and the last two as the other. The first part presents the qualities of the west wind by describing its effects upon the earth, the air and the ocean. The second part expresses the poet's emotional response to and request for the west wind, by speaking directly to the wind and asking for its power. The poem ends up with an optimistic note of confidence and hope. It is an absolute must on the reading list of Shelley's readers. With the noted ending line (i. e., "If Winter comes, can Spring be far behind?"), it is usually read as the author's signature poem. A passionate invocation to the spirit of the west wind, the ode is Shelley's representative work both in theme and form, forcefully prophetic in its fighting spirit and singular in its lyrical beauty. According to Shelley's own accounts, it was his emotional response to a strong hailstorm, in which the poet happened to be swallowed one autumn evening in 1819 on the Arno near Florence. He saw, in the storm of the natural world, an apt metaphor for the storm of revolution in the human world. The poet had been feeling depressed at the triumph of the reactionary Holy Alliance over Napoleon and the French Revolution and was emphatic in his forecast that the storm of revolution would make a powerful comeback yet.

The first stanza describes the power of the west wind and its double role as destroyer (ll. 2 – 5) and preserver (ll. 6 – 12). Line 14 sums up the wind's two basic characteristics, which also constitute the thematic focus of the poem. The second stanza focuses on the adumbration of the wind's power driving clouds before it and bringing storms with it (ll. 15 – 23) with lightning, rain, fire and hail (ll. 23 – 28); it also describes its destructive aspect of "closing night" enveloping all under its dome of a vast tomb (ll. 24 – 25). The third stanza talks about the wind's impact upon the sea, specifically, its impact on the calm of the Mediterranean (ll. 29 – 36) and on the turbulence of the Atlantic (ll. 36 – 42). The Mediterranean sleeps in serenity in summer but is waken up by the wind to see the quivering of the shadows of ancient palaces and towers (ll. 29 – 35) and the Atlantic cleaving asunder into gigantic chasms (ll. 35 – 38). Even the vegetation at the bottom of the sea "grow[s] gray with fear,/tremble[s] and despoil[s] themselves" (ll. 41 – 42). The fourth stanza expresses the poet's emotional response to the west wind. The poet said to the wind (ll. 43 – 47) that he wished to be spirited away like the leaves, to dance like the clouds, to breathe like the waves, and enjoy a share of the wind's strength like the storm though with a lesser degree of freedom of movement. The poet took a nostalgic backward glance at his free, uncontrollable boyhood when he could fly like the wind and even outstrip it in speed (ll. 47 – 51), and wished for the wind to lift him up like a leaf or wave or a cloud (l. 53). But it is only a figment of his imagination, and he had to face "the thorns of life" that he had fallen upon, chained and weighed down, and no longer "tameless, swift, and proud" like the wind (ll. 54 – 56). The last stanza expresses both the poet's request for the wind to help spread the words of his poem "among mankind" and wake it up from its deep stupor (ll. 66 – 69) and his prophecy that spring will come in the wake of winter (l. 70).

"**Ozymandias**" (1818) is a sonnet regarded as one of Shelley's most famous works and is frequently anthologized. Ozymandias was a Greek name for the Egyptian pharaoh Ramesses II (c. 1303 – 1213 BC, pharaoh 1279 – 1213 BC). Shelley began writing his poem in 1817, soon after the announcement of the British Museum's acquisition of a large fragment of a statue of Ramesses II from the 13th century BC, leading some scholars to believe that he was inspired by this. Shelley wrote the poem in friendly competition with his friend and fellow poet Horace Smith (1779 – 1849), who also wrote a sonnet on the same topic with the same title. Both poems explore the fate of history and the ravages of time—that all prominent figures and the empires they build are impermanent and their legacies are doomed to decay and oblivion.

Shelley's political lyrics are among the best of their kind in the whole sphere of European Romantic poetry. He was the first poet in Europe who sang for the working class. **"The Masque of Anarchy"** (1819), written after the Peterloo Massacre of 1819, is the best-known one among his political lyrics. Shelley used "Anarchy" to express the essential nature of the so-called "free competition" under capitalism. The word simply means the tyranny of a handful of oppressors and exploiters over the popular masses. The first part of the work describes a procession of horrible, disgusting masks which may be regarded as an allegorical picture of the contemporary rulers of England. In the second part the poet sang the men of England, their strength and future victory. He called upon them to rise against the oppressors and blood-suckers. In its call for freedom, "The Masque of Anarchy" is perhaps the first modern statement of the principle of nonviolent resistance. The poem was not published during Shelley's lifetime and did not appear in print until 1832. Although Shelley had sent the manuscript in 1819 for publication in *The Examiner*, a leading liberal magazine of the day, it was withheld by Leigh Hunt, who believed that the public were not wise enough to do justice to the sincerity and kind-heartedness of the spirit in the poem.

Shelley's legacy in literary theory is his essay, **"A Defence of Poetry,"** which was written in 1821 and first published in 1840 in *Essays, Letters from Abroad, Translations and Fragments* by Edward Moxon (1801 – 1858) in London. The essay was begun as a light-hearted reply to the magazine article "The Four Ages of Poetry" (1820) by his friend Thomas Love Peacock (1785 – 1866), which humorously argued that the best minds of the future must turn to economic and social sciences rather than poetry. In vindicating the role of poetry in a progressive society and defending the whole notion of imaginative literature and thinking (not just "poetry") within an industrial culture, Shelley came to write his own poetic credo with passionate force and conviction. Against a background of Classical and European literature, he discussed in some detail the nature of poetic thought and inspiration, the problems of translation, the value of erotic writing, the connections between poetry and politics, and the essentially moral nature of the imagination. Shelley associated poetry with social freedom and love. He maintained that poetry, so far from being deteriorated and made powerless by the advance of civilization, was actually the indispensable agent of civilization. He claimed that "poets are the unacknowledged legislators of the world," and that poetry could play a very important part in the spiritual life of society.

20.2.3 John Keats (1795 – 1821)

Keats was, along with Byron and Shelley, one of the main figures of the second generation of Romantic poets, and has always been regarded as one of the principle figures in the Romantic Movement. However, Keats' poems were not well received by critics during his lifetime; his reputation grew after his death and by the end of the 19th century he had become one of the most beloved of all English poets. Keats' stature as a poet has grown steadily through all changes of fashion. Alfred, Lord Tennyson considered him the greatest poet of the 19th century, and Matthew Arnold commended his "intellectual and spiritual passion" for beauty; in the 20th century Keats has been discussed and reconsidered by such critics as T. S. Eliot, Lionel Trilling (1905 – 1975) and Christopher Ricks (1933 –).

Keats was at first apprenticed to learn surgery; yet he had a great passion in poetry. His first extant poem,

"An Imitation of Spenser," was produced in 1814 during his medical training. After that, he devoted more and more time to the study of literature, experimenting with verse forms, particularly the sonnet while he continued his work and medical training at Guy's Hospital (now part of King's College London). In May 1816, Leigh Hunt agreed to publish the sonnet "O Solitude" in his magazine *The Examiner*. It was the first appearance in print of Keats' poetry. 1817 witnessed the publication of Keats' first volume verse *Poems*, which included "I stood tiptoe" and "Sleep and Poetry," and the ending of the poet's medical career. Influenced and inspired by Spenser's *Faerie Queene*, Keats gave up his profession as a surgeon and embarked on writing poetry.

Although the book *Poems* was a critical failure, arousing little interest, Leigh Hunt published Keats' sonnet "On First Looking into Chapman's Homer," foreseeing great things to come. Hunt also introduced Keats to many prominent men in his circle, including Charles Lamb, William Hazlitt and Thomas Barnes (1785 – 1841), the editor of *The Times*. This was a decisive turning point for Keats, establishing him in the public eye as a figure in what Hunt termed "a new school of poetry." (qtd. in Motion, 1997: 130) In 1818, Keats' first long poem *Endymion* came out as a book, which also gave rise to critical denunciation. 1819 saw Keats' high production: he not only composed his six great odes, including "Ode on a Grecian Urn," "Ode on Indolence," "Ode on Melancholy," "Ode to a Nightingale," "Ode to Psyche" and "To Autumn," but also wrote his main poems like "The Eve of St. Agnes," "La Belle Dame sans Merci," "Hyperion," "Lamia" and *Otho the Great*, a play which was critically damned and not performed until 1950. The odes are among Keats' most famous and well-regarded poems. They were written in quick succession during the spring of 1819, except "To Autumn" which was composed in September. Although it is debated in which order they were written, "Ode to Psyche" opened the published series. *Lamia, Isabella, The Eve of St. Agnes, and Other Poems*, the third and final volume Keats lived to see, came out in July 1820, received greater acclaim than *Endymion* or *Poems*, finding favorable notices in both *The Examiner* and *Edinburgh Review*, and would come to be recognized as one of the most important poetic works ever published. In this volume Keats collected both his main poems like "Isabella," "Lamia" and "The Eve of St. Agnes" and all his great odes but "Ode on Indolence."

Keats was prolific during his short career. But his reputation rests on a small body of work, centred on the Odes, and only in the creative outpouring of the last years of his short life was he able to express the inner intensity for which he has been lauded since his death. Keats' ability and talent was acknowledged by several influential contemporary allies such as Shelley and Hunt. His admirers praised him for having developed a style which was more heavily loaded with sensualities, more gorgeous in its effects, more voluptuously alive than any poet who had come before him. Shelley often corresponded with Keats in Rome and loudly declared that Keats' death had been brought on by bad reviews in the *Quarterly Review*. He wrote the despairing elegy *Adonaïs* seven weeks after the funeral and stated that Keats' early death was a personal and public tragedy.

Keats learned the art of poetry mainly from such poets as Spenser, Shakespeare, Milton and the Italian Dante. His poems revealed mastery of form and depth of feeling. The artistic aim in Keats' poetry is always to create a beautiful world of imagination as opposed to the sordid reality of his day. He sought to express beauty in all of his poems. His leading principle is: "Beauty is truth, truth beauty." He expressed the delight which came not only through the eye and the ear but through the senses of touch, taste and smell. His poetry is distinguished by sensuousness and the perfection of form.

Some of Keats' poems touch upon the burning political problems of his day. He showed his dissatisfaction with the society and described the sufferings of the poor people. The democratic views in his poetry offended the aristocratic-bourgeois literary circles. However, Keats voiced his resentment against the rule of the aristocracy and bourgeoisie in a manner different from Byron and Shelley, though he shared a close sympathy with the two in political sentiment. Unlike Byron and Shelley who attempted to remould the contemporary society with both poetry and political action, Keats restricted his application of the principle of liberty to the sphere of art. His pursuit of Beauty in all things bespoke an aspiration for a better life.

Keats' ideas on poetry mainly include his notions of "negative capability," poetic identity, and emphases on the oneness of truth and beauty. To Keats, the "negative capability" is the major quality of a man of achievement: "that is when man is capable of being in uncertainties, mysteries, doubts, without any irritable reaching after fact and reason," as he wrote in a letter to his brothers. In other words, it is the ability to be content with "half knowledge" or ambiguity or refusal to impose one's judgment in the representation of varied human experience. So it leads to the annulment of the self and one's imperfect interpretation. And to annul self requires that one has to have a firm sense of self or identity. Keats saw the achievement of identity as the highest goal of human development. His idea on identity, or "identical soul," places stress on the importance of the world of pains and troubles in the process of schooling one's intelligence so as to make it a soul. Intelligence has to feel and suffer in many different ways and learn to accept one's identity as essential to one's being. This is what he called "spirit-creation" or "soul-making." Keats went through frustrations, failure and misunderstanding in his own life, but he emerged with a firm sense of self. Although he wavered at different moments of his life, he had faith in himself leaving some immortal work behind and winning fame. Of the things that mattered most to him, "Verse, Fame, and Beauty," the first he wrote a good deal of, the second he won, and the third he found in his intense experience with art and life. This leads to his concept of "Truth is beauty, beauty truth" as he expressed it compactly in his "Ode on a Grecian Urn," a hard-won belief that real life is as beautiful and necessary as the eternal beauty in art.

Endymion is a poem of 4,000 lines in four books, written in 1817 and published in 1818. Keats dedicated this poem to Thomas Chatterton. The poem was written in heroic couplets. The story is taken from Greek mythology. The poem starts by painting a rustic scene of trees, rivers, shepherds and sheep. The shepherds gather around an altar and pray to the god of shepherds and flocks. As the youths sing and dance, the elder men sit and talk about what afterlife would be like. However, Endymion, "the brain-sick shepherd-prince" of Mount Latmos, is in a trancelike state, and not participating in their discourse. His sister Peona takes him away and brings him to her resting place where he sleeps. After he wakes, he tells Peona of his encounter with the moon Goddess Cynthia, and how much he loves her. Then Endymion descends to the depths of the earth to find Cynthia. There he encounters a real woman Phoebe and, giving up his pursuit of the ideal, falls in love with her. She, however, turns out to be none other than Cynthia, who, after luring him, weary and perplexed, through "cloudy phantasms," bears him away to eternal life. The poem is a work, rich in luxuriant imagery, of an immature genius, the product of sensation rather than thought. The allegory, which is sometimes obscure, appears to represent the poet pursuing ideal perfection and distracted from his quest by human beauty. The main idea is thus the quest for ideal beauty and perfection.

"Isabella, or The Pot of Basil" is a narrative poem written in 1818 and published in 1820. The story is based on Boccaccio's *Decameron*. Isabella, a young girl of a rich family is in love with a poor servant called Lorenzo. But her worldly, ambitious brothers intend that she shall marry a nobleman. Therefore when they discover her love for Lorenzo they lure him away, murder him and bury his body in a forest. Lorenzo's ghost then appears to Isabella and tells her where he is buried. With the help of her old nurse, she finds his body, severs the head and places it in a pot with a plant of basil over it. Observing how she cherishes the plant, her brothers steal the pot, discover the mouldering head and fly, conscience-stricken, into banishment. Pathetically Isabella mourns her loss, pines away and dies. The basic idea here is sympathy for the oppressed and indignation at the cruelty of the rich. The poet pointed out that the root of the evil lay in the system of exploitation.

"The Eve of St. Agnes," written in 1819 and published in 1820, is a narrative poem consisting of 42 Spenserian stanzas. It was influential in the 19th-century literature. The title comes from the day (or evening) before the feast of Saint Agnes (or St. Agnes' Eve). St. Agnes, the patron saint of virgins, died a martyr in the 4th-century Rome. The eve falls on January 20; the feast day on the 21st. The poem tells a story about a young maiden Madeline. The story is set in a remote period of time, in the depths of winter. Madeline has been told the legend that, on St. Agnes' Eve, maidens may have visions of their lovers. Madeline's lover is Porphyto, who comes from a family hostile to her own. On the Eve of St. Agnes' Day she dreams of him. When she wakes, she finds her lover sitting by her bedside. Then they flee together from the castle.

"The Eve of St. Agnes" paints an idealized picture of the perfect world for human beings. It praises the happy and free love of the young people. With its heightened atmosphere of excitement and passion, the poem is generally regarded as one of Keats' most successful works. Spontaneity of feeling is what the poet tried to capture. The poem reflects the whole spectrum of human emotions from joy to grief and all the shades of color in between. As it is set in medieval times, the poem sounds quaint, new, and full of wonder. Whereas the work is entitled for a virgin martyr, the lovers in the story abandon tradition and elope. The contrast reveals the juxtaposition of the two complementary human traits: reason and passion. The two are mutually dependent, and between them they make life real and viable. The ideal world is one, as the poem illustrates, in which such human feelings enjoy full license. It is in this world, a sanctuary, that the lovers run to live ever happily after, but the misery that the rest of the household suffers testifies that life is not all rosy and that probably the poet is thinking of his own forthcoming tragic end.

It is by his shorter poems that Keats is known to the majority of today's readers. Of his numerous shorter poems, the most important are his sonnets and odes, which show the poet's love for beauty, rich imagination and excellent poetic talent. "Bright Star" and "When I Have Fears," along with "On the Grasshopper and Cricket," are acknowledged as his best sonnets. Keats' odes, as a whole, represent his attempt to create a new type of short lyrical poem, which influenced later generations.

"Ode to a Nightingale," published in 1820, is the best one among his odes and a meditation on the immortal beauty of the nightingale's song and the sadness of the observer, who must in the end accept sorrow and mortality. It consists of eight stanzas of ten lines each. The first stanza expresses the poet's mixed feelings of weal and woe on hearing the nightingale. His heart was aching, and a drowsy numbness was paining his senses, but the bird's song and its happy lot brought joy to the sad poet and enabled him to forget his troubles. The second stanza expresses the poet's desire to lose himself in his cups and escape into "the forest dim" (l. 20) with the bird. The idea to escape is continued into the third stanza, in which the poet felt infinite sorrow at a world "Where youth grows pale, and specter-thin, and dies" (l. 26). It is an obvious reference to his brother's death, his own imminent demise and, by extension, that of all youth in similar circumstances. But as wine was inadequate to sustain the escape, the poet resorted to poetry and hoped to get lost in the vision that poetry inspired. Line 35 contains the famous "tender is the night" which was to become the title of a famous American novel by Scott Fitzgerald (1896 – 1940) in the 20th century. In the fifth stanza the poet visualized himself enjoying the music of the nightingale and the fragrance, "the soft incense" (l. 42), of the vegetation in the bewitching night-enveloped forest. In the sixth stanza, his mirth reached a point where he thought of "easeful death" (l. 52) as an avenue to avoid the harassing human misery, and envisioned the sod that would bury him so that he would become deaf to the everlasting song of the nightingale. The seventh stanza places the pain of life in contrast to the eternal joyful music of the nightingale. The last stanza depicts the fading of the bird-song and the coming back of the poet to face reality, and his feeling of loss and frustration that imagination can offer reprieve for a moment but not for good.

It is said that a nightingale had built its nest near poet's home in the spring of 1819. Inspired by the bird's song, Keats composed "Ode to a Nightingale," which is a personal poem that describes the poet's journey into the state of negative capability. The tone of the poem rejects the optimistic pursuit of pleasure found within Keats' earlier poems and explores the themes of nature, transience and mortality. The nightingale described within the poem experiences a type of death but does not actually die: it is capable of living through its song, which is a fate that humans cannot expect. The poem ends with an acceptance that pleasure cannot last and that death is an inevitable part of life. In the poem, Keats imagined the loss of the physical world and saw himself dead. The contrast between the immortal nightingale and the mortal man, sitting in his garden, is made all the more acute by an effort of the imagination. Many critics favor "Ode to a Nightingale" for its themes but some believe that it is structurally flawed because the poem sometimes strays from its main idea.

"Ode on a Grecian Urn," not well received by Keats' contemporaries, is now considered to be one of the greatest odes in the English language. It also expresses the poet's desire for escape and transcendences. Along with the other odes composed in the spring, the ode indicates that the poet achieved maturity and self-confidence, and was ready to speak with a voice for all humanity as well as himself. It has always been one of Keats' most popular odes as its suggestive profundity appeals for ever to the imagination of the sensitive minds of all generations. The ode suggests that the poet's imagination took wild flights when looking at a Grecian urn. He thought of the urn as a symbol for the joy of eternal life and for the immortalizing power of art and imagination and their useful function, but he also realized that the carved beauty of the urn came to life only with the help of the imagination and that real life was beautiful, too.

Divided into five stanzas of ten lines each, the ode contains the poet's discourse on a series of designs on a Grecian urn. He focused on two scenes—a lover eternally pursuing a beloved without fulfilment, and the villagers about to perform a sacrifice. While the second and third stanzas are about the first scene, the fourth stanza is about the second. The work begins with the poet's speculation over an urn with a legend and figures painted on it and goes on in the following stanza to express his ecstasy on hearing the "unheard melodies" and his joy at the fact that the trees under which the youth stands are forever covered with luxuriant foliage and that, although the young man can never catch up with his "goal" and kiss her, the girl is for ever in sight and the pair is for ever in love. The evergreen branches, the ever new song of the unwearied melodist, the ever panting and ever young lovers, and the eternal human passion—all these in the third stnza leave the poet with a sense of frustration (ll. 4, 11 – 27) and sorrow in comparison (ll. 29 – 30). The first three stanzas thus reveal the power of art immortalizing life and joy. The fourth stanza seems to introduce a different vein of thought on art. Here is on the urn a religious procession, with the priest and the sacrificial heifer, all heading to a green altar of sacrifices. The mind's eye of the poet also saw a little town or a mountain citadel that the crowd left behind, for ever deserted in silence and emptiness. The poet seemed to be musing over the idea that art also immortalizes desolation and prevents fulfillment: there is never consummation of the love between the youth and the girl, the altar can never be reached, the sacrificial ceremony can never be held, and the town or citadel will never be full of people again. Thus the poet saw the limitations and mystery of art. The last stanza records the poet's epiphany, his sudden awareness of art in relation to life, that artistic beauty is a picture of "cold pastoral"; it is always beautiful but lifeless, which can be complemented by real yet transient life; and so "Truth," or real life, is every bit as beautiful as is "Beauty," or art (the urn). Thus the two worlds of art and life are shown to be mutually dependent to reveal their value. The permanence of the world of art is reconciled with the ephemerality of the contingent world of fulfilled life. We will need nothing else to feel happy on earth if we can comprehend this nature of things with the help of such art works as the urn. Hence art as "a friend to man" (l. 48). While he described the various pastoral scenes of love, beauty and joy illustrated on the urn, the poet reflected on the eternal quality of art and the fleeting nature of human love and happiness. The last two lines are particularly well known and their meaning much debated:

"Beauty is truth, truth beauty,"—that is all

Ye know on earth, and all ye need to know.

"Ode on Indolence" describes the state of indolence/laziness and was written during a time when Keats felt that he should devote his efforts to earning an income instead of composing poetry. After finishing the spring odes, Keats wrote in June 1819 that the composition of this poem brought him more pleasure than anything else he had written that year. Unlike the other odes, "Ode on Indolence" was not published until 1848, 27 years after his death.

The poem is an example of Keats' break from the structure of the Classical form. It follows the poet's contemplation of a morning spent in idleness. Three figures—Ambition, Love and Poesy—are presented, all dressed in "placid sandals" and "white robes." The narrator examines each using a series of questions and statements on life and art. The poem concludes with the narrator giving up on having all three of the figures as part of his life. Some critics regard "Ode on Indolence" as inferior to the other five 1819 odes. Others suggest that the poem exemplifies a continuity of themes and imagery characteristic of Keats' more widely-read works, and provides valuable biographical insight into his poetic career.

"Ode on Melancholy" describes the poet's perception of melancholy through a lyric discourse between the poet and the reader, along with the introduction to Ancient Grecian characters and ideals. It consists of three stanzas of ten lines each. Because the poem has fewer stanzas than either "Ode on Indolence" or "Ode on a Grecian Urn," its rhyme scheme appears less elaborate, with the first and second stanzas sharing a rhyme scheme of ababcdecde, while the third takes on one of its own: ababcdedce. As with "Ode on a Grecian Urn," "Ode on Indolence" and "To Autumn," each stanza begins with an abab rhyme scheme and finishes with a Miltonic sestet. The general meter of the poem is iambic pentameter.

"**Ode to Psyche**" is an experiment in the ode genre, and Keats' attempt at an expanded version of the sonnet format describing a dramatic scene. It serves as an important departure from the poet's early poems, which frequently describe an escape into the pleasant realms of imagination. Keats used the imagination to show the narrator's intent to resurrect Psyche and reincarnate himself into Eros (love), which he attempted by dedicating an "untrodden region" of his mind to the worship of the neglected goddess.

"**To Autumn**," the final work of Keats' "1819 odes," marked the end of Keats' poetic career. It is one of the most anthologized English lyric poems and has been regarded as one of the most perfect short poems in the English language. The poem has three eleven-line stanzas which describe a progression through the season, from the late maturation of the crops to the harvest and to the last days of autumn when winter is nearing. The imagery is richly achieved through the personification of Autumn, and the description of its bounty, its sights and sounds. The work has been interpreted as a meditation on death, as an allegory of artistic creation, as the poet's response to the Peterloo Massacre (1819) and as an expression of nationalist sentiment.

Chapter 21 Fiction in the Romantic Age

Together with Wordsworth, Coleridge and Southey, there lived Walter Scott and Jane Austen, who represented the summit of novel-writing in the Romantic age. It is good to note that Scott and Austen differ vastly in their modes of representation. The former's imagination is essentially romantic whereas the latter's is realistic. In fact it was the latter who reasserted the tradition of realism.

21.1 Sir Walter Scott (1771 – 1832)

Walter Scott was a Scottish historical novelist and poet who achieved great success in both poetry and novel and had many contemporary readers in Europe, Australia and North America. In the early phase of his literary career, he wrote poetry and became the most widely-read poet of his day. Then in the last two decades he turned to novel writing and has been universally accepted as the creator and great master of the historical novel not simply in England but in Europe as well. Scott's novels and poetry are still read, and many of his works remain classics of both English-language literature and Scottish literature. These works include the novels like *Ivanhoe*, *Rob Roy*, *Old Mortality*, *Waverley*, *The Heart of Midlothian* and *The Bride of Lammermoor*, and the poem *The Lady of the Lake*.

Scott's literary career began with translating the works by such German dramatists and poets as Goethe and Burger (1747 – 1794). In 1802 – 1803 Scott published his three volumes of *Minstrelsy of the Scottish Ballads*, which he had been collecting among the Scottish people for many years. His first original poem *The Lay of the Last Minstrel* came out in 1805, which was followed by his greatest poem *Marmion* in 1808. Another long poem *The La-*

dy of the Lake appeared in 1810. The two poems aroused Scotland and England to intense enthusiasm and brought unexpected fame to the author. His first novel *Waverley* came out in 1814 and proved a great success. During the following 17 years, Scott wrote on an average nearly two novels per year. His themes are historical. They deal with European history, especially Scottish history and English history.

Marmion: *A Tale of Flodden Field* is an epic poem in six cantos. Marmion is a fictitious character of mixed qualities, a favorite of Henry VIII, proud, ambitious and treacherous, who has tired of one love—a dishonest nun Constance De Beverley—and is in pursuit of the wealthy Lady Clara, who is herself in love with Sir Ralph De Wilton. After much intrige and disguise, during which Clara herslef takes to the convent for a while in refuge from Marmion, and Wilton passes for a parlmer, the action moves to Flodden, with stirring descriptions of the encamped armies, and then of the battle. Marmion is mortally wounded and dies on the battlefield, while De Wilton displays heroism, regains his honor, retrieves his lands, and marries Clara.

The book was a huge and lasting commercial success in both Britain and the United States; yet it did not find favor with the contemporary critics. The introductory letters to Scott's friends, which open each canto, were dismissed as unwarranted intrusions. A hero as flawed as Marmion was also unwelcome at this time and the story was criticized for its obscurity. However, the public enthusiasm for Scott's work was ultimately undimmed and the poem remained popular for over a century.

The Lady of the Lake is a narrative poem set in Scotland. It is composed of six cantos, each of which concerns the action of a single day. The poem has three main plots: the contest among three men—Roderick Dhu, James Fitz-James and Malcolm Graeme—to win the love of Ellen Douglas (the lady of the title and daughter of the outlawed Lord James of Douglas), the feud and reconciliation of King James V of Scotland and James Douglas, and a war between the lowland Scots led by James V and the highland clans led by Roderick Dhu of Clan Alpine. The lively narrative evokes highland scenery and manners, and contains various poetic interludes. The poem was tremendously influential in the 19th century, and inspired several composers, including the Austrian Schubert (1797 – 1828) and the Italian Rossini (1792 – 1868). By the 19th century, it was much less popular. However, it continued to be a standard reading in elementary schools until the early 20th century.

Scott is remembered chiefly for historical novels. His novels cover a long period of time, ranging from the Middle Ages up to the 18th century. They may be divided into three groups according to their subject matter—the group on the history of Scotland, the group on English history and the group on the history of the other European countries.

The first group is the earliest and largest group of Scott's historical novels. The well-known in this group are the "Waverley" novels like *Old Motality*, *Rob Roy*, *The Heart of Midlothian* and *The Bride of Lammermoor*. Among them *Rob Roy* is the best one. The central idea of these novels is how the Scottish people fight against the English government. Walter Scott praised the Scottish people's love for liberty and independence. *Old Mortality* (1816), with "The Tale of Old Mortality" as its original title, is set in the period 1679 – 39 in southwest Scotland, and forms, along with *The Black Dwarf*, the first series of Scott's *Tales of My Landlord*. *The Heart of Midlothian* (1818) was originally published in four volumes as the second series of *Tales of My Landlord*. The title of the book refers to the Old Tolbooth prison, which is located at the time in the heart of the Scottish county of Midlothian. The background event is the Porteous Riots in 1736. The novel is chiefly a record of the gruesome details of the killing of the Captain of the City Guards, Captain John Porteous, who had ordered the soldiers to fire into the crowd. *The Bride of Lammermoor* (1819) is set in the Lammermuir Hills of southeast Scotland and, together with *A Legend of Montrose*, was published as the third series of *Tales of My Landlord*. Scott indicated that *The Bride of Lammermoor* was based on an actual incident. It tells of a tragic love affair between young Lucy Ashton and her family's enemy Edgar Ravenswood. As with all the Waverley Novels, the novel was published anonymously.

Tales of My Landlord is a series of novels written by the historical novelist that form a subset of the so-called Waverley Novels. There are four series: the first three series came out in 1816, 1818 and 1819 respectively as mentioned above; the fourth and last series was published in 1832 and contains such novels as *Count Robert of Paris* and *Castle Dangerous*. So *Tales of My Landlord* actually refers to seven novels, each series composed of two novels, or just one in the case of the second. Of all the seven novels, *The Heart of Midlothian* and *The Bride of Lammermoor* have been the most successful, while *Old Mortality* is considered by modern critics to be among the author's best works. The fourth series was the least successful.

The tales were supposed to be collected from the fictional landlord of the Wallace Inn at Gandercleugh, compiled by Peter Pattieson, the assistant of Jedediah Cleishbotham, and edited and sent to the publisher by Cleishbotham, a schoolmaster and parish clerk of Gandercleugh. Hence the title of the series—"Tales of My Landlord," which is simply a misnomer as the author himself admitted, for the tales were not told by the landlord; nor did the landlord have any hand in them at all.

The Waverly Novels refer to the long series of Scott's novels released from 1814 to 1832, which describe the vicissitudes of the upper classes, the uprisings of the suffering people, the ceaseless border wars, and the life of the Puritan period. Chronologically, they are *Waverley* (1814), *Guy Mannering* (1815), *The Antiquary* (1816), *The Black Dwarf*, *Old Mortality*, *Rob Roy* (1817), *The Heart of Midlothian*, *The Bride of Lammermoor*, *A Legend of Montrose*, *Ivanhoe* (1820), *The Monastery* (1820), *The Abbot* (1820), *Kenilworth* (1821), *The Pirate* (1822), *The Fortunes of Nigel* (1822), *Peveril of the Peak* (1822), *Quentin Durward* (1823), *St. Ronan's Well* (1824), *Redgauntlet* (1824), *The Betrothed* (1825), *The Talisman* (1825), *Woodstock* (1826), *The Fair Maid of Perth* (1828), *Anne of Geierstein* (1829), *Count Robert of Paris* (1832) and *Castle Dangerous* (1832). These novels influenced such famous world authors as Victor Hugo (1802-1885), George Eliot, Tolstoy and James Fenimore Cooper (1789-1851). And American literature would have looked totally different if Scott had not played his part in its creative endeavors. The title "Waverly" came from Scott's first novel, the three-volume *Waverly*, which remained on the best-seller list for over a decade and has become the best known of his works as it lends its title to a series of later novels.

Waverley tells a romantic story set sixty years back from the author's day, during Pretender Prince Charlie's rebellion of 1745, a time of change. The Stuarts are challenging the reigning Hanoverians. Edward Waverley, a romantic young man, has been brought up partly by his Hanoverian father, partly by his uncle, a rich landlord of Jacobite leanings. He is therefore ambivalent in politics and wavers between the reigning King George and the ambitious Prince Charles Edward of the Stuarts. Waverley is commissioned in the army in 1745 and gets a job in George II's dragoons stationed in Scotland, as his father serves in a ministry. He visits his uncle's friend the Baron Bradwardine, a kind-hearted but pedantic old Jacobite, and attracts the interest of his daughter Rose. Impelled by curiosity, he visits Donald Bean Lean, a highland freebooter, and Fergus MacIvor, a local clan chieftain loyal to the cause of the Stuarts. Waverley falls in love with the latter's sister, Flora MacIvor, whose beauty and ardent loyalty to the the Stuarts appeal to his romantic diposition. These visits, unwise in a British officer at a time of acute political tension, compromise Waverley with his colonel. Through the intrigues of Donald Bean Lean, he is accused of fomenting mutiny in his regiment and is cashiered and arrested. Waverley is rescued by the action of Rose Bradwardine and, inflenced by a sense of unjust treatment, by Flora's enthusiasm, and by a kind reception by the Prince, he joins the Jacobite forces and swears allegiance to the Stuarts. The Prince's bid for the throne fails at the battle of Culloden. Whereas Fergus, convicted of treason, is captured and meets his end bravely, Waverley is pardoned with the help of an English Colonel saved by him in a battle before. He eventually regains the favor of the king, inherits his father's family wealth, and marries Rose Bradwardine.

Waverley is one of the best plotted of Scott's novels, every strand well knitted into the story, and the pace graduated carefully from the slow beginning to the tumultuous end. Equally skilful is the progress of Waverley from his woolly-minded ignorance at the opening to the knowledge of the world he acquires from experience. In this first novel, Scott sounded the theme of the oppositon of romance and realism which was to reappear in many of his later works, though the irony with which romantic pretensions are undercut is rarely better deployed.

Rob Roy is set against the backdrop of the Jacobite Rebellion of 1745, which aimed to restore the Stuart monarchy in the person of James Edward, the "Old Pretender," son of the deposed James II. The tale is told in the first person by a young Englishman, Francis (Frank) Osbaldistone. A would-be poet, Frank falls out with his father William due to his reluctance to enter the family business. Frank is sent north to Northumbria to stay with his Jacobite uncle, Sir Hildebrand Osbaldistone, and his place in William's counting house goes to Sir Hildebrand's scheming son Rashleigh. Frank falls in love with Sir Hildebrand's niece Diana Vernon, who lives in Osbaldistone Hall. Her father Sir Frederick, a proscribed Jacobite, lives there too in the guise of a monk Father Vaughan. Sir Frederick has destined Diana for a convent unless she marries one of Sir Hildebrand's six sons. Diana, then, cannot listen to Frank's suit but, when Rashleigh flees to Scotland with vital financial documents vital to the honor and economic solvency of Frank's father William, she assists Frank in his attempts to restore his father's honor and credit. Frank enlists the help of Bailie Nicol Jarvie, a Glasgow business correspondent of his father, and both proceed to the Highlands to bid Rob Roy, a political dependent of the Vernons, to intervene. Rashleigh is compelled to restore the company assets, and Frank returns to England where he is reconciled with his father. There is much confusion as the action shifts to the beautiful mountains and valleys around Loch Lomond. Meanwhile, the Jacobite rebellion breaks out. Sir Hildebrand's other five sons are all killed in the fighting, and he himself dies of grief shortly afterwards. Rashleigh, who has become an informer, is killed by Rob Roy during an attempt on Frank's life. Sir Frederick escapes to France, leaving Diana free to decide her future. The path is thus clear for Frank to inherit Osbaldistone Hall and marry Diana.

The novel is a brutally realistic depiction of the social conditions in Highland and Lowland Scotland in the early 18th century. Some of the dialogue is in Scots, and the novel includes a glossary of Scottish words. Critical response to *Rob Roy* was almost unanimously favorable. For his power of characterization, Scott was now frequently compared with Shakespeare, with particular praise reserved for Bailie Nicol Jarvie and Andrew Fairservice, Frank's shrewd but cowardly manservant. Though Rob Roy is not the lead character (in fact, the narrative does not move to Scotland until halfway through the book), his personality and actions are key to the development of the novel. The novel was a tremendous commercial success, the original print run of 10,000, a huge figure for the time, being bought up in two weeks. The book was loosely adapted into a film in 1995.

The novels of the second group, i. e., the novels on English history, were written to represent stages of English history, covering the days after the Norman Conquest, the life during the Tudor Dynasty and the Stuart rule, the English Revolution and the Restoration Period. The best known in this group is *Ivanhoe*.

Ivanhoe (1819) is set in the late 12th century, when the English people, or Anglo-Saxons, led a hard life under the rule of their Norman Conquerors. It has been credited for increasing interest in romance and medievalism. The hero Wilfred of Ivanhoe is the son of Cedric, a Saxon nobleman. In the hope of restoring the Saxon dynasty one day, Cedric wishes to marry his ward Rowena, a descendant of Alfred the Great, to Athelstane of Coningsburgh, a descendant of Edward the Confessor. Ivanhoe's love for Rowena, however, threatens these plans, leading Cedric to disinherit him. Ivanhoe joins the Third Crusade, and, fighting alongside Richard the Lionheart in the Holy Land, wins the King's flavor. The novel begins with Ivanhoe's return to England, where Prince John is plotting to depose his brother Richard, who has been taken captive in Austria on his way home from the Crusades.

On his way to a great tournament at Ashby-de-la-Zouch, Ivanhoe visits his father's house disguised as a pilgrim. Here he saves the life of Isaac, a rich Jew of York, by warning him of a planned ambush. The book was written and published during a period of increasing struggle for emancipation of the Jews in England, and there are frequent references to injustice against them. At Ashby, Ivanhoe, with the help of the King who has returned to England in disguise, vanquishes all supporters of King John (1166 – 1216, king 1199 – 1216), including his great personal enemies, the Templar Sir Brian de Bois-Guilbert and the brutal baron Front-de-Boeuf. Ivanhoe is wounded in the tournament and nursed back to health by Isaac's daughter Rebecca. Bois-Guilbert and Front-de-Boeuf then assist a mercenary leader Maurice de Bracy in a plan to abduct Rowena. Her traveling party, which includes Cedric, Athelstane, Isaac, Rebecca and the still-recovering Ivanhoe, is attacked and all are led captive to Front-de-Boeuf's Castle of Torquilstone. Here Rowena and Rebecca courageously resist the advances of, respectively Maurice de Bracy and Bois-Guilbert, who has become enamored of the Jewess. The castle is successfully besieged by a band of Saxons and outlaws, led by Locksley (alias Robin Hood) and King Richard himself, and the prisoners are liberated except Rebecca, whom Bois-Guilbert carries off to the Preceptory of Templestowe.

The unexpected arrival at Templestowe of the Grand-Master of the Knights Templar leads to a charge of witchcraft against Rebecca, who only manages to escape immediate execution by demanding trial by combat. At the last moment, Ivanhoe appears as her champion to face a reluctant Bois-Guilbert who has been commanded to represent the Grand-Master's order. At the first pass, Bois-Guilbert falls dead from his horse, unwounded but "a victim to the violence of his own contending passions." At the end, Richard reconciles Ivanhoe and Cedric, Athelstane withdraws his claim to Rowena's hand, and Ivanhoe and Rowena get married. Rebecca, stifling her love for Ivanhoe, accompanies her father to Spain, where they hope to find a more tolerant society. The happy ending of the novel is actually the outcome of the compromise between the Anglo-Saxon lords and the Norman King Richard I (1157 –

1199, king 1189 – 1199). Here Richard I is depicted as a chivalric knight, a brave and just man, representing those of the Norman lords who are far-sighted and sympathetic with the Saxon people's aspirations for a peaceful life and who are in favor of the union of the Normans and Saxons. Another character worth mentioning is the legendary Robin Hood. Scott's characterization of Robin Hood in *Ivanhoe* helps shape the modern notion of this figure as a cheery noble outlaw.

Ivanhoe was a great success. John Henry Newman (1801 – 1890) claimed that Scott "had first turned men's minds in the direction of the Middle Ages," while Carlyle and Ruskin made similar assertions of Scott's overwhelming influence over the revival based primarily on the publication of this novel. (Chandler, 1965: 330) Thackeray's *Rebecca and Rowena* (1850) is an amusing sequel to, and aritical reinterpretation of, this novel. *Ivanhoe* sold at a phenomenal rate. Within less than two weeks, the entire first printing of 10,000 copies was exhausted and the demand for more copies put the printers under serious pressure. Translated into numerous languages, it marked the beginning of Scott's European vogue and the emergence of the historical novel as an international phenomenon.

In this novel, as in Scott's other novels, there are descriptions of various strata of people. Compared to the vivid pictures of other characters, Ivanhoe, the hero of the novel, is also a rather pale figure who acts only as a link between the various characters and events in the novel. *Ivanhoe*, for its realistic description of the life of feudal England, is the high watermark of Scott's fame as an author of historical novels.

Among the novels of the third group, i. e., the novels on the history of the other European countries, the best-known one is *Quentin Durward* (1823), one of the most vigorous and readable of Scott's novels. It is set in the 15th-century France and Burgundy. It is Scott's first venture onto the mainland of Europe, and his story of a young Scots soldier of fortune serving in the guard of King Louis XI (1423 – 1483, king 1461 – 1483) has an enthusiastic reception in Paris. As in many of Scott's novels, the plot deals with the breakdown of traditional chivalric values and the opposition (and here, the reconciliation) of romance and reality.

Scott was the first novelist to recreate the past. His novels combine historical fact with romantic imagination and give a picturesque representation of many historical personages and events. In Scott's novels, historical events are closely interwoven with the fates of individuals. The plot unfolds itself through the interaction between historical life and individual life, thus giving a view "of individuals as they are affected by the public strife and social divisions of the age."

The nominal heroes of Scott's novels, usually young men of noble birth, are often thrown into close companionship with the ordinary people and go through a series of hardships and adventures. But these heroes are usually pale figures, whose actual function in the novels is to hold together the numerous incidents of the plot and introduce other characters far more interesting than themselves.

Scott was mindful of the role and fates of the ordinary people. The numerous pen-portraits of the people from different social strata constitute an important characteristic in Scott's works. However, Scott was conservative in politics. His conservatism showed itself in his opposition to "extremes" in the people's struggles, and compromise was regarded by him as the best means in solving social contradictions.

Besides romantic imagination, Scott also relied upon careful studies and investigations into the detail of historical life. Scott's novels are the developments of the realistic novels by Fielding and Smollett. They paved the way for the development of the realistic novel of the 19th century. In a sense, Scott's literary career marked the transition from romanticism to realism in English literature of the 19th century.

21.2 Jane Austen (1775 – 1817)

While Walter Scott was laying the foundations of his large family estates and recounting the story of battles, chivalry, royalty and brigandage, a quiet sunny little woman, almost unmindful of the great world, was enlivening her father's parsonage and writing about the clergy, the old maids, the short-sighted mothers, the marriageable daughters, and other people that figure in village life. This cheerful, sprightly young woman was Jane Austen.

Austen is one of the great masters of the English novel. She was the first important English woman novelist and the founder of the novel which deals with unimportant middle class people and of which there are many fine examples in later English fiction. She was almost uninfluenced by the current fashions in fiction or by the revolutionary ideas. Austen's novels are simple stories of the lives and thoughts of the commonplace people of the upper-middle class. Her works criticized the Sentimental novels in the late 18th century and were part of the change to the 19th-century realism. She wrote about typical people in everyday life. This gave the English novel its first distinctly modern character. Austen's stories are often comic and about moral problems. They show how women depended on marriage for social standing and economic security.

Austen was very modest about her own genius. She once famously described her work as "the little bit (two Inches wide) of Ivory, on which I work with so fine a brush, as produces little effect after much labor." (Jones, 2003: 80) Austen's major novels include *Northanger Abbey*, *Sense and Sensibility* (1811), whose story took place in southern England in the 1790s and is mostly about two sisters and their life and loves, *Pride and Prejudice* (1813), *Mansfield Park* (1814), *Emma* (1816) and *Persuasion*, which was written shortly before the author's death and published posthumously with *Northanger Abbey* in 1818. Of these six novels *Mansfield Park* was the most successful during the author's lifetime, but *Pride and Prejudice* is universally acknowledged as Austen's masterpiece. *Emma* is a comedy about Emma Woodhouse, a rich and beautiful young lady growing up in the fictional community of Hartfield in the 19th-century England, and about the troubles she causes when she tries matchmaking. *Northanger Abbey*, probably the earliest of Austen's completed works, is a gentle satire on the mystery tale of haunted castles. Its purpose is to ridicule the popular tales of romance and terror, and to contrast with these the normal realities of life.

Austen also wrote some early works represented by *Lady Susan* (written probably in 1793 – 1794), and an unfinished novel *The Watsons* between the writing of *Northanger Abbey* and the revision of *Sense and Sensibility*. She had been working on a new novel *Sanditon* but left it unfinished when she died. Austen's works are perfect, and there is no choosing between them for one who enjoys her quiet irony and her simple delicate analysis of character. There are no heroic passions or astounding adventures. With the publishers she had little success. *Pride and Prejudice* went begging for sixteen years; and *Northanger Abbey* was sold for a trivial sum to a publisher, who laid it aside and forgot it until the appearance and moderate success of *Sense and Sensibility* in 1811. An anonymous article in the *Quarterly Review*, following the appearance of *Emma* in 1815, full of generous appreciation of the charm of the new writer, was the beginning of Austen's fame.

Pride and Prejudice was originally a youthful work entitled *First Impressions*. The story is developed around the Bennet family, especially the love story of the second daughter Elizabeth, i. e., her prejudice and her lover Darcy's pride. This book tells us a great deal about different attitudes toward marriage in Austen's time. Elizabeth's attitude, which is not built upon wealth and money, but on spiritual understanding of each other, is praised by the writer.

The plot is thin, but around it Austen wove vivid pictures of everyday life of simple country society. Through the description of the daily talks and doings of young men and women, she painted very real and interesting characters. The major plot evolves around the love story of Elizabeth and Darcy. Darcy, a young man coming from an aristocratic background, behaves arrogantly toward those below him in social rank. He despises the Bennets as vulgar and beneath him. For the same reason he alienates his friend Mr. Bingley from Jane Bennet. So Elizabeth harbors a suspicion of Darcy's class and does not think much of him at first. Her prejudice deepens when she hears Wickham (who has been brought up by his family) viciously slander Darcy, claiming that the aristocrat has mistreated him. Later Elizabeth visits Darcy's estate and learns about the genial side of the man. Her prejudice is disarmed when Wickham elopes with her kid sister Lydia and Darcy intervenes to put things to right. He seeks Wickham out and pays his debts on condition that he marry Lydia, which the villain does. The warm, caring side of Darcy's that the whole incident reveals changes Elizabeth's mind about the man. The other plots that interweave with the major one include the hurtful but eventually happy love and marriage of Bingley and Jane, the humdrum, probably dreary prospect of the married life of the Collins, the eloped Wickham and Lydia destined to lifelong wretchedness and a probable unhappy resolution, and the often ignored miserable marriage of the older Bennets.

The portrayal of the characters is amazingly varied and colorful. Austen was at her best in writing about women, especially young girls. The gallery of women in the novel is simply glittering. Jane Bennet is a serene, reticent beauty; Elizabeth the spirited, vocal beauty, one of the most endearing girls in English literature; Lydia a spoiled brat, innocent and hopeless silly and romantic; Charlotte Lucas, plain, practical, and mistress of her life; Mrs. Bennet, silly but devoted to her daughters and determined to marry them off to happiness. There are also the worldly Bingley sisters, the haughty Lady Catherine de Bourgh, and her listless daughter Anne de Bourgh. It is the panoramic view of the female gender in the world of men, the inside-track examination of its motives and behavior so true of the womankind, that keeps attracting eternal attention. In addition, the portraits of the men are no less noteworthy. These include the complexities of Darcy's personality, the eccentric Mr. Bennet, the good-natured, impressionable Mr. Bingley, the mediocre Mr. Collins—a mixture of pomposity and humility, and of course Mr. Wickham, the rake and the villain of the novel. It is not so much the artistic virtuosity of the portrayals that impresses as the very humanity that the gallery represents.

Jane Austen was one of the realistic novelists. She drew vivid and realistic pictures of everyday life of the country society in her novels, but Austen's work has a very narrow literary field. She confined herself to small country parishes, whose simple country people became the characters of her novels. Her writings cover just that section of society to which she belonged—the country gentry and their lives in the rural village setting. There is hardly any aristocrat like a lord of the manor, or a poor peasant to feature as her major characters. She was so acquainted with the life of the country and its gentry that she had at her fingertips every detail that she might need for her plot interest. Within her own field, she was unrivaled. Austen's novels, moreover, show a wealth of humor, wit and delicate satire. Her plots are straight-forward; there is little action. Her characters are like real living persons, with faults and virtues mixed as they are in real life. Her prose flows easily and naturally. Her dialogues are admirably true to life.

Chapter 22 Essays in the Romantic Age

It may be noted that the first decades of the 18th and 19th centuries alike witnessed new births in essay writing. As is mentioned in the previous part of this book, Addison and Steele socialized the literary form in the early 18th century, brought it into everyday life and made it familiar and delightful to the multitude. Then it was imitated in the hands of such writers as Fielding, Johnson, Goldsmith and others. So the essay remained popular, though less distinguished, throughout the century of its birth. Early in the 19th century it became more definitely a means of intimate self-expression in the hands of Charles Lamb, William Hazlitt, De Quincey and Leigh Hunt. These essayists were much influenced by the French Revolution in politics and by the Romantic Movement in literature. They did not write according to the old rules and models of Classicism but developed a kind of familiar essay, in which they freely expressed their own personality. Of these four, Charles Lamb remains the most beloved, not only among his contemporaries, but in all English prose literature.

22.1 Charles Lamb (1775 – 1834)

Lamb was an English poet, playwright, literary critic and, above all, essayist. He is famous for the delicacy of his prose and the personal charm of his observations. His great works include *The Essays of Elia* (1823), a collection of essays, and *Tales from Shakespeare* (1807), a children's book. Different from the Romantic poets, who were interested in nature and country life, Lamb felt more at home in the city than in the wild nature. Therefore the subjects of his essays are often drawn from the richness of London life. He showed us a romantic imagination which could find its stimulus not only in nature and in country life but also in society and people. Lamb has been generally considered the finest familiar essayist in England. The familiar essay is characterized by its relaxed style, its conversational tone and its wide range of subject matter.

Lamb began to write at East India House and published his collected works in 1818, which contained poems, plays, a novel and his excellent literary criticism. Lamb's real fame came in 1820, when he began to contribute "Essays of Elia" to the London Magazine. Under the pseudonym Elia, Lamb wrote about a wide variety of subjects. His essays are distinguished for the combination of nostalgia, humor and refined observation. One of his best-known essays is "Dream-Children: A Reverie."

Lamb's literary career can be roughly divided into three periods and his works are classified into three groups accordingly. During the period before 1803, Lamb mainly wrote poems on various subjects. Among them the best-known ones are "The Old Familiar Faces," included in his collaborative work with Charles Lloyd (1775 – 1839) *Blank Verse* (1798), the lyrical ballad "Hester" (1803), and the elegy "On an Infant Dying as Soon as Born" (1827), which is probably the author's finest poem. Besides, he produced a sentimental romance *The Tale of Ro-*

samund Gray and Old Blind Margaret (1798) and a poetical drama *John Woodvil* (1802) in these years. From 1803 to 1820, Lamb devoted largely to literary criticism. His first successful literary venture is *Tales from Shakespeare*. In 1808 came out his *Specimens of English Dramatic Poets Who Lived about the Time of Shakespeare*, which offers readers much information about Elizabethan poets and had noticeable influence on Keats' poetic writing. Then from 1820 till his death, Lamb wrote a series of essays which are collected in his *Essays of Elia* and *Last Essays of Elia* (1833). The two collections contain more than 50 essays on various topics.

The Essays of Elia is a volume of Lamb's first series of essays which appeared in the *London Magazine* between 1820 and 1823. The personal and conversational tone of the essays has charmed many readers; the essays "established Lamb in the title he now holds, that of the most delightful of English essayists." (Moody, 1918: 330) The author himself is the Elia of the collection, and his sister Mary is "Cousin Bridget." Charles Lamb first used the pseudonym Elia for an essay on the South Sea House, where he had worked decades earlier; Elia was the last name of an Italian clerk who worked there at the same time as the author, and after that essay the name stuck. The essays in the collection are all cast as if written by Elia, but they are not reliably autobiographical, even when seeming so. The fanciful, old fashioned character of the narration is maintained throughout. He is, in Lamb's words, "a bundle of prejudices" with a strong liking for the whimsical, the quaint, and the economic. The tone is never didactic or seriously philosophical, and all the more disturbing aspects of life are avoided. The style is very literary and carefully wrought, filled with archaisms and with echoes of Lamb's master Sterne. Some of the best essays are "Some of the Old Benchers of the Inner Temple," "Christ's Hospital," "The South Sea House," "Mr Battle's Opinions on Whist," "Dream Children" and "A Dissertation on Roast Pig." A falling off in the quality of *Last Essays of Elia* is very apparent. That it did not sell well greatly discouraged the author. Lamb's essays were very popular and were printed in many subsequent editions throughout the 19th century.

Tales from Shakespeare, also known as *All the Tales from Shakespeare*, is generally accepted as Lamb's second best-known work, only next to his essays; yet it is a collaborative work of Charles Lamb and his sister Mary Lamb (1764 – 1847), of which the tragedies were reproduced by the former and the comedies by the latter, and its success is attributable more to the sister, whose name did not appear on the title page of the first few editions, than to Charles. The work, designed to make Shakespeare familiar to the young, reduced the archaic English and complicated storyline of Shakespeare to a simple level that children could read and comprehend.

Humor is the most striking feature of Lamb's essays. Charles Lamb was a humorist and a master of puns and jokes, which abound in his essays. But at the core of his humor lies an honest, good soul, pressed by domestic tragedy and wearied by daily drudgery. Therefore in his essays laughter is often mingled with tears and there is sadness behind his humor. By his humor he sometimes broke the ice of commonplace, monotony and hypocrisy of the upper society and expressed the sorrows and pleasures of the common people.

Lamb was also a romanticist. Through his writing he sought a free expression of his own personality and wove romance into the daily life. His essays are intensely personal, which are an excellent picture of the author and humanity. But his romanticism is different from that of Wordsworth: Wordsworth was the romanticist of nature while Lamb was the romanticist of the city. Whereas the former drew inspirations from the mountains and lakes, the latter's imagination was inspired by the busy life of London.

Lamb was especially fond of old writers. His writings are full of archaisms, interspersed with quotations from his favorite authors but always faithful to his own personality. They are highly artistic and inimitable.

Last but not least, Lamb's essays are marked by relaxed style, conversational tone and wide range of subject matter.

22.2　William Hazlitt (1778 – 1830)

Hazlitt was an English literary critic, social commentator and philosopher, who is remembered most for his humanistic essays and literary criticism. Placed in the company of Samuel Johnson and George Orwell, he is now considered one of the great critics and essayists of the English language. Yet his work is currently little read and mostly out of print. During his lifetime he befriended many literary figures both at home and abroad, including Charles and Mary Lamb, Stendhal (1783 – 1842), Samuel Taylor Coleridge, William Wordsworth and John Keats. As an essayist, Hazlitt ranks high in English literature. W. E. Henley (1849 – 1903) has made an interesting comparison between Lamb and Hazlitt, saying that "[t]he best of it all (i. e. the best of English prose of the early 19th century), perhaps, is the best of Lamb. But Hazlitt's for different qualities, is so eminent and shining a second that I hesitate as to the pre-eminency. Probably the race is Lamb's. But Hazlitt is ever Hazlitt, and at his highest moments Hazlitt is hard to beat, and has not these many years been beaten."

Hazlitt was one of the representatives of Romantic criticism, in which individual taste took the place of universal reason as a foundation of literary criticism. His well-known critical works include *Characters of Shakespeare's Plays* (1817), *The Spirit of the Age* (1825), *Lectures on the English Poets* (1818), which contains a series of brilliant essays on Chaucer, Shakespeare, Milton, Pope and Burns and sums up the poetic achievement of England up to the 18th century, *Lectures on English Comic Writers* (1819) affording an evaluation of the Restoration comic drama, and *Lectures Chiefly on the Dramatic Literature of the Age of Elizabeth* (1820), in which Hazlitt gave a clear interpretation of the works of the other dramatists of Shakespeare's day.

Characters of Shakespeare's Plays is a collection of essays which comment not only upon Hamlet, Macbeth and other fictional heroes that appear in the plays, but also upon the distinctive qualities of each major drama (including the dramatic structure and poetry as well as the manner in which the characters were acted on stage), and more generally upon the magnanimity of Shakespeare's imagination. Especially notable is the essay on Coriolanus, which considers the affinities between poetic imagination and political power. Hazlitt rebuked Samuel Johnson for his unimaginative treatment of Shakespeare, and attempted a more flexibly sympathetic appreciation. In this book, Hazlitt discussed each of Shakespeare's plays and helped the reader to have a better understanding of Shakespeare as a poet and as a dramatist who sees life from many angles. The great German poet Heine (1797 – 1856) said that, up to his time, Hazlitt's was the best comment on Shakespeare.

The book consists of 32 essays on the plays themselves, a "Preface," an essay on "Doubtful Plays of Shakespeare" and one on the "Poems and Sonnets," each essay constituting a chapter. As two of the essays encompass five of the plays, the plays discussed amount to 35 in number. Though Hazlitt could find much to appreciate in the comedies, the tragedies (particularly *Macbeth*, *Othello*, *King Lear* and *Hamlet*) seemed to him inherently more important. His comments on the tragedies are often integrated with his ideas about the significance of poetry and imaginative literature in general. As he expressed it at the end of "Lear," tragedy describes the strongest passions, and "the greatest strength of genius is shewn here in describing the strongest passions: for the power of the imagination, in works of invention, must be in proportion to the force of the natural impressions, which are the subject of them." (Hazlitt, 1818: 177) In style and length the essays in the book resemble those of Hazlitt's miscellaneous collection *The Round Table* (1817), a collaborative work with Leigh Hunt, which followed the model for periodical essays established a century earlier in *The Spectator*.

Characters of Shakespear's Plays was composed in reaction to the Neoclassical approach to Shakespeare's plays typified by Dr. Johnson. It was among the first English-language studies of Shakespeare's plays to follow the manner of German critic A. W. Schlegel (1767 – 1845), and, with the work of Coleridge, paved the way for the increased appreciation of Shakespeare's genius that was characteristic of the later 19th-century criticism. It was also the first book to cover all of Shakespeare's plays, intended as a guide for the general reader.

The Spirit of the Age: Or, Contemporary Portraits is a collection of essays presented as a portrait gallery of the eminent writers of Hazlitt's time—Wordsworth, Coleridge, Byron, Southey, Scott, Malthus (1766 – 1834), Charles Lamb and several others, whom Hazlitt believed to represent significant trends in the thought, literature and politics of his time. The essays combine character-sketches with lively critical assessments of the subjects' works and summaries of their reputations, placed in the context of the political and intellectual ferment of their times. They are strongly animated by Hazlitt's political loyalties, especially in the sustained assault upon the Tory critic Gifford for his "ridiculous pedantry and vanity." In this sense, the verdicts on these writers show Hazlitt a discriminating critic.

The Spirit of the Age is one of Hazlitt's most successful books and frequently judged to be his masterpiece, "the crowning ornament of Hazlitt's career, and... one of the lasting glories of nineteenth-century criticism." (Kinnaird, 1978: 301) Hazlitt's experience as a literary, political and social critic contributed to his solid understanding of his subjects' achievements, and his judgements of his contemporaries were later often deemed to have held good after nearly two centuries. Despite its uneven quality, the book has been generally agreed to provide "a vivid panorama of the age." (Wardle, 1971: 406) Yet, missing an introductory or concluding chapter, and with few explicit references to any themes, it was for long also judged as lacking in coherence and hastily thrown together. More recently, critics have found in it a unity of design, with the themes emerging gradually, by implication, in the course of the essays and even supported by their grouping and presentation.

The most interesting part of Hazlitt's work is to be found in his miscellaneous familiar essays, collected under the titles of *Table Talk* (1821 – 22), *The Plain Speaker* (1826), *Sketches and Essays* and *Winterslow* (both in 1839, posthumously). In writing these essays, Hazlitt laid down a topic and then expanded upon it by piling up intimate observations and vivid examples, expressed in "literary-colloquial English." His personal experiences, his spirit of independence, his sensitive imagination and his mastery of the Standard English vocabulary all find excellent expression, and Hazlitt's own direct, vigorous personality emerges full and alive from between the lines. The lovely pieces of prose have become an integral part of the treasury of English literature. The best of Hazlitt may be found among such essays as "My First Acquaintance with Poets,". "On Going a Journey," "The Feeling of Immortality in Youth," "On Reading Old Books," "On Reading New Books," "Of Persons One Would Wish to Have

Seen," "On Taste," "On Familiar Style," "The Sick Chamber" and "The Fight."

22.3　James Henry Leigh Hunt (1784 – 1859)

James Henry Leigh Hunt, best known as Leigh Hunt, was an English essayist, critic and poet, and another representative writer of the Romantic school. His life was that of unceasing literary labor. As a poet he is chiefly remembered for *The Story of Rimini* (1816), a narrative poem based on the tragic story of Paolo and Francesca, two Italian lovers of the 13th century, and written in "free and idiomatic use of language" and the run-on couplets. His short poems include "Abou Ben Adhem" and "Jenny Kissed Me." But his real strength is to be found in prose. He was a born journalist and essayist, editing and writing for a series of periodicals.

Hunt's principal works of literary criticism include *Imagination and Fancy* (1844), which draws interesting parallels between painting and poetry, *Wit and Humor* (1846), which contains well-chosen examples from English poets, and *A Jar of Honey from Mount Hybla* (1848), *Table Talk* (1851) and *The Old Court Suburb* (1855). His *Autobiography* (1850) is also a memorable work.

The importance of Leigh Hunt lies chiefly in his development of the light miscellaneous essays, in his recognition of the genius of Shelley and Keats, in his influence on Keats' early poetical career, and in his critical works.

22.4　Thomas Penson De Quincey (1785 – 1859)

De Quincey, the English essayist and critic, is remembered chiefly for his masterpiece *The Confessions of an English Opium-Eater* (1821), which describes his experiences as an opium addict. Many scholars suggest that De Quincey inaugurated the tradition of addiction literature in the West in publishing this work. The book consists of three parts and the appendix. The first part is an autobiographical account of the author's early life, telling of his running from school, his trip through Wales and his stay in London, and showing his sympathy for the simple people of the underworld, especially for the poor, homeless girl Ann. The second part "The Pleasures of Opium" and the third part "The Pains of Opium" deal with the effects of opium upon the author's sensitive imagination, chiefly in the form of grotesque dreams, which are described with a "poetical prose."

De Quincey shaped his recollections into literary art. He is famous for the ornate descriptions of his fantasies and dreams. The major flaw of his style is discursiveness. Like Lamb, he was profoundly influenced by the gorgeous prose of the 17th century. His work marked a great turn in English prose style from plain to ornate prose-writing. He is one of the representative writers of English Romantic prose.

Exercises

I. Multiple choices

1. *Lyrical Ballads* is the joint work of William Wordsworth and his friend _____, another great Romantic poet.

　　A. S. T. Coleridge　　　　　　　　B. John Keats
　　C. P. B. Shelley　　　　　　　　　D. Walter Scott

2. S. T. Coleridge's masterpiece is _____.

Part Six　The Romantic Period

　　A. "I Wondered Lonely as a Cloud"　　B. "A Red, Red Rose"
　　C. "The Solitary Reaper"　　D. "The Rime of the Ancient Mariner"
3. *Lyrical Ballads* marked the beginning of the _____ in England.
　　A. Romantic Movement　　B. Realism
　　C. Renaissance　　D. Enlightenment Movement
4. According to William Wordsworth, the purest poetry was written in the _____ words.
　　A. fascinating　　B. simplest
　　C. vigorous　　D. rhythmical
5. William Wordsworth, as a great poet of nature, was the first to find words for the most elementary sensations of man face to face with _____.
　　A. social reality　　B. political struggles
　　C. natural phenomena　　D. bourgeois morality
6. "The Rime of the Ancient Mariner" is basically a Christian story, which also plants _____ in the readers' mind as to whether faith serves any purpose in life at all.
　　A. idealism　　B. beliefs
　　C. mysticism　　D. doubts
7. In "The Rime of the Ancient Mariner" the ancient mariner is seen all alone on a wide, wide sea, presenting a vivid, pathetic picture of _____, trying to make sense of his world over which he has not the slightest control, and generating a frame of reference for himself.
　　A. an existentialist　　B. a realist
　　C. a bourgeois　　D. a romanticist
8. _____ is a dream-poem, which is not about the Mongolian king at all but really about the mystery of poetic creation.
　　A. "The Rime of the Ancient Mariner"　　B. "Ode to a Nightingale"
　　C. "Kubla Khan"　　D. "Dejection: An Ode"
9. _____ is the work of a lonely and meditative mind. Its subject is the poet's sad awareness that he was losing his creative powers.
　　A. "The Rime of the Ancient Mariner"　　B. "Ode to a Nightingale"
　　C. "Kubla Khan"　　D. "Dejection: An Ode"
10. S. T. Coleridge's most important prose work is *Biographia Literaria, or Biographical Sketches of My Literary Life and Opinions*, which afforded the new Romantic poetry a new principle of _____, whose task was not to judge but to appreciate and interpret.
　　A. creation　　B. criticism
　　C. imagination　　D. reflection
11. _____ was given the title of the poet laureate by the authority in 1843.
　　A. Robert Southey　　B. Samuel Taylor Coleridge
　　C. William Wordsworth　　D. Percy Bysshe Shelley

12. _____'s prose work is far better than his poetry. His *Life of Nelson* is still read.

    A. Robert Southey   B. Samuel Taylor Coleridge

    C. William Wordsworth   D. Percy Bysshe Shelley

13. Lord Byron is chiefly known for his two long poems, one is *Childe Harold's Pilgrimage* and the other is _____.

    A. *Don Juan*   B. *Lyrical Ballads*

    C. *Paradise Lost*   D. *Prometheus Unbound*

14. The term "Lake School" was applied to S. T. Coleridge, _____, William Wordsworth, and sometimes to De Quincey.

    A. Charles Lamb   B. John Keats

    C. Robert Southey   D. Percy Bysshe Shelley

15. The hero in _____, a Spanish youth of aristocratic birth, is made to go through many adventures and participate in different historical events so that readers can get a broad panorama of the social life of the time.

    A. *Childe Harold's Pilgrimage*   B. *Don Juan*

    C. *Decameron*   D. *Prometheus Unbound*

16. All the following works were produced by Percy Bysshe Shelley except _____.

    A. *Queen Mab*   B. *The Revolt of Islam*

    C. *A Defense of Poetry*   D. *Lyrical Ballads*

17. Besides his lyrical drama *Prometheus Unbound*, Percy Bysshe Shelley also wrote short poems on nature and love, which form an important part of his literary output. _____ is one of his best short lyrics.

    A. "A Red, Red Rose"   B. "Ode to a Nightingale"

    C. "On a Grecian Urn"   D. "To a Skylark"

18. _____ can be read as Percy Bysshe Shelley's signature poem. It is his representative work both in theme and form, forcefully prophetic in its fighting spirit and singular in its lyrical beauty.

    A. "To a Skylark"   B. "Ode to a Nightingale"

    C. "The Cloud"   D. "Ode to the West Wind"

19. _____ was Percy Bysshe Shelley's emotional response to a strong hailstorm, as Shelley himself put it, in which he happened to be swallowed one autumn evening in 1819 on the Arno near Florence.

    A. "To a Skylark"   B. "Ode to a Nightingale"

    C. "The Cloud"   D. "Ode to the West Wind"

20. Influenced and inspired by Edmund Spenser's *Faerie Queene*, John Keats gave up his profession as a _____ and embarked on writing poetry.

    A. civil servant   B. teacher

    C. surgeon   D. farmer

21. In 1820 came John Keats' third and last volume of poems, which contains his main poems like "Isabella," "Lamia" and _____.

    A. "Endymion"   B. "On First Looking into Chapman's Homer"

C. "The Lady of the Lake" D. "The Eve of St. Agnes"

22. John Keats expressed compactly in his _____ his concept of "Truth is beauty, beauty truth," a hard-won belief that real life is as beautiful and necessary as the eternal beauty in art.

   A. "Psyche" B. "Ode to a Nightingale"
   C. "Ode on a Grecian Urn" D. "On Melancholy"

23. The listed famous odes were all written by John Keats except _____.

   A. "Ode to Autumn" B. "Ode to the West Wind"
   C. "Ode on a Grecian Urn" D. "Ode on Melancholy"

24. Walter Scott's novels may be divided into three groups according to their subject matter, i. e. the group on the history of Scotland, the group on the history of England and the group on the history of the other _____ countries.

   A. North American B. South American
   C. Asian D. European

25. The best known of Walter Scott's novels on English history is _____.

   A. *Ivanhoe* B. *Waverly*
   C. *Quentin Durward* D. *Rob Roy*

26. *Ivanhoe*, for its realistic description of the life of feudal England, is the high watermark of _____'s fame as an author of historical novels.

   A. Walter Scott B. Jane Austen
   C. Charles Lamb D. George Eliot

27. The title character of *Ivanhoe* is actually a pale figure who acts only as _____ between the various characters and events in the novel.

   A. a narrator B. a link
   C. a listener D. a mixer

28. _____ was the founder of the novel which deals with unimportant middle class people.

   A. Walter Scott B. Charles Lamb
   C. Jane Austen D. William Hazlitt

29. *Pride and Prejudice* is the masterpiece of _____, the first important English woman novelist.

   A. Charlotte Brontë B. George Eliot
   C. Jane Austen D. Elizabeth Browning

30. Romanticism prevailed in England during the period of 1798 – 1832, beginning with the publication of _____ in 1798, ending with Walter Scott's death in 1832.

   A. *The Pickwick Papers* B. *Lyrical Ballads*
   C. *Ivanhoe* D. *Pride and Prejudice*

31. The story of *Pride and Prejudice* is developed around the Bennet family, especially the love story of the second daughter _____, i. e., her prejudice and her lover's pride.

   A. Elizabeth B. Charlotte

C. Lydia   D. Jane

32. The Romantic Age in England is an age of _____. Many young enthusiastic writers turn to _____ as a happy man to singing.

   A. drama and poetry; drama and poetry   B. drama; drama
   C. prose; prose   D. poetry; poetry

33. The great literary impulse of the Romantic Age is the impulse of _____ in a wonderful variety of forms.

   A. individualism   B. realism
   C. humanism   D. rationalism

34. Walter Scott is the creator and a great master of the _____. His novels give a panorama of feudal society from its early stages to its downfall.

   A. realistic novel   B. historical novel
   C. poetic novel   D. detective novel

35. _____'s novel is the consummation and development of two different trends of English literature of the 18th and 19th centuries, i. e., of Realism and Romanticism. He is often accepted as a transitional figure in English literature.

   A. Charles Dickens   B. D. H. Lawrence
   C. Walter Scott   D. Henry Fielding

36. In his poems William Wordsworth aimed at simplicity and purity of the language. It was his theory that the language spoken by _____ when purified from its defects, was the best of all.

   A. the peasants   B. the noble
   C. the scholars   D. the educated

37. Romanticism as a literary movement came into being in England early in the latter half of the _____.

   A. 18th century   B. 17th century
   C. 19th century   D. 16th century

38. Early in the 19th century the _____ became more definitely a means of intimate self-expression in the hands of Charles Lamb, Willliam Hazlitt, De Quincey and Leigh Hunt.

   A. novel   B. poetry
   C. drama   D. essay

39. William Hazlitt's well-known critical works include *The Characters of Shakespeare's Plays*, *Lectures on the Dramatic Literature of the Age of Queen Elizabeth*, *Lectures on the English Poets*, *Lectures on English Comic Writers* and _____.

   A. *Table Talk*   B. *The Spirit of the Age*
   C. *Sketches and Essays*   D. *The Plain Speaker*

40. _____ is a volume of Charles Lamb's first series of essays which appeared in the *London Magazine* between 1820 and 1823.

   A. *Tales from Shakespeare*   B. *The Spirit of the Age*
   C. *The Essays of Elia*   D. *Characters of Shakespear's Plays*

II. Blank-filling

1. The Romantic Age in England was, like the _____ Age, distinctively an age of poetry. It was regarded as the _____ great age in English literary history.

2. The glory of the Romantic Age is in the poetry of Walter Scott, _____, S. T. Coleridge, Robert Southey, Lord Byron, _____ and John Keats.

3. William Wordsworth is the leading figure of the _____, the focal voice of the period.

4. William Wordsworth's poetry is distinguished by the _____ and purity of his language.

5. William Wordsworth's theory and practice in poetical creation started from a _____ with the social reality under capitalism, and hinted at the thought of "back to _____" and "back to the patriarchal system of the old time."

6. "Lines Composed a Few Miles above Tintern Abbey" well illustrates William Wordsworth's idea of poetry as "the powerful overflow of _____" "recollected in _____."

7. The works of S. T. Coleridge naturally divide themselves into three classes: the poetic, the _____ and the _____, corresponding to the early, the middle and the later periods of his career.

8. "The Rime of the Ancient Mariner" tells a strange story in the four-line ballad stanza form and the atmosphere and the beauty of _____ and imagery make the poem stand alone of its kind.

9. In "The Rime of the Ancient Mariner" the old sailor's world is a(an) _____ world, indifferent, naturalistic, and basically Godless, in which man is utterly thrown upon himself for survival.

10. If Mathew Arnold's "Dover Beach" is a faithful record of how people felt in the mid-19th century, S. T. Coleridge's _____ anticipated it by a whole period of 50 years.

11. According to _____, the poet was a creator and the critic was an assistant in the work of creation.

12. _____ is Lord Byron's masterpiece, a great comic epic of the early 19th century.

13. The protagonists in Lord Byron's major works like *Childe Harold's Pilgrimage* and *Don Juan*, are all archetypes of the _____ hero.

14. Lord Byron created a hero of his own type, the _____ hero, handsome, chivalrous, energetic, pathetic, lonely, remorseful over a sin, gloomy and misanthropic, sexually free, and capable of generous acts and magnanimity.

15. *Childe Harold's Pilgrimage* is written in _____ stanza.

16. John Keats was one of the most important figures of the early nineteenth-century _____. His poetry is distinctive for its _____, physical concreteness, colorful imagery, and closely-knit construction.

17. Percy Bysshe Shelley's legacy in literary theory is his prose work _____.

18. The Romantic era can be considered as indicative of _____.

19. John Keats' leading principle is: "_____"

20. Of the things that mattered most to John Keats, "_____, Fame, and _____," the first he wrote a good deal of, the second he won, and the third he found in his intense experience with art and life.

21. The poem _____ contains the famous "tender is the night" which was to become the title of a famous American novel by Scott Fitzgerald in the 20th century.

22. It is good to note that Walter Scott and Jane Austen differ vastly in their modes of representation. Scott's imagination is essentially _____ whereas Austen's is _____. In fact it was _____ who reasserted the tradition of realism.

23. The themes of Walter Scott's novels are historical. They deal with European history, especially the Scottish history and the _____ history.

24. The central idea of Walter Scott's novels on the history of Scotland is how the Scottish people fight against _____ government. The author praised the Scottish people's love for _____ and _____.

25. The nominal hero of Walter Scott's novel, usually a young man of _____ birth, is often thrown into close companionship with the _____ people and goes through a series of hardships and adventures, and thus acts only as a _____ between the various characters and events in the novel.

26. Different from the Romantic poets, who were interested in nature and country life, Charles Lamb felt more at home in the _____ than in the wild nature. Therefore the subjects of his essays are often drawn from the richness of _____ life.

27. Charles Lamb's _____ essay is characterized by its relaxed style, its conversational tone, and its wide range of subject matter.

28. William Wordsworth's greatest work, _____, was completed in 1805, though it was not published until after his death.

29. One of S. T. Coleridge's greatest works is _____, which tells of a sailor who kills an albatross and for that crime against nature endures terrible punishments.

30. The best examples of Percy Bysshe Shelley's poems are: _____, *The Revolt of Islam*, _____, _____, and *Adonis*.

III. Term definition

1. Romanticism
2. Historical novel
3. Poet laureate
4. Lake Poets/Lake School
5. Negative capability
6. Byronic hero
7. Ode
8. Lyric
9. Imagery

IV. Short-answer questions

1. What is William Wordsworth's theory about the sources of poetry?
2. What are the features in Lord Byron's poetry?
3. What are John Keats' ideas on poetry?
4. What are the features of Walter Scott's historical novels?
5. What are the features of Charles Lamb's essays?

V. Essay questions

1. Give a brief introduction to the English literature in the Romantic Age.
2. Comment on William Wordsworth.
3. Analyze William Wordsworth's theory of nature and its importance to human life demonstrated in his famous

poem "Lines Composed a Few Miles above Tintern Abbey."

4. Analyze S. T. Coleridge's "The Rime of the Ancient Mariner" from the thematic perspective.

5. "Dejection: An Ode" is the work of a lonely and meditative mind. Its subject is the poet's sad awareness that he was losing his creative powers. Analyze the poem stanza by stanza to illustrate how the subject is presented by S. T. Coleridge.

6. The theme of *Prometheus Unbound* is borrowed from the Greek tragedian Aeschylus' play *Prometheus Bound*. But the two are different not in one way. Analyze how Percy Bysshe Shelley's masterpiece departs from its classic counterpart basically in its ethos as well as its substance.

7. "Ode to the West Wind," with its well-renowned ending, has been an absolute must on the reading list of Percy Bysshe Shelley's readers. It can be read as his signature poem. Take the poem as a whole and analyze why it is universally accepted as Shelley's representative work both in theme and form.

8. The same desire for escape and transcendences is expressed in "Ode to a Nightingale" and "Ode on a Grecian Urn." Analyze the poems and explain how the theme is reflected by the poet.

9. The portrayal of the characters in *Pride and Prejudice* is amazingly varied and colorful. Analyze and interpret how Jane Austin made it.

Part Seven　The Period of Realism

(1832 – 1902/1837 – 1901)

Chapter 23　Critical Realism

23.1　Background

After the Napoleonic Wars (1803 – 1815), England began enjoying affluence as a result of relative peace and the advances in science and technology. The country changed from an agricultural nation to an industrial one. It became more urbanized, cities grew in size, and villages declined. Roads developed, canals were built, and so were railways and steamships. National economy picked up at a high speed, education became more general, popular literacy increased, and health and hygiene improved. The spirit of this age can be summarized as "progress" or "reform." On the one hand, during the early two decades or so after 1832, there appeared one important chain of events, the Chartist Movement, as a result of the sharp contradiction between labor and capital. Though the movement declined in 1858 marked by the breaking-up of the National Chartist Association, it eventually forced the ruling classes in England to make certain concessions like the Repeal of the Corn Laws in 1846 and the passage of the Ten Hours Act in 1847. On the other hand, from the 1850s to the 1870s, rapid scientific progress had its strong impact upon philosophy and religion of the day. The discoveries in geology and astronomy led to new concept of time and space and disbelief in the traditional Christian picture of paradise, purgatory and hell. Then Darwin's *On the Origin of Species* (1859) and *The Descent of Man* (1871) introduced the new biological theory of evolution and discredited the biblical story of God's creation of the world and of man and woman. Therefore four things of social and political forces stood out—democracy, education, comparative peace, and rapid progress in arts, science and mechanical inventions. To read the literature of this period, one need bear in mind not simply these generalities but the specific features that constitute what has come to be known pejoratively as "Victorianism," which include the growth of the middle class (chiefly the capitalists), the development of a very conservative kind of morality, the predominance of the moral aesthetic that proved binding to most Victorian writers, the wide currency of utilitarianism, the advent of the theory of evolution, and the faith in progress and a huge sense of moral earnestness.

All these directly or indirectly found their expression in the literary works of the age. For, contrary to the Romanticist's turning back to the past and nature through imagination, the realists wanted a truthful representation in their works of contemporary life and manners. They thought of their method as observational and objective. They believed in science and showed their deep concern for the reality of the society.

23.2 Realism

English Critical Realism as a new literary trend flourished in the 1840s and the early 1850s. It found its expression in the form of novel. The Critical Realists, most of whom were novelists, described with much vividness and artistic skill the chief traits of the English society and criticized the capitalist system from a democratic viewpoint. They not only gave a satirical portrayal of the bourgeoisie and all the ruling classes, but also showed profound sympathy for the common people. In their best works, the greed and hypocrisy of the upper classes were contrasted with the honesty and good-heartedness of the obscure "simple people" of the lower classes. Hence humor and satire abounded in the English realistic novels of the 19th century. Critical Realism revealed the corrupting influence of the rule of cash upon human nature. Here lay the essentially democratic and humanistic character of Critical Realism. But the Critical Realists did not find a way to eradicate the social evils they knew so well. They did not realize the necessity of changing the bourgeois society through conscious human efforts. They were unable to find a good solution to the social contradiction. Their works often started with a powerful exposure of the ugliness of the bourgeois world and ended up with a happy ending or an impotent compromise.

The major contribution made by the 19th-century English Critical Realists is their perfection of the novel. The greatest English Realist of the time was Charles Dickens. Some other novelists, who produced great realistic works during this period, include William Makepeace Thackeray, Charlotte Bronte, Emily Bronte, Elizabeth Gaskell, George Eliot and Thomas Hardy. Like the realists of the 18th century, the 19th-century Critical Realists made use of the broad canvas of the novel for full and detailed representations of social and political events, and of the fate of individuals and of whole social classes. But they went a step further in that they not only pictured the conflicts between separate individuals who stood for definite social strata, but also showed the broad social conflicts over and above the fate of mere individuals. With their artistic representation of vital social movements such as Chartism and their vivid description of dramatic conflicts of the time, the 19th-century realistic novels become "the epic of the bourgeois society."

23.3 Literary Currents

The Victorian Age was largely an age of prose, especially of the novel. The main stream was Critical Realism. Such great novelists as Dickens, Thackeray, Charlotte Bronte, Elizabeth Gaskell, George Eliot and Thomas Hardy were all Critical Realists. Their masterpieces are commonly acknowledged as English realistic classics in novel. Poetry in this period, to some extent, also reflected the crying social contradictions, yet it seldom touched on the serious problems. It mainly concerned itself with the poet's purely personal tastes or spiritual questionings. The most important poet of the age was Tennyson; next to him were Robert Browning and his wife Mrs. Browning. Essay-writing was characterized by social criticism in this period. The important essayists who criticized the evil of the capitalist society were Thomas Carlyle, John Ruskin and Mathew Arnold.

At the end of the 19th century, there emerged some other literary trends in English literature, including Naturalism represented by George Gissing, George Moore (1852 – 1933) and later Arnold Bennett, New Romanticism with Robert Louis Stevenson as the representative, and Aestheticism and Decadence, which proclaimed the "art for art's sake" theory and nurtured literary figures like Algernon Charles Swinburne, Walter Pater and Oscar Wilde.

This period also witnessed the emergence of the working class literature. The Chartist writers introduced into literature a new theme, i. e., the struggle of the proletariat for its rights. The greatest of Chartist poets was Ernest Jones (1819 – 1869).

Chapter 24 Critical Realist Novels

In between the Chartist writers and the more conservative poets and essayists there were a number of novelists, who had a world of sympathy for the miseries of the poor laboring masses and cried out loud against social injustice, but did not approve of the use of violence to right the social wrongs and therefore feared rather than welcomed the Chartist Movement. These novelists include chiefly Dickens and Thackeray, the Bronte sisters and Mrs. Gaskell, George Eliot of a slightly later date, and Thomas Hardy at the end of the century. They have been known as "Critical Realists" in the sense that they were strongly critical of the social reality of their day but did not want to overthrow the existing social order and so could not see a way out of the terrible situation.

The Victorian period witnessed three major phases of growth in novel. The early phase covered the years from the 1830s to the middle of the century when the English society began to feel the impact of change but still managed to keep the old values intact. Industrialization and capitalism had begun to bring wretchedness into the country, but life had not become totally impossible. Optimism was apparently one of the salient features in the works produced in the period. Writers like Charles Dickens were aware of modern ills which they lost no time to castigate, but still wrote with the notion that the world was basically good and could become better. Then came the mid or High Victorian phase of the 1870s when the country had changed from an agricultural nation to an industrial one. Life improved, problems appeared with the progress of civilization, minds became confused as a result of Darwinism, and cries of different dimensions were right down the road. This was a period of dichotomy and high complexity. Writers, George Eliot in particular, sensitively portrayed a mortal world in which good and evil co-existed and each received with time what was its due. In this world people felt the manipulation of the forces out of their control, but they still had room for free choice. Readers would meet evil deeds and evil people but seldom a total villain. Despite some ruthless censure, the works still expressed the faith in human nature and the goodness of a moral society. However, the later phase, stretching from 1880s onward, saw dramatic changes. What had appeared in Dickens and Eliot as a silhouette of the impending crisis became dazzlingly sharp in the vision of later novelists such as Thomas Hardy. Man became insignificant in a world cold and indifferent and probably Godless. He was impotent in face of the overwhelming odds of fate and struggled in vain for survival. What was in store for him was nothing but frustration and despair if not always exactly death. There arrived the age of Naturalism, which was chiefly represented more by George Gissing than by Hardy.

Victorian novels have some salient features in common. They all try to teach as well as to entertain. They are essentially urban, reflecting the values of the middle class. Moreover, they have the pattern of spiritual conversion built into their textual fabric, exhibit a strong sense of history, and see home and marriage as sacred. All great Victorian novels follow the moral standard: Good triumphs over evil, good is praised, and bad castigated (though

Wuthering Heights is not exactly in keeping with this pattern). Formally, the city metaphor recurs through them, and so does symbolic baptism. And despite departures such as Dickens' occasional romantic and half-surrealist methods, social realism remains the Victorian novelists' predominant mode of representation of life. The main point of view employed in Victorian novels is the third-person omniscient, the unlimited vision of which helps to paint the broad canvas of life.

24.1　Charles Dickens (1812 – 1870)

Dickens is commonly acknowledged as the greatest of the Critical Realists and the greatest novelist of the Victorian era. He was brought into the first rank of the most popular novelists of his day by the publication of *The Pickwick Papers* in 1837. His life ever since was a story of work without rest. Dickens created some of the world's best-known fictional characters. His works enjoyed unprecedented popularity during his lifetime. By the 20th century critics and scholars had recognized him as a literary genius. His novels and short stories enjoy lasting popularity. In 2002, Dickens was number 41 in the BBC's poll of the 100 Greatest Britons.

Dickens was a prolific writer. Despite his lack of formal education, he produced 15 novels, five novellas, hundreds of short stories and non-fiction articles. In his works Dickens gave readers a most vivid picture of the daily life of the ordinary people of his time. Moreover, he edited a weekly journal for 20 years as well as lectured and performed extensively. He campaigned vigorously for children's rights, education and other social reforms.

Although Dickens' first book *Sketch by Boz* came out in 1836, his literary success began with the publication of *The Pickwick Papers*. Within a few years he had become an international literary celebrity, famous for his humor, satire and keen observation of character and society. His novels, most published in monthly or weekly installments, pioneered the serial publication of narrative fiction, which became the dominant Victorian mode for novel publication. The installment format allowed Dickens to evaluate his audience's reaction, and he often modified his plot and character development based on such feedback.

Dickens' literary career could be roughly divided into three periods (or two periods with the year 1850 as a dividing point). The three-period division is accepted here. The first period (1836 – 1841) was marked for youthful optimism. Dickens believed that all the evils of the capitalist world would be remedied if only men treated each other with kindliness, justice and sympathetic understanding. He thought that the social problems would be solved if only every employer reformed himself according to the model set by the benevolent gentlemen in his novel and if only the rich used their power and wealth sympathetically to assist the poor to escape from poverty. This naïve optimism is the characteristic of the petty-bourgeois humanitarians of his time. The main novels written in this period are *The Pickwick Papers*, *Oliver Twist* (1838), Dickens' first true novel according to some critics, *Nicholas Nickleby* (1838 – 39) and *The Old Curiosity Shop* (1841).

The second period (1842 – 1850) was a period of excitement and irritation. In 1842 Dickens made a trip to America. Before the visit, he thought of the United States as a world in which there were no class divisions and human relations were humanitarian. But what impressed him most during his visit there was the rule of the dollar and the enormously corruptive influence of wealth and power. Vulgar selfishness, which prevailed everywhere, concealed the fine qualities of the people. Dickens' naïve optimism toward the capitalist society was profoundly shaken. The main novels produced in this period are *Martin Chuzzlewit* (1843 – 44), *Dombey and Son* (1848) and *David Copperfield* (1850).

The third period (1850 – 1870) was a period of intensifying pessimism. The year 1850 marked the coming of Dickens' culmination in writing. The author, consciously and subconsciously, showed himself more and more at odds with the bourgeois society and more and more aware of the absence of any readily available alternative. His main novels produced in this period are *Hard Times* (1854), *A Tale of Two Cities* (1859) and *Great Expectations* (1861).

The Pickwick Papers (*The Posthumous Papers of the Pickwick Club*), written for publication as a serial, is a sequence of loosely-related adventures and a typical picaresque novel like Nashe's *The Unfortunate Traveler*, Smollett's *The Adventures of Roderick Random* and Cervantes' *Don Quixote*. The action is given as occurring between 1827 and 1828, though critics have noted some seeming anachronisms. The protagonist Mr. Samuel Pickwick is a kind and wealthy old gentleman, and the founder and perpetual president of the Pickwick Club. He often gets himself involved in unpleasant situations as a result of his good-heartedness. To extend his researches into the quaint and curious phenomena of life, he suggests that he and three other "Pickwickians"—Mr. Nathaniel Winkle, Mr. Augustus Snodgrass and Mr. Tracy Tupman—should make journeys to remote places from London and report their findings to the other members of the club. The story thus evolves round Mr. Pickwick's adventures with his fellowmen. Their travels throughout the English countryside by coach provide the chief theme of the novel. A distinctive and valuable feature of the work is the generally accurate descriptions of the old coaching inns of England.

The main literary value and appeal of the novel is formed by its numerous memorable characters. Each character in *The Pickwick Papers*, as in many other Dickens' novels, is drawn comically, often with exaggerated personalities. Alfred Jingle, who joins the cast in the second chapter, provides an aura of comic villainy. He is a strolling actor and charlatan, noted for telling bizarre anecdotes in a distinctively extravagant, disjointed style. His devious tricks repeatedly put the Pickwickians in trouble. Further humor is provided when the comic cockney Sam Weller, makes his advent in the tenth chapter of the novel. First seen working at the White Hart Inn in The Borough, Weller is taken on by Mr. Pickwick as a personal servant and companion on his travels and a source of idiosyncratic proverbs and advice, and provides his own oblique ongoing narrative on the proceedings. The relationship between the idealistic and unworldly Pickwick and the astute cockney Weller has been likened to that between Don Quixote and Sancho Panza. In their wanderings, they meet many tragic-comical circumstances owing to their unpractical illusion, their credulity and their naïve aspirations to correct all the evils of the world. Therefore, they often look funny, almost foolish, but the author meant to arouse readers' sympathy and admiration for their simplicity and essential goodness. The brilliant portraits of Pickwick and Sam Weller account a great deal for the popularity of the book.

The Pickwick Papers gives a rather comprehensive picture of the early 19th-century England and affords readers a whole gallery of vivid portraits of the petty-bourgeoisie. Though the plot is formless, the whole thing is extremely interesting, funny and vividly real with its comic episodes. In the novel there are the farcical depiction of an election contest, the mockery of army officers, the ridicule of law courts and lawsuits, the vivid description of the debtor's prison, the satire on money worship in a bourgeois society, and the penetrating exposure of the parliamentary system of England. But the novel does not seem to show deep hatred for the bourgeois society as a whole, and humor rather than satire dominates the novel.

Oliver Twist tells the story of an orphan boy, the title character of the book. Born in a workhouse and of unknown parentage, Oliver Twist is brought up under miserable conditions. After experiencing an unhappy apprenticeship to an undertaker, he runs away to London, where he falls into the hands of a gang of thieves. The head of the thieves is the old Jew Fagin. The other chief members are the burglar Bill Sikes, his mistress Nancy, and the "Artful Dodger," an impudent young pickpocket. Oliver is trained to be a pickpocket. Soon, he is sent on the first mission to pick pockets with the Artful Dodger and Charley Bates. Dodger and Charley steal the handkerchief of an old gentleman named Mr. Brownlow, and promptly flee. So Oliver is caught instead and taken to the magistrate. But he is cleared by a bookstall holder, who saw Dodger commit the crime. Although Mr. Brownlow takes Oliver home, the thieves kidnap him and make him join them again. Monks, who turns out to be Oliver's half-brother, helps the thieves in keeping Oliver in the gang, in order to ruin him and obtain the whole of his father's property. One day, Oliver is made to help one of the thieves in breaking into a lady's house. He gets wounded and comes into the hand of Miss Rose and her guardian Mrs. Maylie, who kindly treat him. Later on, Nancy reveals to Rose that Monks is aware of Oliver's parentage and wishes all proof of it destroyed, and that there is some relationship between Oliver and Rose herself. They make some inquiry about the matter. Unfortunately, Nancy's action is discovered by Fagin, who naturally tells Sikes about it. Nancy is brutally murdered by Sikes. At the end of the novel the thieves in the gang get their just deserts and Oliver's half-brother Monks is compelled to confess his evil doings and then put into prison. Oliver is adopted by Mr. Brownlow.

The novel is a powerful exposure of the bourgeois society. It shows the extreme brutality and corruption of the oppressors and their agents under the mask of philanthropy. Dickens gave vivid descriptions of the sufferings of the poor and oppressed. However, while sympathizing with the miseries of the people, the author did not know what or who was responsible for such miseries and even cherished illusions about the rich, idle and benevolent people like Mr. Brownlow. He believed that the social problems would be solved if only every employer followed the example set by "good gentlemen" like Brownlow.

David Copperfield is regarded by many as Dickens' masterpiece and semi-autobiographical work. It was written at a time when the author's creative powers had reached their height. Like most of his works, it originally appeared in the serial form. In the preface to the 1867 edition, Dickens wrote, "like many fond parents, I have in my heart of hearts a favorite child. And his name is David Copperfield." The story is told in the first person, through the mouth of the hero. Dickens made good use of his own life experiences to expose the social evils of his day. The book has always been a favorite with a wide public.

The hero David Copperfield is a posthumous child. His mother marries again when David is quite young. His stepfather Mr. Murdstone is a vile-natured man. He, in the guise of education, tortures David and drives the gentle weak mother to an early grave. Then David is taken from school and sent to work as a child-laborer in a blacking factory. He lives in poverty and misery. But, later, he runs away and throws himself on the mercy of his aunt Getsy Trotwood, an eccentric but good-hearted old lady, who adopts David and sends him to a good school. Thereafter David begins a new life.

After leaving school, David begins to study law. He meets his former friend Steerforth, who comes from a rich family, and introduces him to Mr. Peggotty—David's former kindly housekeeper Clara Peggotty's brother—and his family, including his nephew Ham and a petty orphan girl called Emily, who has been engaged to Ham. The handsome villain Steerforth induces Emily to run away with him under a promise of marriage, which he does not intend to fulfill. Then he abandons her, and is shipwrecked and drowned off Yarmouth on his return to England. Ham is drowned in an attempt to save Steerforth. Emily is found by Mr. Peggotty, and they, together with Wilkins Micawber—David's former tragicomic landlord—and his family, emigrate to Australia, where they live a happy life. Meanwhile, David has undergone a series of love adventures. He falls in love with and gets married to a petty, empty-headed girl called Dora. But soon his child-wife dies and he marries Agnes, the daughter of his aunt's lawyer Mr. Wickfield. He is now a famous writer and achieves the happy ending of his adventures. Besides the main line, there is a sub-plot of Uriah Heep, the main antagonist of the second half of the novel. Heep is a disturbing young man who serves first as secretary and then as partner to Mr. Wickfield. An archetypal hypocrite, he appears to be extremely self-deprecating and talks constantly of being humble, but gradually reveals his wicked and twisted character. He gains great power over Wickfield and several others, but is finally discovered by Wilkins Micawber to be guilty of multiple fraud by forging Mr. Wickfield's signature, thus misappropriating the personal wealth of the Wickfield family and the portfolios entrusted to the lawyer by others, including £ 5000 belonging to Betsey Trotwood, fooling Wickfield into thinking he has committed this act while drunk, and blackmailing him. Heep is forced to return the forged documents and stolen capital; he is thus defeated but not prosecuted. He is later imprisoned for an (unrelated) attempted fraud on the Bank of England. He nurtures a deep hatred for David Copperfield and many others.

Dickens' democratic viewpoint is apparently seen in this novel. Almost all the aristocratic and bourgeois characters in it are either scoundrels, or liars or moral weaklings. It is the lower petty-bourgeois and proletarian characters, such as Micawber and the Peggotty family who win the love and sympathy of readers. This shows Dickens' sympathy for the working people.

Hard Times appraises the English society and is aimed at highlighting the social and economic pressures of the times. It was not greatly popular in its day, but gained a considerable reputation in the 20th century partly through the admiration of George Bernard Shaw and Frank Raymond Leavis (1895 – 1978). The novel follows a classical tripartite structure, and the titles of each book are related to the saying from the *Bible* "whatsoever a man soweth, that shall he also reap." Book I is entitled "Sowing," Book II is entitled "Reaping," and the third is "Garnering."

Thomas Gradgrind, a citizen of Coketown, a northern industrial city, is a misguided exponent of utilitarianism, who believes in facts and statistics and brings up his children Tom and Louisa accordingly, ruthlessly suppressing the imaginative sides of their nature. As a result, Tom becomes a mean, selfish and dishonest young man. He commits theft. For this he is caught and hustled out of the country. Louisa is sacrificed in marriage to Bounderby, a man 30 years older, though she does not love him. After marriage, she feels unhappy and is tempted by James Harthouse, who takes advantage of her unhappy life with her husband and attempts to seduce her. The better side of her nature is awakened at this experience, and at the crisis she flees for protection to her father, who in turn is awakened to the folly of his system and shelters her. Louisa separates forever from her husband. The unhappy state of his children opens the father's eyes to the knowledge that life contains sentiments as powerful as facts.

This novel makes a fierce attack on the bourgeois system of education and bourgeois utilitarianism. In this novel, Dickens also described the Chartist Movement. He showed that the Chartist Movement was the just struggle of the workers for better conditions, and expressed his sympathy for the workers.

Great Expectations, the best of Dickens' novels according to some critics, is successful in psychological description. It is a satire on the society and those people who dream to enter the higher society. The hero, a poor village boy Pip, is asked to accompany a rich old lady and play with her. The lady is half-crazed by the desertion of her lover on her bridal night, and in order to revenge herself, has brought up an adopted daughter Estella to use her beauty as a means of torturing men. Pip falls in love with Estella, but the girl is very proud and cold to him because of his lower social position. The boy determines to become a rich gentleman. He is secretly assisted by an unknown benefactor. Then he enters the high society. But finally his unknown benefactor proves to be an escaped convict. After the convict has been caught by the policemen, the great expectations of the young man fade away and he returns to labor in the countryside.

Great Expectations is a bildungsroman. It tells a story of a young man growing from innocence to experience, from immaturity to maturity. Pip's spiritual odyssey begins in the form of a quest for self-identity and for his true father. He learns humility, accepts guilt, retrieves lost values and grows up eventually. Pip's experience reveals the spiritual poverty of the time and the terrible moral decline, which results from the 19th-century mechanical civilization. The novel has been regarded as a 19th-century fable of a young man rising from rags to riches. What's more, it transcends its time and space and becomes a fable for all humanity for all time.

The novel is well structured. The 58 chapters fall roughly into three sections. The first section, stretching from the first chapter to the seventeenth, begins with Pip inadvertently saving Magwitch and ends with the recapture of the prisoner. Here Pip is innocent and lives an enjoyable life with the similarly innocent Joe. The second section, covering the following 39 chapters, is the main part of the work. Pip now gets an unexpected offer and goes away to become a gentleman in London. He acquires great expectations, refines his manners and tastes, and feels ashamed of Joe's company. The section ends with the appearance of his true benefactor Magwitch. Then the last two chapters make up the third section, which begins with Pip's sudden brain fever, falling into a coma, a symbolic kind of death of "the gentleman" in him, and surviving to face the new phase of his life. Pip comes back to Joe and recognizes his own roots in the country, and gets united with Estella who turns out to be Magwitch's lost daughter.

The story is typically Victorian. It reflects such basic issues of the era as dehumanization that follows in the wake of industrialization, the sense of spiritual devastation, the quest for identity, and the Victorian emphasis on the home and the hearth.

Dickens' novels, telling much of the unhappy experiences of his own childhood, offer a most complete and realistic picture of the English bourgeois society of his age. It is a world thronged with the diverse specimens of humanity, i. e., characters from all walks of life. It is a world where readers can get a bird's-eye view of the English life then. All the different decades overarching the whole historical period of his creative life get their share of description and offer a historical backdrop for his writings, which reflect the protest of the people against the capitalist exploitation and criticize the vices of the capitalist society.

Dickens' protagonists come close in type to the modern existentialist hero except for their happy ending. The archetypal Dickensian hero/heroine is often an orphan or a child whose parents, though still alive, are as good as dead to them. In these protagonists there is a visible silhouette of young Dickens suffering in a blacking shoe factory or visiting his father in a debtors' prison. They find themselves alone in a heartless world, without family love and any sense of security, ignored by society, and struggling against malignant odds for survival. They go through the phase of despair, the downward movement to Hell, but manage to come back up. Even though his archetypal themes include dehumanization, alienation and quest for self-identity—all modern in nature, Dickens was essentially Victorian, and his optimism did not allow him to go beyond the limitations of his age.

The success of Dickens' novels also lies in his character-portrayal. Not only are the major characters in his novels very carefully delineated and given distinctive individual characteristics but also his minor figures create in the reader's mind strong impressions of their personalities. Some of Dickens' characters are really such "typical characters under typical circumstances" that they become proverbial or are representative of a whole group of similar persons. Besides, Dickens worked intensively on developing arresting names for his characters that would reverberate with associations for his readers and assist the development of motifs in the storyline. To cite one of numerous examples, the name Mr. Murdstone in *David Copperfield* conjures up twin allusions to "murder" and stony coldness.

Dickens was a great humorist and his novels are full of humor. Dickens' humor has something to do with his optimistic outlook on life and society. One notable feature of his humorous narratives is his adroitness at creating the grotesque effect from some of his characters. His skill of exaggeration plays a valuable part so that many of his characters appear like caricatures; in such cases the evil is all evil while the good is all good. Associated sometimes with the grotesque is the melodramatic, another notable feature of Dickens' humorous narratives. Dickens was skilled in the use of melodrama. His unique manipulation of plot, masking, and disguised identities all conspire to give his works an exceptionally charming melodramatic effect. The incoherence, the medley of characters, the jumbling of situations, and the juxtaposition of diverse classes and backgrounds all serve well to contribute to the effect.

Dickens was a great satirist and his works abound in satire. He was highly critical of his age. Social criticism is a hallmark of all his works. He was supremely human and keenly sensitive to the problems of his age and the plight of the common people. He spearheaded his biting attacks toward the English law and the prison system. He had no faith or trust in philanthropy and evangelical religion or in any organized social reform. Dickens' literary style is also a mixture of fantasy and realism. His satires of British aristocratic snobbery—he called one character the "Noble Refrigerator"—are often popular. Comparing orphans to stocks and shares, people to tug boats, or dinner-party guests to furniture are just some of Dickens' acclaimed flights of fancy.

Dickens is not especially known for the construction of plot in his novels. There is in his novels often more than one minor thread of story beside the major one, and these threads are generally very loosely woven together. He seemed to love a complicated and involved plot. In fact, the plots of Dickens' mature works are always complex and complicated, crisscross with surprises and abound in grotesquery and melodrama. His plots were carefully constructed, and he often wove elements from topical events into his narratives.

In almost every one of Dickens' novels there is a happy ending, which points to the author's optimism which is an admirable thing for a Critical Realist because that means he still had his hopes after seeing the gloomy world all around him on the one hand and, as a petty-bourgeois intellectual, could not overstep the limits of his class on the other hand.

Dickens was essentially an intuitive artist. Spontaneity was his trade mark. Even when he became more conscious in his structural planning, he never lost this primal quality of his creative genius. Generally, his early works are more spontaneous than his later ones. Then, probably because his themes become more serious and probably as a result of his improved craft, his writings show more and more signs of conscious designing in conception, his plot interest thickens even more, and his talent at creating events and situations reveals itself at its best.

Dickens was also famous for his adroit use of language. On the whole he had a richness of expressions and generally succeeded in using the right words and phrases at the right moments for the right characters to attain the right effects.

24.2 William Makepeace Thackeray (1811 – 1893)

Thackeray was another representative of Critical Realism in the 19th-century England, second only to Dickens. He has been valued as a great social realist, moralist and satirist. He won due respect from many admirers and impacted quite a few distinguished writers in his lifetime. He wrote mainly about the upper and the upper-middle society, but he touched upon the life of the poor in some of his writings as well. He worked hard all through his career.

Thackeray's first literary success came with a series of satirical sketches entitled *The Snobs of England*, later collected under the title *The Book of Snobs* (1848). This book gives a satirical description of the ruling class in England. In the 1840s Thackeray already established his reputation as a good realistic writer. *Vanity Fair*, which marked the peak of his literary career, came out in 1847. This was followed by his two other important works of social criticism—*Pendennis* (1850) and *The Newcomes* (1855)—and his two historical novels—*Henry Esmond* (1852) and its sequel *The Virginians* (1859)—and other novels. His later works show a sign of weakening in ideological depth and artistic power.

Vanity Fair is Thackeray's masterpiece. Its title was taken from Bunyan's *The Pilgrim's Progress*. With the subtitle "A Novel without a Hero," the author probably intended not to portray individuals, but the bourgeois and aristocratic society as a whole. With scathing irony he exposed the vices of this society—hypocrisy, money-worship and moral degradation.

The story is set at the time of the Napoleonic Wars and gives a satirical picture of a worldly society, which Thackeray intended to be applied to his own times. The main plot centers on the story of two women—Amelia Sedley and Rebecca Sharp. Both of them are typical women in a bourgeois society, in sharply different ways. Rebecca Sharp is crafty, unscrupulous, resourceful, while Amelia Sedley is simple, sentimental, weak, but good at heart. The story begins with the departure of the two girls from their school in a London suburb, where they have studied for six years. Amelia is the daughter of a wealthy merchant, and Rebecca (Becky) is an orphan. Rebecca is determined to worm her way into the upper society at all costs. First she attempts to entrap Amelia's brother Joseph for a husband, but she fails. Then she manages to become governess in Sir Pitt Crawley's family. She soon gains the favor of her master, who is so captivated by her charm that he proposes to her after his wife dies. But Rebecca has to give up this good chance, because she has been already secretly married to the old man's younger son Rawdon, who has the bright prospect of inheriting his aunt's property. But Rawdon's aunt disinherits him on account of his marriage to a dowryless girl. So Rebecca's hopes of being married to a rich man are dashed.

Amelia is engaged to the dashing and self-obsessed Captain George Osborne, whose family are close to the Sedley family. Soon Amelia's father becomes bankrupt and George's rich father forbids George to marry Amelia, who is now poor. Since George and Amelia were raised in close company and were childhood sweethearts, George defies his father and gets married to Amelia. When the British troops are sent to the Continent, George goes to war and is killed in the battle of Waterloo. Amelia, left pregnant, returns to live in genteel poverty with her parents, spending her life in memory of her husband and care of her son. William Dobbin, George Osborne's best friend, has been in love with Amelia. After George's death, Dobbin pays for a small annuity for Amelia and expresses his love for her. But Amelia, who cannot forget about George, does not return Dobbin's love. Saddened, Dobbin goes with his regiment to India for many years.

Becky, after having Rawdon's son, continues her ascent first in post-war Paris and then in London where she is patronized by the rich and powerful Marquis of Steyne. She and Rawdon appear to be financially successful, but at the summit of their social success, Rawdon is arrested for debt. Becky does not bail him out, so he applies to his brother's wife. When he returns home, he finds Becky having an affair with Steyne, and divorces her. Then Becky leaves England and wanders the continent.

A few years later, Rebecca meets her former friend Amelia again. Amelia still holds the dear memory of her dead husband George. But Rebecca discloses an old secret. She shows Amelia a letter written to her by George. In his letter, George asks Rebecca to elope with him on the eve of the battle of Waterloo. Finally realizing that George was not the perfect man she always thought, Amelia agrees to marry Dobbin and returns to England. Becky and Amelia's brother Joseph now live together and stay in Europe until Joseph dies, leaving his property to her. At the end of the novel, Becky returns to England and tries to live there like a lady.

Superficially, *Vanity Fair* is concerned with the lives of the two major characters. However, the author did not just deal with their or anyone's individual lives. The two plotlines tell really separate stories touching on each other only tangentially. Thackeray kept afloat before him a larger narrative design than his story apparently warrants. It is the broad sweep of life, with all the dynamics and logistics associated with life, especially that around London, that the novel sees as its narrative focus. All individual experiences, however distinguished they are from the rest of the cast, all individual events, however significant in history or otherwise, all people who appear as major or minor figures—all details receive coverage not as isolated and particularized but as indispensable parts of a panoramic canvas, the Vanity Fair of the notorious 19th-century London. The novel presents a true-to-life picture of the upper class of England in the early decades of the 19th century and attacks the social relationship of the bourgeois world by satirizing the individual in the different strata of the upper society. It is a world where money grubbing is the main motive for all members of the upper class. Rebecca Sharp is a classic example of this money-grubbing instinct. Everyone wishes to gain something in the novel and acts almost in the same manner as Rebecca. The character of Rebecca Sharp is drawn with admirable skill.

The story is narrated in the third person. The third-person narrator as the author's identical surrogate acts omnisciently, privy to the most hidden part of his characters' soul, and keeping everything well under control. Nowhere else in the English novel has the third-person narrative achieved such a superb effect ever since Henry Fielding first theorized about it. The narration is interspersed with the authorial comments. The author kept popping up in the middle of the storytelling process to offer comments on the happenings of the moment. He came in either as "I" or as "we." Sometimes he would talk directly with the reader, addressing him as "you" often as if he was familiar with his audience, and betraying to him some confidential information on a character, a group, a scenario, or some gossip or popular opinion going around the social circles of London of the time.

Another feature concerning the narrative strategies of the novel is the smooth prose of a retrospective soliloquy. Thackeray was an eloquent discursive chatter. *Vanity Fair* reads like a long soliloquy, with the author looking around and recollecting, enveloping and submerging all people and incidents in an atmosphere of his choosing.

Like Dickens, Thackeray was one of the greatest Critical Realists of the 19th-century Europe. But, unlike Dickens who often employed the grotesque and the melodramatic and appeared sentimental in his novel writing, Thackeray firmly kept to social realism and took it upon himself to paint the immense panorama of real life. He painted life as he saw it. With his precise and thorough observation, and rich knowledge of social life and of the human heart, the pictures in his novels are accurate and true to life. To Thackeray the concern of the novel was solely with real life and real people.

Thackeray was a satirist. His satire was subtle and delicate but caustic and effective. He wished to offer chances for readers to tell the true from the sham. He kept his characters under scrutiny so that any deviation from accepted moral values or any antics of theirs would not escape his ironic, critical censure. In this sense, Thackeray was also a moralist. His aim was to produce a moral impression in all his novels. He made morality the topmost of his concerns. As his age was squeamish about certain subjects, he endeavored to conform to social convention and avoid offending the prevailing tastes. He inherited Fielding's social realism but rejected his "immorality." He regarded himself as a preacher crying out sermons for the world. This attitude won him admiration from his readers.

24.3 George Eliot (1819 – 1880)

George Eliot is the pseudonym of Mary Anne Evans, who was an English novelist, journalist and translator, and one of the three Victorian novelists representing the three phases of the period: Dickens the early phase, George the middle and Thomas Hardy the late. Eliot, essentially a pastoral novelist, represented the more somber and contemplative mode of perception of High Victorian period. One thing that made her so prominent is the fact that she incorporated most of the 19th-century ideas in her works. She was a great moralist, a great moral force for her time, and a philosophical novelist.

George Eliot used the male pen name, as she herself explained, to ensure her works would be taken seriously. Female authors were published under their own names in Eliot's time, but Eliot wanted to escape the stereotype of women only writing lighthearted romances. She also wished to have her fiction judged separately from her already extensive and widely known work as an editor and critic. An additional factor in her use of a pen name may have been a desire to shield her private life from public scrutiny and to prevent scandals attending her relationship with the married George Henry Lewes (1817 – 1878), with whom she lived for over 20 years.

George Eliot began her literary career with the completion in 1856 of her first piece of fiction, a long story titled "The Sad Fortunes of the Reverend Amos Barton," which was followed by two other stories—"Mr. Gilfil's Love Story" and "Janet's Repentance" (both published in 1857). The three were published together in one volume in 1858 under the title of *Scenes of Clerical Life*. *Adam Bede* (1859) is Eliot's first full-length novel and it was followed rapidly by *The Mill on the Floss* (1860) and *Silas Marner* (1861). These three novels deal chiefly with rural life, drawn from the author's own experience and observations in her earlier years in the country. In these works moral problems are discussed and psychological analyses of characters are emphasized. In 1871 – 72 appeared in installments *Middlemarch*, one of Eliot's last novels and a work of maturity, which is sometimes considered the author's greatest work. Eliot produced altogether seven novels, most of which are set in the provincial England and known for their realism and psychological insight.

Thematically, George Eliot was chiefly concerned with individual choices. Her characters are making choices in this or that way, and her plots develop with choices. Exploring the idea of the moral processes which man and his society go through in their development, Eliot studied the classes and individuals in relation to their environment and the effect that their interaction had on each other. It is her belief that the individuals have some limited freedom of will and that their choices define their personalities and their relationship to the controlling organic society. There are redemption, salvation, and reward and punishment for good or bad choices. Choices must be measured against a moral standard to see whether they contribute to the greatest good for the greatest number. There is pain involved in making the right choice. People live by the consequences of their actions; responsibility for a person's life and fate rests solidly with the individual. Individual growth should facilitate social evolution, and morality depends on the regulation of human feelings. Her emphasis on the individual has to do with her agnosticism: she did not know for sure whether there was a supreme being and where the reward or punishment came from. There was a strong hint of a broad determinism in George Eliot. She saw heredity as one factor affecting a person's life. With Eliot's writing the transition from Critical Realism to naturalism began in English literature.

Middlemarch*: A Study of Provincial Life* represents the Victorian realistic rather than emotional response to life. It is a novel with a panoramic view of the life of many persons of different types in an early 19th-century fictional English provincial town of Middlemarch. These many persons in the story form several different threads loosely linked with one another. In spite of the looseness of construction, the novel is George Eliot's great novel and altogether a superb demonstration of her solid realism because many characters of different types are vividly portrayed and many social problems are discussed in the course of portrayals of these characters, and one gets a broad realistic picture of the society in a provincial town, a miniature of the 19th-century England. Here the town booms, bustling with activity and going onward toward a hopeful future. Its spectrum of life is complete with all shades of feeling, all kinds of people, and all patterns of behavior. Virtue coexists with vice. Anachronistic pseudoscience lingers alongside the cutting-edge research of the day. All the segments of society interact; all the people mix and juxtapose. Life is vividly lived and characters of blood and flesh walk out of the pages to face the readers and audience.

The scene is laid during the years of the agitation immediately preceding the first Reform Bill. The principle thread of story has to do with Dorothea Brooke, an ardent, intelligent, idealistic young woman under the negligent though affable care of her eccentric uncle. Out of respect and love, Dorothea marries the middle-aged scholar Mr. Casaubon, but her exuberance is thwarted by Casaubon's "devotion" to his research and singular want of emotion. The marriage proves intensely unhappy; Dorothea realizes during a disastrous honeymoon in Rome that her husband's scholarly plans to write a great work, a "Key to all Mythologies," are doomed, as are her own aspirations to share and aid his intellectual life, and her respect for him gradually turns to pity. She is sustained by the friendship of Casaubon's young cousin Will Ladislaw, a lively, lighthearted, good-natured young man, detested by her husband. The two fall in love with each other but neither bares his/her heart. Nevertheless, Casaubon begins to suspect his wife of having questionable feelings for Ladislaw. Just before he dies, he adds a codicil to his will that his wife will lose her fortune if she marries Ladislaw. As a consequence, Dorothea renounces Casaubon's fortune. She and Ladislaw at last confess their love to each other and get married. In addition to the major plot, there are four other complimentary storylines, including the story of the young doctor Tertius Lydgate whose aspirations for scientific progress fail to materialize as a result of his marriage to the materialistic-minded Rosamond Vincy, the tale of old Mr. Featherstone who leaves nothing at death to his impatient expectant relatives, the story of Fred Vincy in love with Mary Garth, and that of the banker Bulstrode who is torn between his immoral business ethics and his religious spirit. Therefore the theme of the novel may be "egoism" and "frustration."

Adam Bede, George Eliot's first novel, was immediately acclaimed for its realism, for its picturesque portrayal of rural life, and for its humor. The plot was suggested by a story told to the author by her Methodist aunt Elizabeth Evans of a confession of child-murder made to her by a girl in prison. The action takes place at the end of the 18th century. The title character Adam Bede is a village carpenter, an honest young man, who is always ready to help the weak and the suffering. He falls in love with a village girl called Hetty Sorrel, pretty, vain and self-centered, the niece of the genial farmer Martin Poyser of Hall Farm. But the girl does not love him. She wishes that her husband would be rich and have high social position. So she gives her heart to a selfish young squire Arthur Donnithorne, who has no intention to marry her but just flirts with her. She is seduced and deserted by Arthur. Broken-hearted, the girl consents to marry Adam. But before the marriage, she finds that she is pregnant. She goes to look for Arthur. As she can't find him she leaves the baby in a wood and, later, returns to find it dead. So Hetty is arrested and put into prison for murdering the child. In prison she is visited and comforted by her cousin Dinah Morris, a young Methodist woman preacher, whose strong, serious and calm nature is contrasted with Hetty's throughout the novel. Dinah makes Hetty repent. Hetty's sentence is commuted to transportation and a few years later she dies on her way home. Then Adam discovers that Dinah loves him; his brother Seth, who has long and hopelessly loved Dinah, resigns her to him unselfishly. At the end of the novel Adam and Dinah are united.

In this novel, George Eliot portrayed two pairs, Arthur and Hetty on the one hand, and Adam and Dinah on the other. The first are described to be always thinking of their own interest without any consideration of others, while the second are praised for their high moral principles which guide their conduct for the good of others and of themselves. *Adam Bede* shows that George Eliot was influenced by bourgeois positivism.

The Mill on the Floss is a tragic book about the tragic lives of the people made tragic by their time. It evolves around the tragic story of a brother and a sister, Tom and Maggie, who are children of an ignorant and obstinate but honest well-to-do miller Mr. Tulliver. Tom is a prosaic youth, narrow of imagination and intellect, animated by conscious rectitude and a disposition to control others. Maggie is, in contrast, highly strung, intelligent, emotional, and, as a child, rebellious. From this conflict of temperaments, and from Maggie's frustrate sense of purpose, spring much of her unhappiness and the ultimate tragedy. Several years later, Maggie grows into a beautiful girl and falls in love with a young man called Philip Wakem, the deformed son of a neighboring lawyer. The lawyer is the object of Mr. Tulliver's suspicion and dislike, which develop into hatred when Tulliver is made bankrupt as a result of litigation in which the lawyer is on the other side. Tom, loyal to his father, learns of their secret meetings, interferes and makes Maggie promise not to see Philip any more. There comes dissension between brother and sister. Then one day, Maggie is going to visit her cousin Lucy. On her way, she meets Lucy's suitor Stephen. When they go boating on the Floss, the young man, attracted by Maggie's beauty, asks her to marry him. Maggie rejects him. Tom hears of the matter. He suspects that his sister has been making love with Lucy's lover Stephen. So he drives Maggie out of the house, and the girl is ostracized by the society of St. Ogg's. She and her mother take refuge with a loyal friend of her childhood. Only Lucy, Philip and the clergyman Dr. Kenn show sympathy. The situation seems without issue, but in the last chapter a flood descends upon the town, and Maggie, whose first thought is of her brother's safety, courageously comes back in a boat to rescue him from the mill. There is a moment of recognition and reconciliation before the boat overturns, and both, locked in a final embrace, are drowned.

The Mill on the Floss is autobiographical in a sense. Maggie's attending an evangelical school and her alienation from her brother are both directly borrowed from the author's own life. George Eliot attended one such school at 13 and infuriated her brother later in life when she started keeping house with George Henry Lewis without a formal marriage ceremony. She might have written the novel to please her brother and offer reconciliation with her apology.

The characterization of Maggie and Tom reveals Eliot's mature craftsmanship as a conscious artist. Maggie is a token of Eliot's success in creating one of the full-scale heroines in the English novel. The girl is described to be more like her father, proud, obstinate, "that pitiable, furious bull entangled in the mesh of a net." Always feeling the constraints, she looks like a lovely wild animal and is natural in her responses, but with the restrictive influence of St. Ogg's society, she is losing her native endowments. Life is so dreary and humdrum that there is not much that Maggie can do but dream and romanticize herself out of it. In Maggie, we can see the author's moral principles, but her tragedy shows the irreconcilability of a gifted and noble-minded personality with the bourgeois reality represented by the dull and narrow-minded persons. Described to be more like his mother, Tom is quite different from Maggie. He is conventional and works with numbers rather than with imagination and feelings. He honors respectability and fits in with the Victorian system of values. His life is an emotional vacuum. Eager for success and social arrival, he conforms, craves for approval and works hard. Rigid, insensitive, relentless, and capable of cruel behavior, he has no sign of warmth and understanding in him. His heart seems hardened, either as a hereditary trait, or as a result of seasoning by the cold reality of life.

The two opposite characters represent the antithesis between two important faculties of the human mind: the imaginative and the rational. The contrast may serve to make a statement about the Victorian life that society encourages conformity and censures dissent, that it values social arriving and despises uniqueness and difference, and that the life of imagination is useless, outrages public taste, and "brutalizes" social taste in general. The contrast may also reveal the author's ambivalence. On the one hand, Eliot admired Maggie for what she is, her whims, her daydreams and fantasies, and her asceticism and self-renunciation. On the other hand, she seemed to be interested in Tom's success story and tended to identify with Tom, whose values are more in agreement with the Victorian time. George Eliot might have the Victorian disapproval of art and imagination in mind in her painting of the two portraits. Her novel may have been an indication of her divided allegiances to her moral aesthetic and her private vision as a writer.

The contrast between country and town is also loaded with meaning. The mill on the river as a symbol offers food for thought. The adequate, detailed descriptions of the mill and the Tullivers illustrate the author's backward glance at the past and her longing for a pastoral, emotional life of the good old days. As a counterfoil to the country, the town of St. Ogg's is complacent and domineering. With its dominion it is a well-organized society with its rigid self-righteous values, always ready to jump at any deviations from their norm and lash out against dissent. Dull in mind and spirit, and utilitarian and anti-intellectual, St. Ogg's offers no room for the life of imagination, and readily smothers any tendency toward natural, emotional responses to life.

Silas Marner tells the story of a weaver called Silas Marner, who has been forced to leave his native town by a false charge of theft and settles in another village. Then he works very hard and earns a lot of gold. But his gold is stolen by the second son of Squire Cass, the town's leading landowner. For this he suffers a mental stupor. One cold winter evening, a baby girl crawls into his hut. Silas Marner adopts her. This gives a new meaning to his life. Sixteen years later, his adopted daughter grows up into a very beautiful girl, and is about to be married. The draining of a pond near his hut reveals the body of the squire's second son, with the stolen gold. The squire's elder son now acknowledges himself to be the father of the girl by a secret marriage, but the girl refuses to leave Silas Marner. They live happily together. As an outwardly simple tale of a linen weaver, the novel is notable for its strong realism and its sophisticated treatment of a variety of issues ranging from religion to industrialization to community.

George Eliot had a big heart. She could be ruthless in her criticism of human foibles and flaws, but she exhibited a high degree of tolerance and understanding. She felt that people were basically not bad, they were just weak, and she had a large-souled sympathy for the weak. No character of hers is a total villain without any virtue, there is really no grotesque in her works, and it is difficult to find a fussy scene in her writings.

George Eliot is regarded as a social historian. She saw the presentation of society in all its aspects and with all its segments as a novelist's legitimate province. The major events of the time and the major ideas of the period all found their way into her works. Evolution, religious revival such as the rise of evangelism, utilitarianism, positivism and agnosticism all get their share of space in her fictions. In addition, she wrote in earnest to record change. Many of her works were set in the past instead of being contemporaneous. She often felt strangely inspired by the recollections in their literary endeavors and found these highly expedient to help highlight the present.

George Eliot was basically a psychological realist and noted for her masterly psychological descriptions. She is accepted as the precursor of the psychological novel. In her intellectual meditations, she looked deep into the nature of social life and man's relationship to his localized conditions. To her the human milieu helps define human motivations and sheds light on the inner consciousness. She enjoyed detecting and explicating why people behave the way they do and do what they do.

George Eliot had rich humor and keen observation, and her characters are real men and women of her time. Her novels, for the most part, describe the rural life and deal with moral problems. She wrote very faithfully about the ordinary people like farmers, weavers and other handicraftsmen, and she fully realized that the working people like Adam Bede and Silas Marner were much better than the landed aristocracy. The women characters in George Eliot's works mostly enjoy happy endings. They either marry or become dependent on men. For as Eliot said on one occasion, the best a woman can do is to be a wife and mother. The way Eliot handled women's dilemma is exquisite and has won respect and admiration from the feminists.

Eliot's novels are very philosophical. The philosophy she preached is idealistic. She placed social classes and individual interaction under scrutiny, and made in-depth philosophical, intellectual deliberations. She believed that all contradictions of social life could be solved by converting mankind to the religion of humanity. Besides, George Eliot's prose is rich and flowing. As she was fond of painting, her style frequently shows the tableau effect.

24.4 The Bronte Sisters

Charlotte Bronte (1816 – 1855) was an English novelist and poet, and the eldest of the three Brontë sisters who survived into adulthood and whose novels have become classics of English literature. She produced four impressive novels—*The Professor* (1857), *Jane Eyre* (1847), *Shirley* (1849) and *Villette* (1853). Charlotte differed vastly from her sister Emily in inspiration and imagination. Whereas she was close to her age in values and technique, Emily went ahead of her time and transcended it in her concerns. Charlotte quoted her own experience faithfully as her novels all more or less walk directly out of her life, but Emily allowed her mind to take wild flights wherever its muses took it.

Jane Eyre, Charlotte's masterpiece, proved to be a great success from its first publication and has remained one of the most captivating stories across the world. It tells a fascinating story of suffering, love and growth. The heroine Jane Eyre is a penniless orphan and has been left to the care of her uncle Mr. Reed. Unfortunately, her uncle soon dies and she has to stay with her aunt Mrs. Reed at Gateshead Hall. Jane suffers immensely from the neglect and malice of her aunt's family, which eventually rouses Jane's defiant spirit. One day when a cousin knocks her to the floor she fights back. To punish her, Mrs. Reed sends her to the gloomy room where Mr. Reed has died. After experiencing a nervous breakdown and an emotional outburst, Jane is sent to a mental institution Lowwood Institution, where she first studies and then becomes a teacher. Later, Jane takes a job offer as a governess at Thornfield Hall and falls in love with Mr. Rochester, the owner of the Thornfield manor. But while they are about to hold their wedding ceremony in the church, Jane learns that Rochester has got a wife who is mad and locked in a private room. Shocked by the news, the sorely disappointed Jane leaves in disgust and despair, almost dies, and is picked up by the pious St. John Rivers and his sisters. With St. John's help, Jane gets the job of a teacher in a village school. But she finds herself in an emotional tug of war: torn between her love for Rochester and St. John. Then just as she is about to accept St. John's proposal and gets ready to go with him to India, she seems to hear a call coming across space from Rochester and goes back to Thornfield, only to find Rochester's manor all devastated in a fire that his mad wife has set on it and Rochester blinded in his attempt to save his wife in the fire. Jane and Rochester get married and begin a new chapter in their life. At the end of the story, Mr. Rochester's sight is partially restored and they live happily.

Jane Eyre is a typical Victorian book. Charlotte Bronte, like Dickens and Thackeray, gave us realistic pictures of the social life of the 19th century. The virtues and qualities that the novel tries to exemplify and disseminate are all of its age. These include society, family, morality, love and responsibility. One of the central themes of the book is the criticism of the bourgeois system of education. Another problem raised by Charlotte in the novel is the position of women in society. Jane Eyre maintains that women should have equal rights with men. Moreover, the world of *Jane Eyre* is still a moral universe where God is in heaven and all is well below. It is a world radically different from that of her sister's *Wuthering Heights*. There are abuses and manifestations of evil, but man is still spiritually strong enough to challenge and overcome these, and comes out winner. Individuals still possess the will to victory, and personal efforts still make a difference in one's life. She attacked the evils in the bourgeois society. But her realism was colored by the petty-bourgeois society. She believed that education was the key to all social problems, and that, by the improvement of the school system, most of the social evils could be removed. Hearth and home is still valued and love and devotion of a romantic nature still exist to enrich and revitalize the human existence.

The novel is basically autobiographical. Although she denied that Jane Eyre was like her, Charlotte Bronte did pour a great deal of her own experience into the story, such as the life at Lowood Institution and the life as a governess. Jane, like Charlotte, never succumbs to the forces trying to manipulate and hold her in leash. The sense of immediacy, the veiled success story of a self-made individual, the regenerating, ennobling power that lies hidden in the deepest recesses of both personalities—all these have endowed the story with eternal charm. Jane Eyre is Charlotte Bronte's means of recapping and reliving her own life in a vicarious manner.

The book is well remembered for its characterization. The portrayal of Jane Eyre particularly possesses an eternal appeal. The resilience of the human spirit and its indomitable nature as Jane exhibits break through the pages and keep its incredible hold on the imagination of the readers for all time. Jane is neither good-looking nor rich. She is in fact the first image of an ugly duckling in the English literary history. Her success story of rising from her poor social status fascinates readers immensely. In addition, *Jane Eyre* is unique in its gradual revelation of the rich and complex inner world of its heroine. Every incident centers on Jane's response and subsequent action, and is therefore colored heavily by the subjectivity of the forward-looking young woman.

The power of the story stems also from its description of the intensity of the human passion. Jane's warm and genuine passion touches the human heart in a peculiar way. The mutual attraction she and Rochester feel for each other is not so much romantic as it is based on the unique strength of character that they share. Jane's love for Rochester is based on her morality and integrity. It is by the sheer force of her passionate character that she conquers her readers as well as Rochester and St. John Rivers. Rochester, cynical, arrogant and swashbuckling, tends to put people off when he first appears. He may have been a dissolute rake. However, under such a calm appearance hides an eternally fervent heart. Rochester falls in love with the governess and the two get close and married in the end. It is the emotional intensity of the relationship that holds them together and enthralls readers.

The story is told in the first person singular. The first-person narrative exhibits the Victorian intimacy between the writer and the reader, and makes the story successfully attract its readers. The narrator tells the story in a tone expecting agreement every step of the way. The story, told chronologically, reads like an enchanting five-act play with the different phases of Jane's life well represented in Gateshead, Loowood, Thornfield, Norton and Ferndean. Each of these chains up with and leads naturally to the next, the links being forged by a subtle amalgam of Jane's passion and reason. Each and every one of these phases constitutes some test of her personality and all work toward painting her full portrait in some helpful way. There is a continual atmosphere of suspense keeping the readers riveted on the anxious lookout for what may lie down the road. And all through the diverse periods of Jane's life, there is the single presiding consciousness, that of Jane's, that ensures the unity of the narrative and the totality of its vision and effect.

The appeal of the novel, to some extent, comes from Jane's emotional dilemma, which is a permanent attraction for the reader. Jane is pulled apart between two extremes of the human emotional spectrum: the explosive physical and sexual energy of Rochester and the gentle but equally coercive spiritual sublimity of St. John Rivers. Both offer irresistible attraction, but meet with her rejection. Though St. John's spiritual and rational appeal eventually loses out to the prodigious physicality and the vibrant earthliness that Thornfield and Rochester represent, it is in fact a changed, more balanced, spiritually regenerated Rochester that draws Jane back to the fallen garden of an ancient manor-house. For Jane, reason is in harmony with passion.

The novel is also characterized by symbolism. The whole story reads like a fairy tale. One may call it Cinderella story or another Bunyan allegory. The story is immensely enriched by its apt use of symbols. For instance, the sun and the moon, representing the male and female principles respectively, associate closely with Rochester and Jane, and the two planets meet at Ferndean as the two people do. In addition, the Gothic atmosphere, the melodramatic elements, the juxtaposing of the prudent with the unscrupulous, and of virtue with sin, and the extremes of religious devotion and secularism—all these serve to help achieve the artistic effect of the novel admirably well.

Emily Bronte (1818 – 1848) was a novelist and poet, and the second eldest of the three Bronte sisters who survived into adulthood and whose novels have become classics of English literature. She is chiefly remembered for her only novel *Wuthering Heights* (1847), one of the best novels in English literature.

Wuthering Heights "violated" Victorian values and tastes and spoke ahead of its time. It tells a story of tragic love. Wuthering Heights is the name of a grange in a mountainous area. The hero Heathcliff, a gypsy foundling, is picked up by Mr. Earnshaw, the owner of the grange, on the way home and brought up together with his own children. When Mr. Earnshaw dies, his son Hindley bullies and insults Heathcliff. He drives him from their company to the servants' and compels him to work hard out of doors. Heathcliff and Catherine, the daughter of the family, have loved each other since their childhood. But their pure love is crushed by the brother Hindley, because he considers it a shame on the family to let a gipsy marry his sister. Unable to bear the insult, Heathcliff leaves Wuthering Heights and joins the army. Three years later, he becomes a wealthy man and comes back, only to find that his sweetheart has already been married to young Edgar Linton of another farm, Thorncross Grange. He goes to see Catherine and revives her old flame for him but torments her ruthlessly, taking advantage of Edgar's sister Isabella's innocent love for him. In the meantime, he stays with Hindley at Wuthering Heights, tricks him into gambling, and encourages him to slide to alcoholism. Soon Hindley loses his farm out to Heathcliff and dies miserably, leaving his son, young Hareton, behind. Catherine's emotional upheaval causes the premature birth of her daughter Cathy and sends the mother to her early grave. Deserted by Heathcliff, Isabella ends up giving birth to a weakling son Linton, sends him back to her brother, and dies. Heathcliff sends his man over to claim his son, Little Linton, and take him back to Wuthering Heights. Ten years later, Heathcliff takes revenge upon the younger generation. He treats Hareton very cruelly and compels Cathy to marry his own sickly son Linton. After Edgar dies in misery, Heathcliff successfully owns two properties. However, with the death of Heathcliff's only son, the widowed Cathy falls in love with Hareton. Although Heathcliff tries to destroy the love between them, Hareton and Cathy get united after Heathcliff dies. Thus Heathcliff's lifetime revenge turns out to be futile and meaningless.

The chief charming of *Wuthering Heights* lies in the psychic complexities of the two major characters, Catherine and Heathcliff. The author managed to dive into the innermost recesses of the human soul, find the most clandestine of all human psychic secrets, and locate it as a confused bundle of psychic energy, or what Sigmund Freud defined as "instinctive impulse" or id. She recognized this as the fountain of all human physical and spiritual vitality, and succeeded in giving it form in the description of the irrational, mysterious, and hidden features of the two major characters. Although it may be read as a story of revenge, a story that the maltreated poor Heathcliff struggles and schemes to get even with his wealthy oppressors and succeeds, the novel is essentially a conventional mode of addressing a mystery, and not tenable enough to explain the tragic end of Heathcliff. He never feels any gratification at the defeat of his enemies and never gloats over his trophies. All worldly gains seem to be beside the point to him. He loves Catherine with all his heart and soul, even after she gets married to Linton. However, he takes advantage of Isabella's innocence and love for him and elopes with her and makes her pregnant. He knows well that his lost love is never retrievable, but cannot offer himself or Catherine a peaceful life. Heathcliff is a perpetual loser. Catherine lives in a state of confusion. At first, she does not know whom she should marry—she loves the "dirty," unkempt Heathcliff dearly at the bottom of her heart, but feels drawn to the gentle, cultured life of the Lintons. Then she becomes the young mistress of Thorncross Grange, but never feels happy without Heathcliff around. In effect, the two characters appear often as if stripped naked and revealing their native essence to a bewildered world. In Heathcliff, one cannot find any trace of knowledge of human values. He hates concepts like duty, humanity, pity, or charity, and is absolutely disgusted with tradition and morality. He quarrels with God for depriving him of his beloved and needs no Christian burial after his death. Catherine, though educated and acquainted with human values and tastes like decency, compassion and occasional conformity with accepted morality, is every bit as wild and wayward as her surroundings and goes way beyond the pale of the established norms while she is her right self. They both are children of nature and represent the archetypal, elemental forces of existence, and body forth emotional abstractions. With the two dominating the lives of the people on the granges, everybody else is torn between the natural and supernatural and distorted so that they appear to be perverts and grotesques. To some extent, it is the major characters' love, hate and suffering, which often assume superhuman and supernatural proportions, that the novel appeals to its readers for ever.

Wuthering Heights paints a veritable portrait of an amoral universe. It is a world of man, not of God. Although religion and worship are touched upon, they appear to be distorted and even discredited. Nature here is no longer quite as Wordsworth saw it. It appears to be indifferent, self-sustaining, roughly resembling the one that Coleridge first delineated in "The Rime of the Ancient Mariner." In the meantime, it is the scramble and squabble between human beings that take the center stage of the narrative. All the Victorian virtues such as money, class and love are presented in a non-Victorian, highly idiosyncratic way. God seems to have forgotten this nook of His world, and there is nothing that can be seen as the frame of reference. The novel is not about who is right and who is wrong. For matters pertinent to right or wrong belong to a world upon which God still smiles. Emily Bronte spoke ahead of her time and the Zolan naturalist idea of the amoral universe works differently from the Victorian temper.

The narrative strategy is also worth mentioning. The story stretches over a period of thirty years but the narrative covers only about the events of the last year of Heathcliff's life and fleshes out the details of the previous years' life at the grange through Nelly's flashbacks. These flashbacks, along with Lockwood's third-person-narration and Victorian common-sense comments or questions, present readers a double perspective, mutually complimenting, and providing an additional avenue of reading and looking at the story. The strategy also proffers a good deal of leeway for the author to maneuver and manipulate so as to achieve the superb effect of juxtaposing the past with the present and footnoting the behaviors which might have been difficult to understand. In addition, *Wuthering Heights*, along with *Jane Eyre*, brings to the novel the introspection and an intense concentration on the inner life of emotion which before them was the province of poetry alone.

Anne Bronte (1820 – 1849), the youngest sister of the three Brontë sisters, was also a novelist and poet. She published two novels and a volume of poetry titled *Poems by Currer, Ellis, and Acton Bell* (1846), a collaborative work with her sisters. Her first novel *Agnes Grey* (1847) is based upon her own experiences as a governess, while her second and last novel *The Tenant of Wildfell Hall* (1848) is considered to be one of the first sustained feminist novels. Like her poems, both her novels were first published under the masculine penname of Acton Bell. Since Anne's novels are not so good as those by her two elder sisters, space lacks here for a detailed introduction to her.

24.5 Elizabeth Gaskell (1810 – 1865)

Elizabeth Cleghorn Gaskell, often referred to simply as Mrs. Gaskell, was an English novelist and short story writer. Mrs. Gaskell was an active humanitarian and the message of several of her novels was the need for social reconciliation, for better understanding between employers and workers, between the respectable and the outcasts of society. She was a keen observer of human behavior and speech, among both industrial workers in Manchester and farming and country-town communities, and a careful researcher of the background and technicalities of her novels. She had a natural gift for storytelling, although she was at first uncertain in plot creation and given to melodramatic devices.

Mrs. Gaskell was one of the first English writers to describe in a novel the class struggle between the workers and the capitalists in "the Hungry Forties." Her novels offer a detailed portrait of the lives of many strata of society, including the very poor, and are of interest to social historians as well as lovers of literature. Living in Manchester, the center of British industry then, Mrs. Gaskell had a firsthand knowledge of the conditions of the working class, on which her first novel *Mary Barton* (1848) focuses. Gaskell also wrote a humorous novel called *Cranford*

(1853), which gives an account of the small affairs of a country village Cranford with sympathy, keen observation and humor, and thus presents a vivid picture of the provincial petty-bourgeois society.

In her later years, Mrs. Gaskell retreated from Critical Realism owing to her petty-bourgeois views of life and her inability to side with the revolutionary working class. Her novel *North and South* (1855) marked a turning point in her literary creation, for in this novel she abandoned Critical Realism for a kind of writing more acceptable to the bourgeois public. Besides, Mrs. Gaskell was a friend of Charlotte Bronte. Her *Life of Charlotte Bronte* (1857) is one of the best biographies in English literature.

Mary Barton: *A Tale of Manchester Life* is undoubtedly the author's best novel and one of the most important social novels of the 19th century. Severely criticized by bourgeois critics as a book hostile to the employers, the novel was admired by Carlyle and Dickens and translated into several languages, including Finnish and Hungarian. It offers a realistic description of the social and political life of that period. The theme here is the class struggle and conflicts between the workers and the capitalists. The background of the story is Manchester in the "Hungry Forties" and the acute poverty of the unemployed mill-hands. Mary Barton is the daughter of an active and embittered worker and trade unionist John Barton. She has attracted Henry Carson, son of one of the employers, and, flattered by his attentions and the hope of a grand marriage, has repulsed in his favor her faithful admirer Jem Wilson, a young engineering worker. A group of workmen, exasperated by the failure of the employers to consider their grievances, decide to kill young Carson, who has mocked their attempts to reach an understanding, as a warning to his class, and the lot falls on Barton to do the deed. When Carson is shot dead, suspicion falls on Jem Wilson since Carson was his rival. So Jem is arrested. Mary, who has by now realized that it is Jem whom she loves, discovers that her father is the real murderer. She is now faced with having to save her lover without giving away her father. She travels to Liverpool to find Will Wilson, Jem's cousin and a sailor, who was with him on the night of the murder. Will arrives in court to testify, and Jem is found guiltless. Crushed by his remorse, John Barton confesses to the fiercely vindictive old father of Henry Carson, wins his forgiveness and dies soon afterwards in his arms. At the end of the novel, Mary and Jem get married and have a little child.

In this novel, Mrs. Gaskell showed great sympathy for the workers. She highly praised the workers' struggle against the capitalists. But, like Charles Dickens, she had her own limitation. Her petty-bourgeois philanthropy made her look for means of reconciliation between the working class and the bourgeoisie.

24.6 George Meredith (1828 – 1909)

Meredith was an English novelist and poet. All his life, he kept writing and published a number of poems and novels. He wrote mainly about the life of the polite society with some interest in the portrayal of the inner world of man. With psychological analysis he exposed the faults and prejudices of the upper class. Like most of his contemporaries, Meredith was a moralist of a kind. He portrayed a world of moral choice, in which man is at least partly in control and life is still changeable at will. That shows the optimistic spirit he felt about his time. To him, effort and exertion are honorable and body forth the highest of moral duties. Courage is virtue and weakness sin. People should take care of their own lives. So, like George Eliot, Meredith was a realist and psychologist; but unlike George Eliot who used tragedy to teach a moral lesson, Meredith depended more upon comedy, making vice not terrible but ridiculous.

As a bourgeois intellectual, Meredith assumed an attitude of objectivism, which plays an important part in his novels. He constructed a type-man as a hero, and made this type express his purpose and meaning. So his characters seldom speak naturally as George Eliot's do; they are more like Browning's characters in packing a whole paragraph into a single sentence or an exclamation. In terms of the craft of fiction, Meredith tended to talk and tell instead of letting his characters reveal themselves. For instance, he made frequent speeches in *The Egoist* about Willoughby's thought and action, but failed to place the hero on stage to act out his own drama. As a result, Willoughby becomes a flat character and a one-dimensional image and as such leaves little or no impression after his story is closed. This can be one of the weaknesses that have affected Meredith's permanence. As a bourgeois intellectual, Meredith also agreed with the other realists like Charles Dickens that the capitalist society would bring human beings into a dead end; he could not find a proper solution to the social problems. He completely inherited Thackeray's tradition and sarcastically described the upper class of the English society.

However, Meredith's works meet with popular neglect and indifference. The first reason may be that Meredith was not very easy to read. This is especially true to his later works when his financial security allowed him to ignore public tastes and write as he pleased. His vocabulary becomes more fastidious, his syntax more sophisticated, and his symbolism more deliberate and idiosyncratic. His characterization may be another reason—the readers do not often see dynamic, vivacious and endearing characters in his works.

Meredith's main novels include *The Shaving of Shagpat* (1856), *The Ordeal of Richard Feverel* (1859), *Beauchamp's Career* (1875) and *The Egoist* (1879), of which the last is Meredith's best and more carefully planned than his other novels, superior in strength and brilliance.

The Egoist describes how a self-centered aristocrat skillfully wins others' sympathy and love, and exposes how, under the influence of bourgeois individualism and egoism, man's soul is corrupted. The work is well known for its deep psychological analysis of the characters. The hero, the Egoist himself, is Baronet Willoughby Patterne, rich and handsome, with a high position in the country, but totally blind to his own arrogance and to the needs of the women he loves. Laetitia Dale, an intelligent young woman past her first bloom, has loved Willoughby for many years, and his vanity has been flattered. But he ignores Laetitia's devotion and proposes to Constantia Durham, who soon finds out his selfish nature and jilts him. Thus humiliated, Willoughby tries to win and marry Clara Middleton. Clara, bewitched by Willoughby's charm and surroundings, becomes engaged to him, but soon perceives his intention of directing and molding her. Then she attempts to free herself from the entanglements of the engagement, which forms the main theme of the book. Clara envies but cannot emulate Constantia, and Willoughby struggles frantically against an incredible second jilting. Clara is meanwhile seeing more and more of Vernon Whitford, a poor and earnest young scholar. Willoughby feels the threat and proposes to Laetitia, who rejects him out of pride. Then Clara marries the scholar. With this additional humiliation, Willoughby persists and eventually wins the hand of Laetitia.

The theme of will runs through the whole novel. Willoughby possesses a strong self-will. He must be in control. His is a will that enslaves and ensnares others and makes life difficult for others. Clara has her own will, too. It seems fragile, but it knows what it wants. It finally asserts and frees itself from its fetter. Like Clara, the other people in Willoughby's world do not submit to his and anybody's will willingly, either. They struggle to extricate themselves from control and achieve self-growth. Thus will and choice abound in Meredith's fictional world.

24.7 Samuel Butler (1835 – 1902)

Butler was an English novelist and essayist who published a variety of works. He was so learned and was interested in so many things such as religion, revolution, Italian culture, biology, classical studies and biography that he epitomized the explosive intellectual energy of the Victorian period. The multitude of his writings reveals that he was mostly concerned with the notion of evolution and the Christian faith. Most of Butler's works are essays. He made prose translations of the *Iliad* and *Odyssey*, which remain in use to this day. Butler's novels include *Erewhon* (1872), *Erewhon Revisited* (1901) and *The Way of All Flesh* (1903), which criticize the bourgeois society from the viewpoint of a bourgeois intellectual. His novels are imbued with pessimism. They are the remarkable achievements of the English realistic literature at the end of the Victorian age. Except Hardy, no other writer exposed the capitalist system more mercilessly than Butler. Butler pointed out that bourgeois morality and its whole life system would lead to the corruption of human beings. As a matter of fact, he was an excellent psychological novelist and gave minute descriptions of what his characters say or do. As a literary figure, Butler is also remembered for his use of antiphrasis in his writings.

Erewhon is a satirical work, with the European countries, especially England, as its butt. The word "Erewhon" is an anagram of "nowhere." The narrator Higgs crosses a range of mountains and comes upon the undiscovered country of Erewhon. He is first thrown into jail, where he is helped by his beautiful girl jailer Yram (the anagram of Mary). In his release he is lodged with Mr. Nosnibor (the anagram of Robinson) and his family. In this society morality is equated with health and beauty, and crime with illness. The Unborn select their parents, who have to endure their selection. The Musical Banks produce a currency which is venerated but not used. The development of machinery, which had at one stage threatened to usurp human supremacy, had led to a civil war and is now forbidden. The country is ruled by so-called philosophers and prophets, who are merely faddists and fanatics. When he is threatened with prosecution for contracting measles, the narrator announces that he will visit the air-god and end the terrible drought; with Nosnibor's daughter, he escapes in a balloon to England and gets married to her.

The Way of All Flesh, Butler's masterpiece and semi-autobiographical novel published posthumously, tells a story about the Pontifex family over a stretch of four generations. The narrator is a family friend named Overton, who knows the family history well. The story is a family chronicle written by the narrator. Old Mr. Pontifex expects to make his son George a publisher, which he succeeds. When he becomes the head of the household, George would like his son Theobald to be a clergyman. The young man resists in vain as the father threatens to disown him, and ends up becoming one. When Theobald receives his own living, he is chosen by Christina, one of the daughters of an old clergyman, and marries her. They have three children. Ernest is the youngest and his story takes up most of the space of the book. Young Ernest is mistreated both at home by his father and in school by his tyrannical schoolmaster. Physically weak and mentally moody, the lonely boy receives attention from his kind aunt Althea, who decides to get to know whether the boy deserves her legacy after she leaves the scene. Althea leaves her money secretly with her friend Edward Overton, who henceforth becomes Ernest's "guarding angel." With Althea around,

Ernest begins to develop his own personality. When in college he meets a humbug and is cheated out of his inheritance from his grandfather. It is also there that he gets involved in a charge of assault and serves a prison term. On his release Ernest plunges into a disastrous union with Ellen, the frivolous maid of his father's house; and they get engaged in tailoring and running a shop. However, in due course Ernest discovers that Ellen is both a bigamist and an alcoholic. Overton at this point intervenes and pays Ellen a stipend, and she happily leaves for America. By that time Ernest and Ellen have already had two children. Afraid that he might mistreat his own kids, Ernest arranges for them to be taken care of in a loving home. He becomes a bachelor, and, with the money his aunt Alethea leaves to him, devotes himself to literature and writes well in a London flat.

Brilliant with wit and irony, the novel mainly tells the story of Ernest—his unhappy childhood, the hypocrisy of his parents, his learning of scholasticism in a school, his profession as a hypocritical clergyman, his love for a girl, his failure in literary pursuits, his flat life after marrying a worldly woman, and his happy and comfortable life after he accidentally gets legacy from his aunt. The theme of money runs through the whole novel. The hero's father thinks that money is the most sacred thing given by God. The hero notices that people around him are all anxious to get money. The hero himself also has a strong desire to become rich and wealthy.

The Way of All Flesh is a typical Victorian book. First, the name of the major character, Ernest, represents one important Victorian feature of life: there was a good deal of earnestness then, especially on the part of the thinking segment of the population. Then there is the importance of the family which was considered as another prominent feature of Victorian life: life was so challenging and confusing that the Victorians found hearth and home a sanctuary to retreat to after an impossible day. In addition, the book reveals the widespread influence of the theory of evolution on people's lives then. Butler was at odds with the theory of natural selection which he considered as "bad human philosophy." He stressed the effects of conscious striving and the formation of habits as a process of continuous transmission of memory from generation to generation. This became the core of his "unconscious memory." Butler's ideas on evolution included "habit as inherited memory" and "cunning," or will, or striving in lieu of the blind chance of the Darwinian "natural selection." He could not conceive of a universe where man is passive and has no power to shape his own life. In his opinion, man is creative, learns to be master of his environment, and passes his effort on to the next generation as part of a sustained human upward. In *The Way of All Flesh*, there is the inherited habit, the effect of the will, and the link between generations through unconscious memory. The older Pontifexes are depicted so as to illustrate the importance of heredity. Ernest grows to be a replica of his great-grandfather, but manages to go beyond that. He goes through phases of growth. As a product of heredity, he is frustrated with his life and driven by desire to move forward. But he fails all the way, picks up wisdom through trails and errors, and achieves maturity as a distinct moral, ethical being. He exemplifies Butler's theory that the human will shapes human life, and striving ensures the onward progress of human evolution. Furthermore, the novel is characterized by the religious doubt and the problem involving faith. Ernest, in his painful growing up, shares actually all the doubts of his creator such as his skepticism about resurrection.

Last but not the least, *The Way of All Flesh* expresses the author's bitter hatred for the hypocritical morality and constitutes a ruthless attack on what has later come under fire—Victorianism—with its hypocrisy, self-righteousness, self-deception, and its moral degeneration. That is why Butler may also be considered as the first anti-

Victorian.

24.8　Thomas Hardy (1840 – 1928)

Hardy was an English novelist and poet and one of the representatives of English Critical Realism at the turn of the 19th century. A Victorian realist in the tradition of George Eliot, he was influenced both in his novels and in his poetry by Romanticism, especially by William Wordsworth. Hardy was also greatly influenced by Charles Dickens, like whom, he was highly critical of much in the Victorian society, though he focused more on a declining rural society.

Hardy began his literary career with poetry. He wrote poetry throughout his life and regarded himself primarily as a poet. However, he gained fame as a novelist initially. His first collection of poetry did not come out until 1898 when almost all of his fictional works had been published. His poetry was not as well received during his lifetime. It was rediscovered in the 1950s, when the author's poetry had a significant influence on the Movement poets of the 1950s and 1960s, including Philip Larkin.

Hardy himself divided his novels and short stories into three groups: romances and fantasies, novels of ingenuity, and novels of character and environment (also called Wessex novels). He classified as his first series *A Pair of Blue Eyes* (1873), *The Trumpet Major* (1880), *Two on a Tower* (1882), *A Group of Noble Dames* (1891, a collection of short stories) and *The Well-Beloved* (1892 – 97), while those works like *Desperate Remedies* (1871), *The Hand of Ethelberta* (1876), *A Laodicean* (1881) and *A Changed Man, The Waiting Supper and Other Tales* (1913, a collection of short stories and novelettes) were put in the second group.

The last and most significant group includes *Under the Greenwood Tree* (1872), *Far from the Madding Crowd* (1874), *The Return of the Native* (1878), *The Mayor of Casterbridge* (1886), *The Woodlanders* (1887), *Wessex Tales* (1888, a collection of short stories), *Tess of the D'Urbervilles* (1891), *Life's Little Ironies* (1894, a collection of short stories) and *Jude the Obscure* (1896). Among them the best known should be *Tess of the D'Urbervilles* and *Jude the Obscure*. The stories in this group are all set in the semi-fictional region that Hardy named Wessex, and have become known as the "Wessex novels." Hardy's Wessex, based on the medieval Anglo-Saxon kingdom, eventually came to include the counties of Dorset, Wiltshire, Somerset, Devon, Hampshire and much of Berkshire, in southwest and south central England. As these novels all relate to the life of this one particular region, Hardy started off the tradition of "regional novels." All of these books, of great quality and high seriousness, pushed the author to the forefront of the later 19th-century fiction, and placed him among the supreme masters of fiction in world literature. They are all tragedies of a kind, which explore tragic characters struggling against their passions and social circumstances, and in which Hardy truthfully depicted the impoverishment and decay of small farmers. These laborers are mercilessly exploited by the rich land owners. Hardy was sad to see the decline of the patriarchal mode of life in rural England. This is one of the reasons for the growing pessimism in his novels, which shows that mankind is subjected to the rule of some hostile and mysterious fate.

Hardy published 40 short stories, most of which were collected in the four collections mentioned above—*Wessex Tales*, *A Group of Noble Dames*, *Life's Little Ironies* and *A Changed Man, The Waiting Supper and Other Tales*. The stories vary considerably in content, form and style, and in many cases demonstrate a high degree of skill, but

Hardy's reputation in this field has never approached his reputation as a novelist or poet.

Tess of the D'Urbervilles: A Pure Woman Faithfully Presented is the most pastoral of Hardy's novels. Its plot centers on the tragic occurrences of the title character's life. Tess comes from a farmer's family, the Durbeyfields. Her father learns one day that they are the descendants of the ancient family, the D'Urbervilles, and forces her to go in contact with Alec D'Urberville, a wealthy villain, in quest of the family genealogy. Before long Tess is seduced by Alec and gives birth to a child, who dies soon. In order to support the family, Tess goes out to find work on a dairy farm, where she meets Angel Claire. The two fall in love with each other and become engaged. On their wedding-night, the honest girl confesses to her husband that she has been seduced by a man and given birth to a child. Her husband cannot accept the fact, so he abandons her and goes abroad. Then Alec takes advantage of the Durbeyfields' poverty and continues to harass Tess. Again to support the family, Tess gives in and lives with Alec. Some years later, Angel returns and wants Tess to come back to him. Tess then murders Alec and runs away with Angel. They manage to hide for a while in a wood before they come to Stonehenge, where she is arrested. Tess is hanged later. The novel is a classic Aristotelian tragedy. The tragedy of Tess not simply exposes the wickedness of the oppressors represented by Alec but also condemns the hypocritical moral of the society. More importantly, Hardy expressed his sympathy for the poor people represented by Tess and her family.

What dominates the world of *Tess of the D'Urbervilles* is "fate," "destiny" or "chance" as it is variously called. The novel represents the forces beyond human control but controlling the lives of the humans. It emphasizes predestination, whose design of darkness no amount of human effort can alter. The work offers cogent proof that chances play a significant part in Hardy's fictional world. Chances serve to illustrate a pattern of cosmic behavior, i. e. to stand ever opposed to individual endeavors and do all in its power to thwart them. For Hardy this "cosmic irony" decides the fact that there would be only eternal misery in life and no hope for a better eventuality. The spirit of determinist defeatism soaks all the way throughout the story.

Tess of the D'Urbervilles reflects the spirit of the age. It is set in a period when modern civilization starts to encroach the pastoral village life. Agriculture and dairy farms are being replaced, and the railway threatens the existence of the village—the backbone of rural life. The spread of literacy (Tess speaks two dialects), the presence of the threshing machine, and the way Londoners handle milk are just some of the indicators of the outside world impinging upon the pastoral scene. The plains are darkening. Nature stops being benevolent and caring, and so does God. Life becomes cold and indifferent, man's ethical being dwindles, and humans are as powerless as are so many flies. In this condition they struggle in vain to survive. As the sword of Fate hangs over the Durbeyfields from the very beginning, Tess' tragedy is an inevitable ending.

Tess of the D'Urbervilles is one of a series of books about women by men, all of which could be called "feminist"—*Madame Bovary* (1857) by Flaubert (1821 – 1880), *Anna Karenina* (1878) by Tolstoy, *Maggie: A Girl of the Streets* (1893) by Stephen Crane (1871 – 1900) and *Sister Carrie* (1900) by Theodore Dreiser (1871 – 1945). Among those men's works written about the lot of women in western culture during the time between the mid-19th century and the First World War, *Tess of the D'Urbervilles* is one of the best. Hardy himself thought of it as his best novel.

The characterization of the novel is also worth mentioning. Tess incarnates the earth; Alec stands as its antagonist. The contrast and conflict between the two signifies the tension of the age. Tess is like a pagan goddess, a willow wand symbolic of pre-Christian fertility. She is all pastoral, almost a nature goddess, with her open nature, her impulses and her sensuality. Spontaneous and romantic, she is the veritable picture of eternal womanhood, femaleness, and tenderness and love. She represents the Arcadian tradition of rural life. Alec, on the other hand, is a product of the industrial age. He makes himself rich through money-lending and usury. Amoral, hard-headed and sexually aggressive, he has nothing in common with Tess. He is, if anything, whatever she is not in the final analysis. Their contact is tangential, i. e. no more than financial. One needs money and the other has it. Alec sees and seizes his opportunity when the Durbeyfields are in a bad shape. Thus his move toward Tess assumes the stature of a historical struggle between two ages and two lifestyles. He must spoil the natural beauty, and must break its token and spell—Tess. The city must invade the country, and the latter must give in and succumb.

Angel Claire can be obnoxious as a sexist rotter. He himself admits having an affair with a woman but could not forgive Tess for having been raped and borne a child, and therefore abandons her. Claire never once sees that his own affair with another woman is in any way comparable to young Tess' seduction by Alec. His highest concern is whether or not he will "forgive" Tess. He does so because he falls in love with his own romanticized ideal milkmaid, and condemns Tess for not being what he has dreamed. Like most of Hardy's characters, he has no choice; he is acting from his whole background and the character which it has developed. At the end, Claire redeems himself. He repents his abandonment of Tess and "forgives" her, and he will now, a sadder and wiser man, make a life with Tess' sister Liza-Lu as Tess hoped.

Jude the Obscure is Hardy's last but has been seen by many critics as his best novel. It is the most urban and most contemporaneous of all the novels by Hardy. Here the author indicted the class system and Christianity which Oxford represents in particular and probably also the institution of marriage. The book is so titled because it is about the life of a common person who is normally neglected and forgotten. Here is a specimen of Hardy's subtle irony. What he calls "the Obscure" turns out to be a typical Victorian. The novel is set in the backwater of Wessex, and, in the author's words, tells a story "of a deadly war between flesh and spirit," a frightful piece of incredible horrors, dealing symbolically with a period of serious dislocation at all conceivable levels of English life. Jude Fawley, a Wessex villager, is a stonemason with aspirations for Christminster (Hardy's coined name for Oxford) religious scholarship. His family has been under a curse that no marriage can end happily. Jude works and reads avidly. He meets Arabella Donn, a sexy country girl, and is tricked into marrying her. Soon Arabella deserts him. Jude finds work in Christminster and meets Sue Bridehead, his cousin. Sue has been a school teacher under principal Phillotson, who is physically repulsive and much older than Sue. Sue and Phillotson get married, but the unhappy woman leaves her husband and goes to Christminster, where she finds Jude. They fall in love with each other, get married and have children. The marriage proves repugnant to society, which ostracizes the two from normal social connections. Jude finds it difficult to get a job, and his hope to become a priest is dashed. Arabella resurfaces with their son, Father Time by name, and dumps him to Jude. Life becomes increasingly hard for the family. One night Jude and Sue go out, leaving Father Time to take care of his siblings, and come back only to find that Father Time has killed all the kids and then taken his own life. Sue is inconsolable. Believing that the family curse is at work, she goes back to Phillotson and reunites with him, feeling thoroughly subdued. The desperate Jude never recovers from the family tragedy. He falls seriously sick and dies wretchedly, not yet 30. Arabella alone wins out, triumphant and happy in a different surrounding.

Jude the Obscure is in fact Hardy's version of naturalism, which explains why morality does not appear as important in Hardy's as it is in George Eliot's works. The immense feeling of pessimism and grimness is one of the features of the novel that tells it apart from the traditional Victorian realist novels. No longer purely Victorian, it shows Hardy in the process of edging toward the modern novel, of which Kafka (1883 – 1924), Conrad, Joyce and Woolf represented the epitome. In this sense, the novel has been called a transitional one.

As is the case with *Tess of the D'Urbervilles*, *Jude the Obscure* is noted for its characterization, especially of the three major characters. The two women, Arabella and Sue, can be seen to embody the two aspects of Jude's nature. Arabella, almost a sex animal, is all flesh and desire whereas Sue, essentially bodiless, is all intellect and frigidity. Arabella is sometimes regarded as the true heroine of the novel as she seems to succeed and have the final word in the end. She reacts to life intuitively. The universe does not concern her; it is with living happily that she is solely preoccupied. She represents the highest degree of physicality. She keeps sidetracking Jude from his quest for goals of a higher order, and inadvertently helps to destroy him. She is the instrument of the vicious universe set on playing a cosmic joke upon the helpless human. It is, in fact, not her destroying Jude; it is the cosmic forces coupled with Jude succumbing to his baser instincts that kill him off. Her triumph and Jude's defeat prove that it is the "fittest to survive," which is a recurrent theme in Hardy.

Sue's problem is both personally and socially induced. She is well-educated, intelligent, and independent as she is trained to make a living for herself. She has an autistic, narcissistic soul which she needs to keep down to be happy with Jude. She is Jude's equal except that the man is too physical for her. Sex is on the whole detestable to her. Hardy portrays Sue as a kind of naked Venus, a specimen of purity and virginity, qualities to which her last name, Bridehead, offers cogent testimony. She is dammed as she is unable to come to terms with society. She is not a traditional woman; she is not the marrying type. She is a feminist of a kind. Her image represents the growth of a modern female self-awareness in the last few decades of the 19th century. She is probably the first modern woman to appear in English fiction. However, she gradually gives in, sets up house with Jude and has children. Her search together with Jude for meaning and value turns out to be circular: they end up where they first started. She, together with Jude, can be regarded as a precursor to modern existentialists.

Jude is one of the most complex characters in the 19th-century English fiction. The most primitive, the lowest socially of all Hardy's characters, and having the least heroic about him, he is nonetheless the stuff of a hero. He has dreams but is never able to fulfill them; he has talents but is never given recognition for them. Jude's failure proves a couple of notions of wide currency at the time: the theory of evolution, and the naturalistic thesis about man and his life. Jude's downfall is inevitable because of his lower instinctive impulses and his inability to strike a balance between reason and emotion. It is the result of the "deadly war between flesh and spirit" that rages in him. Jude is divided and hovers between the two of them and attracted to both at the same time. He becomes a lost soul in the cold wide world, with no place to belong in. With little free will, he is lonely, weak, and incapable of any self-defence. He is a rootless traveler through modern life, a modern existentialist. Jude has serious flaws in his personality. His judgment is not sound; he fails to understand the nature of the universe and its motives and stumbles along and keeps making the wrong choices. The diagnosis of his tragedy is an interesting psychological study of human nature. His is a case study of Everyone in all time and space. The element of its timelessness comes through well enough to make the novel a solid presence in world literary history.

As Hardy was a determinist in his stance on the nature of life and the cosmos, fatalism is strongly reflected in his writings. The underlying theme of Hardy's novels is the struggle of man against the mysterious force which rules the world, brings misfortune into man's life and predetermines his fate. In Hardy's world man is totally helpless and insignificant, and God is vengeful and powerful and takes delight in making humans suffer. He sees human as mere stakes in His game of dice. Happiness, if there is anything like this, is only a rare, occasional occurrence in the ambient gloom of the universe. So the fictional world of Hardy is amoral in nature, where "the President of the Immortals" (in his own words) sits high up on the throne, hostile often or nonchalant at best to the human world. In his works the strong elements of naturalism is combined with a tendency towards symbolism. These defects spoil the main realistic effect of his art.

Hardy's stories appeal to the readers not so much by means of their plots as through the pathos of the emotional tangle, in which his characters get involved invariably and from which they find it impossible to extricate themselves. The pitch of their emotional suffering awakens a warm echo in the human bosom, and jerks out genuine, sincere tears. In this fictional world humans get caught up in the web of Fate, or the malignant universe, or forces, the only job of which is to debilitate and devastate human lives. There is no free will, circumscribed as it is by society. There is no belonging. Hardy's characters travel incessantly and never get anywhere. This is pretty much the essential situation which his novels try to adumbrate.

Hardy appeared to be fascinated at a minute study of the psychology of his characters. He not only took immense delight in dealing with the psychic oddities of his fictional men and women, but also made a meticulous effort to trace a real sequence of psychological cause and effect and explore human motives and acts. In his portrayal of the inner world, with its passions and its perversity, Hardy was a romanticist rather than a realist both in outlook and technique, venturing at times as far as to employ the melodramatic. This is a feat that indicates Hardy's empathy with the modern spirit. For one thing, he was sensitive enough to notice the variety of psychic eccentricities that were to assume the dimension of grotesquery in *Winesburg, Ohio* (1919) by Sherwood Anderson (1876 - 1941) and, for another, he was beginning to take a serious look into the interior of man rather than rest content with the tradition of representing the mere externals of life.

Hardy had a strong sense of humor and often described nature with charm and impressiveness. His language possesses a silent power and charm. It may not be the most exquisite, but it simply touches the mind and the senses. His prose is studded with rhetorical device, poetic imagery, and metaphors, and is richly connotative. Reading him, one feels the sublimity, the terror, the vastness, the obscurity, and the fascination that can stem only from the panorama of life. In novel-writing, Hardy was also famous for his uneven style. Occasionally, his prose shows an uneducated man's appreciation for the long or 12-letter words. He never said anything simply if he could help it. His ideas are not always lucid, and his plots may occasionally jump and dislocate.

Victorianism killed Hardy the novelist. Although he made a great success in the field of novels, Hardy had to give up writing novels after 1898 and turned to poetry again because he was accused of immorality and the malicious criticism was overpowering. Hardy's poetry likewise expresses his critical attitude toward the society, and his success in verse is comparable to that in prose fiction. Hardy published eight volumes of poetry, including *Wessex Poems* (1898), *Poems of Past and Present* (1902), *Time's Laughingstocks and Other Verses* (1909), *Satires of Circumstance* (1914), *Moments of Vision* (1917), *Late Lyrics and Earlier with Many Other Verses* (1922), *Human Shows, Far Phantasies, Songs and Trifles* (1925) and *Winter Words in Various Moods and Metres* (1928). The *Collected Poems* (1930), published posthumously, contains over 900 poems of great variety and individuality, yet consistent over more than 60 years in their attitudes to life and fate. Probably the most remarkable are in the group of poems written in recollection of his first wife (i. e., "Poems of 1912 – 13" in *Satires of Circumstance*). Hardy followed William Wordsworth and Robert Browning in his endeavor to write in a language close to that of speech, and he abhorred, to use his own words, "the jeweled line." He experimented constantly with rhythms and stresses and verse forms, disliking and avoiding any facile flow. His famous verse works include *Poems of Past and Present* and the epic drama *The Dynasts*. The latter is a vast work in blank verse and prose. It occupied Hardy for many years and came out in three volumes in 1904, 1906 and 1908 respectively. He wrote one other poetic drama *The Famous Tragedy of the Queen of Cornwall* (1923).

Chapter 25 Victorian Poetry

Following the magnificent achievements of Romantic poetry, the Victorian poetry in many aspects showed a further development of themes and attitudes first explored by the Romanticists. The Victorians valued mainly "applied" poetry (as against "pure" or "absolute" poetry), applied in the sense of being useful in inculcating moral lessons or enforcing established values and tastes, or simply as a means of diversion and entertainment. Although this affected poetic creation, the Victorian poets, including Tennyson, Browning, Arnold, Gerard Manley Hopkins (1844 – 1889) and Arthur Hugh Clough (1819 – 1861), managed to speak both in a public and a private voice to meet both the need of the audience and that of their own visions.

Much Victorian poetry gave expression to optimism and progressive vitality of the age. The great poets like Alfred Tennyson and Robert Browning often celebrated the great occasions and achievements of the era. They began writing poetry in emulation of the major Romantic poets. For instance, Tennyson's early poetry was strongly influenced by Byron, Scott and Keats, while Browning's chief model was Shelley. Victorian poetry, as a whole, is remarkably varied and diverse.

25.1 Alfred, Lord Tennyson (1809 – 1892)

Tennyson was recognized among his contemporaries as the greatest poet of the Victorian England and is still a welcome presence on the poetic scene, though the verse revolution of the first 20th century after his death was spearheaded essentially against traditional poetics, the sum total of which he seemed to represent. His lyrical genius has proved fascinating and charming.

Tennyson's poetic output was vast and extremely varied; he wrote lyrics, dramatic monologues, plays, long poetic narratives, elegies and poems commemorating specific occasions. Tennyson published his first independent volume of poetry in 1830. But this collection and the one coming out two years later were not well received by the reviewers. It was the publication of the two-volume *Poems* in 1842 that brought a great success to Tennyson and established his position as a poet of the first rank in English literature. His main poetic works include his four longer poems (poetic narratives) in the middle years of his poetic career—*The Princess* (1847), *In Memoriam* (1850), *Maud* (1855) and *Idylls of the King* (1859 – 85)—and his lyrics like "Break, Break, Break" (1842), "The Lotus-Eaters" (1832) and "Ulysses" (1842). Tennyson was made Poet Laureate of Great Britain and Ireland after Wordsworth in the year his famous *In Memoriam* came out. In addition to *Maud* and *Idylls of the King*, Tennyson also published poetic works like *Enoch Arden* (1864) during his tenure as Poet Laureate.

The Princess: *A Medley* is a long poem of more than 3,000 lines written in blank verse. It tells a love story set in the Middle Ages. The major theme—domestic joy and sorrow—is a modern notion encased in subject of the past. Princess Ida becomes a devotee of women's rights, abjures marriage and founds a university for girls to promote her ideals of women's rights. The prince, to whom she was engaged in childhood, enters the university in the disguise of a girl and is detected by the two tutors, who, from different motives, conceal their knowledge. The deceit is presently detected by Ida, but not before the prince has had occasion to rescue her from drowning. Her determination is unshaken, and a combat ensues between fifty warriors led by the prince and fifty led by Ida's brother. The prince and his men are defeated and wounded. The princess turns the university into a hospital to take care of the wounded, and the prince eventually wins Ida. The poem is made up of a series of idylls, and some vignettes are inserted here and there to highlight the events such as the prince's seizures, the complex relationships of the prince and the princess with their friends and families, and the victory of love. The work is not a straightforward narrative but a medley of idylls—lyric, descriptive, domestic and epic.

In Memoriam A. H. H. is written in stanzas of four octosyllabic lines rhyming abba, and is divided into 132 sections of varying length. It was written in memory of A. H. Hallam, a young man of great promise and an intimate friend of Tennyson, who died young at Vienna. But it is not so much a single elegy as a series of poems written over a considerable period, inspired by the changing moods of the author's regret for his lost friend, expressing his own anxieties about change, evolution and immortality, the last a subject which continued to perturb him deeply. The poem is therefore a record of the poet's spiritual odyssey and recovery of his faith in immortality from his grief over his physical loss.

Tennyson's friend Hallam died when he was just beginning to realize his promise in the prime of his years. His death both enraged and perplexed the poet so that he saw God as remote and death final. He was pained by the irreparable sense of loss and saw no hope of ever uniting with his best friend. He sank to wild despair. But by and by he was beginning to feel the strength of man's inward sense of immortality, and indicate his inclination to identify Hallam with Christ in spirit who may save him. He yearned for mythical contact with the spirit of the lost one and felt the need to revive love as the universal law. He searched for signs of immortality in himself, experienced a swing of woods of content and despair, and suddenly felt a presence when he reread Hallam's letters. Now aware of the continuity of existence, he experienced a brief communion with the universal spirit, of which Hallam's spirit existed as an indistinguishable part. He felt assured that the world was full of immortal love and became affirmative in attitude.

In formal terms *In Memoriam* is a highly personal elegy. It is true that the poem is an elegy similar to Milton's *Lycidas* and Shelley's *Adonaïs*. The pattern of elegiac is visible. There is the progression from the feeling of loss and grief to final triumph of love and affection over sorrow and death. But it was Tennyson's own experience of conversion that supplied the structural pattern of his poem. There is the power of the mythical, the vision of the dead, and the communication between souls. Tennyson did not follow strictly the traditional elegiac pattern such as taking the impersonal direction of the pastoral elegy as Milton or Shelley did.

Maud is a monodrama in sections of different meters, in which the narrator, a man of morbid temperament, describes the progress of his emotions. His family is ruined and his father is killed by the old lord of the Hall. However, he falls in love with the lord's daughter Maud. And their love affair meets with an objection from Maud's brother, who wishes her to marry a vapid "new-made" lord. Although the narrator gets triumph at winning Maud, he flees abroad and gets mad later. At the end of the story the young man recovers himself and finds an outlet for his emotions by taking part in a war. The poem contains several of Tennyson's best lyrics like "I have led her home" and "Come into the garden, Maud." But some contemporary critics found it obscure or morbid, due to its "faith in war as the unique social regenerator" and its emphasis on blood-shedding as a cure for disappointed love.

The Idylls of the King is one of the three major epics produced during the Victorian period, the other two being Robert Browning's *The Ring and the Book* and Gerard Manley Hopkins' *The Wreck of the Deutschland* (composed 1875 – 1876; published 1918). *The Idylls of the King*, containing twelve books based mainly on Thomas Malory's *Morte d'Arthur*, presents the story of Arthur, from his first meeting with Guinevere to the ruin of his kingdom and his death. The protagonists are Arthur and Guinevere, Launcelot, and Elaine, but the design embraces the fates of various minor characters. The adultery of Guinevere and Launcelot is seen as one of the forces that destroy the idealism and bright hopes of the Round Table, and the scene in which the guilty Guinevere "groveled with her face against the floor" before Arthur to listen to his long denunciatory speech was received with great enthusiasm; his forgiveness of her moved the poet himself to tears.

The Idylls of the King is the poet's effort to awaken responsive echoes in modern bosoms to an ancient tale of heroism and woe, the strengths and weaknesses of which might still be relevant to the life of his age. It reveals two voices, or "dissociated sensibility," the public alongside the private. The evident purpose of the sustained poetic endeavor is to glorify the progress of his age, laud Prince Albert and Queen Victoria as idealized rulers, and commend the major Victorian virtues to cater to the needs of a people clamoring for guidance. These virtues include domestic virtues, the emphasis on the home, family affections and love, hero-worship, the identity of the self, self-realization through duty and service, moral earnestness, positive achievements, and others. The epic stresses the importance of love and conjugal harmony as the basis of sound civilized life, and can be seen as a series of love stories—devotion to love in "Lancelot and Elaine," adulterous passion in "Lancelot and Guinevere," the lawless passion of Isolt and Tristram, and the triangle of Mark, Isolt and Tristram which mirrors that of Arthur, Guinevere and Lancelot and which crushes the king's ideal in "The Last Tournament," the wiles of the flesh in "Merlin and Vivien," the betrayal of faith in "Pellas and Ettaire," and marital disharmony in "The Marriage of Geraint" and "Geraint and Enid." In this sense, it was the work of a poet laureate serving his monarch and his people. However, through the depiction of these stories, Tennyson also tended to tell readers that illicit love would lead to the downfall of a civilization. *The Idylls of the King* constitutes an oblique warning to and a criticism of his society as well. The poet managed to express in the series of idyllic pictures his private vision that the ills of his age, the frenzied getting and spending and the threat of materialism to the life of the soul, the increasingly overwhelming middle-class philistinism in tastes and values, and the weakening or the loss of faith all might lead to the decline of the civilization that the Victorians had been busy building.

In his poetry, Tennyson spoke mainly to his own age, the Victorian period. He was a prophet, offering love to his people at a time when the world was becoming amoral and indifferent and alienation was keenly felt all around. He placed abundant emphasis on love, duty and allegiance, and on marriage and home and children. For him, love is an ethical force and man's redeeming grace, and can make or mar a civilization; marriage and home bring happiness, quiet and comfort, and makes life worth living. Tennyson has no patience with any form of social interruption of genuine love. In fact, a recurrent theme in his works has been the frustration of a pure love.

Tennyson's genius was primarily lyrical. He had a genius for evoking moods and states of mind in his poems. He was able to create a sense of nostalgia, a wistful longing for the past or for remote experiences. His lyric genius shines through his nature poetry, his incidental and occasional poetry, and his long poetic narratives. Tennyson's nature poetry is a faithful and fascinating description of the English country life with its sights, sounds, scents and habits. It is characterized by the imitation of the sounds of the English birds like the lark's song, the woodpecker's laughter, the jay's whistle and the owl's shriek, which display the poet's delicate sense of sound and power of onomatopoeia, the representation of nature's infinitude embodied in the sea, the sky, the stars and space, and the display of the fine and exquisite mind of a poet conscious of the spirituality of nature and sensitive to the juxtaposition and contrast between the ephemeral and the eternal, and the infinitesimal and the infinite, which nature reveals for man. Tennyson's incidental and occasional poetry is also full of lyric beauty. The Roman inscriptions aptly condensed, the felicity of Horatian odes, and the unmistakable urbanity in taste all leave a lasting impression on readers. The lyrical note resounding through Tennyson's poetic narratives (like *In Memoriam*) lies in the poet's deep sense of bereavement, the depth of despair that kills all joy in life, the childhood memories and half-forgotten dreams that keep flooding back to torment the mind, the moan of the sea, and the cry of a child lost at midnight. Tennyson was a great master of the sounds and rhythms of the English language. His poetic techniques like the music of his language, his exquisite handling of the poetic tricks such as alliteration and anaphora, and his dexterous use of vowels are all instrumental in enhancing the lyric beauty of his poetry.

In addition, some of his poems deal with the main political, religious and scientific issues of his day. His poems reflect his conservative ideas and idealization of the bourgeois social reality.

25.2 The Brownings

Robert Browning (1812 – 1889) was an English poet and playwright and one of the foremost Victorian poets. As a poet, he was considered second only to Tennyson in his own day and is now almost equally well-known as Tennyson in England and elsewhere. Whereas he was looked up as a prophet advocating courage and striving in his own time, nowadays he is remembered for a couple of things he did for modern poetry—his experiment and use of the dramatic monologue and his contribution to the discovery of the mythical method and symbolism in the writing of psychological poetry. Robert Browning's poems are known for their irony, characterization, dark humor, social commentary, historical settings, and challenging vocabulary and syntax.

Robert Browning was optimistic and believed in the progress of mankind. His conception of life is basically idealistic and hopeful. His poetry represents the exuberant and optimistic spirit of his time, and is full of the zeal and gusto that he hoped people should have to brave ever new life. His watchword is "strive." He was famous then for his concept that the joy of life lies in the living and that it is striving that makes life meaningful. His poetry celebrates the passion and the intensity of feeling alive and active. His is a perfect moral world where God is in heaven and all is well here on earth. His world is full of prophets, artists, lovers and doers of great deeds for whom exerting one's best offers the greatest gratification for the soul. Life is a kind of struggle through which people prove their worth; it is a struggle toward perfection that probably will never materialize. For Browning's is the philosophy of the imperfect, of "success in failure." In his opinion, man is imperfect, which the poet chooses to see as an asset rather than anything else: the craving for improvement drives man for ever onward. In keeping with the spirit of his time, Browning offered a kind of philosophy which touched the hearts of the Victorians and excited and inspired them to experience life with courage and hope.

Browning began the new modern psychological poetry. He made the dramatic monologue a norm as a poetic form for presenting the internal world of the characters. His poems provide scenarios in which a character is made to speak out his mind and thus reveal his inner psychology. This has a strong modern ring because it often resembles a stream-of-consciousness style in modern writing. It represents a jump in perception on the part of the artist from writing about the externalities of the life and people to the scrutiny and exploration of the inner consciousness of the characters. Browning was realistic, much concerned with presenting facts and analyzing human psychology. His realism and psychology have made it possible for modern people to discover the use of symbol and myth. Browning embraced realism and opposed the use of myth as overt subject matter. His poetic creation reveals a visible direction that he tried to take toward a psychological use of myth. Myth in Browning is used to make a statement about the nature of life; it is not to be taken literally.

Both Browning's thought and poetry are characterized by modernity, which is illustrated by his notion of relativism and his emphasis on intuition and divided self. Relativism holds that truth has more than one facet to show for human understanding at one time and is therefore not absolute. This is a new awareness in the history of human epistemology. In this sense, *The Ring and the Book* is a good illustration. The story is enveloped in so many layers of falsehoods and obscurities, and so many people speak out about the case—the two halves of Rome, the victims, the victimizer, the lawyers, the church and the government—that the truth of the murder case is almost lost in the maze of the views thus presented. The poet seemed to tell readers that it was difficult if not impossible to see reality and truth in its totality and finality, which is, in a way, ahead of his time. Browning believed in human instinct and the power of the unconscious, and saw intuitive experience as the best gateway to knowledge. This has to do with the supreme importance he attached to the individual soul and to individualism. He stressed the harmony between the senses and the intuitions in an artist and felt that a poet should be a seer speaking intuitively. With tradition as its weapons, intellect was to Browning directly antithetical to human instinct. Most of his major characters perceive the world intuitively and act accordingly. They tend to "go against the flow," and behave like non-conformists and rebels. As to the subject of the divided self, Browning proved himself to be one of the most sensitive literary artists of time. There was a visible double awareness in him: he felt pulled in two directions in the tug of war between commitment and private vision. On the whole Browning leaned toward commitment and disapproved strongly of the aesthetic movement. Advocating the principle that art is founded in reality, he saw as doomed to failure anyone who places undue emphasis on self-indulgence and self-expression. It is true that Browning was torn between his divided allegiances, and this represented in his portrayal of characters. His world is peopled with characters whose consciousness and unconsciousness, intellect and imagination, external world and inner world are all at work to divide them into two halves, and whose divided selves keep on interacting with each other and finding a way of addressing their dilemmas.

Browning's major works include his collections of monologues such as *Men and Women* (1855), *Dramatic Lyrics* (1842) and *Dramatic Romances and Lyrics* (1845), and his longest, ambitious and monumental work *The Ring and the Book* (1868 – 1869). His best-known short poems are "My Last Duchess" (the most famous one among his poems), "Home Thoughts, from Abroad," "Meeting at Night," "One Word More," "By the Fireside" and "The Last Ride Together."

The Ring and the Book, Robert Browning's masterpiece, is an epic-length poem in blank verse, or more specifically, a verse novel, in 12 books, totaling over 21000 lines, twice as long as *Paradise Lost*. The poem, published in four monthly installments from 1868 to 1869, was a critical and popular success and established Browning's contemporary reputation.

The "Ring" of the title is a figure for the process by which the artist transmutes the "pure crude fact" of historical events into living forms, or it represents the gold of the truth which is so difficult to get at. As the goldsmith, in making a gold ring, moulds the ring with alloy first and then has to get rid of the alloy before he can get the ring out, the poet tries to reach the truth through a process in which he disengages falsehood from fact. The falsehoods come from many perspectives which the poem presents with multiple points of view. The "Book" is a collection of documents relating to the Italian murder trial of the late 17th century on which the poem is based. Browning found the volume on a market stall in Florence and offered it to several of his acquaintances before finally deciding to use it himself. In writing the poem, Browning did not take much interest in the Greek myths and mythical heroes; he felt drawn to little-known people and incidents. There are no King Arthur and his knights as in Tennyson and no Greek celebrities as in Matthew Arnold. By taking those much less-known characters and plots from the past, Browning did a good job of relating the past to the present and teaching a moral lesson.

The story goes as follows. Pietro and Violante Comparini are a middle-aged childless couple living in Rome. Their income could only be secured after Pietro's death if they had a child; so Violante buys the child of a prostitute and passes it off as her own. The adopted child Pompilia is later married to Count Guido Franceschini, an impoverished nobleman from Arezzo. The marriage is unhappy, and the Comparinis, disappointed by life in Arezzo, return to Rome and sue Guido for the restoration of Pompilia's dowry on the grounds of her illegitimacy, which Violante now reveals. Pompilia herself eventually flees from Arezzo in the company of a young priest Giuseppe Caponsacchi. Guido pursues them and has them arrested on the outskirts of Rome; as a result, Caponsacchi is exiled to Civita Vecchia for three years, and Pompilia is sent to a covenant while the lawsuits are decided. But then she is released into the custody of the Comparinis because she is pregnant. A fortnight after Pompilia gives birth to her child, she and her adopted parents are murdered by Guido and four accomplices. The five murderers are arrested. Although Guido claims justification on the grounds of his wife's adultery, they are convicted and sentenced to death. Guido then pleads exemption for himself, but his appeal is rejected and the five are executed.

In Browning's poem, the story is told by a succession of speakers including citizens of Rome, the participants themselves, the lawyers and the pope, each of whose single, insufficient perceptions combines with the others' to form the "ring" of the truth. This design represents Browning's response to a number of pressing concerns in his own creative life and in contemporary philosophies of art and religion. He saw "truth" as both absolute (in its divine essence) and relative (in its human manifestation); the artist partakes of either quality, all means of expression such as language being an inadequate "witness" to the true life of the imagination, just as historical witnesses give a partial and inadequate account of "real" events.

The Ring and the Book is a typical Victorian work because it exemplifies some of the qualities which characterize the era, including the Victorian emphasis on the family, filial piety, marriage and fidelity, and maternal love. Pompilia is a pattern of virtue. She is a good daughter, a good wife and a good mother. There is spacious room and soul for genuine love. She is instinctual, innocent and pure, and too good for the world in which she lives. As such she lives forever at the tender mercies of the hostile forces of society. Her husband Count Guido Franceschini is her antithesis in every possible sense. Just as Pompilia is an etherized spirit, he is all materialized, self-serving, always scheming and calculating, and thoroughly adept in exploiting social institutions to his best advantage. There is nothing like love in him. Marriage is to him just another way of getting rich quick, and connubial faith means exactly nothing to him. He is altogether the authentic embodiment of conscious intellect at which Browning spearheaded his scathing satire. Cruel, violent and malignant, Count Guido is an archetypal specimen of human evil.

Here the government, the church, the legal system and the popular opinion are either too corrupt and too self-centered or too nonchalant and apathetic to care about the fate of an insignificant individual. This represents Browning's social criticism. The poem also bodies forth the poet's aesthetic principle. For Browning, the artist receives his inspiration and sanction for his creation from God, directed by "a Hand/Always above my shoulder," and creates to "[r]epeat God's process in man's due degree." He has a commitment to fulfill to human society: he mediates between the divine and the human and justifies God's ways to man.

All in all, in its immense but ordered size and scope, in the vitality of its characters and the rich evocation of time and place, and in its magnificently troubled exposition of the relation between sign and significance, the poem stands at the center of Browning's achievement.

Elizabeth Browning (1806 – 1861) was one of the most prominent poets of the Victorian era and even more famous than her husband Robert Browning at her death. She was predominantly a socially engaged realist. Her poetry was emotionally charged, rhetorically exquisite and morally correct, and therefore widely popular in Britain and the United States during her lifetime. She is remembered for such poems as "How Do I Love Thee?" (Sonnet 43, 1845) and *Aurora Leigh* (1856).

Elizabeth was introduced to prominent literary figures of the day such as William Wordsworth, Samuel Taylor Coleridge, Alfred Tennyson and Thomas Carlyle in the 1830s, when her first adult collection *The Seraphim and*

Other Poems (1838) came out. She wrote prolifically between 1841 and 1844, producing poetry, translation and prose. Her volume *Poems* (1844) brought her great success. During this time she met and corresponded with the writer Robert Browning, who admired her work. Her well-known *Sonnets from the Portuguese* (1850), 44 in total, records her love with Robert Browning. Her prolific output made her a rival to Tennyson as a candidate for poet laureate when Wordsworth died. Her later and most ambitious work *Aurora Leigh* is an epic novel/poem of modern English life. Its hero is a social reformer and humanitarian of aristocratic lineage while the heroine is a young poetess, in large part a reflection of Mrs. Browning's own personality. The work addresses the problem of a Victorian woman who wants to be a socially involved poet and yearns for freedom. It was warmly received in its day and is becoming increasingly popular now.

Elizabeth also campaigned for the abolition of slavery and her work helped influence reform in the child labor legislation. However, she was brought up in a strongly religious household, and much of her work carries a Christian theme. Elizabeth's writing had a major influence on prominent writers of the day, including the American poets Edgar Allan Poe (1809 – 1849) and Emily Dickinson (1830 – 1886).

25.3　Matthew Arnold (1822 – 1888)

Arnold was an English poet and critic. His achievements in poetry and criticism are impressive. Arnold lived in an era of change in thought and feeling. As England was growing increasingly affluent and the middle class was getting increasingly powerful, values were undergoing a drastic change. The old absolutes seemed to be dying out, but the new ones were having a hard time getting born. With the ideas of evolution up in the air, faith was losing its hold upon popular imagination, and the mythic center that could unify and hold beliefs and values together was fast disappearing. There was no spiritual calm or cheerfulness based on faith; doubts and feelings of discouragement set in. Everything appeared to be "sick." As a poet, Arnold intuited the ills of his society and had a significant message for his people. The poetic characters, such as the weary and suicidal Empedocles, the retiring monks in "The Grande Chartreuse," the "I" of "Lines Written in Kensington Gardens" who sees a huge world that roars by and feels so helpless, and the lonely though indomitable Romantic poets in the "Memorial Verses," are all the author's spokesmen.

Arnold's career as a writer may be roughly divided into four phases—the 1850s, the 1860s, the 1870s and the 1880s. Most of his poems appeared during the 1850s: a volume entitled *The Strayed Reveler and Other Poems*, published in 1849, was followed by *Empedocles at Atna, and Other Poems* (1852), *Poems* (1853), *Poems: Second Series* (1855) and *Merope, a Tragedy* (1858). During the 1860s the focus of Arnold's writing distinctly shifted from poetry to literary and social criticism despite the publication of *New Poems* (1867). In 1865 the first series of his *Essays in Criticism* was published and *Culture and Anarchy*, a fierce attack on middle-class materialism and narrow-mindedness, came out in 1869. In the 1870s Arnold devoted himself mainly to writing about education and religion. In the 1880s he returned to literary criticism and wrote the second series of his *Essays in Criticism*, published soon after his death in 1888.

Arnold keenly felt the sadness of his age, and his poetry expressed his feelings adequately. Many of his poetical works express a tone of regret, disillusion and melancholy. His poems, such as "The Scholar-Gypsy" (1853),

"Empedocles at Atna" (1852), "Dover Beach" (1867), "Lines Written in Kensington Gardens," "Thyrsis" (1867) and "Stanzas from the Grande Chartreuse" (1855), all reveal the intensity of a melancholy that had been widely felt but had awaited apt articulation. Arnold responded to the call of his age and represented "the main movement of mind of the last quarter of a century." He did it so well that he was and has been known ever since as the Victorian poet of loneliness. This unhappiness had to do with his sense of religious frustration and the highly critical stance he took toward his un-poetical age. His has proved to be one of the best verse products coming out of the Victorian period. Arnold had faith in the permanence of his poetry. He tried to fuse Tennyson's poetical sentiment with Browning's intellectual vigor and abundance, and made the best of his poetic endowment to reflect the Victorian temper. As a result, he received recognition as poet number three of his time immediately after Tennyson and Browning.

In his maturity Arnold turned increasingly to prose, writing essays on literary, educational and social topics that established him as the leading critic of the day. His lectures on translating Homer, with his definition of "the grand style," were published in 1861. In addition to *Essays in Criticism* Arnold published *On the Study of Celtic Literature* (1867), which caused Oxford to establish a chair of Celtic studies. *Culture and Anarchy* was followed by *Friendship's Garland* in 1871 and *Literature and Dogma*, a study of the interpretation of the *Bible*, in 1873.

As a social critic, Arnold was worried about the direction which England was taking, one along which the middle class was trying to push the country forward. As a matter of fact, the increasingly wealthy and powerful class was leading the country in a wrong direction. England followed the gospel of getting ahead in the world and wallowed in money and material things. Its tastes were vulgar and low. Showing little or no appreciation for the arts, it impacted all levels of social life vigorously with its tantalizing materialism, and vehemently championed individual license. In his critical works, Arnold sharply criticized the provincialism, philistinism, sectarianism and utilitarian materialism of English life and culture, and argued that England needed more intellectual curiosity, more ideas, and a more comparative, European outlook. The critic, he said, should be flexible, tactful and free of prejudice; his endeavor should be "to see the object as in itself it really is." Arnold's fame as a critic grew steadily.

Essays in Criticism was published in three series in 1865, 1888 and 1910 respectively. In the book Arnold stated his three standards of judgment on poetry. They are the moral, the aesthetic and the sociological. The title of the book was adopted by F. W. Bateson (1901 – 1978) for a periodical founded in 1951, in which Bateson intended to combine "social relevance" and "scholarly standards," and in which the influence both of Arnold and of *Scrutiny*, a Cambridge periodical which ran for 19 volumes, 1932 – 53, may be detected.

Culture and Anarchy, containing many of Arnold's central critical arguments, is his finest work dealing with the whole structure of English civilization and culture. According to him, the English society of his time was composed of "Barbarians, Philistines and Populace." By "Barbarians" he meant the aristocratic classes, who were crude in soul in spite of their fine clothes, airs and graces. The "Philistines" are the middle-class merchants and manufacturers, who were wealthy, but vulgar, narrow-minded and self-satisfied. Both the aristocrats and the middle-class owners were opposed to "sweetness and light" (i. e. culture). But Arnold's deepest contempt and most frequent attack was directed to the middle-class "Philistines." Although his satire and criticism of the English middle class were forceful, his tone was lighter than those of Carlyle and Ruskin. His prescription for the social ills of the English society was moral education and open-mindedness. He criticized the English middle class in order to open their minds to new ideas. He believed that the world of the future would be a middle-class world and the middle class could be educated to be better qualified for the task of governing the country.

As a prose-writer, Arnold is distinguished by his clear and polished style and his sober, scientific spirit, here and there enlivened by humor. He is one of the great literary critics of England.

Chapter 26 Victorian Essays

With the development of capitalism, social problems became acute, especially those caused by the cleavage between wealth and poverty, the conflict between labor and capital, and by child labor, the sordid working and living conditions of the laboring people, economic depressions, mass unemployment and the workers' demand for political rights. Reform Bills were passed in Parliament to pacify the indignation of the workers and avoid a revolution, but things did not improve for all that. It was with these social problems that the English prose-writers of the period were chiefly concerned. Victorian essays were rich and varied. In no other period were so many great writers writing so much powerful and exquisite prose at the same time. These included, among others, Matthew Arnold, Thomas Carlyle, John Ruskin, Thomas Macaulay (1800 – 1859), John Stuart Mill, and a whole group of religious people associated with the Oxford Movement. Among them, Carlyle, Ruskin and Arnold were famous for their social criticism, while Macaulay upheld the interests of the bourgeoisie in power with his essays and histories.

26.1 Thomas Carlyle (1795 – 1881)

Carlyle was a Scottish philosopher, satirical writer, essayist and historian. His reputation as social prophet and critic, and his prestige as historian, were enormous during his own time. He was considered one of the most important social commentators of his time and presented many lectures during his lifetime with certain acclaim in the Victorian era. George Eliot once wrote that "there is hardly a superior or active mind of this generation that has not been modified by Carlyle's writings," and he was later described by Yeats in his *Autobiography* as "the chief inspirer of self-educated men in the eighties and early nineties." In the 20th century, his reputation waned, partly because his trust in authority and admiration of strong leaders were interpreted as foreshadowing of Fascism.

Carlyle's first original work *Sartor Resartus: The Life and Opinions of Herr Teufelsdrockh* (1833 – 1834) appeared in a magazine, but it was regarded by both readers and critics as a difficult and eccentric work and was not published in book form until 1838. It was the publication of *The French Revolution: A History* (1837) a year earlier that established Carlyle's literary reputation as a great writer. Then from 1837 to 1840 Carlyle gave four series of lectures, and one of these he published in 1841 was *On Heroes, Hero-Worship, and the Heroic in History*, which is perhaps the most well-known of his works. Carlyle's growing concern with the "condition of English question" induced him to write a series of pamphlets on the social problems of the "Hungry Forties": *Chartism* (1839), *Past and Present* (1843) and *Latter-Day Pamphlets* (1850). Carlyle also produced two biographies: *Letters and Speeches of Oliver Cromwell* (1845) and *The History of Frederick the Great* (1858 – 1965). They are his longest works and in the two works he illustrated in detail his theory of hero-worship. Besides, it is worth noting that Carlyle's position as a leader of literature was well established from 1843 onwards and that his house was the resort of many of the most brilliant men of the time.

Carlyle's most famous works, *Sartor Resartus* and *Past and Present*, were his obvious attempts to move the nation in the direction he would like it to follow. **Sartor Resartus: The Life and Opinions of Herr Teufelsdrockh** is a satirical novel. "Sartor Resartus" means "tailor retailored/re-patched/re-clothed," and Herr Teufelsdrockh is an imaginary professor. The book consists of two parts. The first part is a discourse on the philosophy of clothes, which are symbols for forms, titles, ceremonies, creeds, institutions, space, time and matter that are merely the coverings of reality; the second part is the biography of Herr Teufelsdrockh himself, which is in some measure the author's autobiography, telling how he faces the Everlasting No, the power of skepticism and denial, and how he reaches the Everlasting Yes, the significance of human value in work. The prose is highly characteristic, dotted with capital letters, exclamation marks, phrases in German, compound words of the author's own invention, wild apostrophes to the Reader, apocalyptic utterances, and outbursts of satire and bathos. It is an early example of what came to be known as "Carlylese."

Past and Present is essentially a repetition of the ideas in *Sarter Resartus*. The book was written when England was going through a severe economic depression. In this and another pamphlet *Chartism*, Carlyle criticized and exposed the deception of Malthus' theory. He showed his anger to the inequality between the poor and the rich. He expressed his sympathy for the poor workers and supported the Chartist Movement.

The French Revolution: A History is not a mere record of "things as they were," but a romantic work, a prose epic written from the heart of an artist. It is in three volumes, "The Bastille," "The Constitution," and "The Guillotine," and opens with the death of Louis XV (1710 – 1774, king 1715 – 1774) in 1774. The history described in the work covers the reign of Louis XVI (1754 – 1793, king 1774 – 1791), the fall of the Bastille, the trial and execution of Louis XVI and his queen Marie Antoinette, the reign of terror and the rise of Napoleon. It is a work of great narrative and descriptive power, and was greatly admired by Dickens and was in part the inspiration of *A Tale of Two Cities*. From a great mass of historical details Carlyle selected only those outstanding figures and picturesque incidents and painted a gallery of vivid portraits and pictures. So the effect of the whole book is not unlike a historical drama, in which the characters of history "haste stormfully across the astonished Earth." In the book Carlyle preached a sermon on eternal justice: "Whatsoever a man soweth, that shall he also reap." All wrong-doing is inevitably followed by vengeance, and nemesis is sure to follow the abuse of power or the neglect of the responsibilities by those in whom power has been placed by Providence. Carlyle stood on the side of the oppressed and gave a solemn warning to the ruling classes of England to mend their ways lest the tremendous upheaval that had happened in France should take place in their own country in just the same terrible manner.

On Heroes, Hero-Worship, and the Heroic in History is a course of six lectures delivered in 1840. In this series Carlyle elaborated his view that "Universal History, the history of what man has accomplished in this world, is at bottom the History of … Great Men." According to Carlyle, history is merely the record of the thoughts and actions of heroes, and the quality of heroism can show itself in any sphere of human activity; the decisive element in history is the individual leadership of genius and the business of the common people is to acknowledge and obey the hero. Carlyle summed up history in six divisions: the Hero as Divinity, the Hero as Prophet, the Hero as Poet, the Hero as Priest or Religious Leader, the Hero as Man of Letters and the Hero as King. To him, democracy was an evil thing. He believed in a benevolent despotism of great men and taught people to sit at the feet of heroes if they were to find salvation.

Carlyle had the merit of having opposed the bourgeoisie in literature at a time when the official English literature was completely dominated by the bourgeois attitudes, tastes and ideas, and in a manner which at moments was even revolutionary. In all his writings criticism of the present is closely bound up with a curiously unhistorical glorification of the Middle Ages, something that frequently occurred with English revolutionaries and some of the chartists. While in the past he admired at least the classic epochs of a definite phase of social development, the present brought him to despair, and he was terrified of the future.

Carlyle handled the English language as if it were completely raw material which he had to recast from the ground up. Archaic words and expressions were revived and new ones invented in the German manner. This new style was often over-inflated and tasteless, but at times brilliant and always original.

Carlyle's prose style is unique in its own way. He never spoke but to amaze his readers and audience. Words rolled out as if out of a sense of urgency. His attempt to handle the language so as to make it do the most effective work was both deliberate and successful. His symbols, his use of personae and his self-protections are among the best qualities of his prose that have caught on. In addition, Carlyle's talk is fiercely denunciatory and movingly eloquent. His prose is emotional and forceful, notable for irony, humor, pathos, eloquence, metaphor and picturesque expression, but sometimes it lacks clearness or ease.

26.2 John Stuart Mill (1806 – 1873)

Mill was an English philosopher, feminist and political economist, and an influential contributor to social theory, political theory and political economy. He has been called the most influential English-speaking philosopher of the nineteenth century. Mill's conception of liberty justified the freedom of the individual in opposition to unlimited state control. Mill expressed his view on freedom by illustrating how an individual's drive to better his station and for self-improvement is the sole source of true freedom. Only when an individual is able to attain such improvements, without impeding others in their own efforts to do the same, can true freedom prevail. Mill's linking of freedom and self-improvement has inspired many. By establishing that individual efforts to excel have worth, he was able to show how they should achieve self-improvement without harming others or society at large.

Mill's emphasis on individual freedom constituted an important part of the 19th-century English liberalism. This aspect of his thinking is expounded in another important work *On Liberty* (1859). The essay explains the relations between society and the individual. What Mill tried to say here is that society would do well to leave the individual alone rather than compel everyone to conform to the opinion of the majority. Enforced conformity subjugates the individual who is in fact more important than social institutions. In connection with the issue is the subjugation of women, which Mill personally witnessed and experienced in his love and marriage and felt most keenly about. He explained his unequivocal position on the issue in his famous work *The Subjection of Women* (1869) and has been seen as a champion of women's liberation. His *Autobiography* (1873), a classic of its genre, describes his intellectual and moral development from his earliest years to his maturity.

Mill was a proponent of utilitarianism, a well-known utilitarian philosopher. He made the utilitarian philosophy more human and better and thus pushed utilitarianism to its new phase. His revision of utilitarianism is mainly recorded in one of his most significant works *Utilitarianism* (1861 – 63).

Although his main area of focus was philosophy, political economy and political science, Mill had close connection with the literary world of his day and exerted quite a measure of influence on the Victorian writing. His thought has offered an approach to understanding the literature of the period.

26.3 John Ruskin (1819 – 1900)

Ruskin was both the leading Victorian critic of art and an important critic of society. His life was spent in traveling, lecturing and writing. He wrote on subjects as varied as geology, architecture, myth, ornithology, literature, education, botany and political economy. His writing styles and literary forms are equally varied. Ruskin penned essays and treatises, poetry and lectures, travel guides and manuals, letters and even a fairy tale. The elaborate style that characterized his earliest writing on art was later superseded by a preference for plainer language designed to communicate his ideas more effectively. In all of his writings, Ruskin emphasized the connections between nature, art and society. He also made detailed sketches and paintings of rocks, plants, birds, landscapes, and architectural structures and ornamentation.

Ruskin's literary career can be roughly divided into three phases. At first he was preoccupied with problems of art, which is well expressed in *Modern Painters*, a work of encyclopedic range in five volumes, coming out respectively in 1843 (Volume I), 1846 (Volume II), 1856 (Volumes III and IV) and 1860 (Volume V). *Modern Painters* began as a defence of contemporary landscape artists, J. M. W. Turner (1775 – 1851) in particular, against the attacks on their paintings made by the conventional critics of the day. Ruskin's plan was to show his artists' "Superiority in the Art of Landscape Painting to all the Ancient Masters Proved by Examples of the True, the Beautiful and the Intellectual." The work involved Ruskin in problems of truth in art and in the ultimate importance of imagination.

During the 1850s Ruskin's principal interest shifted from art to architecture, especially to the problem of determining what kind of society is capable of producing great building. *The Stone of Venice*, a work in three volumes coming out in 1851 (Volume I) and 1853 (Volumes II and III), is an architectural study in which immense original scholarship is put to moralistic use. What the author wanted to revive was the kind of society that had produced Gothic architecture. His concern was more to change industrial society than to revive the Gothic style. However, in this work and the other (i. e., *The Seven Lamps of Architecture*, 1849) Ruskin glorified Gothic architecture, a style distinguished by its high and sharply-pointed arches, which had prevailed in Western Europe from the 12th to the 16th centuries. Such was the influence of these two books that the author's enthusiasm for Gothic architecture had provoked a revival of buildings in that style in many parts of Europe and America.

After 1860 the critic of art became an outspoken critic of laissez-faire economies. Ruskin turned his attention to social problems, and his literary career witnessed a transition from art criticism to social criticism. To do what he could to alleviate the misery of people's life became his mission. He lectured to workers and wrote articles on social reforms. In 1860 a series of his essays on political economy appeared in *The Cornhill Magazine* (1860 – 1975) edited by Thackeray. These essays were later published in *Unto This Last* (1862) and *Munera Pulveris* (1872). *Unto This Last*, *Munera Pulveris* and *Sesame and Lilies* (1865, 1871) are three of Ruskin's major writings criticizing English social, economic and political life. They are characterized by the author's penetrating insight into the social evils under capitalism and his humanitarian approach to the questions of labor and wealth.

Ruskin's transition to social criticism caused a change in his style. What had been gorgeous and rhythmical now became simple and eloquent—so as to appeal to a wider audience. His social and aesthetic thoughts have exerted deep influence on such writers and poets as William Morris (1834 – 1896), the Pre-Raphaelites, Oscar Wilde, Bernard Shaw and D. H. Lawrence.

Chapter 27　Literary Trends at the End of the 19th Century

Together with the main stream of Critical Realism, there emerged several other literary trends at the end of the 19th century. Naturalism, which was not so typical, nurtured writers like George Gissing, George Moore (1852 – 1933) and later Arnold Bennett. New Romanticism, with Robert Louis Stevenson as the representative, was another literary trend prevailing during the period. Then Aestheticism and Decadence, which proclaimed the "art for art's sake" theory, came into the literary scene. The most important representatives are Algernon Charles Swinburne, Walter Pater and Oscar Wilde.

27.1　Naturalistic Trend

In the latter part of the 19th century, naturalism flourished in America with the influence of Zola's biological and social determinism. But somehow it did not get a foothold in England. There was, strictly, nothing in the English fiction like the naturalist works by Emile Zola (1840 – 1902). Although Gissing, Moore and Bennett may come close to the label, their tone is muted. What they tried to do was open a window in the area of subject matter and show the writers that there existed available for representation a new matter—the lowest of the life in social life. Gissing was more representative as far as the English naturalism is concerned.

George Gissing (1857 – 1903) was an English novelist who published 23 novels between 1880 and 1903, including his first novel *Workers in the Dawn* (1880) and his best-known novels, *The Nether World* (1889), *New Grub Street* (1891) and *The Odd Women* (1893). Gissing was not happy with his world. His mind yielded to the stresses of life, and became warped and impulsive. The world was not good enough for him. It was "preposterous" and "sordid," and the common people, for whom his inherited middle-class gentility and his classical education made for his inveterate bias and scorn, were to him "base," "mean" and "vulgar." Influenced by the naturalist notion of man and his life, he wrote about poverty, but his works tend to leave the impression that he was fleeing from it rather than fighting and offering a way out. But it is good to note that he was important as a writer in the English literary history. He was the one who, going against the grain, ruthlessly exposed the corruption and evil which he thought lay at the core of social life then. He did a few things for which he is well remembered today. For instance, he created the image of the alienated hero in the 19th-century fiction, and was about the only author of his time writing in the vein of naturalistic, scientific realism. He tried to offer a scientific analysis of life, describing man as trapped in environment and heredity.

Today, Gissing is most remembered for his novel **New Grub Street**. The story is about the world of literary artists of the time. Here the author depicted the struggle for life, the jealousies and intrigues of the literary world of his time, and the blighting effect of poverty on artistic endeavor. The main theme is the contrast of the career of Jasper Milvain, the facile, clever, selfish and unscrupulous writer of reviews (who accepts the materialistic conditions of literary success), with those of more artistic temperaments. Among these are Edwin Reardon, the author of two fine works, who is hampered by poverty and by the lack of sympathy of his worldly wife, the generous but poor scholar Harold Biffen, and the learned pedant Alfred Yule, who is rendered rancorous and sardonic by constant disappointment. Jasper, materialistically-minded, has no misgivings whatever about breaking a woman's heart. He proposes to Yule's daughter and assistant Marian, who passionately loves him, only because he knows that she is going to be an heiress of £ 5000, but he has no scruples distancing her on learning that she will inherit nothing. Soon he turns his attention to her cousin Amy, Reardon's young widow, and sees his marriage to her as his gateway to success since she has received a legacy. Amy agrees to marry him because he wrote a good review to honor her late husband Reardon. This materialist and money-minded opportunist manages to achieve social arrival at the expense of his conscience as an artist.

In contrast, Edwin Reardon is more sensitive and loyal to his own voice and less accommodating, and lives a life of dire poverty and struggles in vain for a more comfortable creative milieu. He has to work as a clerk and face the constant hostility and antipathy of his worldly wife. He needs Amy to be his muse, but gets no inspiration from her. Moreover, Amy takes their son Willie with her and goes to live with her mother. Then Amy inherits some money and wants to come back and help him. But the proud Reardon declines the offer despite the coercive effort of his friend Harold Biffen to persuade him to give Amy a positive response. Biffen's is a rare cultured voice of understanding. Reardon and Amy achieve final reconciliation because their dying son Willie insists on it and Reardon is so sick that he knows he does not have long to live. A foil to Jasper, Reardon is an idealist to whom artistic integrity means everything. He is self-destructive and takes delight in self-destruction. Losing contact in his little room, he becomes an alienated urban man, an existentialist. Ultimately he is all alone and makes a choice that concerns himself. There is, in his personality, a silhouette of George Gissing himself. The mood of the book is downright gloomy. It is utter despair that Gissing tried to peddle to his readers. Although he wrote about the dilemma of the poor artists, Gissing's topmost concern was here still with the middle class, for the people who suffer most in the novel are those who have known better days.

New Grub Street is not about artists, art and writing; it is chiefly about money and social poverty, and about the intricate relationship between money and art. Thematically, Gissing saw work as important, but the work as he portrayed it does not succeed. This is anti-Victorian. Success for Gissing means not exactly money and prestige though there is in him veneration for money; he retained his own values and vision as an artist. He did not see society as beneficial as did George Eliot, but he felt that it stopped the clock and failed to progress. Gissing's naturalist novel freezes things and offers no hope, no solution, but the dead end. In addition, *New Grub Street* simply describes people and events, yet offers little or no psychological depth.

27.2 New Romanticism

New Romanticism was another literary trend prevailing at the end of the 19th century. New Romantic writers opposed the idea that art reflects life reality. They thought that the task of art should nourish readers' imagination and therefore laid emphasis upon the invention of exciting adventures and fascinating stories to entertain the reading public. They did not admit any connection between art and morality. Stevenson is the representative of New Romanticism in English literature.

Robert Louis Stevenson (1850 – 1894) was a Scottish novelist, poet, essayist and travel writer. In view of his short career, his literary output is amazingly fabulous. His writings include novels, travels, short stories, essays and poems. His novels deal with adventures; his essays are familiar, and expressive of the joy of living; his poems like "A Child's Garden of Verse" interpret the fancies of childhood.

Stevenson's imagination was rich and flighty; his pen kept on writing. His works offer at once a high moral sense and a gospel of joy and happiness for all. They have always provided immense entertainment and have never ceased to enrich the human mind and uplift the human morale. In more ways than one Stevenson went against the Victorian "grain." Whereas most of his fellow writers kept to the moral aesthetic and realism, he veered in a different direction: he wrote romances to season the parochial, down-to-earth lifestyle of his age with a touch of envisaging power to enliven his readers and widen their vistas of life. His principles were lofty and noble. He became immensely popular with his contemporaries who had been through so much change and chaos and had been craving for some freshening means to spirit them away from the humdrum world even for a moment. This they found in grateful Stevenson. Stevenson is best remembered for *Treasure Island* (1883) and *The Strange Case of Dr. Jekyll and Mr. Hyde* (1886).

Treasure Island first came out as a serial in a boys' periodical and was then reissued in book form in 1883. It was acknowledged as Stevenson's best-known work. The romance is set in the 18th century. It describes the surprising adventures of a young man named Jim. It tells of how the young man helps Trelawney (a squire) and Livesey (a doctor) overcome many difficulties and obstacles in securing the treasure left by a captain on an island. The novel has been a popular one ever since its publication. The late Victorian period was beset with a multitude of problems, and the common run of mankind suffered poverty and indignity. Stevenson's *Treasure Island* came at a time when the hopeless were daydreaming for comfort and relief of some kind. In addition, from a perspective of universal applicability, the novel satisfies the perennial human desire for unexpected wealth.

The Strange Case of Dr. Jekyll and Mr. Hyde is a novella about a London lawyer named Gabriel John Utterson who investigates strange occurrences between his old friend Dr. Henry Jekyll and the evil Edward Hyde. Jekyll is a physician who discovers a drug by which he can create for himself a separate personality (Hyde) that absorbs all his evil instincts. The physician assumes this personality from time to time, but afterwards the drug loses its efficacy in restoring his original form and character. Then Dr. Jekyll commits suicide.

The work is commonly associated today with the Victorian concern over the public and private division, individual's sense of playing a part and the class division of London. However, after stage and film productions of the story, the plot has become simplified and misrepresented as merely good versus evil. In this case, there are two personalities within Dr. Jekyll, one apparently good and the other evil. The impact of the work is such that it has become a part of the language, with the very phrase "Jekyll and Hyde" coming to mean a person who is vastly different in moral character from one situation to the next.

Stevenson's style is always simple, but often perfect. Both in his manner and in his matter he exercised a profound influence on the writers of romance at the turn of the 19th century.

27.3　Aestheticism and Decadence

Aestheticism is a term given to a movement, a cult, a mode of sensibility which blossomed in the 1880s. Fundamentally, it expressed the point of view that art was self-sufficient and needed serve no other purpose than its own end. The major implication of the new aesthetic standpoint was that art had no reference to life, and therefore had nothing to do with morality. Swinburne proclaimed the "art for art's sake" theory. While Walter Pater advocated the view that life itself should be treated in the spirit of art.

Aestheticism in poetry was closely identified with the Pre-Raphaelites and showed a tendency to withdrawal or aversion. Many poets of the period strove for beautiful musical effects in their verses rather than for sense. They aspired to sensuousness and revived archaistic modes and archaic language. They also revived an extensive use of classical mythology as a framework for expressing ideas. The two most important representatives of Aestheticism in English literature are Walter Pater and Oscar Wilde.

Decadence in English literature reflected the crisis of the bourgeois culture. It opposed the democratic and socialist ideals. Writers of this group upheld the bourgeois individualism. Their slogan was "art for art's sake." They could see the social evils, but they didn't think it possible to remove those evils and make life fair and just. They thought that the world was suffering from an incurable disease. Their writings were like groans of desperate patients. The ideas, moods and behavior of Decadence were manifested, beginning in the 1860s, in the poems of Algernon Charles Swinburne, and in the 1890s by writers like Oscar Wilde, Arthur Symons (1865 – 1945), Lionel Johnson (1867 – 1902) and Ernest Dowson (1867 – 1900). The representative literary productions are Wilde's novel *The Picture of Dorian Gray* and play *Salome*, and many other poems of Ernest Dowson.

27.3.1　Algernon Charles Swinburne (1837 – 1909)

Swinburne early acquired an intimate knowledge of Greek, French, Italian as well as English literatures, and his models in literary creation were Greek drama, Victor Hugo, Shelley and Shakespeare. Of his own time, he regarded Dante Gabriel Rossetti (1828 – 1882) and Charles Baudelaire (1821 – 1867), the French poet and author of *Flowers of Evil* (1857), as his brother-poets.

Swinburne wrote a number of plays, including his first book *The Queen Mother, Rosamond: Two Plays* (1861), which attracted no attention, *Atalanta in Calydon* (1865) and a trilogy of Mary Queen of Scots. He also produced several books of literary criticism like *Essays and Studies* (1875) and *Miscellanies* (1886). However, Swinburne was mainly a lyric poet. His mastery of metrical skill, versatility in the use of lyric forms and unconventional choice of themes made him an aesthete. His poems, together with those of Rossetti and others, foreshadowed the literary trend of Decadence and "art for art's sake," represented by Oscar Wilde in the 1890s.

Atalanta in Calydon is a poetical drama in the classical Greek form, with choruses, based on the Greek mythological story about Atalanta. The play made him a poet of renown. According to Greek mythology, Atalanta is a girl given up by her father and is suckled by a she-bear. She grows up in solitude, but her beauty attracts many admirers. She asks her suitors to run a race with her. If any of them reaches the goal before her, he is to be her husband; but all whom she leaves behind are to be killed with her dart. As she is almost invincible in running, many suitors perish in the attempt. Then comes her last suitor and would-be husband, a young man called Milanion. Before the pursuit, Aphrodite, the goddess of beauty and love, has given him three golden apples. As soon as the race begins, he throws down the golden apples, and Atalanta, charmed at the sight, stops to gather them, so that Milanion arrives first at the goal and wins her in marriage. Later on, a wild boar ravages the country of Calydon. Atalanta is invited to take part in the hunt of the Calydonian boar. She is the first to wound it and wins its head as the prize.

The work brought Swinburne fame and was highly praised for its successful imitation of Greek models, though the subject had not been treated by any Greek dramatist. Some critics pointed out its antitheism, and William Michael Rossetti (1829 – 1919) compared it to Shelley's *Prometheus Unbound*.

Swinburne's main lyrics were collected under the general title of *Poems and Ballads*, the three volumes of which came out in 1866, 1878 and 1889 separately. The poems witnessed the author's great skill in using a variety of meters and rhyme schemes, the musical effect of his combinations of melodious vowels and consonants, and his selection of colorful language and vivid imagery. The two themes frequently dealt with in the lyrics are love and death. His free choice of subjects and frank treatment of passion are meant to be an expression of defiance to the hypocrisy and philistinism of the Victorian England, though in his resistance against the bourgeois convention he went to the length of Aestheticism.

27.3.2 Walter Pater (1839 – 1894)

Pater was an English essayist, literary and art critic and writer of fiction. He produced a series of essays on Leonardo da Vinci (1452 – 1519), Botticelli (c. 1445 – 1510), Michelangelo (1475 – 1564) and the other Italian artists and writers from the 14th century to the 16th. All these essays were collected in his masterpiece *Studies in the History of the Renaissance* (1873). The "Conclusion" of the book became a kind of manifesto of the aesthetic movement in English literature. His other works include *Marius the Epicurean* (1885), a philosophical novel and Pater's intellectual autobiography set in the third century, *Imaginary Portraits* (1887) and *Appreciations* (1889). Theoretically, Pater held that the sole duty of an aesthete was to develop his aesthetic sensibilities and enjoy all possible varieties of artistic and sensuous experience.

27.3.3 Oscar Wilde (1854 – 1900)

Wilde was an Irish playwright, novelist, essayist and poet, and the representative among the writers of Aestheticism and Decadence. After writing in different forms throughout the 1880s, he excelled in his writings and became one of London's most popular playwrights in the early 1890s. He is remembered for his epigrams, his novel *The Picture of Dorian Gray* and his plays.

From the 1880s to the 1890s, Wilde wrote and published all his major works including a collection of poetry titled *Poems* (1881), which shows his discipleship to Swinburne, Rossetti and Keats, two collections of fairy tales (*The Happy Prince and Other Tales*, 1888; and *A House of Pomegrnates*, 1891), a collection of short stories *Lord*

Arthur Savile's Crime and Other Stories (1891), a series of critical essays collected in *Intentions* (1891), his only novel *The Picture of Dorian Gray* (1891), his best-known comedies (*Lady Windermere's Fan*, 1893; *A Woman of No Importance*, 1894; *An Ideal Husband*, 1895; and *The Importance of Being Earnest*, 1895), the tragedy *Salome*, which was written originally in French and published in English translation in 1894, and *The Ballad of Reading Gaol* (1898) inspired by his prison experience.

Wilde was Pater's favorite disciple. He was greatly influenced by Pater and determined to put Pater's doctrine into practice, and eventually became a spokesman for the aesthetic movement in England. He followed Pater in his literary and art criticism and even went further by declaring that art did not reflect life but life imitated art. He appeared to hold that art should not begin with the study of life but with what is untrue and does not exist. In his essays and lectures he expounded the theory of "art for art's sake," and his fiction is devoted to the propaganda of this principle.

Wilde's works reflect the degradation of bourgeois culture at the beginning of the epoch of imperialism. The two typical works witnessing Wilde's decadent literary trend are his only novel *The Picture of Dorian Gray* and his tragedy *Salome*, which is about the horrible sadism of an ancient Jewish woman. His poems are also decadent; and his comedies and fairy tales expose the corruption of the bourgeois society. Thus nearly all the literary works express the author's dissatisfaction with the society of his time.

Wilde's comedies are acknowledged as his greatest contribution to English literature. They expose the ugly life picture of the upper class of the English bourgeois society and are noted for the witty paradoxes and epigrams in the dialogues and the cleverly constructed plots. For instance, *The Importance of Being Earnest*, Wilde's masterpiece in drama, mercifully exposes the hypocrisy of the upper society in the Victorian England. His fairy tales like "The Devoted Friend," "The Happy Prince," "The Nightingale and the Rose," and others are written in a graceful style and well remembered for the author's sympathy with the sufferings of the poor and his contempt for the greed and selfishness of the rich. *The Ballad of Reading Gaol* reveals his concern for the inhuman prison condition in Britain. "The Soul of Man under Socialism" (1891), an essay of social criticism, indicates his dissatisfaction with the bourgeois society and his naive aspiration toward socialism, though he had not a clear idea of what socialism was and very probably wished for a society which would give him the personal freedom which he desired.

The Picture of Dorian Gray is a typical decadent novel describing the author's aesthetic view and immoralism. The novel is full of vivid descriptions of the depraved life, heinous crimes and divided personality of the hero Dorian Gray. Gray is a handsome but immoral young hedonist whose immorality leaves no trace in his physical appearance, but is reflected in his portrait which becomes uglier and uglier. When he thrusts the portrait, he kills himself and then the portrait recovers its beauty. In this novel, the hero's appearance does not reflect his immorality but his portrait reflects it. Only from the portrait of the hero can we see what kind of person he is. Here Wilde wanted to show that art was above life and that it could reflect things more faithfully than reality.

Exercises

I. Multiple choices

1. Contrary to the _____ turning back to the past and nature through imagination, the realists wanted a

Part Seven The Period of Realism

truthful representation in their works of contemporary life and manners.

A. Romanticists'
B. Classicists'
C. Sentimentalists'
D. Neoclassicists'

2. The main point of view employed in Victorian novels is the _____ omniscient, the unlimited vision of which helps to paint the broad canvas of life.

A. third-person
B. multiple
C. second-person
D. first-person

3. All great Victorian novels, probably with _____ as an exception, follow the moral standard: Good triumphs over evil; good is praised, and bad castigated.

A. *David Copperfield*
B. *Jane Eyre*
C. *Wuthering Heights*
D. *A Tale of Two Cities*

4. Written for publication as a serial, _____ is a sequence of loosely-related adventures and a picaresque novel like Thomas Nashe's *The Unfortunate Traveler* and Cervantes' *Don Quixote*.

A. *The Old Curiosity Shop*
B. *David Copperfield*
C. *Great Expectations*
D. *The Pickwick Papers*

5. _____ is the "benevolent gentleman" produced by Charles Dickens in *Oliver Twist*.

A. Mr. Steerforth
B. Mr. Peggotty
C. Mr. Brownlow
D. Mr. Nathaniel Winkle

6. Telling the story in the first person, through the mouth of the hero, _____ makes good use of the author's own life experiences to expose the social evils of his day.

A. *David Copperfield*
B. *The Pickwick Papers*
C. *Oliver Twist*
D. *A Tale of Two Cities*

7. Which of the following works is NOT written by Charles Dickens? _____.

A. *David Copperfield*
B. *Sense and Sensibility*
C. *Great Expectations*
D. *A Tale of Two Cities*

8. In _____ the unhappy state of the main characters—a brother and a sister—opens their father's eyes to the knowledge that life contains sentiments as powerful as facts.

A. *The Old Curiosity Shop*
B. *Dombey and Son*
C. *Great Expectations*
D. *Hard Times*

9. _____ is successful in psychological description and the best of Charles Dickens' novels according to some critics.

A. *Great Expectations*
B. *The Pickwick Papers*
C. *Oliver Twist*
D. *A Tale of Two Cities*

10. The main plot of *Vanity Fair* centers on the story of two women Amelia Sedley and _____.

A. Rebecca Sharp
B. Silas Marner
C. Mary Barton
D. Hetty Sorrel

11. George Eliot's first three stories were published together in one volume in 1858 under the title of _____.

A. *Adam Bede* B. *The Mill on the Floss*
C. *Scenes of Clerical Life* D. *Silas Marner*

12. _____, essentially a pastoral novelist, represented the more somber and contemplative mode of perception of High Victorian period.

A. Charles Dickens B. Thomas Hardy
C. Jane Austen D. George Eliot

13. The title of the novel _____ was borrowed by Thackeray from *The Pilgrim's Progress* by John Bunyan.

A. *The Book of Snobs* B. *The Newcomes*
C. *Esmond* D. *Vanity Fair*

14. The title character of *Adam Bede* is a _____, an honest young man, who is always ready to help the weak and the suffering.

A. miller B. village carpenter
C. preacher D. weaver

15. _____ is basically autobiographical; although its author denied that, she did pour a great deal of her own experience into the story.

A. *Jane Eyre* B. *Wuthering Heights*
C. *Middlemarch* D. *Adam Bede*

16. *Mary Barton* contains a vivid picture of the class conflicts between _____ and was severely criticized by bourgeois critics as a book of hostile to the employers.

A. the workers and the capitalists B. the peasants and the landlords
C. the revolutionaries and the cavaliers D. the slaves and the slavers

17. John Barton and Mary Barton, the main characters in *Mary Barton*, are _____.

A. husband and wife B. father and daughter
C. brother and sister D. mother and son

18. The only novel written by Emily Brontë is _____.

A. *Jane Eyre* B. *Wuthering Heights*
C. *The Professor* D. *Adam Bede*

19. Mrs. Gaskell's novel _____ marked a turning point in her literary creation, for in this novel she abandoned Critical Realism for a kind of writing more acceptable to the bourgeois public.

A. *Cranford* B. *Life of Charlotte Bronte*
C. *Mary Barton* D. *North and South*

20. In *In Memoriam*, a poem written in memory of the poet's beloved friend and college-mate, _____ interpenetrated the theme—the question of the immortality of the soul.

A. Alfred Tennyson B. Robert Browning
C. Thomas Hardy D. James Joyce

21. The culmination of the novelist Thomas Hardy's literary career is marked by the two greatest works—_____ and *Jude the Obscure*.

Part Seven　The Period of Realism

  A. *Under the Greenwood Tree*　　　　　　B. *A Pair of Blue Eyes*

  C. *Tess of the D'Urbervilles*　　　　　　D. *The Return of the Native*

22. English Critical Realism, as a new literary trend, flourished in the 1840s and the early1850s. It found its expression mainly in the form of _____.

  A. poetry　　　　　　B. novel

  C. drama　　　　　　D. essay

23. _____ abound in the best works of the realist writers. This is one of the important features of the realistic novel of the 19th century.

  A. Fantasy and romance　　　　　　B. Horror and psychological analysis

  C. Humor and satire　　　　　　D. Individuality and philosophy

24. The greatest English Critical Realist of the 19th century is _____.

  A. Charles Dickens　　　　　　B. William Thackeray

  C. Thomas Hardy　　　　　　D. George Eliot

25. In _____ Charles Dickens made good use of his own life experiences to expose the social evils of his day. Some critics regard the novel as the author's semi-autobiography. The story is told in the first person, through the mouth of the hero.

  A. *David Copperfield*　　　　　　B. *Hard Times*

  C. *Great Expectations*　　　　　　D. *A Tale of Two Cities*

26. As Thomas Hardy was a determinist in his stance on the nature of life and the cosmos, _____ is strongly reflected in his writings.

  A. Romanticism　　　　　　B. fatalism

  C. humanism　　　　　　D. Modernism

27. Robert Browning's great contribution to the English poetry is his _____, i. e., poems in which a character or a situation is expressed by words put into the mouth of the character himself.

  A. improvement of sonnets　　　　　　B. heroic couplets

  C. dramatic monologues　　　　　　D. rhyme scheme

28. _____ is the last and one of the greatest of Victorian novelists. His literary career is divided sharply between his Victorian novels and his post-Victorian poetry.

  A. Charles Dickens　　　　　　B. William Thackeray

  C. Thomas Hardy　　　　　　D. George Eliot

29. _____ is the most contemporaneous of all Thomas Hardy's novels. It is an indictment against the class system and Christianity which Oxford represents in particular and probably also the institution of marriage.

  A. *Jude the Obscure*　　　　　　B. *Tess of the d'Urbervilles*

  C. *The Return of the Native*　　　　　　D. *Far from the Madding Crowd*

30. Among George Meredith's main novels _____ is the best one.

  A. *The Ordeal of Richard Feverel*　　　　　　B. *Beauchamp's Career*

  C. *The Way of All Flesh*　　　　　　D. *The Egoist*

31. Oscar Wilde is the representative among the writers of Aestheticism and Decadence, a spokesman for the school of _____.

  A. "Art for Morality's Sake"   B. "Art for Truth's Sake"

  C. "Art for Art's Sake"   D. "Art for Individuals' Sake"

32. Alfred Tennyson interpenetrated the theme—the question of the immortality of the soul in _____, a poem written in memory of the poet's beloved friend and college-mate.

  A. *In Memoriam*   B. "Ulysses"

  C. "The Tiger"   D. "London"

33. _____ was the work that first made Charles Dickens famous as a popular writer of novel.

  A. *Great Expectations*   B. *The Pickwick Papers*

  C. *Hard Times*   D. *Oliver Twist*

34. Which of the following CANNOT be included in the Critical Realists of the Victorian Period? _____.

  A. Charlotte Bronte and Emily Bronte   B. Charles Dickens and William M. Thackeray

  C. Thomas Hardy and George Eliot   D. D. H. Laurence and James Joyce

35. _____, Samuel Butler's masterpiece, tells a story about the Pontifex family over a stretch of four generations.

  A. *Jane Eyre*   B. *Wuthering Heights*

  C. *Adam Bede*   D. *The Way of All Flesh*

36. _____ was made poet laureate in 1850 when William Wordsworth died, the year in which his famous *In Memoriam* came out.

  A. Robert Browning   B. Matthew Arnold

  C. Alfred Tennyson   D. Percy Bysshe Shelley

37. _____ began the new modern psychological poetry and made the dramatic monologue a norm as a poetic form for presenting the internal world of the characters.

  A. William Wordsworth   B. Robert Browning

  C. Alfred Tennyson   D. Percy Bysshe Shelley

38. In _____ Matthew Arnold stated his three standards of judgment on poetry, which are the moral, the aesthetic and the sociological.

  A. *On the Study of Celtic Literature*   B. *Literature and Dogma*

  C. *Essays in Criticism*   D. *Culture and Anarchy*

39. _____, containing many of Matthew Arnold's central critical arguments, is his finest work dealing with the whole structure of English civilization and culture.

  A. *On the Study of Celtic Literature*   B. *Literature and Dogma*

  C. *Essays in Criticism*   D. *Culture and Anarchy*

40. _____ was written to prove, with the help of portraits of heroes, the author's favorite view of history: "The history of the World is the Biography of Great Men."

  A. *Sartor Resartus*   B. *Heroes and Hero-Worship*

C. *The French Revolution* D. *Past and Present*

41. _____'s most famous works, *Sartor Resartus* and *Past and Present*, are his obvious attempts to move the nation in the direction he would like it to follow.

    A. Thomas Carlyle B. Matthew Arnold
    C. John Ruskin D. Thomas Macaulay

42. Today, George Gissing is most remembered for his novel, _____, which simply describes people and events, yet offers little or no psychological depth.

    A. *Treasure Island* B. *Atalanta in Calydon*
    C. *New Grub Street* D. *The Picture of Dorian Gray*

43. _____, Robert Louis Stevenson's best-known work, is set in the 18th century and describes the surprising adventures of a young man named Jim.

    A. *Treasure Island* B. *Atalanta in Calydon*
    C. *New Grub Street* D. *The Picture of Dorian Gray*

II. Blank-filling

1. During the early two decades or so after 1832, in England there appeared one important chain of events, _____, as a result of the sharp contradiction between labor and capital.

2. Charles Darwin's *On the Origin of Species* and *The Descent of Man* introduced the new biological theory of evolution and discredited the biblical story of _____ of the world and of man and woman.

3. The realists thought of their method as observational and _____.

4. The Victorian novels are essentially urban, reflecting the values of the _____ class.

5. The main point of view employed in Victorian novels is the _____ omniscient, the unlimited vision of which helps to paint the broad canvas of life.

6. Charles Dickens thought that the social problems would be solved if only every employer reformed himself according to the model set by the _____ in his novel and if only _____ used their power and wealth sympathetically to assist _____ to escape from poverty.

7. The subtitle of *Vanity Fair* is _____, which, according to some critics, implies that the writer's intention was not to portray individuals, but the bourgeois and aristocratic society as a whole.

8. In spite of the looseness of construction, _____ is George Eliot's great novel because many characters of different types are vividly portrayed and many social problems are discussed in the course of portrayals of these characters, and one gets a broad realistic picture of the society in a provincial town of the 19th-century England.

9. William Thackeray's first literary success came with a series of satirical sketches entitled *The Snobs of England*, later collected under the title _____.

10. George Meredith wrote mainly about the life of the polite society with some interest in the portrayal of the _____ world of man.

11. George Eliot's major thematic concern relates to _____. All her novels are full of making choices, and her plots develop with choices.

12. _____, George Eliot's first novel, was immediately acclaimed for its realism, for its picturesque por-

trayal of rural life, and for its humor.

13. _____ is a tragic book about the tragic lives of people made tragic by their time. It evolves around the tragic story of a brother and a sister, Tom and Maggie, who are children of an ignorant and obstinate but honest well-to-do miller Mr. Tulliver.

14. _____ describes how a self-centered aristocrat skillfully wins others' sympathy and love, and exposes how, under the influence of bourgeois individualism and egoism, man's soul is corrupted. The work is well known for its deep _____ analysis of the characters.

15. What dominates the world of _____ is "the President of the Immortals," or maybe variously called "fate," "destiny" or "chance."

16. The Victorians valued mainly "applied" poetry (as against _____ poetry), applied in the sense of being useful in inculcating moral lessons, or enforcing established values and tastes, or simply as a means of diversion and entertainment.

17. _____ tried to fuse Alfred Tennyson's poetical sentiment with Robert Browning's intellectual vigor and abundance, and made the best of his poetic endowment to reflect the Victorian temper. As a result, he received recognition as poet number three of his time immediately after Tennyson and Browning.

18. Oscar Wilde's comedies are acknowledged as his greatest contribution to English literature. His best-known comedies include *Lady Windermere's Fan*, *A Woman of No Importance*, *An Ideal Husband* and _____ (1895).

III. Term definition
1. English Critical Realism
2. Dramatic monologue
3. Bildungsroman
4. Narrative
5. Foil
6. Symbol
7. Symbolism
8. Pre-Raphaelites
9. Aestheticism
10. Decadence
11. Regional novel
12. Idyll
13. Psychological novel

IV. Short-answer questions
1. What are the major features of Charles Dickens' novels?
2. How did Thomas Hardy himself divide his novels?
3. What are the features of William Thackeray's novels?
4. What are the features of George Eliot's novels?
5. What are the themes of *Tess of the d'Urbervilles*?
6. What are the writing features of George Meredith's fiction?
7. What are the salient features of the Victorian novels?
8. What are the features of Thomas Hardy's novels?
9. What are the writing features of Thomas Carlyle?

V. Essay questions
1. Give a brief introduction to the English literary currents of the Victorian period.

2. Describe the growth of the Victorian novel.

3. Charles Dickens' great works, produced in different periods of his literary career, well expressed the trace of the author's thought. Summarize one or two salient features in each period and interpret it/them through analyzing the most representative work(s) of the period.

4. Make a comment on *The Mill on the Floss* from the perspective of characterization.

5. List the salient features of *Jane Eyre* and give some interpretation according to your understanding.

6. List the salient features of *Wuthering Heights* and give some interpretation according to your understanding.

7. List the salient features of *Jude the Obscure* and give some interpretation according to your understanding.

8. Introduce *The Way of All Flesh* from the perspective of philosophy.

Part Eight　The Early Twentieth Century

Chapter 28　Introduction

28.1　Background

For Britain, the 20th century was generally a time of decline of the national fortune and power. The first disturbing factor was imperialism, which naturally fostered the two world wars. These two world wars cost Britain not only many lives but also much of its property. In order to pay for the wars, Britain had to give up many of its investments at home and abroad. Its industrial equipment became old-fashioned and lagged behind that of US, Germany and even Japan. This, in turn, resulted in its economic depression and momentous changes in social and political life. In addition, the struggle for women's rights was reaching a climax, the movement for Irish independence gained momentum, and the laboring class made important gains in political power and living standards. All these worked together to give rise to the loss of Britain's dominant position in world politics.

The rapid development of science and technology in the last years of the 19th century and the early decades of the 20th century led on the one hand to great gains in material wealth and large-scale agricultural and industrial production, and on the other hand it resulted in the worldwide mass unemployment and especially the wholesale massacre and destruction during World War I. Consequently, much skepticism and disillusionment spread among the post-World-War-I generation throughout the world and on the European and the North American continents in particular. Many educated people turned to conservatism, to traditional Christian religion (Catholicism), whereas many others, attracted to Marxism and to the Soviet regime, turned to the left, to socialism and communism.

The influence of the theory of evolution advanced by Charles Darwin in the mid-19th century greatly shook the orthodox Christian belief in God and the creation of the world was gradually replaced either by complete atheism or by faith in all sorts of myths of the Oriental or Occidental origin. In the field of psychology, the influence of Carl Jung (1875 – 1961) and especially of Sigmund Freud with his theory of the subconscious mind and dreams was strongly felt and actually penetrating to many British authors of the 20th century, particularly those of the 1920s like James Joyce and Virginia Woolf who tried the "stream-of-consciousness" method in prose fiction.

The status of the arts and literature was beginning to undergo a process of redefining. The alienation of the artist, first evident in the Victorian Aestheticism, now became a widely felt impulse among the artistically minded people. The French symbolists and the Modernist masters such as James Joyce and Thomas Mann (1875 – 1955) all exhibited their penchant to writing regardless of popular tastes. There was a strong sense of disaffection and a huge drive for change in the literary circles. The important developments in the fields like anthropology and philosophy were also exerting a far-reaching influence on literary creation. The multi-volume *The Golden Bough* (1911 – 1915) by James Frazer (1854 – 1941) and the new concept of time of Henry Bergson (1859 – 1941), like Sigmund Freud's *Interpretation of Dreams* (1913) in psychology, contributed in large measure to the forthcoming artistic and literary experimentation. Although nothing major occurred before the 1920s, a lot was going on in the first years of the 20th century. The Edwardians and the Georgians, not responsive enough to the change in taste and values, continued to write in the transitional period. They did their part for English literature.

28.2 Literature

In drama, the English literature of the early 20th century produced two important realist writers—William Butler Yeats and Bernard Shaw. Yeats dealt realistically with the daily life of the Irish country people in his plays (Irish drama). Exploring in his plays a range of social themes like militarism, education, women's situation, and the like, Shaw became another dramatic giant in English literature after William Shakespeare. His plays witnessed a revival of English drama after centuries of relative silence.

The greatest poets in this period are William Butler Yeats and T. S. Eliot. Yeats was awarded the Nobel Prize for literature in 1923. Although he was distinguished as a playwright, especially of verse drama, his fame rested chiefly on his poetry. His early poetry was appreciably influenced by the Aestheticism of the Pre-Raphaelites and the symbolism from France, while his later poetry definitely betrayed his inclination toward Modernism. T. S. Eliot (1888 – 1965) considered him to be the greatest English-speaking poet of his age. T. S. Eliot was also a great critic and fine playwright. He was the chief leader among the writers during the first half of the 20th century. His *The Waste Land* (1922) expresses the temper of his age, the spiritual disease of the 20th century. He is accepted as the experimentalist of Modernist poetry in the English language. He won the Nobel Prize for literature in 1948.

The novelists of the early 20th century can be roughly divided into two groups, the realists and the Modernists. The remarkable one among the first group should be John Galsworthy, who has been noted for portraying the history of English bourgeois life in his famous trilogies, especially in his first trilogy *The Forsyte Saga*. In other words, Galsworthy inherited the traditions of Critical Realism of the Victorian period represented by Dickens. The representative writers of the second group mainly include D. H. Lawrence, James Joyce and Virginia Woolf. What they shared in their novels is that all of them took interest in describing what is happening in the minds of their characters. They insisted that fiction should explore the depths and recesses of personality, revealing an unending stream of impression, feelings and thoughts. In this sense, Lawrence was perhaps an exception. He too looked inward, not to show us a stream of impressions as Virginia Woolf did, but to explore those mysterious areas of feeling.

Chapter 29 Drama in the Early 20th Century

After Sheridan and Oliver Goldsmith, English drama experienced a general decline. In the first half of the 19th century the English theater saw no remarkable performance except Shelley's *The Cenci* (1819). Although many wrote for the theater, including Alfred Tennyson and Matthew Arnold, English drama did not show signs of improvement until after the 1860s, when some commendable though modest efforts began to appear. There were T. W. Robertson (1829 – 1871), trying to bring life and realism to the stage in such works as *Caste* (1867), Henry Arthur Jones (1851 – 1929), who began to put on the "problem play," and Arthur Pinero (1855 – 1934). Pinero attempted to delineate real life situations in his works and became a bridge between the past and the new stage, of which George Bernard Shaw was the legitimate representative. Pinero was a popular playwright of manners in his time, and some of his works are still staged occasionally today. He was serious with his business of writing, and often envisioned the whole complexity of his dramatic scenario before he put it down on paper. He said that he always managed to meet his characters and talk with them and get to know them inside out before he began to portray them and assign them the right place in his works. In the area of comedy, the verbal wit experienced a revival in the comedies of W. S. Gilbert (1836 – 1911) and A. S. Sullivan (1842 – 1900). Oscar Wilde made his presence well felt with his comedies around the time. But for all that, English drama did not quite regain its value until George Bernard Shaw came on the scene.

George Bernard Shaw (1856 – 1950) was the greatest dramatist in the English literature in the 20th century. He was awarded the Nobel Prize in Literature in 1925 for his contributions to literature and an Oscar in 1938 for his work on the film *Pygmalion*, which was adapted from his play of the same title. Shaw followed the great tradition of realism in his dramatic writing. His influence on Western theatre, culture and politics stretched from the 1880s to his death in 1950.

Shaw began his literary career as a novelist and produced five novels from 1879 to 1883, but all these works were turned down at first by the publishers: *Immaturity* was written in 1879 but not printed until 1931; *Cashel Byron's Profession* was completed in 1882 but published in 1886; *An Unsocial Socialist* was written in 1883 and did not come out till 1887; *The Irrational Knot* was written in 1880 and published late in 1905; *Love Among the Artists* was produced in 1881 and published in the United States in 1900 and in England in 1914. In 1885 Shaw took interest in critical essays and became first a critic of music and then a theatre critic. He was highly critical of the Victorian-era productions of Shakespeare, and specifically denounced the dramatic practice of editing Shakespeare's plays, whose scenes tended to be cut in order to create "acting versions." Much of Shaw's music criticism, ranging from short comments to the book-length essay *The Perfect Wagnerite* (1898), extols the work of the German composer Richard Wagner (1813 – 1883). He considered Wagner's four-part opera *Der Ring des Nibelungen* (*The Ring of the Nibelung*), a work of genius and reviewed its London premieres in detail. Beyond the music, he saw it as an allegory of social evolution where workers, driven by "the invisible whip of hunger," seek freedom from their wealthy masters. Shaw's writings about music gained great popularity because they were understandable to the average well-read audience of the day. All of his music critiques have been collected in *Shaw's Music: The Complete Musical Criticism of Bernard Shaw* (1989). As a drama critic for the *Saturday Review*, a post he held from 1895 to 1898, Shaw championed Henrik Ibsen (1828 – 1906) whose realistic plays scandalized the Victorian public. His influential *Quintessence of Ibsenism* was written in 1891. Shaw's greatest gift was for the modern drama. He began writing plays in 1892 and produced more than 60 plays, including *Man and Superman* (pub. 1903, perf. 1905), *Mrs. Warren's Profession* (pub. 1898, perf. 1902), *Major Barbara* (perf. 1905, pub. 1907), *Saint Joan* (perf. 1923, pub. 1924), *Caesar and Cleopatra* (perf. 1899, pub. 1901) and *Pygmalion* (pub. 1913, perf. 1913). With his range from biting contemporary satire to historical allegory, Shaw became the leading comedy dramatist of his generation and one of the most important playwrights in the English language since the 17th century.

Shaw also took an active part in the socialist movement and made a careful study of the works of Marx and Friedrich Engels (1820 – 1895), yet he failed to grasp the necessity of a revolutionary reconstruction of the world. As a young man raised in poverty, Shaw embraced socialism and became an early and lifelong force in the Fabian Society, a highly influential British organization, founded in 1884, to promote a gradual, as opposed to revolutionary, socialism, which was the foundation for the British Labor Party in 1900. He tirelessly wrote and spoke on behalf of its wide-ranging vision to transform the British society, advocating a minimum wage for the working class, universal healthcare, women's right to vote, and the abolition of hereditary privilege. He edited the classic text "Fabian Essays in Socialism" (1889), and helped create the London School of Economics and Political Science from a bequest by an early Fabian in 1895. He publicly opposed Britain's entry into both World Wars.

As a playwright, Shaw drew the attention of his audience to the serious social problems of his time. He did not move chiefly by plot interest. In his opinion, a good play is good not so much because its plot piques the restless curiosity of its audience as because it presents the conflict of ideas to provoke thinking. For him, no play can be serious without serious discussions of grave problems of life.

Shaw's literary career can be divided into three periods. The first period stretched from 1879 to 1901. Shaw produced his five novels, some of his critical essays on music and drama, and the plays which fall into three groups: "Unpleasant Plays," "Pleasant Plays" and "Three Plays for Puritans." These plays were all produced in the 1890s. Shaw's "Unpleasant Plays" include *The Philanderer* (pub. 1898, perf. 1902), *Mrs. Warren's Profession* and his first play *Widower's Houses* (perf. 1892, pub. 1893). His "Pleasant Plays" are *Arms and the Man* (perf. 1894, pub. 1898), *Candida* (perf. 1894, pub. 1898), *The Man of Destiny* (perf. 1897, pub. 1898) and *You Never Can Tell* (pub. 1898, perf. 1899). *Arms and the Man* marked Shaw's dramatic maturity. Among his "Three Plays for Puritans" are *The Devil's Disciple* (perf. 1897, pub. 1901), *Captain Brassbound's Conversion* (perf. 1900, pub. 1901) and *Caesar and Cleopatra*. During the second period, which covered the years between 1901 and 1913, Shaw produced works like *Man and Superman*, *John Bull's Other Island* (perf. 1904, pub. 1907), *Major Barbara*, *Pygmalion*, and others. The third period of Shaw's literary career ended in 1929. In this period, he completed the well-known works like *Heartbreak House* (pub. 1919, perf. 1920), *Saint Joan* and *Back to Methuselah* (pub. 1921, perf. 1922).

The subjects in Shaw's dramatic works cover a wide range of social life. These include slum landlordism in *Widower's Houses*, the rise of Protestantism in England and nationalism in Europe in *Saint Joan*, monarchy and democracy in *The Apple Cart* (perf. 1928, pub. 1929), Irish grievances against English rule in *John Bull's Other Island*, his views on prostitutes and prostitution in *Mrs. Warren's Profession*, and on the Life Force and creative evolution in *Man and Superman* and *Back to Methuselah*, and his attack on the movement of Christian socialism in *Candida*, on evangelism in *Major Barbara*, on inequality between social classes and censure of middle-class morality in *Pygmalion*, on pre-war spiritual poverty in Europe and the shallow Victorian work ethic in *Heartbreak House*, and on Victorian conventions such as home, romantic love, military glory, and idealism in *Arms and the Man*.

Man and Superman: A Comedy and a Philosophy, probably Shaw's masterwork, is a four-act play and an extensive farce that contains an amusing amalgam of diverse doctrines, notions that the author gleaned from Bunyan, Goethe, Tolstoy, Wilde, Ibsen, Plato, Shelley, Marx, Friedrich Nietzsche (1844 – 1900) and Arthur Schopenhauer (1788 – 1860). Its dominant idea is the Life Force. In his 37-page preface, Shaw claimed that it had always been the woman who took the initiative in the business of love and sex from the beginning of time. The man was to put the food on the table, but the woman was to continue the race. The story pivots on John Tanner, who takes it upon himself to turn all the values upside down. His book *The Revolutionist's Handbook and Pocket Companion* holds in contempt all possible established concepts and practices such as humor, marriage, law, democracy and faith. In addition, it speculates about the features of the Superman. Tanner is appointed along with his antithesis, the conventional Roebuck Ramsden, as Miss Ann Whitefield's guardian. Ann, emblematic of the female vessel for the birth of the Superman and the Life Force, tries to entrap him in marriage, but he is not willing to be her prey. He runs away. Ann, with the Life Force in her, follows close at his heels through the English Channel to the other European countries and catches him in Spain. Reluctantly he submits and admits to her, "The Life Force enchants me: I have the whole world in my arms when I clasp you."

The play demonstrates Shaw's optimism about the future that stems from his belief in creative evolution. As Shaw saw it, the only hope was the superman through eugenic breeding (i. e. with mother-woman Ann and artist-man Tanner). This notion bodies forth Shaw's positive morality and his denial of pessimistic Schopenhauer's philosophy. Shaw admired Darwin's theory of evolution and satirized brutally liberal politics (especially the anarchy of the bad-tempered socialist Christian Mendoza). There is also an expression of Shavian feminism, which is, taken as a whole, a complicated, obscure sort of feminism. This is expressed in the female charaters like Ann and Violet. Ann looks like a new woman, assertive, sure of herself, aggressive, and independent in her will and determinism. Violet is her opposite. Although Violet has the courage to break the taboo and have pre-marital sex, she takes orders from her man and does not recognize the new moral standard with which Tanner tries to justify her act.

Major Barbara is a three-act play written and premiered in 1905 and first published in 1907. It portrays the conflict between spiritual and worldly power embodied in Barbara Undershaft, an idealistic young woman Major in the Salvation Army in London, and her machiavellian father Andrew Undershaft. Barbara is engaged in helping the poor as an official. For many years she and her siblings have been estranged from their father, who now reappears as a millionaire armaments manufacturer. The father gives money to the Salvation Army, which offends Major Barbara, who does not want to be connected to his "tainted" wealth. However, the father argues that poverty is a worse problem than munitions, and claims that he is doing more to help society by giving his workers jobs and a steady income than Major Barbara is doing to help them by giving them bread and soup. This play came before the British society had fully experienced the massive scale of the human cost from modern industrial weapons and warfare, which would soon change during the coming carnage of World Wars I and II.

Mrs. Warren's Profession was first performed in London in 1902. The profession in the title refers to prostitution. The story centers on the relationship between Mrs. Kitty Warren and her daughter Vivie. Mrs. Warren, a former prostitute and current brothel owner, is described as "on the whole, a genial and fairly presentable old blackguard of a woman." Vivie, an intelligent and pragmatic young woman, has just graduated from university and come home to get acquainted with her mother for the first time in her life. The play focuses on how their relationship changes when Vivie learns what her mother does for a living. It explains why Mrs. Warren became a prostitute, condemns the hypocrisies relating to prostitution, and criticizes the limited employment opportunities available for women in the Victorian Britain.

Pygmalion, a great comedy, was first performed in Vienna in 1913 and published in London in 1916. It is named after the king of Cyprus in the Greek mythology. Pygmalion, the mythological character, falls in love with his own sculpture, which has been endowed with life by Aphrodite and transformed into the flesh and blood of Galatea. The general idea of the myth is a popular subject for the English playwrights of the Victorian era, some of whom exerted great influence on Bernard Shaw.

The play describes the transformation of a Cockney flower girl Eliza Doolittle into a passable imitation of a duchess by the phonetician Professor Henry Higgins, who undertakes this task in order to win a bet and to prove his own points about English speech and the class system: he teaches her to speak standard English and introduces her successfully to social life, thus winning his bet, but she rebels against his dictatorial and thoughtless behavior, and "bolts" from his tyranny. The play ends with a truce between the two of them, as Higgins acknowledges that she has achieved freedom and independence and emerged from his treatment as a "tower of strength: a consort battleship." It is added in the postscript that Eliza marries the docile and devoted Freddy Eynsford Hill. The play is a sharp lampoon of the rigid British class system of the day and a commentary on women's independence. *My Fair Lady*, the 1957 musical version, makes the relationship between Eliza and Higgins significantly more romantic.

Shaw was a Critical Realist writer. His plays, dealing with contemporary social problems, bitterly criticize and attack English bourgeois society. They explore a range of social themes, including militarism, education, and the situation of women, and tear away the mask of capitalism and deeply expose the social conflicts. In their realism and wit, Shaw's plays are largely comedies of ideas in the French dramatist tradition of Moliere and mark a turning to realism and naturalism that is increasingly to dominate English drama.

Shaw was a humorist. He managed to produce amusing and laughable situations. He delighted in ridiculing, up-setting, scandalizing and astonishing his public. He presented many of his characters as fools. The humor of Shaw always has a touch of satire—a sharp lash that he used with superb skill for exposing and discrediting vice or folly of the age.

Chapter 30 The Edwardians

In her famous essay "Modern Fiction," Virginia Woolf singled out three novelists of the first years of the 20th century for analysis and branded them as "Edwardians," a nomenclature not favorable in meaning. She was especially relentless when discussing one of these, Arnold Bennett, the other two being H. G. Wells and John Galsworthy. Her major complaint was about their over-emphasis on the description of externalities in their representation of life rather than on the internal world of man which she thought should take precedence over anything else in novel-writing. The authors, who wrote and made their names in this "Edwardian" period when King Edward VII (1841 – 1910, king 1901 – 1910) was on the throne, also included Joseph Conrad whose novels came close to Mrs. Woolf's definition of the modern novel, Rudyard Kipling, a poet and prose writer, whose writings are brilliant but sometimes exhibit a degree of imperialistic arrogance and racial bias, and E. M. Forster, probably one of the first writers then sensitive to and aware of the change which materialized into Modernism in the works of Mrs. Woolf, James Joyce and D. H. Lawrence.

30.1　Arnold Bennett (1867 – 1931)

Bennett is best known as a novelist and came under the influence of Zolan naturalism and the writings of the Russian writer Turgenev (1818 – 1883). He also worked in other fields such as journalism, propaganda and film.

Bennett won a literary competition hosted by a magazine in 1889 and was encouraged to take up journalism full-time. In 1894, he became assistant editor of the periodical *Woman*. He noticed that the material offered by a syndicate to the magazine was not very good, so he wrote a serial which was bought by the syndicate. He then wrote another about the mysterious disappearance of a German prince, which was published in 1902 as a novel titled *The Grand Babylon Hotel*. His first novel *A Man from the North* was published to critical acclaim in 1898 and he became editor of the magazine. From 1900 he devoted himself full-time to writing, giving up the editorship. He continued to write journalism despite the success of his career as a novelist.

Bennett wrote over thirty novels and a miscellany of other writings including a popular play. He is famous for his "Five Towns" stories, all of which are based on the pottery towns of modern England. They include *Anna of the Five Towns* (1902), *The Old Wives' Tale* (1908), and The Clayhanger Trilogy—*Clayhanger* (1910), *Hilda Lessways* (1911) and *These Twain* (1915). The descriptions in these novels are true-to-life, naturalistic reproductions of the life in the towns with its faith, stench, poverty, and the overall tedium and gray ugliness that characterized this segment of English society. With the exception of *Anna of the Fives Towns*, which focuses more on one individual's fortune, all the other tales offer a panoramic view of the life of this wretched part of English society. As well as the novels, much of Bennett's non-fiction works have stood the test of time. One of his most popular non-fiction works is the self-help book *How to Live on 24 Hours a Day* (1910). Additionally, extracts from his diaries are often quoted in the British press.

Anna of the Five Towns centers on Anna Tellwright, daughter of a wealthy but miserly and dictatorial father, living in the Potteries area of Staffordshire, England. Her activities are strictly controlled by the Methodist church. The novel tells of Anna's struggle for freedom and independence against her father's restraints, and her inward battle between wanting to please her father and wanting to help Willie Price whose father Titus Price commits suicide after falling into bankruptcy and debt. Anna is courted by the most eligible bachelor Henry Mynors in the town and agrees to be his wife, much to her young sister Agnes' pleasure. Although she discovers in the end that she loves Willie Price, Anna does not follow her heart, for he is leaving for Australia, and she is already promised to Mynors.

The Old Wives' Tale deals with the lives of two very different sisters, Constance and Sophia Baines, following their stories into old age from their youth when they work in their mother's draper's shop. Set in Burslem and Paris, it covers a period of about 70 years from roughly 1840 to 1905.

The book consists of four parts. The first part "Mrs. Baines" details the adolescence of both Sophia and Constance, and their life in their father's shop and house (a combined property). The father is ill and bedridden, and the main adult in their life is Mrs. Baines, their mother. At the end of this part, Sophia (whose name reflects her sophistication, as opposed to the constant Constance) has eloped with a travelling salesman. Constance meanwhile marries Mr. Povey, who works in the shop. The second part "Constance" details the life of Constance from that point forward up until the time she is reunited with her sister in old age. Her life, although outwardly prosaic, is nevertheless filled with personal incident, including the death of her husband Mr. Povey and her concerns about the character and behavior of her son. The third part "Sophia" carries forward the story of what happened to Sophia after her elopement. Abandoned by her husband in Paris, Sophia eventually becomes the owner of a successful pensione. The last part "What Life Is" details how the two sisters are eventually reunited. Sophia returns to England and the house of her childhood, where Constance still lives.

The Clayhanger Family is a series of novels published between 1910 and 1918. Though the series is commonly referred to as a "trilogy," it actually consists of four books—*Clayhanger*, *Hilda Lessways*, *These Twain* and *The Roll-Call* (1918); the first three novels were released in one single volume as *The Clayhanger Family* in 1925. The novels are a coming-of-age story following Edwin Clayhanger as he leaves school, takes over the family business and falls in love. They are set in Bennett's usual setting of "the Five Towns," a thinly-disguised version of the six towns of "the Potteries" which amalgamated into the borough (and later city) of Stoke-on-Trent. Buildings described in the novels are still identifiable in Burslem, which is the fictional "Bursley."

In ***Clayhanger***, the title character is not fully aware of his father's history—his supporting the extremely poor family even during his early childhood, and his rising to become one of the key men in the "Five Towns." Therefore Clayhanger rather takes for granted much of his family's affluence and influence. He allows his ambition to become an architect to be overruled by his domineering father Darius and becomes instead an unwilling (and underpaid) office junior in his father's printing business. He does mildly revolt against his father and his family. While he is capable of seeing through the many hypocrisies of the Victorian England, he does not confront them or become his own man until his father's final illness and death hand him control of his business. The triumph of the book is not in outlining Edwin Clayhanger's escape from the respectable bourgeoisie but in detailing its effect on his life and his submission to it.

Hilda Lessways parallels Edwin Clayhanger's story from the point of view of his eventual wife Hilda. It recounts the story of her coming of age, her working experiences as a shorthand clerk and keeper of a lodging house in London and Brighton, her relationship with George Cannon that ends in her disastrous bigamous marriage and pregnancy, and finally her reconciliation with Edwin Clayhanger. Meanwhile, the novel is in part a re-telling of the plot of *Clayhanger* and includes some scenes from the earlier book from Hilda's perspective. While Bennett makes no direct references to the social and political emancipation of women that was taking place during the period of the novel, the character of Hilda combines the determination of a young woman for self-expression with the disempowerment imposed on her by social norms.

These Twain chronicles the married life of Edwin and Hilda. Edwin, now released from the controlling influence of his father, finds himself free to run his business and his life, a freedom that is diminished by his wife's caprices. He does not enjoy an entirely happy marriage: Hilda does not conform to the stereotype of a submissive wife, which is partly why Edwin married her. It is also suggested that the marriage is based on sexual compatibility, and, as a result, its problems are outside the bedroom. Hilda, who is rescued from virtual destitution by Edwin through their marriage, and who already has a child, is not a figure of passive gratitude, and has opinions on matters such as Edwin's business, which would normally be a wholly male preserve. Edwin has his doubts about their union, and is brought to (mostly impotent) anger by his wife just as he was by his father. The book shows how Hilda and Edwin attempt to compromise. It is suggested that they had both become perhaps too set in their ways before their marriage, even though each was in some way "saved" by their union.

The Roll-Call concerns the young life of Clayhanger's stepson George, who is an architect and represents what his stepfather Edwin Clayhanger wished to become. The central character displays an unattractive arrogance because of the wealth behind him. In an early chapter, he thinks about adding electric light to his London dwelling and decides that he—or rather, his stepfather—can well afford it. The author seemed to have felt that the children of the successful bourgeoisie, unless their excesses were suppressed as Edwin's were, would become spoilt.

Bennett was a careful "scientific" observer, an efficient recorder and a good story-teller. Reading him can be a good rewarding experience. In addition to the enjoyment one can never fail to derive from the tales, one can get an authentic version of the reality at the turn of the 20th century. Indeed, Bennett could serve as a social historian of some kind. One of the things he did not do well, however, was his failure to sense the wind of change already beginning to blow in the new century, and this incurred a very dear price he had to pay in fame and historical placement. As a matter of fact, Bennett took an immense delight in the minute and accurate portrayal of the exterior details of life, told his stories with a calm countenance and took care to avoid comments, and stopped right at the point when the interior of the human soul got involved. This does not mean that the writer had no compassion; Bennett had plenty of it as he said in his journals to the effect that compassion was the hallmark of greatness for a writer. His objective documentation of life was all right as a manner of literary creation—so akin to that of Trollope's—until Mrs. Woolf stood out to say that it was not. Her comments upon his works, which began a new epoch in literary history, sent Bennett all the way down to the nadir of his reputation, from which he had yet to recover.

30.2 Rudyard Kipling (1865 – 1936)

Kipling was an English short-story writer, poet and novelist, and one of the most popular writers in the United Kingdom in both prose and verse in the late 19th and early 20th centuries. He was awarded Nobel Prize for Literature in 1907 and became the first English-language writer to receive the prize and its youngest recipient to date. He was also sounded out for the British Poet Laureateship and on several occasions for a knighthood, both of which he declined.

Kipling's works include fictions like *The Jungle Book* (1894), *Kim* (1901) and "The Man Who Would Be King" (1888), and poems like "Mandalay" (1890), "Gunga Din" (1890), "The Gods of the Copybook Headings" (1919), "The White Man's Burden" (1899) and "If—" (1910). Basically a short-story writer, Kipling is regarded as a major innovator in the art of the short story, which as a genre throve after he enriched it with his craft. Kipling's stories are mostly set in India and cover areas such as India, South Africa, South America and London. His subjects are highly inclusive, touching on diverse social manners.

Kipling is best known for his ***The Jungle Book***, a collection of stories about a white child left in an Indian jungle but surviving the inclement environment in the company of his jungle folk—the wolves, bears, tigers, panthers and elephants. The child Mowgli, brought up by Mother Wolf, lives as one of the wolf pack in the brute world for seventeen years before he meets his mother Messua and returns finally to the man pack to which he belongs. The tales in the book (and also those in *The Second Jungle Book* which followed in 1895, and which includes five further stories about Mowgli) are fables, using animals in an anthropomorphic manner to give moral lessons. The book has become a classic of its own kind, offering good reading matter for all readers—as a fable for children and as a book of wisdom for adults. It is even good for scholars and philosophers as they can read and meditate upon the nature of the human condition. What detracts from its value as a classic is the fact that Kipling, with his imperialistic and white chauvinistic attitude, revealed a strong racial bias here. Mowgli may be seen as a white man trying to make out in an inferior milieu in which white virtues cannot take root.

"**The Man Who Would Be King**" is a novella about two British adventurers in British India who become kings of Kafiristan, a remote part of Afghanistan. The story was inspired by the exploits of an Englishman James Brooke (1803–1868) and by the travels of an American adventurer Josiah Harlan (1799–1871). It incorporates a number of other factual elements such as locating the story in eastern Afghanistan's Kafiristan and the European-like appearance of many of Kafiristan's Nuristani people. The story was first published in *The Phantom Rickshaw and Other Eerie Tales* (Volume Five of the *Indian Railway Library*, published in 1888).

"**The White Man's Burden**" is notorious for the author's blatant, repellent show of Anglo superiority. The poem was originally published with the subtitle "The United States and the Philippine Islands." Through "Burden," Kipling tended to reflect the subject of American colonization of the Philippines, recently won from Spain in the Spanish-American War. The poem consists of seven stanzas, following a regular rhyme scheme. It appears to be a rhetorical command to white men to colonize and rule other nations for the benefit of those people (both the people and the duty may be seen as representing the "burden" of the title).

Although the poem mixes exhortation of empire with somber warnings of the costs involved, imperialists within the United States of America understood the phrase "white man's burden" as justifying imperialism as a noble enterprise. Because of its theme and title, the poem has become emblematic both of Eurocentric racism and of Western aspirations to improve and industrialize the developing world. A century after its publication, the poem still rouses strong emotions and can be analyzed from a variety of perspectives.

30.3 John Galsworthy (1867–1933)

Galsworthy was one of the most prominent English novelists in the early 20th century. He received the Nobel Prize for literature in 1932. With 17 novels, 28 plays and a dozen volumes of short stories and miscellaneous writings to his credit, Galsworthy was one of the most prolific writers of the period. He inherited the tradition of Critical Realism of the Victorian period represented by Charles Dickens and kept to his traditional way of writing amid the engulfing din of a new way of literary expression—Modernism. Coming from a wealthy Forsyte-like family, he wrote a good deal of his own life into his fiction. His themes focus on the lives and experiences of the rich men of property, their selfishness, their philistinism, their decadence, depravity and decline, and their fierce conflict with the workers. Galsworthy wrote in such a way that his readers can never feel let down to look for entertainment and moral guidance in reading him. He is noted for portraying the history of the English bourgeois life in his famous trilogies, especially in his first trilogy *The Forsyte Saga*.

Galsworthy's major works are his three trilogies, in which he dealt with several generations of a distinguished wealthy bourgeois family. They are *The Forsyte Saga* (1906 - 1921), *A Modern Comedy* (1924 - 1928) and *The End of the Chapter* (1931 - 1933). The first trilogy includes *The Man of Property* (1906), *In Chancery* (1920) and *To Let* (1921), and two interludes—*The Indian Summer of a Forsyte* (1918) and *Awakening* (1920). The second includes *The White Monkey* (1924), *The Silver Spoon* (1926) and *Swan Song* (1928). The third consists of *Maid in Waiting* (1931), *The Flowering Wilderness* (1932) and *Over the River* (1933).

The Forsyte Sage, as with many of Galsworthy's other works, deals with social class, upper-middle class lives in particular. Although sympathetic to his characters, the author highlighted their insular, snobbish and acquisitive attitudes and their suffocating moral codes. He is viewed as one of the first writers of the Edwardian era who challenged some of the ideals of society depicted in the preceding Victorian literature. The trilogy is an extended treatment, resumed in *A Modern Comedy*, of the history of the Forsyte family from the late Victorian period through the end of WWI. The story covers all the vicissitudes relating and leading up to the final conclusion of the family drama. It narrates in fact the complexities of the experience of one particular social class—the industrialists, parasites, and their like—and the scenes culled from their lives. The major character here is Mr. Soames Forsyte, the nephew of old Jolyon. The story of **The Man of Property** evolves around Soames and his sense of property. Soames lives in London surrounded by his prosperous old uncles and their families. He is a successful solicitor and a man of property. His relationship with his wife Irene is strained because he sees her as just another piece of his property. He represents the sum total of the vices of the capitalist rich—selfishness, greed, hypocrisy and tyranny. The beautiful Irene falls in love with Bosinney, the fiancé of young Jolyon's daughter, but returns to Soames when Bosinney is killed in a street accident. *The Man of Property* established the author's fame as a prominent novelist and marked the peak of Critical Realism in all Galsworthy's works. It criticizes the possessive instinct of the Forsytes and its effects upon the family relationships. Soames' sense of property is the buff of the author's satire and criticism. But the dominant critical note here becomes softened in the later works of the first trilogy.

In **In Chancery**, Soames divorces Irene and marries a French girl Annette Lamotte. They have a daughter named Fleur. Irene, after 12 years of solitude, is married to young Jolyon, the prodigal son who runs away from his arranged marriage at the beginning of the saga. She gives birth to a son named Jon. However, Soames still cherishes a passion for Irene. **To Let** tells the story of the next generation: Soames' daughter Fleur and Irene's son Jon meet by chance and fall in love at first sight. The union being impossible, Jon leaves for America in despair, and the equally sad Fleur is married off to Michael, the heir to a baronetcy. After young Jolyon dies, Irene leaves to join Jon in America. The desolate Soames learns that his wife is having an affair with a Belgian, and discovers that Irene's house Robin Hill—the country house he built for Irene—is empty and to let. He is left contemplating all that he has lost. The novel thus concludes the Forsyte Saga.

As a dramatist, Galsworthy, in his 28 plays, as in his novels, realistically dealt with the social problems of his time. His play writing began with *The Silver Box* (1906), one of his two best-known plays. It is a play about theft in which the author employed a favorite device of "parallel" families, one rich one poor. This is the first of a long line of plays on social and moral themes. Galsworthy's reputation as a dramatist became firmly established with his other best-known play *The Strife* (1909), an examination of men and managers in industry.

A Critical Realist in the early 20th century, Galsworthy directed his attack and satire toward the propertied class in his realistic novels. While exposing the well-to-do and diagnosing the social disease, he penetrated into the subtle windings of the human heart and drew human passions with psychological depth. But his criticism of the upper class is limited to the spheres of ethics and aesthetic only. He suggested no remedies of social problems. His aim was to dethrone his own class in society.

Galsworthy is also noted for his style, which is marked by its strength and elasticity, by its powerful sweep, brilliant illustrations and deep psychological analysis. His language is concise, clear and straightforward.

30.4　H. G. Wells (1866 – 1946)

Herbert George Wells was a novelist-reformer. He is best remembered for his achievement in science fiction and his prophecies about the outbreak of the two world wars, which reveal his rich imaginative powers. Wells is acknowledged as one of the founding figures of science fiction, along with Jules Verne (1828 – 1905) and Hugo Gernsback (1884 – 1967). In actuality, he wrote more than science fiction. His literary writings can be divided into three groups—science fiction, social satire, and novels of ideas. He wrote over 100 volumes, of which over 50 are novels, and a few are collections of short stories and other miscellanies. Wells was nominated for the Nobel Prize in Literature in four different years. Like Bennett and Galsworthy, he wrote in the tradition of realism.

Wells' earliest specialized training was in biology, and his thinking on ethical matters took place in a specifically and fundamentally Darwinian context. He was also from an early date an outspoken socialist, often (but not always, as at the beginning of the First World War) sympathizing with pacifist views. His later works became increasingly political and didactic. Novels like *Kipps: The Story of a Simple Soul* (a 1905 social novel) and *The History of Mr. Polly* (a 1910 comic novel), which describe lower-middle-class life, led to the suggestion, when they were published, that he was a worthy successor to Charles Dickens, but Wells described a range of social strata and in *Tono-Bungay* (1909), which is a semi-autobiographical novel and has been called "arguably his most artistic book," even attempted a diagnosis of the English society as a whole. (Smith, 1986: 174)

Through his science fiction, Wells took his readers with him in his visionary flights through space and time, and offered them an ample opportunity to observe life from different spatial and temporal perspectives. His stories serve a serious purpose of social satire at the same time they entertain. Wells' prophetic faculty was simply amazing. He visualized man's flight long before the first airplane was born and man's space travel over 60 years prior to the first human landing on the moon. And he foresaw the possibility of a nuclear war. His major works in science fiction include *The Time Machine* (1895), probably his best effort in this field, *The War of the Worlds* (1898), describing as it does the honors of a Martian invasion of the earth, *The First Men in the Moon* (1901), with its description of life on the moon not substantially different from modern men's actual discoveries on it, *The Island of Doctor Moreau* (1896) as well as *The Invisible Man* (1897). The titles alone suggest the author's immense influence on subsequent works, some of which are often but dim replicas of the great master's visions.

The Time Machine is a novella, whose protagonist is an English scientist and gentleman inventor living in the Victorian England and identified by a narrator simply as the Time Traveller. The narrator recounts the Traveller's lecture to his weekly dinner guests that time is simply a fourth dimension, and his demonstration of a tabletop model machine for travelling through it. He reveals that the Traveller has built a machine capable of carrying a person through time and returns at dinner the following week to recount a remarkable tale, becoming the new narrator. In the new narrative, the Time Traveller first tests his device with a journey that takes him to A. D. 802,701, where he meets the Eloi, a society of small, elegant, childlike adults. Then he travels further ahead to roughly 30 million years from his own time, where he sees some of the last living things on a dying Earth. His travels cover strange adventures and end up with his going back to the machine and returning to the Victorian time, arriving at his laboratory just three hours after he originally left. Interrupting dinner, he relates his adventures to his disbelieving visitors, offering as evidence two strange white flowers that Weena, an Eloi woman, whom he saved from drowning and with whom he developed an innocently affectionate relationship, put in his pocket. The original narrator then takes over and relates that he returns to the Time Traveller's house the next day, finding him preparing for another journey. He reveals that, though he promises to return in a short period of time, the Time Traveller has never returned.

Wells is generally credited with the popularization of the concept of time travel by using a vehicle that allows an operator to travel purposely and selectively forwards or backwards in time. The term "time machine" is now almost universally used to refer to such a vehicle. *The Time Machine* has since been adapted into two feature films of the same name, as well as two television versions, and a large number of comic book adaptations. It has also indirectly inspired many more works of fiction in many media.

30.5 Joseph Conrad (1857 – 1924)

Conrad was a Polish-British writer and one of the greatest novelists in the English language. He was more a transitional figure than any Edwardian. He exhibited a close affinity in temperament with the rising generation of Modernists. His preeminence in English literature relates to the fact that, coming in between the two periods, he acted as a bridge, a liaison, thus helping English literature enter a new phase.

In his literary endeavors Conrad drew mostly on his personal experiences on the sea and in the remote parts of the world as well as on the national experiences of his native Poland. His short stories and novels reflect aspects of a European-dominated world. Conrad possessed an unusual power to dramatize such scenes as related to typhoons and such secrets as hidden in the woods. He represented them in an entrancing manner compounded of authentic details and a rich romantic flavor. Appreciated early on by literary critics, his fiction and nonfiction have since been seen as almost prophetic, in the light of subsequent national and international disasters of the 20th and 21st centuries.

Conrad's works are heavily Modernistic in theme and form, though they still contain elements of the 19th-century realism. Conrad is considered an early Modernist. His narrative style and anti-heroic characters have influenced many authors, including T. S. Eliot, William Faulkner (1897 – 1962), Graham Greene, and more recently Salman Rushdie (1947 –). Many films have been adapted from, or inspired by, Conrad's works. One of the salient features of his fiction is the strikingly permeating sense of disjunction and fragmentation that characterizes the

Modernist works. Conrad wove adroitly into a coherent whole disparate stories that different people tell from different perspectives, so that stories appear within the story dotted with endless discursive digressions. He intended to replicate both the sense of mystery inherent in life and the diverse phases of the mind in a manner very close to being impressionistic. He tried to bring out his theme by means of the momentary impressions it leaves on the mind. This manner of representation enabled the writer to approach the various facets of truth at various moments in his various moods. Another feature of Conrad's fiction is the psychological explorations and the focus on the interiority of the characters. There is seen in his characters the perpetual feeling of solitude and alienation, the craving for human connection, friendship and compassion which are, however, always conspicuously absent from life. The longing for understanding or luck, if they ever come, seems to come always when it is too late for any good.

Conrad was a unique, gifted novelist. He wrote a great number of novels such as *Almayer's Folly* (1895), *The Outcast of the Islands* (1896), *The Nigger of the Narcissus* (1897), *Lord Jim* (1900) and *Typhoon* (1902), and a good many novellas and short stories, one of which is *The Heart of Darkness* (1902). He also wrote an autobiography, adding to the impressive total of over 30 volumes of writing that he did over a period of some thirty years. Conrad's fiction falls roughly into three groups—the sea fiction, the forest fiction and the social fiction. A good number of his novels and novellas are set on the sea which is his major source of subjects and inspiration. *Lord Jim* and *The Heart of Darkness* are both among his most fascinating and powerfully influential works.

Lord Jim relates the tragic, highly moral story of the title character. Jim is chief mate on board the Patna, an ill-manned ship carrying a party of Muslim pilgrims in Eastern waters. He is young, idealistic, and a dreamer of heroic deeds. When the Patna threatens to sink, Jim joins the other officers who escape in the few lifeboats, and leaves the helpless pilgrims on the ship. Although the Patna does not sink and the pilgrims are rescued, Jim feels guilty and spends his lifetime redeeming the sin he commits at the moment of cowardice and moral defection. What happens to Jim thereafter is related by an observer Marlow. Jim, alone among the crew, remains to face the court of enquiry, deeply disturbed at his defection from a code of conduct dear to him. Condemned by the court and stripped of his papers, he tries to disappear, moving from place to place whenever his past threatens to catch up with him. He searches for anonymity and the chance to redeem himself. Through Marlow's intervention Jim is sent to a remote trading station in Patusan. His efforts create order and well-being in a previously chaotic community and he wins the respect and affection of the people and is honored as "Lord Jim." He has achieved some sense of peace, but the memory of his jump is still with him. When Gentleman Brown and his gang of thieves arrive to disrupt and plunder the village, Jim begs the chiefs to spare them, pledging his own life for their departure. But Brown behaves treacherously and a massacre takes places. Jim feels he has only one course of action; rejecting the idea of flight he delivers himself up to Chief Doramin, whose son was a victim of the massacre. Doramin shoots him and Jim willingly accepts this honorable death.

The story is not presented in the chronological order. It looks like a hotchpotch, or a fish cut up into pieces and placed tail over head in a frying pan. The narrative chaos is, however, well deliberated upon and carefully designed. The different parts of the story are nicely tied together with the help of well planted leads and dexterous foreshadowings. This peculiar narrative scheme serves the purpose to help increase the tension and suspense and the sense of mystery with which the story is enveloped. It is also designed to do a much more important job: to examine the different aspects of Jim's complex inner world of guilt and faith in rebirth, and paint a better picture of his soul struggling through self-censure and pain to redemption, regeneration and spiritual serenity. The disjunctiveness and disorderliness vanish when all the loose ends as part and parcel of a unity are tied up in a knot, tidy and neat enough to knead the reader's bits of impressions into a totality of awareness. Here Conrad took over from George Eliot and Henry James and developed their hitherto not yet well heeded tradition of the psychological novel. Another thing to note is the varying points of view used for the three sections of the book. In the first section, an omniscient narrator helps reveal Jim's interiority for the readers. In the second section, a first-person point of view is employed from chapter 5 and carries the story through chapter 35. The last section wraps up the narrative in flashbacks with the help of letters and manuscripts.

The Heart of Darkness, a novella, adds as it does the term "the heart of darkness" to the modern literary critical idiom and offers an important theme to literature in general. On board a boat anchored peacefully in the Thames the narrator Marlow tells the story of his voyage to Africa, the continent whose shape resembles that of the human heart, and the heart of which is Congo. Traveling in Africa to join a cargo boat, Marlow grows disgusted by what he sees of the greed of the ivory traders and their brutal exploitation of the natives. The trip to Congo as described in the book is not just a trip; it proves to be an attempt on the part of the traveler at self-exploration and self-analysis. As the story goes, the narrator sees the extent of devastation to which the white colonialists have subjected the continent. He learns about Kurtz, the most brutal and atrocious of these colonialists, a dying man who has been there for years, pillaging, cheating and killing large numbers of the local people, and has made himself a veritable satanic demigod figure there. But the man presents a psychological complexity himself. Born of English and French parentage, Kurtz bodies forth the sum total of western education. As a young adventurer, he had his ideal and ambition to come and "civilize" the African "primitives." But the thirst for power and wealth has pushed him into the abyss of crime and punishment. In a very real sense, he has also been a spiritual victim of his own greed, robbery and eternal loneliness. The narrator sees him dying with screams, "Horror, horror!" condemning probably both himself and the system he represents, the one that has made him suffer inordinately and successfully ruined his life.

Formally, the novella effectively employs an amalgam of the symbolic, impressionistic and fragmentary modes of perception and presentation to dive little by little into the quagmire of guilt and despair of the man's heart and reveal the deep-seated horrors of a soul completely gone evil and unredeemable. Thematically, the man is clearly made out to represent the guilty conscience of the colonialists, in whose heart of hearts lies nothing but darkness. The narrator discovers through Kurtz that the heart of the Europeans is all darkness and that the heinous crimes they have committed against humanity prove themselves to be the very savages who Kurtz once suggested in a report to one international organization should be exterminated. The book is thus a thorough condemnation of the criminal behavior of the colonialist powers. Its rich load of meaning has been well excavated from different perspectives, including the social, the historical, the mythological, or the psychological.

30.6 E. M. Forster (1879 – 1970)

Forster was an English novelist, short story writer, essayist and librettist. He is best known for his ironic and well-plotted novels examining class difference and hypocrisy in the early 20th-century British society. The writers, Forster felt sensitively, would have to go down another avenue and the novels would have to be written in a different way if they were true to the new experience of the new age. In his collection of speeches, *Aspects of the Novel* (1927), he well expounded the idea that the novel should not merely follow the common tradition of telling a story but should be written differently. This idea coincides with the stance which Virginia Woolf held in her criticism on the Edwardians.

In actual writing, however, Forster was in essence a transitional figure in between literary periods. His subjects touch upon such themes as the inner world of man, the sense of estrangement and alienation, and the relationship between man and nature, all themes that smell strongly of Modernism. *A Room with a View* (1908) is Forster's most optimistic work while *A Passage to India* (1924) is his greatest success.

A Passage to India, written in the traditional manner, tries to represent and explore the psychological facet of man. On the one hand, it claims that hope stems from the human connection or "communion" by means of which man can vanquish hopelessness. On the other hand, it seems to be saying that it is impossible for the East and the West to connect with each other as there is no road leading from Britain to India and there exists in fact a vast void of nothingness beneath the deceptive surface of the rush and bustle of life. This suggests Forster's awareness of the nihilist spirit engulfing the first years of the 20th century. One striking feature of the novel is its symbolism. Its three sections—the mosque, the cave and the temple—constitute an adequate expression of its plot priorities—the possibility, the barrier and the opposition—all pertinent to the connection of the two hemispheres; they manage to leave a faint ray of hope for the readers. In addition, Forster hooked and held attention often by means of his spectacular plot interest. His authorial comments and advice often smacked strongly of Fielding and Thackeray.

30.7 Katherine Mansfield (1888 – 1923)

Mansfield is the pen name of Katherine Mansfield Beauchamp Murry. She was a prominent Modernist writer of short fiction. Her achievement in the area of the short story has been such that she represents a milestone in the history of the genre.

Mansfield was born and brought up in colonial New Zealand. At the age of 19, she left New Zealand and settled in the United Kingdom, where she became a friend of Modernist writers such as D. H. Lawrence and Virginia Woolf. A year later, Mansfield began writing, drawing profusely from her recollections of her childhood, her family and her native city. The stories of this nature include her best work "Prelude" (1918), and other works like "At Bay," "The Garden Party" and "Her first Ball." Mansfield's subjects are more about individuals than direct social concerns. She found value in personal responses and impressions and tried to derive "the real thing" from these reflections. In formal aspects, Mansfield placed more focus on the excavation of the psychology of her characters rather than on the detailed description of the exteriors. Sensitive to the change in values and tastes of the time, she employed the impressionist mode of representation at times. There is not much of a plot, or coherent narrative in her stories. Her handling of space and time, as she did with her "The Daughters of the Late Colonel" (1902), indicates that she was not indifferent to the rising Modernist mode of writing. Her collections of short stories include *Bliss and Other Stories* (1920), *The Garden Park and Other Stories* (1922), *The Dove's Nest and Other Stories*

(1923) and *Something Childish and Other Stories* (1924). Her critical writings, over 100 in number, are collected in her *Novels and Novelists* (1930).

Chapter 31 The Georgians and the War Poets

Between 1910 and 1920 during the so-called "Georgian" period (1910 – 1936) when George V (1865 – 1936) was on the throne, a group of lyrical poets were active on the English literary scene. The term "the Georgians" came from a series of five anthologies named *Georgian Poetry*—*Georgian Poetry 1911 – 12* (1912), *Georgian Poetry 1913 – 15* (1915), *Georgian Poetry 1916 – 17* (1917), *Georgian Poetry 1918 – 19* (1919) and *Georgian Poetry 1920 – 22* (1922)—edited by Edward Marsh (1872 – 1953) and showcasing the poets' works. The Georgian poets include John Drinkwater, W. H. Davies, Water de la Mare, Edward Thomas, Rupert Brooke, and even Robert Graves, who had a long and complex career. Some of D. H. Lawrence's lyrics were also included in the Georgian anthologies, though these were different and superior. The Georgians rejected the avant-garde aesthetic kind of poetry of the last decade of the 19th century and turned back to tradition. They observed poetically nature, love and rural traditional English life, and wrote about these in a style gentle, less self-conscious and more easily approachable. They sang sweet pastoral songs in praise of the temporal serenity and stability that England had enjoyed before WWI and offered an avenue of escape for the people in the period of chaos after it. These poets were capable of sentimental lapses and skilled in traditional metrics. Receiving warm welcome from the general readers, they sold enviously well. But they were harshly criticized later for their want of depth in thought and feeling. The Georgians lost their vogue in the 1920s when the pastoral mode of writing was out of place and a wind of change started blowing on the post-WWI scene. The imagist movement had already started, and Modernism was fast burgeoning into shape. From then on Yeats and Eliot began their domination, and the Georgians were ignored for some three decades. Then the poets of the 1950s veered away from High Modernism and Dylan Thomas and turned to tradition, dredging in their literary endeavors these Georgians from the deeps of oblivion. The famous American Robert Frost (1874 – 1963) was in England around this time and also became a Georgian as well: he was probably the best of the group.

Meanwhile, during and after WWI, there were a host of war poets in England, including Edward Thomas, Rupert Brooke, Edmund Blunden, David Jones and Wilfred Owen. They wrote about the war and their poetry is characterized by poignant immediacy. Most of the poems are short but vital and intense. As the dehumanizing technology deprived man of his history-making role, man lost his control of the war and his self, and was no longer heroic. As a consequence, there was no epic to come out. But as the poets fought and died in the trenches, their responses to the reality of war were vigorous and emotionally loaded. Actually, the Georgians are hard to separate from the war poets, or vice versa, as they wrote in the same context.

31.1 W. H. Davies (1871 – 1940)

Davies was a Welsh poet and writer, one of the most popular poets of his time as well as a well-known figure among the Georgian Poets. The principal themes in his works are observations about the hardships in life, the ways in which the human condition is reflected in nature, his own tramping adventures and the various characters he met. He wrote hundreds of brief and simple nature lyrics. Almost all of his poetry belongs to quiet traditionalism, and many of them do not have any distinction. His first volume of poetry *The Soul's Destroyer and Other Poems* came out in 1905. This was followed by several other volumes and growing praise from writers such as Edward Thomas; he made many friends in the literary and artistic world. His best-known poems record his sharp and intense response to the natural world. In 1923 he married a girl much younger than himself, and he told the story of his extraordinary courtship in *Young Emma*, posthumously published in 1980. His *Complete Poems*, with an introduction by O. Sitwell (1892 – 1969), appeared in 1963.

31.2 Walter de la Mare (1873 – 1956)

Walter de la Mare was an English poet, short story writer and novelist. He belonged rather to the 19th century than to the 20th, chiefly on account of his romantic temper in poetry, so that he has been sometimes called "the belated last poet of the romantic tradition." (qtd. in Barfield, 1973: 75) Remembered chiefly as a poet, for both adults and children, de la Mare was fluent, highly inventive, technically skilful, and unaffected by fashion. In his favorites themes of childhood, fantasy, and the numinous, commonplace objects and events are invested with mystery and often with an undercurrent of melancholy. Especially in the few poems that brought him fame he distinguished himself with the infusion of magic and mystery that reminded one of Coleridge and Keats. He is probably best known for his works for children and for his poem "**The Listeners**." In the poem readers are introduced into the magic land in which a traveler knocks several times "on the moonlit door" and, receiving no response except from "a host of phantam listeners" "in the lone house," he shouts in the silence: "Tell them I came," but "no one answered,/That I kept my word." This episode that seems to take place out of time and space and to exist for only a few brief moments hearkens back to "The Rime of the Ancient Mariner" and "The Eve of St. Agnes." Equally shrouded in mystery is "All That's Past," another simple lyric tracing back to the undated past, in which the first stanza out of three contains such strange charm that it sounds a jarring note in the age of Modernist poetry which fell under the influence of the Metaphysical poetry of the 17th century.

Walter de la Mare also wrote some subtle psychological horror stories, amongst them "Seaton's Aunt" and "Out of the Deep." His 1921 novel *Memoirs of a Midget* won the James Tait Black Memorial Prize for fiction and his post-war *Collected Stories for Children* won the 1947 Carnegie Medal for British children's books.

31.3 Philip Edward Thomas (1878 – 1917)

Edward Thomas was an Anglo-Welsh poet, essayist and novelist, and the most appreciated Georgian poet. His lucid nature poems impressed W. H. Auden and other poets of a later generation. His poetic career began in 1914 when he experienced a creative outburst. Most of Thomas' poetry was published posthumously; a few pieces appeared under the pseudonym "Edward Eastaway" between 1915 and 1917. *The Poems of Edward Thomas* (1978) is the fullest among Edward Thomas' various collections. His theme is the natural world and his work shows a loving and accurate observation of the English pastoral scene, combined with a bleak and scrupulous honesty and clarity. His mood is basically melancholy. Like Robert Frost, Edward Thomas advocated the use of natural diction and of colloquial speech rhythms in metrical verse. He also wrote a number of "war poems" that portray, among other things, his love for his country. So he is commonly considered a war poet, although few of his poems deal directly with his war experiences.

In "**Adlestrop**" (1915) the poet sits in late June at a station, the train draws up, but no one stirs. It leaves the platform bare and the rest of the world—the station, the willows, willow-herb, grass, the meadowsweet, haycocks, cloudlets, and him—"still and lonely." Then he hears the sweet soothing voice of a blackbird and becomes aware of the faint but sure chorus of all the birds in Oxfordshire and Gloucestershire. He feels that he is not still and lonely after all with this musical backdrop for his existence. "**The Owl**" (1915) sketches the poet's fear of loss and death and suffering that the war and poverty may bring to his fellow creatures. Here the poet turns in after a tiring night trip in the cold North wind, and enjoys now the comforts of life—food, warmth and the rest, but the plaintive strains of the owl keep reminding him of the hardships of the night that he has been through. The same dominant ideas of solitude and warm humanity mingle with a touch of despair and noble heroism in his poem "Rains" (1916).

Living a couple of years longer to witness its disastrous impact on human life, Thomas was different from Rupert Brooke in his representation of the war. His war poems reveal his tragic awareness of the devastating and debilitating effects of wars. "**As the Team's Head Brass**" (1917) is set in the fields where the ploughman is working with his team of horses. The poet-narrator sits by and talks with him. The farmer complains about the war killing his fellow farmers and his working mates and leaving farm work undone and making life impossible. There is mention of casualties and injuries. The ploughman sounds like a philosopher when he says, "[i]f we could see all might seem good" (l. 32), revealing the unpredictability of life and the helplessness of the humans. The poem is noted for its symbolism. The blizzard that fells the tree and the lovers who disappear and resurface can both be symbolic in a way. The former can be seen as a symbol of the war, while the lovers, leaving the scene at the beginning when the subject of the war is about to be brought up and returning in the end when the subject is closed with the ambiguous vision of a better world, could signify the life force that may be eclipsed for a while but always manages to endure.

31.4 John Drinkwater (1882 – 1937)

Drinkwater was a prolific English poet, dramatist, critic and actor. His first volume of *Poems* appeared in 1903. His works appeared in all five volumes of *Georgian Poetry*, and were collected in 1933 in *Summer Harvest*. In 1907 Drinkwater founded the company which later became the Birmingham Repertory Theater. He wrote many plays, including *Abraham Lincoln* (1918), *Oliver Cromwell* (1921), *Mary Stuart* (1922) and a successful comedy *Bird in Hand* (1927). He also wrote stories and plays for children, and produced critical studies of Swinburne, Byron, Shakespeare, and others.

Drinkwater was possibly the most representative of the so-called "Georgian Poets" at their worst. He wrote on very conventional themes in traditional verse form and had little to distinguish himself with. However, there was a quiet and contemplative dignity in a short poem like "Reciprocity," in which he tried to meditate on common natural phenomena like meadows and stars and trees.

31.5 Rupert Brooke (1887 – 1915)

Brooke, probably the typical Georgian in feeling and style, was noted for his idealistic war sonnets, especially "The Soldier" (1914). He was also known for his boyish good looks, which were said to have prompted the Irish poet W. B. Yeats to describe him as "the handsomest young man in England." (Jones, 1999: 304) His two volumes of verse are *Poems 1911* (1911) and *1914 and Other Poems* (1915). The latter was especially popular in the 1920s.

Brooke's vision of war was clearly Romantic. In contrast to the modern view that debunks and de-romanticizes war and heroism, Brook felt that war was a purifier, and death was heroic. There is a good deal of ebullience and naïve appreciativeness in his poetry. "**The Soldier**" is a good illustration. Here the poet-soldier faces death with joy. There is no fear, no regret and no hesitation. He has but his country in mind, with her flowers, her love, her air, rivers and suns, thoughts, sights and sounds, happy dreams, laughter, "and gentleness,/In hearts at peace, under an English heaven." He is part and parcel of his native England for which he dies willingly. His country purifies, so do war and death; his heart will shed away all evil, and become "[a] pulse in the Eternal mind." There is no thought of self but a lot of gratitude and appreciation for what his country has done for him. The poet-soldier believes that his death will add credit to his beloved motherland.

The heroic spirit that Brooke's sonnets manage to exalt and beautify has been prized greatly by his countrymen in times of crisis like wars, and he has been regarded as a token of the continuity of the nation's patriotic tradition. His poetry is somehow crude in diction but rich and touching in the sentiments that the poet felt genuinely from the bottom of his soul.

31.6 Wilfred Owen (1893 – 1918)

Owen was an English poet and soldier, one of the leading poets (probably the finest war poet) of WWI. His war poems were composed between January 1917 when he was first sent to the Western Front and his death in November 1918. The best of his works were written during a period of intense creativity from August 1917 to September 1918. His *Collected Poems* appeared in 1920. Among his best-known works, most of which were published posthumously, are "Dulce et Decorum est" (published 1920), whose Latin title is taken from the Roman poet Horace and means "it is sweet and honorable," "Insensibility," whose title refers to the fact that the soldiers have lost the ability to feel due to the horrors which they faced on the Western Front during WWI, "Anthem for Doomed Youth" (1917), "Futility" (1918) and "Strange Meeting" (1918).

Owen's poetry is noted for its abundance of compassion and its technical achievements, one of which is the para-rhyme or off-rhyme he pioneered. For Owen, there was no time for gradual growth; his was a forced maturity. His sensitive mind faced a sudden and drastic combination of stimulus and challenge, and met it with an admirable creative outburst. The spark of originality illumines all his poetry so that it will ever shine among the greatest of war poems. His shocking, realistic war poetry on the horrors of trench and gas warfare was heavily influenced by his friend and mentor Siegfried Sassoon (1886 – 1967), and stood in stark contrast both to the public perception of war at the time and to the confidently patriotic verse written by earlier war poets such as Rupert Brooke.

Owen called his poems elegies which he felt might be consolatory to posterity though not to his generation. What he focused on in his writing was the overall reality of civilized life, one grim aspect of which is hidden and should be revealed in full. For Owen, that aspect was war, which, along with "the pity of war," is his major theme. Owen condemned war. There is an arid irony in his poetry. The sonnet "**Anthem for Doomed Youth**" is a good example of Owen's way of writing an elegy for the war dead. Instead of the consolation that an elegy normally offers, the sonnet is informed with incontrollable anger and accusation throughout. The title itself is anger poeticized. There is boundless compassion in the "anthem" and equally boundless wrath at the fact that the war dooms the youth to premature death. The octave raises a question, the answer to which is condemnation of war. The war scenes are vivid to the senses and increase the awareness of war as evil as the lines keep piling up on top of each other. The sestet is about a memorial but Owen represented it in his unique way, for he felt that the grief caused by such an atrocity was not to be palliated by anything conventional. The war is not just and justifiable, death is not to be glossed over, and both should be remembered. For youths killed on the battlefield there is no need for a conventional memorial service, because it tends to put the dead in requiem and the living in forgetfulness. There is no need for bells, candles, flowers and the pall. Instead, Owen urged remembrance and compassion as reflected in such actions as the shining of the boys' eyes, the paling of the girls' cheeks, the tenderness of patient minds, and the slow drawing-down of blinds (which probably signals the fact that sadness must end as well). The note of warning is evident in the sonnet. Owen's originality here as indeed in most of his works lies in this, that he projected himself into the facts and conveyed his sentiment effectively with images and symbols of his own, drawn from his own experience of actual war life, rather than resorted to readily available traditional stereotyped ones.

Owen's famous poem "**Strange Meeting**" is a good expression of "the pity of war." The meeting is strange because it occurs in Hell between the ghosts of two dead soldiers. The two fought on opposing sides and one of them, the speaker, killed the other. Now that they end up where they are in the same plight, the speaker says that there is no cause to mourn now. But the other seems to disagree. For him there is, in fact, though it is pointless to him now. The cause to mourn for him is the life, his life cut short and wasted, and the hopelessness to get it back. His life was once good: he made the best of it—the joy and the sorrow of it all. People might laugh at his joy, but his sorrow must die with him now. It is the sorrow that he keenly feels as he died without telling the truth about the "pity of war, the pity war distilled." As a result, nations progress but continue to war with one another; people both wise and courageous continue to march into Hell. He would rather enlighten and save them from bloodshed with his own death in the way—he hints—Jesus did for mankind. The implication is that the war is senseless, causing senseless deaths, and people fail to see this and continue the senseless mutual slaughter. Here lies the pity of war. This is an elegy not just for one person but for all, not just for one period but for all time.

"Strange Meeting" is characterized by the innovative rhyme pattern known as para-rhyme or "the half rhyme" or "off-rhyme," or two words with the same consonants but different vowels that match with one another at the end of the lines. The poem introduces it for the first time in the English literary history. In the poem the end words of every two lines rhyme with each other in this "half" way: "escaped" with "scooped," "groined" with "groaned," "bestirred" with "stared" and so on right up to the end of the work with fair regularity. The immediate effect of this scheme is the feeling of something left imperfect, shortchanged, or to be desired, and of the possibility of setting things to rights. This form matches the theme perfectly well: war cuts short lives that have yet to be fully lived, and people do not seem to be aware of it, which is "the pity of war." Owen's off-rhyme has influenced later writers including the 1930s'.

31.7 David Jones (1895 – 1974)

Jones was probably the only soldier-poet who wrote about the war in an epic manner. His well-known *In Parenthesis*, a Modernist work by all standards, was begun in 1929 over ten years after WWI and was published in 1937. It is a long poem-prose—as there is both prose and poetry in it—with some plot interest. The "writing" describes an experience equally powerful as poets Wilfred Owen and Siegfried Sassoon experienced it but well mediated and mellowed by space and time. Jones was able to see the war from an epic perspective, encase it in the mythic milieu of Welsh-Arthurian mythology, and endow it with some universal and historical dimension of significance. But he also felt the lack of the epic nature of the war: he was conscious that man was controlled rather than controlling in the game, and it was difficult to paint him in a heroic color the way Homer does Odysseus in his *Odyssey*. Jones' soldiers do not know where to go and what to do except as told; they are moved around and struggle but are unaware that they have already been wrapped up in death's embrace. There is not much debunking of the war in the way Jones wrote about it. It is an experience removed from its immediate milieu and replayed in the mind over and over so that it has lost its sting. The retrospective poet was able to see and tell about it in a detached, distant, manner.

31.8 Robert von Ranke Graves (1895 – 1985)

Robert Graves was an English poet, novelist and critic. He was also a prominent translator of Classical Latin and Ancient Greek texts; his versions of *The Twelve Caesars* (121 AD) and *The Golden Ass* (the only Ancient Roman novel in Latin to survive in its entirety, whose date of composition is uncertain) remain popular, for their clarity and entertaining style. Graves was awarded the 1934 James Tait Black Memorial Prize for his historical novels—*I, Claudius* and *Claudius the God*.

Graves' output is prodigious. During his long life Graves produced more than 140 works, including many volumes of poetry, essays, fiction, biography, and works for children, and many free translations from various languages. He saw himself primarily as a poet, and wrote some of his prose reluctantly for financial reasons, but much of it is of lasting quality. His powerful autobiography *Goodbye to All That* (1929), a memoir of his early life (including his role in WWI), is an outstanding example of the new freedom and passionate disillusion of the post-war generation. He wrote many novels, most of them with a historical bias like *I, Claudius* and *Claudius the God* (both 1934). Notable among his non-fiction works is his speculative study of poetic inspiration *The White Goddess* (1948), which argues that true poets derive their gifts from the Muse, the primitive, matriarchal Moon Goddess, the female principle, once dominant but now disastrously dispossessed by male values of reason and logic. His *Collected Poems* of 1955 confirmed a worldwide reputation; the most recent volume of *Collected Poems* appeared in 1975. Since his early days, Graves, partly through voluntary exile, avoided identification with any school or movement, speaking increasingly with a highly individual yet ordered voice in which lucidity and intensity combine to a remarkable degree. His love poems, some of his best-known and most distinctive works, are at once cynical and passionate, romantic and erotic, personal and universal. He has also written ballads, songs for children, dramatic monologues, narratives and poetic anecdotes; his technique is not experimental, but the classical precision of his verse is rarely archaic.

The poet Graves began as a Georgian, embraced Metaphysical values in midstream, but turned back to his earlier forms of writing in the latter part of his long and complex career. His early works shared the Georgian rural serenity and simplicity though he took inspiration from Celtic legends and models like John Skelton (c. 1463 – 1529), and wrote in a romantic vein. Some of his early poems were included in the Georgian anthologies. He went to the war and came alive, only to write about it to escape from the traumatizing war experience. This went on until he met the American poet Laura Riding (1901 – 1991) in the mid-1920s and got in touch with the Fugitives like John Crowe Ransom (1888 – 1974). Then sensitive to the change in the 1920s, he and Riding published *A Survey of Modernist Poetry* (1927), contributed to the Metaphysical revival, and wrote the poems that were to make his fame. He was influenced by John Crowe Ransom and e. e. cummings (1894 – 1962). Graves attempted successfully to stay away from the Modernist or avant-garde rhetoric so much up in the air at his time. Imagism, T. S. Eliot and Ezra Pound (1885 – 1972), and even the New Criticism all failed to impress him. His style continued to be elegant, coherent and discursive despite Eliot's paramount influence of impersonality and parataxis. Love was his major theme until the late 1940s when his book *The White Goddess: A Historical Grammar of Poetic Myth* (1948) appeared in print. Through his synthesis of his myth, he hoped to achieve a primordial kind of unity as a stay against modern chaos. In the mid-20th-century endeavor of the Movement poets, Graves' reputation grew as he became one of the poets the younger generation admired.

"**Down, Wanton, Down!**" (1933) is a typical Graves poem both in theme and form. The theme is about lust and love; the form is traditional with its graceful regularity, but full of Metaphysical wit and conceits. The work is a knotted puzzle that takes a good deal of intellectual energy to unravel. The "wanton" in the title is in fact lust which, as the poem moves, takes the form of phallus. The first two stanzas refer to acts of sexual intercourse while the remaining three read the phallus a lecture on how lust repels love and beauty. The implication seems to be that love may not be able to endure as it is nearly always associated with lust. "The White Goddess" (1953) embodies Graves' faith in the Great Mother, the female principle she represents, and his view that poetry needs her help to recover its lost vitality. The poem alludes to the poet's book by the same title.

31.9 Edmund Blunden (1896 – 1974)

Blunden was both a Georgian poet who wrote nature poetry and a poet of WWI. He wrote of his experiences in the war in both verse and prose. For most of his career, Blunden was also a reviewer for English publications and an academic in Tokyo and later Hong Kong. He ended his career as Professor of Poetry at the University of Oxford.

Although his early pastoral pieces resemble somewhat the poems of W. H. Davies on the country scene, his quiet, contemplative and nostalgic lyrics like "Forefathers" and "Almswoman" show his genuine affection and admiration for simple, old laboring folk rather than mere descriptions of natural beauty in poems like "The Pike" and "The Midnight Skaters." ***Undertones of War*** (1928) is his best-known work and chief record of his experience on the Western Front. It was written chiefly in prose but interspersed with short poems. In this book and in other poems on the war Blunden generally avoided descriptions of physical horror and outrage, but often very quietly, indirectly and yet unmistakably he condemned the barbarity and the terrible destruction caused by war. His first *Collected Poems* appeared in 1930. Further volumes of his own poems were collected as *Poems 1930 – 1940*; a study of Hardy appeared in 1941, and a biography of Shelley in 1946. *After the Bombing* (1950), another volume of poems, is more contemplative and searching than his previous works. He was appointed professor of poetry at oxford in 1966. Throughout his working life as a teacher and scholar Blunden produced a wide variety of critical and editorial works, with an emphasis on John Clare (1793 – 1864), who wrote powerfully of nature, of a rural childhood, and of the alienated and unstable self, the Romantics, and his fellow war poets. Although heralded as one of the leaders of the Georgians, he belonged to no group; his precise natural imagery is, in his best work, fused with his own moods and attitudes, and with those of the countrymen and countrywomen who inhabit his landscape. After many years in the making, Blunden's reputation stands high.

Chapter 32　The 1920s' Literature

The most important developments in the field of philosophy and psychology during the 1920s that impacted literary creativity and criticism should be Bergson's notion of time and Freud's theory of psychoanalysis. Bergson's philosophical theory touches upon such topics as time, memory and consciousness. To Bergson time is not to be merely measured in clock time, or the traditional representations of hours, months, and years. Instead of being mere extended images of space, time as Bergson saw it is continuous, an indivisible continuity, a succession of qualitative changes which melt into and permeate one another, without precise outlines, and without any tendency to externalize themselves in relation to one another. This is time in the mind, subjective in nature, or psychological time, indicating the incessant flow of the consciousness. In keeping with this new concept, true reality—the self—exists in psychological time; selfhood continues its existence in memory; typical memory is unconscious memory, which is the most perfect union of past and present and reflects the true nature of the soul. In order to achieve self-recognition, man must peek through the thick curtain of the "superficial self" and remove the many tiers of barriers between reality and consciousness so as to reveal the ever fluid nascent consciousness, thought and feeling, along with the intrinsic internal relations. Bergson found the conventional novel wanting in this, that, instead of seeing a character as a process of ceaseless becoming, it fails to get at the true nature of things and represent true reality, as it treats time as mere space and renders "a slice of life" in a superficial, chronological or sequential order. Thus the stream-of-consciousness method soon appeared as a new mode of representing human experience, and Bergson's philosophy of time helped pave the way for the rise of Modernism or stream-of-consciousness literature.

Freud's theory of "the subconscious," exploring man's irrational behavior, added impetus to the emergence of the new form of literary expression. According to Freud, the human psyche consists of two parts—the "ego" and the "id" or the instinctual impulse. The ego is both consciousness and subconsciousness while the id, the storehouse of all basic human instincts, is the most nebulous, unapproachable part of the human body. The id, as part of the subconscious, is repressed by the consciousness and the ego, both of which keep to logic and order. As repressed desires are often sexual by nature, the growth of sexual consciousness constitutes, as Freud saw it, one important aspect of human development. Freud's interpretation of dreams fascinated many writers. A dream, Freud found, is the process in which the human subconscious becomes active, and the "psychological self" tries to assert itself by getting rid of external inhibitions. Though still repressed to some extent, this assertion serves as some form of satisfaction to the subconscious. Dreams have their own language and syntax as a result of the compromise between the conscious and the subconscious. This theory of psychoanalysis offered the latitude for writers to explore and describe the new area of experience, the human subconscious, and led straight to the advent of the stream-of-consciousness literature of the 1920s. Freudian influence on the field of literature was not just limited to creative literary endeavors of the time; it impacted literary criticism on no small way. Beginning with Virginia Woolf's criticism of the Edwardians, new critical standards was set, whereby a new system of critical values evolved and got enforced and a clear line of demarcation was drawn between traditional and modern novels. The new critical system depreciated and disparaged the conventional novels for placing focus solely on the externalities of life; it helped promote the modern way of expression and its emphasis on the excavation of the inner world of man.

Against this philosophical and psychological background, there emerged literary innovations of almost all kinds. Writers and sensitive minds began to take a fresh look at man and his life, and discovered substantive changes in the relationships between man and man, between man and nature, and between man and self. The various levels of tension that these caused, the absurdity of life, the growing sense of alienation, the evil side of nature and the existentialist crisis of man—all these came to the surface crying for attention and gave rise inevitably to the diverse attitudes of negativity such as pessimism, nihilism and existentialism (that came later in time). These feelings permeated the literary works of the period. Modernist masters were busy writing, and the works of permanent power and appeal came out in print in quick succession. In the field of novel, James Joyce's *Ulysses*, Virginia Woolf's *Mrs. Dalloway* and *To the Lighthouse*, Thomas Mann's *The Magic Mountain* (1924) and *Remembrance of Things Past* (1913 – 1927) by Marcel Proust (1871 – 1922), also translated as *In Search of Lost Time*, were out there, and in the field of poetry T. S. Eliot and William Butler Yeats were the most prominent of all to make their voices heard. All these combined well with other efforts such as the works of Ernest Hemingway and William Faulkner to shine forth the splendor of Modernism, which as a movement was international in scope and served well to reflect and record the temper of the times. The impact Modernism has had on literary history as a whole cannot be underrated. The major authors and their masterpieces that came out of it were all among the greatest ever produced in history, and some of these such as *Ulysses* and *The Waste Land* have become milestones in world literature, comparable in power and permanence to Homer's *Odyssey* or Dante's *The Divine Comedy*, or Shakespeare's *Hamlet*. After ranging for over a decade the Modernist momentum began to taper off, and the early years of the 1930s saw a new scenario of life, a new awareness and a new vision burgeoning into shape—Postmodernism.

32.1 Novel

The 1920s novel in English literature is characterized by Modernism with the writers like D. H. Lawrence, James Joyce and Virginia Woolf as the representatives. What these writers shared in their works was that all of them turned their interest to describe what was happening in the minds of their characters. They insisted that fiction should explore the depths and recesses of personality, revealing an unending stream of impression, feelings and thoughts. In this sense, Lawrence is perhaps an exception. He too looked inward, not to show us a stream of impressions as Virginia Woolf does, but to explore those mysterious areas of feeling.

32.1.1 D. H. Lawrence (1885 – 1930)

Lawrence was an English novelist, poet, playwright, essayist, literary critic and painter as well. His collected works, among other things, represent an extended reflection upon the dehumanizing effects of modernity and industrialization. In them, some of the issues Lawrence explored are emotional health, vitality, spontaneity and instinct. Lawrence's opinions earned him many enemies and he endured official persecution, censorship, and misrepresentation of his creative work throughout the second half of his life, much of which he spent in a voluntary exile which he called his "savage pilgrimage." At the time of his death, his public reputation was that of a pornographer who had wasted his considerable talents. E. M. Forster, in an obituary notice, challenged this widely held view, describing him as the "greatest imaginative novelist of our generation." Later, the influential Cambridge critic F. R. Leavis championed both his artistic integrity and his moral seriousness, placing much of Lawrence's fiction within the canonical "great tradition" of the English novel.

Lawrence placed emphasis on the depiction of the inner world and the irrational and called for the emancipation of the id. He was heavily influenced by Freudianism, yet different from Freud in that he hated the tyranny of reason and the rational in life. To Lawrence the great and the beautiful come from within the inner soul, not from the progress of society and science. The evil of modern mechanical civilization lies in its ruthless violation of the human soul, harnessing it to social, economic and political commitments, and depriving it of its original, pious ability—the instinct to love in a pure and sincere way, thus totally dehumanizing man. To Lawrence, what was detestable in Freudianism was its clinical quality, and its rationalization of love, which disappeared from life because of Freud's loquacious theorizing about it. This was an intolerable sacrilege that Lawrence felt that modern science had committed against life. Because of the pressure and the corrupting effect of modern civilization, man began to love rationality, human relationship became alienated and cold, and the process of depersonalization intensified. What essentially set Lawrence off from Freud was the novelist's faith in will as against Freud's belief in reason, which is a moot point traceable further back in western cultural history. Although they differed in approach, they agreed upon the principle—the significance of the subconscious and the irrational, and so in the final analysis there was no essential discrepancy in their positions. In literary writing Lawrence called for the restoration of man's true selfhood to its pristine purity. For him, the most sacred thing is love, and the sacred can be realized only in the love between a man and a woman. Only in love can man restore his true emotional self. Sex is the highest expression of individuality, and modern man's tragedy lies in seeing sex as the fulfillment of an animal desire and in repressing love's irrationality. Lawrence regarded sex as his religion, saw the essence of religious experience as one's own experience, and felt that the emotion that makes humans human should exist independent of traditional and social conscience and commitment. All his life Lawrence wrote to censure modern western society and communicate his prophetic— though a little desperate and decadent—vision that the end of western civilization is in sight, man should live in the primitive way, and his new life should begin with the freedom of sex. Besides, Lawrence's close attachment to his mother led him to the complexities of human love. His paternal background set the realistic tone in his representation of life. Thus reading Lawrence can be a very intriguing experience: often it is a painting of one or more aspects of love set against a gray backdrop of real life. His stories are all well set in their locales and reflect the life of his time well.

Lawrence was a versatile genius. In addition to novels for which he is mainly renowned, he also excelled in the short story and poetry. His major short stories include "Odor of Chrysanthemums" (1911) "Daughters of the Vicar" (1914), "The Ladybird" (1923) and "The Rocking-Horse Winner" (1926). His poetry is thematically similar to his novels, dwelling on love, maternal love ("End of another Home Holiday" among others), and on nature as a counterpoint to the human loss of innocence and instinctive response (*Birds, Beasts, and Flowers*, 1923). In poetry, he wrote rhymeless, stanzaless free verse, and gave priority to the representation of human feelings rather than to poetic form and structure. His poetry, often rough with signs of hasty composition, offers an index to his own experiences, feelings, and responses to life in general. During his lifetime and even afterwards Lawrence was a controversial figure because of his frank treatment of sex and outspoken insistence upon a need for a readjustment in the relationship between the sexes.

Lawrence began his publication with a group of poems in 1909, which was followed by a series of his famous novels. His first novel *The White Peacock* appeared in 1910. Three years later in 1913, he published *Sons and Lovers*, perhaps his most popular novel. In 1915 *The Rainbow* came out. The novel is probably Lawrence's best novel and marked the culmination of his literary career. It broke away from the author's early tradition and showed a strong tendency toward Modernism. Lawrence produced his other works, including *Women in Love* (1920), *Aaron's Rod* (1922), *Kangaroo* (1923) and *The Man Who Died* (1929) before *Lady Chatterley's Lover*, his most controversial novel, was put in print in 1928. Love is the major theme of Lawrence's novels. *Sons and Lovers* treats of a mother's dominant and debilitating love over the sons, *The Rainbow* and *Women in Love* deal with the possible unconscious influences on human relationships, marriage and personal fulfillment, and *Lady Chatterley's Lover* praises genuine unfettered love between a man and a woman.

Sons and Lovers is often taken to be largely autobiographical, its subject matter paralleling much of the author's early life. It tells the story of a coal miner's family with the third child Paul as the central character. The work is perhaps the first English novel with a truly working-class background. The thread of the story evolves around Paul's love for the two girls Miriam and Clara as well as his love for his mother Mrs. Morel, a sensitive and high-minded woman better educated than her husband. Mr. Morel, the bread-earner of the family, is a collier crude in taste and drinks heavily. The Morels are not on good terms with each other. Baffled and thwarted, Mr. Morel is sometimes violent while Mrs. Morel, disappointed and embittered, rejects her husband and turns all her love towards her children, particularly her sons William and Paul. She struggles with poverty and meanness of her surroundings to keep herself and her family "respectable" and is determined that her boys will not become miners. William does well, gets to London, but develops pneumonia and dies there young. Numbed by despair, Mrs. Morel gets roused only when Paul, now her only attention and care, also falls ill. She nurses him back to health and their attachment deepens subsequently. So when Paul meets Miriam and falls in love with her, Mrs. Morel fears that Miriam will exclude her and therefore tries to break up their relationship. As a result, Paul turns away from Miriam and becomes involved with Clara Dawes, a married woman separated from her husband. But his affair with Clara peters out when she returns to her husband. Meanwhile Mrs. Morel is ill with cancer and suffers so much that Paul gives her an overdose of morphine to end her pain. With his mother's death, Paul gets free from her control. He resists the urge to follow her "into the darkness" and, with a great effort, turns towards life.

The theme of *Sons and Lovers* is usually said to concern the effect of mother-love upon the development of a son, i. e. the "Oedipus Complex" and its negative impact upon human growth. The story is visibly Oedipal in the son's hate for the father and his over-dependence on his mother. The father's being driven out of the family's emotional life and the fact that Paul has to live separately from his father after his mother's death—these are somewhat parallel to the ancient Oedipus' behavior. Paul's psychically erratic love for his over-assertive and possessive mother is another, more significant, indication of the Oedipus complex at work. The son is all the time aware of the presence of her mother as a shaping factor in his life, yet there is nothing he can or indeed would be willing to do about it. He allows his whole emotional being to be dominated by his mother's love, and leaves little or no room in his heart for any other involvement. He is plunged in the depths of despair when he finds himself facing the spiritual vacuum that his bereavement generates for him. So the novel ends on a tragic note. Its description of the mother-son relationship is an eye-opener and a reminder of the complexities of the human psyche. It is a post-Freudian book.

The Rainbow tells the story of three generations of the Brangwen family, a dynasty of farmers and craftsmen who live in the east Midlands of England, on the borders of Nottinghamshire and Derbyshire, particularly focusing on the individual's struggle for growth and fulfillment within the strictures of English social life. The book spans a period of roughly 65 years from the 1840s to 1905 and shows how the love relationships of the Brangwens change against the backdrop of the increasing industrialization of Britain.

The book opens with the marriage of Tom Brangwen, a hard-working, well-to-do farmer in Nottinghamshire, to a Polish refugee and widow Lydia Lensky. There is a very vivid description of how Tom, at first not on good terms with Anna, Lydia's daughter by her first husband, gradually develops into full sympathy for the child. Then it deals with Anna's destructive, battle-riven relationship with her husband Will Brangwen, Tom's nephew and a lace-designer and wood carver. Although Will and Anna are very much in love at first, Anna gets tired of their love and concentrates her attention on the bringing-up of her six children. The latter half, the last and probably the most famous part, of the book, is about Will and Anna's daughter Ursula and her struggle to find fulfillment for her passionate, spiritual and sensual nature against the confines of the increasingly materialist and conformist society around her. Detailed accounts are given of her love affair with Anton Skrebensky, a British soldier of Polish ancestry, of her brief lesbian adventure with her class-mistress Winifred Inger during her last two terms at high school, and of her miserable experience as an elementary school teacher of unruly children in the small town of Ilkeston. In all these episodes the inner workings in Ursula's mind are so vividly and minutely presented that they remind readers of the great novels of psychological analysis such as Flaubert's *Madame Bovary* and the works of Dostoyevsky (1821 – 1881) and Leo Tolstoy. Freud's influence is also distinctly visible. *The Rainbow* ends with Ursula watching a rainbow towering over the Earth, promising a new dawn for humanity: "She saw in the rainbow the earth's new architecture, the old, brittle corruption of houses and factories swept away, the world built up in a living fabric of Truth, fitting to the over-arching heaven."

Through the marital relations and love lives of the three generations in the Brangwen family, Lawrence reflected the woman's dissatisfaction with the mere physical love of either the husband or the lover and thus represented his recurrent view on love and sex and marriage. *The Rainbow* is remarkable for its study of the recurrence of love and conflict within the marriages it describes, for its attempt to capture the flux of human personality, and for its sense of a mystic procreative continuity within the "rhythm of eternity" both of the seasons and the Christian year.

The Man Who Died is a short novel that was originally written in two parts and published in 1929. The first part was written in 1927 after Lawrence's trip to some Etruscan tombs with his friend Earl Brewster (1878 – 1957), a trip that encouraged the author to reflect upon death and myths of resurrection. The second part was added in 1928 during the author's stay in Gstaad, Switzerland. "The Escaped Cock" was always Lawrence's preferred title for this tale but it has been printed under the present title by some later publishers.

The novel gives the biblical story of resurrection, an unusual yet charming twist. After Jesus' death, as the story goes, the crucified person dies and is interred as Christ, but Jesus the man does not die. This man, now nameless, admitting the mistake that he has made acting as Christ, comes to the shrine of the Egyptian fertility goddess, learns the secret of sex from a fair-haired priestess of the goddess and discovers his own love as a human being. He is thus restored to the innocence of his consciousness and gets to know his mistake in having led humankind astray. He learns that the salvation of the soul lies in intimate living and becomes Jesus after Christ's resurrection.

Lady Chatterley's Lover helped mar and make Lawrence's reputation. It is a story about natural spontaneous love and warm, personal contact. Lady Connie Chatterley is sexually thirsty. She has not had good sex for ten years as her husband Sir Clifford Chatterley is paralyzed from waist down due to a war wound. She has had some sterile contact with the playwright Michaelis, a family friend, and adoration from the artist Duncan, another family connection, but neither can give her what she desperately needs—genuine love and a true marriage. Her chance meeting with Oliver Mellors, the gamekeeper on her family forest grounds, offers her a gleam in an otherwise totally dreary milieu of gloom. The two find irresistible mutual attraction and have many sexually exhilarating trysts and intimate sexual encounters in the natural setting of the woods. Eventually they decide to stop the hide and seek and get married regardless of everything.

Lawrence's detailed and poetic descriptions of sexual union, and his uncompromising use of four-letter words, caused the book (long available in foreign editions) to be unpublishable in full in England until 1960 when Penguin Books took the risk of producing a complete text.

32.1.2 Virginia Woolf (1882 – 1941)

Woolf is regarded as one of the main exponents of Modernism and one of the great 20th-century innovative novelists associated with the stream-of-consciousness technique. What makes Woolf's fiction distinctive is its attempt to go beyond what she regarded as the tyranny of plot, to get close to life as it is actually experienced. To Woolf, the world in which we live is disjunctive, fragmentary and disorderly. Chaos is so ubiquitous that an ordered world as imposed from outside like a mythic center is nothing but an illusion. The purpose of the Modernist writings is to reveal the true nature of the modern human condition and its disconcerting absence of meaning, purpose and order. Characterization rather than plot thus becomes the topmost concern for writers, and sequential time gives way to psychological time, as the age of Modernism is one of psychological depths and not so much one of actions as of opinions of actions. Woolf, along with her fellow Modernists, made for the triumph of internalization and showed new maps of the mind with their vivid pictures of self-consciousness. They made it their job as Modernists to seek order and form in a world in which neither seemed clearly present. In a sense, the works of Woolf represent the sum total of the Modernist art of novel-writing. They reveal the author's compulsion to recreate the human spiritual experience through art, to increase the popular recognition of the subconscious and the irrational behavior of man at the mercy of the irrational emotions and impulses, and to generate a psychological shock effect on the readers at large. They offer a new vision of character. For Woolf, art is important because it gives meaning to life, helps conquer the inevitable disillusionments of life and provides the fulfillment of happiness that nothing else can offer. In other words, art time conquers real time. She believed that art could create a man-made paradise. The way to do it is through catching the ideal moments of an otherwise disappointing life and making them enjoyable with the medium of language. Those moments, "moments of epiphany" in Joyce's description, or "moment of being" in Woolf's, when the mind lives life to the fullest, can bring people happiness and pleasure and help them peek at the "order" absent from real life, and get through the surface to the very nature of things. These moments, measured personally and freed of linearity, are the telescoping of the past, the present and the future in one. They represent stasis in flux, time out of time, spatialized, involving the transfiguration of the ordinary world. These are the times when one experiences release and unity. Woolf's works are a record of those moments in the lives of her characters. As it is evident that these moments are not always enough to sustain human morale in face of adversity, the fate of a number of Woolf's characters such as Septimus in *Mrs. Dalloway* and Roda in *The Waves* is inevitably tragic in the end.

It was not until the publication of her second novel that Woolf began to try, as an experiment, a new creative method. She tried her best to reduce the element of plot in the novel, to adopt the stream of consciousness, or interior monologue, in her novels, and to explore problems of human personality and personal relationships. The novel *Mrs. Dalloway* (1925) made her reputation as an important psychological writer, a reputation made secure by the later works like *To the Lighthouse* (1927) and *The Waves* (1931), in which she introduced her characters not to the reader but to the other characters in the novel so that the reader gets a kaleidoscopic view with the mobility of the waves in the sea.

Woolf was a prolific writer. She produced a good number of novels and short stories as well as hundreds of essays of critical acumen. She also left a rich legacy of volumes of diaries and letters. Her major novels include *Jacob's Room* (1922), *Mrs. Dalloway*, *To the Lighthouse*, *The Waves*, *The Years* (1937) and *Between the Acts* (1941); it was *Mrs. Dalloway*, *To the Lighthouse* and *The Waves* that established her reputation. Her famous literary commentaries such as "Modern Fiction" (1924) serve as solid spade work for the rise and dissemination of the Modernist spirit in her time. Woolf was also an influential feminist. Her two essays—*A Room of One's Own* (1929) and *Three Guineas* (1938)—are taken as classics of the feminist movement, the first of which contains the author's famous dictum: "A woman must have money and a room of her own if she is to write fiction."

In her essay "Modern Fiction" Woolf located the major weakness of the traditional novel in its focus on depicting exterior details but ignoring any dip into the inner world of man. She felt that traditional novelists tried to meet the tyrannical need for plot interest, creating probable, impeccable tragedies, comedies and love stories with characters well dressed like real people, while life could be very different and could be represented radically differently.

For Woolf, the human mind received every day "a myriad of impressions" which do not always provide the right stuff for any plot interest in a tragedy or comedy or a love story, nor lead to any logical traditional endings. Life appeared to her like "a luminous halo" that envelopes people all the time in their waking consciousness. In her incisive criticism, she singled out for her point of analysis Arnold Bennett, who she said did the best job as expected of the best craftsman in painting externalities, but made no effort to touch the human consciousness. Branding him and Galsworthy and Wells as Edwardians and materialists, she compared them to the "spiritual" James Joyce whose focus is the exact opposites of theirs—the flow of the mind.

Mrs. Dalloway is mainly about one day in the life of the middle-aged Mrs. Clarissa Dalloway in relation to those connected with her. It is narrated with the stream-of-consciousness method, pure and simple, and there is not much of plot interest. Mrs. Dalloway is the upper-class housewife of a British Member of Parliament. On this fine June day she is out shopping to get ready for her evening party. She feels happy to be out in the fresh air, seeing people and hearing the boisterous bustle of London. There she meets an old acquaintance and thinks for a while of his ever sick wife. She sees a limousine and speculates about the passenger inside. The things around activate her memory and send her back to her youth, her husband and her lesbian-oriented daughter whose tutor-friend is a religious fanatic. She thinks of love, her uncertainty of love for her husband and daughter and theirs for her, her old-time crush on the two men—her present husband Richard and Peter Walsh who left for India after her marriage— and her own unnatural love for Sally, a girl friend. The point that keeps recurring in her mind is: what would have happened had she not married Richard for the security and social position that she thought he would give her as a hopeful cabinet minister or a prime minister? She feels trapped.

While Mrs. Dalloway is down-town, Septimus Smith is sitting in a park with his wife Lucrezia. His odd behavior and talk of suicide frighten her. Septimus, a war hero, has almost everything to make him and his wife happy— a good job and the promise his employer keeps talking about that he has, but he feels sad as he sees nothing but horror and hypocrisy in the world he lives in. He has visions from a dead war comrade and detests the doctor who comes to help him. Lucrezia takes him to a distinguished psychiatrist Sir. Bradshaw, who advises moving him away to "a quiet rural area."

When Mrs. Dalloway is home, her husband is away to lunch with a woman she never likes, and presently Peter comes for a visit. Peter asks her if she is happy, and is surprised to see her so engrossed in her party. He has led a more tangled life, having divorced, returned to London and fallen in love with another woman. Now Mrs. Dalloway's party is in progress and turns out to be a complete success with both the incumbent prime minister and her former lover Peter Walsh present for her. Then she hears of Septimus' suicide and feels deeply affected: she feels "like him." Looking back at her own life, Mrs. Dalloway realizes that she has existed for others, snobbish, trivial and neurotic, no longer the "Clarissa" that she was, having sacrificed her ties with Peter and Sally. She is getting old, but Peter feels still attracted to her.

In the novel two narrative threads intertwine relating to Clarissa and Septimus. Woolf exhibited her consummate craftsmanship in forestalling any possible impression of structural dislocation. The unity of the novel is first ensured by the similarity in character between the two major figures. Some other tricks are also at work to connect the two worlds. One of these is using something the people from the different spheres share somehow as a common experience—a car, a plane, a child, a singer, or chiming clocks. Then there is the author's deft choice of the linkage between the streams of consciousness of different people. The jumps from person to person and from one thing to another are well smoothed out to avoid possible bumping ruggedness in the narrative terrain. Thus one thing leads naturally to another and the narrative flows smoothly on and on. In *Mrs. Dalloway*, memory plays an important role in the author's manipulation of the stream of consciousness. In addition, the party serves well as an effective wire-puller, tying up all the loose threads in a closely knit knot. The major characters all appear, either physically or in the conversations, giving the story a wonderful sense of inclusiveness and finality. What also deserves attention is the ever present narrator, whose voice directs and screens the thoughts of the characters for the readers.

To the Lighthouse, a stream-of-consciousness narrative, draws powerfully on the author's recollections of family holidays at St. Ives, Cornwall, although the setting is ostensibly the Hebrides Islands; her parents, as Woolf acknowledged, provided the inspiration for the maternal, managing, gracious, much-admired Mrs. Ramsay, and the self-centered, self-pitying, poetry-reciting, absurd and tragic figure of the philosophy professor Mr. Ramsay, who become the focus of one of her most profound explorations of the conflict between the male and female principles.

The novel is in three sections, of which the first and longest, "The Window," describes a summer day, with the Ramsays on holiday with their eight children and assorted guests, including the plump and lethargic elderly poet Augustus Carmichael, the young woman artist Lily Briscoe, who represents in part the struggle and cost of female creativity, and the graceless lower-middle-class academic Charles Tansley. A party is going on at the Ramsays' summer cottage house on the Isle of Skye in the Hebrides Islands. Family tension centers on the desire of the youngest child James to visit the lighthouse and his father's apparent desire to thwart him: the frictions of the day are momentarily resolved around the dinner table. After dinner, the children are put to bed and the guests are gone, and Mrs. Ramsay joins her husband in the library, knitting while he reads. She is thinking. Sitting by the window at nightfall, she sees the waves splashing at the shoreline, and her mind suddenly spirits itself, over and beyond the cares and worries of her real world, away to another, the one in the distance where the lighthouse stands, and where she finds everything pure, transparent and full of celestial happiness. In that brief moment or a "moment of being," Mrs. Ramsay experiences the very taste of bliss and the true union of the self with the world. Her soul relishes the moment of serenity in a transcendental fashion and feels the utmost gratification. Now she is renewed and reenergized enough to face life again with confidence and hope.

The second section, "Time Passes," records with laconic brevity the death of Mrs. Ramsay and of her children, and dwells with desolate lyricism on the abandoning of the family home and its gradual postwar reawakening. They never return to their summer cottage and a lot occurs within the many years after they come back from the summer. Mrs. Ramsay dies, so do some of her children in childbirth or the war, among whom is her son Andrew killed in the war. The summer house stands in sore neglect—the wallpaper peeling down, with rust, mildew, spider webs and dust everywhere. Then with the war over, the Ramsays come back with some friends like the poet Carmichael and the painter Lily Briscoe. The section is important as a testing of the ideals in the book. It is an observation of what happens to the question of the androgynous vision first raised in section one, an observation from an esthetic distance, with the real focus not so much on inter-personal relationships as on a look at the human and

— 269 —

non-human world. "Nothing" seems to be the key word here. The total fracture and horror and the insensibility of death and nature, the fall of the wallpaper, the mildewed books, the separation, the ending of human assumptions, nature's indifference—all these denote a tension between the aesthetic as fixity and the existential as process and the connection between them. This section as a whole reads like a poetic interlude with important family events inserted in square brackets.

The last section, "The Lighthouse," describes the exhausting but finally successful efforts of Lily, through her painting of the cottage, to recapture the revelation of shape-in-chaos which she owes to the vanished Mrs. Ramsay, and the parallel efforts of Mr. Ramsay, Camilla and James to reach the lighthouse. The son is put in charge of the preparations. The family trip is successful, despite the undercurrents of rivalry, loss and rebellion that torment them, and ends with the happy Mr. Ramsay praising his son for a job well done. In this section Lily experiences a moment of ecstasy, a sense of a vision fulfilled. She feels at one with all time and is filled with sympathy for the human condition. Thus she is able to finish her painting, which embodies a perfect aesthetic view, acts as a mediating medium between real life and the human ideal, and indicates the success of art patterning or subordinating the world. It means that Woolf had not by this point of her career accepted the world yet.

To the Lighthouse represents a heroic exploration and re-creation of the bereavements and (real or imagined) tyrannies of the past; it also displays Woolf's technique of narrating through stream of consciousness and imagery at its most assured, rich and suggestive. The novel is noted for its thematic and structural unity. In thematic terms the novel advocates the author's unique vision of art and literature. This has been defined as the androgynous vision, or one that combines both the female and the male principles in artistic creation. Neither principle alone will produce the best work of art. The opposition of the two genders is illustrated in the antithetical character traits of Mrs. Ramsay versus Mr. Ramsay. The latter is all logic and reason while the former is all imagination. The man is scientific and metaphysical while the woman is intuitive, mythical and metaphoric. The contrast between the two is obvious. The first section depicts Mrs. Ramsay sitting there watching the lighthouse and lost in thought. She is the feminine all through. As the center of attention in this part of the book, she organizes everything and takes care of meticulous details. But as her vision is limited and dependent on male intelligence, she fails in many things: the dinner is tedious; her effort to bring pairs together ends in no marriage; and her plan to visit the lighthouse never materializes. Lily in the first section is probably too heavily influenced by Mrs. Ramsay to complete her painting. But she feels the two principles at once in her viewpoint, which makes her the stuff for an ideal artist in the final section of the book. Her androgynous vision matures in the final stroke, i. e. the line she draws in the middle of the picture, which appears final and symmetrical.

32.1.3 James Joyce (1882 – 1941)

Joyce was the founder of stream of consciousness. He tried not merely to describe how a character might think, but also to present a record of the character's thoughts. He wrote only and always about Dublin. He devised ways of expanding his accounts of Dublin, however, so that they became microcosms, small-scale models, of all human life, of all history and all geography. Indeed that was his life's work, to write about Dublin in such a way that he was writing about all of human experience.

Joyce was serious about both his thematic and technical concerns. In thematic terms, he never forgot to promote the spiritual freedom of his native country with his writings. Irish nationalism features prominently in his works. Although overshadowed sometimes with minute depiction of life in its variegated forms, the theme of Irish discontentment and struggle for freedom always appears as a clear narrative thread. Joyce had in mind to authentically reflect the mood of his country and his people. His love for the common people was also well expressed in his works. He found great value in love and compassion. He loved life itself and believed that love made life worth living and made man invincible. Meanwhile, Joyce was preoccupied with art and its mission in life. He took nothing short of the whole of life as the province of his fictional representation—history, philosophy, art and literature, man, his nature, and his cosmos, human epistemology and ontology, psychology, the psychic fabric of man, and the list can go on and on for ever. But it is conspicuous that one thing always stands out in bold relief on his fictional canvas, that is, art and its relation to life.

In technical terms, Joyce is well known for his frank representation of reality. He embraced realism against romanticism. He was outspoken and insisted on portraying all the aspects of man—the good as well as the evil side. For Joyce, characterization mattered more than plot. His descriptions of the sex encounters, the details of the human body, and the impure thoughts that flit through the minds of his characters proved to be repulsive and infuriating to the conservative taste at the time. Joyce is also noted for his adroit use of the stream-of-consciousness technique and his contribution to its subsequent popularity as an effective stylistic medium. In addition, Joycean language has always been a topic of immense interest to people. It is poetic, accurate, forceful, connotative, rhythmic, musical, picturesque, aptly polyglottic, and humorous beyond description. Thus by pushing both thematic and formal boundaries infinitely further back, he has become "the writers' writer" in literary history.

Joyce's major novels include *Dubliners* (1914), *A Portrait of the Artist as a Young Man* (1916), *Ulysses* (1922) and *Finnegans Wake* (1939). His novels such as *Ulysses* and *Finnegans Wake* made a complete change in the form and structure of fiction and had a decisive impact on the development of the stream of consciousness or interior monologue, despite their tremendous difficulties in reading comprehension caused by Joyce's employment of his special dream language, Homeric myth, puns, Roman Catholicism, Irish Folklore, scholastic philosophy, and so forth.

Dubliners, Joyce's first published book, is a collection of 15 stories, the most famous of which are "The Dead" and "Araby." Focusing on life in Dublin, the stories follow a pattern of childhood, adolescence, maturity and public life, culminating with the longest, "The Dead," frequently described as "the finest short story in English." Joyce intended the stories to be a "chapter of the moral history" of Ireland, set them in Dublin "the center of paralysis" which is dismal, dreary and dull, and wrote them in what he called "a style of scrupulous meanness." Although the narrators of the stories are different, they are all in essence the fictional externalizations of the author's inner world and the process of his emotional and psychic growth. The major characters are basically out of the same mold—they aspire for something infinitely better than their lot has offered them. Because of Joyce's frankness and his insistence on publishing without deletion or alteration, he found himself in the first of what would be several battles with publishers who refused to print his work without excisions, as well as the focus of a brief campaign for freedom to publish.

A Portrait of the Artist as a Young Man is largely autobiographical with Stephen Dedalus as the author's surrogate. It takes a close look at Stephen's striving for and attainment of psychological maturity from childhood through young manhood, and examines the development of the author's own artistic sensibility. The book ends with Stephen locating his ideal in artistic creation and asserting his belief that self-exile offers the way for him to realize it. So he leaves for Europe. The novel consists of five chapters, each of which covers one phase of the major character's growth. Here the experimentation lies principally in its prose style changing as the novel progresses to mirror the growth and development of Stephen's mind. Though not as innovative as the later works, the novel foreshadows many of the themes and verbal complexities of *Ulysses*.

Finnegans Wake is a prose work, in which Joyce adopted a special dream language without punctuation and displayed humor and lyrical beauty in spite of the obscurity of the novel. The novel was written in a unique and extremely difficult style, making use of endless puns and wordplay, coined words, riddles, allusions, and around 40 languages besides English. It is a tremendous performance, a book about everything. It represents a radical departure from the novelistic tradition and has been seen as an extreme illustration of the Modernist stance that the modern novel no longer places its emphasis on story-telling.

The novel is circular in structure, with no beginning or end. It is an account of a night, or rather one night's dream of the protagonist Humphrey Chimpden Earwicker, a Dublin tavern-keeper, in whose consciousness all recorded history finds a meaning and a home. The first reading may be confusing as the readers find it difficult to decide on the identity of the major dreamer: a character in the book or the author himself. There are 17 chapters in the book, each of which depicts one of the 17 phases of a dream. Each phase varies with its twists and turns, the substance of the dream keeps changing every moment, and no dream occurrence receives long coverage. The description of the dream state reaches perfection and reveals a profundity, the depth of which is simply unfathomable.

It is interesting that "wake" is not only the Irish term for funeral, but also a part of the verb "awaken." Thus the novel is concerned with the death and rebirth of Finnegan, a builder of cities and a Dublin bricklayer, a compound of all the heroes of myth. So the central theme is a cyclical pattern of history, of fall and resurrection, though the book is thematically all-inclusive: the past, the present, and the future, all essential human relationships such as those between man and woman, age and youth, life and death, and love and hate.

While *Finnegans Wake* writes about a Dublin night which begins at dusk and ends at daybreak, **Ulysses** paints its daytime cityscape and describes the experiences of a few people during the day of Thursday, June 16, 1904 and the few hours early the next morning. The day was chosen because, as some people speculate, it was the one on which the author met his future wife, but as others say, it was the day on which she became unfaithful to him for the first time. The novel is made up of 18 chapters in three parts with a varying number of chapters in each. Part 1 is composed of the first three chapters, focusing on one of the major characters, Steven Dedalus; part 2, the next twelve chapters, is devoted mainly to Leopold Bloom, the dominant figure in the novel; and part 3, the last three chapters, tells the meeting of the three characters as well as Molly's inner thoughts. The novel consists in the scenes in which the three major characters appear alone or with others, and records, among other things, their inner world and their sensual impressions.

Like *A Portrait of the Artist as a Young Man*, *Ulysses* also tells Joyce's own story. The author wrote a good deal of his life into the novel. But *Ulysses* is just a veiled autobiography, for here Joyce created two characters as his surrogates instead of one. He appears as Steven most of the time and as Bloom some of the time, while Molly offers a faint, leery image of his wife. Many descriptions of Steven and his life have a solid basis in Joyce's actual life experiences. In addition, *Ulysses* can be seen as a blue book to Dublin, Joyce's beloved city. In the course of the story a public bath, a funeral, a newspaper office, a library, public houses, a maternity hospital and a brothel are visited. A number of other Dublin scenes and characters are introduced. It is a Dublin from past to present, from cradle to grave, a Dublin that could be replicated, as some people say, with the help of the descriptions of it in *Ulysses* if ever by any chance it should vanish from sight.

Ulysses is a perfect book of the echoes and parallels of Homer's *Odyssey*. It is original in the use of language and told chiefly through the consciousness of the principle figure. The novel describes a single day in the life of three Dubliners made to correspond to the three main characters of *Odyssey*. Its structure bears a striking resemblance to that of *Odyssey*. The various chapters roughly correspond to the episodes of the classic, Stephen representing Telemachus, Bloom Odysseus, and Molly Penelope. Echoing the three-sectional narrative of *Odyssey*, in which the first part relates the story of Telemachus (Odysseus' son) venturing out to look for his father, the second part the wanderings of Odysseus on the sea in his attempt to get back home, and the third the final happy family reunion, *Ulysses* begins with Steven going out, continues with Bloom roaming around but always with his mind riveting on his wife Molly, and concludes with the two men meeting the woman in a resemblance of a family reunion. The author deliberately built in some hints in the title—Ulysses is derived from *Ulixes*, the Latin name for Odysseus—and the wanderings of the major figures, and adroitly imbedded some allusions to the Homeric classic. This makes *Ulysses* a highly allusive and symbolic novel.

In thematic terms, the novel mainly focuses on Bloom's fate. The man is going through a slough of despond but sees no rescue from either angel or man. His despair is traceable to the death of his son that still rankles in his memory. His present life is anything but happy. There does not seem much for him to look forward to in the future. His mood of gloom and loneliness is well integrated with the temper of modern times. But the good part of the story is that all is not lot. He is not giving up on his marriage. This positive gesture echoes Molly's conscious response and provides a ray of hope in the end for them both. There is reason to believe that the man and his wife will surmount the barrier of alienation and come together to live happily again. Here Joyce attempted to affirm the indomitable human spirit. He highlighted selfless love of the common people.

In terms of characterization, the novel is unique and impressive. For one thing, the three major characters represent three different human archetypes in education, taste, and attitude toward life, with Steven the most cultured, Bloom in the middle of the social and educational ladder, and Molly settling comfortably at the bottom. Together the three represent the modern humankind and the strands of modern sensibility. The book thus offers both a reflection of human nature and its universal application and makes an acrid comment upon modern life. For another, the book manages to flesh out Bloom with the help of the other characters such as Steven and Molly. Bloom is a person of an exceptionally complex texture. There exist in him the two polar extremes of intellectual and worldly character traits, which are represented respectively by Stephen and Molly. He is, like Stephen, knowledgeable and learned in his own way, a thinking kind of person whose excessive thinking weakens and turns him into a morose person. Meanwhile, like Molly, he is unwilling to give up on life. He hates Molly for her infidelity, but loves her and cares about his life with her. There is still such physicality in him that he is not indifferent to love and sex.

In terms of style, Joyce had diverse literary devices and tricks up his sleeves to promote effect. He could be poetic as when he dealt with Steven, yet lyrical and harmonious as with Bloom with the use of alliteration and a lively, rhythmic mode of expression to adumbrate various kinds of depression and anxiety. Joyce's diction varies well and consistently with different characters. Meanwhile, the novel employs a variety of techniques, especially those of interior monologue and of parody. Chapters differ in their dominant stylistic features: some employ direct narration, others use stream of consciousness, and still others indulge in the parody of many nonfiction forms such as newspaper headlines, mystery plays and slapsticks, pedagogic questions and answers. There is also the parody of literary style and authors such as the funny narrator in chapter 9 of part 2, the writer for a women magazine in chapter 10 of part 2, the series of authors and weeklies in chapter 11 of part 2, and the elegant journalistic style in chapter 2 of part 3. The multiple narrative points of view and the constant change of styles meet the need for conveying a variety of information and depicting fresh details from different sources. The change marked Joyce's deliberate innovative effort with a new literary technique. *Ulysses* is the first stream-of-consciousness novel in the English literary history. Although there is lucid direct telling in some portions of the book, most of the story is narrated in the stream-of-consciousness manner.

32.2 Poetry

The 1920s poetry is also labeled as Modernism. The greatest representatives are William Butler Yeats and T. S. Eliot, who dominated the first half of the 20th century. T. S. Eliot was a great poet, playwright and literary critic, and the chief leader among the writers during the first half of the 20th century. He is accepted as an experimentalist of Modernist poetry in English language and most remembered for his poetic works like *The Waste Land* and *Four Quartets* (1943). Eliot was awarded the Nobel Prize for literature in 1948 "for his outstanding, pioneer contribution to present-day poetry." He was a US citizen till 1927 when he was naturalized by the British government. So he is sorted into American literature and a detailed study of him is not arranged in this book.

William Butler Yeats (1865 – 1939) was a playwright, essayist and poet with volumes of writing in all three genres, but his reputation has been built mainly on his poetry. He was once praised as the greatest English-speaking poet of his age by T. S. Eliot and is generally considered one of the two or three greatest English language poets of the 20th century. In a sense, modern English poetry began with Yeats as much as it did with T. S. Eliot and Ezra Pound. He lived and wrote in a period of transition. He came on the scene in between Swinburne and T. S. Eliot. Yeats was awarded the Nobel Prize for literature in 1923.

Yeats was a prolific writer. His works fall into three categories—poems, plays and essays. The poetic works are decidedly in the majority, including *The Wanderings of Oisin and Other Poems* (1889), *In the Seven Woods* (1903), *The Green Helmet and Other Poems* (1910), *Poems Written in Discouragement* (1913), *Responsibilities: Poems and a Play* (1914), *The Wild Swans at Coole* (1917), *Michael Robartes and the Dancer* (1920), *Seven Poems and a Fragment* (1922), *The Cat and the Moon and Certain Poems* (1924), *October Blast* (1927), *The Tower* (1928), *The Winding Stair and Other Poems* (1929), *Words for Music Perhaps and Other Poems* (1932), *Wheels and Butterflies* (1934), *The King of the Great Clock Tower* (1934), *A Full Moon in March* (1935), *New*

Poems (1938) and *Last Poems and Two Poems* (1939). Yeats' publications of essays include those collections like *Ideas of Good and Evil* (1903), *Discoveries* (1907), *Per Amica Silentia Lunae* (1918), *The Cutting of an Agate* (1919) and *On the Boiler* (1939). His major plays are *The Countess Kathleen* (1892), *The Land of Heart's Desire* (1894), *Cathleen ni Houlihan* (1902), *On Baile's Strand* (1904) and *Deirdre* (1907). These and his other plays are known for their innovation of the fairyland atmosphere and of the supernatural in the Irish legends and folklore, while many of his verse dramas are celebrated for the beautiful passages of lyrical poetry to be found in them. Their atmosphere also lies in the part they played as one of the mainstays in the Irish literary theater, particularly at the Abbey Theater in Dublin.

Yeats had a long poetic career and is generally considered one of the few writers who completed their greatest works after being awarded the Nobel Prize. Stretching from the 1880s and 1890s to the 1930s, his poetic career can be divided roughly into four broad phases. In the first phase he was interested in the Irish folklore and wrote his early romantic dreamy poems. The writings like *The Wanderings of Oisin* are peerless portraits of the romantic and dreamy Celtic twilight. What he read and experienced especially in the 1890s—his contact with some Pre-Raphaelites, his visit to his mother's home place Sligo in the west Ireland, and his reading of Standish O'Grady and some translations of Gaelic poetry—all featured in the love poems of his early fuzzy romanticism. Poems like "The Stolen Child," "The Rose of the World" and "The Lake Isle of Innisfree" among the finest of all time are all dreamy lyrics, evocative and nostalgic, and intriguing to read. "The Lake Isle of Innisfree" is typical in describing his beloved Sligo in its slow pace and natural imagery. His experience in the beautiful county colors much of the poem. There is also a good deal of Irish myth and Irish landscape description in such poems as "The Rose of the World" and "The Man Who Dreamed of Faeryland." He would have gone down in history as a significant late Victorian poet had he not written anything else.

The second phase covered the first two decades of the 20th century when he was involved in the Irish nationalism and discovered Ireland as a literary subject and composed works to express support for Irish nationalism and the Irish struggle for national independence. The writings produced in this period are romantic by and large, but colored now with a heavy touch of realism. His famous poem "September 1913" turns out to be a watershed in his poetic composition. It is a bitter satire on the mood of his people. Although devoted to his country's struggle for independence, Yeats felt somehow disillusioned by the apathy of his countrymen. His contempt was obvious for the frenzy of the popular—especially the middle class'—getting and spending, which he saw as a life devoid of dignity or nobility of spirit. Other poems that came out of the period such as "Easter 1916" also echoed his strong nationalist feelings.

The third and a new phase, in which Yeats' style became more distinctive, followed in the 1920s. A substantive change came about in the nature of his poetry, for he embraced the new values of the new verse and became a major voice along with T. S. Eliot and Ezra Pound in representing the spirit of the time. T. S. Eliot's rediscovery of the Metaphysical poets and Ezra Pound's Imagist endeavor, now underway as the first chapter of modern poetry, both impacted the older poet. *The Green Helmet* and *Responsibilities* reveal clearly that he had left the 19th century behind and that, for him, the phase of "Romantic Ireland" was over as he declared in his "September 1913." From then onward volumes poured out that were to establish him as a major poet of the 20th century. These include

Michael Robartes and the Dancer, *The Tower* and *The Winding Stair*, the last two representing Yeats at his best. "Leda and the Swan," "The Second Coming" and "Sailing to Byzantium" that came out of the period are all among the greatest poems of the 20th century. They constitute part of Yeats' system. "Leda and the Swan," especially a Miltonic sonnet, tells the Greek myth of the seduction of Leda, the Spartan queen, by the God of gods, Zeus, who takes on the form of a swan. The tone of the poem illustrates the poet's attitude of disapproval, even antagonism, to the divine act. "Sailing to Byzantium" is a four-stanza poem about the agony of old age and the wish for immortality, achievable by way of art and poetry.

In the last phase of his career, stretching from 1928 till his death, Yeats' style underwent another substantive change. Imitating folk ballads, he wrote some simple, pleasant, unornamented poems like *Crazy Jane*, *Lapiz Lazuli* and *Long-Legged Fly*. All of these are affirmative in attitude and ebullient with a sense of pride which endows tragedy with meaning and chaos with order. The **"Crazy Jane" series**, eight poems in all, are among the most memorable and probably the greatest of Yeats' poems. Here Yeats seemed to put his "system" aside and faced life on its at once physical and philosophical levels of meaning. The gist of Jane's story is that, when young, the girl overflows with passion and ignores the advances of a divinity student in favor of Jack the journeyman, the person who is full of animal spirit. They enjoy love to the fullest extent. As soon as the student becomes a holy cleric (and finally a bishop), he has Jack banished, but Jane's fidelity remains. Time flies, Jane becomes old, ugly and poor, and the Bishop is now interested in her soul. Jane does not believe in his nonsense and holds to her view of life as before. There is a touching existential ring about Jane's craziness about life: joy exists beyond tragedy. The style is in the form of a ballad, all simple, limpid and intense "words for music." The first of these eight poems "Crazy Jane and the Bishop" tells Jane's feeling of disgust at the Bishop's vicious remark about her and Jack living like beasts together. In the second poem, "Crazy Jane Reproved," Jane ignores what people say about her and goes on loving the roaring, ranting journeyman. The third, "Crazy Jane on the Day of Judgment," in the form of a conversation between Jane and a "he" (the bishop, or God, or the conventional lot all taken together), recounts two views on love with Jane reaffirming her thirst for passionate love and living regardless of all consequences. The fourth, "Crazy Jane and Jack the Journeyman," reiterates Jane's stance on passion and love. The fifth, "Crazy Jane on God," is about Jane's love of joy in passional experience without moral considerations. In the sixth, "Crazy Jane Talks with the Bishop," Jane tells the man now concerned with her soul that, though she lives in a sty, her soul is clean and safe. The seventh, "Crazy Jane Grown Old Looks at the Dancers," presents Jane as a spectator-commentator and restates that passion may be destructive like "the lion's tooth," but it is the only thing that makes life worth living. The last of these, "Crazy Jane on the Mountain," continues Jane's role as an observer, jealous, reminiscent, grieving for the loss of youth, but still aching for passional experience. The overall impression that the "Crazy Jane" series makes is that the devil-may-care style of hard living is its own reward and its own justification if needed, which is a concept of life essentially secular in nature.

Yeats was a symbolist poet in that he used allusive imagery and symbolic structures throughout his career. He chose words and assembled them so that, in addition to a particular meaning, they suggest other abstract thoughts that may seem more significant and resonant. His use of symbols is usually something physical that is both itself and a suggestion of other, perhaps immaterial, timeless qualities.

Unlike other Modernists who experimented with free verse, Yeats was a master of the traditional forms. The impact of Modernism on his writings can be seen in the increasing abandonment of the more conventionally poetic diction of his early works in favor of the more austere language and more direct approach to his themes that increasingly characterizes the poetry and plays of his middle period, including the volumes like *In the Seven Woods*, *Responsibilities* and *The Green Helmet*. His later poetry and plays are written in a more personal vein, and the works written in the last twenty years of his life include mention of his son and daughter, as well as meditations on the experience of growing old. In his poem, "The Circus Animals' Desertion," he described the inspiration for these late works.

Chapter 33 The 1930s' Literature

In the history of Europe and America the 1930s witnessed the Great Depression in economy and the emergence of fascism in politics. The UK was not fortunate enough to escape from their catastrophic effect. Like other European countries, it experienced an economic recession and social and political upheavals. The decade thus, as W. H. Auden described it, was one of "crisis and dismay" in British history. In the meantime, new ideas about possible changes were up in the air. Marxism became a fashion, with Freudianism still active, both appealing to the literary circles as well as the people in general. Literary expression underwent a significant change. It acquired a clearer social function. High Modernism began to give way to something new. Writers found it fascinating to write differently. So by the 1930s Virginia Woolf had written her more plot-intense *The Years* (1937), quite a departure from her other works like *The Waves*, and T. S. Eliot had begun composing his more personal and more reflective *Four Quartets*, different and more enduring to the readers than his previous works.

33.1 Poetry

In the 1930s' English poetry, Modernism, still lingering and haunting, was no longer binding. Yeats and Eliot proved to be both repellent and attractive. The new generation of poets did not approve of the prevailing pessimistic view of life and man. They believed in the ameliorating capacity of art. For them, the Modernist demand on art and artists was too rigorous, and they had a strong desire to blaze a trail of their own. As a result, they rebelled against the older tradition. Some of them, like the Auden group, tried to write a more approachable poetry of ordinary life and speech so as to reach out to a more politically minded audience. These poets did not care much whether they were perfect in form. They agreed that art and poetry should be distinct from the previous mode of creation.

Poetic writings of this decade were diverse and numerous. Yeats and Eliot were still writing. So were the Georgians. W. H. Auden was already eye-catching with the publication of several poetic books. He caught the sensibility of his age and influenced and inspired the young poets collected later in the so-called Auden group. Together with the group, he became the mainstay of the decade's poetry. Alongside there was William Empson who persevered in his New Critical or Metaphysical mode of writing regardless of the dominant temper of the time. In the mid-1930s, a new force became visible on the scene. Young Dylan Thomas and George Barker (1913 – 1991) and the Surrealists reacted vehemently to the Modernist and Audenian ways of writing and started what has come to be known as the Romantic revival. The movement continued to gather momentum in the next decade until the 1950s when its excesses enraged the still younger generation, essentially the Movement poets such as Philip Larkin and Donald Davie, and gave way to the postwar new wave of writing.

There were no important poems coming out of the following war period but some expressions of religious despair, a movement called the "New Apocalypse" movement dealing with the subconscious elements of human nature. These poems either urged people to accept the irrational and myth as the basis of life or expressed the sense of forthcoming crisis, human vulnerability, and compassion for human suffering. But, as a whole, they were of no significance.

33.1.1 The Auden Group

The Auden Group is the name given to a group of British and Irish writers active in the 1930s, including W. H. Auden, Louis MacNeice, Cecil Day-Lewis, Stephen Spender, Christopher Isherwood, and sometimes Edward Upward (1903 – 2009) and Rex Warner (1905 – 1986). They were occasionally called simply the Thirties poets.

The Auden Group was not a group or a movement in the sense of being organized as such. The four poets, Auden, Day-Lewis, MacNeice and Spender, were in the same room only once in the 1930s, for a BBC broadcast in 1938 of modern poets (also including Dylan Thomas and others who were not associated with the Auden Group). This event was so insignificant that Day-Lewis evidently forgot it when he wrote in his autobiography *The Buried Day* (1960) that the four were first together in 1953. The connections between the individual writers, as friends and collaborators, were, however, real. Auden and Isherwood produced three plays and a travel book. Auden and MacNeice collaborated on a travel book. As undergraduates, Auden and Day-Lewis wrote a brief introduction to the annual Oxford Poetry. Auden dedicated books to Isherwood and Spender. Day-Lewis mentioned Auden in a poem. But the whole group never operated as such.

The group became first known through the two anthologies edited by Michael Roberts (1902 – 1948)—*New Signatures* (1932) and *New Country: Prose and Poetry by the Authors of New Signatures* (1933), whose emphasis was on the newness of the writers included. Although many newspaper articles and a few books appeared about the Auden Group, the existence of the group was essentially a journalistic myth, a convenient label for poets and novelists who were approximately the same age, who had been educated at Oxford and Cambridge, who had known each other at different times, and who had more or less left-wing views ranging from MacNeice's political skepticism to Upward's committed communism. These poets not only shared basically the same kind of experience but also went through roughly the same process of growth. They began with the Modernists, some Romantics and probably D. H. Lawrence very much in their minds, and moved to embrace the socially and politically engaged verse that was largely written for the consumption of the working class, then felt disappointed and disillusioned, and moved on to a new phase at the end of the decade. It was a generation of divided allegiances and consciences, sore in midst of a tug of war between the forces pulling them in two directions of writing in the service of society versus writing in the private mode. All these phases are adequately reflected in the works of such poets as Spender, Lewis, MacNeice, John Lehmann (1907 – 1987), Glyn Jones (1905 – 1995), and Geoffrey Grigson (1905 – 1985) who was to be one of the most severe critics of Dylan Thomas.

The poets of this group were brilliant and anxious young men with a huge sense of mission to help change their society. All of them were acutely self-conscious that they had insights to offer. Although working on their own, the group shared the notion of writing poetry about different subjects in different ways from the first-generation Modernists. They would like to take poetry out of the hands of an elite readership to the masses and move it out of the obscurity into which the Modernist artifice of ellipsis, paratactic syntax, and learned allusions had thrown it. They used ordinary speech to write a poetry that verged on propaganda and placed their art at the service of a new life. Their separate efforts were concerted by the cementing influence of W. H. Auden, from whom all the rest of the group received inspiration and learned to write. They read him carefully, "shuddered" at his haunting powers, smelt "a change of air," and saw the "beginning of good."

33.1.1.1 W. H. Auden (1907 – 1973)

Auden was the most important poet of the post-T. S. Eliot generation (or the 2nd-generation Modernists) and its acknowledged leader and spokesman. He is also regarded by many critics as one of the greatest writers of the 20th century. Auden was an Anglo-American poet. He left Europe for America in 1939 and became a US citizen in 1946. He was an influence over American poetry of the 1940s and 1950s.

Auden's works are noted for their stylistic and technical achievement, their engagement with moral and political issues, and their variety in tone, form and content. His poetry is the record of his thoughts and experiences in the different phases of his life. Its central themes are love, politics and citizenship, religion and morals, and the relationship between unique human beings and the anonymous, impersonal world of nature. His early poetry is political. Vibrant and powerful partly because it is shocking and violent, it tries to analyze the ills of his time from a Freudian and Marxist perspective. From the late 1930s he changed to a more religious view of life and the world, focusing more on personal responsibility and traditional values. Later in his career, he came to realize that evil will be here to stay and that times may change but not the brutal nature of existence, as is evident in his "The Shield of Achilles" (1955). Suspicious of all attempts to reform life, he sought solace in love and friendship and religious feeling. Naturally, Auden is best known for the love poems such as "Funeral Blues" (whose early version was published in 1936, but final, familiar form was first published in *The Year's Poetry* in London in 1938), the poems on political and social themes such as "September 1, 1939" and "The Shield of Achilles," the poems on cultural and psychological themes such as *The Age of Anxiety* (1947), and the poems on religious themes such as *For the Time Being: A Christmas Oratorio* (1944) and *Horae Canonicae*—a series of poems written between 1949 and 1955.

In formal terms Auden was always a consummate artist, gleaning from all possible traditions and coalescing them well in his versification. His facile combination of high art with popular and colloquial elements constitutes a special fascination. His poetry is well known for its variety of styles and forms, its musical aspect, and its comic element and light touch. Thoughtful, playful and deep, it can awaken echoes when read at different times and by different people. There is a lot of power and permanence in the man. Reading him is similar to reading T. S. Eliot: the readers enjoy both what he says and how he says it and feel instantly that they are in contact with genius. This is particularly true of early Auden.

Auden's early poetry was written in the tone of a young prophet. As one of the disaffected young men, Auden saw an England where "nobody is well," and demanded action and attention to meet the exigencies of his time. He felt that English energy was decaying. It might take a revolution to renew that energy and save English values and standards. Writers could criticize the old and envision a new life. Young Auden described himself as a "pink liberal." His politics seemed to be Marxist, though in retrospect it was more accurately that of a radial liberal. His *The Orators* (1932), while attacking the injuries of the 1930s, clearly projects the daydreams of urgent social change and suggests the cures for the ills. The most belligerent of all Auden's works in the period is perhaps his "A Communist to Others" (1933). Here the poet saw a world floundering. He called for alliance with the workers, satirized the stance of liberal intellectuals as false and harmful, and felt the future belonged to the working class. His poems like "1929," "Spain 1937" and "September 1, 1939," and his drama *The Dance of Death* (1933) in which Karl Marx appears toward the end, all illustrate the sincere social concern on the part of the author.

Auden changed in his attitude toward Marxism at the end of the 1930s. He was in the US and began a new writing phase. 1940 could be a watershed in Auden's life. The fight in him seemed to be tapering off to a calmer observation, then to some philosophical rumination. Auden became conservative, wrote religious poetry and was therefore regarded by some critics as a Lost Leader. A careful reading of his works after 1940 will reveal a different facet, maybe a deeper layer, of the poet's mind at work. He switched his focus to the analysis of human foibles but managed to retain his quest for ideal life in his poetry. From the 1940s on, he took interest in the ideas of Soren Kierkegaard (1813 – 1855), the existentialist Danish philosopher, and his contemporary, Reinhold Niebuhr (1892 – 1971), the American theologian, and frequently alluded to the former's notion of man concerned with his nature and salvation and the latter's concept of man's moral dilemma in his later poetry. For Auden, humans have their own problems, through which they struggle. They may succeed or fail in the struggle but they listen to no other warnings but the choice of their own will all the time. They are not perfect. In his poetry, Auden dissected man's weaknesses and expressed his quest for an ideal existence that is morally higher and nobler. The best of Auden is impersonal, viewing the human condition at a distance. In the poems produced after he settled down in the US, including the long poems like *New Year Letter* (1941), *The Sea and the Mirror* (1944), *For the Time Being* and *The Age of Anxiety*, Auden did not sound as resolute as he had used to be. It might have to do with the emigration. The last phase of his career, with volumes of verse such as *About the House* (1967) and *City without Walls* (1969), reveals a consummate style of personal tone and easy informality. Later in life Auden seemed to think that poetry was ineffectual to make things happen.

Basically a poet, Auden was a multi-talented writer. Other areas of his interest included plays, social criticism, travelogues and war reportage. His major books of verse include *Poems* (1930), *The Orators*, *On this Island* (1937), *Another Time* (1940), *Nones* (1951), *About the House* and *City without Walls*. The best of his criticism was collected in *The Dryer's Hand* (1962). Auden was always prolific, especially so in the decade of the 1930s when he published the majority of his most exciting works in nine volumes.

"Spain" (1937) was written during the Spanish Civil War and is regarded by some as one of the most important literary works in English which emerged from that war. Auden published two versions of the poem, first as a pamphlet *Spain* (1937) and then in revised form and titled "Spain 1937" in his book *Another Time*. The poem is primarily a call to action and showcases Auden at his most radical and revolutionary. It consists of 92 lines and can be divided roughly into three parts. The first part (ll. 1 – 24) relates both the good and evil aspects of the past and puts today's struggle in a proper historical perspective. The second part (ll. 25 – 68) deals with the sense of confusion and lots of orientation on the part of modern people who find themselves, all of a sudden, completely thrown upon their own to shift for survival. The third part (ll. 69 – 92) envisions tomorrow and its glory. Tomorrow is the future with advances in science, medicine, life in general, love and romance, "but today the struggle" (l. 80). Today people face increasing casualties, personal debates, the expedient means of relief, a dying and desperate reality, and a history not to be able to help or pardon our inadequacies to deal with our problems. There is a keen sense of frustration and disillusionment. Basically the tone is pessimistic, hopeless, but with an acute awareness of one's historic responsibility and implied intention to try to do one's best.

"**Muse des Beaux Arts**" (French for "Museum of Fine Arts") is a well-known short poem, written in December 1938 while Auden was staying in Brussels, Belgium with Christopher Isherwood. It was first published under the title "Palais des beaux arts" (Palace of Fine Arts) in the Spring 1939 issue of *New Writing*, a Modernist magazine edited by John Lehmann. Then it appeared in the book *Another Time* in 1940. The poem is written in the conversational style which Auden is noted for. It is radically different in its tone. It is mainly about the painting *The Fall of Icarus* by the Flemish painter Pierter Breughel (1520 – 1569), which is based on a mythological story in Ovid's *Metamorphoses* (8 AD) describing the fall of Icarus from the sky. While Ovid's original portrays the amazement of the plowman, the shepherd and the fisherman who stand by and look on the macabre scene with compassion for the downfall of their fellow human being, Breughel's painting represents them as being apathetic: the plowman may have heard the splash of the fall but it does not concern him as an important failure, for he turns away and goes on with his plowing. Neither does the death bother the ship as it sails on calmly. Auden here satirized "the human position" to human suffering as represented in Breughel's painting: the position from which mutual love and compassion are conspicuously absent. This Auden saw as an essential weakness of human nature that needs addressing. The idea of love here is social by nature.

"**September 1, 1939**" was written on the occasion of the outbreak of World War II and first published in *The New Republic* issue of 18 October 1939. A year later, it was collected and published in book form in Auden's collection of poetry *Another Time*. The poem deliberately echoes the stanza form of W. B. Yeats' "Easter, 1916," another poem about an important historical event. Like Yeats', Auden's poem moves from the description of historical failures and frustrations to a possible transformation in the present or future. Until the two final stanzas, the poem briefly describes the social and personal pathology that has brought about the outbreak of war: first the historical development of Germany "from Luther until now," next the internal conflicts in every individual person that correspond to the external conflicts of the war. Much of the language and content of the poem echoes that of C. G. Jung's *Psychology and Religion* (1938).

The Age of Anxiety: A Baroque Eclogue, whose title became a popular phrase describing the modern era, was written mostly in a modern version of Anglo-Saxon alliterative verse. It is a long poem composed of six parts. Set in a wartime bar in New York City, it deals, in eclogue form, with man's quest to find substance and identity in a shifting and increasingly industrialized world. The poem was awarded the Pulitzer Prize for Poetry in 1948. It inspired a 1949 symphony—Symphony No. 2, *The Age of Anxiety*, for Piano and Orchestra—by composer Leonard Bernstein (1918 – 1990), and a 1950 ballet by Jerome Robbins (1918 – 1998) based on the symphony.

Another Time is a book of Auden's shorter poems written between 1936 and 1939, except for those already published in the two travel books in prose and verse, *Letters from Iceland* (1937), a collaborative work with MacNeice, and *Journey to a War* (1939). These poems are among the best-known of his entire career. *Another Time* is divided into three parts, "People and Places," "Lighter Poems" and "Occasional Poems." The first part includes such poems as "Law, say the gardeners, is the sun," "Oxford," "Herman Melville," "The Capital," "Voltaire at Ferney," "Muse des Beaux Arts," "Dover," and many others. The second part contains "Miss Gee," "O tell me the truth about love," "Funeral Blues," "Roman Wall Blues," "The Unknown Citizen," "Refugee Blues," and other poems. The poems like "Spain 1937," "In Memory of W. B. Yeats," "September 1, 1939," "In Memory of Sigmund Freud," and others make up the third part of the book.

Auden's influence on a succeeding generation of poets was incalculable, comparable only with that, a generation earlier, of Yeats (to whom Auden himself paid homage in "In Memory of W. B. Yeats," 1939). His progress from the engaged, didactic, satiric poems of his youth to the complexity of his later works offered a wide variety of models—the urbane, the pastoral, the lyrical, the erudite, the public, and the introspective mingle with great fluency. He was a master of verse form and accommodated traditional patterns to a fresh, easy and contemporary language.

33.1.1.2 Frederick Louis MacNeice (1907 – 1963)

MacNeice was an Irish poet and playwright. His body of works was widely appreciated by the public during his lifetime, due in part to his relaxed, but socially and emotionally aware style. Never as overtly (or simplistically) political as some of his contemporaries, his works show a humane opposition to totalitarianism as well as an acute awareness of his Irish roots. MacNeice has been regarded as second only to Auden in achievement in his generation of poets. Like his contemporaries, he wrote some didactic lyrics in keeping with the period spirit, but was not extreme in terms of social engagement.

MacNeice made the acquaintance of Auden and Spender at Oxford. He was never leftist in his belief and felt no need to change it as did his other Oxford friends. His association with them was actually a careless affair: his poems appeared in *Oxford Poetry: 1929* along with those by Auden, Spender and Day-Lewis; his book of poems *Blind Fireworks* came out in 1929 when he was at Oxford. MacNeice became known as a poet through his contributions to *New Verse* and his *Poems* (1935). His subsequent volumes of poetry include *The Earth Compels* (1938), *Autumn Journal* (1939), a long personal and political meditation on the events leading up to Munich, *Plant and Phantom* (1941), *Springboard* ("1944), *Holes in the Sky* (1948), *Autumn Sequel* (1954) and *The Burning Perch* (1963). He wrote about his world to reveal its ills and problems, and also to appreciate and celebrate life.

MacNeice's early works reveal a technical virtuosity, a painter's eye for an image, humor, and an impulse towards making sense of what he later called the "drunkenness of things being various." Suspicious of all rigid systems, whether political or philosophical, he worked to establish some pattern from life's flux. He used most of the classic verse forms, but his distinctive contribution was his deployment of assonance, internal rhymes, and half-rhymes, and ballad-like repetitions that he had absorbed from the Irishry of his childhood.

MacNeice was a many-talented writer. He was also renowned as an outstanding writer of radio documentaries and radio parable plays. These include *Christopher Columbus* (1944) and his most powerful dramatic work *The Dark Tower* (1947). In addition, he translated some Aeschylus and Goethe, and produced an amount of literary criticism as well. Although overshadowed in the 1930s and 1940s by Auden, and later by critical fashion, his reputation was revived by the 1966 publication of his *Collected Poems*, edited by E. R. Dodds (1893 – 1979).

33.1.1.3 Stephen Spender (1909 – 1995)

Spender was an English poet, novelist and essayist who concentrated on themes of social injustice and the class struggle in his works. He was appointed the 17th Poet Laureate Consultant in Poetry to the United States Library of Congress in 1965.

Spender began his literary career with novel writing in 1929. His first work, a novel, was not published until 1988, under the title *The Temple*. The novel is about a young man who travels to Germany and finds a culture at once more open than England's—particularly about relationships between men—and showing frightening anticipations of Nazism, which are confusingly related to the very openness the main character admires. His early poetry, notably *Poems* (1933), was often inspired by social protest. He wrote a lot of poetry in the 1930s, including some Marxist poems and patriotic sonnets, which emphasize social over individual priorities. His social concern was deep and genuine, and his poetry could be topical and doctrinaire. "The Pylons" (collected in *Poems*), using images like the pylons and aircraft as symbols of hope, is the reason why the Auden group became also known as "the Pylon Poets." His verse is testimony to his spiritual odyssey in that decade. Living in Vienna his convictions found further expression in *Vienna* (1934), a long poem in praise of the 1934 uprising of Austrian socialists, and in *Trial of a Judge* (1938), an anti-Fascist drama in verse. *The Still Center* (1939), another volume of his poems, came out after he did propaganda work in Spain for the republican side during the Spanish Civil War. His other books of verse include *Poems of Dedication* (1947), *Collected Poems 1928 – 1953* (1955) and *Collected Poems 1982 – 85* (1985).

Spender also published a critical work, *The Destructive Element* (1935), largely on Henry James, T. S. Eliot and W. B. Yeats and their differing responses to a civilization in decline, which ends with a section called "In Defence of a Political Subject," in which he discussed the work of Auden and Upward and argued the importance of treating politico-moral subjects in literature. A gradual shift in his political allegiances may be seen in his poetry and critical works. In addition, Spender was co-editor of two important journals, *Horizon* (1939 – 41) and *Encounter* (1953 – 67).

33.1.1.4 Cecil Day-Lewis (1904 – 1972)

Day-Lewis was a distinguished Anglo-Irish poet of his age. He was professor of poetry at Oxford from 1951 to 1956, the first poet of distinction holding the post since Mathew Arnold. He met Auden at Oxford, with whom he edited *Oxford Poetry* (1927), and became associated with the Auden group there. He was politically active in the 1930s, writing for the *Left Review*, supporting the Left Book Club and speaking at meetings. He joined the Communist party in 1936 and in 1937 edited a socialist symposium *The Mind in Chains: Socialism and the Cultural Revolution*. These preoccupations are reflected in his *Transitional Poem* (1929), *From Feathers to Iron* (1931) and *The Magnetic Mountain* (1933), which have a strong revolutionary flavor, prophesying a new dawn: "We shall expect no birth-hour without blood." *The Magnetic Mountain* was significant at the time of its publication on account of the "social reference" contained in many of the poems therein. Day-Lewis was appointed Poet Laureate in 1968. All his life he looked up to Thomas Hardy as his model. From the late 1930s onward, he composed mostly in the 19th-century modes.

33.1.2 Dylan Marlais Thomas (1914 – 1953)

Dylan Thomas was a great Welsh poet and writer, who wrote exclusively in the English language. He has been acknowledged as one of the most important Welsh poets of the 20th century and noted for his original, rhythmic and ingenious use of words and imagery. He became popular in his lifetime and remained so after his premature death in New York City. In his later life he acquired a reputation, which he encouraged, as a "roistering, drunken and doomed poet." Although Thomas refused to align with any literary group or movement, he is viewed as part of Modernist and Romantic movements, especially the latter.

The fresh voice of Thomas burst out in the mid-1930s. This has come to be known as the Romantic revival of the 1930s. The revival became a trend partly because people still loved the Romantic mode and feeling, partly because Thomas and his associates like George Barker, Ruth Pitter (1897 – 1992), Kathleen Raine (1908 – 2003), Lawrence Durrell, Vernon Watkins (1906 – 1967), and Sydney Keyes (1922 – 1943) were brought up in the Romantic traditions, which include the concept of nature as sacred and mystical, pastoral lyricism, emotional outburst, meditation, the self, the subconscious and the irrational, the intuitive and visionary powers of the mind, and the power of the imagination. The poets had little sympathy for Auden and Empson's Metaphysical kind of poetry and tended to use a florid and melodious diction. They were sensitive to Blake, Wordsworth and Whitman. The Romantic revival gathered momentum in the 1940s until it became too dominant for the next generation, that of the 1950s, to tolerate. Then a reaction set in, and the phase of Movement poetry began.

Thomas was a precocious Neo-Romantic poet capable of wild flights of imagination and meaningful recollections. He was rich and wild in imagination even when he was a boy. He was fascinated with the power of words and their sensory appeal. His great literary passions included James Joyce, Gerard Manley Hopkins and D. H. Lawrence. Although he rebelled against T. S. Eliot and Auden, these Modernist masters left their imprint on him as well. He admired John Donne for his clever conceits. He was sensitive to the influences of Freud and modern psychology. From surrealism he learned but he was not part of that movement. Thomas became known with the publication of his *Eighteen Poems* (1934) and *Twenty-Five Poems* (1936). Some of his early poems were published in T. S. Eliot's *Criterion*, a British literary magazine published from October 1922 to January 1939. *The Map of Love* came out in 1939, *Deaths and Entrances* in 1946, and his final *Collected Poems 1934 – 1952* in 1952. Thomas was also an accomplished prose writer. His first published prose work was *After the Fair*, printed in *The New English Weekly* on 15 March 1934. The later prose works like *Portrait of the Artist as a Young Dog* (1940), a mock-Joycean autobiography, *Under Milk Wood* (1954), a popular play, and *Quite Early One Morning* (1954) show that he was capable of writing moving short stories.

Thematically, Thomas' works chiefly cover subjects like birth, life, love, sex and death. Childhood is one of his favorite subjects. He wrote quite a bit about the unborn child in its ovular, embryonic and fetal stages. He loved describing the beauty of the natural landscape. And there are of course love and sex. His other subjects include human relationships (such as friendship and tyranny), poetry as a craft and the poetic process, war and man's inhumanity, and God (faith and reason and free thought). Basically, Thomas focused on the unity of life, the continuous process of life, death and new birth. To him man gets born from the mother's womb and begins dying at that very moment. So he derived consolation from the unity of man with nature, present with past, and life with death, and refused to mourn the death of a child as he put it in a poem. Thomas' poetry possesses a strong pristine quality, singing without reserve of primitive desires, and pushing these forcefully into the human consciousness. There is also a kind of despair and determinism that reminds one of the religious nature of his philosophy. Many of Thomas' famous poems exhibit his awareness of life's mutability and his sadness about it.

Thomas' works, especially his early poems, seem to portray a "womb and tomb" situation of his—and, by extension, human—existence, and represent the chaotic world in which he and his fellow men had to face the destructive powers trying to control them. There are dreams and madness, ghosts and vampires and witches. The forces in control of man are associated often with sex and occasionally with the atrocity of war. It is a world of terror, a nightmarish one, because not supported by faith. Thomas did not hide the facts of life, however painful they are; he accepted them. At the bottom of his soul lies his yearning for affirmation. He made it clear that his poetry is "the record of my individual struggle from darkness toward some measure of light." Death, he believed, could be transcended. His rhetoric is bardic and rapt, and in his message shines forth the persevering human spirit in face of encroaching darkness. Some of his oft-anthologized poems include "Poem in October," "A Refusal to Mourn the Death by Fire, of a Child in London," "Fern Hill" and "Do Not Go Gentle into That Good Night."

In terms of poetic forms, Thomas' poetry abounds in complex, unexpected images. He was good at weaving threads of different colors skillfully into the tapestry of his poetry, be they from the *Bible*, Welsh legends, Freudianism, Metaphysical wit, Modernism, symbolism, or surrealism. He was meticulously careful with his sound effect, syntactical effectiveness, and the moving power of his images. His language is emotionally loaded and pregnant with meaning. One major feature of his poetry is its unconventionality, its rebelliousness against accepted usages, which accounts for his obscurity.

All in all, Thomas' verbal style played against strict verse forms. His images were carefully ordered in a patterned sequence, and his major theme was the unity of all life, the continuing process of life and death and new life that linked the generations. Thomas saw biology as a magical transformation producing unity out of diversity, and in his poetry sought a poetic ritual to celebrate this unity. He saw men and women locked in cycles of growth, love, procreation, new growth, death and new life. Therefore, each image engenders its opposite.

33.1.3 Sir William Empson (1906 – 1984)

Empson was an English literary critic and poet, widely influential for his practice of closely reading literary works, a practice fundamental to New Criticism. His best-known work is his first, *Seven Types of Ambiguity*, published in 1930. He was listed by Jonathan Bate (1958 –) among the three greatest English literary critics of the 18th, 19th and 20th centuries, the other two being Samuel Johnson and William Hazlitt.

As a poet, Empson wrote mainly a New Critical kind of poetry, exemplifying the major features of the New Critical poem. This kind of poetry keeps the basic Modernist but abandons or tones down other High Modernist features such as extreme fragmentation, paratactic syntax, ellipsis, symbolism and myth, cross-culturalism, and allusions. As a result, it is cautious and traditional, less revolutionary and disorienting, and was more amenable to all tastes and more popular with the rising younger generation of the 1940s. Empson paid a good deal of attention to the poem as a well-wrought urn, with its coherent form, coherent images and figures, rhymes and stanzas, and integrated attitude and vision. His works are basically rational, witty, rigorous in meters and stanzas, and are strewn with metaphors often very difficult to understand. He was particularly good at using puns and paradoxes and concepts or terms from modern physics and mathematics. All these have made for his obscurity. There are traces of Metaphysical influence in his poetry. By the age of thirty Empson had written most of his poems. He published two volumes of verse, *Poems* (1935) and *The Gathering Storm* (1940). *Collected Poems* (revised) appeared in 1955.

As a literary critic, Empson was a student of I. A. Richards who contributed a good deal to the rise and growth of the New Criticism. He developed Richards' critical thought in his famous critical work *Seven Types of Ambiguity* (1930), a trail blazer in itself both in subject and exposition, which impacted poetry writing and criticism in some way. His other critical works include *Some Versions of Pastoral* (1935), *The Structure of Complex Words* (1951) and *Milton's God* (1961), which are not quite comparable in conception and execution to his *Seven Types of Ambiguity*.

33.2 Fiction

The 1930s' fiction appeared to be atavistic. The writers of the decade were no longer "Modernists." They reverted back to the traditional plot and characterization which Modernist masters had despised and almost discarded, in spite that they still inherited certain formal features of the previous generation. In other words, the 1930s' fiction went beyond the Modernist endeavor and back to the traditions of the Victorian and still earlier periods. This was an obvious reaction to the Modernist innovations. It is noticed that C. P. Snow came closer to George Eliot, John Galsworthy and Arnold Bennett in style; Joyce Cary seemed to be imitating Lawrence Sterne, Henry Fielding and Charles Dickens; and Graham Greene appeared to be kith and kin of Wilkie Collins (1824 - 1889), Louis Stevenson and early Joseph Conrad. As to Ivy Compton-Burnett, she did not go even one step beyond 1910, and George Orwell sought help and found value in the naturalistic styles of George Gissing and Emile Zola. The writers of this period seemed to agree that the experimentation of the 1920s was over and outdated and that the best course of action for them was to retreat from its adventurous endeavor. Such rhetoric as technique, experiment and form almost vanished. The modern artistic novel seemed to have few or no worshipers in this period.

The common feature shared by the works of the 1930s' writers is their limited scope in subject matter and length. Within a different context, the writers of this decade focused more on Britain and felt less concerned with "international" or European literary creativity. If Joyce, Woolf, and Lawrence and Conrad thought not only of Britain, and if their novels tended to be "international" both in theme and form, the writers such as Graham Greene and Evelyn Waugh were preoccupied more with native, local, parochial matters. They refused to deal with serious international crises in their fiction. Meanwhile, the writers of this decade became more "introverted" as a consequence of the huge external changes and their successive increasing pressure. They seemed to feel that engagement with life and its major problems leads to a dead end, whereas detachment offers a refuge and an avenue to safety. So they tried to avoid handing subjects like world wars with their sound and fury and the disaffection and despair that stemmed from the big changes. They found, instead, the areas of personal interest fascinating. There is, incidentally, little mention of contemporary occurrences in the works of writers such as Bowen, Compton-Burnett and Evelyn Waugh. Samuel Beckett and Graham Greene were among the few who dealt with subjects both of a personal and social nature.

There were quite a few names out of the period that demand attention. These include Aldous Huxley, George Orwell, Evelyn Waugh, Graham Greene, Christopher Isherwood, Joyce Cary, C. P. Snow and Compton-Burnett, and the famous Samuel Beckett as well.

33.2.1 Aldous Leonard Huxley (1894 – 1963)

Aldous Huxley was an English writer, philosopher and a prominent member of the Huxley family. Versatile and prolific, he wrote copiously on a variety of topics and in a variety of literary genres, and achieved an international renown for himself. Although he is seen as a minor novelist, he did help reflect, in his moderate, sometimes distorting fashion, the spirit of his century, and was nominated for the Nobel Prize in Literature in seven different years. His well-known novels include *Crome Yellow* (1921), *Point Counter Point* (1928) and *Brave the New World* (1932).

Early in his career Huxley edited the magazine *Oxford Poetry* and published short stories and poetry. He had already published three volumes of verse and a volume of stories before *Crome Yellow*, a country-house satire, came out, which earned him reputation for precocious brilliance and cynicism. During the 1920s and 1930s when he and his wife lived first in Italy and then in France, he wrote much fiction, including a collection of stories *Mortal Coils* (1922) and such novels as *Antic Hay* (1923), set in postwar London's nihilistic bohemia, *Those Barren Leaves* (1925), set in Italy, and *Point Counter Point*, in which were recognized portraits of D. H. Lawrence as Rampion and John Middleton Murry (1889 – 1957) as Burlap. His most enduringly popular work *Brave New World* was followed by *Eyeless in Gaza* (1936). Huxley's literary reputation deteriorated when he left in 1937 for California, partly for the sake of his eyes, partly in disillusion with the failure of the peace movements of Europe, partly in search of new direction. He continued to write in many genres. His subsequent novels include *After Many a Summer* (1939), in which Gerald Heard (1889 – 1971) appears as the mystic Propter, *Time Must Have a Stop* (1944), *Ape and Essence* (1948), *The Genius and the Goddess* (1955), and *Island* (1962), an optimistic Utopia. His other works include essays, historical studies, travel works and *The Devils of Loudun* (1952), a study in sexual hysteria which became the basis of the play *The Devils* (1960) by John Whiting (1917 – 1963). Huxley was a humanist, pacifist and satirist. He later became interested in spiritual subjects such as parapsychology and philosophical mysticism, in particular, Universalism. *The Doors of Perception* (1954), a wide-ranging output of essays, and *Heaven and Hell* (1956) describe his experiments with mescalin and LSD. By the end of his life, Huxley had been widely acknowledged as one of the pre-eminent intellectuals of his time.

Although *Brave New World* has an assured place as a popular classic, Huxley's other novels have proved difficult to "place" as literature. Their mixture of satire and earnestness, of apparent brutality and humanity, have led some to dismiss them as smart and superficial, a symptom rather than an interpretation of a hollow age; others have seen them as brilliant and provocative "novels of ideas" written by a man who was not by nature a novelist, but who helped to liberate a generation by shedding light "in dark places."

Brave the New World, set in a dystopian London, has been seen as Huxley's best literary effort. It basically tells the story of a Savage in confrontation with a well-developed civilized society. The Savage is brought to London and feels intrigued in a world so new to him. Here he sees a scientifically planned social order in which people live in content with their assigned places in society. He learns that the people are all born from incubators, brought up in nurseries, classified from birth in keeping with their prenatal manipulated levels of intelligence, and conditioned through education so that they are happy with their social placement. This is what, as he comes to see it, generates an ideal social stability so absent from human life everywhere else. Then the Savage discovers to his great dismay that something absolutely essential to meaningful life is missing from the new world, i. e. individual identity and freedom, love, and independent thinking. He decides to denounce the scientifically imposed order of peace and harmony. He feels so frustrated and incapable of handling the stress that he finds his easy exit out of it in suicide. The novel paints a picture of horror of a future that Huxley envisages will be forthcoming with science and civilization fast advancing, totalitarianism steadily taking over, and natural human life and human nature itself ever on the defensive retreat in face of fatal threat. Huxley apparently deemed it impossible to shake off the shadow of his prophetic vision, and so he painted an even more dreadful picture about the future human condition in his *Brave the New World Revisited* (1958). Here the author made his final plunge in the abyss of pessimism, decadence and despair, from which he never recovered. *Brave the New World* is in essence an acrid satire in which the author managed to bring his mature powers into play for the best effect possible for his art. Though it deserves a commendable mention, as a creative endeavor, its vision is flawed. The author's view of life and its prospect is somewhat morbid and as such lacking in creditability.

33.2.2 George Orwell (1903 – 1950)

Orwell is the pen name of Eric Arthur Blair, who was an English novelist, essayist, journalist and critic. His work is marked by lucid prose, awareness of social injustice, opposition to totalitarianism, and commitment to democratic socialism. He is commonly ranked as one of the most influential 20th-century English writers and chroniclers of the English culture and best known for the dystopian novel *Nineteen Eighty-Four* (1949) and the allegorical novella *Animal Farm* (1945), both of which well illustrate his preoccupation with political considerations and his disappointment at communism as he saw it practiced in the Soviet Union then. His non-fiction works, including *The Road to Wigan Pier* (1937), documenting his experience of working-class life in the north of England, and *Homage to Catalonia* (1938), an account of his experiences in the Spanish Civil War, are widely acclaimed, as are his essays on politics, literature, language and culture. Orwell's works continue to influence popular and political culture, and the term "Orwellian"—descriptive of totalitarian or authoritarian social practices—has entered the language together with several of his neologisms, including "cold war," "Big Brother," "Thought Police," "Room 101," "doublethink" and "thoughtcrime." In 2008, *The Times* ranked him the second on a list of "the 50 greatest British writers since 1945."

Animal Farm is a satire in fable form on revolutionary and post-revolutionary Russia, and by extension, on all revolutions. Here the human society is likened to the animal world. The plot is well designed to approximate and satirize Stalin (1878 – 1953) and his system. The novel begins with the Old Major, an old boar, relating his ideal of an animal society in which the human rule is done away and all animals live in equality and happiness. This inspires the Animalist revolution that drives all the humans out of the farm, so that all the animals can live in equality and bliss. Then a rift occurs between the two leading boars, Snowball and Napoleon. Napoleon, ruthless and cynical, drives Snowball, the idealist, away to establish himself as the absolute ruler. He betrays Old Major's ideal and even signs a business contract with his human neighbors. All the animals are thus placed back in square one and suffer enslavement as before. The hint at Stalin as Napoleon is obvious. The ideal may be the initial communism, the two boars and their quarrel may be intended to replicate the historical scenario between Trotsky (1879 – 1940) and Stalin, and the contract may refer to the Soviet-German pact that was signed before the outbreak of WWII. It is no wonder that *Animal Farm* played an important part in the post-WWII anti-Soviet campaign.

Nineteen Eighty-Four best illustrates Orwell's anti-tyranny stance. It is a nightmare story of totalitarianism of the future and one man's hopeless struggle against it and final defeat by acceptance. It is set in Oceania, a fictional country-world where everything is regulated from above—love, marriage, speech and language, thinking, and history. Independent thinkers are burned to ashes; human movement is closely monitored by the thought police; and social life is all gloom and terror. The tyrant is known as "Big Brother," and the common man is Winston Smith, a member of the Outer Ring of the party. Winston cherishes an ideal of his own, keeps a secret journal, falls in love with Julia and makes her his mistress, and so breaks all the taboos. He is arrested by the secret police, made to suffer incredibly, and has to submit to the authority of the ruler to save his neck. The spearhead of the novel is once again pointed directly at the Soviet Union. Orwell was one of the disillusioned Western intellectuals first enamored with and then alienated from the Soviet Union and its ideal. He was probably the most vehement and aggressive of the turncoats.

Nineteen Eighty-Four is a warning of the possibilities of the police state brought to perfection, where power is the only thing that counts, where the past is constantly being modified to fit the present, where the official language, "Newspeak," progressively narrows the range of ideas and independent thought, and where Doublethink becomes a necessary habit of mind. It is a society dominated by slogans like "War is Peace, Freedom is Slavery, Ignorance is Strength" and controlled by compulsory warship of the head of the Party, Big Brother. The novel had an extraordinary impact, and many of its phrases and coinages (including its title), as is previously mentioned, passed into the common language, although the precise implications of Orwell's warning (and it was a warning, rather than a prophecy) have been subjected to many different political interpretations.

33.2.3　Evelyn Waugh (1903 – 1966)

Waugh was an English writer of novels, biographies and travel books; he was also a prolific journalist and reviewer. His best-known works include the early satires *Decline and Fall* (1928) and *A Handful of Dust* (1934), *Brideshead Revisited* (1945) and the Second World War trilogy *Sword of Honour* (1952 – 61). As a writer, Waugh is recognized as one of the great prose stylists of the English language in the 20th century. He inherited the British literary satirical tradition and wrote caustic satires in his life. Most of his novels are modeled on the constant thematic and structural pattern that an innocent young man experiences his rise and fall in a world of evil and treachery. Simple, honest and naïve, the young man, still emotionally growing, easily becomes a tragic plaything in the hands of the evil powers he comes in contact with.

The satiric power in Waugh's novels is derived from a number of exquisite devices that he employed at will. One of these is his use of the protagonists like Paul in *Decline and fall*, Adam in *Vile Bodies* (1930) and Tony in *A Handful of Dust* as a means to reveal the direct contrast between the alarming social corruptions on the one hand and the total helplessness of the good and innocent folks on the other. Another is his skilful use of the pastoral and the lyric touches in the portrayal of evil characters, which brings out the contrast between good and evil in bold relief. Also, he mentioned serious matters such as death in a factual and indifferent tone and backed out of the scene in detachment to allow the characters to mention a grave subject in a very brief manner; in this way, the nonchalance of a cold universe is effectively revealed. The other notable is his use of verbal irony as a way of self-exposure and self-censure, which is especially powerful in handling the silly and evil characters. Moreover, Waugh was capable of blending the comic within the tragic and remorseless in his attacks upon the evil and the absurd in life, which won him a place in the literature of his age.

Decline and Fall, Waugh's first important novel, was published with great success. The title is a contraction of *The History of the Decline and Fall of the Roman Empire* (1776 – 1788) by Edward Gibbon (1737 – 1794) as well as an allusion to *The Decline of the West* (1918, 1922) by the German philosopher Oswald Spengler (1880 – 1936), which first appeared in an English translation in 1926 and which argues, among other things, that the rise of nations and cultures is inevitably followed by their eclipse. Waugh read both Gibbon and Spengler while writing his first novel. The story is based in part on the author's own schooldays at Lancing College, undergraduate years at Hertford College, Oxford, and his experience as a teacher at Arnold House in north Wales. It is a social satire that employs the author's characteristic black humor in lampooning various features of the British society in the 1920s.

The novel tells the sad story of a modest and unassuming theology student Paul Pennyfeather. Paul falls victim to the drunken antics of the Bollinger Club and is subsequently expelled from Oxford for running through the grounds of Scone College without his trousers. Having thereby defaulted on the conditions of his inheritance, he is forced to take a job teaching at an obscure public school in Wales called Llanabba, run by Dr Fagan. Attracted to the wealthy mother of one of his pupils, Pennyfeather becomes private tutor to her boy Peter and then engaged to be married to her—the Honorable Mrs. Margot Beste-Chetwynde, who later becomes "Lady Metroland" and appears in Waugh's other novels. Pennyfeather, however, is unaware that she makes her fortune by selling the virginity of poor girls and is a criminal running a "white-slave" trade. Arrested on the morning of the wedding, after running an errand for Margot related to her business, Pennyfeather takes the fall to protect his fiancée's honor and is sentenced to seven years in prison for traffic in prostitution. Margot marries another man with government ties and he arranges for Paul to fake his own death and escape. In the end Paul returns to where he started. He studies under his own name at Scone, having convinced the college that he is the distant cousin of the Paul Pennyfeather who was sent down previously. The novel ends as it started, with Paul sitting in his room listening to the distant shouts of the Bollinger Club.

The novel seems to be saying that in a world which is by and large amoral, Paul, as an insignificant common person, lives at the tender mercies of the people who have the power and privilege to do as they please. He is, as his last name suggests, mere feathers and worth no more than a penny. Margot and her minister-husband can "kill" and "resurrect" a human life the way jugglers and God figures do, whereas the average run of mankind is supposed to run their show like funny, wretched puppets. One important stylistic feature to note here is the matter-of-fact tone in which the good number of references are made to the variety and the severity of the vices that exist in the different government agencies and the rich segments of society. The plainness of the narrative style contrasts beautifully well with the force of satire that it generates.

33.2.4 Henry Graham Greene (1904 – 1991)

Graham Greene was an English novelist and author regarded by some critics as one of the greatest writers of the 20th century in English literature. Although his reputation was at its highest in the contemporary period and has been seen as one major postwar novelist, he was closely associated with the 1930s in which some of his major works were written. Combining literary acclaim with widespread popularity, Greene acquired a reputation early in his own lifetime as a great writer, both of serious Catholic novels and of thrillers (or "entertainments" as he termed them); however, even though shortlisted in 1967, he was never awarded the Nobel Prize for Literature.

Through 67 years of writings which include over 25 novels, Greene explored the ambivalent moral and political issues of the modern world, often through a Catholic perspective. His thematic focus remained constant all through his long and productive life. He was probably one of the best of his generation to depict the dilemma in which modern man has managed to land himself in. Greene's subjects may appear to be wide-ranging—strikes, political assassinations, world finance, the Spanish Civil War, the Vietnam-French conflicts, pre-Castro Cuba, the pre-Independence Congo, faith and religion, socialism, and Marxism. But no matter what he wrote about, be it different people, places or events, careful perusal will reveal his all-time concern with man, his condition, his fallen state, his moral quandary, his social and ethical problems, his psychic conflicts, the temptation of evil, and the sordidness and meaninglessness of his life as a whole. Generally Greene's early novels are more religious-oriented while his contemporary works cover a variety of subjects of political interest. His mode of representation is peculiar, rendering the whole and the general truth through the portrayal of a part and the specific. Often set in an exotic milieu, where violence and crimes are the order of the day, his stories mostly center on a petty common person lost in an odd labyrinth of an environment and shifting the best he can for himself. Very prolific and popular, Greene kept writing right up to the end of his life. He won for himself a prominent place in history. His major works include *The Power and the Glory* (1940), *The Heart of the Matter* (1948) and *The Human Factor* (1978).

The Power and the Glory is seen as Greene's most successful work. The title is an allusion to the doxology often recited at the end of the Lord's Prayer: "For thine is the kingdom, the power, and the glory, forever and ever, amen." It was also published in the U.S. initially under the name *The Labyrinthine Ways*. The novel tells the story of an outlaw Roman Catholic priest in the Mexican state of Tabasco during the 1930s, when the Mexican government was trying to suppress the Catholic Church.

Set in Mexico, which Greene visited in 1938, at a time of religious persecution in the name of revolution, the novel describes the last desperate wanderings of the Whisky priest (so nicknamed as he drinks) as outlaw in his own state. The story starts with the arrival of the priest in a country town in an area where Catholicism is outlawed, and then follows him on his trip through Mexico, where he tries to minister to the people as best as he can. He is also haunted by his personal demons, especially by the fact that he fathered a child in his parish some years ago. He meets the child, but is unable to feel repentant about what happened. Rather, he feels a deep love for the evil-looking and awkward little girl and decides to do everything in his power to save her from damnation. He is contrasted with Padre José, a priest who has been forced by the government to renounce his faith and marry a woman and lives as a state pensioner, with "the gringo," bank robber, murderer and materialist, and with the lieutenant, portrayed as an angry idealist and "a good man," who pursues the Whisky priest and eventually captures and puts him to death.

The lieutenant has had bad experiences with the church in his youth. He thinks that all members of the clergy are fundamentally evil and believes that the church is corrupt and does nothing but provide delusion to the people. So there is a personal element in his search for the Whisky priest. Cold and inhumane, though morally irreproachable, the lieutenant puts into practice a demonic plan of taking hostages from villages and shooting them, if it proves that the Whisky priest has sojourned in a village but is not denounced.

During his journey the Whisky priest also encounters a mestizo who later reveals himself to be a Judas figure. In his flight from the lieutenant and his posse, the Whisky priest escapes into a neighboring province, only to reconnect with the mestizo, who persuades the priest to return to hear the confession of a dying man. Though the priest suspects that it is a trap, he feels compelled to fulfill his priestly duty. As a consequence, he is captured by the lieutenant, who admits that he has nothing against the priest as a man, but he must be shot "as a danger." The lieutenant is convinced that he has "cleared the province of priests." In the final scene, however, another priest arrives in the town, which, among other possible readings, suggests that the Catholic Church cannot be destroyed.

The Power and the Glory well illustrates Greene's religious concern. The structure of the story approximates very much that of the biblical story: Jesus (the priest) is betrayed by Judas (the mestizo), and is sentenced reluctantly by the Roman general Pilate (the lieutenant). The Whisky priest is human rather than a paragon of virtue, but he is not totally without any redeeming quality. He keeps his unswerving faith in God, stays awake and aware of his religious duties, and is equal to the occasion, at the critical moments of his life, when he feels called upon to behave the way a hero and a martyr is supposed to do. He knows, for instance, that he will meet with danger if he agrees to go back with the mestizo, but he feels bound by his sense of duty and cannot bring himself to do otherwise. He dies, but reappears in the end as Jesus is resurrected in the *Bible*. The lieutenant possesses a uniqueness of his own: he is persistent and earnest to a fault, but does not lose the sense of justice and compassion. What he shares with the priest is the love that fills both hearts and their sensitivity to love. Their encounter in prison, though grief, exemplifies the spiritual communion possible to achieve between human beings. When the priest says to the lieutenant, "You are a good man," and when the lieutenant replies, "You are not a bad person either," the understanding and friendship that they manage to achieve exhibit the best effect of human connection in life. The mestizo is to the priest more or less what the biblical Judas is to Jesus Christ. He promises to be good and faithful as Judas does, and betrays the holy man all the same in the end. Like many of Greene's works, the novel combines a conspicuous Christian theme and symbolism with the elements of a thriller. In 1941, it received the British literary award the Hawthornden Prize and was chosen by *Time* magazine in 2005 as one of the hundred best English-language novels since 1923.

33.2.5 Women Writers

The 1930s witnessed the rise of some women writers after Virginia Woolf and Katherine Mansfield. These writers include Ivy Compton-Burnett, Elizabeth Bowen, Rebecca West, and others. Although their works are different in theme and form, they have one thematic focus—women and their lives and their inner world—in common.

33.2.5.1 Dame Ivy Compton-Burnett (1884 – 1969)

Ivy Compton-Burnett was an English prolific writer, producing a total of 20 novels in her long career. She began to publish in the 1920s, but came to prominence in the next decade. Her subject matter focused on the late-Victorian upper class with which she was fully acquainted. She was preoccupied with the depiction of the life of the English country gentility in the period stretching from the latter half of the 19th century through the early years of the 20th century. Going through the period of both financial and moral decline, this class experienced a grotesque and absurd phase of life of tyranny, guilt, violence and incest that occurred in their closed and narrow circle. Compton-Burnett's characters often appear larger than life, behaving in ways exaggerated, boldly envisioned, yet humanly conceivable.

Compton-Burnett is noted for her careful handling of language, her exquisite choice of words and her adept manipulation of dialogues so as to help push the story steadily to its climax and achieve the best possible narrative effect in plot structuring and portrayal of characters. In theme Compton-Burnett did not go beyond the early 20th century. Her major works include *Men and Wives* (1931), *A House and Its Head* (1935), *A Family and a Fortune* (1939), *Manservant and Maidservant* (1947) and *Two Worlds and Their Ways* (1949), among which *Manservant and Maidservant* is acknowledged as her best.

33.2.5.2 Dame Rebecca West (1892 – 1983)

Rebecca West, the adopted name of Cicely Isabel Fairfield, was a British author, journalist, literary critic and travel writer. A prolific, protean author who wrote in many genres, West was committed to feminist and liberal principles. She enjoyed high esteem in her time as one of the best journalists and one of the most sensitive and observant literary critics. She was one of the earliest writers who became aware of the power and permanence of the rising generation of writers still struggling then such as James Joyce. Her systematic comments upon Henry James, James Joyce and D. H. Lawrence reveal her acute critical acumen rare for her time. She reviewed books for *The Times*, the *New York Herald Tribune*, the *Sunday Telegraph*, and the *New Republic*, and she was a correspondent for *The Bookman*. Her major works include *Black Lamb and Grey Falcon* (1941), a two-volume study of the Yugoslav nation, *A Train of Powder* (1955), her coverage of the Nuremberg trials, *The Return of the Soldier* (1918), her first and Modernist WWI novel, and the "Aubrey trilogy" of autobiographical novels including *The Fountain Overflows* (1956), *This Real Night* (1984) and *Cousin Rosamund* (1985). In 1947 *Time* called West "indisputably the world's number one woman writer." She was made CBE in 1949 and DBE in 1959 in recognition of her outstanding contributions to the British letter.

33.2.5.3 Elizabeth Bowen (1899 – 1973)

Bowen was an Anglo-Irish novelist and short story writer. She was greatly interested in "life with the lid on and what happens when the lid comes off," in the innocence of orderly life, and in the eventual, irrepressible forces that transform experience. She also examined the betrayal and secrets that lie beneath the veneer of respectability. In terms of theme, she kept one thing always topmost in her mind—the adumbration of young women's life and their emotional world. Although she wrote basically in the traditional manner, she was hypersensitive to the perspective influence of the Modernist innovation in the craft of fiction and tried to delineate the inner world in a fresh and minute way. She was an admirer of film and influenced by the filmmaking techniques of her day. The locations in which Bowen's works are set often bear heavily on the psychology of the characters and on the plots. Her critical observations on the craft of the novel have been of value to later literary criticism. Her major novels are *The Death of the Heart* (1938) and *The Heat of the Day* (1949). The latter is a war novel which is considered one of the quintessential depictions of London atmosphere during the bombing raids of World War II. Her work on literary criticism "The Novelist's Craft" (1956) is an important work on novel-writing.

33.2.6 The Leftist-oriented Writers

The 1930s was a decade in which leftist-oriented writings bloomed in Europe and in England as well. The severity of the crisis and the extent of suffering of the people and the subsequent spread of the influence of the Soviet Union and Marxism colored literary creativity so much that social concern became the major thematic focus for a good number of leftist and proletarian writers in their creative endeavors. These include, J. B. Priestley, Christopher Isherwood, Lewis G. Gibbon, Walter Greenwood, and others. Whereas the writers like Lewis G. Gibbon and Walter Greenwood made the voice of protest of the working class well heard, such writers as J. B. Priestley and Christopher Isherwood all tried to respond in their unique way to the new zeitgeist of the new decade. The weakness that detracted from their permanence was probably their over-emphasis on the effect of propaganda at the expense of the quality of their works as art.

33.2.6.1 Lewis Grassic Gibbon (1901 – 1935)

Lewis Gibbon was the pseudonym of James Leslie Mitchell, a Scottish writer. He attracted attention from his earliest attempts at fiction, notably from H. G. Wells, but it was his trilogy entitled **A Scots Quair** (1946), and in particular its first book *Sunset Song* (1932), with which he made his mark. *Sunset Song* is widely regarded as an important classic (voted Scotland's favorite book in a 2005 poll supported by the Scottish Book Trust and other organizations) but opinions are more varied about the other two—*Cloud Howe* (1933) and *Grey Granite* (1934). *A Scots Quair*, with its combination of stream of consciousness and lyrical use of dialect, is considered to be among the defining works of the 20th-century Scottish Renaissance. It tells the story of Chris Guthrie, a young woman growing up in the northeast of Scotland in the early 20th century. All three parts of the trilogy have been turned into serials by BBC Scotland. *Spartacus* (1933), a novel set in the famous slave revolt, is his best-known full-length work outside this trilogy. Besides, Gibbon also wrote some short stories, which were collected posthumously in *A Scots Hairst* (1969), and essays.

33.2.6.2 Walter Greenwood (1903 – 1974)

Greenwood was an English novelist and playwright, best known for his first and socially influential novel **Love on the Dole** (1933), which is about the destructive social effects of poverty in his home town. The novel was a critical and commercial success, and a huge influence on the British public view of unemployment. It even prompted the parliament to investigate, leading to reforms. The popularity of the novel, which was adapted as a play that had successful runs in both Britain and the United States, meant Greenwood would not have to worry about employment again.

Although he never matched the success of *Love on the Dole*, Greenwood produced a succession of novels during the 1930s: *His Worship the Major* (1934), *The Time is Ripe* (1935), *Standing Room Only* (1936), *Cleft Stick* (1937), *Only Mugs Work* (1938), *The Secret Kingdom* (1938) and *How the Other Man Lives* (1939). His works produced after WWII include the *Trelooe* trilogy—*So Brief the Spring* (1952), *What Everybody Wants* (1954) and *Down by the Sea* (1956)—and a few plays: *Cure for Love* (1945, filmed in 1950), *Too Clever for Love* (1952) *and Saturday Night at the Crown* (1958).

33.2.6.3　J. B. Priestley (1894 – 1984)

John Boynton Priestley was an English novelist, playwright and broadcaster. He lived a long and productive life. His multi-volume output includes novels, plays and critical commentaries. Priestley was a realist. He was concerned with the human condition in the years of the Depression and wrote about the worries and fears of the lower strata of society in face of joblessness and bankruptcy. His works of the period spearheaded their critical edge against the ills of society. His Yorkshire background is reflected in much of his fiction, notably in **The Good Companions** (1929), a tragic-comic story of success and pain. The novel is Priestley's most popular and successful literary effort. It first brought him to wide public notice and has been long on the top of the best-sellers' list.

Basically a novelist, Priestley also wrote a good number of plays, the most famous of which include *Dangerous Corner* (1932) and *An Inspector Calls* (1945). Many of his plays are structured around a time-slip, and he went on to develop a new theory of time, with different dimensions that link past, present and future. He was popular as a playwright for over 20 years in the West End of London theaters.

In 1940, Priestley broadcast a series of short propaganda talks that were credited with saving civilian morale during the Battle of Britain. His left-wing beliefs brought him into conflict with the government, but influenced the birth of the Welfare State.

33.2.6.4　Christopher Isherwood (1904 – 1986)

Isherwood was an English novelist and a left-oriented realist in the 1930s, who wrote his best works in the decade. He focused his creative energies on the depiction of the social and political problems of his day and supported all the causes of a leftist orientation. He became an active member of the Audenic group and wrote political plays in collaboration with Auden.

The 1930s was Isherwood's "European" period in which he wrote his famous works such as those relating the Berlin stories. After his immigration to the US in the late 1940s, his "American" period began. All his works share one feature: they are all in a way tied up with an individual's quest for truth about life and about self. Isherwood was essentially autobiographical. Some of his characters and some of the narrators of his stories are clearly his own representations. Isherwood is a highly readable writer. His most famous works are his **Berlin stories** that appear in his novels like *Mr. Norris Changes Trains* (1935), *Goodbye to Berlin* (1937) and *The Berlin Stories* (1946). Having lived in pre-Hitler Berlin for over three years (1929 – 1933), he learned about the city and its psychology from inside. *Goodbye to Berlin*, probably the most renowned of all his works, is a coherent amalgam of several "loosely connected" diaries and sketches, and a short novel, with an overlapping cast of characters.

Exercises

I. Multiple choices

1. After R. B. Sheridan and Oliver Goldsmith, English _____ experienced a general decline.
   A. poetry　　　　　　　　　　　　　　　B. drama
   C. novel　　　　　　　　　　　　　　　　D. literature

2. *The Forsyte Saga* is the best of _____'s three trilogies and has been regarded as his masterpiece.

  A. John Galsworthy   B. D. H. Lawrence
  C. James Joyce   D. Oscar Wilde

 3. _____'s play *Mrs. Warren's Profession* belongs to his "Plays Unpleasant." In this play the author accused the bourgeoisie of making profit by fostering prostitution.
  A. William Shakespeare   B. R. B. Sheridan
  C. Bernard Shaw   D. Henry Fielding

 4. _____ is probably Bernard Shaw's masterwork. The play is an extensive farce that contains an amusing amalgam of diverse doctrines.
  A. *Mrs. Warren's Profession*   B. *Arms and the Man*
  C. *Widower's Houses*   D. *Man and Superman*

 5. Arnold Bennett was famous for his _____, which include *Anna of the Five Towns*, *The Old Wives' Tale* and *The Clayhanger Trilogy*.
  A. "Five Towns" stories   B. trilogies
  C. "Five Prophetic" stories   D. interior monologues

 6. In her famous essay "Modern Fiction," _____ singled out three novelists of the first years of the 20th century for analysis and branded them as "Edwardians," a nomenclature not favorable in meaning.
  A. James Joyce   B. T. S. Eliot
  C. Virginia Woolf   D. Bernard Shaw

 7. E. M. Forster was probably one of the first writers then sensitive to and aware of the change which materialized into _____ in the works of Virginia Woolf, James Joyce and D. H. Lawrence.
  A. Realism   B. Modernism
  C. Sentimentalism   D. Postmodernism

 8. Rudyard Kipling is best known for _____, a tale of a white child left in an Indian jungle but surviving the inclement environment in the company of his jungle folk—the wolves, bears, tigers, panthers and elephants.
  A. *The Heart of Darkness*   B. *The Waves*
  C. *In Chancery*   D. *The Jungle Books*

 9. _____ inherited the tradition of Critical Realism of the Victorian period represented by Charles Dickens.
  A. John Galsworthy   B. D. H. Lawrence
  C. James Joyce   D. Oscar Wilde

 10. _____ established John Galsworthy's fame as a prominent novelist and marked the peak of Critical Realism in all his works.
  A. *In Chancery*   B. *To Let*
  C. *The Silver Box*   D. *The Man of Property*

 11. John Galsworthy's play writing began with _____, one of his best-known plays.
  A. *In Chancery*   B. *To Let*
  C. *The Silver Box*   D. *The Man of Property*

 12. Which of the following is NOT H. G. Wells' science fiction?

A. *The Time Machine* B. *The War of the Worlds*

C. *The First Men in the Moon* D. *The Heart of Darkness*

13. _____ is best remembered for his achievement in science fiction and his prophecies about the outbreak of the two world wars.

A. John Galsworthy B. H. G. Wells

C. Rudyard Kipling D. Oscar Wilde

14. *Lord Jim* and _____ are both among Joseph Conrad's most fascinating and powerfully influential works.

A. *A Passage to India* B. *The Rainbow*

C. *The Heart of Darkness* D. *The Jungle Books*

15. _____, written by E. M. Forster in the traditional manner, tries to represent and explore the psychological facet of man.

A. *A Passage to India* B. *The Rainbow*

C. *The Heart of Darkness* D. *The Jungle Books*

16. E. M. Forster claimed in _____ that hope stemmed from the human connection or "communion" by means of which man can vanquish hopelessness.

A. *A Passage to India* B. *The Rainbow*

C. *The Heart of Darkness* D. *The Jungle Books*

17. Sensitive to the change in values and tastes of the time, Katherine Mansfield employed the _____ of representation at times.

A. impressionist mode B. traditional mode

C. naturalistic mode D. expressionistic mode

18. Rupert Brooke, whose vision of _____ was clearly Romantic, became famous for "the very few incomparable _____ sonnets" that he wrote in 1914.

A. love, love B. war, war

C. nature, nature D. death, death

19. Which of the following is NOT Robert Graves' work?

A. "Down, Wanton, Down!" B. "As the Team's Head Brass"

C. *Claudius the God* D. *The White Goddess*

20. Walter de la Mare is probably best known for his works for children and for his poem _____.

A. *Abraham Lincoln* B. "The Soldier"

C. *In Parenthesis* D. "The Listeners"

21. Walter de la Mare, chiefly on account of his _____ temper in poetry, has been sometimes called "the belated last poet of the _____ tradition."

A. realistic, old B. modernist, new

C. romantic, romantic D. sentimentalist, sentimentalist

22. Which of the following is NOT the Georgian poet?

A. Walter de la Mare B. W. H. Davies

C. John Drinkwater   D. William Butler Yeats

23. The most important developments in the field of philosophy and psychology during the 1920s that impacted literary creativity and criticism should be _____ notion of time and _____ theory of psychoanalysis.

A. Bergson's, Freud's   B. Einstein's, Jung's
C. Newton's, Freud's   D. Bergson's, Marx's

24. D. H. Lawrence was heavily influenced by Freudianism. He placed emphasis on the depiction of the inner world and the irrational and called for the emancipation of the _____.

A. ego   B. superego
C. reason   D. id

25. D. H. Lawrence's close attachment to his mother led him to the complexities of human love, and his paternal background set the _____ tone in his representation of life.

A. romantic   B. realistic
C. modern   D. irrational

26. _____ is D. H. Lawrence's semi-autobiographical novel and perhaps also his most popular novel.

A. *The Rainbow*   B. *Lady Chatterlay's Lover*
C. *Sons and Lovers*   D. *Women in Love*

27. Almost the whole of James Joyce's masterpiece _____ is devoted to the narration of one day's life of a Jewish advertisement-canvasser Leopold Bloom in Dublin, the Irish capital.

A. *Finnegans Wake*   B. *A Portrait of the Artist as a Young Man*
C. *Dubliners*   D. *Ulysses*

28. _____, James Joyce's first published book, is a collection of 15 stories, the most famous of which are "The Dead" and "Araby."

A. *Finnegans Wake*   B. *A Portrait of the Artist as a Young Man*
C. *Dubliners*   D. *Ulysses*

29. *Finnegans Wake* is an account of a night; or rather one night's dream of the protagonist _____, a Dublin tavern-keeper, in whose consciousness all recorded history finds a meaning and a home.

A. Molly   B. Finnegan
C. Humphrey Earwicker   D. Steven Dedalus

30. *Mrs. Dalloway* is _____'s first completely successful novel in the author's "new" style of the "stream of consciousness."

A. James Joyce   B. Virginia Woolf
C. D. H. Lawrence   D. John Galsworthy

31. In her essay _____, Virginia Woolf located the major weakness of the traditional novel in its focus on depicting exterior details but ignoring any dip into the inner world of man.

A. *A Room of One's Own*   B. "Modern Fiction"
C. *Three Guineas*   D. *Between the Acts*

32. *Mrs. Dalloway* is mainly about _____ in the life of the middle-aged Mrs. Clarissa Dalloway in relation

Part Eight The Early Twentieth Century

to those connected with her.

  A. one day   B. three days

  C. one year   D. one night

33. John Galsworthy is one of the most prominent of the 20th-century _____ writers in English literature.

  A. realistic   B. romantic

  C. naturalist   D. aesthetic

34. The Nobel Prize winners for literature do NOT include _____.

  A. Bernard Shaw   B. T. S. Eliot

  C. John Galsworthy   D. Oscar Wilde

35. During his lifetime and even afterwards _____ was a controversial figure because of his frank treatment of sex and his outspoken insistence upon a need for a readjustment in the relationship between the sexes.

  A. Charles Dickens   B. D. H. Lawrence

  C. Thomas Hardy   D. George Eliot

36. Bernard Shaw was the greatest dramatist in the English literature in the 20th century. He followed the great tradition of _____ in dramatic writing.

  A. realism   B. modernism

  C. aestheticism   D. romanticism

37. W. B. Yeats' works fall into 3 categories—poems, plays and essays, among which the _____ are decidedly in the majority.

  A. poems   B. essays

  C. plays   D. essays and plays

38. *The Tower* and _____ represent W. B. Yeats at his best.

  A. *Michael Robartes and the Dancer*   B. *The Wild Swans at Coole*

  C. *The Winding Stair*   D. *In the Seven Woods*

39. _____ was NOT written by D. H. Lawrence.

  A. *The Rainbow*   B. *Lady Chatterlay's Lover*

  C. *Sons and Lovers*   D. *Ulysses*

40. _____ was generally accepted as the founder of "stream of consciousness." His novels made a complete change in the form and structure of fiction and had a decisive impact on the development of the "stream of consciousness" or "interior monologue."

  A. James Joyce   B. T. S. Eliot

  C. Oscar Wilde   D. Bernard Shaw

41. _____ was the most important poet of the post-T. S. Eliot generation, or the 2nd-generation Modernists, and its acknowledged leader and spokesman.

  A. W. B. Yeats   B. Dylan Thomas

  C. Oscar Wilde   D. W. H. Auden

42. W. H. Auden's major books of verse include _____, *On this Island, Another Time, About the House*,

and others.

A. *The Dryer's Hand* B. *The Orators*
C. *The Dance of Death* D. *For the Time Being*

43. The Auden Group is the name given to a group of British and Irish writers active in the 1930s that mainly included W. H. Auden, Louis MacNeice, Cecil Day-Lewis and _____.

A. W. B. Yeats B. Dylan Thomas
C. William Empson D. Stephen Spender

44. _____ is William Empson's best-known work.

A. *The Structure of Complex Words* B. *The Gathering Storm*
C. *Seven Types of Ambiguity* D. *Milton's God*

45. Aldous Huxley's well-known novels include *Crome Yellow*, _____ and *Brave the New World*.

A. *Mortal Coils* B. *The Doors of Perception*
C. *Point Counter Point* D. *Oxford Poetry*

46. _____, Evelyn Waugh's first important novel, smacks strongly of black humor.

A. *A Handful of Dust* B. *Decline and Fall*
C. *The Decline of the West* D. *The History of the Decline and Fall of the Roman Empire*

II. Blank-filling

1. In the first half of the 19th century the English theater saw no remarkable performance except Percy Bysshe Shelley's _____.

2. Thematically, *Man and Superman* demonstrates Bernard Shaw's _____ about the future that stems from his belief in creative evolution.

3. Arnold Bennett was famous for his "Five Towns" stories, all of which are based on the _____ of modern England.

4. Arnold Bennett's _____, instead of the other tales among the "Five Towns" stories, focuses more on one individual's fortune.

5. Arnold Bennett was a careful "scientific" observer and an efficient recorder. His _____ of life was all right as a manner of literary creation until Virginia Woolf stood out to say that it was not.

6. Virginia Woolf complained that the so-called "Edwardians," including Arnold Bennett, H. G. Wells and John Galsworthy, overemphasized the description of _____ in their representation of life instead of the internal world of man which she thought should take precedence over anything else in novel-writing.

7. *The Jungle Books* is written in the tradition of _____ fables, with each one of its chapters in obvious contrast to the _____ world.

8. John Galsworthy's themes focus on the lives and experiences of the rich men of _____, their selfishness, their philistinism, their decadence, depravity and decline, and their fierce conflict with the workers.

9. John Galsworthy is noted for portraying the history of the English bourgeois life in his famous _____, especially in the first one *The Forsyte Saga*.

10. As a dramatist, John Galsworthy, in his 28 plays, as in his novels, realistically dealt with the _____

Part Eight The Early Twentieth Century

of his time.

11. H. G. Wells has been regarded as one of the founding figures of _____, which reveals his rich imaginative powers.

12. One of the salient features of Joseph Conrad's fiction is the strikingly permeating sense of disjunction and fragmentation that characterizes the Modernist works. The author weaves adroitly into a coherent whole _____ that different people tell from different perspectives, so that stories appear within the story dotted with endless discursive digressions.

13. *Lord Jim* is not presented in the _____ order. It looks like a hotchpotch, or a fish cut up into pieces and placed tail over head in a frying pan.

14. The novella *The Heart of Darkness* adds as it does the term "_____" to the modern literary critical idiom and offers an important theme to literature in general.

15. *A Room with a View* is E. M. Forster's most optimistic work, while _____ is his greatest success.

16. In formal aspects, Katherine Mansfield placed more focus on the excavation of the _____ of her characters rather than on the detailed description of the exteriors.

17. Edward Thomas, like Robert Frost, advocated the use of natural diction, and of _____ speech rhythms in metrical verse.

18. Wilfred Owen's major theme is war and "_____."

19. For D. H. Lawrence, _____ is the highest expression of individuality, and modern man's tragedy lies in seeing it as the fulfillment of an animal desire and in repressing love's irrationality.

20. What makes Virginia Woolf's fiction distinctive is its attempt to go beyond what she regarded as the tyranny of _____, to get close to life as it is actually experienced.

21. In thematic terms *To the Lighthouse* advocates the author's unique vision of art and literature, which has been defined as the _____ vision, or one that combines both the female and the male principles in artistic creation.

III. Term definition

1. The Auden Group
2. The Edwardians
3. Epiphany
4. Fragmentation
5. The Georgians
6. Interior monologue
7. Modernism
8. Nobel Prizes
9. Parody
10. Psychoanalysis
11. Science fiction
12. Stream of consciousness

IV. Short-answer questions

1. What are the writing features in Bernard Shaw's plays?
2. What are John Galsworthy's writing features?
3. What is D. H. Lawrence's view on love and sex?
4. What is Virginia Woolf's notion of art?

V. Essay questions

1. Give a brief introduction to D. H. Lawrence's *Sons and Lovers*.

2. Give an account of D. H. Lawrence's difference from Sigmund Freud in his stance on psychoanalysis as a theory.

3. Give a brief introduction to Virginia Woolf's *To the Lighthouse*.

4. Comment on the major features in James Joyce's works.

5. Introduce *Ulysses* from the perspectives of content, theme, characterization and style.

6. Comment on William Butler Yeats' poetic career.

7. Comment on the shift in W. H. Auden's tone of poetry.

8. Give a brief introduction to Aldous Huxley's *Brave the New World*.

Part Nine The Postwar Period

Postwar Britain experienced immense changes. Democratization and socialization occurred, values were shifting, and class differences became less acute. Relative affluence was returning, and a "welfare" state was in the works. The postwar period is sometimes known as the second Elizabethan era. Prosperity returned in the 1950s and London remained a world center of finance and culture, though the nation was no longer a major world power. People tended to value the day-to-day experience and take it easy. It became apparent that the new period called for its own literary expression. The writers who had emerged in the prewar decades found the postwar mood no longer congenial to their imaginative endeavors. Some of them were losing critical favor; and some literary periodicals were shutting down. Literary tastes underwent some drastic change. High Modernism with its formal innovations was felt to be out of date, and people began to look backward beyond James Joyce and T. S. Eliot to a time, the 18th and the 19th centuries, when there was a good story telling in fiction. There was little demand for adventure but a strong desire for the traditional and the familiar forms.

Chapter 34 Postwar Poetry

The postwar scene of English poetry was a colorful one. For one thing, the Modernist poets and works were still highly visible. Robert Graves and William Empson were popular and attractive. The Metaphysical style, which T. S. Eliot did much to resurrect and revive, was still in vogue. The Romantics of the previous decades like Dylan Thomas and Edith Sitwell (1887 – 1964), and also many younger poets continued to write in the same vein. For another, a new generation was emerging. Literary historians have tended to label the new poets of the 1950s all including Philip Larkin, Donald Davie and Thom Gunn as part of what has come to be known as the Movement poetry, while in actuality different groups existed and tried to exhibit their own identities. Other contemporary poets active on the literary scene include Charles Tomlinson, Ted Hughes and Geoffrey Hill since the 1960s and 1970s, and the even younger ones of the later period such as Tony Harrison, Seamus Heaney, Craig Raine and James Fenton.

34.1 The Movement Poetry

The term, "the Movement," first appeared in 1954 in an article by J. D. Scott, the literary editor of the *Spectator*, who was discussing the features of the new poetry of postwar Britain. Although it was used there in a jocular manner, the label sank deep in memory and gained wide currency. The Movement poets were first made known as a group in an anthology entitled *Poets of the 1950s* (1955) edited by D. J. Enright (1920 – 2002) and again in another better-known anthology *New Lines* (1956) by Robert Conquest (1917 – 2015). Then the rest of the world as well as Britain became alert that a new frame of reference had appeared for gauging the mood of postwar Britain.

The Movement poets included, among others, Philip Larkin, Donald Davie, D. J. Enright, Thom Gunn, Robert Conquest, John Wain, Elizabeth Jennings (1926 – 2001), Kingsley Amis and John Holloway (1920 – 1999). These poets wrote in a dramatically different way from the poets of the war years. Fed up with the experimental Romantic efforts of Dylan Thomas and his contemporaries to shape life and the world, they reacted strongly by veering in a new direction and came to grips downright with their new, different reality. They were concerned with the social changes that postwar Laborite Britain was going through, and tried to examine life in an honest, realistic manner. In addition, they felt the acute need to cater to a broader readership than the Modernist endeavor had served, and they could be anti-intellectual and anti-cultural in their stance. Most of the younger poets of the 1950s were either part of the Movement or shared its values.

What the Movement poets reacted particularly against was Dylan Thomas' kind of Romantic vision of things, his arrangement of complex, unexpected images, and his abandoning strict verse forms. They chose, instead, the traditional rational forms of communication as exemplified by the minor Augustans of the 18th century. The rebellion against Dylan Thomas and his generation of poets was actually part of the larger postwar reaction to the dominance of T. S. Eliot and the Metaphysical mode of writing as shown in the works of William Empson.

The Movement poets shared some essential literary features and qualities in their works. They were, for instance, self-expressive, intuitive, obscure, experimental, realistic, and concerned with formal control. Their style is generally plain, direct, deflated, personal and formal. Their diction is lean and spare. There is not much room for Dylan Thomas' Romantic rhetoric of his mysticism or Empson's elaborate punning. The Movement poets regarded T. S. Eliot and Ezra Pound as continental influences and appreciated much better A. E. Housman (1859 – 1936), Thomas Hardy, the Georgians and the 18th-and 19th-century poets such as Thomas Gray, William Cowper and William Wordsworth.

The Movement poetry tended to be depressing in mood and tone. This was in part traceable to the quandary in which they found themselves in postwar Britain. The writers of the period were caught in a dilemma: they thought the Socialist ideals all right, but lacked a strong faith in them. There is a good deal of hurt and pain and fear in their works. The Movement took English poetry along a road that Dylan Thomas and his followers had never thought of traversing. It is necessary to add that the Movement poets wrote also novels and literary criticism and that the group was heterogeneous in ideas and practices rather than monolithic in any sense of the term.

34.1.1 Philip Larkin (1922 – 1985)

Larkin was an English poet, novelist and librarian, and the dominant figure of the Movement poetry. He published four books of poetry altogether, including *The North Ship* (1945), *The Less Deceived* (1955), *The Whitsun Weddings* (1964) and *High Windows* (1974). It was his second collection of poems that brought him to prominence. Early in his career, he also wrote some novels, including *Jill* (1946) and *A Girl in Winter* (1947). Larkin was under the influence of both William Butler Yeats (as is evident in *The North Ship*) and Thomas Hardy (as revealed in *The Less Deceived* and *The Whitsun Weddings*) before he found his mature style. He was a landmark in the literary history of his country. Together with his contemporaries such as Kingsley Amis, Donald Davie and Thom Gunn, he wrote a new kind of poetry in order to be true to the spirit of his age. He did his best to help revive the 18th-and 19th-century literary tradition of his country and oppose what the Movement termed foreign influences such as that of the High Modernists—T. S. Eliot's or Ezra Pound's. He was offered, but declined, the position of Poet Laureate in 1984 when John Betjeman (1906 – 1984) died.

Larkin's poetry has been characterized as combining "clarity," "an ordinary, colloquial style," a "quiet, reflective tone," "ironic understatement" and a direct engagement with commonplace experiences. Larkin rejected Dylan Thomas' kind of Romantic vision of things. His poetry is plain in style, almost free from metaphors and melodious rhetoric. His subject is daily life as being lived by the common people. He generally painted life in drab and gloomy colors. There is a good deal of disillusionment, skepticism and helplessness in his works.

Larkin's poems normally begin with the poet-speaker observing some object or person or place or anything from the external world and then move on with his inspired deliberations. Larkin is mostly personal and even confessional in tone, with the "I" frequently featuring as the speaker and clinging to his own voice and view obdurately. His power lies in the fact that his personal truth often coincides with public truth and becomes identical with it.

"**Poetry of Departures**" (1955) basically talks about two possible courses of action for human beings to take in life. One is romantic and the other is realistic. The romantic one thrills as it is everyone's dream, audacious, purifying and elemental. But it is "artificial," not practical enough, not quite in keeping with common sense. Ultimately life is not always swashbuckling, not always heroic. Very often, it is humdrum, drab, and dreary with everything, bed, books, china, "in perfect order." It is, in a word, not exciting, but we have got to live with that. The title of the poem, which has little physical connection with its content, metaphysically sums it up well: The poet would "depart" from the road taken, take the realistic course of action, and write realistically about life here and now.

Larkin's poetry is generally short and lyrical. He saw something, described it and reflected on it. For instance, when he saw a couple of young people together somewhere, he would guess that they are making out, the girl is wearing some protection, and they are feeling the bliss of hot and wet love and sex. Then reflection cuts in. That kind of bliss, he would tell us, is the paradise that old people always dream of, the kind of bliss he had when he was young forty years ago. Then in the midst of the thought of joy and abandonment, the poet, now no longer young, thought of the high church windows, its glass, the blue sky beyond, and the nothingness that stretches endless still beyond that. Thus beginning with a sort of nostalgia, a sense of loss, the poet turned back to himself, now over sixty years old. For the poet-speaker, nothing is going to happen ever again except, probably, death, which is one of Larkin's recurring themes and subjects. The sense of bliss led suddenly, abruptly, to a sense of horror of having to face eternity. This would be possibly the experience that people have reading his famous poem—"**High Windows**."

"**Home Is So Sad**" conveys an acute sense of being deserted, lonely, disillusioned, and nostalgic for the good old days never to return. The "home" of the poem used to be a joyous and hopeful place that strove upward. There were pictures, cutlery, music in the piano, and, of course, people. Now though the things are still there, the home withers and stops trying to be a better place. The ending is full of longing for the lost past, and of a desperate clinging to it and reluctance to part with it. All this is amply delineated with that terse yet fully loaded "That vase." The tone verges almost on being sentimental. But a different interpretation could be that such warmth of feeling could indicate the resilience of a mind against overwhelming odds.

34.1.2 Donald Davie (1922 – 1995)

Davie was another English Movement poet and literary critic, whose poems in general are philosophical and abstract, but often evoke various landscapes. Davie rediscovered the values of the minor 18th-century poets like William Cowper, Oliver Goldsmith, George Crabbe and Isaac Watts, and made these predominant for the Movement poetry. He became a neo-Augustan. What impressed him about Augustan poetry was the intrinsic connection between its moral and formal concerns. Davie did not like the Modernist-Symbolist ideas about poetry; he showed his firm opposition to the Confessional poets like Robert Lowell (1917 – 1977), Sylvia Plath (1932 – 1963) and Theodore Roethke (1908 – 1963) and to the great masters such as W. B. Yeats and T. S. Eliot. However, he was very sympathetic to Ezra Pound's poetry, which he thought had been unfairly misunderstood, and he also wrote some poems akin to the Confessional poetry in tone. His great influences were F. R. Leavis and Yvor Winters (1900 – 1968). His major works have been included in such volumes as *Brides of Reason* (1955), *Selected Poems 1950 – 1970* (1972), *Three for Water Music and the Shires* (1981), *Collected Poems 1970 – 1983* (1983), *To Scorch or Freeze* (1988), and *Collected Poems* (1990). Much of Davie's poetry has been compared to that of the traditionalist Philip Larkin, but other works are more influenced by Ezra Pound. He is featured in the *Oxford Book of Contemporary Verse* (1980).

Davie was a moralist all his life. He believed that, in face of the philistine modern world, the poet had a clear social purpose to accomplish as a moralist and write in a form that would help people get to know their place in the world and the general scheme of things better. Poetry was a means of discovering universal truths and offering a space to "the man going mad" in the universe. Davie's style is therefore connected with morality. He held that the formal control of rhyme, meter and syntax should help affirm moral values. His devotion to traditional forms was life-long and unflinching. His syntax is impeccable, and his diction chaste by and large though, with time, some relaxation has been observed. Davie's attitude toward language is clear. The key word he used in his first book of criticism about poetry is "chastity." He felt that language and syntax needed purifying. The perfection of the word served to strengthen social and moral law and helped man to come to terms with himself.

Davie wrote to grapple with the reality of his time. His subjects mostly relate to England. To him the present—post-imperial Britain—was vulgar, and devoid of virtue, and hope was "a sickly dream." Modern life was cramped with its "small and mean utilities." England needed to affirm the values of the past as it is now experiencing a serious moral decay. As a matter of fact, Davie was conservative and traditional. Although he offered a variety of images in his works—elegant angels caught in song, the clink of coins in his father's pocket, or the jingle of harness when a horse moves, his poetry is often concerned with geography and history and as such is analytical, dry and knotty, and not easy to read. Davie took a huge interest in American culture as well, which is well expressed in his works like "Sequence to Francis Parkman" (1961), "Goodbye to the USA" series, and some others.

Davie was capable of self-criticism. While raving against the decadent London which he saw as a symbol of the depravity of the present, he was sober enough to know that depravity existed not just in the external world but also inside his head and heart. The readers of his "Revulsion" and "St. Paul's Revisited" will readily see the point clearly.

Davie was a passionate and truly caring critic of his time. He often wrote on the technique of poetry and frequently discussed poetry, poets and poetic forms. His critical works such as *Purity of Diction in English Verse* (1953) and *Articulate Energy: An Inquiry into the Syntax of English Poetry* (1958) did a lot toward helping establish the poetic values of the Movement poets. However, as a poet and critic of importance of his time, Davie has not always been fully appreciated. He expressed his frustration at what he called "the inattentive world" when he said later in life that he wrote to the Glory of God which was the one and only justification for him. Faith became more and more important as he grew older. He was an example of intellectual courage and integrity of his age. Davie's criticism, like his poetry, is also characterized by his interest in modernist and pre-modernist techniques.

34.1.3 Thom Gunn (1929 – 2004)

Thomson William Gunn, or Thom Gunn for short, was an Anglo-American poet who was praised for his early verses in England, where he was associated with the Movement. He was one of the finest poets of his time. Gunn was educated at Cambridge and came under the influence of William Empson, R. F. Leavis, and the Metaphysical school of poetry. The Augustan virtues of moral responsibility and formal virtuosity, so pervasive in England in the 1950s, left its permanent imprint on his work, too. But when he moved to America later, he was influenced by the American poets like William Carlos Williams (1883 – 1963). His poetry has changed significantly both in theme and style over the years ever since. Although he kept his traditional meters and rhymes, his later poetry moved toward a looser, free-verse style, and his subjects, his diction, and his vision of life and man have revealed clear Williamsian features.

Gunn kept writing and publishing all his lifetime. His major works include such volumes of verse as *Fighting Terms* (1954), *The Sense of Movement* (1957), *My Sad Captains* (1961), *Touch* (1967), *Moly* (1971), *Jack Straw's Castle* (1976), *The Passages of Joy* (1982), in which his homosexuality was openly acknowledged, and *The Man with Night Sweats* (1992), his most famous work, containing several powerful poems about AIDS. After relocating from England to San Francisco, Gunn wrote about gay-related topics—particularly in *The Man with Night Sweats*—as well as drug use, sex and his bohemian lifestyle. A change soon became visible. What is worth noting is that Gunn's poetry defies neat classification on the whole.

Gunn is one of those on the contemporary scene who touch people with the beauty of their art and the impact of their power. Gunn's is a very exquisite sensibility. He is not unlike Philip Larkin in his mode of poetic creation. Generally he observed life, and then contemplated and drew out the hidden moral that he felt existed in life and experiences. The sense of immediacy of the experience is often undercut by the sudden distancing that comes with the deliberation, but the poetic effort manages to exert a subtle impact on the readers' mind. Here we see the influence of the Metaphysical and the Augustan art at work.

In **"Considering the Snail"** (1956), the poet-speaker sees a snail trying to worm through a tunnel of wet grass blades all night. Drenched all over but moved by some desire and purpose, it has kept crawling and groping in the dark. The poet begins to wonder what power is propelling it forward. The world of the snail is dark and rainy and full of unknowns like in "a wood." Hence it offers obstacles to progress. The snail, living in its world which is also devoid of compassion and camaraderie, is solitary; its survival and progress depend solely on its own effort and determination, but it struggles onward. Through the depiction of the snail's world, the poem seems to imply aloneness and resilience in the modern human life. It is hard to define which one of these is a more positive postulate for life. Aloneness, which constitutes a major condition of modern life, may be construed as negative in terms of human and social interrelatedness, but it could also be seen as an index to the human insistence on individuality and self-assertion.

"My Sad Captains" (1956) is another example of the poet's early works, these works of the 1950s and early 1960s, which were written in the tone of "Considering the Snail." The captains in the poem are warriors of a distant past. They do not appear to the mind of the poet until late at night when they begin to shine as stars. Their force may have been "wasteful," and their efforts may have been repeated, impetuous and sad "failures." But these people have tried and lived and left a scratch on the stone of eternity. They still live "perfectly embodied" in the minds of people like the stars revolving "with disinterested/hard energy." This is a paean to human striving. Failure or otherwise is neither here nor there in evaluating human lives. What matters most is the fact that living consists in striving. Like the snail braving the unknown in "Considering the Snail," the captains of the past may not have gotten anywhere in their world of "chaos," but they had that desire, that passion, that drive, which alone defines the worth of human existence. The title denotes the warmth that the poet felt toward their memory and the sympathy with which he identified himself with them.

Gunn's poems since the 1970s illustrate some change in the poet's vision if not exactly in his style. **"From the Wave"** is a good example. Here the poet saw the surfers (or probably himself as one of them) riding on the wave and moving with it, and achieving triumph and possession. They curl their feet, balance their weights by imitating the wave, turning half wave and half men and turning into seals, and come back in success. The essential difference in vision between this poem and the ones discussed above is that, although here exists the oneness of the human with the natural world, the surfers manage to keep their minds as against "the mindless heave" of the wave and keep their distinctness when the wave loses its. Based on the observation of human existence, Gunn dealt in this poem with the paradox of the vexed relationship between the self and the world, and by extension between the self and the community. Self-assertion is essential, but is meaningful only against the backdrop of contact and fellowship, which signifies, sadly but unavoidably, the surrender of a patron of one's self.

34.2 Poetry since the 1960s and 1970s

English poetry of the 1960s and 1970s was on the whole a reaction to the Movement poetry of the previous decade. The poets of these two decades exhibited something in common like attacking the Movement poetry and being open to influences abroad like Robert Lowell, John Berryman (1914 – 1972), Ezra Pound, William Carlos Williams and Wallace Stevens (1879 – 1955). The tension, that coheres in their works, between the strong influences of the native English styles (such as the elegiac and the baroque) and those from outside, American as well as European (Modern and Postmodernist), proves to be a source of fascination to the readers. The major poets of the period are Geoffrey Hill, Ted Hughes, Charles Tomlinson and C. H. Sisson (1914 – 2003).

34.2.1 Alfred Charles Tomlinson (1927 – 2015)

Charles Tomlinson was a British poet and translator, and also an academic and artist. He had been sensitive to the influences of various poetic traditions and styles, which include, among others, Augustan poetry, Ezra Pound, Wallace Stevens, Hart Crane (1899 – 1932) and William Carlos Williams. Tomlinson is noted for his sensory observations, suggestive imagery and moral insistence. His poetry has won international recognition and has received many prizes in Europe and the United States. He was once an Honorary Fellow of the American Academy of the Arts and Sciences and of the Modern Language Association, and was made CBE in 2001 for his contribution to literature.

Tomlinson's first book of poetry *Relations and Contraries* came out in 1951, followed by another two books of verse—*The Necklace* (1955) and *Seeing is Believing* (1958). In the following two-odd decades before the publication of his *Collected Poems* (1985), he published *American Scenes and Other Poems* (1966), *The Way of a World* (1969), *Written on Water* (1972), *The Way In and Other Poems* (1974), *Selected Poems 1951 – 1974* (1978) and *Notes from New York and Other Poems* (1984). In 1997 his *Selected Poems: 1955 – 1997* appeared in print and it was another decade later that his *New Collected Poems* (2009) came out.

"**The Atlantic**" is a poem describing the motions of a wave. It begins with the onrush of the wave from the ocean toward the shore, its foam and its billowing, and its reaching the shore. It relates how the wave interacts with the sunlight, "dyeing the uncovering beach/With sunglaze," before it is pulled back to where it comes. Having depicted the movement of the wave in minute detail and successfully drawing the attention of the readers to it, the poem seems to conclude on a meditative note, with a moral for the readers: "That which we were,/Confronted by all that we are not,/Grasps in subservience in replenishment." It sounds a little reproachful and somewhat edifying, reproachful almost in a Thoreauvian sense that people define themselves by external measures rather than internal, and edifying that they should locate resources for growth within themselves.

34.2.2 Ted Hughes (1930 – 1998)

Hughes was an incredibly prolific English poet, translator, editor and children's book author. He was appointed Poet Laureate in 1984, a post he held until his death. His forays into translations, essays and criticism were noted for their intelligence and range. He is frequently ranked as one of the best poets of his generation and one of the 20th-century greatest writers. In 2008 *The Times* ranked Hughes the fourth on its list of the "50 greatest British writers since 1945."

In his lifetime Hughes published such unprecedented best-selling volumes of poetry as *The Hawk in the Rain* (1957), *Lupercal* (1960), *Crow* (1970), *Moortown Diary* (1979), *Selected Poems 1957 – 1981* (1982), *Wolfwatching* (1989) and *Birthday Letters* (1998), as well as many beloved children's books, including *The Iron Man* (1968). With Seamus Heaney, he edited the popular anthologies *The Rattle Bag* (1982) and *The School Bag* (1997). Named executor of Plath's literary estate, he edited several volumes of her work. Hughes was married to the American poet Sylvia Plath (1932 – 1963) from 1956 until her suicide in 1963. His part in the relationship became controversial to some feminists and some American admirers of Plath. His last poetic work *Birthday Letters* explores their complex relationship. These poems make reference to Plath's suicide, but none addresses directly the circumstances of her death. A poem discovered in October 2010, *Last letter*, describes what happened during the three days before her death. Hughes also translated works from Classical authors, including Ovid and Aeschylus. His posthumous publications include *Selected Poems 1957 – 1994* (2002), an updated and expanded version of the original 1982 edition, and *Letters of Ted Hughes* (2008), showcasing Hughes' voluminous correspondence. The publication of Hughes' *Collected Poems* (2003) provided new insights into the poet's writing process.

The Hawk in the Rain secured Hughes' reputation as a poet of international stature. His poetry signaled a dramatic departure from the prevailing modes of the period. He marshaled a language of nearly Shakespearean resonance to explore themes which were mythic and elemental. Working in sequences and lists, Hughes frequently uncovered a kind of autochthonous, yet literary, English language. According to Peter Davison (1928 – 2004) in the *New York Times*, Hughes "searches deep into the riddles of language, too, those that precede any given tongue, language that reeks of the forest or even the jungle. Such poems often contain a touch—or more than a touch—of melodrama, of the brutal tragedies of Seneca that Hughes adapted for the modern stage."

Hughes was born in Yorkshire, and his father was a veteran from World War I. These facts became two important factors in his poetic career. Yorkshire with its crude and cruel natural landscape and the war with its atrocities and casualties both impressed Hughes' poetic imagination and decided in large measure his thematic concerns. Hughes' works deal in the main with existence. He focused on the struggle for survival and the pain and suffering that come along with it. His world, especially in his early poetry, is one "red with tooth and claw," and there is not much of a hope there. To read Hughes' poetry is to enter a world dominated by nature, especially by animals. This holds true for nearly all of his books, from *The Hawk in the Rain* to *Moortown Diary* and *Wolfwatching*. Hughes' love of animals was one of the catalysts in his decision to become a poet. Hughes once confessed that he began writing poems in adolescence when it dawned upon him that his earlier passion for hunting animals in his native Yorkshire ended either in the possession of a dead animal or at best a trapped one. He wanted to capture not just live animals, but the aliveness of animals in their natural state: their wildness, their quiddity, the fox-ness of the fox and the crow-ness of the crow. However, Hughes' interest in animals was generally less naturalistic than symbolic. Using figures such as "Crow" to approximate a mythic everyman, Hughes' works speak to his concern with the vatic, even shamanic powers of poetry.

"**Pike**" (1959) describes a world of horror. Pikes are killers from birth with their "malevolent aged grin," stalking the marine world and terrorizing it. The poet kept three of these at one time behind glass and found, very soon, two of these swallowed by the other. And he found, on another occasion, two fish trying to swallow each other because they spared nobody including their own kind. This resembles the world of "Relic," which is a fully drawn naturalistic one. The connotation that we derive from many of Hughes' works like this tends to be that the world of nature is similar to and suggestive of human nature.

Crow is a sequence Hughes started writing in 1966. His thematic focus is reinforced by the poems in this book. The idea came from his acquaintance with an American painter who wanted Hughes to write about his drawings of the crow. Hughes made good use of the opportunity to illustrate his own ideas about the world and life in general. He wove a story into his writings about the pictures: Nightmare is skeptical about God's wisdom of creating the world, and is challenged to do better. So Nightmare brings Crow into being to play with God. God and Crow then engage each other in different difficult situations from which Crow emerges more intelligent. The world of Crow is full of pain and anguish, and the occurrences here are often grotesque and brutal. Crow is an unpleasant creature, mean, aggressive and violent, but he manages to survive the worst of any existential experiences. The readers tend to have mixed feelings toward Crow, feelings of both dislike and affection. Hughes probably suggested that there was something of the creature in all of us.

The poems in *Moortown* do no less to body forth the poet's vision of existence. "**Birth of Rainbow**," a poem collected in the book, portrays a world so harsh and cruel that survival would be a miracle. Rainbow is the name of a calf. It is so called because its mother happens to stand at the end of the rainbow at its birth. The place of birth is a snow-covered ridge. The time is when a hailstorm is coming. The calf gets born, the cow eats up the blood, and both are left to shift for themselves when the people run for shelter in face of a forthcoming storm. If rainbow signifies God's presence and His protection as it normally does to people, then the birth of the calf Rainbow occurs in the absence of both.

34.2.3 Sir Geoffrey William Hill (1932 – 2016)

Geoffrey Hill has been considered to be among the most distinguished poets of his generation and was called the "greatest living poet in the English language." (Lezard, 2013) In June 2010 Hill was elected Professor of Poetry in the University of Oxford. Then he was knighted in the 2012 New Year Honors for services to literature. Hill wrote to reveal the extent of human suffering and the evil of the human heart. To him evil comes from the human heart. It is the heart that betrays and persecutes, and causes pain. Although he was capable of compassion, Hill's tone is generally harsh and condemnatory. He did not spare himself in his censure of human behavior.

Hill's poems are impersonal, objective, well-made artifacts. His language is rich and complex, and his syntax can be disjunctive. Some of his works reveal the imprint of such American poets as Allen Tate (1899 – 1979) and Robert Lowell (especially of the latter's early works). The influence of the Metaphysical poets is clearly visible. One other important influence on him is William Butler Yeats. Hill had a strong sense of history. His themes are predominantly historical and religious, many of the poems brooding over the violence of the near and distant past. Hill tried to establish a connection between the present and the legendary and mythic past. The past serves to illustrate how the present has come to be what it is, and how human nature and human behavior never seem to change for the better.

Hill's first volume of poetry *For the Unfallen* came out in 1959. His important poems in the 1960s are the eight sonnets in the sequence *Funeral Music*. Recording the statements of the people executed in the medieval England, the poems harp on themes such as pain and despair, self-sacrifice, and belief in god. *King Log* was published in 1968, which was followed by *Mercian Hymns* (1971) and *Tenebrae* (1978). *Mercian Hymns* consists of prose poems celebrating Offa, a presiding genius of the West Midlands, and possesses a mythical dimension that mirrors modern life. Hill's long poem *The Mystery of the Charity of Charles Peguy* (1983) is a densely allusive meditation on the life, faith and death of the French poet Charles Peguy (1873 – 1914). *Cannon* (1996), a volume in which distinct poetic sequences are interwoven, mulls over the political and religious history of England, and denounces what it takes to be the corruption of recent public life.

"**September Song**" (1968), fully loaded both in meaning and tone, is about the gassing of the Jews in the Nazi concentration camps. The fury is toned down so that what is left is simply a flat, almost matter-of-fact, narrative. One of the victims was a child born on June 19, 1932. The idea of the cruel existence for the child hovers silently over every line and every word. The poet's voice was muffled because he felt so overwhelmed and so aghast at man's inhumanity to man. The child's misfortune was all caused from the outset by his fellow creatures: he was first "undesirable" to his parents (probably) and then to his persecutors, the Nazis. The usually joyous season (September) becomes murderous and the beautiful roses turn ruthless. There is no longer God's plenty; there is only more evil and pain than people can handle. The poet felt so much about the child's death that he thought he had died. The fact is that the poet was born on June 18, 1932. In making an elegy for himself, he had one for all of his own kind.

Hill also wrote some books of literary criticism, including *The Lords of Limit* (1984), *The Enemy's Country* (1991), *Style and Faith* (2003) and *Collected Critical Writings* (2008). The social context of poetry and the responsibilities of the poet are minutely described in the first two.

34.3 Younger Poets of the Later Period

Younger poets like Tony Harrison, Seamus Heaney, Craig Raine, James Fenton, and Jon Stallworthy (1935 – 2014) who is noted for his themes of love and family with its joys and sorrows, belong properly to the later period. Their poetry is often humorous, satiric and quasi-popular as they are anxious to reach a wide audience.

34.3.1 Tony Harrison (1937 –)

Harrison is an English poet, translator and playwright. He is one of Britain's foremost verse writers and many of his works have been performed at the Royal National Theatre. He is noted for controversial works such as the poem "V" (1985), as well as his versions of dramatic works from Middle English *The Mysteries*, from French Moliere's *The Misanthrope*, and from ancient Greek such as the tragedies *Oresteia* and *Lysistrata*. He is also noted for his outspoken views, particularly those on the Iraq War. Harrison is renowned for his independent voice and impassioned commentary on public affairs.

Harrison stands apart from his contemporaries in both theme and style. In subject, he writes about his own life and family experiences. In attitude, he is a working-class poet, demotic and subversive. Memories of his working-class childhood and family life provide the material for much of his poetry, although he has travelled widely and his works also reflect experiences of Africa, the Soviet Union and America. In style, Harrison is classic with his iambs, couplets, his 16-line sonnets, which contrast with and are often ridiculed (or seemingly so) by his subject. It is also worth noting that Harrison introduced into poetry the colloquial speech, his father's working-class speech. In his effort to speak for his father's class, Harrison often goes an extra mile to court the possible danger of formal awkwardness that the incongruity between subject and style may generate. The classy classic iambs contrast nicely with the uneducated speech they encase. Both his original works and his translations show a great facility in rhyme and a skilful adaptation of colloquial style. His most famous work is a continuous long sequence of poems entitled *The School of Eloquence* (1976, 1978, 1981, 1987).

Harrison is class-conscious and proud of his working-class background. "**Heredity**" (1978), a poem of two couplets, is a good example. Its first couplet is apparently a reproduction of someone's question about the origin of his poetic talent. The query—"How you became a poet's a mystery! /Wherever did you get your talent from?"—itself is a composite of admiration and disbelief. It is direct and blunt, but not without a note of flattery, probably asked by a condescending middle-class sycophant and snob. The second couplet is an answer caustic and poignant with a huge sense of pride: "I say: I had two uncles, Joe and Harry—/one was a stammer, the other dumb." The vehemence of the reply may suggest a mild degree of self-consciousness and self-defensiveness, which reinforces the note of pride.

Harrison's works dealing with his personal relationship with his parents are most moving. The poet portrays the bond that existed between him and his parents in a heartwarming tone. In "**Long Distance**" (1981), for instance, he talks about his father—the old man's bereavement, his genuine love for his dead wife, his longing to join her in the other world, and his "dumb" way of handling his emotion—probably his incommunicativeness—in such a way that it reveals the intense love that the son feels for both his parents and his pride of having had them as parents.

34.3.2 Seamus Justin Heaney (1939 – 2013)

Seamus Heaney, an Irish poet, playwright, translator and lecturer, is acknowledged by some critics as "the best Irish poet since W. B. Yeats" and one of the greatest contemporary English poets. He was awarded the Nobel Prize in Literature in 1995 and the Lifetime Recognition Award from the Griffin Trust for Excellence in Poetry in 2012.

In the early 1960s, Heaney became a lecturer in Belfast after attending university there and began to publish poetry. He was a professor at Harvard from 1981 to 1997 and its Poet in Residence from 1988 to 2006. From 1989 to 1994, he was also the Professor of Poetry at Oxford. Heaney's literary papers are held by the National Library of Ireland. His works have been among the most profusely commented upon of his contemporaries. His main volumes of verse include *Death of a Naturalist* (1966), *Door into the Dark* (1969), *Wintering Out* (1972), *North* (1975), *Field Work* (1979), *Sweeney Praises the Trees* (1981), *Station Island* (1984), *The Haw Lantern* (1987), *Seeing Things* (1991), *Sweeney's Flights* (1992), *The Spirit Level* (1996), *Electric Light* (2001), *District and Circle* (2006) and *Human Chain* (2010). His highly praised translation of the Anglo-Saxton epic *Beowulf* came out in 1999.

Heaney was well known for writing about the common people of his land. From the outset of his career he was determined to speak for the voiceless and the oppressed very much like Tony Harrison. He wrote a lot about these people. His thematic concerns cover his celebration of the rural people with their crafts and skills and their contribution to communal life, his native land's long history of invasion and violence from which he drew, and his search for salvation for his country as well as for himself as an artist. The meticulous care with which he depicted the daily life and routine activity of the common people shows his deep love for the lower class.

What appears to dominate Heaney's poetry is to find "a door into the dark" which is good enough for the redemption of all humans as well as himself. He seemed to have found it in what he called "displacement." One may have to be displaced the way Wordsworth was from one's good place of nature and move to live somewhere else in order to retain sanity and help achieve salvation. Self-exile is a form of displacement whereby to find freedom. James Joyce and some of the other "familiar ghosts" from Heaney's own past or Irish literary history in *Station Island* (1984) offer him good advice in this regard. Joyce went away but returned a faithful émigré to his native land in his literary creations. This is "epiphany" for Heaney. Heaney did not seek escape in space. He banished himself into time and imagination. Thus he wrote about his land's history of violence and hoped to make the past usable as a foil and a mirror to the present. In poem after poem, such as "Shoreline," "Ocean's Love to Ireland," "Bog

Oak," "For the Commander of the 'Eliza'" and "At a Potato Digging," Heaney kept revealing the persistent horror of the human condition. In poems like "Punishment," "The Tollund Man" and "Bog Queen," the connection and comparison between the past and the present illustrate Heaney's overriding concern with the perennial tragic nature of human life. Heaney's flight into the past is also footnoted in his fascination with the legendary Irish King Sweeney. In addition, poetry and imagination also offer the poet a place where to displace and relocate himself; and language can also be an avenue of self-exile. This is evident in such volumes of verse as *Wintering Out*, *North* and *Field Work*. The image of self-exile on the sea in "Casualty" appears once again when the readers hear Joyce speak in the last section of *Station Island*. Heaney had been searching, probing, engraving his own signatures, and speaking on his own frequencies. Writing is his way of coping and helping to cope. When read this way, Heaney assumed an immensely new magnitude as an Anglo-Irish poet.

"The Forge" (1969) focuses on a blacksmith, working away at his forge. The poet's observation of the forge is all inclusive, the old axes, the iron hoops, the hammer and the anvil's short-pitched ring, the sparks spreading out like a fantail, the hissing sound of the new shoe toughening in water, and the blacksmith diffusing himself into the different shapes of his products amid the dint which is music to the poet's ear. The blacksmith is gratified to hear the clatter of hoofs and know that he has done his bit to keep the "traffic flashing in rows." To the poet the forge possesses a metaphysical dimension of significance: it is a holy place with its anvil immovably set in the center as an alter; it is "a door into the dark," through which people explore the origin and mystery of human life.

"Digging" (1964) is vastly suggestive; it has been read as Heaney's statement of purpose for his career or his intention to excavate the past and history. But it could be understood on a mere physical level. It is a paean of the hardworking older generations. It was digging that they did, but they did it happily to perfection. And perfection in anything is not easy to come by. The middle seven stanzas out of the nine of the poem, all devoted to the minute description of the father and grandfather's labors, reveal the deep admiration and love Heaney had for his at once extraordinary and ordinary ancestors. "Mother of the Groom" (1972) is another poem showing Heaney's love and admiration for the common people.

34.3.3 Craig Anthony Raine (1944 –)

Craig Raine is a highly imaginative and inventive English poet. Along with Christopher Reid (1949 –), he is the best-known exponent of Martian poetry or the Martians, after the title of his second volume of verse *A Martian Sends a Postcard Home* (1979). The Martians are ingenious in their poetic expression. They say things in ways totally odd to the readers. It is true that they set out to describe this ordinary world, but they end up making it out as if it were a strange and alien one. Reading Raine can be quite a demanding but delightful mental exercise. The effect is often funny and even ridiculous, but it is rewarding. Raine is fascinated with John Donne's works and is very much influenced by the latter's Metaphysical wit. His poetry exhibits a tremendous amount of wit and ingenuity in the use of his singular metaphors. He seems to play with his readers with his magic wand of poetry that changes the familiar into the unfamiliar, deals out riddles and demands their imagination to figure out the answers to these problems. In this way he manages to make a much deeper impression upon the readers' minds than by merely using the language and rhetoric already well known to them. Raine is well known for his unexpected metaphors. James Joyce's "descriptive lust" holds a special appeal to his imagination. Raine is certainly inventive, experimental and even idiosyncratic in his "descriptive lust." He suggests rather than tells in a blunt way. Raine's poems on his childhood and family bespeak the impact of Robert Lowell's *Life Studies* (1959) as well.

"The Onion, Memory" (1978) is full of descriptions that border on elaborate riddles. The scenario here is that of a man revisiting his ex-wife. The couple walk the "old ground" together, which is another way of saying "recollecting life." The recollection is suggested rather than directly presented, embodied as it is in an odd but interesting formula of "objective correlative." They go through the old places where they used to go when still married: the road with its tractor ruts, the green commons, the village bakery, a hotel dining room, then going back home, with wind howling outside and jelly stored away in the fridge, doing what they used to do at homes, one slicing onions and one sewing up dresses, recalling the past that makes the speaker feel sad, thinking how time steals by and life is unfulfilled. The poem ends up with the speaker stumbling into the washing on the line and imagining that he sees ghosts and death there. The mood is touching as it involves human softness in feeling and a pathetic desire that life cannot fulfill. It is in fact a tragic theme in the disguise of a grotesque, playful exterior form. Here lies the tension between the funny art form and the serious subject that it tries to address.

The poem is noted for its imagery, the knotted "metaphors" that readers have to work through. It is its use of so many metaphors that helps hide beneath the jocular surface an emotional tangle: a painful nostalgia, a backward glance of yearning, a deep sigh of remorse, and a tragic sense of the irretrievability of the past and the emotional hell of the present. The image of "the dinosaur" may connote the duration of their divorce or some degree of nostalgic backward glance. The grass on the green is probably a reminder of their first kiss there or doing something else intimate as lovers or indicating what they feel about each other at the moment. The dough going through the baking process is seen as a shortened human life journey from crib to coffin, suggesting the sense of transience, helplessness and regret that they have not done better in life. The flowers are all the beautiful images of the hotel maids waiting at the dinner table, where the uncooked herrings blink a tearful eye, the candles palpitate, and Russian violinists "bow and scrap" on the tape. The dining scene is a medley of joy and grief. The trees, sword grass, white thorns, all bow to force (of the wind) and control, and the jelly in the fridge seems to suggest order and self-control that bring a sense of balance. The onion symbolizes memory probably because of its multiple layers and its lasting poignant smell. The memory of the past reveals the humanity in both man and woman.

"A Martian Sends a Postcard Home," the title poem of Raine's second volume of verse, is the poet's signature work and a graphic illustration of the Martian poetry. It describes an alien's perception of the people and things on the earth. It is distorted and bizarre, but tremendously intriguing. This Martian sees everything familiar to the earthlings and describes it in a way that often requires an effort for humans to understand.

34.3.4 James Fenton (1949 –)

Fenton is an English poet, journalist and literary critic. Though he is predominantly a satirist, the main stylistic influence on his work is W. H. Auden. Fenton is, like Auden, a consummate artist. His styles range all the way from open form to regular meters and rhymes. He can be obscure sometimes. His output is small, but it is unique and powerful. His poetry is often "narrative," telling a story in a compressed way. It presents facts but refuses to moralize; Fenton would like the readers to digest those facts alone. This objectivity has to do with the poet's interest in the world around him. The fact that he went as a journalist to Vietnam, Cambodia and Germany in the

1970s and to the Far East in the 1980s has proved significant to his poetic creation. He has learned from those areas of intense human conflict and suffering about the negative side of the world and felt the horror of its darkness.

Fenton began his literary career early in his first year at university with the sonnet sequence *Our Western Furniture* (1968), which was awarded the Newdigate Prize. The book largely concerns the cultural collision in the 19th century between the United States and Japan, and displays in embryo many of the characteristics that define Fenton's later works, such as technical mastery combined with a fascination with issues that arise from the Western interaction with other cultures. Fenton became an occasional war reporter in Vietnam during the late phase of the Vietnam War which ended in 1975. His experiences in Vietnam and Cambodia from 1973 form a part of his reportage *All the Wrong Places: Adrift in the Politics of the Pacific Rim* (1988). *The Memory of War: Poems 1968 – 1982* (1982) ensured his reputation as one of the greatest war poets of his time. Fenton was appointed Oxford Professor of Poetry in 1994, a post he held till 1999. In 2007 he was awarded the Queen's Gold Medal for Poetry.

"**A German Requiem**" (1981) is one of Fenton's most famous poems. A requiem is a ritual, a special mass, to pacify the spirits of the dead. The poem describes a ritual of this kind that helps people remember to forget so as to assign the souls of the victimized Jews to oblivion and eternal rest, and make it more possible to live their own lives as well. Although there is no direct reference to the Jews killed during WWII except for the names of the dead and the oblique mention of "so many died" and Jewish Passover, it is meant to be an elegy to those innocent victims of the Nazi holocaust. The poem can also be seen as an indication of the poet's awareness of the transitoriness of life and the inevitable, enduring menace of morality. The sense of helplessness is so acute that people have to forget the shadow in order to enjoy the sun. In other words, there is so much pain for the living to face the dead that they "must forget" in order to move on. The poignancy of the poem stems not so much from the depiction of the details of the holocaust as from the agonized effort to desist from recollection.

"A German Requiem" begins with a reference to the workmen leveling off the old "houses" and "streets" of the graveyard. The dismantling is an attempt to forget. The speaker is tongue-tied: "Oh, if I were to begin to tell you/The half, the quarter, a smattering of what we went through!" But he did not even try to begin to tell. The people find peace not so much for the dead as for themselves when they annually meet once or twice to remember in order to forget for the rest of the year. They find it easier and better for the living to let go of the memory of the past. There is a touch of pathos both in the imagined reproach on the part of the dead for forgetting them, and in the sense of helplessness on the part of the living for having to come to terms with the fact in this way that their loved ones are dead ("It is not what he wants to know. /It is what he wants not to know. /It is not what they say. /It is what they do not say" [ll. 76 – 80]).

"**Wind**" (1983), another famous poem, is a powerful indictment against human nature as the source of pain and suffering. It consists of four quatrains. The first stanza is well loaded. The opening line, "this is the wind, the wind in the field of corn," is physical enough, but what follows immediately gives the wind and the field of corn a metaphorical significance: the crowds fleeing from a major disaster down valleys and dry riverbeds (probably real-life scenes that Fenton saw with his naked eyes in his career as a journalist) appear to be the "corn" in the field subject to the threat of a ruthless coercive power of which "the wind" stands as a symbol. The nature of the disaster is anybody's guess. A nuclear holocaust has been suggested as apt enough to fit the category of "major." In fact, it could be anything that would present a "major" threat to human existence (such as biochemical weaponry). The second stanza further defines the wind as a rumor of "something" that threatens to bring "fire and sword" to the world and so horrifies its inhabitants. The next stanza is also rich enough to warrant more than one interpretation. For one thing, it seems to relate one of the speaker's own experiences: it could be a war scene that he witnessed. It could also be his vision of the primordial, probably biblical past when human nature is not capable of change for the better. A thousand years is as meaningful and meaningless as two seconds in terms of human change as it never occurs. The last stanza touches further on human nature and the nature of human life. It raises a question that the humankind might become self-knowing enough to ask; the implication is that most probably they will not ask, as the very fact of asking indicates that they can become better. If they ever ask, the question is self-reflexive and self-critical; it is about the nature of the "smithy" of "the hilt of the sword": the evil sword is manufactured by the human mind and heart and is then out of control. As to the common run of mankind, they are the powerless "corn" at the tender mercies of the wind.

Chapter 35 Postwar Fiction

After WWII most English writers chose to focus on aesthetic or social rather than political problems. Such novelists as Henry Green (1905 – 1973), Ivy Compton-Burnett and Lawrence Durrell, though they made their presence already felt in the 1930s, tended to cultivate their own distinctive voices, while others, especially the representatives of the "Angry Young Men" like Kingsley Amis and Alan Sillitoe, expressed a deep dissatisfaction with the British society. The postwar fiction is mainly marked by a number of highly individual novelists. They are chiefly Anthony Burgess, Iris Murdoch and the Nobel Prize winners in Literature, including Elias Canetti, William Golding, V. S. Naipaul and Doris Lessing. The glory of the postwar fiction is also seen in the writers like Anthony Powell, who continued to work in the expansive 19th-century tradition, producing a series of realistic novels chronicling life in England during the 20th century.

35.1 "Angry Young Men"

The young writers of the 1950s, very often "scholarship boys," were the rising members of the lower middle class. They were normally iconoclastic and against established standards. Ambitious and disillusioned, they lashed out against contemporary society in their works. In formal terms they were in revolt against the high literary ideals of Modernism and wrote in a deliberately vulgar, comic and satirical vein. They created characters that represented their radical, parochial attitudes and became known as "Angry Young Men."

The epithet "Angry Young Men" was originally a journalistic term used to describe a group of playwrights and novelists of the mid-1950s, but it has also come to refer loosely to the major characters that these authors have created. For instance, Jim Dixon in *Lucky Jim* by Kingsley Amis, Joe Lunn in *Scenes from Provincial Life* (1950) by William Cooper (1910 – 2002), and Joe Lampton in *Room at the Top* (1957) by John Gerald Braine (1922 – 1986)—all these, authors and characters alike, come under the label of "Angry Young Men." John Wain and Colin Wilson (1931 – 2013) were also connected with this group. John Osborne's Jimmy Porter in his play *Look Back in Anger*, Alan Sillitoe's Arthur Seaton in his novel *Saturday Night and Sunday Morning* and Philip Larkin's John Kemp in his *Jill*, all from the working class, fit well in here, too. Although it is sometimes said to derive from the title of a work by the Irish writer Leslie Paul (1905 – 1985), *Angry Young men* (1951), the term "Angry Young Men" came to be widely used only after the publication of Osborne's play *Look Back in Anger* in 1957, which gives manifest expression to the disaffection of the postwar generation. The term, always imprecise, began to have less meaning over the years as the writers to whom it was originally applied became more divergent, and many of them dismissed the label as useless.

35.1.1 Sir Kingsley William Amis (1922 – 1995)

Kingsley Amis was an English novelist, poet and critic. His biographer Zachary Leader (1946 –) (2006: 1) claimed that Amis was "the finest English comic novelist of the second half of the 20th century." In 2008, *The Times* ranked Amis the thirteenth on its list of the 50 greatest British writers since 1945. As a novelist, Amis was a leading figure of "Angry Young Men" group, and as a poet, he was considered to be one important member of the Movement poetry coterie.

Amis tried to explore the social problems of his age and developed his personal signature with time. Both funny and serious, presenting serious problems in a funny way, Amis' kind of comedy leans toward black humor and has this knack of making his readers first laugh but then experience the pathos of the situation or the person that they laugh at. Amis was both good at choosing his comic subject and at its effective portrayal. His common practice is to draw caricatures by means of exaggeration so that his characters often appear at once real and improbable. His plots are fascinating though often slim. When the decade of the 1950s was left behind, Amis had already made himself famous and rich, and as such he lost his aggressive satirical edge and stopped being neither young nor angry. His humor dimmed as well in time.

Amis was a prolific writer. He produced more than 20 novels, six volumes of poetry, a memoir, various short stories, and some other writings. His works extend into many genres—poetry, novels (science fiction and mystery), short stories, essays and criticism, food and drink writing, anthologies, and radio and television scripts. Amis began his literary career with poetic writing. His poetry is known for its typically straightforward and accessible style; yet it, like his novels, often masks a nuance of thought. After publishing several volumes of verse like *Bright November* (1947) and *A Frame of Mind* (1953), he got down to novel writing. He is chiefly known as a comedic novelist of the mid- to late-20th-century British life.

Amis' first and perhaps most famous novel *Lucky Jim* came out in 1954. It was perceived by many as part of the Angry Young Men movement of the 1950s which reacted against the stultification of conventional British life, though the author himself never encouraged this interpretation. Amis' other novels of the 1950s and the early 1960s similarly depict situations from contemporary British life, often drawn from the author's own experiences. *That Uncertain Feeling* (1955) centers on a young provincial librarian and his temptation towards adultery; *I Like It Here* (1958) presents Amis' contemptuous view of "abroad," tracing his own travels on the Continent with a young family; *Take a Girl like You* (1960) steps away from the immediately autobiographical, but remains grounded in the concerns of sex and love in ordinary modern life, tracing the courtship and ultimate seduction of the heroine Jenny Bunn by a young schoolmaster Patrick Standish.

With *The Anti-Death League* (1966), Amis began to show some of the experimentation with content, if not with style, which would mark much of his work in the 1960s and 1970s. Amis' departure from the strict realism of his early comedic novels is not so abrupt as might first appear. He had avidly read science fiction since a boy and had developed that interest into the Christian Gauss Lectures of 1958 while visiting Princeton University. The lectures were published in that year as *New Maps of Hell: A Survey of Science Fiction*, a serious but light-handed treatment of what the genre had to say about man and society. Amis was particularly enthusiastic about the dystopian works and in *New Maps of Hell* coined the term "comic inferno" to describe a type of humorous dystopia, particularly as exemplified in the works of Robert Sheckley (1928 – 2005). Amis further displayed his devotion to the genre in editing the science fiction anthology series *Spectrum* I – V.

Though not explicitly science fiction, *The Anti-Death League* takes liberties with reality not found in Amis' earlier novels and introduces a speculative bent into his fiction, one which would continue to develop in his other genre novels, such as *The Green Man* (1969) (mystery/horror) and *The Alteration* (1976) (alternative history). Much of this speculation was about the improbable existence of any benevolent deity involved in human affairs. In *The Anti-Death League*, *The Green Man*, *The Alteration* and elsewhere, including poems such as "The Huge Artifice: an interim assessment" and "New Approach Needed," Amis showed frustration with a God who could lace the world with such cruelty and injustice, and championed the preservation of ordinary human happiness—in family, in friendships, in physical pleasure—against the demands of any cosmological scheme.

During this time, Amis had not turned completely away from the comedic realism of *Lucky Jim* and *Take a Girl like You*. *I Want It Now* (1968) and *Girl, 20* (1971) both depict the "swinging" atmosphere of London in the late 1960s, in which Amis certainly participated, though neither book is strictly autobiographical. *Girl, 20* is framed in the world of classical (and pop) music, of which Amis was not a part—the book's relatively impressive command of musical terminology and opinion shows both Amis' amateur devotion to music and the almost journalistic capacity of his intelligence to take hold of a subject which interested him. That intelligence is similarly on display in the presentation of ecclesiastical matters in *The Alteration*, when Amis was neither a Roman Catholic nor a devotee of any Church.

Throughout the 1950s, 1960s, and 1970s, Amis was also regularly producing essays and criticism, principally for journalistic publication. Some of these pieces were collected in *What Became of Jane Austen? and Other Essays* (1970), in which Amis' wit and literary and social opinions were on display. Amis' opinions on books and people tended to appear conservative, and yet, as the title essay of the collection shows, he was not merely reverent of "the classics" and of traditional morals, but was more disposed to exercise his own rather independent judgment in all things.

Amis' literary style and tone changed significantly after 1970, with the possible exception of *The Old Devils* (1986), a Booker Prize winner. Several critics accused him of being old fashioned and misogynistic, while others said that his output lacked the humanity, wit and compassion of earlier efforts. This period also saw Amis the anthologist, a role in which his wide knowledge of all kinds of English poetry was on display. *The New Oxford Book of Light Verse* (1978), which he edited, was a revision of the original volume done by W. H. Auden. Amis took the anthology in a markedly new direction: Auden had interpreted light verse to include "low" verse of working-class or lower-class origin, regardless of subject matter, while Amis defined light verse as essentially light in tone, though not necessarily simple in composition. *The Amis Anthology* (1988), a personal selection of his favorite poems, grew out of his works for a London newspaper, in which he selected a poem daily and presented it with a brief introduction.

Amis was shortlisted for the Man Booker Prize three times in his writing career for *Ending Up* (1974), *Jake's Thing* (1978) and finally winning the prize for *The Old Devils* in 1986.

Lucky Jim follows the exploits of the title character James (Jim) Dixon, a reluctant medieval history lecturer in a provincial university. The novel pioneers the characteristic subject matter of the time: a young man making his way in a postwar world that combines new and moribund attitudes. It is a satirical comedy, which spearheads its satiric edge against the high-brow academic set seen through Jim's eyes, a world of fakes in which Jim Dixon lives. Dixon is a northern, grammar school-educated, lower middle class young man. He is uneasy with the pseudo-intellectual values he meets in academic society. The action takes place towards the end of the academic year. Dixon is concerned about losing his position at the end of his probationary first year, for he made an unsure start in the department. In his attempt to be awarded tenure, he tries to maintain a good relationship with his head of department, Professor Welch, a well-to-do, malicious, scheming academic, whose word can make or mar Jim's career at the college. He must also, to establish his credentials, ensure the publication of his first scholarly article, despite having little time remaining.

Dixon struggles with an on-again off-again "girlfriend" Margaret Peel, a neurotic and self-serving fellow lecturer, whose attachment makes Jim miserable beyond words. Margaret is recovering from a failed suicide attempt, in the wake of an unsuccessful relationship with a boyfriend. She employs emotional blackmail to appeal to Dixon's sense of duty and pity to keep him in an ambiguous and sexless relationship. Professor Welch holds a cultural evening that seems to be an opportunity for Dixon to advance his standing amongst his colleagues but this goes dreadfully wrong when Dixon gets drunk and burns his host's bedclothes. At the evening party Dixon meets Christine Callaghan, a young Londoner and the latest girlfriend of Professor Welch's son, Bertrand, who is an amateur painter, a fake bohemian, a calculating lover, as well as an aggressive social climber, competing with Jim both in love and job hunting. After a bad start, Dixon realizes he is attracted to Christine, who is far less pretentious than she initially appears. Dixon's obvious attempts to court Christine upset Bertrand, who is using his relationship with her, to reach her well-connected Scottish uncle, who is seeking an assistant in London. Dixon rescues Christine from the university's annual dance when Bertrand treats her badly. They get close to each other, but have to part company under the pressure of Margaret and Bertrand.

The novel reaches its climax during Dixon's public lecture on "Merrie England," which tends to extol Professor Welch's views but backfires as Dixon, having attempted to calm his nerves with an excess of alcohol, uncontrollably begins to mock Welch and everything else that he hates. Dixon finally loses his job. Welch, not unsympathetically, informs him his employment will not be extended. Christine's uncle, who reveals a tacit respect for Dixon's individuality and attitude towards pretension, offers him the coveted assistant job in London, which pays much better than his lecturing position. Dixon then meets Margaret's ex-boyfriend, who reveals that he was not exactly her boyfriend at all. And the two realize that the suicide attempt was faked to emotionally blackmail both men. Dixon feels he is free of Margaret and has the last laugh when Christine decides to pursue her relationship with him, for she discovered that Bertrand was also pursuing an affair with the wife of one of Dixon's former colleagues. The two decide to leave for London.

The comedy of *Lucky Jim* is Dixon's rebellion against the cant and pretension he meets in academic life and the uncontrolled escalation of this from private fantasy to public display. The novel ends with him in possession of a measure of affluence, the London life he craves and the girl. Jim is lucky indeed. With its farce, acute social observation, and linguistic subtlety all in one, the work has proved to be one of the great books of the 1950s.

The characterization of the protagonist is a great success. Jim is not really a much better person in behavior than the bunch of fakes around him. In fact he is a fake himself, capable of compromising his integrity. He does not want Margaret, but he could, even willingly, walk into her trap. He hates Professor Welch's guts, but he accepts his manipulation. He is anti-intellectual, but he is intellectually thinking. He does not seem to deserve the luck that comes his way. What is saving in him, however, is his better nature, from which comes his self-knowledge. He knows that he is a sham himself, and feels bad about it. He has an inner world where he lives a self-critical life. He is slightly better because he is less false and more capable of self-mockery. Whereas the world around is all pretences, Jim manages to retain an ounce of spontaneous and authentic humanity, which tells him apart from those about him. In addition, Jim is brilliant in terms of intellection. His speech at the college festival shines with the radiance of his intellectually thinking mind. Although he makes no big effort toward his success, he is thinking. So he knows about his world and knows how to hit the nail on the head. He knows what to do and how to do it. He is half drunk, but it is exactly at such moments that he becomes strangely lucid, loosens up from traditional inhibitions, and intuits the verities of life in general and college life in particular. Incidentally, that scene has become Kingsley Amis' best creative effort and one of the most unforgettably comic in recent literary history. Jim is no fool as he appears to be. The phoniness aground drives him crazy. He is an angry young man. His disaffection leads to self-revelation.

Amis was a pace setter for the fiction of his age. His Jim Dixon is an archetypal creation, a new hero for fiction. Graceless, yet sensitive and tough in contact with the phony, this character is a specimen of an angry man, representing the whole group of fictional protagonists that were to people the novels of the time. In a very real sense, the fictional Jim Dixon also bodies forth the temper of the young generation of intellectuals of the 1950s, educated in grammar schools, struggling and disaffected, and angry in a world into which they had a hard time fitting. But as was the case with his creator, Jim Dixon is going through a phase of his life; people can predict with a degree of safety that with time he will get established and stop being young and angry.

35.1.2 John Barrington Wain (1925 – 1994)

John Wain was an English poet, novelist and critic. For most of his life, he worked as a freelance journalist and author, writing and reviewing for newspapers and the radio. Wain was one of those postwar novelists who turned away from the prewar craze for experimentation and went back to the 18th-century tradition of a good storytelling. His concern is with the life of the present, where he tended to find man wanting in dignity and moral worth in face of adversity. His vision of life is basically tragic that life is suffering and survival is difficult. His plot is solid and peopled with well delineated characters. His hero is usually a modern man, a sensitive rebel, yet an effete person not dynamic enough to chart out the course of his own life.

Wain was often referred to as one of the "Angry Young Men." Indeed, he did contribute to *Declaration* (1957), an anthology of manifestos by writers associated with the philosophy, and a chapter of his novel *Hurry on Down* was excerpted in a popular paperback sampler, *Protest: The Beat Generation and the Angry Young Men* (1958). Wain was also associated with the Movement poetry. Here lies the similarity between Wain and Kingsley Amis and Philip Larkin, good friends of Wain's for a time, who were also associated, with equal dubiousness, with the "angries." Aside from their poetry, it may be more accurate to refer to these three, as was sometimes done at the time, as "The New University Wits," writers who desired to communicate rather than to experiment, and who often did so in a comic mode. However, they all became more serious after their initial works.

Wain produced more than a dozen novels, among which the notable ones are *Hurry on Down* (1953), *Strike the Father Dead* (1962), *The Pardoner's Tale* (1978), *Young Shoulders* (1982), and his Oxford Trilogy—*Where the Rivers Meet* (1988), *Comedies* (1990) and *Hungry Generations* (1994). He was also a prolific poet and critic, with critical works on such writers as Arnold Bennett, Samuel Johnson and William Shakespeare. Among the other writers about whom he wrote are the Americans Theodore Roethke and Edmund Wilson. Wain is still known for his poetry and literary interests, though his works are no longer as popular as they were. Critical remarks about Wain by Amis and Larkin in their posthumously-published letters may have contributed to dimming his reputation.

Wain's first novel **Hurry on Down** is a comic picaresque story about an unsettled university graduate who rejects the standards of conventional society. The protagonist Charles Lumpley well interprets the author's portrayal of a modern man. Charles is very much like Kingsley Amis' Jim, not happy with his life, hating his lot, and resenting all that is middle class and commonplace. He drifts through life, changing jobs as his survival requires and getting what he needs by any means, fair or foul. He is, in a word, a picaresque hero, basically kind and malleable enough to cope with the "slings and arrows" of the world. The novel borrows from the 18th-century two important narrative tricks: the structural device of chaining events together and the authorial intrusion. A similar rebellion against established values occurs in *Strike the Father Dead*, a tale of a young jazzman Jeremy Coleman's rebellion against his conventional father, who is a professor of classics and a token of prewar values. The son is not happy under his father's thumb and wants to be a jazz pianist and live a life of his own. He struggles, succeeds in life and learns about it.

The Pardoner's Tale, probably Wain's most tragic novel, entwines two stories well in one artistic framework: the first-person narrative of Gus Howkins, an elderly man estranged from his wife, and a third-person story about the major character Giles Hermitage, a writer working on the Howkins story. Giles Hermitage is a sensitive, lonely individual, depressed and spiritually poor, and assailed by a deathwish. He tries to survive through art. As a novelist, he endeavors to make sense of his life and the world through his creations. He gets in contact with a woman Mrs. Chichester-Redfern, whose experience in life is similar in nature to his and who would like to get some answers to her questions about her life through art as well. She would like the novelist to write a story in which her husband, who has deserted her, would feature as a suffering individual. She is clearly the emblem of the death force. Her daughter Diana is her opposite. She accepts life and is lively, jumping from one man's bed to another and feeling fulfilled. At the bottom of Diana's life, however, something vital is missing, too, as her life is sheer existence, with no intimacy, not much of an attachment, but a good deal of alienation and the feeling of being bottled up in her own cosmos. The whole novel is set in a gloomy milieu of sterility and meaninglessness. Here stands Wain, the man postmodern in spirit.

35.1.3　Alan Sillitoe (1928 – 2010)

Sillitoe was an English novelist, poet and essayist, and one of the "Angry Young Men" of the 1950s. He disliked the label, as did most of the other writers to whom it was applied. Sillitoe was a prolific writer. During his literary career he produced dozens of novels, more than a dozen volumes of poetry, several collections of short stories, some essays, and other works. He is best known for his first novel *Saturday Night and Sunday Morning* (1958) and the early short story "The Loneliness of the Long Distance Runner," published in 1959 as part of a short story collection of the same title. In 1997 Sillitoe was elected a Fellow of the Royal Society of Literature.

Sillitoe's first volume of verse *Without Beer or Bread* came out in 1957, which was followed by his much-praised novel *Saturday Night and Sunday Morning*. A year later, his first collection of short stories *The Loneliness of the Long Distance Runner* was published, whose title story is a first-person portrait of a rebellious and anarchic Borstal boy with a talent for running who refuses both literally and metaphorically to play the games of the establishment. The story was adapted into films in 1962. Then a large number of woks came out in succession in the following decades, including the novels like *Key to the Door* (1961), *The Death of William Posters* (1965), *A Tree on Fire* (1967), *A Start in Life* (1970), *The Flame of Life* (1974), *The Widower's Son* (1976), *The Storyteller* (1979), *Her Victory* (1982), *The Lost Flying Boat* (1983), *Down from the Hill* (1984), *Life Goes On* (1985), *Out of the Whirlpool* (1987), *The Open Door* (1989), *Birthday* (2001) and *A Man of His Time* (2004), the volumes of poetry like *Storm: New Poems* (1974), *Barbarians and Other Poems* (1974), *Sun Before Departure: Poems, 1974 – 1982* (1984), *Tides and Stone Walls: Poems* (1986), *Three Poems* (1988) and *Collected Poems* (1993), the collections of short stories like *The Ragman's Daughter and Other Stories* (1963), *Men, Women and Children* (1973), *Down to the Bone* (1976), *The Second Chance and Other Stories* (1981), *The Far Side of the Street: Fifteen Short Stories* (1988) and *New and Collected Stories* (2005), and the collections of essays like *Mountains and Caverns: Selected Essays* (1975). His 1995 autobiography *Life without Armor* was critically acclaimed on publication and offers a view into his squalid childhood. In 2007 he completed and published *Gadfly in Russia*, an account of his travels in Russia spanning 40 years. Sillitoe was celebrated in the Soviet Union as a spokesman for the oppressed worker in the West in the 1960s and was invited to visit the country several times. In 2008, to mark the author's 80th birthday, London Books republished *A Start in Life* as part of its London Classics series.

Among the clusters of contemporary literary constellations, Sillitoe seemed to be solitary in his creative endeavors. He leaned toward neo-Marxism in his stance. Running counter to the vogue of the neo-picaresque and other contemporaneous traditions, he persevered in his effort to affirm the value of his class and wrote exclusively about the life of his class, the working class. He seemed to have inherited the tradition of the proletarian writers of the 1930s and embraced the contemporary "new left" current of thinking that sought to keep the working class aware of its own identity in face of modern temptations and distractions. But he wrote differently. He managed to turn the proletarian type of propagandist discourse into an engaging fictional narrative. He wrote as a novelist does, not as a propagandist. Sillitoe thus, among the writers of "Angry Young Men," stood out as particularly unique in his thematic focus.

The protagonists in Sillitoe's works are mostly angry young men, coming from working family backgrounds and working mostly in factories. They are sorely frustrated and furious with their lot. However, they are not molded on the same fictional pattern as are the characters of some other "angry young men" type. They are, in a word, not angry in the same way Osborne's Jimmy Porter or Amis' Jim Dixon is. Sillitoe's young men are always part of their class. They do not move upward out of their social stratum; they are temporarily lost, feel extremely unhappy and behave in an odd or even grotesque manner, but whatever extravagance they exhibit, the bottom line is that they do not leave their class. Their spiritual odyssey generally begins with their loss of direction, sliding downhill and wallowing in meaninglessness, and groping in alienation and woe until they see the glimmer of light at the end of their long tunnel. Then they manage to overcome their geocentricism, place themselves back in their social group and experience salvation through positive and balanced self-realization. They always find rebirth of a kind in affiliation. Sillitoe' fiction covers basically the growth of their class consciousness and the journey that they traverse from benighted aloneness to solid belonging. Sillitoe extolled the working class and its virtues such as mutual love, solidarity and hard work.

Saturday Night and Sunday Morning is Sillitoe's best novel. Influenced in part by the stripped-down prose of Ernest Hemingway, the book conveys the attitudes and situation of a young factory worker faced with the inevitable end of his youthful philandering. As with John Osborne's *Look Back in Anger* and John Braine's *Room at the Top*, the real subject of the novel is the disillusionment of postwar Britain and the lack of opportunities for the working class. The novel was adapted as a film in 1960.

The book, as the title clearly indicates, consists of two parts, "Saturday Night" and "Sunday Morning." It describes the life of the protagonist Arthur Seaton, a dissatisfied young Nottingham factory lathe worker, who is, like Sillitoe's other protagonists, a working man rather than a rising member of the lower middle class. When he appears on "Saturday Night," Arthur is twenty-one years old, physically strong and full of ideas about life. It is apparent that he feels that he is the victim of a gross injustice, the nature of which, however, he cannot define. To him, society, employers and tradition and all the rest of whatever he vaguely lumps together as life—all these seem to form a conspiracy against him. He rebels against all indiscriminately and indiscreetly. Nothing is sacred to him; no one deserves his love; and all wrongs him one way or another. He becomes self-indulgent and cares only about his petty interests. He goes to pubs, drinks profusely, goes fishing and moves in and out of relationships. A girl named Doreen Greatton is devoted to him, but he finds her distasteful and does nothing to return her warm love. At the same time he takes an immense delight in perversity, keeping tryst with married young women (in fact two sisters), and successfully courting disaster. So, on one of the Saturday nights, he is soundly beaten up by one of the husbands and ends up his weekend in wounds and agony. He touches hell in his life. This proves to be a blessing in disguise, however, as it makes him think good and deep. Now back to square one in life, he is awake enough to size up his situation. His "Sunday Morning" begins in self-censure and self-loathing. He hurls at himself all the negativity that he has done at life and is bent on self-improvement. He recalls his life at the village where his grandfather lived and worked as the village blacksmith. He sinks himself back into the wholesome milieu of nature, fishing and meditating. And he finally patches up with Doreen and confirms his love for her. Then comes the point at which he experiences a kind of regeneration when he goes and visits his aunt Ada, whose large-hearted love is the fitting symbol of a class and his community. The end of the novel finds him well reoriented and poised at the threshold of his new life.

35.2   Other Writers on the Postwar Literary Scene

Besides the "Angry Young Men," there are a number of other writers, who have made great contributions to the postwar fiction. They are Elias Canetti, William Golding, V. S. Naipaul and Doris Lessing, who were all awarded the Nobel Prize in Literature, and John Fowels, Lawrence Durrell, Anthony Burgess, Iris Murdoch, and Muriel Spark. Then there are those writers who, although they made their presence felt in the 1930s, became really established in the postwar years. They are Anthony Powell, Joyce Cary and C. P. Snow. In age they were of the 1930s generation, but they did their most important work in the 1940s and 1950s. Although few of the writers of the recent period have come up with masterworks comparable in stature to those of the 1920s, they have done their best to add to the success of English fiction.

35.2.1   Lawrence George Durrell (1912 – 1990)

Lawrence Durrell was an expatriate British novelist, poet, dramatist and travel writer, though he resisted affiliation with Britain and preferred to be considered cosmopolitan. It has been posthumously suggested that Durrell never had British citizenship, though, more accurately, he became defined as a non-patrial in 1968, due to the amendment to the Commonwealth Immigrants Act 1962. Hence, he was denied the right to enter or settle in Britain under new laws and had to apply for a visa for each entry.

Although Durrell was first recognized as a poet, his poetry has been overshadowed by his novels. As he lived mostly in the eastern Mediterranean, his works are set basically there. In 1935 Durrell's first novel *Pied Piper of Lovers* was published. Around this time he chanced upon a copy of the novel *Tropic of Cancer* (1934) by Henry Miller (1891 – 1980) and wrote to Miller, expressing intense admiration for his novel. Durrell's letter sparked an enduring friendship and mutually critical relationship that spanned 45 years. The two got on well as they were exploring similar subjects. Durrell's next novel *Panic Spring* (1937) was heavily influenced by Miller's work. So was his first novel of interest *The Black Book: An Agon*, which was published in Paris in 1938 and did not appear in Britain until 1973; it is a mildly pornographic fantasia, peopled by prostitutes and failed artists. During World War Two, Durrell served as a press attaché to the British Embassies, first in Cairo and then Alexandria. In Alexandria he met Eve (Yvette) Cohen, a Jewish woman and native Alexandrian, who was to become his model for the character Justine in the tetralogy *Alexandria Quartet*, his most famous work, which consists of *Justine* (1957), *Balthazar* (1958), *Mountolive* (1958) and *Clea* (1960). With the publication of *Justine* Durrell achieved his fame as a novelist.

The first three novels of **Alexandria Quartet** tell essentially the same story but from different perspectives, a technique Durrell described in his introductory note in *Balthazar* as "relativistic." Only in the final novel *Clea* does the story advance in time and reach a conclusion. Overall, it is a bewitching story with its maze of interrelationships, its mystery of a political conspiracy unraveled in a slow, agonizing suspense, its plain and bold sexuality and voluptuousness. Its scope and its fast-moving pace hook and hold the readers at its tender mercies.

The tetralogy deals with events around the 1930s and the 1940s, some time before, during, and after the end of WWII in the beautiful, exciting and decadent Egyptian city Alexandria. The major characters include the narrator L. G. Darley, an Anglo-Irish school teacher and budding writer, his Greek mistress Melissa, the British ambassador Mountolive, the British intelligence agent Pursewarden, the French artist Clea, and the Jewish Justine. All are bound together in a web of political and sexual intrigue. Living in Alexandria, the narrator picks up wisdom in love and life and learns about the art of writing. His love life constitutes in a way his odyssey to self-realization and recognition of the need for art. This aspect of his experience is intricate and intriguing. Altogether he has three love affairs with Melissa, Justine and Clea respectively, besides the secret one with Amaril, a romantic gynecologist. The political side of the story relates to the espionage and counter-espionage between the Copts and the Muslims. The Copts plot to protect their interests against their enemies by providing aid to the establishment of Israel in Palestine. Darley is in fact a British agent as Justine is a Coptic one. At the beginning of the story, he prepares himself to become a novelist and write a "Once upon a time" kind of story. He meets Percy Pursewarden, who eventually becomes a mentor figure in his career. Darley takes interest in Justine, the wife of a Coptic banker and conspirator, and tries to get to know her through reading and writing about her and through physical contact with her. He has an affair with her and, when the affair fails, he withdraws to an island to meditate and sort out his experiences and thoughts. Justine both hurts and teaches him so that he gets ready to embrace art as a liberating force. He falls in love with Clea, who leads him to selfless love. It is Pursewarden and Clea who help Darley into a mature writer.

Sexual love is one of the major themes of the tetralogy. The *Quartet*, full of sexual encounters, is an investigation of modern love and an exploration of sex in all its aspects. The presentation of its variety is such that people tend to get the impression that the world of Durrell's is one of total depravity and decadence. Almost all of Durrell's characters are steeped in his debased and debasing milieu, and hopelessly egocentric. They love themselves more than anything else. Their sexual love seems to be a kind of quest for the salvation of their selfhood, rather than as a means to connect with their fellow creatures and the world in general so as to endow their lives with meaning. Such love fails because it never goes beyond the physical to reach the spiritual plane, and it limits rather than liberates the humanity of the "lovers." No love in the whole of the *Quartet* has produced any positive effect on any lover's life.

Another major and perhaps more important theme of the *Quartet* is art as a way leading to salvation. Durrell made it clear through his artist characters. There are quite a few of them, trying to solve the mystery of life and find the truth about it. There is Justine's first husband Jacob Arnauti, who tries to probe into Justine's psychic world through writing about her. His book *Moeurs* fails in its purpose because his perception is marred: he overlooks Justine's wound left by the death of her child. Then there is the narrator Darley, who does not always comprehend what he observes, and Pursewarden, whose notebooks indicate that he suffers from and becomes well aware of the pain of physical self-love. Pursewarden sees truth through art. As he writes, his personality grows and ultimately transcends his art. His is to Durrell the vision of the artist as seer. Clea, relating herself to Justine (love) and Pursewarden (art), locates in between and beyond, manages to achieve the unity of love and art and live beyond both, and thus best exemplifies Durrell's theme that art purifies as well as manures the psyche, and that art is the only way to fulfillment.

The *Quartet* impresses critics by the richness of its style, the variety and vividness of its characters, its movement between the personal and the political, and its exotic locations in and around the city which Durrell portrayed as the chief protagonist: "The city which used us as its flora—precipitated in us conflicts which were hers and which we mistook for our own: beloved Alexandria!" *The Times Literary Supplement* review of the *Quartet* stated: "If ever a work bore an instantly recognizable signature on every sentence, this is it." In 2012, the Nobel Records were opened after 50 years and it was revealed that Durrell was among a shortlist of authors considered for the 1962 Nobel Prize in Literature, along with John Steinbeck (winner), Robert Graves, Jean Anouilh and Karen Blixen. It was decided that "Durrell was not to be given preference this year" probably because "they did not think that *The Alexandria Quartet* was enough, so they decided to keep him under observation for the future." Also a candidate in 1961, Durrell had in the previous year been ruled out because he "gives a dubious aftertaste ⋯ because of [his] monomaniacal preoccupation with erotic complications." (Flood, 2013)

35.2.2 Sir William Gerald Golding (1911 – 1993)

William Golding was a British novelist, playwright and poet. He is best known for his first novel *Lord of the Flies* (1954), which established him as a rising star on the scene and paved the way for him to win the Nobel Prize for literature in 1983. In 1980 he was awarded the Booker Prize for literature for his novel *Rites of Passage* (1980), the first book of his sea trilogy *To the Ends of the Earth*, the other two of which are *Close Quarters* (1987) and *Fire down Below* (1989). In 2008, *The Times* ranked Golding the third on its list of "the 50 greatest British writers since 1945."

Golding produced more than ten novels during his lifetime. Besides those mentioned above, there are *The Inheritors* (1955), *Pincher Martin* (1956), *Free Fall* (1959), *The Spire* (1964), *The Pyramid* (1967), *The Scorpion God* (1971), *Darkness Visible* (1979), *The Paper Men* (1984) and *The Double Tongue* (published posthumously in 1995). *The Inheritors* tells of man's brutal extermination of his gentler ancestors. The intrinsic cruelty of man is at the heart of Golding's novels. *Pincher Martin* records the delusions experienced by a drowning sailor in his last moments. *Free Fall* explores the issue of free choice as a prisoner held in solitary confinement in a German POW camp during WW II looks back over his life. *The Spire* follows the building (and near collapse) of a huge spire onto a medieval cathedral. Here the spire symbolizes both spiritual aspiration and worldly vanity. In *The Pyramid* three separate stories in a shared setting, a small English town in the 1920s, are linked by a narrator, and *The Scorpion God* consists of three novellas, the first set in a prehistoric African hunter-gatherer band, the second in an ancient Egyptian court and the third in the court of a Roman emperor. *Darkness Visible* is about a terrorist group, a paedophile teacher, and a mysterious angel-like figure who survives a fire in the Blitz (the period of strategic bombing of the UK by Nazi Germany during WW II). *The Paper Men* is about the conflict between a writer and his biographer; and *The Double Tongue*, Golding's final novel, tells the story of the Pythia, the priestess of Apollo at Delphi.

Golding often presented isolated individuals or small groups in extreme situations, dealing with man in his basic condition stripped of trappings, and creating the quality of a fable. His vision is consistent. He would like to examine man's weakness in anatomic precision. His insights have been eye-opening enough to warrant the awarding the Nobel Prize in literature to him. His novels are set usually in a place far from "the old world": either on a wild island as is in *Lord of the Flies*, or on a rock in the Atlantic as in *Pincher Martin*, or in a primitive world as in *The Inheritors*, or a medieval town as in *The Spire*. Golding's theme is the dark side or evil of human nature. These all are adequately illustrated by *Lord of the Flies*.

Lord of the Flies describes a group of boys stranded on a tropical island reverting to savagery. The story is simple in plotline. A group of boys aged 6 to 12 are left on a desert island as a result of a plane crash. Completely on their own in a world where there is no adult guidance and supervision, the children begin to take life into their own hands. As they differ on the issue of how to live as a group, they take different courses of action. Ralph, the leader figure, would like to establish law and order, but Jack Merridew wants to go hunting and killing. The latter forms his own separate group and leads some boys away. Soon the two distinct notions of life and modes of behavior come to clash with each other, and things begin to happen at an amazing rapidity. First Piggy gets killed by Roger, Jack's "executioner." Then Simon is murdered. Jack gets the upper hand, and Ralph has to hide himself to run from his hot pursuit. The twins, Sam and Eric (known as Samneric) are threatened with torture if they refuse to tell on his whereabouts. Jack's gang sets the island on fire in order to drive Ralph out in the open. The fire catches the attention of a passing ship, which then comes over to stop their barbarism and take them back to their country.

Lord of the Flies is certainly a Golding's "fable," a veiled story about the truth of human existence, or exactly, about the nature of man. It is generally, as is the case with *Aesop's Fables*, timeless and placeless because of the universally applicable nature of the verities revealed. Instead of recreating and replicating their civilized way of life in a new, bleak environment as Robinson Crusoe does, the boys in *Lord of the Flies* simply return to the primitive, pristine state of human existence and mentality, and repeats the dark, tragic side of human history of tyranny, violence, fanaticism, intolerance and confrontation. Thirsty for power and blood, and resorting to barbaric ritual and superstitions, they fight and kill each other, thus revealing the naked heart of darkness that exists at the center of their beings. This may be called in Christianity "Original Sin" or simply evil, which resides as part of the human consciousness and breaks out loose to do irreparable damages whenever and wherever possible.

The employment of symbolism is a salient feature of the novel. The title and the boys are both symbolic. The "Lord of the Flies" may allude to the biblical Beelzebud or the Greek mythic Zeus or the tattoo that Jack and his group have come to worship, and indicates the devil figure, the source of evil. Hence the novel is just about this devil that lives in all humans. Although the boys, not fully initiated into the adult world, are naïve, they are not innocent in the Adamic sense: Adam and Eve do not have any knowledge, but the boys do. They represent clear categories of human attributes. Ralph is reason incarnate, Jack primitive passion, Piggy moral awareness, and Simon conscience and thinking. In these terms their interaction assumes the immediate significance of a society in operation. In other words, their world is a society in miniature. As their behavior becomes atavistic and their passion overwhelms their reason, human degeneration and dehumanization occur. Piggy's death signals the boys' loss of control over their lives and returning to barbarism, and Simon's being murdered, or rather, the death of conscience, marked the beginning of the reign of darkness. Piggy's glasses are also symbolic. That he loses them one at a time suggests the boys' gradual loss of values and sense of direction. In addition, the individual events incorporate symbolism. Ralph's obsession of keeping a fire going, for example, can be a sign of hope of rescue and eventual survival.

Due to Golding's use of symbolism and other literary devices, *Lord of the Flies* can be differently interpreted by different readers. To some readers, the novel is not in a totally pessimistic tone. The story tells a truth, one that keeps haunting the readers, but it does so to alert them to a brutal fact about man and his life that humans tend to ignore and forget. It does not mean to denigrate the human race; as a mater of fact, the end of the story connotes some hope of survival and good. The boys fail to behave better, as the captain of the rescuing ship says, but there is room for improvement as they are allowed to live and learn. Once they merge back into the civilization from which they were wrenched off for a while, the boys may become more responsible and conscionable. To other readers, the story embodies a different kind of outlook on man and his world: If one sees the boys' desert island as a microcosm for the human world, of which the rescuing adults are a part, then nothing would stop the adults grabbing at each other's throats if evil continues to grow in their hearts. Golding seemed to tell the dismal truth about the human situation in the form of a fable. Then there is reason to see the story as pessimistic.

35.2.3 Anthony Burgess (1917 – 1993)

John Anthony Burgess Wilson, who published under Anthony Burgess, was an English novelist, literary critic and composer. From relatively modest beginnings in a Catholic family in Manchester, he eventually became one of the best-known English literary figures of the latter half of the 20th century. Although Burgess was predominantly a comic writer, his dystopian satire *A Clockwork Orange* (1962) remains his best-known novel. In 1971 the novel was adapted into a highly controversial film, which Burgess said was chiefly responsible for the popularity of the book. Burgess produced numerous other novels, including the Enderby quartet—*Inside Mr. Enderby* (1963), *Enderby Outside* (1968), *The Clockwork Testament, or Enderby's End* (1974) and *Enderby's Dark Lady, or No End of Enderby* (1984)—and *Earthly Powers* (1980), regarded by most critics as his greatest novel. He wrote librettos and screenplays as well as studies of classic writers, notably James Joyce. Burgess also composed over 250 musical works; he sometimes claimed to consider himself as much a composer as an author, although he enjoyed considerably more success in literary writing.

Burgess' first published fiction is his Malayan trilogy *The Long Day Wanes*, including *Time for a Tiger* (1956), *The Enemy in the Blanket* (1958) and *Beds in the East* (1959). It was the author's ambition to become "the true fictional expert on Malaya." In these works, Burgess was working in the tradition established by Kipling for British India, and Conrad and William Somerset Maugham (1874 – 1965) for Southeast Asia. Burgess operated more in the mode of Orwell, who had a good command of Urdu and Burmese (necessary for Orwell's works as a police officer) and Kipling, who spoke Hindi (having learnt it as a child). Like his fellow English expats in Asia, Burgess had excellent spoken and written command of his operative language(s), both as a novelist and speaker, including Malay.

Burgess' repatriate years (c. 1960 – 69) produced *The Right to an Answer* (1960), which touches on the theme of death and dying, *One Hand Clapping* (1961), a satire on the vacuity of popular culture, *The Worm and the Ring* (1961), which had to be withdrawn from circulation under the threat of libel action from one of Burgess' former colleagues, a school secretary, *A Clockwork Orange*, and *Nothing like the Sun: A Story of Shakespeare's Love Life* (1964), which, drawing on the biography *Shakespeare, Man and Artist* (1938) by Edgar Innes Fripp (1861 – 1931), is a fictional recreation of Shakespeare's love-life and an examination of the supposedly partly syphilitic sources of the bard's imaginative vision, and won critical acclaim and placed Burgess among the first-rank novelists of his generation.

M/F (1971) was listed by the writer himself as one of the works of which he was most proud. *Beard's Roman Women* (1976) was revealing on a personal level, dealing with the death of his first wife, his bereavement, and the affair that led to his second marriage. In *Napoleon Symphony: A Novel in Four Movements* (1974), Burgess brought Napoleon Bonaparte to life by shaping the structure of the novel to *Eroica* symphony (completed 1804; performed 1805) by Ludwig van Beethoven (1770 – 1827). The novel contains a portrait of an Arab and Muslim society under occupation by a Christian western power (Egypt by Catholic France). In the 1980s, religious themes began to feature heavily in Burgess' novels such as *Man of Nazareth* (1979), *Earthly Powers* (1980) and *The Kingdom of the Wicked* (1985). Though Burgess lapsed from Catholicism early in his youth, the influence of the Catholic "training" and worldview remained strong in his work all his life. This is notable in the discussion of free will in *A Clockwork Orange*, and in the apocalyptic vision of devastating changes in the Catholic Church, due to what can be understood as Satanic influence, in *Earthly Powers*.

Burgess kept working through his final illness and was writing on his deathbed. The novel *Any Old Iron* (1988) is a generational saga of two families (one Russian-Welsh, the other Jewish), encompassing the sinking of the Titanic, World War I, the Russian Revolution, the Spanish Civil War, World War II, the early years of the State of Israel, and the rediscovery of Excalibur. *A Dead Man in Deptford* (1993), about Christopher Marlowe, is a companion novel to *Nothing like the Sun*. The verse novel *Byrne: A Novel* (1995) was published posthumously. Burgess' other novels include *The Doctor is Sick* (1960), *Devil of a State* (1961), *The Wanting Seed* (1962), *Honey for the Bears* (1963), *The Eve of St. Venus* (1964), *A Vision of Battlements* (1965), *Tremor of Intent: An Eschatological Spy Novel* (1966), *Abba Abba* (1977), *1985* (1978), *The End of the World News: An Entertainment* (1982), *The Pianoplayers* (1986) and *Mozart and the Wolf Gang* (1991).

Burgess also made contributions to critical studies. His *English Literature: A Survey for Students* (1958, revised 1974), was aimed at newcomers to the subject. He followed this with *The Novel Today* (1963) and *The Novel Now: A Student's Guide to Contemporary Fiction* (1967). He wrote the Joyce studies *Here Comes Everybody: An Introduction to James Joyce for the Ordinary Reader* (also published as *Re Joyce*) and *Joysprick: An Introduction to the Language of James Joyce* (1973). His 1970 *Encyclopædia Britannica* entry on the novel (under "Novel, the") is regarded as a classic of the genre. Burgess wrote full-length critical studies of William Shakespeare, Ernest Hemingway and D. H. Lawrence, as well as *Ninety-nine Novels: The Best in English since 1939* (1984).

Burgess' dystopian novel **A Clockwork Orange** was inspired initially by an incident during the Second World War in which his wife Lynne was robbed, assaulted and violated by deserters from the US Army in London during the blackout. The event may have contributed to her subsequent miscarriage. The book is an examination of free will and morality. The young anti-hero Alex, captured after a short career of violence and mayhem, undergoes a course of aversion therapy to curb his violent tendencies. This results in his defenselessness against other people and paralysis to enjoy some of his favorite music that, besides violence, was an intense pleasure for him. Near the time of publication the final chapter was cut from the American edition of the book. Burgess had written the novel with twenty-one chapters, meaning to match the age of majority. "21 is the symbol of human maturity, or used to be, since at 21 you got to vote and assumed adult responsibility," Burgess wrote in a foreword for a 1986 edition. Needing a paycheck and thinking that the publisher was "being charitable in accepting the work at all," Burgess accepted the deal and allowed *A Clockwork Orange* to be published in the US with the twenty-first chapter omitted. The 1971 film adaptation by Stanley Kubrick (1928 – 1999) was based on the American edition, and thus helped to perpetuate the loss of the last chapter.

35.2.4 Dame Muriel Spark (1918 – 2006)

Muriel Spark was a Scottish novelist, who began her literary career as editor and biographer, working for the Poetry Society and editing its *Poetry Review* from 1947 to 1949. She turned to fiction after winning the *Observer* short-story competition in 1951. Her first novel *The Comforters* was published in 1957. It featured several references to Catholicism and conversion to it, although its main theme revolved around a young woman who becomes aware that she is a character in a novel. *The Ballad of Peckham Rye* (1960), a bizarre tale of the underworld, mixing shrewd social observation with hints of necromancy, is perhaps her best-known work. Her next novel *The Prime of Miss Jean Brodie* (1961) is a disturbing portrait of an Edinburgh schoolmistress and her group of favored pupils. The author displayed originality of subject and tone, making extensive use of flashforwards and imagined conversations in the novel.

Spark was made Dame Commander of the Most Excellent Order of the British Empire in 1993, in recognition of her services to literature, and was twice shortlisted for the Booker Prize, in 1969 for *The Public Image* (1968) and in 1981 for *Loitering with Intent* (1981), which contains many autobiographical references to the author's early career. As a matter of fact, the problems of biography and autobiography form the subject of *Loitering with Intent*. The novel was reprinted in 2001 in the US and in 2007 in the UK. *The Public Image* is set in Rome and concerns Annabel Christopher, an up-and-coming film actress, who carefully cultivates her image to keep her career on course, managing to mask her lack of talent. In 1998, Spark was awarded the Golden PEN Award by English PEN for "a Lifetime's Distinguished Service to Literature." Ten years later, in 2008 *The Times* ranked Spark the eighth on a list of "the 50 greatest British writers since 1945." In 2010, Spark was shortlisted for the Lost Man Booker Prize of 1970 for *The Driver's Seat* (1970), a novella which was advertised as "a metaphysical shocker," and is indeed in the psychological thriller genre, dealing with themes of alienation, isolation and loss of spiritual values.

35.2.5 Doris May Lessing (1919 – 2013)

Doris Lessing was a British novelist, poet, playwright, librettist, biographer and short story writer. She was awarded the 2007 Nobel Prize in Literature. In awarding the prize, the Swedish Academy described her as "that epicist of the female experience, who with skepticism, fire and visionary power has subjected a divided civilization to scrutiny." Lessing was the eleventh woman and the oldest person ever to receive the Nobel Prize in Literature, and the third-oldest Nobel laureate in any category. In 2008, *The Times* ranked her the fifth on a list of "the 50 greatest British writers since 1945."

Lessing is one of the most successful prolific British novelists of the recent decades. By the time of her death, more than 50 of her novels had been published. Her major novels include *The Grass is Singing* (1950), *The Golden Notebook* (1962), *Briefing for a Descent into Hell* (1971), *The Diaries of Jane Somers* (1983 – 1984), *The Good Terrorist* (1985), *The Fifth Child* (1988), the *Children of Violence* series (1952 – 1969), including *Martha*

Quest (1952), *A Proper Marriage* (1954), *A Ripple from the Storm* (1958), *Landlocked* (1965) and *The Four-Gated City* (1969), and the five novels collectively known as *Canopus in Argos: Archives* (1979 – 1983)—*Shikasta* (1979), *The Marriages Between Zones Three, Four and Five* (1980), *The Sirian Experiments* (1980), *The Making of the Representative for Planet 8* (1982) and *The Sentimental Agents in the Volyen Empire* (1983).

Lessing's fiction is commonly divided into three distinct phases: the phase on the Communist theme (1944 – 1956), when she was writing radically on social issues, to which she returned in *The Good Terrorist*, the phase on the psychological theme (1956 – 1969), when she was writing about the inner world of women and sometimes concerning anti-communism, and the phase after the 1970s, when she was exploring the Sufi theme in the social or soft science fiction like the *Canopus in Argos* series or, as she preferred to put it, "space fiction." Basically a realist, Lessing took interest in writing in the mythic mode in the 1970s. In the 1980s she reverted back to the realistic mode, though still exhibiting some traces of fantasy at times. Since the 1990s she had been writing a good number of short stories. Lessing's themes are wide and varied: social problems, political concerns, racial questions, and feminist views on life and love relationships, but she focused mostly on black-white relations and on the life of the woman in a male-oriented world. Her commitment to life and society is evident in all her fiction.

Lessing's first novel *The Grass Is Singing* and the collection of short stories *African Stories* (1964) are set in Southern Rhodesia (now Zimbabwe). Her *Canopus* sequence was not popular with many mainstream literary critics. It presents an advanced interstellar society's efforts to accelerate the evolution of other worlds, including the Earth. Using Sufi concepts, the series of novels also utilizes an approach similar to that employed by the early 20th-century mystic G. I. Gurdjieff (1866/1877? – 1949) in his work *All and Everything*. Lessing's interest turned to Sufism after coming to the realization that Marxism ignored spiritual matters, leaving her disillusioned. Her earlier works of "inner space" fiction like *Briefing for a Descent into Hell* and *Memoirs of a Survivor* (1974) also connect to this theme.

Lessing's best-known work **The Golden Notebook** is the longest and most ambitious work she had ever attempted to write. This book explores mental and societal breakdown. It also contains a powerful anti-war and anti-Stalinist message, an extended analysis of communism and the Communist Party in England from the 1930s to the 1950s, and a famed examination of the budding sexual and women's liberation movements. It is a masterpiece in portraiture of the manners, aspirations, anxieties and the particular problems of the times in which we live. Different from some scholars who consider it a feminist classic, the author herself thought highly of its theme of mental breakdowns as a means of healing and freeing one's self from illusions. She also regretted that critics failed to appreciate the exceptional structure of the novel. She explained in *Walking in the Shade* that she modeled Molly partly on her good friend Joan Rodker, the daughter of the Modernist poet and publisher John Rodker (1894 – 1955).

The Golden Notebook is a daring narrative experiment. Here the multiple selves of Anna Freeman Wulf are rendered in astonishing depth and detail. Anna is a middle-aged contemporary woman in a male world. She is an expatriate single parent with a 13-year-old daughter Jane to support and depend on emotionally. She, like Lessing herself, strives for ruthless honesty as she aims to free herself from the chaos, emotional numbness, and hypocrisy afflicting her generation. A writer of a commercially successful book on the royalties of which she lives, Anna now keeps four notebooks, which have different covers. In the one with a black cover, she reviews the African experience of her earlier years. In the red-covered one, she records her political life, her disillusionment with communism. In the yellow-covered one she writes a novel in which she creates a female character Ella as her alter ego. And in the blue one she keeps a personal diary, which covers her present life experiences and thoughts. Finally, in love with an American writer and threatened with insanity, Anna tries to bring the threads of all four books together in a golden notebook and reflects the inner life of women who want to live freely. Anna's best friend is Molly Jacobs, a Jewish actress and a single parent as well, whose adult son is blind from his suicide attempt and tries to make everyone miserable. Molly was once involved in communist cultural activities. Anna and Molly are striving for self-fulfillment in a world in which life for women is a struggle. Anna's American boyfriend Saul Green can be a difficult person, but he proves to be a source of support for Anna. Both Anna and Molly try desperately to find meaning in relationships as well as in social work.

The Golden Notebook is a great success in terms of characterization, the characterization of Anna in particular, which is, to a great degree, attributed to the medium of the four notebooks and the supportive portrait of Molly. The notebooks help reveal Anna's personality graphically. One of these records her political experience: she has been a liberal, a communist and a disillusioned idealist. Another portrays her as an individual: independent, free, and wishing to attain the freedom that the male gender enjoys in life. One other shows her engaged in self-scrutiny: placing herself as Ella in an imagined scenario and examining the Anna-Ella parallel for self-searching. Ella is Anna in disguise. She looks like her creator, living through similar experiences—a writer, divorced, depressed and on the brink of collapse because of a failed relationship. Ella suffers disorientation and is saved by a new attachment to an American. Anna's imaginative effort offers a chance of distancing herself from the confused mess of her real life and seeing things from a different approach. Then, there is Molly, her duplicate of sorts in actual life, warm, vibrant, sharing the same convictions and struggling for self-realization. The two women lean on each other. Anna ends up achieving salvation both in life and in writing. In a way the portrayal of Anna represents the author's independent-minded response to women's life in the modern world.

The novel is unique and intriguing in structure. It reads like a novelist writing about a novelist, with stories within the story and novels within the novel. Each of the notebooks is divided into four sections, the last of which forms part of the major portion of the book, and the major portion is prefaced with a "Free Woman" section. And the section, also called "the Golden Notebook," attempts to weave the disparate narrative threads about the different Annas in the four notebooks into a recognizable web. The novel ends up with a "Free Woman" section. It sounds complicated, but it works well for structuring the development of the story. Moreover, all four notebooks and the frame narrative testify to the themes of Stalinism, the Cold War and the threat of nuclear conflagration, and women's struggles with the conflicts of work, sex, love, maternity and politics. However, Lessing herself in the preface claimed that the most important theme in the novel was fragmentation, the mental breakdown that Anna suffers, perhaps from the compartmentalization of her life reflected in the division of the four notebooks. Her relationship and attempt to draw everything together in the golden notebook at the end of the novel are both the final stage of Anna's intolerable mental breakdown and her attempt to overcome the fragmentation and madness.

35.2.6 Dame Jean Iris Murdoch (1919 – 1999)

Iris Murdoch was an Irish-born British novelist and philosopher, best known for her novels about good and evil, sexual relationships, morality, and the power of the unconscious. Her first published novel *Under the Net* (1954) was selected in 1998 as one of Modern Library's 100 best English-language novels of the 20th century. In 1987, she was made Dame Commander of the Order of the British Empire. In 2008, *The Times* ranked Murdoch the twelfth on a list of "the 50 greatest British writers since 1945."

Murdoch was influenced by the French existentialist-philosopher Jean-Paul Sartre (1905 – 1980). She was a philosopher-writer; yet her novels, in their attention and generosity to the inner lives of individuals, follow the tradition of novelists like Dostoyevsky, Tolstoy, George Eliot and Marcel Proust, besides showing an abiding love for Shakespeare. Murdoch devoted herself wholly to writing and was very prolific. During her lifetime she produced over twenty novels, including *Under the Net*, *The Sandcastle* (1957), *The Bell* (1958), *A Severed Head* (1961), *The Black Prince* (1973) and *The Sea, the Sea* (1978).

There is great variety in Murdoch's achievement. The richly layered structure and compelling realistic comic imagination of *The Black Prince* are very different from the early comic work *Under the Net* or *The Unicorn* (1963). *The Unicorn* can be read as a sophisticated Gothic romance, or as a novel with Gothic trappings, or perhaps as a parody of the Gothic mode of writing. *The Black Prince* is a study of erotic obsession, and the text becomes more complicated, suggesting multiple interpretations, when subordinate characters contradict the narrator and the mysterious editor of the book in a series of afterwords. Though novels differ markedly and her style developes, themes recur. Her novels often include upper-middle-class male intellectuals caught in moral dilemmas, gay characters, refugees, Anglo-Catholics with crises of faith, empathetic pets, curiously knowing children and sometimes a powerful and almost demonic male enchanter who imposes his will on the other characters—a type of man Murdoch is said to have modeled on her lover, the Nobel laureate Elias Canetti. Murdoch was awarded the Booker Prize in 1978 for *The Sea, the Sea*, a finely detailed novel about the power of love and loss, featuring a retired stage director who is overwhelmed by jealousy when he meets his erstwhile lover after several decades apart. An authorized collection of her poetic writings, *Poems by Iris Murdoch*, appeared in 1997. Several of her works have been adapted for the screen, including the British television series of her novels *An Unofficial Rose* (1962) and *The Bell*.

Murdoch's fourth and finest novel **The Bell** is an artistic rendering of myth and reality well intertwined. The story is set in a lay religious community established by the middle-aged Michael Meade at his ancestral estate Imber Court, close to the Imber Abbey of which Mother Clare is the Abbess. It is by and large a community of misfits, social or spiritual or both, soul-sick and at odds with the world. These include Nick and Catherine Fawley, twin brother and sister in their late twenties, Toby Gashe, a boy of eighteen about to go to Oxford, Paul and Dora Greenfield, the unhappily married couple, and James Tayper Pace, an energetic settlement worker (the only exception here as he is a man of faith). Meade was once a schoolmaster and had a homosexual relationship with his pupil Nick Fawley. When he sees Toby in the group, he fails to resist the temptation to kiss him. This infuriates and saddens Nick. Young Catherine, a neurotic, about to become a nun, loves Meade in secret. Young Dora, who has been away because she was unhappy with her marriage, comes to join her middle-aged husband and learns about an ancient legend. As the legend goes, a 14th-century Imber nun took a lover, the Imber Abbey was thus placed under a curse, and the bell of the Abbey fell into the lake. Meade's community, believing a new bell would do it good, plans to install one. Then Toby discovers the old bell by accident and schemes with Dora to replace the new bell with the old one. They inadvertently sound the old bell and foil their own design. The bell installation ceremony is not to come off anyway because Nick plots for the new bell to fall again into the lake. The community disintegrates. Catherine survives her suicide attempt but becomes mentally weak. Nick commits suicide. Toby is sent home. Mother Clare and Pace dissolve the Imber Court. Meade leaves for London, and so does Dora for a new chapter in her life.

Love or failure of love is the major theme of the novel, which is represented by the two major characters, Michael Meade and Dora Greenfield, the one demonstrating the failure of love and the other the saving grace of love. Both survive the dissolution of the Imber Court community as they are awake to the importance of love in life. Meade is a good man. He had studied for a religious call, but when he was schoolmaster he was led into a homosexual relationship by his pupil Nick Fawley, and lost his chance to become a priest. Now Meade establishes Imber Court and sees it as a fulfillment of his religious aspiration. Dora is a loving person and enjoys being loved. She represents the life impulse in the novel along with Mother Clare. The novel probably focuses on the idea that love saves. Its fitting symbol is the bell. The bell embodies a curse—suppression of love—which only love can remove. As it is "the voice of love," its burial at the bottom of the lake suggests the absence of love in the community, which may be the root cause of the spiritual sickness affecting the members there. Its projected reinstallation indicates the members' growing awareness of the importance of love and their dire need for it. They would like to become normal and merge back into the life of general humanity. The ancient story of the bell, which has survived the obliteration of time, may connote the fact that love is highly necessary for the spiritual wellness of all people of all time and that the community needs nothing else as the effective cure for its disease. By the same token, the failure of the reinstallation is pregnant with meaning, too. It means that love is not easy to come by and that regeneration is a difficult undertaking. Therefore, it is educational to those anxious about renewal and eager to turn over a new page in life. One of these people is Meade, who becomes a better person. The other is Dora, who has now a new life to look forward to. The tragedy of the twin brother and sister is a moral story about love and life as well.

The Bell is a success in terms of characterization. Since the story is really more about Michael Meade, he is the focus of the author's portrayal. Meade is a good person suffering from spiritual and physical self-denial. He needs to pick up some essential qualities in order to heal himself and become whole. Mother Clare acts as a spiritual guide. She is the affirmer of faith and selfhood on the basis of her love of god, who inspires Meade to establish the Imber Court, and whose nunnery in its close vicinity forms a foil to Meade's court in self-fulfillment. Dora is a mentor figure for Meade as well. Full of enthusiasm about life, she offers an example of living in a vital and vibrant manner, independent in opinion, free of inhibitions, and believing in staying truly alive. Nick is Meade's warner, his negative mirror image, who teaches him to act differently. As he is basically a man of faith and an eager and perceptive learner, Meade is able to grow in self-knowledge and moral strength and survive the traumatic experience of his life.

35.2.7 John Robert Fowles (1926 – 2005)

John Fowles was an English novelist of international stature. He was named one of "the 50 greatest British writers since 1945" by *The Times*. His major novels include *The Collector* (1963), *The Magus* (1966), *The French Lieutenant's Woman* (1969), *The Ebony Tower* (1974) and *Mantissa* (1982). He also produced a miscellany of other things such as poetry, short fiction, essays and philosophy.

Fowles' works reflect the influence of Jean-Paul Sartre and Albert Camus (1913 – 1960), among others; he has been, in a very serious sense, regarded as a postmodernist novelist. He enjoyed experimenting with a number of important things relating to fiction such as points of view, the notion of time, metafiction, parody, the ways a story ends, and emphasis on his characters' efforts to internalize their harrowing experiences. Fowles was a popular novelist as well. He never failed to fascinate his readers; reading him can always be an enjoyable experience. His works have been translated into many languages, and several adapted as films. His stories are basically traditional in nature, or love stories in its various forms, which present little or no obscurity in comprehension. There seems to be some kind of pattern that underpins his stories: the hero undertakes a quest with the guidance of some wise man, and finds the woman he loves and becomes spiritually whole.

In late 1960, though he had already drafted *The Magus*, Fowles began working on *The Collector*, which is about a lonely young man Frederick Clegg, who works as a clerk in a city hall and collects butterflies in his spare time. The novel was adapted as a feature film by the same name in 1965. British reviewers accepted the novel as an innovative thriller, but several American critics detected a serious promotion of existentialist thought. When the paperback rights were sold in the spring of 1963, it was "probably the highest price that had hitherto been paid for a first novel." The success of the novel encouraged Fowles to devote himself full-time to a literary career. Afterwards, he set about collating all the drafts he had written of what would become his most studied work *The Magus*, based in part on his own experiences in Greece. *The Magus* is an instant best-seller that was directly in tune with the 1960s "hippie" anarchism and experimental philosophy. It was followed by *The French Lieutenant's Woman*. Fowles' later fictional works include *The Ebony Tower*, a collection of five novellas and short stories with interlacing themes, each built around a medieval myth, *Daniel Martin* (1977), *Mantissa*, which consists entirely of a presumably imaginary dialogue in a writer's head between himself and an embodiment of the Muse Erato after he wakes amnesiac in a hospital bed, and *A Maggot* (1985), an 18th-century murder mystery that makes use of contemporary documents. *Daniel Martin* is a long, self-searching, semi-naturalistic, semi-experimental account of a screenwriter Daniel and his relationships with Hollywood, capitalism, art and his sister-in-law. It is set in a wide variety of locations, ranging from opening sequences in Devon and Oxford to a closing sequence in the ruins of Palmyra. The novel uses both first and third person voices, whilst employing a variety of literary techniques such as multiple narratives and flashback.

The French Lieutenant's Woman established Fowles' international reputation. It was translated into more than ten languages and was adapted as a feature film in 1981. The book is a Victorian romance with a postmodern twist that was set in Lyme Regis, Dorset, where Fowles lived for much of his life. It builds on Fowles' authority in the Victorian literature. The novel explores Charles Smithson's relationship with Sarah Woodruff, whom he falls in love with. Charles, the protagonist, is a true-to-form Victorian gentleman and amateur naturalist, expecting to inherit a title and wealth from his uncle and get married to a rich young lady Ernestina Freeman. Then he meets Sarah Woodruff, a woman of disrepute, who is said to have been a mistress for a French lieutenant. Hence her nickname, the French lieutenant's woman. She is unusually pretty and her gloom adds remarkably well to her attraction. Charles seeks the advice of the doctor Dr. Grogan, the prototype of a modern psychologist, and learns more about her. He feels so irresistibly drawn to her with time that his passion soon amounts to obsession. He has an affair with her in a hotel and becomes the object of the vicious scandal that his servant spreads about him. The event discredits him thoroughly in the eyes of his leisured class so that he is ruined and ostracized. When he packs up and goes to the hotel for Sarah, however, he is dismayed to find her already gone. Then he spends a long time and does everything humanly possible to search for her and finds her eventually. The story ends, as the book suggests, in three different ways:

a) Charles does not visit Sarah, but immediately returns to Lyme to reaffirm his love for Ernestina. They marry, though the marriage never becomes particularly happy, and Charles enters a trade under Ernestina's father Mr. Freeman. The narrator pointedly notes the lack of knowledge about Sarah's fate. Charles tells Ernestina about an encounter which he implies is with the "French Lieutenant's Woman," but elides the sordid details, and the matter is ended. The narrator dismisses this ending as a daydream by Charles, before the alternative events of the subsequent meeting with Ernestina are described. This first ending is a semblance of verisimilitude in the traditional happy ending found in actual Victorian novels.

b) Charles and Sarah have a rash sexual encounter in which Charles realizes that Sarah was a virgin. Reflecting on his emotions during this, Charles ends his engagement to Ernestina and proposes to Sarah through a letter. Charles' servant Sam fails to deliver the letter and, after Charles breaks his engagement, Ernestina's father disgraces him. His uncle marries and his wife bears an heir, ensuring the loss of the expected inheritance. To escape the social suicide and depression caused by his broken engagement, Charles goes abroad to Europe and America. Ignorant of Charles' proposal, Sarah flees to London without telling her lover. During Charles' trips abroad, his lawyer searches for Sarah, finding her two years later living in the Chelsea house of the painter and poet Dante Gabriel Rossetti, where she enjoys an artistic, creative life. Sarah shows Charles the child of their affair, leaving him in hope that the three may be reunited.

c) The narrator re-appears outside the house at 16 Cheyne Walk and turns back his pocket watch by fifteen minutes. Events are the same as in the second-ending version until Charles meets Sarah, when their reunion is sour. The new ending does not make clear the parentage of the child and Sarah expresses no interest in reviving the relationship. Charles leaves the house, intending to return to the United States, wondering whether Sarah is a manipulative, lying woman who exploited him.

In terms of characterization, the major characters like Charles Smithson and Sarah Woodruff stand out. Charles, not happy with his life, good and well provided as he is, embodies the nascent half-awareness of the modern man. He may not know what he wants exactly, but he is searching. The fact that he feels the monotony of his humdrum existence is an evident signal that he is thirsting for change. At first he may just experience this feeling at the subconscious level of his being, but he becomes increasingly aware of his emotional quandary when he comes in contact with Sarah Woodruff, who proves to be an odd fascination that he finds impossible to shake off. Then when he meets her again at the mysterious Undercliff, he is hopelessly carried away. He feels the magnetism of her tug so much that he forgets everything—his proper behavior, his commitments and his future—just so as to enjoy the self-gratification that the moment can offer. Thus torn between his love for the rich yet conventional Ernestina and the mysterious, irrational, but erotically captivating Sarah Woodruff, he experiences a fall and a rise, a fall from his present secure status and a rise to the attainment of his full self-knowledge and psychic maturity. Although he suffers total disgrace and isolation, he feels good and happy and would have lived for the rest of his life in perfect contentment had Sarah not deserted him. Charles is a bundle of contradictions. On the one hand, he is rational enough to know that he should marry Ernestina and keep his position. On the other hand, he is emotionally drawn to the unknown course of life to which Sarah is pulling him. He has his internal fight and decides to take the road not taken and brave the dangers of a new world ahead. His quest for Sarah is actually a quest for self-identity. Sarah attracts a good deal of attention. She is a sensitive woman, with an independent spirit. She may even be seen as the prototype of the emerging modern woman, or a precursor to feminism. She chafes in her social bracket and struggles to assert her presence. Sarah does not care about what society thinks of her, but enjoys the license that the title "the French lieutenant's woman" gives her. She is, in the opinion of her society, already a whore, the lowest of the low among women so that society cannot be just and good to her anyway. Whatever she may do would not help her because she is already "formulated" like a helpless insect "sprawling on a pin."

The French Lieutenant's Woman is a typical example of metafiction. All through the work, the author keeps telling the readers (and throwing in all sorts of reminders such as Hitler, radar and TV) that, although the story is about the Victorian England, his is a fictional story, not a reality. Furthermore, contrary to the traditional realist fiction which looks like reality, the story of *The French Lieutenant's Woman* is an obvious parody of the Victorian, traditional realistic, narrative method; it is good story telling until the author feels the urge to jog his readers out of their comfortable mode of reception and their anxious search for the real story. He does this by alerting them to the fact that their search will end in failure as there is nothing like the real story. Thus, as noted earlier on, the novel offers a number of endings instead of only one, just to make it difficult, if not entirely impossible, for the readers to locate and pin down the real story.

35.2.8　Sir Vidiadhar Surajprasad Naipaul (1932 –)

V. S. Naipaul is a Trinidad-born British novelist and travel writer. He is known for his early comic novels set in Trinidad, his later bleaker novels of the wider world, and his autobiographical chronicles of life and travels. In 2001 he was awarded the Nobel Prize in Literature. The Swedish Academy praised his work "for having united perceptive narrative and incorruptible scrutiny in works that compel us to see the presence of suppressed histories." However, his fiction and especially his travel writing have been criticized for their allegedly unsympathetic portrayal of the Third World.

Naipaul has published more than 30 books, both of fiction and nonfiction, over some 50 years. His first three books are all comedies of manner, which are set in Trinidad. They are *The Mystic Masseur* (1957), a novel which was filmed in 2001, *The Suffrage of Elvira* (1958), a comic novella about a rural election in Trinidad, and *Miguel Street* (1959), a series of stories. His next novel *A House for Mr Biswas* (1961), also set in Trinidad, traces the fortunes of its mild hero, a portrait inspired by Naipaul's father, from birth to death; he progresses from the job of sign-writer to that of journalist, is trapped into marriage and almost absorbed by his wife's vast family, but continues to bid for independence, symbolized by the house which he acquires shortly before his death. The novel describes the dissolution of a whole way of life, as the younger members of the family depart for new educational opportunities in Europe. After completing *A House for Mr Biswas*, Naipaul spent the next five months in the Caribbean. As a result of this trip, he wrote *The Middle Passage: Impressions of Five Societies—British, French and Dutch in the West Indies and South America* (1962), his first travel book. In this book, Naipaul portrayed the West Indies as islands colonized only for the purpose of employing slaves for the production of other peoples' goods. *Mr. Stone and the Knights Companion* (1963), his only attempt at a novel set in Britain with white British characters, was followed by *An Area of Darkness* (1964), the resulting book of his one-year visit to India and his highly controversial and critical account of India. In late 1964, Naipaul was asked to write an original script for an American movie and the result was a novella named "A Flag on the Island," later published in *A Flag on the Island* (1967), a collection of short stories set in the West Indies and London. His next novel *The Mimic Men* (1967) is set on a fictitious Caribbean island. From this time on Naipaul's works became more overtly political and pessimistic.

Naipaul's fiction produced in the 1970s includes *In a Free State* (1971), winner for Booker Prize, which explores problems of nationality and identity through three linked narratives (i. e., three short stories with the last one also titled "In a Free State"), *Guerrillas* (1975), a portrait of political and sexual violence in the Caribbean, and *A Bend in the River* (1979), an equally horrifying portrait of the emergent Africa. Naipaul's intense, broad and predominantly melancholy experience of human nature in the modern world may also be seen in the travel books and works of political journalism which have provided a background for his fiction. These, besides *The Middle Passage* and *An Area of Darkness*, include *The Return of Eva Perón and the Killings in Trinidad* (1980), *Among the Believers: An Islamic Journey* (1981), and *A Turn in the South* (1989), which is about evangelical Christianity in the southern states of the USA. *The Overcrowded Barracoon and Other Articles* (1972) is a collection of personal and political articles. Naipaul's recurrent themes of political violence, innate homelessness and alienation inevitably give rise to comparisons with Joseph Conrad. *The Enigma of Arrival* (1987), which sows a softening of mood and tone, is a semi-autobiographical novel describing a young Trinidadian's arrival in the post-imperial England and his sense of settling into a rural landscape which he has previously known only through literature and art: Naipaul himself, like his narrator, lived for many years in rural Wiltshire on a decaying estate. Naipaul's fiction produced in the 1990s and 2000s are *A Way in the World* (1994), *Half a Life* (2001), *The Nightwatchman's Occurrence Book: And Other Comic Inventions (Stories)* (2002) and *Magic Seeds* (2004).

The Mimic Men broke new ground for Naipaul. It does not unfold chronologically. Its language is allusive and ironic, its overall structure whimsical. It has strands of both fiction and non-fiction, a precursor to other Naipaul novels. It is intermittently dense, even obscure, but it also has beautiful passages, especially descriptive ones of the fictional tropical island of Isabella. The subject of sex appears explicitly for the first time in Naipaul's work. The plot, to the extent there is one, is centered around a protagonist Ralph Singh, an East Indian-West Indian politician from Isabella. Singh is in exile in London and attempting to write his political memoirs. Earlier, in the immediate aftermath of decolonization in a number of British colonies in the late 1950s and early 1960s, Singh has shared political power with a more powerful African Caribbean politician. Soon, the memoirs take on a more personal aspect. There are flashbacks to the formative and defining periods of Singh's life. In many of these, during crucial moments, whether during his childhood or married life or political career, he appears to abandon engagement and enterprise. These, he rationalizes later, belong only to fully-made European societies. When it was published, the novel received generally positive critical notice.

All the narratives in *In a Free State* describe displaced characters like a servant from Bombay transported to Washington, a lost and angry West Indian youth in London, and two whites in a hostile African state. **"In a Free State,"** the title novella, is about two young expatriate Europeans driving across an African country, which remains nameless but offers clues of Uganda, Kenya and Rwanda. The novella speaks to many themes. The colonial era ends and Africans govern themselves. Political chaos, frequently violent, takes hold in newly decolonized countries. The young, idealistic, expatriate whites are attracted to these countries, seeking expanded moral and sexual freedoms. They are rootless, their bonds with the land tenuous; at the slightest danger they leave. The older, conservative, white settlers, by contrast, are committed to staying, even in the face of danger. The young expatriates, though liberal, can be racially prejudiced. The old settlers, unsentimental, sometimes brutal, can show compassion. The young, engrossed in narrow preoccupations, are ill-informed of the dangers that surround them. The old are knowledgeable, armed and ready to defend themselves. The events unfolding along the car trip and the conversation during it become the means of exploring these themes.

35.2.9　Joyce Lunel Cary (1888–1957)

Joyce Cary was an Anglo-Irish novelist and artist. His major works include two trilogies. The first trilogy consists of *Herself Surprised* (1941), *To Be a Pilgrim* (1942), and *The Horse's Mouth* (1944), which is chiefly concerned with the life of the artist Gulley Jimson; the second is a study of politics, including *Prisoner of Grace* (1952), *Except the Lord* (1953) and *Not Honor More* (1955). The major theme of the novels, which exhibit a vast range of characters, is the necessity for individual freedom and choice.

During WWI Cary served with a Nigerian regiment fighting in the German colony of Cameroon. His short story "Umaru" (1921) describes an incident during this period in which a British officer recognizes the common humanity that connects him with his African sergeant. In 1920, Cary obtained a literary agent and some of the stories he had written in Africa were sold to *The Saturday Evening Post*, an American magazine, published under the name "Thomas Joyce." This provided Cary with enough incentive to resign from the Nigerian service. Cary worked hard on developing as a writer, but his brief economic success soon ended as the *Post* decided that his stories had become too "literary." He worked at various novels and a play, but nothing sold. Finally, in 1932, Cary managed to publish *Aissa Saved*, a novel that drew on his Nigerian experience. The book was not particularly successful, but sold more than the author's next novel *An American Visitor* (1933), even though that book had some critical success. His third novel *The African Witch* (1936) did a little better.

Although none of Cary's first three novels was particularly successful critically or financially, they are progressively more ambitious and complex. Indeed, *The African Witch* is so rich in incident, character and thematic possibility that it over-burdens its structure. Cary understood that he needed to find new ways to make the narrative form carry his ideas. *Mister Johnson* (1939) was written entirely in the present tense. Although now regarded as one of his best novels, it sold poorly at the time. Cary's early "African" novels—*Aissa Saved*, *An American Visitor*, *The African Witch* and *Mister Johnson*—show with shrewd sympathy the relations between Africans and their British administrators. Cary contemplated a trilogy of novels based on his Irish background. *Castle Corner* (1938) did not do well and Cary abandoned the idea. But *Charley Is My Darling* (1940), about displaced young people at the start of World War II, found a wider readership, and the memoir *A House of Children* (1941) won the James Tait Black

Memorial Prize for best novel.

Then Cary undertook his great works examining historical and social change in England during his own lifetime. The First Trilogy (1941 – 44) finally provided Cary with a reasonable income, and *The Horse's Mouth* (1944) remains his most popular novel. Cary's pamphlet "The Case for African Freedom" (1941), published by Orwell's Searchlight Books series, had attracted some interest, and the film director Thorold Dickinson (1903 – 1984) asked for Cary's help in developing a wartime movie set partly in Africa. In 1943, while writing *The Horse's Mouth*, Cary travelled to Africa with a film crew to work on *Men of Two Worlds* (1946). Cary travelled to India in 1946 on a second film project with Dickinson, but the struggle against the British for national independence made movie-making impossible, and the project was abandoned. *The Moonlight* (1946), a novel about the difficulties of women, ended a long period of intense creativity for Cary. *A Fearful Joy* was published in 1949. Cary was now at the height of his fame and fortune. He began preparing a series of prefatory notes for the re-publication of all his works in a standard edition published by Michael Joseph (1897 – 1958).

Cary also visited the United States, collaborated on a stage adaptation of *Mister Johnson*, and was offered a CBE, which he refused. Meanwhile he continued work on the three novels that make up the Second Trilogy (1952 – 55). In 1952, Cary had some muscle problems which resulted in a wasting and gradual paralysis. As his physical powers failed, Cary had to have a pen tied to his hand and his arm supported by a rope to write. Finally, he resorted to dictation until unable to speak, and ceased writing for the first time since 1912. His last work *The Captive and the Free* (1959), the first volume of a projected trilogy on religion, was left unfinished at his death.

35.2.10 Charles Percy Snow, Baron Snow (1905 – 1980)

C. P. Snow was an English physical chemist and novelist who also served in several important positions in the British Civil Service and briefly in the UK government. He is best known for his series of novels known collectively as *Strangers and Brothers*, and for *The Two Cultures*, a lecture in which he lamented the gulf between scientists and "literary intellectuals."

Snow's first novel *Death under Sail* (1932) was a detective story, which was followed by *New Lives for Old* (1933), and *The Search* (1934), which deals with the frustrations of a scientist's life. In 1975 he wrote a biography of Anthony Trollope (1815 – 1882). His *Strangers and Brothers* includes *The Light and the Dark* (1947), *Time of Hope* (1949), *The Masters* (1951), *The New Men* (1954), *Homecomings* (1956), *The Conscience of the Rich* (1958), *The Affair* (1959), *Corridors of Power* (1963), *The Sleep of Reason* (1968) and *Last Things* (1970). In these works Snow depicted intellectuals in academic and government settings in the modern era. The best-known of the sequence is *The Masters*, which deals with the internal politics of a Cambridge college as it prepares to elect a new master. Having all the appeal of an insider's view, the novel depicts concerns other than the strictly academic that influence the decisions of supposedly objective scholars. In 1974, Snow's novel *In Their Wisdom* (1974) was shortlisted for the Booker Prize. In *The Realists* (1978), an examination of the work of eight novelists—Stendhal, Balzac, Charles Dickens, Dostoevsky, Leo Tolstoy, Benito Pérez Galdós (1843 – 1920), Henry James and Marcel Proust—Snow made a robust defense of the realistic novel.

On 7 May 1959, Snow delivered an influential Rede Lecture called *The Two Cultures*, which provoked "widespread and heated debate." Subsequently published as *The Two Cultures and the Scientific Revolution*, the lecture argues that the breakdown of communication between the "two cultures" of modern society—the sciences and the humanities—is a major hindrance to solving the world's problems. For Snow, the quality of education in the world was on the decline. For example, many scientists have never read Charles Dickens, but artistic intellectuals are equally non-conversant with science. He specifically condemned the British educational system, as it had, since the Victorian period, over-rewarded the humanities (especially Latin and Greek) at the expense of scientific education. He believed that in practice this deprived British elites (in politics, administration and industry) of adequate preparation for managing the modern scientific world. By contrast, Snow said, German and American schools sought to prepare their citizens equally in the sciences and humanities, and better scientific teaching enabled the rulers of those countries to compete more effectively in a scientific age. Later discussion of *The Two Cultures* tended to obscure Snow's initial focus on differences between British systems (of both schooling and social class) and those of competing countries.

35.2.11 Anthony Dymoke Powell (1905–2000)

Anthony Powell was an English novelist best known for his twelve-volume work *A Dance to the Music of Time*, published between 1951 and 1975. His major work has remained in print continuously and has been the subject of TV and radio dramatizations. In 2008, *The Times* named Powell one of "the 50 greatest British writers since 1945."

Powell began publishing his literary works in the early 1930s. Such novels as *Afternoon Man* (1931), *Venusberg* (1932) and *From a View to a Death* (1933) are all good social satires. His ambitious work **A Dance to the Music of Time** consists of four trilogies that cover the 30-odd years' experiences of the protagonist's life. Likening life to a dance in which both meaningful rhythm and fickle whirling around occur at intervals, the series is essentially comic-tragic, indicating that tragedy inheres in comedy, and genuine anxiety and sorrow lie beneath a gracefully surface of humor and even playfulness. The first trilogy (1951–1955)—*A Question of Upbringing* (1951), *A Buyer's Market* (1952) and *The Acceptance World* (1955)—covers the protagonist Nicholas Jenkins' life from 1921 through the early 1930s. He is in school, goes through college, makes friends, falls in love and gets close to the leftist forces at the beginning of the 1930s. The second trilogy (1957–1962)—*At Lady Molly's* (1957), *Casanova's Chinese Restaurant* (1960) and *The Kindly Ones* (1962)—is about Jenkins' experiences in the rest of the decade of the 1930s: his emerging as a straggling novelist, his marriage to a girl of noble parentage and his young adulthood brought to conclusion by a combination of events such as the rise of Fascism, the Spanish Civil War, the abdication of King Edward VIII (1894–1972, king 1936) and the outbreak of WWII. The third trilogy (1964–1968)—*The Valley of Bones* (1964), *The Soldier's Art* (1966) and *The Military Philosophers* (1968)—relates the story of his six years' military service, and the last trilogy (1971–1975)—*Books Do Furnish a Room* (1971), *Temporary Kings* (1973) and *Hearing Secret Harmonies* (1975)—records his life after the war when he resumes his work as a novelist and meets his surviving friends. The war leaves behind a war-torn London and a Britain both happy and sad, more on the sad side perhaps in its elegiac mood.

The multi-volume fiction is noted for its rich gallery of people, over 200 in number, its bewitching plot interest, and its fascinating language with its numerous allusions and metaphors. No less impressive is its subtle balance between immediate involvement and attachment in judgment, and its biting social censure and satire. The books serve well as a social-historical record of the country or a fictional approximation of that exceptional phase of history. Though not strictly autobiographical, the work is heavily personal in nature as the author obviously wrote a good deal of himself into the history.

35.2.12　Elias Canetti (1905 – 1994)

Elias Canetti was a German language author, born in Bulgaria, and later a British citizen. He was a modernist novelist, playwright, memoirist and non-fiction writer. He won the Nobel Prize in Literature in 1981, "for writings marked by a broad outlook, a wealth of ideas and artistic power." He is known chiefly for his celebrated tetralogy of autobiographical memoirs of his childhood and of pre-Anschluss Vienna including *The Tongue Set Free* (1977, tr. 1979), *The Torch in My Ear* (1980, tr. 1982), *The Play of the Eyes* (1985, tr. 1990), and *The Secret Heart of the Clock* (1987, tr. 1989), for his modernist novel *Auto-da-Fé* (1935, tr. 1946), and for *Crowds and Power* (1960, tr. 1962), a study of crowd behavior as it manifests itself in human activities ranging from mob violence to religious congregations.

Chapter 36　Postwar Drama

The decades of the 1930s and 1940s were a dull and uninspired period for English drama. Its progress slowed down somehow after the success of Bernard Shaw's brilliant plays. The theater was either flooded with stereotyped social plays, or with some left-oriented and political dramas that were not well balanced in their thematic and artistic concerns; they reflected the formal aspect of the dramatic art. Although there were some experimental efforts in some small theaters, and some occasions to offer opportunities for new works to appear on stage, these did not get far in their endeavors. Thus the department of drama seemed again to lag a few steps behind the other literary divisions like poetry and fiction when the postwar era set in. However, it did not stay that way for long. The dramatic giant Samuel Beckett soon appeared and towered above his contemporaries. He helped revive English drama after Shaw with his amazing successes on the postwar stage. Beckett is considered the greatest exponent of the theater of the absurd. His uncompromisingly bleak, difficult plays (and novels) depict the lonely, alienated human condition with compassion and humor. Meanwhile, some other important, younger playwrights followed in his footsteps and pushed the theater further forward. There were Arnold Wesker, John Osborne, a chanticleer of some kind to his generation of writers, and Harold Pinter and Tom Stoppard, who were to pick up where the older dramatists left off and make headway in their unique fashion.

Absurdist plays explore the absurd nature of the human condition. The world that the drama of the absurd tries to delineate seems to be one in which God no longer smiles upon the humankind, and man is thrown back upon himself for survival. As a result, modern man feels an acute sense of futility and meaninglessness, and sees no light at the end of the tunnel. This is the basic factor that helps decide the tragic theme of the drama of the absurd. However, the absurd dramatists chose to present the sorry plight of man in a humorous vein, in the form of black comedy, so that people watch and laugh, then feel the pain and achieve a heightened awareness of the nature of their lives. Such plays are therefore often tragic-comedies. The 1950s and the first part of the 1960s was the period in which the drama of the absurd prospered as a fashion. It tapered off then and melted into the genre as an intrinsic part of its warp and woof. Latecomers such as Tom Stoppard tried to reinvent it, but then decided to change gears after a moderate degree of success in their absurdist endeavors. While Pinter and Stoppard, along with Beckett, are labeled under the umbrella of the theater of the absurd, Osborne and Wesker were more associated with kitchen sink drama, another major element of the postwar period, though they did have something in common with absurdist playwrights.

36.1 Samuel Barclay Beckett (1906 – 1989)

Samuel Beckett was an Irish expatriate avant-garde novelist, playwright, theatre director and poet, who lived in Paris for most of his adult life and wrote in both English and French. Many of Beckett's works were written in French and translated into English. He was one of the key writers in the "Theatre of the Absurd." His work became increasingly minimalist in his later career. Beckett was awarded the 1969 Nobel Prize in Literature "for his writing, which—in new forms for the novel and drama—in the destitution of modern man acquires its elevation." He is widely regarded as the most important post-Shaw playwright and one of the most influential writers of the 20th century.

Beckett was a monumental figure in postwar English theater. He was instrumental in revitalizing the fine dramatic traditions by bringing in an existentialist and absurdist element, and ushering in the era of the drama of the absurd in recent literary history. His works offer a bleak, tragicomic outlook on human nature, often coupled with black comedy and gallows humor. He was heavily influenced by James Joyce's Modernist experimentation and the French existentialist philosophy. He is considered one of the last Modernists. As an inspiration to many later writers, he is also sometimes considered one of the first Postmodernists. Within his long and productive career overarching half a century from the 1930s through the postwar period, he wrote works that are strongly suggestive of the two prominent literary phases—Modernism and Postmodernism, and this feature has helped make him a truly seminal figure in the literature of his century. The novels that he wrote in the 1930s, comic, mature and philosophical satires on social life, constitute part and parcel of the literary milieu of that age. As a playwright, Beckett helped bring the drama of the absurd into existence in the 1950s and 1960s. He is also well renowned for his daring formal experimentation.

Beckett was greatly concerned with the human condition. Through his experience in daily life and during WWII in particular, he learned about the nature of modern life and man's lot in the universe. He came to sense acutely the absurdity of human life and its purposelessness, and understand well the human dilemma in a basically Godless world. His basic thematic focus is to throw in relief modern man's rootlessness, want of identity, and hopelessness. The frustration, the agony, the spiritual dearth that people experience—all these generated a sense of urgency in Beckett to bring the problem to light in a form, every bit absurd as life itself, so that people would see the true nature of their condition better and do something about it. This was also probably the reason for the advent of the absurd drama as well as the absurd novel in the West of the 1960s.

Beckett stood in the forefront of the Absurd tradition. The basic tenor of his tone falls in step with the modern human experience that man's life seems to be all a cosmic joke. His protagonists are made out to be shiftless and effete creatures: such a character appears, for instance, in his "The End," in which the man finds it difficult either to live or die and so waits for death all day. They are clownish, often ridiculous in action and speech, pathetically obdurate in temperament, but they do not strike people as totally worthless and despicable. In this sense they reveal the basic plight of modern man's condition, of which many are unaware though already suffering in it. In a word, they are all existentialists of a kind trying to make sense of their senseless lives. They may embody the inquisitive, questing spirit of the intellectually thinking section of the humankind, never ready to settle for anything short of the absolute truth and certitude. They feel homeless, insecure and indecisive as to whether "to be or not to be." But they do not die; they just manage to hang on there with their incessant questioning. Their physical and spiritual bleakness is often indicated in a Beckett play by means of a bleak setting with little in the background except for a tree or a road, and there is little or no room for maneuver or any initiative for change. The plot is slim and its events are wanting in coherent or casual relationship. There is little activity of significance, yet often a good deal of talking that leads nowhere, and a good deal of questioning that gets no definitive answers. Yet the talking goes on, so does the questioning. Thus Beckett's drama exhibits a kind of symbolism too deep sometimes to fathom easily. They are often capable of more than one interpretation. Beckett helped break the back of the realistic tradition.

Becket's earliest works are generally considered to have been strongly influenced by James Joyce. They are erudite and seem to display the author's learning merely for its own sake, resulting in several obscure passages. The opening phrases of the short-story collection *More Pricks than Kicks* (1934) anticipate aspects of Beckett's later works: the physical inactivity of the character, the character's immersion in his own head and thoughts, and the somewhat irreverent comedy of the final sentence. Similar elements are present in his first published novel *Murphy* (1938), whose opening sentence hints at the somewhat pessimistic undertones and black humor that animate many of Beckett's works: "The sun shone, having no alternative, on the nothing new." *Watt* (1953), written while Beckett was in hiding in Roussillon during World War II, is similar in terms of themes but less exuberant in its style. It explores human movement as if it were a mathematical permutation, presaging Beckett's later preoccupation—in both his novels and dramatic works—with precise movement.

After World War II, Beckett turned definitively to the French language as a vehicle. It was this, together with the "revelation" experienced in his mother's room in Dublin (in which he realized that his art must be subjective and drawn wholly from his own inner world), that resulted in the works for which Beckett is best remembered today. In the 15 years after the war, Beckett produced four major full-length stage plays: *Waiting for Godot* (1954), *Endgame* (1957), whose original French version is *Fin de partie* (1957), *Krapp's Last Tape* (1959) and *Happy Days* (1961). These plays, which are often considered, rightly or wrongly, to have been instrumental in the so-called "Theatre of the Absurd," deal in a very blackly humorous way with themes similar to those of the roughly contemporary existentialist thinkers. Broadly speaking, the plays deal with the subject of despair and the will to survive in spite of that despair, in the face of an uncomprehending and incomprehensible world. The words of Nell—one of the two characters in *Endgame* who are trapped in ashbins, from which they occasionally peek their heads to speak—can best summarize the themes of the plays of Beckett's middle period: "Nothing is funnier than unhappiness, I grant you that. …Yes, yes, it's the most comical thing in the world. And we laugh, we laugh, with a will, in the beginning. But it's always the same thing. Yes, it's like the funny story we have heard too often, we still find it funny, but we don't laugh any more."

Beckett's outstanding achievements in prose during the period were the three novels *Molloy* (1955), whose original French version came out in 1951, *Malone Dies* (1956), whose original French version is *Malone meurt* (1951), and *The Unnamable* (1958), whose original French version is *L'innommable* (1953). In these novels—sometimes referred to as a "trilogy," though this is against the author's own explicit wishes—the prose becomes increasingly bare and stripped down. *Molloy*, for instance, still retains many of the characteristics of a conventional novel (time, place, movement and plot) and it makes use of the structure of a detective novel. In *Malone Dies*, movement and plot are largely dispensed with, though there is still some indication of place and the passage of time; the "action" of the book takes the form of an interior monologue. Finally, in *The Unnamable*, almost all sense of place and time are abolished, and the essential theme seems to be the conflict between the voice's drive to continue speaking so as to continue existing, and its almost equally strong urge towards silence and oblivion. Despite the widely held view that Beckett's works, as exemplified by the novels of this period, are essentially pessimistic, the will to live seems to win out in the end.

After these three novels, Beckett struggled for many years to produce a sustained work of prose, a struggle evidenced by *Stories and Texts for Nothing*, a collection of three short stories ("The Expelled," "The Calmative" and "The End," all written in 1946) and the thirteen short prose pieces he named "Texts for Nothing" (1950 – 1952). In the late 1950s, however, he created one of his most radical prose works, *Comment c'est* (1961), its English version *How It Is* published in 1964. This work relates the adventures of an unnamed narrator crawling through the mud while dragging a sack of canned food. It was written as a sequence of unpunctuated paragraphs in a style approaching telegraphese. *How It Is* is generally considered to mark the end of his middle period as a writer.

Throughout the 1960s and into the 1970s, Beckett's works exhibited an increasing tendency—already evident in much of his work of the 1950s—towards compactness. This has led to his works sometimes being described as minimalist. The extreme example of this, among his dramatic works, is the 1969 piece *Breath*, which lasts for only 35 seconds and has no characters. In his theatre of the late period, Beckett's characters—already few in number in the earlier plays—are whittled down to essential elements. The ironically titled *Play* (1962), for instance, consists of three characters immersed up to their necks in large funeral urns. The television drama *Eh Joe* (1966) is animated by a camera that steadily closes in to a tight focus upon the face of the title character. The play *Not I* (1973) consists almost solely of, in Beckett's words, "a moving mouth with the rest of the stage in darkness." Many of these later plays explore memory, often in the form of a forced recollection of haunting past events in a moment of stillness in the present. They also deal with the theme of the self confined and observed. Beckett's most politically charged play *Catastrophe* (1982) deals relatively explicitly with the idea of dictatorship. After a long period of inactivity, Beckett's poetry experienced a revival during this period in the ultra-terse French poems of *mirlitonnades*, with some as short as six words long. These defied Beckett's usual scrupulous concern to translate his work from its original into the other of his two languages; several writers have attempted translations, but no complete version of the sequence has been published in English. Among Beckett's numerous works, such novels as *Murphy*, *How It Is*, *Watt* and the trilogy *Molloy*, *Malone Dies* and *The Unnamable*, and the plays like *Waiting for Godot*, *Endgame* and *Krapp's Last Tape* are accepted as his major ones.

Waiting for Godot, the most famous of all Beckett's plays, was voted "the most significant English language play of the 20th century." It is Beckett's translation of his own original French version ***En attendant Godot*** (1952) and is subtitled (in English only) "a tragicomedy in two acts." In the play, two tramp characters Vladimir and Estragon wait endlessly and in vain for the arrival of a mysterious personage named Godot, while disputing the appointed place and hour of his coming. The work is thematically concerned with man's salvation through God's grace. There are strong biblical references throughout, but Beckett's powerful and symbolic portrayal of the human condition as one of ignorance, delusion, paralysis and intermittent flashes of human sympathy, hope and wit has been subjected to many varying interpretations since the play's 1953 premiere. The play consists of two acts. Its plot is slim enough. The two tramps come together and wait for Godot, though neither is sure whether they are doing the right thing. On one occasion they want to hang themselves, but decide to wait for Godot first. Then Pozzo comes up driving his servant Lucky; the tramps wrangle with Pozzo about his treatment of Lucky, but the subject gets nowhere eventually. Pozzo would sell Lucky. Lucky weeps but kicks Estragon when the latter helps wipe his tears. Estragon weeps. Pozzo complains about Lucky making life intolerable for him, and the tramps abuse Lucky for doing that. Pozzo philosophizes on the haphazard nature of life, is praised by the tramps, and orders Lucky to dance for them for their appreciation. Estragon mocks at Lucky's dance but fails to imitate it. Pozzo orders Lucky to think for the group, and Lucky comes up with incoherent words on God, Hell, sport and the suburbs and is silenced by the others who seize his hat. Pozzo and Lucky leave. Then a boy comes to say that Godot will come next morning. Estragon decides to leave barefoot, and the two separate for the night. When they meet again it is the following evening. The boots are still there. They talk of the day before, but cannot recall much. Then they think they hear voices of the dead around them and try to outspeak them. They remember talking nonsense yesterday and doing that for the past fifty years. They find the boots and Lucky's derby hat, and play exchanging hats for a while. Then Pozzo and Lucky appear again, with Pozzo blind, now dragged by a mute Lucky. The tramps want to help as members of the human race, but fall down while trying to raise Pozzo. They call Pozzo "all humanity," and suddenly get up without difficulty. Pozzo says that life is momentary and time does not matter, and then leaves with Lucky. Days and nights pass, the boy comes and goes with messages, Godot does not appear, and the tramps decide to hang themselves again if Godot does not come the next night. They end up saying where they are.

In terms of theme, *Waiting for Godot* depicts a world that goes through a phase of crisis of faith. Godot, the miniature of God in fact, never appears despite the long anxious waiting on the part of the tramps. No one is sure any more whether God still exists, and all are worried that He does not care any more about his creatures, even though He may be around somewhere. He has already shown his indifference to man's lot, feeling no love and compassion for humanity, or the need to communicate with it. He may have condemned the human species without good reason and have pushed it over to the abyss of agony and suffering. The play has been seen as the most effective of its kind as a drama of the absurd.

Waiting for Godot is devoid of either sense or action in the traditional sense of the terms. It seems to be a monstrous pile of nonsense, filled with a whole lot of "sound and fury," but "signifying nothing." A striking sense of absurdity and sterility keeps assailing the readers as well as the audience. Yet the nonsense that people read or hear is not entirely without its redeeming virtue: it amuses and, more importantly, forces people to think good and deep about the questions that keep popping up: why do these people behave the way they do? Don't they inhabit the same universe as we do? Then the sense of absurdity begins to break through, and the readers and the audience begin to relate to the absurdity of the existence of the characters. They begin to sense it existing in their own lives and realize the absurd nature of the human condition in general. In terms of action, although there is a lot of movement, there is little activity that makes sense or leads to any visible result. This indicates clearly the lack of sense and purpose in human existence.

36.2　Harold Pinter (1930 – 2008)

Harold Pinter was an English playwright, screenwriter, director and actor. He was one of the most gifted playwrights of the 1950s and 1960s and one of the most influential modern British dramatists. His writing career spanned more than 50 years. His best-known plays include *The Birthday Party* (1958), *The Caretaker* (1960), *The Homecoming* (1965) and *Betrayal* (1978), each of which he adapted for the screen. His screenplay adaptations of others' works include *The Servant* (1963), *The Go-Between* (1971), *The French Lieutenant's Woman* (1981), *The Trial* (1993) and *Sleuth* (2007). He also directed or acted in radio, stage, television and film productions of his own and others' works. Pinter was awarded the Nobel Prize in literature in 2005.

Pinter wrote prolifically on various subjects. His major plays such as *The Birthday Party*, *The Caretaker* and *The Homecoming* have all become classics. Thematically, Pinter was chiefly concerned with people's internal fabric of fears, desires, guilt and sexual drives that debilitate and jeopardize their chances of survival. His plots follow a general pattern: people live a well-ordered life, often within an enclosed space like a room, where they live as if they played games; then some outsider kicks in to break their external peace and offers a backdrop against which they splatter the complexities of their true inner landscape of negativity. Subsequently some violent mental battle ensues, truth is let out, and a psychic breakdown is experienced. This happens over and over in his works such as *The Room* (1957), *The Birthday Party*, *The Caretaker* and *The Homecoming*. Since the 1980s Pinter has switched gears and veered radically toward the political arena.

Pinter is noted for his superb stagecraft. For one thing, he was good at keeping his audience in suspense. *The Birthday Party*, for instance, includes such features as the fluidity and ambiguity of time, place and identity, and the disintegration of language. People are mystified by the identities of Stanley and the two visitors. Very little of the expository information in the play is verifiable; it is often contradicted by the characters and otherwise ambiguous, and, therefore, one cannot take what they say at face value. *The Homecoming*, where Max (the patriarch of the family) presents an exciting psychic enigma, is also a highly ambiguous, an enigmatic, and even a cryptic play. In the 1960s, when first encountering the play, its earliest critics complained that, like Pinter's other plays as perceived then, *The Homecoming* seemed, in their words, "plotless," "meaningless" and "emotionless" (lacking character motivation), and they found the play "puzzling"; later critics argue that the play evokes a multiplicity of potential meanings, leading to multiple interpretations. For another, Pinter's works are characterized by the effective use of irony. People say one thing and mean another. Their communication is in fact a miscommunication as the readers need to detect the truth between the lines and beneath the surface. The irony of his characters' lives lies in this, that they all seem contented and all right whereas the truth is just the opposite. Hence the need for a medium, in the form of an outsider, to externalize their inner texture. There is, in addition, Pinter's language to consider. Pinter was exceptionally good at using tricks such as pauses, silences and double entendres to convey the ironic aspect of people and life. He handled his dramatic language to help achieve his thematic purpose. For Pinter, the speech people hear indicates what is not heard and it is a cover-up of some kind for the true meaning, or in his words, "a constant stratagem to cover nakedness." He felt that the biggest game in drama was to uncover the naked truth about life and people.

The Birthday Party is Pinter's second full-length play and one of his best-known and most-frequently performed plays. Although its hostile London reception almost ended the author's playwriting career, the play is considered "a classic" and has been described by Martin Esslin (1918 – 2002) as an example of the Theatre of the Absurd. It is about Stanley Webber, a former piano player in his late thirties, who lives in a rundown boarding house, run by Meg and Petey Boles, in an English seaside town. Stanley eases himself comfortably into the company of his landlady Meg as her surrogate son. He is feeling fine with his routine manner of behavior, indulging in his fantasies, exchanging trivialities with his hosts and flirting a little with Meg. Now two men, Goldberg and McCann, suddenly appear at this rundown seaside home and pose a threat to Stanley's well established way of life. The outsiders seem to have been looking for Stanley. But Stanley feels that they have come to cart Meg off in a wheelbarrow. Then Lulu, a young woman in her twenties, comes into the midst of this group and flirts with the men. Meg holds a birthday party for Stanley, at which the two strangers try between them to torment Stanley mentally. Stanley behaves in an odd way, first beating a drum at a wild tempo and marching around the room, and then appearing in a game of the blindman's bluff. When the lights come back on, he appears, with his glasses broken, all over Lulu, who lies on a table. The next morning he comes out neatly dressed and expressionless. Then he is taken downstairs by the visitors and put in a waiting car. Before they leave for a healer, Meg's husband calls out to Stanley to stand up to them and not let them do with him as they please.

The play is rich enough to warrant multiple interpretations. Some see it as symbolic of human growth; others explain it away with the idea of art being encroached upon by worldliness; still others regard the intrusion of Goldberg and McCann as bodying forth of the shaping influence in the modern west—the Judaic-Christian faith, destroying Stanley's—modern man's—self-constructed life of complacency. In addition, there is also the notion that Staley may have been suffering from the agony of some childhood guilt and needs an outlet for his strenuous Oedipus impulse. The play leaves its audience often with a number of queries that need to be worked out after the curtain falls.

The Homecoming, probably Pinter's masterwork, is a two-act play written in 1964 and was first published in 1965. The original Broadway production won the 1967 Tony Award for Best Play. Its 40th-anniversary Broadway production at the Cort Theatre was nominated for a 2008 Tony Award for "Best Revival of a Play." Set in North London, the play has six characters. Five of these are men who are related to each other: Max, a retired butcher; his brother Sam, a chauffeur; and Max's three sons, including Teddy, an expatriate American philosophy professor, Lenny, who appears to be a pimp, and Joey, a would-be boxer in training who works in demolition. The only woman character is Teddy's wife Ruth. The play concerns Teddy and Ruth's "homecoming," which has distinctly different symbolic and thematic implications. Here the peace and stability of the home of men is jeopardized by the visiting woman Ruth. Max lives together with his brother Sam and his two sons, Lenny and Joey, in a shabby North

London house. Ruth comes with Teddy to visit her father-in-law's house and begins to interact with the males under the same roof. She is such a life force, with such a robust sexual and emotional energy, and proves herself to be such an enigma to them all that this thirty-year-old woman successfully jogs them all out of their set ways and brings them inside out. Her dominance is multiple. She exercises her emotional control over her father-in-law, her psychological power over the homosexually-oriented Lenny and her irresistible sexual appeal over the boxer Joey, the most physical of the three brothers. Max, the seventy-year-old, is shaken out of his patriarchal authority and his happy illusion about his happy past, and is reduced to an absolutely abject condition when he crawls over to Ruth for a kiss in the end. Even Uncle Sam feels impelled to come out with the truth about Max's wife—her promiscuity. Teddy, Ruth's intellectual husband, stands aloof and looks on when all the men seem to pay their advances to her. He even helps his brother Lenny arrange for her prostitution. Thus Ruth the outsider eventually comes out as the person in control and the hitherto "happy" household disappears. She does not go with her husband Teddy when he departs for the United States. She stays to be a prostitute for the family.

36.3　Sir Tom Stoppard (1937 –)

Tom Stoppard is a Czech-born British playwright and screenwriter, knighted in 1997. He has received one Academy Award and four Tony Awards. He has been a key playwright of the National Theatre and is one of the most internationally performed dramatists of his generation. He was sensitive to the profound influence of the tradition of the absurd drama of the older generation writers such as Samuel Beckett and Eugene Ionesco (1912 – 1994), and wrote to continue it in his own manner in the English theater. The play that made his name as an absurd dramatist was his comedy *Rosencrantz and Guildenstern Are Dead* (1967). It was the point at which he steadily climbed to the peak of his absurd dramatist career in the 1970s.

Stoppard has written prolifically for radio, screen and stage, finding prominence with plays such as *Rosencrantz and Guildenstern Are Dead*, *Every Good Boy Deserves Favor* (1977), *The Real Thing* (1982), *Arcadia* (1993), *Indian Ink* (1995), based on his 1991 radio play *In the Native State*, *The Invention of Love* (1997) and *The Coast of Utopia* (2002), and the television play *Professional Foul* (1977). *The Real Thing* examines the nature of honesty, and its use of a play within a play is one of many levels on which the author teases the audience with the difference between semblance and reality. *Arcadia* concerns the relationship between past and present, order and disorder, certainty and uncertainty. It has been acclaimed by many critics as Stoppard's masterpiece and as the finest play from one of the most significant contemporary playwrights in the English language. *The Invention of Love* portrays the life of poet A. E. Housman, focusing specifically on his personal life and love for a college classmate, and presents the sexual complexities of the Aesthetic movement and conflicts between art and scholarship. *The Coast of Utopia*, the recipient of the 2007 Tony Award for Best Play, is a trilogy of plays: *Voyage*, *Shipwreck* and *Salvage*. The trilogy focuses on the philosophical debates in pre-revolution Russia between 1833 and 1866. Stoppard's major screenplays include *Brazil* (1985), *The Russia House* (1990) and *Shakespeare in Love* (1998), which won seven Academy Awards, including Best Picture, Best Actress (Gwyneth Paltrow) and Best Supporting Actress (Judi Dench).

Stoppard came on the scene at a time when the absurdist drama had had its heyday. He is an iconoclast of his own kind. He is not merely to inherit and follow a great tradition. He sets out to reinvent it so as to give it a new lease of life. Basically absurdist, Stoppard differs from Beckett or Ionesco in his characterization and use of language. He re-creates characters. He borrows characters and plotlines from other writers like Shakespeare, Oscar Wilde and Beckett in a manner known as "travesty" and remakes his borrowings into distinct entities. His characters suffer from despair, but they do not always live on in total gloom. In formal terms, Stoppard deviates from the absurdist tendency to emphasize the deficiency of the communicative power of language in modern life. He stresses its importance to eloquence and cogent reasoning. He loves "language juggling." However, Stoppard's plays have been sometimes dismissed as pieces of clever showmanship, lacking in substance, social commitment, or emotional weight. His theatrical surfaces serve to conceal rather than reveal his views, and his fondness for towers of paradox spirals away from social comment. This is seen most clearly in his comedies *The Real Inspector Hound* (1968) and *After Magritte* (1970), which create their humor through highly formal devices of reframing and juxtaposition. Stoppard himself acknowledges that he started off "as a language nerd," primarily enjoying linguistic and ideological playfulness, feeling early in his career that journalism was far better suited for presaging political change than playwriting.

The accusations of favoring intellectuality over political commitment or commentary are met with a change of tack, as Stoppard produces increasingly socially engaged work. From 1977, he became personally involved with human rights issues, in particular with the situation of political dissidents in Central and Eastern Europe. Themes of human rights, censorship and political freedom now pervade Stoppard's works along with exploration of linguistics and philosophy. *Every Good Boy Deserves Favor*, inspired by a meeting with a Russian exile, is about a political dissident in a Soviet psychiatric hospital and criticizes the Soviet practice of treating political dissidence as a form of mental illness. This play as well as *Dogg's Hamlet, Cahoot's Macbeth* (1979), *The Coast of Utopia*, *Rock' n' Roll* (2006), and two works for television *Professional Foul* and *Squaring the Circle* (1984) all concern themes of censorship, rights abuses and state repression. Stoppard has his moral concerns for man. He does not like to leave man hanging over there in the absurdist void of modern existence. As he has faith in the human potential, man's perseverance and courage to face up to life's challenges, there is always room in his plays for vivacity and a good laugh even in the depths of despair. Stoppard's later works have sought greater inter-personal depths, whilst maintaining their intellectual playfulness. Stoppard acknowledges that he moved away from the "argumentative" works and more towards plays of the heart around 1982, as he became "less shy" about emotional openness. There lies the integration of heart and mind in his works. *The Real Thing* uses a meta-theatrical structure to explore the suffering that adultery can produce and *The Invention of Love* also investigates the pain of passion. *Arcadia* explores the meeting of chaos theory, historiography and landscape gardening. *The Coast of Utopia* is a trilogy of "human" plays.

Rosencrantz and Guildenstern Are Dead, a three-act play, is almost Stoppard's signature play, his first major play to gain recognition. The story of Shakespeare's *Hamlet*, as told from the viewpoint of two courtiers, echoes Beckett in its double act repartee, existential themes and language play. "Stoppardian" became a term describing works using wit and comedy while addressing philosophical concepts. The play established several characteristics of Stoppard's dramaturgy, including his word-playing intellectuality, his audacious, paradoxical and self-conscious theatricality, and his preference for reworking pre-existing narratives. The story is simple in plot. Two minor characters borrowed from *Hamlet*, Rosencrantz and Guildenstern, act as its protagonists. These Elizabethan courtiers are both fitted out with cloak, hat and stick, and a huge leather moneybag. Rosencrantz looks more or less like his comrade Guildenstern. It is difficult to distinguish one of them from the other. They are, however, different in temperament: Rosencrantz is dull, and Guildenstern philosophical. Guildenstern thinks about their destiny, and together they think why they have come there. Then they remember that they have been asked to go to the King's palace for reasons they do not know. They are waiting for somebody to come and tell them about it. While waiting the two play word games, or guess the sides of a coin and gamble a little. But they do not seem to be playing simply to kill time; they are doing so with a sense of urgency that indicates they are using the games as a way of avoiding something. Then the Tragedians come. These are a troupe of six traveling actors, including Alfred, a boy, the player, a horn player, a flutist and a man who moves the cart of props. The player is the spokesperson for the Tragedians; he is a man of few principles. The Tragedians are on their way to court where they are commissioned by Hamlet to act a play of his design. On seeing the two people, they perform for them just to make some money on the side (end of act one). In acts two and three Rosencrantz and Guildenstern go to court to play their parts there in the play. Both serve as Claudius' spies to find out why Hamlet behaves oddly. One of them pretends to be Hamlet so that the other can test him out for an answer to the king's query. Eventually they fall into Hamlet's trap and are condemned to die. At the end of the play, the Tragedians become the pirates, Hamlet escapes amidst the pirates' attack, but the two "spies" disappear, possibly for good.

In thematic terms, the play adumbrates an existentialist and absurdist world in which people seem to suffer from a severe debilitation in action and communication. Rosencrantz and Guildenstern, totally innocent, live in a world so sophisticated for them that they die without even knowing for what they die. In the original—Shakespeare's *Hamlet*—both Rosencrantz and Guildenstern are Hamlet's school friends. They are enlisted in King Claudius' service as spies without knowing what they are really doing. Stoppard apparently used their innocence to approximate modern man's rudderlessness in life. The two innocents play games to pass time, which is clearly inspired by Beckett's *Waiting for Godot*. Stoppard's innocents play meaningless games not so much for fun to kill time as for fending off their inner feelings of despair and doom. They act out their parts of their lives against the backdrop of a desert, or wilderness, painted in bleak expressionistic shapes, where there is no light, hope, nor anything close to salvation. They get involved in Hamlet's confrontation with Claudius, yet they do not know why they are, or what parts are assigned to them. They think they should be informed, but they are so "abandoned" (probably by God in the Godless world) that they get surprisingly little explanation at the end of the play (and for that matter, of their lives). Stoppard made a dexterous use of dislocation to achieve the play's superb comic effect. From his point of view, the sense of disjunction, between hope and fulfillment and the intensity of the anxiety that it generates, constitutes the basic causes for the innocents' pain, their absurd behavior, and the laughter their absurdity evokes among the audience. It is a kind of laughter very much in the nature of the black comedy, which produces an inevitable feeling of sadness at the characters' rootlessness, their having nowhere to belong and their falling into the quagmire of despond. Helpless and desperate in face of malicious odds, these abandoned individuals survive or die all depending on how they shift for themselves, with whatever resources at their disposal. These may include their companionship, mutual compassion, and the amount of sense of humor that they still have for self-mockery in order to keep their sanity. The play reveals Stoppard's consummate skill as a dramatist with which he presented a question of a profound metaphysical nature within the subtle framework of a comedy. Stoppard's ambition is to achieve what he calls "the perfect marriage between the play of ideas and farce or perhaps even high tragedy."

36.4 John James Osborne (1929 – 1994)

John Osborne was an English playwright, screenwriter, actor and critic of the Establishment. In a productive life of more than 40 years, Osborne wrote over twenty plays. He explored many themes and genres, writing for stage and screen. His personal life was extravagant and iconoclastic. He was notorious for the ornate violence of his language, not only on behalf of the political causes he supported but also against his own family, including his wives and children. Osborne's works transformed British theatre. He helped to make it artistically respected again, throwing off the formal constraints of the former generation and turning our attention once more to language, theatrical rhetoric and emotional intensity. He saw theatre as a weapon with which ordinary people could break down the class barriers. However, the works of his kind of authenticity and originality would remain the exception rather than the rule.

Osborne's first play *The Devil inside Him* (1950), a collaborative work, was written when he became involved as a stage manager and acting, joining Anthony Creighton's provincial touring company. His second play *Personal Enemy* (1955) was written with Anthony Creighton (1922 – 2005) (with whom he later wrote *Epitaph for George Dillon* staged at the Royal Court in 1958). *Personal Enemy* was staged in regional theatres before he submitted *Look Back in Anger*.

Look Back in Anger attracted mixed notices but a great deal of publicity. Having depicted an "angry young man" in the earlier play, Osborne wrote about an angry middle-aged man in his next work *The Entertainer* (1957), a three-act play, which is new and nontraditional. The play was first performed on 10 April 1957 at the Royal Court Theatre, London, and starred Laurence Olivier (1907 – 1989) as Archie Rice, a failing music-hall performer. It uses the metaphor of the dying music hall tradition and its eclipse by early rock and roll to comment on the moribund state of the British Empire and its eclipse by the power of the United States, something flagrantly revealed during the Suez Crisis of November 1956 that elliptically forms the backdrop to the play. An experimental piece, *The Entertainer* was interspersed with vaudeville performances. Following *The Entertainer* were *The World of Paul Slickey* (1959), a musical that satirizes the tabloid press, the unusual television documentary play *A Subject of Scandal and Concern* (1960), and the 1962 double bill *Plays for England*, consisting of "The Blood of the Bambergs" and "Under Plain Covers." *Luther*, depicting the life of Martin Luther, the archetypal rebel of an earlier century, was first performed in 1961; it transferred to Broadway and won Osborne a Tony Award. *Inadmissible Evidence* was first performed in 1964. In between these plays, Osborne won an Oscar for his 1963 adaptation of *Tom Jones*. *A Patriot for Me* (1965), drawing on the Austrian Redl case, is a tale of turn-of-the-century homosexuality and espionage which helped to end, along with *Saved* (1965) by Edward Bond (1934 –), the system of theatrical censorship under the Lord Chamberlain. Both *A Patriot for Me* and *The Hotel in Amsterdam* (1968) won Evening Standard Best Play of the Year awards. The latter play features three showbiz couples in a hotel suite, having fled a tyrannical and unpleasant movie producer, referred to as "K. L."

Osborne's plays in the 1970s chiefly include *West of Suez* (1971) which starred Ralph Richardson (1902 –

1983), *A Sense of Detachment* (1972), first produced at the Royal Court in 1972, and *Watch It Come Down* (1976), first produced at the National Theatre. In his later years, Osborne published two volumes of autobiography, *A Better Class of Person* (1981) and *Almost a Gentleman* (1991). *A Better Class of Person* was filmed by Thames TV in 1985. In 1999 the two volumes of autobiography were combined and published under the title "Looking Back—Never Explain, Never Apologize." He also collected various newspaper and magazine writings together in 1994 under the title *Damn You, England*. His last play is *Déjà Vu* (1991), a sequel to *Look Back in Anger*. Osborne is now well remembered for his plays like *Look Back in Anger*, *The Entertainer* and *Inadmissible Evidence*.

Osborne's famous play **Look back in Anger** catches and expresses the mood of his time so well, as *The Catcher in the Rye* (1951) by J. D. Salinger (1919 – 2010) and *Lord of the Flies* by William Golding do respectively for their time, that it has become a landmark of a kind in recent history. It gave rise to the epithet the "Angry Young Man" that has since labeled under its umbrella a number of characters in their works. The play was an immediate commercial success. It transferred to the West End and to Broadway, toured to Moscow and in 1958 a film version was released. It has long been in evidence in London, Paris and New York. It is a work of some power and permanence despite its clear social and political coloring. It turned Osborne from a struggling playwright into a wealthy and famous angry young man and won him the Evening Standard Drama Award as the most promising playwright of the year.

Look back in Anger is largely autobiographical, based on Osborne's time living and arguing with his first wife Pamela Lane in cramped accommodation in Derby. It concerns a love triangle involving an intelligent and educated but disaffected young man of working-class origin (Jimmy Porter), his upper-middle-class, impassive wife (Alison) and her haughty best friend (Helena Charles). It tells a simple but fascinating story. Jimmy has intellectual energy, lots of wit and fire, and an eloquent tongue. He feels unjustly placed in society. And he is angry. He is angry because his father, a man committed to a righteous cause, is left to die in misery. He is angry because he is placed at a disadvantage in his quest for a true and good life. And he is angry with the middle class from which his wife comes. He is up in protest. He lashes out at all that he thinks keeps putting him and people like him down. These include the old social order at large and his upper-middle-class wife Alison at home, and they hear the brunt of his cruel attacks. His friend Cliff Lewis, who stays with the Porters, is milder, more tolerant and a lot less vehement though he is also from similar humble origins. Alison is miserable, Cliff attempts to defend her and keep the peace, but Jimmy remains angry and restless. Helena steps in to cash on the situation. Cliff resents her maneuvering and moves out, and Helena advises Alison to stand up to Jimmy and leave him. Alison, now pregnant, walks out and loses her baby. Then, in utter misery, she comes back to ask Jimmy for forgiveness. Alison's father Colonel Redfern comes for Alison after he learns of the Porters' discord from Helena's telegraph, and finds that he likes his son-in-law. The Porters reconcile with each other, and Helena leaves in disappointment.

In terms of characterization, Jimmy Porter is impressive. Jimmy is a vibrant person, masculine, dynamic, caring, but capable of cruel verbal violence at people and things that he considers less than genuine. He yearns and strives for an authentic existence, dislikes sham morality intensely and loves to grapple with the quintessence of life. He is ever ready to help get rid of injustice and suffering for others as well as for himself. He is adamant as far as his stance on life goes. Jimmy is in a slightly altered sense Professor Higgins in George Bernard Shaw's play *Pyg-*

malion.

The play is symbolic. To begin with, there is the flat of the Porters, a prison cell of a space, confining and constraining, with little hope for an exit or a peek at the world outside. The room defines Jimmy's view of his wretched existence. The church bells that keep ringing when Jimmy is fuming at his injustice are a mild but insistent reminder that faith is more rewarding. There is also the reference to T. S. Eliot, the bad guy, the symbol of conservative values in religion, politics and literary creative endeavor, and to George Orwell, the good guy, emblematic of fellowship and community spirit. These embody the aspects of the values of Jimmy's generation.

36.5 Sir Arnold Wesker (1932 – 2016)

Arnold Wesker was a British dramatist known for his contributions to world drama. He was the author of fifty plays, four volumes of short stories, two volumes of essays, and other assorted writings. His plays have dealt with themes ranging from self-discovery, love, confronting death, political disillusion and much else, and have been translated into 20 different languages and performed worldwide.

Wesker left school at 16 and worked at various jobs before making his name as a playwright. His early plays—*The Kitchen* (1957), *Roots* (1958) and *Their Very Own and Golden City* (1966)—were staged by the English Stage Company at the Royal Court Theatre. His inspiration for *The Kitchen* came when he was working at the Bell Hotel in Norwich, Norfolk. *The Kitchen* first appeared at the Royal Court Theater and was later made into a film. It shows the stresses and conflicts of life behind the scenes in a restaurant, which culminate in tragedy; its use of the rhythms of working life is highly innovative and did much to stimulate the growth of what was to be known, though in a slightly different sense, as kitchen sink drama. *Roots* is also set in Norfolk. It is the second play in the Wesker Trilogy, the other two being *Chicken Soup with Barley* (1956) and *I'm Talking about Jerusalem* (1958). *Roots* focuses on Beatie Bryant as she makes the transition from an uneducated working-class woman obsessed with Ronnie, her unseen liberal boyfriend, to a woman who can express herself and the struggles of her time. It is written in the Norfolk dialect and considered to be another kitchen sink drama by Wesker. *Roots* was first presented at the Belgrade Theatre, Coventry in May 1959 before transferring to the Royal Court Theatre. *The Merchant* (1977), renamed "Shylock" by the author, is a retelling of Shakespeare's *The Merchant of Venice*. In this retelling, Shylock and Antonio are fast friends bound by a mutual love of books, culture and a disdain for the crass anti-semitism of the Christian community's laws. They make the bond in defiant mockery of the Christian establishment, never anticipating that the bond might become forfeit. When it does, the play argues, Shylock must carry through on the letter of the law or jeopardize the scant legal security of the entire Jewish community. He is, therefore, quite as grateful as Antonio when Portia, as in Shakespeare's play, shows the legal way out. The play received its American premiere on 16 November 1977 at New York's Plymouth Theatre. This production had a challenging history in previews on the road, culminating with the death of the exuberant Broadway star Zero Mostel (1915 – 1977), who was initially cast as Shylock. Wesker wrote a book titled *The Birth of Shylock and the Death of Zero Mostel* (1997) chronicling the entire process from initial submissions and rejections of the play through to rehearsals, Zero's death, and the disappointment of the critical reception for the Broadway opening. The book reveals much about the author's relationship to director John Dexter (1925 – 1990), who had been the earliest, near-familial interpreter of Wesker's works, to criticism, to casting, and to the ephemeral process of collaboration through which the text of any play must pass.

Wesker's other major plays include *Chips with Everything* (1962), a study of class attitudes in the RAF (Royal Air Force) during National Service, *The Four Seasons* (1965), which is about a love affair, *Their Very Own and Golden City* (1966) and *The Friends* (1970), both of which deal in different ways with the disappointment of political and social hope, *Caritas* (1981), which shows the spiritual anguish of a 14th-century anchoress who realizes she has mistaken her vocation, and *Annie Wobbler* (1984), one of several one-woman plays.

In 2005, Wesker published his first novel *Honey*, which recounts the experiences of Beatie Bryant, the heroine of his earlier play *Roots*. The novel broke from the previously established chronology. *Roots* was set in the early 1960s and Beatie is 22; in *Honey* she has only aged three years yet the action has been transplanted into the 1980s. Other oddities are that the timeframe includes the Rushdie affair and John Major's fall as recent events and yet the action is concerned with the dotcom boom.

In 2008 Arnold Wesker published his first collection of poetry *All Things Tire of Themselves*. The collection dates back many years and represents what he considered his best and most characteristic poems. Wesker was knighted in the 2006 New Year's Honors list. He was a patron of the Shakespeare Schools Festival, a charity that enabled school children across the UK to perform Shakespeare in professional theatres.

Exercises

I. Multiple choices

1. All the following poets may be classified as the Movement poets EXCEPT _____.
   A. Philip Larkin   B. Donald Davie
   C. Thom Gunn   D. W. H. Auden

2. It was _____, Philip Larkin's second collection of poems, that brought him to prominence.
   A. *The North Ship*   B. *The Less Deceived*
   C. *The Whitsun Weddings* D. *High Windows*

3. After relocating from England to San Francisco, Thom Gunn wrote about gay-related topics—particularly in his most famous work, _____—as well as drug use, sex and his bohemian lifestyle.
   A. *The Man with Night Sweats*   B. *Fighting Terms*
   C. *The Sense of Movement*   D. *My Sad Captains*

4. To read _____'s poetry is to enter a world dominated by nature, especially by animals.
   A. Philip Larkin   B. Seamus Heaney
   C. Ted Hughes   D. W. H. Auden

5. _____ was appointed Poet Laureate in 1984.
   A. Cecil Day-Lewis   B. Sir John Betjeman
   C. Ted Hughes   D. Alfred, Lord Tennyson

6. _____ was an Irish poet, playwright, translator and lecturer, and the recipient of the 1995 Nobel Prize in Literature.

A. Tony Harrison B. Seamus Heaney
C. Ted Hughes D. Geoffrey Hill

7. Along with Christopher Reid, _____ is the best-known exponent of Martian poetry or the Martians, after the title of his second volume of verse *A Martian Sends a Postcard Home*.

A. Tony Harrison B. Seamus Heaney
C. Ted Hughes D. Craig Raine

8. The epithet, "Angry Young Men," was originally a journalistic term used to describe a group of playwrights and novelists of the mid-1950s, but it has also come to refer loosely to the major _____ that these authors have created.

A. characters B. situations
C. stories D. themes

9. As a novelist, Kingsley Amis was a leading figure of the "_____," and as a poet, he was considered to be one important member of the Movement poetry coterie.

A. Black Humor B. Angry Young Men
C. Beat Generation D. the Martians

10. _____ is perhaps Kingsley Amis' most famous novel, satirizing the high-brow academic set of an unnamed university, seen through the eyes of its protagonist, as he tries to make his way as a young lecturer of history.

A. *That Uncertain Feeling* B. *I Like It Here*
C. *Lucky Jim* D. *The Anti-Death League*

11. _____, like Kingsley Amis and Philip Larkin, was associated with both the Movement poetry and the "Angry Young Men."

A. John Wain B. Seamus Heaney
C. Alan Sillitoe D. Ted Hughes

12. _____, the tale of a young boy dealing with the death of loved ones, is probably John Wain's most tragic novel.

A. *Hurry on Down* B. *Strike the Father Dead*
C. *Young Shoulders* D. *The Pardoner's Tale*

13. In 2008, to mark Alan Sillitoe's 80th birthday, London Books republished _____ as part of its London Classics series.

A. *Life without Armor* B. *The Loneliness of the Long Distance Runner*
C. *A Start in Life* D. *Saturday Night and Sunday Morning*

14. _____ is Alan Sillitoe's first and best novel.

A. *Life without Armor* B. *The Loneliness of the Long Distance Runner*
C. *A Start in Life* D. *Saturday Night and Sunday Morning*

15. Lawrence Durrell's tetralogy *Alexandria Quartet* consists of _____, *Balthazar*, *Mountolive* and *Clea*.

A. *Panic Spring* B. *Justine*

C. *The Black Book*   D. *Pied Piper of Lovers*

16. William Golding is best known for his first novel _____, which established him as a rising star on the scene and paved the way for him to win the Nobel Prize for literature in 1983.

    A. *Rites of Passage*   B. *Free Fall*

    C. *Lord of the Flies*   D. *The Spire*

17. In 1980 William Golding was awarded the Booker Prize for literature for his novel _____, the first book of his sea trilogy *To the Ends of the Earth*, the other two of which are *Close Quarters* and *Fire down Below*.

    A. *Rites of Passage*   B. *Free Fall*

    C. *Lord of the Flies*   D. *The Spire*

18. The following works are all Doris Lessing's EXCEPT _____.

    A. *The Grass is Singing*   B. *The Golden Notebook*

    C. *Canopus in Argos: Archives*   D. *Saturday Night and Sunday Morning*

19. Doris Lessing's best-known work _____ is the longest and the most ambitious work the author has ever attempted to write.

    A. *The Grass is Singing*   B. *The Golden Notebook*

    C. *Canopus in Argos: Archives*   D. *Saturday Night and Sunday Morning*

20. V. S. Naipaul is known for his early comic novels set in _____, his later bleaker novels of the wider world, and his autobiographical chronicles of life and travels.

    A. England   B. America

    C. Trinidad   D. Africa

21. _____, winner for Booker Prize, explores problems of nationality and identity through three linked narratives.

    A. *In a Free State*   B. *An Area of Darkness*

    C. *The Mimic Men*   D. *Guerrillas*

22. Although Anthony Burgess was predominantly a comic writer, his dystopian satire _____ remains his best-known novel.

    A. *A Clockwork Orange*   B. *Earthly Powers*

    C. *M/F*   D. *Nothing like the Sun*

23. Anthony Burgess' _____ is regarded by most critics as his greatest novel.

    A. *A Clockwork Orange*   B. *Earthly Powers*

    C. *M/F*   D. *Nothing like the Sun*

24. C. P. Snow is best known for his series of novels known collectively as *Strangers and Brothers*, and for _____, a 1959 lecture in which he lamented the gulf between scientists and "literary intellectuals."

    A. *Death under Sail*   B. *In Their Wisdom*

    C. *The Realists*   D. *The Two Cultures*

25. Although critics have seen his formal experiments in different ways, John Fowles has been, in a very serious sense, regarded as a _____ novelist.

Part Nine The Postwar Period

   A. romantic
   B. realist
   C. postmodernist
   D. modernist

26. John Fowles' major novels include *The Collector*, *The Magus*, _____, *The Ebony Tower* and *Mantissa*.
   A. *The French Lieutenant's Woman*
   B. *Lord of the Flies*
   C. *Saturday Night and Sunday Morning*
   D. *Lucky Jim*

27. _____, who wrote many of his works in French and translated them into English, is considered the greatest exponent of the theater of the absurd.
   A. Kingsley Amis
   B. William Golding
   C. V. S. Naipaul
   D. Samuel Beckett

28. _____ is set in a lay religious community established by the middle-aged Michael Meade at his ancestral estate, Imber Court, close to the Imber Abbey of which Mother Clare is the Abbess.
   A. *The Sea, the Sea*
   B. *The Bell*
   C. *The Black Prince*
   D. *The Unicorn*

29. _____, translated into more than ten languages, established John Fowles' international reputation.
   A. *The French Lieutenant's Woman*
   B. *Lord of the Flies*
   C. *Saturday Night and Sunday Morning*
   D. *Lucky Jim*

30. Joyce Cary's first trilogy (1941–44) consists of _____, *To Be a Pilgrim* and *The Horse's Mouth*.
   A. *The African Witch*
   B. *Mister Johnson*
   C. *Herself Surprised*
   D. *Prisoner of Grace*

31. Anthony Powell is best known for his twelve-volume work _____, published between 1951 and 1975.
   A. *At Lady Molly's*
   B. *A Buyer's Market*
   C. *A Dance to the Music of Time*
   D. *From a View to a Death*

32. As a playwright, _____ helped bring the drama of the absurd into existence in the 1950s and 1960s, and has been regarded as the most important post-Shaw playwright in recent literary history.
   A. Tom Stoppard
   B. Samuel Beckett
   C. John Osborne
   D. V. S. Naipaul

33. Samuel Beckett's outstanding achievements in prose during the middle period of his literary career were the three novels _____, *Malone Dies* and *The Unnamable*, sometimes referred to as a "trilogy," though this is against the author's own explicit wishes.
   A. *Waiting for Godot*
   B. *Endgame*
   C. *Krapp's Last Tape*
   D. *Molloy*

34. Having depicted an "angry young man" in *Look Back in Anger*, John Osborne wrote about an angry middle-aged man in his next work _____, a three-act play.
   A. *Luther*
   B. *The Entertainer*
   C. *Inadmissible Evidence*
   D. *A Patriot for Me*

35. John Osborne won an Oscar for his 1963 adaptation of _____.
   A. *Tom Jones*
   B. *Damn You, England*

C. *The Hotel in Amsterdam*　　　　　　D. *Look Back in Anger*

36. _____ is largely autobiographical, based on John Osborne's time living and arguing with his first wife Pamela Lane in cramped accommodation in Derby.

A. *A Patriot for Me*　　　　　　B. *Damn You, England*

C. *The Entertainer*　　　　　　D. *Look Back in Anger*

37. Harold Pinter's best-known plays include *The Birthday Party*, _____ and *Betrayal*, each of which he adapted for the screen.

A. *Waiting for Godot*　　　　　　B. *The Homecoming*

C. *Rosencrantz and Guildenstern Are Dead*　　　　　　D. *Look Back in Anger*

38. *The Homecoming*, probably _____ 's masterwork, is a two-act play written in 1964 and was first published in 1965.

A. Harold Pinter　　　　　　B. John Osborne

C. Samuel Beckett　　　　　　D. Tom Stoppard

39. The play that made Tom Stoppard's name as an absurd dramatist was his comedy _____.

A. *Arcadia*　　　　　　B. *The Coast of Utopia*

C. *The Invention of Love*　　　　　　D. *Rosencrantz and Guildenstern Are Dead*

40. _____ was the point at which Tom Stoppard steadily climbed to the peak of his absurd dramatist career in the 1970s.

A. *Arcadia*　　　　　　B. *The Coast of Utopia*

C. *The Invention of Love*　　　　　　D. *Rosencrantz and Guildenstern Are Dead*

41. _____, almost Tom Stoppard's signature work, is a three-act play about the story of Shakespeare's *Hamlet*, told from the viewpoint of two courtiers.

A. *Every Good Boy Deserves Favor*　　　　　　B. *The Real Thing*

C. *Rosencrantz and Guildenstern Are Dead*　　　　　　D. *Shakespeare in Love*

42. _____, *I'm Talking about Jerusalem* and *Chicken Soup with Barley* are now grouped as the Wesker Trilogy.

A. *Their Very Own and Golden City*　　　　　　B. *Roots*

C. *The Kitchen*　　　　　　D. *The Merchant*

II. Blank-filling

1. Although Thom Gunn kept his traditional meters and rhymes, his subjects, his diction, and his vision of life and man revealed clear _____ features.

2. Geoffrey Hill wrote to reveal the extent of human suffering and the evil of the _____.

3. In subject and attitude, Tony Harrison is a _____ poet, demotic and subversive.

4. A dominant thematic concern for Seamus Heaney is to find "a door into the dark" which is good enough for the redemption of all humans as well as himself. He seemed to have found it in what he called "_____."

5. James Fenton's poetry is often "_____," telling a story in a compressed way, and presents facts but refuses to moralize; Fenton would like the readers to digest those facts alone.

Part Nine The Postwar Period

6. Among the writers of the "Angry Young Men," Alan Sillitoe stood out as particularly unique in his thematic focus. He wrote exclusively about the life of his class, the _____.

7. The first three novels of *Alexandria Quartet* tell essentially the same story but from different perspectives, a technique Lawrence Durrell described in his introductory note in *Balthazar* as "_____."

8. William Golding's theme is the dark side or evil of _____, which is adequately illustrated by *Lord of the Flies*.

9. William Golding preferred his story to be called "_____," a veiled story about the truth of human existence.

10. *The Golden Notebook* reads like a novelist writing about a novelist, with stories within the story and novels within the novel. Each of the notebooks is divided into four sections, the last of which forms part of the major portion of the book, and the major portion is prefaced with a "_____" section.

11. _____ is set in the Victorian England and its protagonist Charles Smithson is a true-to-form Victorian gentleman, expecting to inherit a title and wealth from his uncle and get married to a rich young lady Ernestina Freeman.

12. _____, a Postmodernist form of writing about fiction in the form of fiction, is a style of fictive narrative that tries to tell the readers that fiction is fiction and is not an illusion of reality as the realists have tried to "deceive" the readers into believing.

13. _____ was to help revive English drama after Bernard Shaw with his amazing successes on the postwar stage.

14. C. P. Snow is best known for his series of novels known collectively as *Strangers and Brothers*, and for _____, a 1959 lecture in which he laments the gulf between scientists and "literary intellectuals."

15. John Osborne's play _____ gave rise to the epithet the "Angry Young Men" that has since labeled under its umbrella a number of characters in their works.

16. Thematically, Harold Pinter was chiefly concerned with people's internal fabric of fears, desires, guilt and sexual drives that debilitate and jeopardize their chances of _____.

17. Harold Pinter's plots follow a general pattern: people live a well-ordered life, often within an enclosed space like a room, where they live as if they played games, and then some outsider kicks in to break their external peace and offers a backdrop against which they splatter the complexities of their true inner landscape of _____.

18. "_____" became a term describing works using wit and comedy while addressing philosophical concepts.

III. Term definition

1. Academy Awards
2. Angry Young Men
3. Black comedy
4. Gallows humor
5. Golden PEN Award
6. James Tait Black Memorial Prizes
7. Kitchen sink drama
8. Man Booker Prize for Fiction
9. Martian poetry or the Martians
10. Metafiction
11. The Movement Poetry
12. Theater of the Absurd

IV. Short-answer questions

1. What are the writing features of Philip Larkin's poetry?
2. What are the writing features of Donald Davie's poetry?
3. What are the thematic concerns in Seamus Heaney's poetry?
4. What are the writing features of Iris Murdoch's novels?
5. *The French Lieutenant's Woman* is a typical example of metafiction. Why?
6. What are the writing features in Samuel Beckett's works?
7. What are the writing features in Tom Stoppard's plays?

V. Essay questions

1. Discuss about both the theme and style in Tony Harrison's poetry.
2. Analyze Craig Raine's "The Onion, Memory" from the perspectives of theme and art form.
3. Give an account of Kingsley Amis' literary career.
4. Give a brief introduction to *Lucky Jim*.
5. Comment on Lawrence Durrell's *Alexandria Quartet* from the thematic and formal perspectives.
6. Comment on William Golding's *Lord of the Flies* from the perspectives of themes and writing techniques.
7. Comment on Doris Lessing's *The Golden Notebook* from the perspectives of content, theme, characterization and structure.
8. Comment on Iris Murdoch's *The Bell* from the perspectives of theme and characterization.
9. Comment on Samuel Beckett's *Waiting for Godot* from the perspectives of theme and sense.
10. Give a brief introduction to *The Birthday Party*.

Glossary

Academy Awards（美国奥斯卡电影金像奖）

The Academy Awards or the Oscars (the official title was rebranded as "the Oscars" in 2013, changed from "the Academy Awards") is an annual American awards ceremony honoring cinematic achievements in the film industry and widely considered to be the most prestigious cinema awards ceremony in the world. The various category winners are awarded a copy of a statuette, officially the Academy Award of Merit, which is better known by its nickname Oscar. The awards, first presented in 1929 at the Hollywood Roosevelt Hotel, are overseen by the Academy of Motion Picture Arts and Sciences (AMPAS). The awards ceremony was first broadcast to radio in 1930 and televised in 1953. It is now seen live in more than 200 countries.

The Oscars is the oldest entertainment awards ceremony; its equivalents, the Emmy Awards for television, the Tony Awards for theatre, and the Grammy Awards for music and recording, are modeled after the Academy Awards. Historically given during the first quarter of a new year, the Oscars honor achievements for cinematic accomplishments for the preceding year. The 88th Academy Awards ceremony was held at the Dolby Theatre in Los Angeles on February 28, 2016. A total of 2,947 Oscars have been awarded since the inception of the award through the 87th.

Aestheticism（唯美主义）

Aestheticism or the Aesthetic Movement was a European phenomenon during the latter 19th century that had its chief headquarters in France. In opposition to the dominance of scientific thinking, and in defiance of the widespread indifference or hostility of the middle-class society of their time to any art that was not useful or did not teach moral values, French writers developed the view that a work of art is the supreme value among human products precisely because it is self-sufficient and has no use or moral aim outside its own being. The end of a work of art is simply to exist in its formal perfection, that is, to be beautiful and to be contemplated as an end in itself. A rallying cry of Aestheticism became the phrase "art for art's sake."

The historical roots of Aestheticism are in the views proposed by the German philosopher Immanuel Kant in his *Critique of Judgment* (1790) that the "pure" aesthetic experience consists of a "disinterested" contemplation of an object that "pleases for its own sake," without reference to reality or to the "external" ends of utility or morality. As a self-conscious movement, however, French Aestheticism is often said to date from the witty defense of Theophile Gautier (1811 – 1872) of his assertion that art is useless. Aestheticism was developed by Baudelaire, who was greatly influenced by Edgar Allan Poe's claim in "The Poetic Principle" (1850) that the supreme work is a "poem *per se*," a "poem written solely for the poem's sake"; it was later taken up by Flaubert, Mallarme (1842 – 1898) and many other writers. In its extreme form, the aesthetic doctrine of art for art's sake veered into the moral and quasi-religious doctrine of life for art's sake, with the artist represented as a priest who renounces the practical concerns of ordinary existence in the service of what Flaubert and others called "the religion of beauty."

The views of French Aestheticism were introduced into the Victorian England by Walter Pater, with his emphasis on high artifice and stylistic subtlety, his recommendation to crowd one's life with exquisite sensations, and his advocacy of the supreme value of beauty and of "the love of art for its own sake." The artistic and moral views of Aestheticism were also expressed by Algernon Charles Swinburne and by the writers of the 1890s such as Oscar Wilde, Arthur Symons and Lionel Johnson, and by the artists like J. M. Whistler (1834 – 1903) and Aubrey Beardsley (1872 – 1898). The influence of ideas stressed in Aestheticism—especially the view of the "autonomy" (self-sufficiency) of a work of art, the emphasis on craft and artistry, and the concept of a poem or novel as an end in itself and as invested with "intrinsic" values—has been important in the writings of prominent 20th-century authors like W. B. Yeats, T. E. Hulme (1883 – 1917) and T. S. Eliot, and in the literary theory of the New Critics.

Alexandrine（亚历山大诗行）

An Alexandrine is an iambic line of six feet with a pause after the first three feet or in the middle of the line. It is common in the German literature of the Baroque period and in the French poetry of the early modern and modern periods. In English it is used as the last line of the Spenserian stanza or as a variant in a poem of heroic couplets, rarely in a whole work. However, the English drama often used the Alexandrine before Christopher Marlowe and William Shakespeare, who replaced it with iambic pentameter. The name is derived from the fact that certain French poems in the 12th and 13th centuries on Alexander the Great were written in this meter. In non-Anglo-Saxon or French contexts, the term dodecasyllable is often used.

Allegory（寓言）

An allegory is a narrative, whether in prose or verse, in which the agents and actions, and sometimes the setting as well, are contrived by the author to make coherent sense on the "literal," or primary, level of signification, and at the same time to signify a second, correlated order of signification.

Allegories can be classified into two main types: a) historical and political allegory, in which the characters and actions that are signified literally in their turn represent, or "allegorize," historical personages and events; b) the allegory of ideas, in which the literal characters represent concepts and the plot allegorizes an abstract doctrine or thesis. Both types of allegory may either be sustained throughout a work, or else serve merely as an episode in a non-allegorical work. In the second type, the sustained allegory of ideas, the central device is the personification of abstract entities such as virtues, vices, states of mind, moods of life, and types of character. In explicit allegories, such reference is specified by the names given to characters and places.

Alliteration（头韵）

Alliteration is the repetition of a speech sound in a sequence of nearby words. The term is usually applied only to consonants and only when the recurrent sound begins a word or a stressed syllable within a word. In Old English alliterative meter, alliteration is the principal organizing device of the verse line: the verse is unrhymed; each line is divided into two half-lines of two strong stresses by a decisive pause; and at least one, and usually both, of the two stressed syllables in the first half-line alliterate with the first stressed syllable of the second half-line. In later English versification, however, alliteration is used only for special stylistic effects, such as to reinforce the meaning, to link related words, or to provide tone color and enhance the palpability of enunciating the words.

Allusion（典故）

An allusion is a passing reference, without explicit identification, to a literary or historical person, place or event, or to another literary work or passage. A literary allusion puts the alluded text in a new context under which it assumes new meanings and denotations. Although an allusion is used to link concepts that the reader already has knowledge of, with concepts discussed in the story, it is not possible to predetermine the nature of all the new meanings and inter-textual patterns that it will generate. Nevertheless, an allusion is bound up with a vital and perennial topic in literary theory, the place of authorial intention in interpretation. Most allusions serve to illustrate or expand upon or enhance a subject, but some are used to undercut it ironically by the discrepancy between the subject and the allusion.

Angry Young Men, the（愤怒的青年）

The epithet "Angry Young Men" is originally a journalistic catchphrase loosely applied to a group of mostly working- and middle-class British playwrights and novelists, who became prominent in the 1950s. The leading members include Kinsley Amis, John Osborne, Alan Sillitoe and Colin Wilson, whose political views were radical or anarchic, and who described various forms of social alienation. Although it is sometimes said to derive from the title of the work *Angry Young Man* by the Irish writer Leslie Paul, the term came to be widely used only after the publication of John Osborne's play *Look Back in Anger* in 1957, which gives manifest expression to the disaffection of the postwar generation.

The young writers under the label of "Angry Young Men," very often "scholarship boys," were the rising members of the lower middle class. They were normally iconoclastic and against established standards. Ambitious and disillusioned, they lashed out against contemporary society. In formal terms they were in revolt against the high literary ideals of Modernism and wrote in a deliberately vulgar, comic and satirical vein. They created characters that represented their radical, parochial attitudes. These characters have also come to be labeled "Angry Young Men." They mainly include Kingsley Amis' Jim Dixon in *Lucky Jim*, William Cooper's Joe Lunn in *Scenes from Provincial Life* and John Gerald Braine's Joe Lampton in *Room at the Top*. John Wain was also connected with this group. John Osborne's Jimmy Porter in his play *Look Back in Anger*, Alan Sillitoe's Arthur Seaton in his novel *Saturday Night and Sunday Morning* and Philip Larkin's John Kemp in his *Jill*, all from the working class, fit well in here, too.

The term began to have less meaning over the years as the writers to whom it was originally applied became more divergent, and many of them dismissed the label as useless.

Antimasque（[带面具的] 滑稽戏）

An antimasque (also spelled anti-masque), a form developed by Ben Jonson and later evolving into a farce or pantomime, is a spectacle of disorder which usually starts or precedes a masque. In the antimasque the characters are grotesque and unruly, the action ludicrous, and the humor broad; it serves as a foil and countertype to the elegance, order and ceremony of the masque proper, and is characterized by impropriety and transformed by the masque into goodness, propriety and order, typically by the King's presence alone. The antimasque was also contrasted with the masque by the use of the lower class as characters. This then was supposed to harmonize with the king and the higher class.

Arthurian Legend（亚瑟王传奇）

Arthurian legend is a group of stories in several languages that developed in the Middle Ages concerning Arthur, semi-historical king of the Britons, and his knights. The legend intricately weaves the ancient Celtic mythology with later traditions around a core of possible historical authenticity. The earliest references to Arthur are found in Welsh sources. The earliest continuous Arthurian-narrative is in *History of the Britons* by the English writer Geoffrey of Monmouth. Here Arthur is identified as the son of the British King Uther Pendragon, and his counselor Merlin is introduced. All later developments of the Arthurian legend are based on Geoffrey's work. An Arthurian tradition also developed in Europe. By 1100 Arthurian romances were known as far away as in Italy. Inspired by chivalry and courtly love, they are more concerned with the exploits of Arthur's knights than with Arthur himself. English Arthurian romances, dating from the 13th and 14th centuries, are concerned with individual knights: Percival and Galahad, the Grail Knights and especially Gawain. The culminating masterpiece of these is the anonymously written *Sir Gawain and the Green Knight*.

Assonance（元韵/类韵）

Assonance is the repetition of similar vowel sounds—especially in stressed syllables—in a sequence of nearby words. It has been an optional poetic device used within and between lines of verse for emphasis or musical effect. Note the recurrent long *i* in the opening lines of Keats' "Ode on a Grecian Urn":

   Thou still unravished br*i*de of qu*i*etness,

   Thou foster ch*i*ld of s*i*lence and slow t*i*me…

Auden Group, the（奥登一族）

The Auden Group is the name given to a group of British and Irish writers active in the 1930s, including W. H. Auden, Louis MacNeice, Cecil Day-Lewis, Stephen Spender, Christopher Isherwood, and sometimes Edward Upward and Rex Warner. They were sometimes called simply the Thirties poets. They also got the nickname "Mac-

Spaunday," which was invented by Roy Campbell in his *Talking Bronco* (1946) after the chief members—MacNeice, Spender, Auden and Day-lewis.

The Auden Group was not a group or a movement in the sense of being organized as such. It became first known through the two anthologies edited by Michael Roberts—*New Signatures* and *New Country: Prose and Poetry by the Authors of New Signatures*, whose emphasis was on the newness of the writers included. Although many newspaper articles and a few books appeared about the Auden Group, the existence of the group was essentially a journalistic myth, a convenient label for poets and novelists who were approximately the same age, who had been educated at Oxford and Cambridge, who had known each other at different times and had more or less left-wing views ranging from MacNeice's political skepticism to Upward's committed communism. These poets not only shared basically the same kind of experience but also went through roughly the same process of growth. They began with the Modernists, some Romantics and probably D. H. Lawrence very much in their minds, and moved to embrace the socially and politically engaged verse that was largely written for the consumption of the working class, then felt disappointed and disillusioned, and moved on to a new phase at the end of the decade. It was a generation of divided allegiances and consciences, sore in midst of a tug of war between the forces pulling them in two directions of writing in the service of society versus writing in the private mode.

The poets of this group were brilliant and anxious young men with a huge sense of mission to help change their society. All of them were acutely self-conscious that they had insights to offer. Although working on their own, the group shared the notion of writing poetry about different subjects in different ways from the first-generation Modernists. They would like to take poetry out of the hands of an elite readership to the masses and move it out of the obscurity into which the Modernist artifice of ellipsis, paratactic syntax and learned allusions had thrown it. They used ordinary speech to write a poetry that verged on propaganda and placed their art at the service of a new life. Their separate efforts were concerted by the emerging influence of W. H. Auden, from whom all the rest of the group received inspiration and learned to write.

Augustan age, the (奥古斯都时代)

The Augustan age is a term derived from the period of literary eminence under the Roman Emperor Augustus (27 BC – AD 14) during which Virgil, Horace and Ovid flourished. In English literature it is generally taken to refer to the early and mid-18th century, though the earliest usages date back to the reign of Charles II. The age is a literary epoch that featured the rapid development of the novel, an explosion in satire, the mutation of drama from political satire into melodrama, and an evolution toward poetry of personal exploration. Augustan writers such as Alexander Pope, Joseph Addison, Jonathan Swift and Richard Steele greatly admired their Roman counterparts, imitated their works, and themselves frequently drew parallels between the two ages. In philosophy, it was an age increasingly dominated by empiricism, while in the writings of political-economy it marked the evolution of mercantilism as a formal philosophy, the development of capitalism and the triumph of trade.

Ballad (民谣)

Ballads are anonymous narrative songs that have been preserved by oral transmission. They originate and are communicated among illiterate or only partly literate people. In all probability the initial version of a ballad was composed by a single author, but he or she is unknown; and since each singer who learns and repeats an oral ballad is apt to introduce changes in both the text and the tune, it exists in many variant forms. Typically, the popular ballad is dramatic, condensed and impersonal: the narrator begins with the climatic episode, tells the story tersely by means of action and dialogue (sometimes by means of the dialogue alone), and tells it without self-reference or the expression of personal attitudes or feelings. Although many traditional ballads probably originated in the later Middle Ages, they were not collected and printed until the 18th century, first in England, then in Germany.

Many ballads employ set formulas (which help the singer remember the course of the song) including a) stock descriptive phrases like "blood-red wine" and "milk-white steed," b) a refrain in each stanza, and c) incremental repetition, in which a line or stanza is repeated, but with an addition that advances the story.

Bildungsroman (教育小说/成长小说)

The term was coined in 1819, legitimized in 1870 and popularized in 1905. The birth of the *Bildungsroman* is normally dated to the publication of *Wilhelm Meister's Apprenticeship* by Johann Wolfgang Goethe in 1795 – 1796. Although it arose in Germany, the *Bildungsroman* has had extensive influence first in Europe and later throughout the world. Thomas Carlyle translated Goethe's novel into English, and after its publication in 1824, many British authors wrote novels inspired by it. In the 20th century, it spread to Germany, Britain, France and several other countries around the globe.

A *Bildungsroman* refers to a novel of formation, a novel of education, or a coming-of-age story, which focuses on the psychological and moral growth of the protagonist from youth to adulthood, and in which, therefore, character change is extremely important. It usually relates the growing up or "coming of age" of a sensitive person who goes in search of answers to life's questions with the expectation that these will result from gaining experience of the world. The genre evolved from folklore tales of a dunce or youngest son going out in the world to seek his fortune. Usually in the beginning of the story there is an emotional loss which makes the protagonist leave on his journey. In a *Bildungsroman*, the goal is maturity, and the protagonist achieves it gradually and with difficulty. The genre often features a main conflict between the main character and society. Typically, the values of society are gradually accepted by the protagonist and he/she is ultimately accepted into society—the protagonist's mistakes and disappointments are over. In some works, the protagonist is able to reach out and help others after having achieved maturity.

There are many variations and subgenres of *Bildungsroman* that focus on the growth of an individual. They include *Entwicklungsroman*, *Erziehungsroman* and *Künstlerroman*. An *Entwicklungsroman*, or a "development novel," is a story of general growth rather than self-cultivation. An *Erziehungsroman*, or an "education novel," focuses on training and formal schooling, while a *Künstlerroman*, or an "artist novel," is about the development of an artist and shows a growth of the self.

Biographical novel (传记体小说)

The biographical novel is a genre of novel which provides a fictional and usually entertaining account of a person's life. This kind of novel concentrates on the experiences a person had during his/her lifetime. The people he/she met and the incidents which occurred are detailed and sometimes trimmings are done to meet the artistic needs of the fictional genre, the novel. Names and accounts may be changed as and when necessary. A very good example of this kind is Oliver Goldsmith's *The Vicar of Wakefield*, which is believed to be the biography of a person the author had known and observed very closely.

Black comedy (黑色喜剧/荒诞喜剧)

A black comedy (or dark comedy) is a comic work that employs farce and morbid humor, which, in its simplest form, is humor that makes light of serious subject matter usually considered taboo. Black comedy corresponds to the earlier concept of gallows humor. It is often controversial due to its subject matter. Some comedians use it as a tool for exploring vulgar issues, thus provoking discomfort and serious thought as well as amusement in their audience. Popular themes of the genre include murder, suicide, depression, abuse, mutilation, war, religion, barbarism, drug abuse, terminal illness, domestic violence, sexual violence, pedophilia, insanity, nightmare, disease, racism, homophobia, sexism, disability (both physical and mental), chauvinism, terrorism, genocide, corruption, torture and crime.

Blank verse (素体诗/无韵诗)

Blank verse consists of lines of iambic pentameter which are unrhymed—hence the term "blank." Of all English metrical forms it is closest to the natural rhythms of English speech, and at the same time more flexible and variously used than any other type of versification. Soon after blank verse was introduced by the Earl of Surrey in his translations of Books 2 and 4 of Virgil's *Aeneid*, it became the standard meter for Elizabethan and later poetic drama, and widely used form for narrative and meditative poems. Much of the finest verse in English—by William Shakespeare, John Milton, William Wordsworth, Alfred Tennyson and Wallace Stevens—has been written in blank verse. A free form of blank verse is still the medium in such 20th-century verse plays as those by Maxwell Anderson (1888–1959) and T. S. Eliot.

Blank verse should not be confused with free verse, which has no regular meter.

Burlesque (滑稽戏)

Burlesque has been succinctly defined as "an incongruous imitation"; that is, it imitates the manner (the form and the style) or the subject matter of a serious literary work or a literary genre, in verse or in prose, but makes the imitation amusing by a ridiculous disparity between the manner and the matter. The burlesque may be written for the sheer fun of it; usually, however, it is a form of satire. The butt of the satiric ridicule may be the particular work or the genre that is being imitated, or the subject matter to which the imitation is incongruously applied, or (often) both of these together.

In a burlesque imitation, the form and the style may be either lower or higher in level and dignity than the subject to which it is incongruously applied. If the form and the style are high and dignified but the subject is low or trivial, we have the "high burlesque"; if the subject is high in status and dignity but the style and manner of treatment are low and undignified, we have "low burlesque."

Byronic hero, the (拜伦式英雄)

The Byronic hero is a variant of the Romantic hero as a type of character, an idealized but flawed character exemplified in the life and writings of Lord Byron, after whom the hero is named. Not only Byron's own persona but also the characters from his writings are considered to provide defining features. The Byronic hero first appeared in Byron's semi-autobiographical epic narrative poem *Childe Harold's Pilgrimage*.

This kind of hero is usually a proud, mysterious rebel figure of noble origin. With immense superiority in his passions and powers, he would carry on his shoulders the burden of righting all the wrongs in a corrupt society. He would rise single-handedly against any kind of tyrannical rules either in government, in religion, or in moral principles with unconquerable wills and inexhaustible energies. The conflict is unusually one of rebellious individuals against outworn social systems and conventions. The historian and critic Thomas Macaulay described the character as "a man proud, moody, cynical, with defiance on his brow, and misery in his heart, a scorner of his kind, implacable in revenge, yet capable of deep and strong affection." (qtd. in Christiansen, 1989: 201)

Canto (诗章/诗篇)

Canto refers to a subdivision of an epic or other narrative poem, equivalent to a chapter in a prose work.

Carpe diem (及时行乐)

Carpe Diem, meaning "to seize the day" or "to make the best of the present moment," is a Latin phrase from one of Horace's *Odes* which has become the name for a very common literary motif, especially in lyric poetry. In a carpe diem poem the speaker emphasizes that life is short and time is fleeting in order to urge his auditor (often represented as a virgin reluctant to change her condition) to make the most of present pleasures. The most celebrated examples in English are Andrew Marvell's "To His Coy Mistress" (1681), and Robert Herrick's "To the Virgin, To Make Much of Time" (1684), which begins with "Gather ye rosebuds, while ye may." In some Christian poems and sermons, the carpe diem motif warns us to prepare our souls for death, rather than our bodies for bed.

CBE (大英帝国司令勋章)

CBE stands for Commander of the Most Excellent Order of the British Empire. It is the third class of award to the Order. The Most Excellent Order of the British Empire (often shortened informally to "Order of the British Empire") is the most junior and most populous order of chivalry in the British and other Commonwealth honors systems. It was established on 4 June 1917 by King George V, and comprises five classes, in civil and military divisions, the most senior two of which make the recipient either a knight if male, or dame if female. There is also the related British Empire Medal, whose recipients are affiliated with, but not members of, the Order. The five classes of award to the Order are, in descending order of seniority: Knight Grand Cross or Dame Grand Cross of the Most Excellent Order of the British Empire (GBE), Knight Commander or Dame Commander of the Most Excellent Order of the British Empire (KBE or DBE), Commander of the Most Excellent Order of the British Empire (CBE), Officer of the Most Excellent Order of the British Empire (OBE) and Member of the Most Excellent Order of the

British Empire (MBE).

Character (人物)

Characters are the persons represented in a dramatic or narrative work, who are interpreted by the reader as being endowed with particular moral, intellectual and emotional qualities by inferences from what the persons say and their distinctive ways of saying it—the dialogue—and from what they do—the action. The grounds in the characters' temperament, desires and moral nature for their speech and actions are called their motivation. A character may remain essentially "stable" or unchanged in outlook and disposition, from beginning to end of a work, or may undergo a radical change, either through a gradual process of development or as the result of a crisis. Whether a character remains stable or changes, the reader of a traditional and realistic work expects "consistency"—the character should not suddenly break off and act in a way not plausible grounded in his or her temperament as we have already come to know it.

E. M. Forster made a distinction between flat characters and round characters. A **flat character** (also called a type or "two-dimensional" character) is built around "a single idea or quality" and is presented without much individualizing detail, and therefore can be fairly adequately described in a single phrase or sentence. A **round character** is complex in temperament and motivation and is represented with subtle particularity; such a character therefore is as difficult to describe with any adequacy as a person in real life, and like real persons, is capable of surprising us.

Children's Laureate (童书桂冠作家)

Children's Laureate is a position awarded in the United Kingdom once every two years to a writer or illustrator of children's books to celebrate the outstanding achievement in the field. The post stemmed from a discussion between the Poet Laureate Ted Hughes and the children's writer Michael Morpurgo (1943 –).

A panel of judges considers nominations from a range of organizations representing librarians, critics, writers and booksellers, including the International Board on Books for Young People. They also consider writers and illustrators nominated directly by children, who now vote online.

The award is funded by several publishing industry and charity sector sponsors, including the Museums, Libraries and Archives Council. The Children's Laureate receives a silver medal at the announcement ceremony. He/She makes frequent public appearances in person and in the media. The current position has been held by Chris Riddell (1962 –) since 9 June 2015.

Closet drama (案头剧)

A closet drama is written in dramatic form, with dialogues, indicated settings and stage directions, but is intended by the author to be read rather than to be performed onstage. Some representative examples in English literature are John Milton's *Samson Agonistes*, Lord Byron's *Manfred* (1816 – 1817) and Percy Bysshe Shelley's *Prometheus Unbound*. Its related form, the closet screenplay, developed during the 20th century. The dichotomy between private "closet" drama (designed for reading) and public "stage" drama (designed for performance in a commercial theater setting) dates from the late 18th century. The practice of circulating plays in written form (printed or handwritten) for literary audiences predates this period, however.

Comedy (喜剧)

In the most common literary application, a comedy is a fictional work in which the materials are selected and managed primarily in order to interest and amuse readers: the characters and their discomfitures engage readers' pleasurable attention rather than profound concern; readers are made to feel confident that no great disaster will occur; and usually the action turns out happily for the chief characters. The term "comedy" is customarily applied only to plays for the stage or to motion pictures. It should be noted, however, that the comic form, so defined, also occurs in prose fiction and narrative poetry. Within the very broad spectrum of dramatic comedy, the following types are frequently distinguished: romantic comedy, satiric comedy, comedy of manners, and farce.

Comedy of humors (幽默喜剧)

The comedy of humors refers to a genre of comedy that focuses on a character or range of characters, each of whom has two or more overriding traits or "humors" that dominate his/her personality, desire and conduct. This comic technique may be found early in Aristophanes (c. 446 – c. 386 BC), but the English playwrights Ben Jonson and George Chapman (c. 1559 – 1634) popularized the genre in the closing years of the 16th century. In the later half of the 17th century, it was combined with the comedy of manners in Restoration comedy (1660 – 1700).

The comedy of humors owes something to the earlier vernacular comedy but more to a desire to imitate the classical comedy of Plautus (c. 254 – 184 BC) and Terence (c. 195/185 – c. 159 BC) and to combat the vogue of romantic comedy, as developed by William Shakespeare. The satiric purpose of the comedy of humors and its realistic method lead to more serious character studies with Ben Jonson's *The Alchemist*. The humors each have been associated with the physical and mental characteristics; the result is a system that is quite subtle in its capacity for describing types of personality.

Comedy of manners (风俗喜剧)

The comedy of manners originated in the New Comedy of ancient Greece in the late 4th century B.C. and at the beginning of the 3rd century B.C. (as distinguished from the Old Comedy represented by Aristophanes) and was developed by the Roman dramatists in the 3rd and 2nd centuries B.C. The plays dealt with the vicissitudes of young lovers and included what became the stock characters of much later comedy, such as the clever servant, old and stodgy parents and the wealthy rival. The English comedy of manners was early exemplified by William Shakespeare's *Love's Labor's Lost* and *Much Ado about Nothing*, and was given high polish in Restoration comedy, which dealt with the relations and intrigues of men and women living in a sophisticated upper-class society, and relied for comic effect in large part on the wit and sparkle of the dialogue and to a lesser degree, on the violations of social standards and decorum by would-be wits, jealous husbands, conniving rivals and foppish dandies. A middle-class reaction against what had come to be considered the immorality of situation and indecency of dialogue in the courtly Restoration comedy resulted in the sentimental comedy of the 18th century. In the latter part of the century, however, Oliver Goldsmith's *She Stoops to Conquer* and Richard Brinsley Sheridan's *The Rivals* and *A School for Scandal* revived the wit and gaiety, while deleting the indecency of Restoration comedy. The comedy of manners lapsed in the early 19th century, but was revived by many skillful dramatists from Oscar Wilde through George Bernard Shaw to Neil Simon (1927 –) and other writers of the present era.

Comic novel (喜剧小说)

A comic novel is a novel-length work of humorous fiction. The famous novels like James Joyce's classic *Ulysses* have been categorized as such. Many well-known authors have written comic novels, including P. G. Wodehouse (1881 – 1975), Henry Fielding, Mark Twain (1835 – 1910) and John Kennedy Toole (1937 – 1969).

Conceit (奇喻)

Originally meaning a concept or image, "conceit" came to be the term for figures of speech which establish a striking parallel, usually ingeniously elaborate, between two very dissimilar things or situations. English poets of the 16th and 17th centuries adapted the term from the Italian "concetto." Two types of conceit are often distinguished by specific names—the Petrarchan Conceit and the Metaphysical Conceit.

The Petrarchan Conceit is a type of figure used in love poems that had been novel and effective in the Italian poet Petrarch, but became hackneyed in some of his imitators among the Elizabethan sonneteers. The figure consists of detailed, ingenious and often exaggerated comparisons applied to the disdainful mistress, as cold and cruel as she is beautiful, and to the distresses and despair of her worshipful lover.

The Metaphysical Conceit is a characteristic figure in John Donne and other Metaphysical poets of the 17th century. It was described by Samuel Johnson as "wit" which is "a kind of discordia concors; a combination of dissimilar images, or discovery of occult resemblances in things apparently unlike. ⋯The most heterogeneous ideas are yoked by violence together." The Metaphysical poets exploited all knowledge—commonplace or esoteric, practical, theoretical, or philosophical, true or fabulous—for the vehicles of these figures; and their comparisons, whether succinct or expanded, were often novel and witty, and at their best startlingly effective.

Consonance (尾韵/辅韵)

Consonance is the repetition of identical or similar consonants in a sequence of nearby words whose vowel sounds are different (e. g. live-love, lean-alone, pitter-patter).

Couplet (偶句/对句)

A couplet is a pair of rhymed lines that are equal in length.

Courtly love (宫廷爱情/典雅爱情)

Courtly love is a doctrine of love, together with an elaborate code governing the relations between aristocratic lovers. It was widely represented in the lyric poems and chivalric romances of western Europe during the Middle Ages.

Decadence (颓废派)

In the latter 19th century, some French proponents of the doctrines of Aestheticism, especially Charles Baudelaire, also espoused views and values that developed into a movement called the "Decadence." The term (not regarded by its exponents as derogatory) was based on qualities attributed to the literature of Hellenistic Greece in the last three centuries B. C., and to the Roman literature after the death of the Emperor Augustus in 14 A. D. These literatures were said to possess the high refinement and subtle beauties of a culture and art that have passed their vigorous prime, but manifest a special savor of incipient decay. Such was also held to be the state of European civilization, especially in France, as it approached the end of the 19th century.

Central to the Decadent movement was the view that art is totally opposed to "nature," in the sense both of biological nature and of the standard, or "natural," norms of morality and sexual behavior. The thoroughgoing Decadent writer cultivated high artifice in his style and, often, the bizarre in his subject matter, recoiled from the fecundity and exuberance of the organic and instinctual life of nature, preferred elaborate dress over the living human form and cosmetics over the natural hue, and sometimes set out to violate what was commonly held to be "natural" in human experience by restoring to drugs, deviancy from standard norms of behavior, and sexual experimentation, in the attempt to achieve "the systematic derangement of all the senses." The movement reached its height in the last two decades of the 19th century. This period is also known as fin de siècle (end of the century), which connotes the lassitude, satiety and ennui expressed by many writers of the Decadence.

Decadence in English literature reflected the crisis of bourgeois culture. It opposed the democratic and socialist ideals. Writers of this group upheld bourgeois individualism. Their slogan was "art for art's sake." They could see the social evils, but they didn't think it possible to remove those evils and make life fair and just. They thought that the world was suffering from an incurable disease. Their writings were like groans of desperate patients. The ideas, moods and behavior of Decadence were manifested, beginning in the 1860s, in the poems of Algernon Charles Swinburne, and in the 1890s by writers like Oscar Wilde, Arthur Symons, Lionel Johnson and Ernest Dowson; the notable artist of the English Decadence was Aubrey Beardsley. The representative literary productions of Decadence in English literature are Oscar Wilde's novel *The Picture of Dorian Gray*, his play *Salome* and many other poems of Ernest Dowson.

Deism (理神论/自然神论)

Deism is a widespread mode of religious thinking that manifested the faith in human reason that characterized the European Enlightenment during the later 17th and the 18th centuries. It has been succinctly described as "religion without revelation." The thoroughgoing deist renounced, as violating reason, all "revealed religion," that is, all particular religions, including Christianity, which are based on faith in the truths revealed in special scriptures at a certain time and place, and therefore available only to a particular individual or group. The deist instead relied on those truths which prove their accord with universal human reason by the fact that they are to be found in all religions, everywhere, at all times. Therefore the basic tenets of deism were, in theory, the elements shared by all particular, or "positive," religions.

The deists held that God indeed is the creator of the universe, but He sets it in motion as a self-regulating mechanism; everything in the universe operated according to natural laws, which could be understood by the human mind. Thus the best way to worship God is to study his handiwork, namely, the natural world and the human world, and to do good things to mankind. Deism simplified the Christian religion in such a way that the rights of religion became consistent with the rights of government and rights of the individual. Deism, as a more intellectualized and liberalized religion, became an antidote to Puritan (of Calvinist) tenets. Many thinkers assimilated aspects of deism while remaining professing Christians.

Diction (文辞)

Diction, in its original, primary meaning, refers to the writer's or the speaker's distinctive vocabulary choices and style of expression in a poem or story. In a secondary, common sense, it means the distinctiveness of speech, the art of speaking so that each word is clearly heard and understood to its fullest complexity and extremity, and concerns pronunciation and tone, rather than word choice and style. This secondary sense is more precisely and commonly expressed with the term enunciation, or with its synonym articulation.

In literature, diction is usually judged with reference to the prevailing standards of proper writing and speech and is seen as the mark of quality of the writing. It is also understood as the selection of certain words or phrases that become peculiar to a writer. A writer's diction can be analyzed under a great variety of categories, such as the degree to which the vocabulary and phrasing is abstract or concrete, Latin or Anglo-Saxon, colloquial or formal, technical or common.

Dirge (挽歌)

A dirge is a versified expression of grief, or a somber song expressing mourning or grief, which is appropriate for performance at a funeral. It differs from the elegy in that it is short, less formal and usually represented as a text to be sung.

Drama (戏剧)

Drama is the form of composition designed for performance in the theater, in which actors/actresses take the roles of the characters, perform the indicated action and utter the written dialogue. In poetic drama the dialogue is written in verse, which in English is usually blank verse and in French is the twelve-syllable line called an Alexandrine. However, almost all the heroic dramas of the English Restoration Period were written in heroic couplets.

Drama, as a literary term, comes from a Greek word meaning action, which is derived from the verb meaning to do or to act. The common alternative name for a dramatic composition is a play. The enactment of drama in theater, performed by actors on a stage before an audience, presupposes collaborative modes of production and a collective form of reception. The structure of dramatic texts, unlike other forms of literature, is directly influenced by this collaborative production and collective reception. The early modern tragedy *Hamlet* by William Shakespeare and the classical Athenian tragedy *Oedipus the King* (c. 429 BC) by Sophocles (496 BC – 406 BC) are among the masterpieces of the art of drama. A modern example is *Long Day's Journey into Night* (1956) by Eugene O'Neill (1888 –

1953).

Drama is often combined with music and dance: the drama in opera is generally sung throughout; musicals generally include both spoken dialogues and songs; and some forms of drama (such as melodrama) have incidental music or musical accompaniment underscoring the dialogue. In certain periods of history (the ancient Roman and modern Romantic) some dramas have been written to be read rather than performed. In improvisation, the drama does not pre-exist the moment of performance; performers devise a dramatic script spontaneously before an audience.

Dramatic monologue (戏剧独白)

A monologue is a lengthy speech by a single person. In a play, when a character utters a monologue that expresses his/her private thoughts, it is called a soliloquy. The dramatic monologue, however, does not designate a component in a play, but a type of lyric poem that was perfected by Robert Browning, a poem delivered as though by a single imagined person, frequently but not always to an imagined auditor: the speaker is not to be identified with the poet, but is dramatized, usually ironically, through his/her own words.

In its fullest form, the dramatic monologue has the following features: a) a single person, who is patently not the poet, utters the speech that makes up the whole of the poem, in a specific situation at a critical moment; b) this person addresses and interacts with one or more other people; but we know of the auditors' presence and what they say and do, only from clues in the discourse of the single speaker; c) the main principle controlling the poet's formulation of what the lyric speaker says is to reveal to the reader, in a way that enhances its interest, the speaker's temperament and character. The third feature—the focus on self-revelation—serves to distinguish a dramatic monologue from its near relation, the dramatic lyric, which is also a monologue uttered in an identifiable situation at a dramatic moment.

The dramatic monologue was employed by many 19th- and 20th-century poets, including Alfred Tennyson, Thomas Hardy, Rudyard Kipling, Robert Frost, Ezra Pound and T. S. Eliot, and several Victorian women poets who found it a useful vehicle for giving voice to women's concerns and repressions.

Dream vision (叙梦寓言诗)

Dream vision (also called dream allegory) is a mode of narrative widely employed by medieval poets: the narrator falls asleep, usually in a spring landscape, and dreams the events he goes on to relate; often he is led by a guide, human or animal, and the events which he dreams are at least in part an allegory. A very influential medieval example is the 13th-century French poem *Roman de la Rose* (*The Romance of the Rose*); the greatest of medieval poems, Dante's *The Divine Comedy*, is also a dream vision. In the 14th-century England, it is the narrative mode of the fine elegy *Pearl*, of William Langland's *Piers Plowman*, and of Geoffrey Chaucer's *The Book of the Duchess* and *The House of Fame*. After the Middle Ages the vogue of the dream allegory diminished, but it never died out, as John Bunyan's prose narrative *The Pilgrim's Progress* and John Keats' verse narrative *The Fall of Hyperion: A Dream* (1819) bear witness. *Alice's Adventures in Wonderland* (1865) by Lewis Carroll (1832 – 1898) is in the form of a dream vision, and James Joyce's *Finnegan's Wake* consists of an immense dream on the part of archetypal dreamer.

Eclogue（田园诗/牧歌）

An eclogue is a poem in a classical style on a pastoral subject. Poems in the genre are sometimes also called bucolics. The terms eclogue, bucolic and idyll have been widely used as synonyms, except that grammarians have made an effort to confine "eclogue" to poems in dialogue form.

Edwardians, the（爱德华时代的小说家）

In her famous essay "Modern Fiction," Virginia Woolf singled out three novelists of the first years of the 20th century for analysis and branded them as "Edwardians," a nomenclature not favorable in meaning. She was especially relentless when discussing one of these, Arnold Bennett, the other two being H. G. Wells and John Galsworthy. Her major complaint was about their over-emphasis on the description of externalities in their representation of life rather than on the internal world of man which she thought should take precedence over anything else in novel-writing. The authors, who wrote and made their names in this "Edwardian" period when King Edward VII was on the throne for a decade, also included Joseph Conrad whose novels came close to Woolf's definition of the modern novel, Rudyard Kipling, whose writings are brilliant but exhibit in some a degree of imperialistic arrogance and racial bias, and E. M. Forster, probably one of the first writers then sensitive to and aware of the change which materialized into Modernism in the works of Virginia Woolf, James Joyce and D. H. Lawrence.

Elegy（挽歌/悲歌）

The classical (ancient Greek and Roman) elegy was any poem written in elegiac meter (alternating lines of dactylic hexameter and pentameter), including the subject matter of change and loss frequently expressed in the elegiac verse form, especially in complaints about love. In Europe and England the term continued to have a variable application through the Renaissance. In the 17th century the word began to be limited to its most common present usage: a formal and sustained lament in verse for the death of a particular person, usually ending in a consolation. Therefore nowadays an elegy is simply defined as a mournful, melancholic or plaintive poem, especially a funeral song or a lament for the dead.

English Critical Realism（英国批判现实主义）

English Critical Realism, as a new literary trend, flourished in the 1840s and the early 1850s. It found its expression in the form of novel typically represented by Charles Dickens' works. Such writers as William Makepeace Thackeray and Thomas Hardy were also representative of the English Critical Realism. The Critical Realists, most of whom were novelists, described, with much vividness and artistic skill, the chief traits of the English society and criticized the capitalist system from a democratic viewpoint. They not only gave a satirical portrayal of the bourgeoisie and all the ruling classes, but also showed profound sympathy for the common people. In their best works, the greed and hypocrisy of the upper classes were contrasted with the honesty and good-heartedness of the lower-class people. Hence humor and satire abounded in the English realistic novels of the 19th century, which revealed the corrupting influence of the rule of cash upon human nature. Here lay the essentially democratic and humanistic character of Critical Realism. But the Critical Realists did not find a way to eradicate the social evils they knew so well. They did not realize the necessity of changing the bourgeois society through conscious human efforts. They were unable to find a good solution to the social contradiction. Their works often started with a powerful exposure of the ugliness of the bourgeois world and ended up with a happy ending or an impotent compromise.

English PEN（英国作家协会）

PEN originally stood for "Poets, Essayists, Novelists," but now it stands for "Poets, Playwrights, Editors, Essayists, Novelists" and includes writers of any form of literature, such as journalists and historians. English PEN is the founding center of PEN International, the worldwide writers' association. The organization promotes freedom of expression and literature across frontiers. English PEN is a registered charity in England and Wales, and is governed by a board of trustees which is elected from and by members. The current President of English PEN is Maureen Freely (1952 –).

Enlightenment（启蒙运动）

Enlightenment was a progressive intellectual movement throughout Western Europe in the 18th century. It was an expression of struggle of the bourgeoisie against feudalism. The enlighteners fought against class inequality, stagnation, prejudices and other survivals of feudalism. They thought the chief means for bettering the society was "enlightenment" or "education" for people. In other words, they believed in the power of reason, and that is why the 18th century has often been called "the Age of Reason."

As a movement, the Enlightenment developed many ramifications. In their attempt to rationalize the government and law, the Enlightenment thinkers regarded government as the political expression of law. And law itself was defined as the "necessary relationships which derive from the nature of things." According to them, the law of all lands was valid only when it conformed to the law which reason perceived in nature. As regards religion, the Enlightenment was completely secular in outlook. The tendency was rather toward deism. In art and literature, what coincided with the Age of Reason was a period called Neoclassicism represented by John Dryden and Alexander Pope in England. These people were on the whole traditionalists and they had a great respect for the Classical artists and authors, and for their rules of their art. They thought that reason and judgment were the most admirable faculties and that decorum was essential.

Epic（史诗）

In its strict sense, an epic or a heroic poem is a long verse narrative on a serious subject, told in a formal and elevated style, and centered on a heroic or quasi-divine figure on whose actions depends the fate of a tribe, a nation, or (in the instance of John Milton's *Paradise Lost*) the human race.

There is a standard distinction between traditional and literary epics. Traditional epics (also called "folk epics" or "primary epics") are written versions of originally oral poems about a tribal or national hero during a warlike age. Among these are the *Iliad* and *Odyssey* that the Greeks ascribed to Homer; the Anglo-Saxon *Beowulf*; the

French *Chanson de Roland* and the Spanish *Poema del Cid* (composed sometime between 1140 and 1207) in the 12th century; and the 13th-century German epic *Nibelungenlied*. Literary epics were composed by individual poetic craftsmen in deliberate imitation of the traditional form. Of this kind is Virgil's *Aeneid*, which later served as the chief model for Milton's literary epic *Paradise Lost*. Literary epics are highly conventional compositions which usually share the following features:

a. The hero is a figure of great national or even cosmic importance.

b. The setting of the poem is ample in scale and may be worldwide or even larger.

c. The action involves superhuman deeds in battle, or a long, arduous and dangerous journey intrepidly accomplished, in the face of opposition by some of the gods.

d. In these great actions the gods and other supernatural beings take interest or an active part.

e. An epic poem is a ceremonial performance, and is narrated in a ceremonial style which is deliberately distanced from ordinary speech and proportioned to the grandeur and formality of the heroic subject and architecture.

Epigram (警句/讽刺短诗)

An epigram is a brief, interesting, memorable, and sometimes surprising or satirical statement, whether in verse or prose. Derived from the Greek word "epigramma" meaning "inscription," this literary device has been employed for over two millennia. It may be on any subject, amatory, elegiac, meditative, complimentary, anecdotal, or (most often) satiric. Martial (between 38 and 41 AD – between 102 and 104 AD), the Roman epigrammatist, established the enduring model for the caustically satiric epigram in verse.

The verse epigram was much cultivated in England in the late 16th and 17th centuries by such poets as John Donne, Ben Jonson and Robert Herrick. The form flourished especially in the 18th century. Matthew Prior (1664 – 1721) was a highly accomplished writer of epigrams, and many closed couplets by Alexander Pope are detachable epigrams.

Epigraph (题词/碑文)

In literature, an epigraph is a phrase, quotation, motto, or poem that is set at the beginning of a literary work, document or component. The epigraph may serve as a preface, as a summary, as a counter-example, or to link the work to a wider literary canon, either to invite comparison or to enlist a conventional context. One of the epigraphs preceding T. S. Eliot's "The Hollow Men" (1925) is a reference to Guy Fawkes Day, when English children carry stuffed effigies, or likenesses, of the traitor Fawkes. The epigraph serves as a motif throughout the poem for the ineffectuality Eliot identifies with his generation of "stuffed men."

Epiphany (顿悟)

"Epiphany" means "a manifestation," which is usually used in Christian theology to signify a manifestation of God's presence within the created world. In the early draft of *A Portrait of the Artist as a Young Man* entitled *Stephen Hero* (published posthumously in 1944), James Joyce adapted the term to secular experience, to signify a sudden sense of radiance and revelation that one may feel while perceiving a commonplace object. Here Joyce defined an epiphany as "a sudden spiritual manifestation," the sudden "revelation of the whatness of a thing," the moment in which "the soul of the commonest object seems to us radiant." Much of Joyce's fiction is built around such special moment of sudden insight, just as William Wordsworth's long autobiographical poem *The Prelude* is constructed around certain revelatory "spots of time."

Epistolary novel（书信体小说）

The word "epistolary" is derived through Latin from the Greek word epistolē, meaning a letter. An epistolary novel refers to a novel told through the medium of letters written by one or more of the characters. Originating with Samuel Richardson's *Pamela*, the epistolary novel was one of the earliest forms of novel to be developed and remained one of the most popular up to the 19th century. It had much influence on Europe. Its reliance on subjective points of view makes it the forerunner of the modern psychological novel.

The advantages of the novel in letter form are that it presents an intimate view of the character's thoughts and feelings without interference from the author and that it conveys the shape of events to come with dramatic immediacy. Also, the presentation of events from several points of view lends the story dimension and verisimilitude. In other words, the epistolary form can add greater realism to a story, because it mimics the workings of real life. It is thus able to demonstrate differing points of view without recourse to the device of an omniscient narrator.

Epithalamion（喜歌/颂歌）

Epithalamion or "epithalamium" (Latin form) is a poem written to celebrate a marriage. The term in Greek means "at the bridal chamber" since the verses were originally written to be sung outside the bedroom of a newly married couple. The form flourished among the Neo-Latin poets of the Renaissance, who established the model that was followed by writers in the European vernacular languages.

Essay（散文）

An essay is any short composition in prose that undertakes to discuss a matter, express a point of view and persuade readers to accept a thesis on any subject, or simply entertain. The essay differs from a "treatise" or "dissertation" in its lack of pretension to be a systematic and complete exposition, and in being addressed to a general rather than a specialized audience. Therefore, the essay discusses its subject in nontechnical fashion, and often with a liberal use of such devices as anecdote, striking illustration, and humor to augment its appeal.

Essays can be divided into the formal and the informal. The formal essay (or article) is relatively impersonal. The author writes as an authority, or at least as highly knowledgeable, and expounds the subject in an orderly way. Examples can be found in various scholarly journals, as well as among the serious articles on current topics and issues in any of the magazines addressed to a thoughtful audience. In the informal essay (or familiar or personal essay), the author assumes a tone of intimacy with his audience, tends to deal with everyday things rather than with public affairs or specialized topics, and writes in a relaxed, self-revelatory, and sometimes whimsical fashion.

Euphuism（尤弗伊斯体/绮丽体）

Euphuism is a conspicuously formal and elaborate prose style which had a vogue in the 1580s in drama, prose fiction and probably also in the conversation of English court circles. It took its name from John Lyly's moralistic prose romance *Euphues*. In the dialogues of this work and of *Euphues and His England*, as well as in his stage comedies, Lyly exaggerated and used persistently a stylized prose which other writers had developed earlier. The style is sententious (that is, full of moral maxims), relies persistently on syntactical balance and antithesis, reinforces the structural parallels by heavy and elaborate patterns of alliteration and assonance, exploits comparisons and the rhetorical question, and is addicted to long similes and learned allusions which are often drawn from mythology and the habits of legendary animals.

Evening Standard Theatre Awards（英国标准晚报戏剧奖）

The Evening Standard Theatre Awards, established in 1955, are presented annually for outstanding achievements in London Theatre. Sponsored by the *Evening Standard* newspaper, they are announced in late November or early December. They are the equivalent of the Broadway theatre Drama Desk Awards.

Experimental literature（试验文学）

Experimental literature refers to written work—usually fiction or poetry—that emphasizes innovation, most especially in technique.

Fable（寓言）

The fable is one of the most enduring forms of folk literature and can be found in the literature of almost every country. As modern researchers agree, it is spread abroad less by literary anthologies than by oral transmission. A fable is a succinct fictional story, in prose or verse, that features animals, mythical creatures, plants, inanimate objects, or forces of nature that are anthropomorphized (given human qualities, such as verbal communication), and that illustrates or leads to an interpretation of a moral lesson (a "moral"), which may at the end be added explicitly as a pithy maxim. A fable differs from a parable in that the latter excludes animals, plants, inanimate objects, and forces of nature as actors that assume speech or other powers of humankind.

Farce（闹剧/滑稽戏）

Farce is a type of comedy designed to provoke the audience to simple, hearty laughter—"belly laughs," in the parlance of the theater. To do so it commonly employs highly exaggerated or caricatured types of characters, puts them into improbable and ludicrous situations, and makes free use of sexual mix-ups, broad verbal humor, and physical bustle and horseplay. Farce was a component in the comic episodes in medieval miracle plays. In the English drama, farce is usually an episode in a more complex form of comedy.

Feature film（故事片）

A feature film is a film (also called a movie or motion picture) with a running time long enough to be considered the principal or sole film to fill a program. The notion of how long this should be has varied according to time and place. According to the Academy of Motion Picture Arts and Sciences, American Film Institute, and British

Film Institute, a feature film runs for 40 minutes or longer, while the Screen Actors Guild states that it is 80 minutes or longer.

The majority of feature films are between 70 and 210 minutes long. *The Story of the Kelly Gang* (1906, Australia) was the first dramatic feature film released (running at approximately 60 minutes), while *The Corbett-Fitzsimmons Fight* (1897, USA) is considered by some as the first documentary feature film (running time is 100 minutes), however it is more accurately characterized as a sports program as it included the full unedited boxing match. The first feature-length adaptation was *Les Misérables* (1909, USA). Other early feature films include *The Inferno (L'Inferno)* (1911), *Quo Vadis?* (1912), *Oliver Twist* (1912), *Richard III* (1912), *From the Manger to the Cross* (1912) and *Cleopatra* (1912).

Foil (陪衬人物)

A foil is a character whose qualities or actions serve to emphasize those of the protagonist or of some other characters by providing a strong contrast with them.

Folktale (民间故事/民间传说)

The folktale, strictly defined, is a short narrative in prose of unknown authorship which has been transmitted orally; many of these tales eventually achieve written form. The term, however, is often extended to include stories invented by a known author, such as "The Three Bears" (1837) by Robert Southey and the story of George Washington (1732 – 1799) and the cherry tree by Parson Weems (1759 – 1825). These stories have been picked up and repeatedly narrated by word of mouth as well as in written form. Folktales are found among peoples everywhere in the world. They include myths, fables, tales of heroes (whether historical or legendary), and fairy tales. Many so-called fairy tales are not stories of fairies but of various kinds of marvels; examples are "Snow White" (1812) and "Jack and the Beanstalk" (1807). Another type of folktale, the set "joke"—the comic (often bawdy) anecdote—is the most abundant and persistent of all; new jokes, or new versions of old jokes, continue to be a staple of contemporary social exchange, wherever people congregate in a relaxed mood.

The same, or closely similar, oral stories have turned up in Europe, Asia and Africa, and have been embodied in the narratives of many writers. For instance, Geoffrey Chaucer's *The Canterbury Tales* includes a number of folktales, among which "The Pardoner's Tale" of Death and the three rioters was of Eastern origin. The standard catalogue of recurrent motifs in folktales throughout the world is the six-volume *Motif-Index of Folk-Literature* (1955 – 1958) by Stith Thompson (1885 – 1976).

Foot (音步)

A foot is the combination of a strong stress and the associated weak stresses which make up the recurrent metric unit of a line. The relatively stronger-stressed syllable is called, for short, "stressed"; the relatively weaker-stressed syllables are called "light," or most commonly, "unstressed." The four standard feet distinguished in English are iamb (an unstressed syllable followed by a stressed syllable), anapest (two unstressed syllables followed by a stressed syllable), trochee (a stressed syllable followed by an unstressed syllable) and dactyl (a stressed syllable followed by two unstressed syllables). Iambs and anapests, since the strong stress is at the end, are called "rising meter"; trochees and dactyls, with the strong stress at the beginning, are called "falling meter." Iambs and trochees, having two syllables, are called "duple meter"; anapests and dactyls, having three syllables, are called "triple meter." It should be noted that the iamb is by far the commonest English foot.

Fragmentation (碎片)

Fragmentation is a term used by Modernists in their writings to depict modern life, which, in their eyes, is fragmented, falling apart. In Modernist works, the framework in its traditional sense is gone, usual connective patterns are missing, and coming in their place are unrelated pieces or dissociated fragments. Consequently, a sense of discontinuity or chaos is projected. The reader has to create meaning out of the chaos.

Gallows humor (绞刑架上的幽默)

Gallows humor is humor about very unpleasant, serious or painful circumstances. Any humor that treats serious matters, such as death, war, disease, crime, etc., in a light, silly or satirical fashion is considered gallows humor. Gallows humor has been described as a witticism in response to a hopeless situation. It arises from stressful, traumatic or life-threatening situations, often in such circumstances that death is perceived as impending and unavoidable.

Genre (类型/体裁)

Genre is a term, French in origin, which denotes types or classes of literature. The genres into which literary works have been grouped at different times are very numerous, and the criteria on which the classifications have been based are highly variable.

A literary genre is a recognizable and established category of written work employing such common conventions as will prevent readers or audiences from mistaking it for another kind. Much of the confusion surrounding the term arises from the fact that it is used simultaneously for the most basic modes of literary art (lyric, narrative/epic, dramatic), for the broadest categories of composition (poetry, prose fiction, drama), and for more specialized subcategories, which are defined according to several different criteria including formal structure (sonnet, picaresque novel), length (novella, epigram), intention (satire), effect (comedy), origin (folktale) and subject-matter (pastoral, science fiction). While some genres, such as the pastoral elegy or the melodrama, have numerous conventions governing subject, style and form, others—like the novel—have no agreed rules, although they may include several more limited subgenres.

Georgians, the (乔治时代的诗人)

The Georgians, named after George V (king 1910 – 1936), were a group of lyrical poets whose works were included in Sir Edward Marsh's *Georgian Anthologies*. They wrote and published mainly between 1910 and 1920. These poets as a group included John Drinkwater, W. H. Davies, Water de la Mare, W. W. Gibbon, Edward Thomas, Rupert Brooke, Robert Graves, Edmund Blunden, and others. Some of D. H. Lawrence's lyrics were also included in the Georgian anthologies, though these were different and superior.

The Georgians rejected the avant-garde aesthetic kind of poetry of the last decade of the 19th century and turned back to tradition. They observed poetically nature, love and rural traditional English life and wrote about these in a style gentle, less self-conscious and more easily approachable. They sang sweet pastoral songs in praise of the temporal serenity and stability that England had enjoyed before WWI and offered an avenue of escape for the people in the period of chaos after it. These poets were capable of sentimental lapses and skilled in traditional metrics. Receiving warm welcome from the general readers, they sold enviously well. But they were harshly criticized later for their want of depth in thought and feeling.

The Georgians lost their vogue in the 1920s when a wind of change started blowing and swept them aside. The pastoral mode of writing was out of place on the post-WWI scene, and a verse revolution was visibly under way. The imagist movement had already started, and Modernism was fast burgeoning into shape. From then on William Butler Yeats and T. S. Eliot began their domination, and the Georgians were ignored for some three decades. Then the poets of the 1950s veered away from high Modernism and Dylan Thomas and turned to tradition, dredging in their literary endeavors these Georgians from the deeps of oblivion. It is good to know that the famous American Robert Frost was in England around this time and became a Georgian as well: he was probably the best of the group.

Golden PEN Award（英国金笔奖）

The Golden PEN Award is a literary award established in 1993 by English PEN, given annually to a British writer for "a Lifetime's Distinguished Service to Literature." The winner is chosen by the Board of English PEN. The award has previously been called the S. T. Dupont Golden Pen Award. The award is one of many PEN awards sponsored by International PEN affiliates in over 145 PEN centers around the world.

Graveyard Poets（墓园派诗人）

The Graveyard Poets, also termed "Churchyard Poets" or "Boneyard Boys," were a number of pre-Romantic English poets of the 18th century who wrote meditative poems, usually set in a graveyard, on the theme of human mortality, in moods which range from elegiac pensiveness to profound gloom. The vogue resulted in one of the most widely known English poems, Thomas Gray's *Elegy Written in a Country Churchyard*. The writing of graveyard poems spread from England to Continental literature in the second part of the 18th century and was represented in America by "Thanatopsis" (1817) of William Cullen Bryant (1794 – 1878). The Graveyard Poets are often recognized as precursors of the Gothic literary genre as well as the Romantic Movement.

Hendecasyllable（十一音节诗句）

The hendecasyllable is a line of eleven syllables, hence the name, which came from the Greek word for eleven. It was used in Ancient Greek and Latin verse as well as in medieval and modern European poetry. The classical hendecasyllable is a quantitative meter used in Ancient Greece in Aeolic verse—the distinct lyric poetry characteristic of the two great poets of Archaic Lesbos, Sappho (sometime between 630 and 612 BC – c. 570 BC) and Alcaeus (c. 620 – 6th century BC), who composed in their native Aeolic dialect—and in scolia (songs sung by invited guests at banquets), and later by the Roman poet Catullus (c. 84 – 54 BC). The meter was imitated in English, notably by Alfred Tennyson, Algernon Charles Swinburne and Robert Frost.

The hendecasyllable is the principal meter in Italian poetry. Its defining feature is a constant stress on the tenth syllable, so that the number of syllables in the verse may vary, equaling eleven in the usual case where the final word is stressed on the penultimate syllable. The verse also has a stress preceding the caesura, on either the fourth or sixth syllable. The most usual stress schemes for the Italian hendecasyllable are stresses on sixth and tenth syllables, and on the fourth, seventh and tenth syllables. Most classical Italian poems are composed in hendecasyllables, including the major works of Dante, Petrarch, Ludovico Ariosto (1474 – 1533), and Tasso. The rhyme system varies from terza rima to ottava, from sonnet to canzone. Since the early 16th century, hendecasyllables have been often used without a strict system, with few or no rhymes, both in poetry and in drama.

The term is sometimes used in English poetry to describe a line of iambic pentameter with an extra short syllable at the end, as in the first line of John Keats' *Endymion*: "A thing of beauty is a joy for ever."

Heroic Couplet (英雄双簧体/英雄双韵体)

Heroic Couplet (or decasyllabic couplet) refers to the rhymed couplet of iambic pentameter. The adjective "heroic" was applied in the later 17th century because of the frequent use of such couplets in heroic (that is, epic) poems and in heroic dramas. This verse form was introduced from France into English poetry by Geoffrey Chaucer and has been in constant use ever since.

High culture (高雅文化)

High culture is a term now used in a number of different ways in academic discourse, whose most common meaning is the set of cultural products, mainly in the arts, held in the highest esteem by a culture. This is also a term used in the era before WWI to describe people of European cultures, as every other culture was considered under-developed and of low culture.

In more popular terms, high culture is the culture of an upper class such as an aristocracy or an intelligentsia, but it can also be defined as a repository of a broad cultural knowledge, a way of transcending the class system. It is contrasted with the low culture or popular culture of, variously, the less well-educated, barbarians, Philistines, or the masses. Still similarities can be noted between high culture and traditional-folk culture as they can be all conceived as the repository of shared and accumulated traditions functioning as a living continuum between the past and the present.

Historical novel (历史小说)

Some realistic novelists, the first and most representative one among whom was Walter Scott in the 19th century, made use of events and personages from the historical past to add interest and picturesque-ness to their narrative. This resulted in the emergence of the historical novel. The historical novel not only takes its setting and some characters and events from history, but also makes the historical events and issues crucial for the central characters and narrative. Some of the greatest historical novels also use the protagonists and actions to reveal what the author regards as the deep forces that impel the historical process.

Horatian satire（贺拉斯式讽刺）

Horatian satire, named after the Roman satirist Horace, playfully criticizes some social vice through gentle, mild and light-hearted humor. Horace wrote satires to gently ridicule the dominant opinions and "philosophical beliefs of ancient Rome and Greece" (Rankin, 2016). Rather than writing in harsh or accusing tones, he addressed issues with humor and clever mockery. Horatian satire follows this same pattern of "gently[ridiculing]the absurdities and follies of human beings." (Drury, 2016) It directs wit, exaggeration and self-deprecating humor toward what it identifies as folly, rather than evil. Its sympathetic tone is common in modern society.

A Horatian satirist's goal is to heal the situation with smiles, rather than by anger. He/She makes fun of the general human folly instead of pointing to any specific follier. "In a work using Horatian satire, readers often laugh at the characters in the story who are the subject of mockery as well as themselves and society for behaving in those ways." (Thomas, 2016) Alexander Pope has been established as an author whose satire "heals with morals what it hurts with wit." (Green, 2016) His is Horatian satire and attempts to teach.

Humanism（人文主义）

The word humanist was coined in the 16th century to signify one who taught and worked in the fields of humanities like grammar, rhetoric, history, poetry and moral philosophy, as distinguished from fields less concerned with the moral and imaginative aspects and activities of man, such as mathematics, natural philosophy, and theology. The humanists wrote many works concerned with educational, moral and political themes, based largely on classical writers like Aristotle, Plato, and above all, Cicero. In the 19th century humanism came to be applied to the view of human nature, the general values, and the educational ideas common to many Renaissance humanists, as well as to a number of later writers in the same tradition.

Nowadays, in a broad sense, the term humanism suggests any attitude which tends to exalt the human element or stress the importance of human interests, as opposed to the supernatural, divine elements or as opposed to the grosser, animal elements. In a more specific sense, humanism suggests a devotion to those studies supposed to promote human culture most effectively, in particular, those dealing with the life, thought, language and literature of ancient Greece and Rome. In literary history the most important use of the term is to designate the revival of classical culture which accompanied the Renaissance.

Typically, Renaissance humanism assumed the dignity and central possibility of human beings in the universe, emphasized the importance in education of studying classical imaginative and philosophical literature, although with emphasis on its moral and practical rather than its aesthetic values, and insisted on the primacy, in ordering human life, of reason (considered the distinctively human faculty) as opposed to the instinctual appetites and the "animal" passions. Many humanists also stressed the need for a rounded development of an individual's diverse powers, physical, mental, artistic and moral, as opposed to a merely technical or specialized kind of training.

Hymn (赞美诗)

A hymn is a type of song, usually religious, specifically written for the purpose of praise, adoration or prayer, and typically addressed to a deity or deities, or to a prominent figure or personification. The term derived from Greek "hymnos," which originally signified songs of praise that were for the most part addressed to the gods, but in some instances to human heroes or to abstract concepts. The early Christian Churches, following classical examples, introduced the singing of hymns as part of the liturgy; some of these consisted of the texts or paraphrases of Old Testament psalms, but others were composed as songs of worship by churchly authors of the time. The writing of religious hymns continued through the Renaissance and was supplemented by a revival of "literary hymn" on secular or even pagan subjects. The tradition of writing hymns on secular subjects continued into the 19th century. The secular hymns were composed to be read rather than sung. They were often long and elaborate compositions that verged closely upon another form of versified praise, the "ode."

Although most familiar to speakers of English in the context of Christian churches, hymns are also a fixture of other world religions, especially on the Indian subcontinent. Hymns also survive from antiquity, especially from Egyptian and Greek cultures. Some of the oldest surviving examples of notated music are hymns with Greek texts. Collections of hymns are known as hymnals or hymn books. Hymns may or may not include instrumental accompaniment.

Idyll (田园诗)

An idyll or idyl is a short poem, descriptive of rustic life in terms of idealized innocence and contentment, written in the style of Theocritus' short pastoral poems, the *Idylls*. Unlike Homer, Theocritus did not engage in heroes and warfare. His idylls are limited to a small intimate world and describe scenes from everyday life. Later imitators include the Roman poets Virgil and Catullus, Italian poet Leopardi (1798 – 1837), and the English poet Alfred, Lord Tennyson (*Idylls of the King*). Goethe called his poem *Hermann and Dorothea* (written 1796 – 97; published 1782 – 84), which Schiller (1759 – 1805) considered the very climax in Goethe's production, an idyll.

The term, together with eclogue and bucolic, is virtually synonymous with pastoral. The difference between these terms lies only in their different origins: idyll came from the title of Theocritus' pastorals, eclogue (literally, "a selection") from the title of Virgil's pastorals, and bucolic poetry from the Greek word for "herdsman."

Iambic pentameter (抑扬格五音步)

Iambic pentameter is a commonly used type of metrical line in traditional English poetry and verse drama. The term describes the rhythm that the words establish in that line, which is measured in small groups of syllables called "feet." The word "iambic" refers to the type of foot that is used, known as the iamb, which in English is an unstressed syllable followed by a stressed syllable. The word "pentameter" indicates that a line has five of these "feet."

Different languages express rhythm in different ways. In Ancient Greek and Latin, the rhythm was created through the alternation of short and long syllables. In English, the rhythm is created through the use of stress, alternating between unstressed and stressed syllables. An English unstressed syllable is equivalent to a classical short syllable, while an English stressed syllable is equivalent to a classical long syllable. When a pair of syllables is arranged as a short followed by a long, or an unstressed followed by a stressed, pattern, that foot is said to be "iambic." A line of iambic pentameter is made up of five such pairs of short and long, or unstressed and stressed, syllables.

Iambic rhythms come relatively naturally in English. Iambic pentameter is the most common meter in English poetry; it is used in many of the major English poetic forms, including blank verse, the heroic couplet and some of the traditional rhymed stanza forms. William Shakespeare used iambic pentameter in his plays and sonnets.

Iambic tetrameter (抑扬格四音步)

Iambic tetrameter is a meter in poetry, which refers to a line consisting of four iambs or iambic feet. The word "tetrameter" simply means that there are four feet in the line. Some poetic forms rely upon iambic tetrameter: triolet, Onegin stanza, Memoriam stanza and long measure (or long meter) ballad stanza.

Imagery (意象)

Imagery is one of the most common terms in criticism and one of the most variable in meaning. Its applications range all the way from the "mental pictures" which, it is sometimes claimed, are experienced by the reader of a poem, to the totality of the components which make up a poem. Three discriminable uses of the word, however, are especially frequent; in all these senses imagery is said to make poetry concrete, as opposed to abstract: a) Imagery, "images" taken collectively, is used to signify all the objects and qualities of sense perception referred to in a poem or other work of literature, whether by literal description, by allusion, or in the vehicles (the secondary references) of its similes and metaphors; b) Imagery is used, more narrowly, to signify only specific descriptions of visible objects and scenes, especially if the description is vivid and particularized; c) Commonly in recent usage, imagery signifies figurative language, especially the vehicles of metaphors and similes. Critics after the 1930s, and notably the New Critics, went far beyond earlier commentators in stressing imagery, in this sense, as the essential component in poetry, and as a major factor in poetic meaning, structure and effect.

Interior monologue (内心独白)

Interior monologue refers to an extended representation in prose or verse of a character's unspoken thoughts, memories and impressions, rendered as if directly "overheard" by the reader without the intervention of a summarizing narrator. The device is distinguished from the dramatic monologue by the fact that the thoughts are unspoken rather than addressed to an auditor. Many modern poems make use of this convention, and it is widely employed in modern fiction, notably in the deliberately incoherent stream-of-consciousness style adopted by Dorothy Miller Richardson (1873 – 1957), James Joyce, and others.

While many sources use "interior monologue" and "stream of consciousness" as synonyms, the *Oxford Dictionary of Literary Terms* suggests, that "they can also be distinguished psychologically and literarily. In a psychological sense, stream of consciousness is the subject-matter, while interior monologue is the technique for presenting it." And for literature, "while an interior monologue always presents a character's thoughts 'directly,' without the apparent intervention of a summarizing and selecting narrator, it does not necessarily mingle them with impressions and perceptions, nor does it necessarily violate the norms of grammar, or logic, but the stream-of-consciousness technique also does one or both of these things." Similarly, the *Encyclopedia Britannica Online*, while agreeing that these terms are "often used interchangeably," suggests, that "while an interior monologue may mirror all the half thoughts, impressions and associations that impinge upon the character's consciousness, it may also be restricted to an organized presentation of that character's rational thoughts."

Irony（反讽）

In Greek comedy the character called the *eiron* was a dissembler, who characteristically spoke in understatement and deliberately pretended to be less intelligent than he was, yet triumphed over the *alazon*—the self-deceiving and stupid braggart. In most of the modern critical uses of the term "irony," there remains the root sense of dissembling or hiding what is actually the case; not, however, in order to deceive, but to achieve special rhetorical or artistic effects. There is verbal irony and structural irony.

Verbal irony is a statement in which the meaning that a speaker implies differs sharply from the meaning that is ostensibly expressed. The ironic statement usually involves the explicit expression of one attitude or evaluation, but with indications in the overall speech-situation that the speaker intends a very different, and often opposite, attitude or evaluation.

While verbal irony depends on knowledge of the fictional speaker's ironic intention, which is shared both by the speaker and the reader, structural irony depends on knowledge of the author's ironic invention, which is shared by the reader but is not intended by the fictional speaker; that is, the author introduces a structural feature that serves to sustain a duplex meaning and evaluation throughout the work. One common literary device of this sort is the invention of a naïve hero, or else a naïve narrator or spokesperson, whose invincible simplicity or obtuseness leads him to persist in putting an interpretation on affairs which the knowing reader, who penetrates to and shares the implied point of view of the authorial presence behind the naïve persona, just as persistently is called on to alter and correct.

James Tait Black Memorial Prizes（詹姆斯·泰特·布莱克纪念奖）

The James Tait Black Memorial Prizes are literary prizes awarded for literature written in the English language. They, along with the Hawthornden Prize, are Britain's oldest literary awards. Based at the University of Edinburgh in Scotland, United Kingdom, the prizes were founded in 1919 by Mrs. Janet Coats Black in memory of her late husband James Tait Black, a partner in the publishing house of A & C Black Ltd.

Juvenalian satire（尤维纳利斯式讽刺）

Juvenalian satire, named after the Roman satirist Juvenal, is more contemptuous and abrasive than the Horatian. Juvenal disagreed with the opinions of the public figures and institutions of the Republic and actively attacked them through his literature. "He utilized the satirical tools of exaggeration and parody to make his targets appear monstrous and incompetent. " (Podzemny, 2016) Juvenalian satire follows this same pattern of abrasively ridiculing societal structures. It addresses social evil through scorn, outrage and savage ridicule. This form is often pessimistic, characterized by irony, sarcasm, moral indignation and personal invective, with less emphasis on humor. Strongly polarized political satire is often Juvenalian.

A Juvenalian satirist's goal is to provoke some sort of change because he/she sees his/her opponent as evil or harmful. A Juvenalian satirist mocks "societal structure, power, and civilization. " (Thomas, 2016) He/she will do this by exaggerating the words or position of his/her opponent in order to jeopardize his/her opponent's reputation and/or power. Jonathan Swift has been established as an author who "borrowed heavily from Juvenal's techniques in[his critique]of contemporary English society. " (Podzemny, 2016) His is Juvenalian satire and attempts to punish.

Kitchen sink realism/kitchen sink drama (激进现实主义/极端现实主义戏剧)

Kitchen sink realism (or kitchen sink drama) is a term applied to a British cultural movement in the late 1950s and early 1960s in theatre, art, novels, film and television plays, whose protagonists are the so-called "angry young men" disillusioned with modern society. Set frequently in poorer industrial areas in the North of England and using the accents and slang heard in those regions, kitchen sink drama depicts the domestic situations of working-class Britons living in cramped rented accommodation and spending their off-hours drinking in grimy pubs, to explore controversial social issues and political controversies ranging from abortion to homelessness. The plays of such representative writers as Arnold Wesker, Shelagh Delaney (1938 – 2011) and John Osborne were written in part as a reaction against the drawing-room comedies and middle-class dramas of Noël Coward (1899 – 1973) and Terence Rattingan (1911 – 1977), and also undermined the popularity of the verse drama of T. S. Eliot and C. Fry. Kenneth Tynan (1927 – 1980) was a principal advocate of this new group of writers.

John Osborne's *Look Back in Anger* is thought of as the first of the genre. The gritty love-triangle in the play takes place in a cramped, one-room flat in the English Midlands. Shelagh Delaney's 1958 play *A Taste of Honey*, which was made into a film of the same name in 1961, is about a teenage schoolgirl who has an affair with a black sailor, gets pregnant and then moves in with a gay male acquaintance; it raises issues such as class, race, gender and sexual orientation. The conventions of the genre have continued into the 2000s, finding expression in such television shows as *Coronation Street* and *EastEnders*.

Lake Poets/Lake School (湖畔派诗人)

The term was applied to Samuel Taylor Coleridge, Robert Southey, William Wordsworth, and sometimes to De Quincey, who lived in the Lake District at the beginning of the 19th century. The expression "Lake School" seems first to appear in the *Edinburgh Review* of August 1817. Lord Byron made play with the term, and in the dedication to *Don Juan* (1819) referred slightly to "all the Lakers. " In his *Recollections of the Lake Poets* De Quincey denied the existence of any such "school. "

Legend (传奇)

A legend is a story or group of stories handed down through popular oral tradition, usually consisting of an exaggerated or unreliable account of some actually or possibly historical person—often a saint, a monarch, or a popular hero. Legends are sometimes different from myths in that they concern human beings rather than gods, and sometimes they have some sort of historical basis whereas myths do not, but these distinctions are difficult to maintain constantly. The term "legend" was originally applied to accounts of saints' lives, but it is now mainly applied to fanciful tales of warriors (e. g. King Arthur and his knights), criminals (e. g. Faust, Robin Hood), and other sinners; or more recently to those bodies of biographical rumor and embroidered anecdote surrounding dead film stars and rock musicians (e. g. John Lennon).

Literary Criticism (文学批评)

Literary criticism is the overall term for studies concerned with defining, classifying, analyzing, interpreting and evaluating works of literature in light of existing standards of taste, or with the purpose of creating new standards. There are two approaches to literary criticism: theoretical criticism and practical criticism. The former proposes an explicit theory of literature, in the sense of general principles, together with a set of terms, distinctions and categories, to be applied to identifying and analyzing works of literature, as well as the criteria (the standards, or norms) by which these works and their writers are to be evaluated. The latter (also called applied criticism) concerns itself with the discussion of particular works and writers; in an applied critique, the theoretical principles controlling the mode of the analysis, interpretation and evaluation are often left implicit, or brought in only as the occasion demand.

Lost Man Booker Prize (未按时颁发的曼布克文学奖)

The Lost Man Booker Prize was a special edition of the Man Booker Prize for Fiction awarded by a public vote in 2010 to a novel from 1970 as the books published in 1970 were not eligible for the Man Booker Prize due to a rules alteration; until 1970 the prize was awarded to books published in the previous year, while from 1971 onwards it was awarded to books published the same year as the award. The prize was won by J. G. Farrell (1935 – 1979) for *Troubles* (1970).

Lyric (抒情诗)

In the original Greek, "lyric" signified a song rendered to the accompaniment of a lyre. In some current usages, lyric still retains the sense of a poem written to be set to music; the hymn, for example, is a lyric on a religious subject that is intended to be sung. The adjective "lyrical" is sometimes applied to an expressive, song-like passage in a narrative poem. However, in the most common use of the term, a lyric is any fairly short poem, consisting of the utterance by a single speaker, who expresses a state of mind or a process of perception, thought and feeling. Many lyric speakers are represented as musing in solitude. In dramatic lyrics, however, the lyric speaker is represented as addressing another person in a specific situation.

Although the lyric is uttered in the first person, the "I" in the poem need not be the poet who wrote it. The lyric genre comprehends a great variety of utterances. Some are ceremonial poems uttered in a public voice on a public occasion. Among the lyrics in a more private mode, some are simply a brief, intense expression of a mood or state of feeling. But the genre also includes extended expressions of a complex evolution of feelingful thought, as in the long elegy and the meditative ode. And within a lyric, the process of observation, thought, memory and feeling may be organized in a variety of ways.

Magical realism/Magic realism/Marvelous realism (魔幻现实主义)

Magical realism, magic realism, or marvelous realism is a style employed in literature, painting and film that, encompassing a range of subtly different concepts, shares an acceptance of magic in the rational world. Of the three terms, Magical realism is the most commonly used, in literature in particular, to portray magical or unreal elements as a natural part in an otherwise realistic or mundane environment.

The terms are broadly descriptive rather than critically rigorous. Matthew Strecher (1999: 267) defined magic realism as "what happens when a highly detailed, realistic setting is invaded by something too strange to believe." Many writers are categorized as magical realists, which confuses what the term really means and how wide its definition is. Magical realism is often associated with Latin American literature, particularly authors including Gabriel García Márquez (1927 – 2014) and Isabel Allende (1942 –).

Man Booker Prize for Fiction (曼布克小说奖)

Originally and formerly known as the Booker-McConnell Prize, after the company Booker-McConnell began sponsoring the event in 1968, the Man Booker Prize for Fiction is commonly called the Booker Prize for short. It is a literary prize awarded each year for the best original novel, written in the English language and published in the UK. The Prize is greeted with great anticipation and fanfare. The winner of the Man Booker Prize is generally assured of international renown and success; therefore, the prize is of great significance for the book trade.

Martian poetry or the Martians (火星派)

Martian poetry was a minor movement in British poetry in the late 1970s and early 1980s. The poets most closely associated with the movement are Craig Raine and Christopher Reid. The Martians are ingenious in their poetic expression. They say things in ways totally odd to the readers. It is true that they set out to describe this ordinary world, but they end up making it out as if it were a strange and alien one.

The term derived from Raine's poem "A Martian Sends a Postcard Home" in which the narrator, a Martian, uncomprehendingly observes human behavior and tries to describe it to his fellow Martians. This drive to make the familiar strange was carried into fiction by Martin Amis (1949 –), including his novel *Other People: A Mystery Story* (1981). The story unfolds from the point of view of a protagonist who is apparently suffering from an extreme form of amnesia which causes her to lose her memory of even basic aspects of human experience. Hence the term "Martianism," coincidentally an anagram of Martin Amis, has been applied more widely to include fiction as well as poetry.

Martian poetry became a popular topic in the teaching of poetry composition to school children. Related to Surrealism, it arose in the context of the experimental poetry of the late 1960s, but also owes a debt to a variety of English traditions including Metaphysical poetry, Anglo-Saxon riddles, and nonsense poetry of Lewis Carroll and

Edward Lear (1812 – 1888). In this context what was distinctive about Martian Poetry was its focus on visual experience. Dr Samuel Johnson's description of the Metaphysical poets' approach where "the most heterogeneous ideas are yoked by violence together" could aptly describe much Martian poetry.

Masque/mask (假面剧)

The masque was inaugurated in Renaissance Italy and flourished in England during the reigns of Elizabeth I, James I and Charles I. In its full development, it was an elaborate form of court entertainment that combined poetic drama, music, song, dance, splendid costuming, and stage spectacle. A plot—often slight, and mainly mythological and allegorical—served to hold together these diverse elements. Professional actors and musicians were hired for the speaking and singing parts. Often, the masquers who did not speak or sing were courtiers. All the players wore masks; hence the title. The play concluded with a dance in which the players doffed their masks and were joined by the audience.

Melodrama (音乐剧/情节剧)

"Melos" is Greek for song, and the term "melodrama" was originally applied to all musical plays, including opera. In scholarly and historical musical contexts, melodramas are dramas of the 18th and 19th centuries in which orchestral music or song was used to accompany the action. Existing in a long timeframe and using a variety of formats, a melodrama is a dramatic or literary work in which the plot, which is typically sensational and designed to appeal strongly to the emotions, takes precedence over detailed characterization. Characters are often simply drawn and may appear stereotyped. In the early 19th-century London, many plays were produced with a musical accompaniment that, as in modern motion picture, served simply to fortify the emotional tone of various scenes.

The term is now also applied as well to stage performances without incidental music, novels, movies, and television and radio broadcasts. In modern contexts, the term "melodrama" is generally pejorative as it suggests that the work in question lacks subtlety, character development, or both. The terms "melodrama" and "melodramatic" are also, in an extended sense, applied to any literary work or episode, whether in drama or prose fiction, that relies on implausible events and sensational action.

Meta-fiction (元小说)

Meta-fiction, a Postmodernist form of writing about fiction in the form of fiction, is a style of fictive narrative that tries to tell the readers that fiction is fiction and is not an illusion of reality as the realists have tried to "deceive" the readers into believing. Unlike the antinovel, or anti-fiction, meta-fiction is specifically fiction about fiction, i.e. fiction which deliberately reflects upon itself. It poses questions about the relationship between fiction and reality, usually using irony and self-reflection, and forces readers to be aware that they are reading a fictional work. Meta-fiction writers feel skeptical about the idea of authentic representation of reality and write novels not so much to tell a story as to shock the readers' expectations. They tend to use burlesque and parody, a manner of writing in which an effort is made to imitate an original in order to poke fun at it or to reveal the discrepancy between the imitation and the original, as a means of subverting the readers' sense of complacency. The term was coined by William H. Gass (1924 -) in a 1970 essay entitled "Philosophy and the Form of Fiction."

Meta-fiction is primarily associated with Modernist literature and Postmodernist literature, but is found at least as early as Homer's *Odyssey*, Chaucer's *The Canterbury Tales* and Laurence Sterne's *Tristram Shandy*. Cervantes' *Don Quixote* is considered to be one of the early examples of meta-fiction as well. In the 1950s several French novelists published works whose styles were collectively dubbed "nouveau roman" (new novel). These "new novels" were characterized by the bending of genre and style and often included elements of meta-fiction. It became prominent in the 1960s, with such works as *Lost in the Funhouse* (1968) by John Barth (1930 -), *Slaughterhouse Five* (1969) by Kurt Vonnegut (1922 - 2007) and *The Crying of Lot 49* (1966) by Thomas Pynchon, and the like.

Metaphor (暗喻/隐喻)

Metaphor is a figure of speech in which a word or expression that in literal usage denotes one kind of thing is applied to a distinctly different kind of thing, without asserting a comparison.

Metaphysical poetry (玄学派诗歌)

The Metaphysical poets appeared in England at about the beginning of the 17th century. The poets as a group include John Donne, George Herbert, Richard Crashaw, Henry Vaughan, Robert Herrick, Thomas Carew, Abraham Cowley and Andrew Marvell. John Donne is acknowledged as the "father of the Metaphysical School" while George Herbert is "the saint of the Metaphysical School." The works of the school are characterized by mysticism in content and fantasticality in form.

The term "Metaphysical" came first from the 17th-century poet-critic John Dryden who, commenting on Donne, felt that Donne loved to play with metaphysics both in his satirical and love poetry, so that his love poems reveal the subtleties of metaphysics instead of focusing on love. Samuel Johnson, the literary dictator of the second half of the 18th century, elaborated Dryden's concept when he criticized Donne and his group for showing off their knowledge rather than describing natural human sentiment in their love poetry. His views later found echoes from such 19th-century critics as William Hazlitt. Thus "Metaphysical" became derogatory, and Metaphysical poetry lay in silence and obscurity for the long period of the 18th and 19th centuries. It managed to recover from this eclipse only in the early years of the 20th century, first anthologized by a well-known scholar Herbert J. C. Grierson and then especially when T. S. Eliot, another literary dictator, took interest in it and brought it back to light. Today the school is so well known that no one ignores it without good reason. And the nomenclature "Metaphysical" has long lost its pejorative denotation and come to mean simply the poems by Donne and his group.

The basic feature of Metaphysical poetry is its "wit" or "conceit." "Wit" here means being clever at "yoking" the most heterogeneous ideas together by violence so as to impress people (to paraphrase Johnson's statement on the subject), and "conceit" denotes a fantastic fancy or way of thinking in the form of peculiar, ingenious, knotty, many-sided metaphors. These are employed along with far-fetched, difficult imagery in the works of Donne and his fellow poets. There is good reason to believe that the poets tried to conquer by sheer unconventionality rather than follow the normal channel of communication. They went out of their way to find a way of expression which demanded the readers to stretch their perspective and imaginative powers to the farthest limit possible to make sense of it. Hence the prophecy of Ben Jonson that this kind of poetry is too difficult for people to catch on in history. Metaphysical poetry has remained unprecedented with virtually no successful followers, and it is often an exacting exercise of the mental powers for those who read it. The reward, however, hard-won often after a battle of wit and intellect, is often a combination of grateful pleasure, gratification and fun.

Meter (格律/节拍)

Meter is the recurrence, in regular units, of a prominent feature in the sequence of speech-sounds of a language. There are four main types of meter in European languages:

a. In Classical Greek and Latin, the meter was quantitative; that is, it was established by the relative duration of the utterance of a syllable, and consisted of a recurrent pattern of long and short syllables.

b. In French and many other Romance languages, the meter is syllabic, depending on the number of syllables within a line of verse, without regard to the fall of the stresses.

c. In older Germanic languages, including Old English, the meter is accentual, depending on the number of stressed syllables within a line, without regard to the number of intervening unstressed syllables.

d. The fourth type of meter, combining the features of the two preceding types, is accentual-syllabic, in which the metric units consist of a recurrent pattern of stresses on a recurrent number of syllables. The stress-and-syllable type has been the predominant meter of English poetry since the 14th century.

Miracle plays, Morality plays, and Interludes (神迹剧、道德剧与幕间剧)

Miracle plays, Morality plays, and Interludes are types of late-medieval drama, written in a variety of verse forms.

The **miracle play** has as its subject either a story from the *Bible*, or else the life and martyrdom of a saint. In the usage of some historians, however, "miracle plays" denote only dramas based on saints' lives, and the term "mystery play" is applied to drama based on the *Bible*.

The **morality plays** are medieval allegorical plays in which personified human qualities act and dispute to present the conflict between good and evil. The usual protagonist represents Mankind or Everyman; among the other characters are personifications of virtues, vices and Death, as well as angels and demons who contest for the prize of the soul of Mankind. A character known as the Vice often plays the role of the tempter in a fashion both sinister and comic; he is regarded by some historians as a precursor both of the cynical, ironic villain and of some of the comic figures in Elizabethan drama, including Shakespeare's Falstaff. The best-known morality play is the 15th-century *Everyman*, which is still given an occasional performance; other notable examples, written in the same century, are *The Castle of Perseverance* and *Mankind* (c. 1470). Prevailing in the Middle Ages, morality plays contribute to the flowering of English drama in the Renaissance England.

Interlude (Latin, "between the play") is a term applied to a variety of short stage entertainments, such as secular farces and witty dialogues with a religious or political point. In the late 15th and early 16th centuries, these little dramas were often performed by bands of professional actors; it is believed that they were often put on between the courses of a feast or between the acts of a longer play.

Modernism（现代主义）

Modernism was a complex and diverse international movement in all the creative arts, originating at the end of the 19th century, and provided the greatest creative renaissance of the 20th century. Therefore the term is generally applied to the wide range of experimental and avant-garde trends in literature (and other arts) of the early 20th century, including Symbolism, Futurism, Expressionism, Imagism, Vorticism, Dadaism, Cubism and Surrealism, along with the innovations of unaffiliated writers.

Modernist writers tended to see themselves as the avant-garde disengaged from bourgeois values, and disturbed their readers by adopting complex and difficult new forms and styles. Modernism has become the synonym of revolution in form and has been called the "tradition of the new." Modernist literature is characterized chiefly by a rejection of the 19th-century traditions and of their consensus between author and reader. In fiction, the accepted continuity of chronological development was upset by Joseph Conrad and Marcel Proust; and William Faulkner, James Joyce and Virginia Woolf attempted new ways of tracing the flow of characters' thoughts in their stream-of-consciousness styles. In poetry, the traditional meters were rejected and free verse became the poets' favor. Ezra Pound and T. S Eliot replaced the logical exposition of thoughts with collages of fragmentary images and complex allusions. Luigi Pirandello (1867–1936) and Bertolt Brecht (1898–1956) opened up the theatre to new forms of abstraction in place of realist and naturalist representation. In a word, the Modernist techniques of juxtaposition and multiple points of view challenge the reader to reestablish a coherence of meaning from fragmentary forms.

Thematically, Modernist writing was predominantly cosmopolitan and often expressed a sense of urban cultural dislocation, along with an awareness of new anthropological and psychological theories. It strove to reflect the 20th century's social and political changes, its dangers and anxieties, its rapid growth in technological and psychological knowledge. It provided fresh ways of looking at man's position and function in the universe. In English, its major landmarks are Joyce's *Ulysses* and Eliot's *The Waste Land*.

Motif and Theme（主旨与主题）

A motif is a conspicuous element, such as a type of incident, device, or formula, which occurs frequently in works of literature. It is also applied to the frequent repetition within a single work of a significant verbal or musical phrase, or set description, or complex of images.

Theme is sometimes used interchangeably with "motif," but the term is more usefully applied to a general concept or doctrine, whether implicit or asserted, which an imaginative work is designed to incorporate and make persuasive to the reader.

Movement Poetry, the（运动派诗歌）

The term, "the Movement," first appeared in 1954 in an article by J. D. Scott, the literary editor of the *Spectator*, who was discussing the features of the new poetry of postwar Britain. Although it was used there in a jocular manner, the label sank deep in memory and gained wide currency. The Movement poets were first made known as a group in an anthology entitled *Poets of the 1950s*, edited by D. J. Enright, and then again in another better-known anthology *New Lines* by Robert Conquest. Then the rest of the world as well as Britain became alert that a new frame of reference had appeared for gauging the mood of postwar Britain.

The Movement poets included, among others, Philip Larkin, Donald Davie, D. J. Enright, Thom Gunn, Robert Conquest, John Wain, Elizabeth Jennings, Kingsley Amis and John Holloway. These poets wrote in a dramatically different way from the poets of the war years. Fed up with the experimental Romantic efforts of Dylan Thomas and his contemporaries to shape life and the world, they reacted strongly by veering in a new direction and came to grips downright with their new, different reality. They were concerned with the social changes that postwar Laborite Britain was going through, and tried to examine life in an honest, realistic manner. In addition, they felt the acute need to cater to a broader readership than the Modernist endeavor had served, and they could be anti-intellectual and anti-cultural in their stance. Most of the younger poets of the 1950s were either part of the Movement or shared its values.

The Movement poets shared some essential literary features and qualities in their works. They were self-expressive, intuitive, obscure, experimental, realistic, and concerned with formal control. Their mood and tone tended to be depressing. Their style is generally plain, direct, deflated, personal and formal. Their diction is lean and spare. Moreover, the Movement poets wrote also novels and literary criticism; and the group was heterogeneous in ideas and practices rather than monolithic in any sense of the term.

Mystery fiction（神秘小说）

Mystery fiction is a genre of fiction typically focused on the investigation of a crime. It is often used as a synonym for detective fiction or crime fiction, i. e., a novel or short story in which a detective (either professional or amateur) investigates and solves a crime mystery. Sometimes mystery books are nonfictional. Mystery fiction can be detective stories in which the emphasis is on the puzzle or suspense element and its logical solution such as a whodunit. It can be contrasted with hardboiled detective stories, which focus on action and gritty realism.

Mystery fiction may involve a supernatural or thriller mystery where the solution does not have to be logical, and even no crime involved. This usage was common in the pulp magazines of the 1930s and 1940s, where titles such as *Dime Mystery*, *Thrilling Mystery* and *Spicy Mystery* offered what at the time were described as "weird menace" stories. This contrasted with parallel titles of the same names which contained conventional hardboiled crime fiction. The first use of "mystery" in this sense was by *Dime Mystery*, which started out as an ordinary crime fiction magazine but switched to "weird menace" during the latter part of 1933.

Narrative（叙事）

A narrative is a story, whether told in prose or verse, involving events, characters, and what the characters say and do. Some literary forms such as the novel and short story in prose, and the epic and romance in verse, are explicit narratives that are told by a narrator. In drama, the narrative is told, but evolves by means of the direct presentation on stage of the actions and speeches of the characters. It should be noted that there is an implicit narrative element even in many lyric poems, of which William Wordsworth's "The Solitary Reaper" is a good example.

Narrative poetry（叙事诗）

Narrative poetry is a form of poetry that tells a story, often making use of the voices of a narrator and characters as well; the entire story is usually written in metered verse. Narrative poems do not have to follow rhythmic patterns. The poems that make up this genre may be short or long, and the story it relates to may be complex. It is usually dramatic, with objectives, diverse characters, and meter. Narrative poems include epics, ballads, idylls and lays.

Some narrative poetry takes the form of a novel in verse. An example of this is *The Ring and the Book* by Robert Browning. A romance is also a narrative poem that tells a story of chivalry. Both *Romance of the Rose* and Alfred Tennyson's *Idylls of the King* are such examples. Although these examples use medieval and Arthurian materials, romances may also tell stories from classical mythology.

Shorter narrative poems are often similar in style to the short story. Sometimes these short narratives are collected into interrelated groups, as with Geoffrey Chaucer's *The Canterbury Tales*. Some literatures contain prose narratives that include poems and poetic interludes; much Old Irish poetry is contained within prose narratives, and the Old Norse sagas include both incidental poetry and the biographies of poets.

Negative capability（客体感受力）

Negative capability is the ability to perceive and to think beyond any presupposition of human nature. It describes the capacity of human beings to transcend and revise their contexts. It further captures the rejection of the totalizing constraints of a closed context, and the ability to experience phenomena free from epistemological bounds, as well as to assert their own will and individuality upon their activity.

The term was first used by the English poet John Keats to describe the quality of selfless receptivity necessary to a true poet and critique those who sought to categorize all experience and phenomena and turn them into a theory of knowledge. In a letter to his brothers (December 1817), he wrote "at once it struck me, what quality went to form a Man of Achievement especially in Literature and which William Shakespeare possessed so enormously—I mean Negative Capability, that is when man is capable of being in uncertainties, Mysteries, doubts, without any irritable reaching after fact and reason." He went on to criticize Coleridge for not being "content with half knowledge"; and in later letters complained of the "egotistical" and philosophical bias of William Wordsworth's poetry. By negative capability, then, Keats seemed to have meant a poetic capacity to efface one's own mental identity by immersing it sympathetically and spontaneously within the subject described, as Shakespeare was thought to have done.

It has recently been appropriated by philosopher and social theorist Roberto Mangabeira Unger (1947 -) to comment on human nature and to explain how human beings innovate and resist within confining social contexts.

Neoclassicism（新古典主义）

In literature, the term refers to the habit of imitating the great authors of antiquity (notably its poets and dramatists) as a matter of aesthetic principle, and the acceptance of the critical precepts which emerged to guide that imitation. Medieval writers had often used classical works for models, but Petrarch in the 14th century was the first to do so because he considered it the only way to produce great literature. The epic, eclogue, elegy, ode, satire, tragedy, comedy and epigram of ancient times all found imitators, first in Latin, then in the vernaculars, and eventually practice was succeeded by precept. At the beginning of the 16th century the recovery of the previously neglected *Poetics* of Aristotle provoked an attempt to establish rules for the use of the ancient genres. The most famous invention was the observance of the dramatic unities of time, place and action, which won great support in France where a new generation of playwrights in the 1620s and 1630s was eager to attract a more educated public.

Neoclassicism is mainly applied to the style of Western literature that flourished from the mid-17th century until the end of the 18th century and the rise of Romanticism. Neoclassical writers believed that literature should both instruct and delight, and the proper subject of art was humanity. They stressed the classical artistic ideals of rules, reason, harmony, balance, restraint, decorum, order, logic, accuracy, serenity, realism and form—above all, an appeal to the intellect rather than emotion. The Restoration in 1660 marked the beginning of the Neoclassical Period in England, whose writers include John Dryden, Alexander Pope, Samuel Johnson, etc.

In the context of art history, the term "Neoclassical" generally refers to the style and aesthetics of a somewhat later period (mid- to late 18th century), when an emphasis on the "antique" ideals of harmony and grandeur emerged in part as a reaction against the excesses of baroque and the triviality of rococo.

Nobel Prizes (诺贝尔奖)

Nobel Prizes were established under the will of Alfred Bernhard Nobel (1833 – 1896), a Swedish chemist distinguished in the development of explosives, by which the interest on the greater part of his large fortune is distributed in annual prizes for the most important discoveries in physics, chemistry, and physiology or medicine respectively, to the person who shall have most promoted "the fraternity of nations" (the Nobel Peace Prize), and to the "person who shall have produced in the field of literature the most outstanding work of an idealistic tendency."

Objective correlative (客观对应物)

An objective correlative is a literary term referring to a symbolic article used to provide explicit, rather than implicit, access to traditionally inexplicable concepts as emotion or color. The term was coined by Washington Allston (1779 – 1843) around 1840 in the "Introductory Discourse" of his *Lectures on Art* and was popularly employed in literary criticism after T. S. Eliot's rather casual introduction into his essay "Hamlet and His Problems" (1919). "The only way of expressing emotion in the form of art," Eliot wrote, "is by finding an 'objective correlative'; in other words, a set of objects, a situation, a chain of events which shall be the formula of that particular emotion; such that when the external facts, which must terminate in sensory experience, are given, the emotion is immediately evoked." Helping define the objective correlative, "Hamlet and His Problems," republished in Eliot's book *The Sacred Wood: Essays on Poetry and Criticism* (1920), discusses the author's view of William Shakespeare's incomplete development of Hamlet's emotions in the play *Hamlet*. According to Eliot, the feelings of Hamlet are not sufficiently supported by the story and the other characters surrounding him. The purpose of the objective correlative is to express the character's emotions by showing rather than describing feelings. Eliot emphasized definiteness, impersonality and descriptive concreteness instead of vagueness of description and the direct statement of feelings in poetry. He insisted that poetry must be impersonal and that the poet should be detached from the depicted character.

Eliot's insistence on impersonality in creating an emotion greatly influenced the formation of the New Critical canon. With the prevalence of New Criticism, T. S. Eliot largely developed his notion of the objective correlative. It is worth noting that Eliot's concept of an outer correlative for inner feelings has been often criticized for falsifying the way a poet actually composes, since no object or situation is in itself a "formula" for an emotion, but depends for its emotional significance and effect on the way it is rendered and used by a particular poet.

Ode (颂诗/颂歌)

An ode is a long lyric poem that is serious in subject and treatment, elevated in style and elaborate in its stanzaic structure. It aims at praising and glorifying an individual, commemorating an event, or describing nature intellectually rather than emotionally. Odes originally were songs performed to the accompaniment of a musical instrument. There are two different classical models: the Greek choral odes of Pindar (c. 522 – c. 443 BC) devoted to public praise of athletes (5th century BC), and Horace's more privately reflective odes in Latin (c. 23 – 13 BC). John Keats wrote many celebrated odes such as "Ode on a Grecian Urn" and "Ode to a Nightingale."

Ottava rima (八行体)

Ottava rima is a rhyming stanza form of Italian origin. Originally used for long poems on heroic themes, it later came to be popular in the writing of mock-heroic works. In its original Italian form ("eighth rhyme"), pioneered by Boccaccio in the 14th century and perfected by Ariosto in the 16th century, it used hendecasyllables, but the English version uses iambic pentameters. Each stanza consists of three alternate rhymes and one double rhyme, following the abababcc pattern. Ottava rima was introduced into English by Thomas Wyatt in the 16th century and later used by Lord Byron in *Don Juan* as well as by John Keats, Percy Bysshe Shelley and William Butler Yeats. The ottava rima stanza in English consists of eight iambic lines, usually iambic pentameters.

Pamphlet (小册子/短论)

A pamphlet refers to a short essay or treatise, usually on a current topic, published without a binding.

Among the first printed materials, pamphlets were widely used in England, France and Germany from the early 16th century, often for religious or political propaganda; they sometimes rose to the level of literature or philosophical discourse. In North America, pre-Revolutionary War agitation stimulated extensive pamphleteering; foremost among the writers of political pamphlets was Thomas Paine (1737 – 1809). By the 20th century, the pamphlet was more often used for informational purposes than for the propagation of controversial positions by government organizations, religious groups and learned societies.

Pamphleteering was a means of propagating new or controversial ideas through the distribution of inexpensive and easily produced tracts or pamphlets. Because the pamphlets were brief and written in a popular style, they enjoyed tremendous circulation. Read aloud in taverns, churches and town meetings, pamphlets became a significant means of mass communication and an essential vehicle for carrying on political debates in colonial America.

Pamphleteering had its roots in English practice, particularly during the religious controversies and political contests of the commonwealth period. Americans continued to engage in pamphlet debates over issues that confronted the new government, especially the question of adopting the Constitution of the United States. Although newspapers were the forum for some of these debates—as was the case with the *Federalist Papers*—political opponents also used pamphlets to promote their points of view. The proliferation of newspapers in the early national period made pamphlet warfare less common, but some writers still used pamphlets to express their positions. Religious enthusiasts, reform groups, and propagators of utopian societies or economic panaceas often found the pamphlet an effective tool. Campaigns flooded the country with pamphlets to augment the circulation of newspapers or to make political attacks. Toward the end of the 19th century, socialists and populists used pamphlets to gain converts. Propagandists during World War I, especially pacifists, utilized the pamphlet to sustain morale or refute criticism. After World War I, pamphlet use declined, but never stopped.

Pamphleteer (小册子作者)

Pamphleteer is a historical term for someone who creates or distributes pamphlets, unbound (and therefore inexpensive) booklets intended for wide circulation. Pamphlets were used to broadcast the writer's opinions: to articulate a political ideology, for example, or to encourage people to vote for a particular politician. During times of political unrest pamphleteers were highly active in attempting to shape public opinion. Thomas Paine's pamphlets were influential in the history of the American Revolutionary War. Another famous pamphleteer was the 17th-century Dutch naval officer Witte Corneliszoon de With (1599 – 1658), who wrote papers mocking and praising his fellow-officers. Poet and polemicist John Milton published pamphlets as well.

Before the advent of telecommunications, those with access to a printing press and a supply of paper often used pamphlets to widely disseminate their ideas. Today's "pamphleteers" might communicate their missives in a blog.

Pantomime (哑剧)

Pantomime is acting on the stage without speech, using only posture, gesture, bodily movement and exaggerated facial expression to mime ("mimic") a character's actions and to express a character's feelings. Elaborate pantomimes, halfway between drama and dance, were put on in ancient Greece and Rome, and the form was revived, often for comic purposes, in Renaissance Europe. Mimed dramas enjoyed a vogue in the 18th-century England, and in modern times the silent movies encouraged a brief revival of the art and produced a superlative pantomimist in Charlie Chaplin (1889 – 1977). In America and many other countries, circus clowns are expert pantomimists, and miming has recently been revived in the theater for the deaf.

Parable (道德性小故事)

A parable is a succinct, didactic story in prose or verse, which illustrates one or more instructive lessons or principles. It differs from a fable in that fables employ animals, plants, inanimate objects, or forces of nature as characters, whereas parables have human characters. The term came from a Greek word, meaning "comparison, illustration, analogy. " It was the name given by Greek rhetoricians to an illustration in the form of a brief fictional narrative. Some scholars of the canonical gospels and the New Testament apply the term only to the parables of Jesus, though that is not a common restriction of the term.

Parody（戏仿）

The term parody was first used to refer to a narrative poem in epic meter, but is not generally restricted in later use. The parodist must both imitate and create incongruity in relation to the pretext, and parody has, contrary to pastiche, traditionally had a comic dimension. In other words, a parody, in current use, is an imitative work, created to mock, comment on or trivialize an original work, its subject, author, style, or some other target by means of satiric or ironic imitation. Parody should be distinguished from satire: the former targets a pre-existing text; the latter persons or events in the real world. Parody is a double-coded form of discourse. The classical mock-epic tradition and Aristophanes' parodies of the tragedies by Euripides (c. 480 – 406 BC) provided early examples of the genre. Liturgical parody and parodies of sacred texts flourished in the Middle Ages. In the 19th century appeared a strong popular tradition of parody. The 20th century again witnessed a renewed interest in parody.

Pastoral（牧歌/田园诗）

The originator of the pastoral was the Greek poet Theocritus, who in the 3rd century B. C. wrote poems representing the life of Sicilian shepherds: "pastor" is Latin for "shepherd." Virgil later imitated Theocritus in his Latin *Eclogues*, and in doing so established the enduring model for the traditional pastoral: a deliberately conventional poem expressing an urban poet's nostalgic image of the peace and simplicity of the life of shepherds and other rural folk in an idealized natural setting. The conventions that hundreds of later poets imitated from Virgil's imitations of Theocritus include a shepherd reclining under a spreading beech tree and meditating the rural muse, or piping as though he would never grow old, or engaging in a friendly singing contest, or expressing his good or bad fortune in a love affair, or grieving over the death of a fellow shepherd. From this last type developed the pastoral elegy, which persisted long after the other traditional types had lost their popularity. Other terms often used synonymously with pastoral are idyll, from the title of Theocritus' pastorals; eclogue (literally, "a selection"), from the title of Virgil's pastorals; and bucolic poetry, from the Greek word for "herdsman."

Pattern/concrete/shape poetry（图案诗/具象诗/形体诗）

Pattern or concrete or shape poetry is poetry in which the typographical arrangement of words is as important in conveying the intended effect as the conventional elements of the poem, such as meaning of words, rhythm, rhyme, and so on. It is sometimes referred to as visual poetry, a term that has evolved to have distinct meaning of its own, but which shares the distinction of being poetry in which the visual elements are as important as the text.

PEN International（国际笔会/世界作家协会）

PEN International, known as International PEN until 2010, is a worldwide association of writers, founded in London in 1921 to promote friendship and intellectual co-operation among writers everywhere. The association has autonomous International PEN centers in over 100 countries. It is the world's oldest human rights organization and the oldest international literary organization.

Other goals of the organization included: to emphasize the role of literature in the development of mutual understanding and world culture; to fight for freedom of expression; and to act as a powerful voice on behalf of writers harassed, imprisoned and sometimes killed for their views.

Persona (人物角色)

A persona, in its everyday usage, is a social role or a character played by an actor. The word is derived from Latin, where it originally referred to a theatrical mask, from which came the term "dramatis personae" for the list of characters that play roles in a drama, and ultimately the English word "person," a particular individual. Its meaning in the latter Roman period changed to indicate a "character" of a theatrical performance or court of law, when it became apparent that different individuals could assume the same role, and legal attributes such as rights, powers and duties followed the role. The same individuals as actors could play different roles, each with its own legal attributes, sometimes even in the same court appearance.

In literature the term is often applied to the first-person speaker who tells the story in a narrative poem or novel, or whose voice we hear in a lyric poem. Although a persona often serves as the "voice" of the writer, it should not be confused with the writer, for a persona may not accurately reflect the writer's personal opinions, feelings, or perspectives on a subject. In English literature, the term has become associated with the work of two modern poets, Ezra Pound and T. S. Eliot. They understood the term slightly differently and derived its use and meaning from different traditions. Eliot had taken over and developed the ironic "I" of Laforgue (1860 – 1887), while Pound worked from Robert Browning's dramatic monologues. Whereas Eliot used "masks" to distance himself from aspects of modern life which he found degrading and repulsive, Pound's personae were poets and could be considered in good part alter-egos who are to be dissociated from "characters." For Pound, the personae were a way of working through a specific poetic problem. In this sense, the persona is a transparent mask, wearing the traits of two poets and responding to two situations, old and new, which are similar and overlapping.

Philosophical novel (哲理小说)

The Philosophical novel refers to a novel in which a significant proportion is devoted to a discussion of the sort of questions normally addressed in discursive philosophy. These might include the function and role of society, the purpose of life, ethics or morals, the role of art in human lives, and the role of experience or reason in the development of knowledge. Philosophical fiction would refer to the so-called novel of ideas, including a significant proportion of science fiction, utopian and dystopian fiction, and Bildungsroman.

Picaresque novel (流浪汉小说)

The Spanish form of the word "picaresque" is "picaresca," which is from "picaro" for "rogue" or "rascal." The picaresque novel is a genre of prose fiction which depicts the adventures of a roguish hero of low social class who lives by his wits in a corrupt society. It, with elements of comedy, is realistic in manner, episodic in structure (that is, composed of a sequence of events held together largely because they happened to one person), and often satiric in aim. This style of novel originated in the 16th-century Spain and flourished throughout Europe in the 17th and 18th centuries. The first, and very lively, English example was Thomas Nashe's *The Unfortunate Traveler*. The picaresque type survived in many later novels and continues to influence modern literature.

According to the traditional view of Thrall and Hibbard (first published in 1936), seven qualities distinguish the picaresque novel or narrative form, all or some of which may be employed for effect by the author: a) A picaresque narrative is usually written in the first person as an autobiographical account. b) The main character is often of low character or social class. He/she gets by with wit and rarely deigns to hold a job. c) There is no plot. The story is told in a series of loosely connected adventures or episodes. d) There is little if any character development in the main character. Once a picaro, always a picaro. His/her circumstances may change but they rarely result in a change of heart. e) The picaro's story is told with a plainness of language or realism. f) Satire might sometimes be a prominent element. g) The behavior of a picaresque hero/heroine stops just short of criminality. Carefree or immoral rascality positions the picaresque hero as a sympathetic outsider, untouched by the false rules of society.

Poet laureate (桂冠诗人)

Poet laureate is an honorary position officially appointed by a government, or conferring institution like a university. The title is given to a poet who receives a stipend as an office of the royal household, his duty (no longer enforced) being to write court odes or to compose poems for special events and occasions. Over a dozen national governments continue the poet laureate tradition. The title in the US was established in 1985 by the US Senate.

Poet Laureate of the United Kingdom (英国桂冠诗人)

The Poet Laureate of the United Kingdom, also referred to British Poet Laureate, is an honorary position appointed by the monarch of the United Kingdom on the advice of the Prime Minister. The role does not entail any specific duties, but there is an expectation that the holder will write verse for significant national occasions. The position has been held by Carol Ann Duffy (1955 –) since May 2009. The United Kingdom also has a "Children's Laureate," currently Chris Riddell (1962 –). Various poets, including Thomas Gray, Walter Scott, Philip Larkin and Seamus Heaney have declined the post.

The role was entitled the Poet Laureate of the Kingdom of England, which grew out of the Court Poet of Medieval England (first appointed in the 12th century), until the Acts of Union 1707, when it became the Poet Laureate of the Kingdom of Great Britain. The present title, Poet Laureate of the United Kingdom, has been used since the Acts of Union 1800.

The post was traditionally held for life, with John Dryden being the only holder to have been dismissed in 1688, due to his refusal to swear an oath of allegiance to the new king William III. From Andrew Motion (1952 –) in 1999, the appointment has been for 10 years.

Pre-Raphaelites (前拉菲尔学派)

Pre-Raphaelites are a group of English artists and writers of the Victorian period, associated directly or indirectly with the self-styled Pre-Raphaelite Brotherhood of young artists founded in 1848 by Dante Gabriel Rossetti, John Everett Millais (1829 – 1896) and William Holman Hunt (1827 – 1910). The aim of the organized Brotherhood was to replace the reigning academic style of painting by a return to the truthfulness, simplicity, and the spirit of devotion which they attributed to the Italian painting before the time of Raphael (1483 – 1520) and the high Italian Renaissance. Although the organization itself lasted only a few years and dissolved in the 1850s, and the original members went their different ways, some achieving considerable commercial success, its influence was enduring, and Pre-Raphaelitism as a broader current survived in the paintings of Edward Burne-Jones (1833 – 1898), the designs of William Morris, and the art criticism of John Ruskin, as well as in the poetry of Christina Rossetti (1830 – 1894), D. G. Rossetti, William Morris and A. C. Swinburne. Pre-Raphaelite poetry is often characterized by dream medievalism, the pictorial realism with symbolic overtones, and the union of flesh and spirit, sensuousness and religiousness notably in D. G. Rossetti's "The Blessed Damozel" (1850), William Morris' *The Defense of Guenevere* (1858) and Swinburne's *Poems and Ballads*.

Prose (散文)

Prose is an inclusive term for all discourse, spoken or written, which is not patterned into the lines either of metric verse or of free verse. It is possible to discriminate a great variety of non-metric types of language, which can be placed along a spectrum according to the degree to which they exploit, and make prominent, modes of formal organization. At one end is the irregular, and only occasionally formal, prose of ordinary discourse. Distinguished written discourse, in what John Dryden called "that other harmony of prose," is no less an art than distinguished verse; in all literatures, in fact, artfully written prose seems to have developed later than written verse. As written prose gets more "literary"—whether its function is descriptive, expository, narrative, or expressive—it exhibits more patent, though highly diverse, modes of rhythm and some other formal features like repetition, balance, and contrast of clauses.

Prose poem (散文诗)

Prose poems are densely compact, pronouncedly rhythmic, and highly sonorous compositions which are written as a continuous sequence of sentences without line breaks.

Prose romance (散文传奇)

Prose romance has as precursors the chivalric romance of the Middle Ages and the Gothic novel of the later 18th century. It usually deploys characters that are sharply discriminated as heroes or villains, masters or victims; its protagonist is often solitary and relatively isolated from a social context; it tends to be set in the historical past, and the atmosphere is such as to suspend the reader's expectations based on everyday experience. The plot of the prose romance emphasizes adventure and is frequently cast in the form of the quest for ideal or the pursuit of an enemy; and the nonrealistic and occasionally melodramatic events are claimed by some critics to project in symbolic form the primal desires, hopes and terrors in the depths of the human mind, and to be therefore analogous to the materials of dream, myth, ritual and folklore.

Psychoanalysis（精神分析/心理分析）

Psychoanalysis is a set of psychological and psychotherapeutic theories and associated techniques, originally popularized by the Austrian physician Sigmund Freud. Since then, it has expanded and been revised, reformed and developed in different directions. In literature, psychoanalysis refers to the study of human psychological functioning and behavior in narrative or characterization. It is a method of investigation of the mind relying on a systematized body of knowledge about human behavior. Its basic tenets include the following: a) besides the inherited constitution of personality, a person's development is determined by often forgotten events in early childhood; b) human attitude, mannerism, experience and thought are largely influenced by irrational drives; c) irrational drives are unconscious; d) attempts to bring these drives into awareness meet psychological resistance in the form of defense mechanisms; e) conflicts between the conscious and the unconscious, or with repressed material can materialize in the form of mental or emotional disturbances such as neurosis, neurotic traits, anxiety, depression, and the like; f) the liberation from the effects of the unconscious material is achieved through bringing this material into the conscious mind.

Psychological novel（心理小说）

A psychological novel is a work of prose fiction which places more than the usual amount of emphasis on interior characterization and on the motives, and internal action which springs from, and develops, external action. The psychological novel is not content to state what happens but goes on to explain the motivation of this action. In this type of writing character and characterization are more important than usual, and the psychological novel often delves deeper into the mind of a character than novels of other genres. So it can also be called a novel of the "inner man." In some cases, the stream-of-consciousness technique, as well as interior monologues, may be employed to better illustrate the inner workings of the human mind at work. Flashbacks may also be featured. While these three textual techniques are also prevalent in "Modernism," there is no deliberate effort to fragment the prose or compel the reader to interpret the text.

The Tale of Genji, written in the 11th-century Japan, has often been considered the first psychological novel. In the West, the origins of the psychological novel can be traced as far back as to Giovanni Boccaccio's 1344 *Elegia di Madonna Fiammetta*, or *The Elegy of Lady Fiammetta* in English; that is before the term psychology was coined.

The first rise of the psychological novel as a genre is said to have started with the English Sentimental novel of which Samuel Richardson's *Pamela* is a prime example. In the French literature, Stendhal's *The Red and the Black* (1830) is often called an early psychological novel. *The Princess of Cleves* (1678) by Madame de La Fayette (1634 – 1693) is also considered an early precursor of the psychological novel. The modern psychological novel originated, according to *The Encyclopedia of the Novel*, primarily in the works of the Norwegian Nobel laureate Knut Hamsun (1859 – 1952)—in particular, *Hunger* (1890), *Mysteries* (1892), *Pan* (1894) and *Victoria* (1898). In the literature of the United States, Henry James, Arthur Miller (1915 – 2005) and Edith Wharton (1862 – 1937) are considered major contributors to the practice of psychological realism.

Regional novel (地域小说)

A regional writer is one who concentrates much attention on a particular area and uses it and the people who inhabit it as the basis for his or her stories. Such a locale is likely to be rural and/or provincial. The regional novel emphasizes the setting, speech and social structure and customs of a particular locality not merely as local color but as important conditions affecting the temperament of the characters and their ways of thinking, feeling and interacting.

Once established, the regional novel began to interest a number of writers, and soon the regions described became smaller and more specifically defined. For example, the novels of Mrs. Gaskell and George Eliot centered on the Midlands; those of the Bronte sisters were set in Yorkshire, Thomas Hardy's in Wessex and William Faulkner's in "Yoknapatawpha County." There were also "urban" or "industrial" novels, set in a particular town or city, some of which had considerable fame in the 19th century. Notable instances are Mrs. Gaskell's *Mary Barton*, Charles Dickens' *Hard Times* and George Eliot's *Middlemarch*.

Renaissance (文艺复兴)

The Renaissance was a European cultural movement whose influence was felt in literature, philosophy, art, music, politics, science, religion, and other aspects of intellectual inquiry. It had its origin in north Italy in the 14th century and spread northward to other European countries like France, Germany, the Low Countries and lastly to England. The Renaissance period is considered the bridge between the Middle Ages and modern history.

The term Renaissance originally indicated a revival of classical (Greek and Roman) arts and sciences after the dark ages of medieval obscurantism. It encompassed innovative flowering of Latin and vernacular literatures. The study and propagation of classical learning and art was carried on by the progressive thinkers of the humanists, who emphasized the capacities of the human mind and the achievements of human culture. In other words, humanists held their chief interest not in ecclesiastical knowledge, but in man, his environment and doings, and bravely fought for the emancipation of man from the tyranny of the church and religious dogmas. In politics, the Renaissance contributed the development of the conventions of diplomacy, and in science an increased reliance on observation. Therefore humanism became the keynote of the Renaissance. At the heart of the Renaissance philosophy was the assertion of the greatness of man.

In different countries, however, the movement occurred in different periods with different emphases. The Renaissance style and ideas were slow to penetrate England, for instance. The English Renaissance dated from the late 15th to the early 17th century. Its beginning is often taken, as a convenience, either to be 1476, when William Caxton introduced a printing press into England, or to be 1485, when the Battle of Bosworth Field ended the Wars of the Roses and inaugurated the Tudor Dynasty. The Elizabethan era in the second half of the 16th century is usually regarded as the height of the English Renaissance. The dominant art forms of the English Renaissance were literature and music. Visual arts in the English Renaissance were much less significant than in the Italian Renaissance. The most important representative during this period in English literature was William Shakespeare. So the culmination of the English Renaissance is also named the Age of Shakespeare.

Revenge tragedy(复仇悲剧)

The revenge tragedy, or revenge play, or the tragedy of blood, is a dramatic genre in which the protagonist seeks revenge for an imagined or actual injury. The term "revenge tragedy" was first introduced in 1900 by A. H. Thorndike (1871 – 1933) to label a class of plays written in the late Elizabethan and early Jacobean eras.

The revenge tragedy derived from Seneca's favorite materials of murder, revenge, ghosts, mutilation and carnage, but while Seneca had relegated such matters to long reports of offstage actions by messengers, the Elizabethan writers usually represented them on stage to satisfy the appetite of the contemporary audience for violence and horror. The common ingredients of the revenge tragedy include: the hero's quest for vengeance, often at the prompting of the ghost of a murdered kinsman or loved one; scenes of real or feigned insanity; a play-within-a-play; scenes in graveyards, several limbs, scenes of carnage and mutilation, etc.

Rhyme(押韵)

In English versification, standard rhyme consists of the repetition, in the rhyming words, of the last stressed vowel and of all the speech sounds following that vowel (e. g. fate-late; follow-hollow). End rhymes, by far the frequent type, occur at the end of a verse-line while internal rhymes occur within a verse-line.

The rhyme consisting of a single stressed syllable is called a masculine rhyme (e. g. still-hill, bore-more) while the rhyme consisting of a stressed syllable followed by an unstressed syllable is called a feminine rhyme (ending-bending). A feminine rhyme, since it involves the repetition of two syllables, is also known as a double rhyme. A rhyme involving three syllables is called a triple rhyme.

If the correspondence of the rhymed sounds is exact, it is called perfect rhyme, or else full or true rhyme. Eye rhyme consists of words whose endings are spelled alike, and in most instances were once pronounced alike, but have in the course of time acquired a different pronunciation.

Rhyme royal(帝王韵)

Rhyme royal (or Rime royal) is a rhyming stanza form that was introduced into English poetry by Geoffrey Chaucer. The rhyme royal stanza consists of seven lines, usually in iambic pentameter. The rhyme scheme is a-b-a-b-b-c-c. In practice, the stanza can be constructed either as a tercet and two couplets (aba bb cc) or a quatrain and a tercet (abab bcc). This allows for variety, especially when the form is used for longer narrative poems. Along with the couplet, it was the standard narrative meter in the late Middle Ages.

Romance(传奇故事)

As a literary genre of high culture, romance or chivalric romance is a type of prose or verse narrative of the life and adventures of a noble hero. As the prevailing form of literature in the aristocratic circles of High Medieval and Early Modern Europe, romances reworked legends, fairy tales and history to suit the readers' and hearers' tastes. The modern image of "medieval" is more influenced by romances than by any other medieval genre, though they, famously burlesqued by Cervantes in *Don Quixote*, were out of fashion around 1600.

Romances were originally written in Old French, Anglo-Norman and Occitan, and in English, Italian and German later. They had in common essential features like lacking general resemblance to truth or reality; containing perilous adventures more or less remote from the ordinary life; exaggerating the vices of human nature and idealizing the virtues; laying emphasis on supreme devotion to a fair lady; choosing knights, men of noble birth skilled in the use of weapons, as the central characters; and having nothing to do with the common people as they are written for the noble class. Thematically, romances fell mainly into three cycles or three groups—"matters of Britain," "matters of France" and "matters of Rome and Greece." The first group mainly focuses on the exploits of King Arthur and his Knights of the Round Table, within which was incorporated the quest for the Holy Grail. The second group mainly centers on the exploits of Charlemagne. The famous work of this group is *Chanson de Roland*. The last group is an endless series of fabulous tales of Alexander the Great and about the Trojan War as well. Among all theses romances the Arthurian Legends are more noteworthy.

Romanticism（浪漫主义）

Romanticism was a movement in literature, philosophy, music and art, which developed in Europe in the late 18th and early 19th centuries. In most areas it was at its peak in the approximate period from 1800 to 1850. Starting from the ideas of Rousseau in France and from the Storm and Stress movement in Germany, it held that Classicism, dominant since the 16th century, failed to express man's emotional nature and overlooked his profound inner forces.

Romanticism stressed intense emotion—especially that experienced in confronting the new aesthetic categories of the sublimity and beauty of nature—as an authentic source of aesthetic experience, and promoted the individual imagination as a critical authority allowed of freedom from Classical notions of form in art. It assigned a high value to the achievements of "heroic" individualists and artists, and emphasized individual values and aspirations above those of society. As a reaction to the Industrial Revolution, to the aristocratic social and political norms of the Age of Enlightenment, and to the scientific rationalization of nature, Romanticism looked to the Middle Ages and to direct contact with nature for inspiration. It not simply considered folk art and ancient custom to be noble statuses but also valued spontaneity.

Romanticism was embodied most strongly in the visual arts, music and literature, but had a major impact on historiography, education and the natural sciences as well. It had a significant and complex effect on politics, and gave impetus to the national liberation movement in the 19th-century Europe. While for much of the period the movement was associated with liberalism and radicalism, its long-term effect on the growth of nationalism was perhaps more significant. In the second half of the 19th century, Realism was offered as a polar opposite to Romanticism. The decline of Romanticism during this time was associated with multiple processes, including social and political changes and the spread of nationalism.

Romanticism as a literary movement made its appearance in England as a renewed interest in medieval literature early in the latter half of the 18th century. With the 1798 publication of William Wordsworth's *Lyrical Ballads* in collaboration with S. T. Coleridge, it began to bloom and found a firm place in the history of English literature. The first three decades of the 19th century recorded the triumph of English Romanticism, whose end was marked by

Walter Scott's death in 1832. The Romantic Age in England, resembling the Elizabethan era, was an age of poetry. Many young enthusiastic writers turned to poetry as a happy man to singing. The glory of the age is seen in the poetry of Wordsworth, Coleridge, Lord Byron, Percy Bysshe Shelley and John Keats.

Science Fiction (科幻小说)

Science fiction is a genre of fiction dealing with imaginative content such as futuristic settings, futuristic science and technology, space travel, time travel, faster-than-light travel, parallel universes and extraterrestrial life. It often explores the potential consequences of scientific and other innovations, and has been called a "literature of ideas." Science fiction includes the following elements: a) a time setting in the future, in alternative timelines, or in a historical past that contradicts known facts of history or the archaeological record; b) a spatial setting or scenes in outer space (e. g. spaceflight), on other worlds, or on subterranean earth; c) characters that include aliens, mutants, androids, or humanoid robots and other types of characters arising from a future human evolution; d) futuristic or plausible technology such as ray guns, teleportation machines and humanoid computers; e) scientific principles that are new or that contradict accepted physical laws, such as time travel, wormholes, or faster-than-light travel or communication; f) new and different political or social systems; h) paranormal abilities such as mind control, telepathy, telekinesis and teleportation; and i) other universes or dimensions and travel between them.

Sentimentalism (感伤主义)

Sentimentalism was a literary tradition followed by some English poets and novelists of the 18th century. It indulged in emotion and sentiment, which were used as a sort of relief for the grief and heartaches felt toward the world's wrongs, and as a kind of mild protest against the social injustice. The writers who followed this tradition criticized the cruelty of the capitalist relations and the gross social injustices brought about by the bourgeois revolutions and the Industrial Revolution. They yearned for the return of the patriarchal times. They thought the bourgeois society was founded on the principle of reason, so they began to react against anything rational and to advocate that sentiment should take the place of reason.

In the English poetry of the 18th century, Sentimentalism first found its full expression in the forties and the fifties in Edward Young's *Night Thoughts* and Thomas Gray's *Elegy Written in a Country Church-yard*. In the later decades of the century, it was found in a number of poems by William Cowper. In fiction, it was first found in *Pamela* by Samuel Richardson. Some other representative novels include Laurence Sterne's *A Sentimental Journey through France and Italy*, Oliver Goldsmith's *The Vicar of Wakefield* and *The Man of Feeling* (1771) by Henry Mackenzie (1745 – 1831).

Soliloquy (独白)

Soliloquy is the act of talking to oneself, whether silently or aloud. In drama it denotes the convention by which a character, alone on the stage, utters his or her thoughts aloud. Playwrights have used this device as a convenient way to convey information about a character's motives and state of mind, or for purposes of exposition, and sometimes in order to guide the judgments and responses of the audience.

A related stage device is the aside, in which a character expresses to the audience his or her thought or intention in a short speech which, by convention, is inaudible to the other characters on the stage. Both devices, common in Elizabethan and later drama, fell into disuse in the late 19th century, when the increasing requirement that plays convey the illusion of real life impelled dramatists to exploit indirect means for conveying exposition and guidance to the audience.

Sonnet（十四行诗）

A sonnet is a lyric poem consisting of a single stanza of fourteen iambic pentameter lines linked by an intricate rhyme scheme, expressing different aspects of a single thought, mood, or feeling, sometimes revolved or summed up in the last lines. Originally short poems accompanied by mandolin or lute music, sonnets are generally composed in the standard meter of the language in which they were written—for example, iambic pentameter in English, and the Alexandrine in French. The form reached its peak with the Italian poet Petrarch, whose *Canzoniere* includes 317 sonnets addressed to his beloved Laura. Sir Thomas Wyatt and Henry Howard, Earl of Surrey, are credited with introducing the sonnet into English with translations of Italian sonnets as well as with sonnets of their own.

There are two major patterns of rhyme in sonnets written in English: the Petrarchan/Italian and the Shakespearean/English. The former consists of an octave, or eight-line stanza, and a sestet, or a six-line stanza. The octave has two quatrains, rhyming abba abba, but avoiding a couplet; the first quatrain presents the theme, and the second develops it. The sestet is built on a few different rhymes, arranged cddcee, cdecde, cdccdc, or cdedce; the first three lines exemplify or reflect on the theme, and the last three lines bring the whole poem to a unified close. Excellent examples of the Petrarchan sonnet in the English language are found in the sonnet sequence *Astrophel and Stella* by Sir Philip Sydney, which established the form in England. There, in the Elizabethan era, it reached the peak of its popularity. The English sonnet, exemplified by the works of William Shakespeare and by Edmund Spenser's *Amoretti*, developed as an adaptation to a language less rich in rhymes than Italian. This form differs from the Petrarchan sonnet in being divided into three quatrains, each rhymed differently, with a final, independently rhymed couplet that makes an effective, unifying climax to the whole. The rhyme scheme is abab cdcd efef gg.

Spenserian stanza, the（斯宾塞诗节）

The Spenserian stanza is a fixed verse form invented by Edmund Spenser for his epic poem *The Faerie Queene*. The stanza has nine lines, each of the first eight lines is in iambic pentameter form, and the ninth line is an alexandrine or an iambic hexameter line. The rhyme scheme is abab bcbc c. Because of its rare beauty, this verse form was much used by nearly all the later poets, especially imitated by the romantic poets of the 19th century.

Stanza（诗节）

A stanza (Italian for "stopping place") is a grouping of the verse-lines in a poem, often set off by a space in the printed text. Usually the stanzas of a given poem are marked by a recurrent pattern of rhyme and are also uniform in the number and lengths of the component lines. Some unrhymed poems, however, are also divided into stanzaic units and some rhymed poems are composed of stanzas that vary in their component lines.

Stream of Consciousness(意识流)

Stream of consciousness is a term used variously to describe either the continuity of impressions and thoughts in the human mind, or a special narrative device used in literature for representing this psychological principle in unpunctuated or fragmentary forms of interior monologue. The term was coined by the philosopher and psychologist William James (1842 – 1910) in *The Principles of Psychology* (1890), in the first sense. The literary sense of the term was introduced in 1918 by May Sinclair (1863 – 1946) in a review of early volumes in Dorothy Miller Richardson's novel sequence *Pilgrimage* (1915 – 1938), which include the first notable English uses of the technique. As used by Richardson, and more famously by James Joyce in his novel *Ulysses*, stream of consciousness represents the "flow" of impressions, memories and sense-impressions through abandoning accepted forms of syntax, punctuation and logical connection. In other words, it is a narrative mode that seeks to portray an individual's point of view by giving the written equivalent of the character's thought processes, either in a loose interior monologue, or in connection to his/her actions. Stream-of-consciousness writing is usually regarded as a special form of interior monologue and is characterized by associative leaps in thought and lack of punctuation.

Stream of consciousness and interior monologue are distinguished from dramatic monologue and soliloquy, which are chiefly used in poetry or drama, and where the speaker is addressing an audience or a third person. In stream of consciousness the speaker's thought processes are more often depicted as overheard in the mind (or addressed to oneself); it is primarily a fictional device. Especially after James Joyce's virtuoso demonstration of its possibilities in the unpunctuated final chapter in *Ulysses*, the stream-of-consciousness method of rendering characters' thought processes became an accepted part of the modern novelist's repertoire, used by Virginia Woolf, William Faulkner, and others.

Style(文风/文体)

Style has traditionally been defined as the manner of linguistic expression in prose or verse—as how speakers or writers say whatever it is that they say. The style specific to a particular work or writer, or else distinctive of a type of writings, has been analyzed in such terms as the rhetorical situation and aim, characteristic diction or choice of words, type of sentence structure and syntax, and the destiny and kinds of figurative language.

In standard theories based on Cicero and other classical rhetoricians, styles were usually classified into three main levels: the high/grand style, the middle/mean style and the low/plain style. The doctrine of decorum, which was influential through the 18th century, required that the level of style in a work be appropriate to the social class of the speaker, to the occasion on which it is spoken, and to the dignity of its literary genre. The modern critic Northrop Frye (1912 – 1991) introduced a variant of this long-persisting analysis of stylistic levels in literature. He made a primary differentiation between the demotic style, which is modeled on the language, rhythms, and associations of ordinary speech, and the hieratic style, which employs a variety of formal elaborations that separate the literary language from ordinary speech. Frye then proceeded to distinguish a high, middle and low level in each of these classes.

Symbol（象征）

In the broadest sense a symbol is anything which signifies something; in this sense all words are symbols. In discussing literature, however, the term "symbol" is applied only to a word or a phrase that signifies an object, a person, a place, or an event that has a meaning in itself and that also stands for something larger than itself, such as a quality, an attitude, a belief, or a value. Some symbols are conventional or public and their further significance is determinate within a particular culture. Poets mostly use such conventional symbols; they also use private or personal symbols, whose significance they largely generate themselves. Once private or personal symbols are employed, the literary work will be hard to interpret.

Symbolism（象征主义）

Symbolism was a late 19th-century art movement of French, Russian and Belgian origin in poetry and other arts. In literature, the style had its beginnings with the publication of *The Flowers of Evil* (1857) by Charles Baudelaire. The works of Edgar Allan Poe, which Baudelaire admired greatly and translated into French, were a significant influence and the source of many stock tropes and images. The aesthetic was developed by Stéphane Mallarmé (1842 – 1898) and Paul Verlaine (1844 – 1896) during the 1860s and 1870s. In the 1880s, the aesthetic was articulated by a series of manifestos and attracted a generation of writers. The term "symbolist" itself was first applied by the critic Jean Moréas (1856 – 1910), who invented the term to distinguish the symbolists from the related decadents of literature and art.

Symbolists believed that art should represent absolute truths that could only be described indirectly. Thus, they wrote in a very metaphorical and suggestive manner, endowing particular images or objects with symbolic meaning. Jean Moréas, in his "Symbolist Manifesto" (1886), announced that symbolism was hostile to "plain meanings, declamations, false sentimentality and matter-of-fact description," and that its goal instead was to "clothe the Ideal in a perceptible form," whose "goal was not in itself, but whose sole purpose was to express the Ideal."

The symbolist poets wished to liberate techniques of versification in order to allow greater room for "fluidity," and as such were sympathetic with the trend toward free verse, as evident by the poems of Gustave Kahn (1859 – 1936) and Ezra Pound. Symbolist poems were attempts to evoke, rather than primarily to describe; symbolic imagery was used to signify the state of the poet's soul.

Synesthesia（共感觉）

Synesthesia, from the Ancient Greek words meaning "union of the senses," is a neurological phenomenon in which stimulation of one sensory or cognitive pathway leads to automatic, involuntary experiences in a second sensory or cognitive pathway. People who report such experiences are known as synesthetes.

Difficulties have been recognized in adequately defining synesthesia: many different phenomena have been included in the term synesthesia, and in many cases the terminology seems to be inaccurate. A more accurate term may be ideasthesia.

Common synesthetic expressions include the descriptions of colors as "loud" or "warm" and of sounds as "smooth." This effect was cultivated consciously by the French Symbolists, but is often found in earlier poetry, notably in John Keats.

Terza rima (三行体/三行诗节押韵法)

Terza rima, whose literal translation from Italian is "third rhyme," was first used by the Italian poet Dante Alighieri for his *The Divine Comedy*. It is a three-line stanza using chain rhyme in the pattern aba bcb cdc ded, etc. Thus the second line of each tercet provides the rhyme for the first and third lines of the next. There is no limit to the number of lines, but poems or sections of poems written in terza rima end with either a single line or couplet repeating the rhyme of the middle line of the final tercet. The two possible endings for the example above are ded e or ded ee. There is no set rhythm for terza rima, but in English, iambic pentameter is generally preferred. In fact, terza rima has been adopted by several poets in English pentameters, notably by P. B. Shelley in his "Ode to the West Wind."

Theater of the Absurd, the (荒诞剧)

The Theater of the Absurd is a term used to characterize the work of a number of European and American dramatists of the 1950s and early 1960s. As the term suggests, the function of such theater is to give dramatic expression to the philosophical notion of the "absurd," a notion that had received widespread diffusion following the publication of Albert Camus' essay "The Myth of Sisyphus" in 1942. Critic Martin Esslin coined the term in his 1960 essay "Theatre of the Absurd." He related these plays based on a broad theme of the Absurd, similar to the way Camus used the term in his 1942 essay. To define the world as absurd is to recognize its fundamentally mysterious and indecipherable nature, and this recognition is frequently associated with feelings of loss, purposelessness and bewilderment. To such feelings, the Theater of the Absurd gives ample expression, often leaving the observer baffled in the face of disjointed, meaningless, or repetitious dialogues, incomprehensible behavior, and plots which deny all notion of logical or "realistic" development, but the recognition of the absurd nature of human existence also provided dramatists with a rich source of comedy, well illustrated in two early absurd plays, Ionesco's *La Cantatrice Chauve* (1948) and Samuel Beckett's *Waiting for Godot*. The Theater of the Absurd drew significantly on popular traditions of entertainment, on mime, acrobatics and circus clowning, and, by seeking to redefine the legitimate concerns of "serious" theater, played an important role in extending the range of postwar drama.

Amongst the dramatists associated with the Theater of the Absurd are Samuel Beckett, Harold Pinter, Tom Stoppard, Eugene Ionesco, Arthur Adamov (1908 – 1970), Edward Albee (1928 –), Albert Camus, and others. The absurdist playwrights in their plays take the form of man's reaction to a world apparently without meaning, and/or man as a puppet controlled or menaced by invisible outside forces. Though the term is applied to a wide range of plays, some characteristics coincide in many of the plays: broad comedy, mixed with horrific or tragic images; characters caught in hopeless situations forced to do repetitive or meaningless actions; dialogue full of clichés, wordplay and nonsense; plots that are cyclical or absurdly expansive; either a parody or dismissal of realism and the concept of the "well-made play."

Tony Award（托尼奖）

The Antoinette Perry Award for Excellence in Theatre, more commonly known informally as the Tony Award, recognizes achievement in live Broadway theatre. Presented by the American Theatre Wing and the Broadway League at an annual ceremony in New York City, the awards are given for Broadway productions and performances, except one for regional theatre. Several discretionary non-competitive awards are also given, including a Special Tony Award, the Tony Honors for Excellence in Theatre, and the Isabelle Stevenson Award. The awards are named after Antoinette Perry (1888 – 1946), co-founder of the American Theatre Wing.

The Tony Awards are considered the highest US theatre honor, the New York theatre industry's equivalent to the Academy Awards (Oscars) for motion pictures, the Grammy Awards for music and the Emmy Awards for television, and the Laurence Olivier Award for theatre in the United Kingdom and the Moliere Award of France.

From 1997 to 2010, the Tony Awards ceremony was held at Radio City Music Hall in New York City in June except in 1999, when it was held at the Gershwin Theatre. In 2011 and 2012, the ceremony was held at the Beacon Theatre. The 67th Tony Awards returned to Radio City Music Hall on June 9, 2013, as did the 68th Tony Awards on June 8, 2014 and the 69th Tony Awards on June 7, 2015. The 70th Tony Awards ceremony was held on June 12, 2016 at the Beacon Theatre.

Tragedy（悲剧）

The term is broadly applied to literary, and especially to dramatic, representations of serious actions which eventuate in a disastrous conclusion for the protagonist.

More precise and detailed discussions of the tragic form properly began with Aristotle's classic analysis in the *Poetics* (4th century B. C.). Aristotle defined tragedy as "the imitation of an action that is serious and also, as having magnitude, complete in itself," in the medium of poetic language and in the manner of dramatic rather than of narrative presentation, involving "incidents arousing pity and fear, wherewith to accomplish the catharsis of such emotions."

Authors in the Middle Ages lacked direct knowledge either of classic tragedies or of Aristotle's *Poetics*. Medieval tragedies were simply the story of a person of high status who, whether deservedly or not, is brought from prosperity to wretchedness by an unpredictable turn of the wheel of fortune. The tragedies of this period owed much to the native religious drama, the miracle and morality plays, which had developed independently of classical influence, but with a crucial contribution from the Roman writer Seneca, whose dramas got to be widely known earlier than those of the Greek tragedians.

Until the close of the 17th century almost all tragedies were written in verse and had as protagonists men of high rank whose fate affected the fortunes of a state. A few minor Elizabethan tragedies had as the chief character a man of the lower class, but it remained for the 18th-century writers to popularize the bourgeois or domestic tragedy, which was written in prose and presented a protagonist from the middle or lower rank who suffers a commonplace or domestic disaster. Since that time most successful tragedies have been in prose and represent middle-class, or occasionally even working-class, heroes and heroines.

Tragedy since WWI has also been innovative in other ways, including experimentation with new versions of ancient types. A recent tendency, especially in the critics associated with the new historicism, has been to interpret traditional tragedies primarily in political terms, as incorporating in the problems and catastrophe of the tragic individual an indirect representation of contemporary social or ideological dilemmas and crises.

Tragicomedy (悲喜剧)

Tragicomedy is a type of Elizabethan and Jacobean drama which intermingles both the standard characters and subject matter and the standard plot-forms of tragedy and comedy. Thus, the important agents in tragicomedy include both people of high degree and people of low degree, even though, according to the reigning critical theory of that time, only upper-class characters are appropriate to tragedy, while members of the middle and lower classes are the proper subject solely of comedy. Also, tragicomedy represents a serious action which threatens a tragic disaster to the protagonist, yet, by an abrupt reversal of circumstance, turns out happily.

Three Unities (三一律)

In the 16th and 17th centuries, critics of drama in Italy and France added to Aristotle's unity of action, which he described in his *Poetics*, two other unities, to constitute one of the rules of drama known as "the three unities." On the assumption that verisimilitude—the achievement of an illusion of reality in the audience of a stage play—requires that the action represented by a play approximate the actual conditions of the staging of the play, they imposed the requirement of the "unity of place" (that the action represented be limited to a single location) and the requirement of the "unity of time" (that the time represented be limited to the two or three hours it takes to act the play, or at most to a single day of either twelve or twenty-four hours). In large part because of the potent example of William Shakespeare, many of whose plays represent frequent changes of place and the passage of many years, the unities of place and time never dominated English Neoclassicism as they did criticism in Italy and France. A final blow was the famous attack against them, and against the principle of dramatic verisimilitude on which they were based, in Samuel Johnson's "Preface to Shakespeare" (1765). Since then, the unities of place and time, as distinguished from the unity of action, have been regarded as entirely optional devices, available to the playwright to achieve special effects of dramatic concentration.

Understatement (降格陈述/低调陈述)

Understatement is a figure of speech which deliberately represents something as very much less in magnitude or importance than it really is, or is ordinarily considered to be. The effect is usually ironic. Its contrary figure is hyperbole which is an overstatement, or the extravagant exaggeration of fact or of possibility. Hyperbole may be used either for serious or ironic or comic effect.

University Wits (大学才子)

The University Wits is a phrase used to name a group of the late 16th-century English playwrights and pamphleteers who were educated at the universities (Oxford or Cambridge) and who became popular secular writers.

The term was not used in their lifetime but coined by George Saintsbury (1845 – 1933), a 19th-century English writer, literary historian and journalist. This diverse and talented loose association of London writers and dramatists set the stage for the theatrical Renaissance of Elizabethan England. They are identified as among the earliest professional writers in English, and prepared the way for William Shakespeare.

Prominent members of this group were Christopher Marlowe, Robert Greene (1558 – 1592) and Thomas Nashe from Cambridge, and John Lyly, Thomas Lodge and George Peele (1556 – 1596) from Oxford. Thomas Kyd is also sometimes included in the group, though he is not believed to have studied at university. While Marlowe was the most famous dramatist among them, Greene and Nashe were better known for their controversial, risqué and argumentative pamphlets, creating an early form of journalism. Greene has been called the "first notorious professional writer."

Edward Albert (1951 – 2006) in his *History of English Literature* (1979: 89) argued that the plays of the University Wits had several features in common: a) There is a fondness for heroic themes, such as the lives of great figures like Mohammed and Tamburlaine. b) Heroic themes need heroic treatment: great fullness and variety, splendid descriptions, long swelling speeches, the handling of violent incidents and emotions. These qualities, excellent when held in restraint, only too often lead to loudness and disorder. c) The style is also "heroic." The chief aim is to achieve strong and sounding lines, magnificent epithets and powerful declamation. This again leads to abuse and to mere bombast, mouthing, and in the worst cases to nonsense. In the best examples, such as in Marlowe, the result is quite impressive. In this connection it is to be noted that the best medium for such expression is blank verse, which is sufficiently elastic to bear the strong pressure of these expansive methods. d) The themes are usually tragic in nature, for the dramatists were as a rule too much in earnest to give heed to what was considered to be the lower species of comedy. The general lack of real humor in the early drama is one of its most prominent features. Humor, when it is brought in at all, is coarse and immature. Almost the only representative of the writers of real comedies is Lyly.

Key to Exercises

Part One The Anglo-Saxon Period

I. Multiple choices

1. D   2. A   3. B   4. C   5. A   6. D   7. B

II. Blank-filling

1. Alfred the Great
2. Norman Conquest
3. Christian/religious
4. *The Song of Beowulf*

III. Term definition

(Omitted.)

IV. Essay questions

(Omitted.)

Part Two The Medieval Age

I. Multiple choices

1. A   2. C   3. B   4. B   5. D   6. A   7. A
8. D   9. B   10. D   11. C   12. A   13. C   14. A
15. C

II. Blank-filling

1. Norman Conquest
2. romances; a noble hero
3. the poor; the rich and the powerful
4. *The Canterbury Tales*
5. Arthur
6. Italian; English
7. the dialect of London
8. pursue earthly happiness; asceticism; humanism
9. unlettered people; professional minstrels; scholarly poets

III. Term definition

(Omitted.)

IV. Short-answer questions

1 – 3 (Omitted.)

4. The stylistic features of ballads may be summarized as follows:

1) Ballads are characterized by a simple, plain language of the common people, which leaves a strong dramatic effect. The simplicity is reflected both in the verse form and the colloquial expressions.

2) The priority of the ballad is the story which deals only with the culminating incident or climax of a plot.

3) Most of the ballads are quasi-historical, such as the ballad "Judas" and "Robin Hood" ballad.

4) Ballads also tell their stories in a highly characteristic way; they are intensely dramatic. To strengthen the dramatic effect of the narration, ballads also make full use of hyperbole; actions and events are much exaggerated.

5) Music has an important influence on the ballads.

6) Another salient feature of the ballad is its use of refrains and other kinds of repetitions.

V. Essay questions

1. *Sir Gawain and the Green Knight*, an important story from the Arthurian legend, is a 4-part/canto verse-romance of 2,530 lines in 101 sections. The first canto deals with the beheading; the second canto tells of the long and arduous trip Gawain makes o the castle; the third canto relates the three days he spends in a bargain with the lord; and the last canto wraps up his trip with his final encounter with the Green Knight and the anti-climatic revelation of the moral of the story.

In structural terms, the narrative is well conceived and neatly knit into an organic unity. The different parts and sections interlock and the threads are pulled together to offer a sense of finality. There is also a fine psychological element that enriches the plot and adds to the characterization. The portrait of Sir Gawain is vivid and fully rounded. There is in him a strange medley of conflicting qualities that makes him perfectly human. He is just a little short of an ideal hero.

Sir Gawain and the Green Knight shares quite a few basic features with Old English poems like *Beowulf*. In line structure and the use of devices such as alliteration, it is notably similar. As it was written in the north Midland dialect, it is less approachable than Chaucer's London dialect.

However, it is one of the most delightful old romances in any language. In form, it is an interesting combination of French and Saxon elements. It is written in an elaborate stanza combining meter and alliteration. At the end of each stanza there is a rimed refrain.

2. The General Prologue is usually regarded as the greatest portrait gallery in English literature. It comprises a group of vivid sketches of typical medieval figures. All classes of the English feudal society, except the royalty and the poorest peasant, are represented by the 30 pilgrims. They range from the knight and squire, and prioress, through the landed proprietor and wealthy tradesman, down to the drunken cook and humble plowman. There are also a doctor and a lawyer, monks of different orders and nuns and priests, and a summoner, a sailor, a miller, a carpenter, a yeoman (a small independent farmer), and an Oxford scholar. In the center of the group is the Wife of Barth, the owner of a large cloth-factory. The pilgrims are people from various parts of England. They serve as

the representatives of various sides of life and social groups and are a microcosm of 14th-century English society. That is why Chaucer was praised by Gorky as the "founder of English realism."

The purpose of the General Prologue is not only to present a vivid collection of character sketches, but also to reveal the author's intention in bringing together a great variety of people and narrative materials to unite the diversity of the tales by allotting them to a diversity of tellers engaged in a common endeavor, to set the tone for the storytelling (one of jollity which accords with the tone of the whole work: that of grateful acceptance of life), to make clear the plan for the tales, to motivate the telling of tales, and to introduce the pilgrims and the time and occasion of the pilgrimage. On the other hand, there is also an intimate connection between the tales and the Prologue, both complementing each other. The Prologue provides a framework for the tales.

Part Three The Renaissance Period

I. Multiple choices

1. B	2. B	3. C	4. D	5. A	6. D	7. C
8. A	9. B	10. A	11. C	12. A	13. B	14. B
15. B	16. A	17. A	18. B	19. B	20. A	21. C
22. D	23. A	24. C	25. C	26. D	27. C	28. B
29. B	30. C	31. D	32. A	33. A	34. A	

II. Blank-filling

1. sonnet
2. Spenser
3. *The Faerie Queene*
4. England
5. humanism
6. poet's poet
7. pastoral
8. sonnets; Spenserian sonnet
9. no place
10. prose romances
11. *Euphues*
12. artistic
13. Danish
14. *Hamlet*
15. humanist
16. rising bourgeoisie
17. individuality
18. individualists
19. Humanism; freedom; independence; earthly life; heavenly life

20. imitation; assimilation.

21. Francis Bacon

22. religious reformation; Martin Luther

23. The Elizabethan drama

24. Christopher Marlowe

25. individual ones; type ones; psychoanalytical

26. dark lady

27. *The Faerie Queene*

28. printing

29. *Doctor Faustus*

30. *Every Man in His Humor*

III. Term definition

(Omitted.)

IV. Short-answer questions

(Omitted.)

V. Essay questions

1 – 2 (Omitted.)

3. In *The Merchant of Venice* Shakespeare conveys several contrasting themes. First, he deals with the theme of justice versus mercy: Shakespeare reveals different aspects of justice versus mercy and suggests, through Portia, that all men should be merciful. Human mercy should follow the example of Divine mercy. There is a further aspect of justice in this case—injustice revealed in the Christians' treatment of the Jews. In this way Shakespeare gives Shylock a motive in wanting his revenge on Antonio.

Then comes the theme of commercial or material values versus love: Shakespeare puts forward the idea that true love is much more worthwhile than money and material values. Antonio epitomizes true love in his friendship for Bassanio, when he is prepared to lay down his life for his friend. Shylock, on the other hand, does not appear to be able to distinguish his values. When he hears that Jessica has run away, he cannot decide which hurts him most: the loss of his daughter or the loss of his money.

Some other contrasting themes include superficial/external beauty versus moral/spiritual beauty or truth (as in the case of the three caskets), and the letters of law versus the spirit of the law.

Part Four The Period of Revolution and Restoration

I. Multiple choices

1. B	2. D	3. B	4. A	5. A	6. C	7. C
8. D	9. D	10. A	11. C	12. B	13. C	14. B
15. C	16. A	17. D	18. D	19. A	20. B	21. D
22. C	23. D	24. B	25. A			

II. Blank-filling

1. 17th
2. mysticism
3. Metaphysical School
4. George Herbert
5. wit
6. love; sacred
7. religious; divorce; political
8. *Paradise Regained*; *Samson Agonistes*
9. Greek
10. *Paradise Lost*; *The Pilgrim's Progress*
11. court
12. realism; directness and simplicity of expression
13. heroic couplet
14. poems; plays
15. political; religious
16. balance
17. intellect

III. Term definition

(Omitted.)

IV. Short-answer questions

(Omitted.)

V. Essay questions

1. In Milton's *Paradise Lost*, Satan is the real hero of the poem. He, like a conquered and banished giant, remains obeyed and admired by those who follow him down to hell. He is firmer than the rest of the angles. It is he who, passing the guarded gates obstacle, makes man revolt against God.

Satan represents the spirit of rebellion against an unjust authority of God. When he gets to the Garden of Eden, he believes in no reason why Adam and Eve should not taste the fruit of the Tree of Knowledge.

Though defeated, Satan prevails, since he has won from God a third part of his angels, and almost all the sons of Adam. Though wounded, he triumphs, for the thunder which hits upon his head leaves his heart invincible. Though feebler in force, he remains superior in nobility, since he prefers independence to happy servility, and welcomes his defeat and his torments as a glory, a liberty, and a joy.

2 – 3 (Omitted.)

Part Five The Age of Enlightenment

I. Multiple choices

1. B   2. C   3. B   4. B   5. D   6. B   7. A

Key to Exercises

8. C	9. D	10. D	11. B	12. C	13. A	14. B
15. A	16. D	17. A	18. B	19. C	20. D	21. C
22. D	23. B	24. A	25. C	26. B	27. A	28. B
29. A	30. C	31. D	32. C	33. A	34. C	35. D
36. A	37. B	38. C	39. D	40. B	41. A	42. A
43. C	44. D					

II. Blank-filling

1. Whigs; Tories
2. moderate group; radical group
3. "Father of English and European Novels"
4. Neoclassical
5. rimed couplet
6. time; place
7. lyric; epic
8. Alexander Pope; heroic couplet
9. ignorance
10. apologia
11. *The Tatler*; *The Spectator*
12. *A Dictionary of the English Language*
13. Samuel Johnson
14. thoughts; feelings
15. *Tom Jones*
16. realistic; realism; real life
17. Neoclassical
18. Smollett
19. Sentimentalism
20. *The Life and Opinions of Tristram Shandy, Gentleman*
21. *The Deserted Village*; *She Stoops to Conquer*; *The Citizen of the World*; *The Vicar of Wakefield*
22. Classicism
23. Romantic
24. individual
25. *The Seasons*
26. *Night Thoughts*
27. "Ode to Evening"
28. *The Village*
29. *The Shepherd's Calendar*
30. lyrics

31. *Songs of Innocence*; *Songs of Experience*

III. Term definition

(Omitted.)

IV. Short-answer questions

1. a. The main literary stream of the 18th century was realism. What the writers described in their works were social realities. The main characters were usually common men. Most of the writers concentrated their attention on daily life.

b. The 18th century was an age of prose. A group of excellent prose writers, such as Addison, Steele, Swift, Fielding, were produced. Novel writing made a big advance in this century. The main characters in the novels were no longer kings and nobles but the common people.

c. In this age satire was much used in writing. Since there was fierce strife of the two political parties in society, nearly every writer of the century was employed and rewarded by Whigs or Tories for satiring their enemies. The English literature of this age produced some excellent satirists, such as Pope, Swift and Fielding.

d. This period was also characterized by the reign of Classicism, best represented by poets like Alexander Pope, and the Pre-romantic poetry with Robert Burns and William Blake as its exponents.

2 – 11 (Omitted.)

V. Essay questions

1 – 9 (Omitted.)

10. Today Goldsmith is chiefly remembered for four books: *The Vicar of Wakefield*, *The Deserted Village*, *She Stoops to Conquer* or *The Mistakes of a Night* and *The Citizen of the World*.

The Vicar of Wakefield is Goldsmith's masterpiece and only novel which definitely established his fame as a writer. It is about a romantic story told in the first person singular by the central character Dr. Primrose, the vicar. It is a Sentimental work based on the moral vision of man as innocent and kind. There is goodness, nobility, and fidelity in life, and old values and verities still function well. In addition, there is such to consider as Goldsmith's wit, humor, his craft of planting ballads and tales within tales, and his philosophical depth, which all make for the fascination it holds for its readers, modern as well as ancient.

In the novel, Goldsmith describes the joys and sorrows of the simple, poor family who represent the oppressed people. The author shows sympathy for the family, and condemns Squire Thornhill, who stands for the cruelty, hypocrisy and moral degradation of the wicked feudal landlord and of the city bourgeoisie. But the solution for the righting of the social wrongs is not satisfactory, for the happy denouement at the end hints the existence of a good and benevolent landlord in the person of Sir William Thornhill whose righteous intervention alone can check the villainy of Squire Thornhill and restore the vicar's family to happiness.

The Deserted Village, written in heroic couplet, is Goldsmith's best poem. It begins with the poet's happy reminiscences of his home village. Then he expresses his lament over the decline of the happy village life. He puts the blame on the enclosure movement. Goldsmith describes how the peasants become homeless and landless, how the poor men become beggars and the poor women become prostitutes.

This poem is a sharp protest against the large scale enclosures of common land for the rich landlords and capitalists. It also reflects the poet's conservative stand, looking backward with nostalgia at the deserted village which merely illustrated the replacement of the feudal countryside by capitalist agriculture.

She Stoops to Conquer is Goldsmith's best comedy. The play is a classic in world theater and ranks among the best English comedies of the 18th century and second only to Sheridan's *The School for Scandal*, and has always been successful when staged.

It is a funny boisterous comedy of melodramatic misunderstandings and has been regarded as one of the most beloved comedies of all time. The humor and humanity of the characters, especially Kate and Tony, adds a touch of immortal power to it. As a satire on the artificial and pretentious behavior of the day, the play exalts the quality of truth and honest feelings. Kate is not dressed in her Sunday best when she wins her man's love, and Marlow loves her for what she is and not as a respectable young lady of standing and expectations. The drama also brings out in full relief the notion of individual choice and right to choose one's own happiness. Tony can be scheming, but he is good-natured essentially, not self-serving and inflicting hurt on others. Goldsmith is generous and tolerant of human foibles and follies; he does not censure or punish any of his characters, but takes pains to see to it that everyone get fair treatment in the end. The way in which the characters interact in their cultured and well-intentioned manner makes for geniality and interpersonal cordiality, helps civilize public behavior, and decrease its violent and crude elements. The salutary influence the play exercised on the 18th century is said to be considerable. In addition, Goldsmith's dialogues are vivacious and immensely humorous, and the whole performance impresses the audience with its vitality and joyful mood.

The Citizen of the World is Goldsmith's collection of familiar essays. It contains 98 essays originally contributed to a magazine. These essays are supposed to be letters written by a Chinese residing in London to his friends in the east. In these letters he describes and criticizes the strange customs of the country or countries where he lived or traveled. Goldsmith voices through the Chinese traveler his satirical comments on the English society of his day. He shows how the English talk so much about political liberty but do not really understand its meaning, how in England money may buy reputation and even a fine monument or an imposing-looking tomb in the Westminster Abbey, how religious worship in English churches is simply a sham and most worshipers go to churches to see the spectacle and listen to music and then dose off during the sermon, how ridiculous the legal processes are and how long-drawn-out lawsuits profit only the lawyers, how hypocrisy exists everywhere in human relationship.

The language used by Goldsmith in these essays is quite effective, lightfully racy and is almost always full of humor and subtle wit. These essays are certainly among the outstanding specimens of English prose of the period.

Part Six The Romantic Period

I. Multiple choices

1. A	2. D	3. A	4. B	5. C	6. D	7. A
8. C	9. D	10. B	11. C	12. A	13. A	14. C
15. B	16. D	17. D	18. D	19. D	20. C	21. D
22. C	23. B	24. D	25. A	26. A	27. B	28. C
29. C	30. B	31. A	32. D	33. A	34. B	35. C

36. A   37. A   38. D   39. B   40. C

II. Blank-filling

1. Elizabethan; second
2. William Wordsworth; Percy Bysshe Shelley
3. English romantic poetry
4. simplicity
5. dissatisfaction; nature
6. emotion; tranquility
7. critical; philosophical
8. music
9. amoral
10. "Dejection: An Ode"
11. Coleridge
12. *Don Juan*
13. Byronic
14. Byronic
15. Spenserian
16. Romanticism; sensual description
17. *A Defense of Poetry*
18. an age of crisis
19. Beauty is truth, truth beauty.
20. Verse; Beauty
21. "Ode to a Nightingale"
22. romantic; realistic; Austen
23. English
24. English; liberty; independence
25. noble; ordinary; link
26. city; London
27. familiar
28. *The Prelude*
29. "The Rime of the Ancient Mariner"
30. *Queen Mab*; *The Cenci*; *Prometheus Unbound*

III. Term definition

(Omitted.)

IV. Short-answer questions

(Omitted.)

V. Essay questions

1. The Romantic Age in England was, like the Elizabethan era, distinctively an age of poetry. It was regarded

as the second great age in English literary history, for poetry is the highest form of literary expression, and seems to have been most in harmony with the noblest powers of the English genius. The glory of the age is in the poetry of Scoot, Wordsworth, Coleridge, Byron, Shelley, Keats, and Southey.

Women novelists appeared in this age. It was during this period that women assumed, for the first time, an important place in English literature. Mrs. Anne Radcliff was one of the most successful writers of the school of exaggerated romance. Jane Austen offered us her charming descriptions of everyday life in her enduring work.

The greatest historical novelist Walter Scott also appeared in this period. His historical novels combine a romantic atmosphere with a realistic description of historical background and common people's life. Scott marked the transition from romanticism to the period of realism after it.

Romantic prose was represented by Lamb, Hazlitt, De Quincey and Hume. Lamb was the best essayist, whose familiar essays are very famous.

2. Wordsworth was the representative of the first generation of Romantic poets, who expressed the deepest aspirations of English Romanticism. He saw nature and man with new eyes. His whole work is an attempt to communicate that new vision.

Wordsworth's poetry is distinguished by the simplicity and purity of language. It was his theory that language spoken by the peasants, when purified from its defects, was the best of all. His theory and practice in poetical creation started from a dissatisfaction with the social reality under capitalism, and hinted at the thought of "back to nature" and "back to the patriarchal system of the old time".

Nearly all of his good poetry was written during the first decade of his literary career (1798 – 1807). His later writings were full of mysticism and many of them unreadable. His *Lyrical Ballads*, the joint work with Coleridge, marked the beginning of the Romantic Movement in England. The poems in *Lyrical Ballads*, the majority of which were written by Wordsworth, were characterized by a sympathy with the poor, simple peasants, a passionate love of nature and, of course, the simplicity and purity of the language.

Wordsworth was at his best in descriptions of mountains and rivers, flowers and birds, children and peasants, and reminiscences of his childhood and youth. He, as a great poet of nature, was the first to find words for the most elementary sensations of man face to face with natural phenomena. The most famous poems in this group are "To the Cuckoo", "Lucy Poems", "I Wondered Lonely as a Cloud", and "The Solitary Reaper".

3 – 9 (Omitted.)

Part Seven The Period of Realism

I. Multiple choices

1. A	2. A	3. C	4. D	5. C	6. A	7. B
8. D	9. A	10. A	11. C	12. D	13. D	14. B
15. A	16. A	17. B	18. B	19. D	20. A	21. C
22. B	23. C	24. A	25. A	26. B	27. C	28. C
29. A	30. D	31. C	32. A	33. B	34. D	35. D
36. C	37. B	38. C	39. D	40. B	41. A	42. C

43. A

II. Blank-filling

1. the Chartist Movement
2. God's creation
3. objective
4. middle
5. third-person
6. benevolent gentlemen; the rich; the poor
7. "A Novel without a Hero"
8. *Middlemarch*
9. *The Book of Snobs*
10. inner
11. individual choices
12. *Adam Bede*
13. *The Mill on the Floss*
14. *The Egoist*; psychological
15. *Tess of the D'Urbervilles*
16. "pure" or "absolute"
17. Matthew Arnold
18. *The Importance of Being Earnest*

III. Term definition

(Omitted.)

IV. Short-answer questions

1, 3–9 (Omitted.)

2. Hardy himself divided his novels into three series. They are romances and fantasies, novels of ingenuity, and novels of character and environment, with the last of greater significance.

V. Essay questions

(Omitted.)

Part Eight The Early Twentieth Century

I. Multiple choices

1. B	2. A	3. C	4. D	5. A	6. C	7. B
8. D	9. A	10. D	11. C	12. D	13. B	14. C
15. A	16. A	17. A	18. B	19. B	20. D	21. C
22. D	23. A	24. D	25. B	26. C	27. D	28. C
29. C	30. B	31. B	32. A	33. A	34. D	35. B
36. A	37. A	38. C	39. D	40. A	41. D	42. B

| 43. D | 44. C | 45. C | 46. B |

II. Blank-filling

1. *The Cenci*
2. optimism
3. pottery towns
4. *Anna of the Fives Towns*
5. objective documentation
6. externalities
7. beast, human
8. property
9. trilogies
10. social problems
11. science fiction
12. disparate stories
13. chronological
14. the heart of darkness
15. *A Passage to India*
16. psychology
17. colloquial
18. the pity of war
19. sex
20. plot
21. androgynous

III. Term definition
(Omitted.)

IV. Short-answer questions
(Omitted.)

V. Essay questions
(Omitted.)

Part Nine The Postwar Period

I. Multiple choices

1. D	2. B	3. A	4. C	5. C	6. B	7. D
8. A	9. B	10. C	11. A	12. D	13. C	14. D
15. B	16. C	17. A	18. D	19. B	20. C	21. A
22. A	23. B	24. D	25. C	26. A	27. D	28. B
29. A	30. C	31. C	32. B	33. D	34. B	35. A

36. D   37. B   38. A   39. D   40. D   41. C   42. B

II. Blank-filling

1. Williamsian
2. human heart
3. working-class
4. displacement
5. narrative
6. working class
7. relativistic
8. human nature
9. a fable
10. Free Woman
11. *The French Lieutenant's Woman*
12. Metafiction
13. Samuel Beckett
14. *The Two Cultures*
15. *Look back in Anger*
16. survival
17. negativity
18. Stoppardian

III. Term definition

(Omitted.)

IV. Short-answer questions

(Omitted.)

V. Essay questions

(Omitted.)

Appendix I List of Nobel Laureates in Literature

1901: Sully Prudhomme (1839 – 1907), French poet and essayist; writing in French; awarded for poetry and essay

Citation: "in special recognition of his poetic composition, which gives evidence of lofty idealism, artistic perfection and a rare combination of the qualities of both heart and intellect"

1902: Theodor Mommsen (1817 – 1903), German classical scholar, historian, jurist, journalist, politician, archaeologist and writer; writing in German; awarded for history and law

Citation: "the greatest living master of the art of historical writing, with special reference to his monumental work, *A History of Rome*"

1903: Bjørnstjerne Bjørnson (1832 – 1910), Norwegian poet, novelist, playwright and lyricist; writing in Norwegian; awarded for poetry, novel and drama

Citation: "as a tribute to his noble, magnificent and versatile poetry, which has always been distinguished by both the freshness of its inspiration and the rare purity of its spirit"

1904: Frédéric Mistral (1830 – 1914), French writer and lexicographer of the Occitan language; writing in Occitan; awarded for poetry and philology

Citation: "in recognition of the fresh originality and true inspiration of his poetic production, which faithfully reflects the natural scenery and native spirit of his people, and, in addition, his significant work as a Provençal philologist"

1904: José Echegaray (1832 – 1916), Spanish dramatist, civil engineer and mathematician; writing in Spanish; awarded for drama

Citation: "in recognition of the numerous and brilliant compositions which, in an individual and original manner, have revived the great traditions of the Spanish drama"

1905: Henryk Sienkiewicz (1846 – 1916), Polish novelist, journalist and philanthropist; writing in Polish; awarded for novel

Citation: "because of his outstanding merits as an epic writer"

1906: Giosuè Carducci (1835 – 1907), Italian poet; writing in Italian; awarded for poetry

Citation: "not only in consideration of his deep learning and critical research, but above all as a tribute to the creative energy, freshness of style, and lyrical force which characterize his poetic masterpieces"

1907: Rudyard Kipling (1865 – 1936), British novelist, short-story writer and poet; writing in English; awarded for novel, short story and poetry

Citation: "in consideration of the power of observation, originality of imagination, virility of ideas and remarkable talent for narration which characterize the creations of this world-famous author"

1908: Rudolf Christoph Eucken (1846 – 1926), German philosopher; writing in German; awarded for philosophy

Citation: "in recognition of his earnest search for truth, his penetrating power of thought, his wide range of vision, and the warmth and strength in presentation with which in his numerous works he has vindicated and developed an idealistic philosophy of life"

1909: Selma Lagerlöf (1858 – 1940), Swedish writer and first female writer to win the Nobel Prize in Literature; writing in Swedish; awarded for novel and short story

Citation: "in appreciation of the lofty idealism, vivid imagination and spiritual perception that characterize her writings"

1910: Paul von Heyse (1830 – 1914), German writer and translator; writing in German; awarded for poetry, drama, novel and short story

Citation: "as a tribute to the consummate artistry, permeated with idealism, which he has demonstrated during his long productive career as a lyric poet, dramatist, novelist and writer of world-renowned short stories"

1911: Maurice Maeterlinck (1862 – 1949), Belgian playwright, poet and essayist; writing in French; awarded for drama, poetry and essay

Citation: "in appreciation of his many-sided literary activities, and especially of his dramatic works, which are distinguished by a wealth of imagination and by a poetic fancy, which reveals, sometimes in the guise of a fairy tale, a deep inspiration, while in a mysterious way they appeal to the readers' own feelings and stimulate their imaginations"

1912: Gerhart Hauptmann (1862 – 1946), German dramatist and novelist; writing in German; awarded for drama and novel

Citation: "primarily in recognition of his fruitful, varied and outstanding production in the realm of dramatic art"

1913: Rabindranath Tagore (1861 – 1941), Bengali-Indian writer and painter and first non-European to win the Nobel Prize in Literature; writing in Bengali; awarded for poetry, novel, drama, short story and music

Citation: "because of his profoundly sensitive, fresh and beautiful verse, by which, with consummate skill, he has made his poetic thought, expressed in his own English words, a part of the literature of the West"

1914: *Not awarded*

1915: Romain Rolland (1866 – 1944), French dramatist, novelist, essayist and art historian; writing in French; awarded for novel

Citation: "as a tribute to the lofty idealism of his literary production and to the sympathy and love of truth with which he has described different types of human beings"

1916: Verner von Heidenstam (1859 – 1940), Swedish poet and novelist; writing in Swedish; awarded for poetry and novel

Citation: "in recognition of his significance as the leading representative of a new era in our literature"

Appendix I List of Nobel Laureates in Literature

1917: Karl Adolph Gjellerup (1857 – 1919), Danish poet and novelist; writing in Danish; awarded for poetry

Citation: "for his varied and rich poetry, which is inspired by lofty ideals"

1917: Henrik Pontoppidan (1857 – 1943), Danish realist writer; writing in Danish; awarded for novel

Citation: "for his authentic descriptions of present-day life in Denmark"

1918: *Not awarded*

1919: Carl Spitteler (1845 – 1924), Swiss poet; writing in German; awarded for poetry

Citation: "in special appreciation of his epic, *Olympian Spring*"

1920: Knut Hamsun (1859 – 1952), Norwegian novelist, poet, dramatist and social critic; writing in Norwegian; awarded for novel

Citation: "for his monumental work, *Growth of the Soil*"

1921: Anatole France (1844 – 1924), French poet, journalist and novelist; writing in French; awarded for novel and poetry

Citation: "in recognition of his brilliant literary achievements, characterized as they are by a nobility of style, a profound human sympathy, grace, and a true Gallic temperament"

1922: Jacinto Benavente (1866 – 1954), Spanish dramatist; writing in Spanish; awarded for drama

Citation: "for the happy manner in which he has continued the illustrious traditions of the Spanish drama"

1923: William Butler Yeats (1865 – 1939), Irish poet and playwright; writing in English; awarded for poetry

Citation: "for his always inspired poetry, which in a highly artistic form gives expression to the spirit of a whole nation"

1924: Władysław Reymont (1867 – 1925), Polish novelist; writing in Polish; awarded for novel

Citation: "for his great national epic, *The Peasants*"

1925: George Bernard Shaw (1856 – 1950), Irish playwright, critic and passionate socialist; writing in English; awarded for drama and literary criticism

Citation: "for his work which is marked by both idealism and humanity, its stimulating satire often being infused with a singular poetic beauty"

1926: Grazia Deledda (1871 – 1936), Italian poet and novelist; writing in Italian; awarded for poetry and novel

Citation: "for her idealistically inspired writings which with plastic clarity picture the life on her native island and with depth and sympathy deal with human problems in general"

1927: Henri Bergson (1859 – 1941), French philosopher; writing in French; awarded for philosophy

Citation: "in recognition of his rich and vitalizing ideas and the brilliant skill with which they have been presented"

1928: Sigrid Undset (1882 – 1949), Danish-born Norwegian novelist; writing in Norwegian; awarded for novel

Citation: "principally for her powerful descriptions of Northern life during the Middle Ages"

1929: Thomas Mann (1875 – 1955), German novelist, short story writer, social critic, philanthropist and essayist; writing in German; awarded for novel, short story, essay

Citation: "principally for his great novel, *Buddenbrooks*, which has won steadily increased recognition as one of the classic works of contemporary literature"

1930: Sinclair Lewis (1885 – 1951), American novelist, short-story writer and playwright; writing in English; awarded for novel, short story and drama

Citation: "for his vigorous and graphic art of description and his ability to create, with wit and humour, new types of characters"

1931: Erik Axel Karlfeldt (1864 – 1931), Swedish poet; writing in Swedish; awarded for poetry

Citation: "The poetry of Erik Axel Karlfeldt"

1932: John Galsworthy (1867 – 1933), British novelist and playwright; writing in English; awarded for novel

Citation: "for his distinguished art of narration which takes its highest form in *The Forsyte Saga*"

1933: Ivan Bunin (1870 – 1953), Russian writer (born in Russian Empire, living in France); writing in Russian; awarded for short story, poetry and novel

Citation: "for the strict artistry with which he has carried on the classical Russian traditions in prose writing"

1934: Luigi Pirandello (1867 – 1936), Italian dramatist, novelist, poet and short story writer; writing in Italian; awarded for drama, novel and short story

Citation: "for his bold and ingenious revival of dramatic and scenic art"

1935: *Not awarded*

1936: Eugene O'Neill (1888 – 1953), American Playwright; writing in English; awarded for drama

Citation: "or the power, honesty and deep-felt emotions of his dramatic works, which embody an original concept of tragedy"

1937: Roger Martin du Gard (1881 – 1958), French novelist; writing in French; awarded for novel

Citation: "for the artistic power and truth with which he has depicted human conflict as well as some fundamental aspects of contemporary life in his novel cycle *Les Thibault*"

1938: Pearl S. Buck (1892 – 1973), American writer; writing in English; awarded for novel and biography

Citation: "for her rich and truly epic descriptions of peasant life in China and for her biographical masterpieces"

1939: Frans Eemil Sillanpää (1888 – 1964), Finnish writer; writing in Finnish; awarded for novel

Citation: "for his deep understanding of his country's peasantry and the exquisite art with which he has portrayed their way of life and their relationship with Nature"

1940: *Not awarded*

1941: *Not awarded*

1942: *Not awarded*

1943: *Not awarded*

1944: Johannes Vilhelm Jensen (1873 – 1950), Danish writer; writing in Danish; awarded for poetry

Citation: "for the rare strength and fertility of his poetic imagination with which is combined an intellectual curiosity of wide scope and a bold, freshly creative style"

1945: Gabriela Mistral (1889 – 1957), Chilean poet-diplomat, educator and feminist; writing in Spanish; awarded for poetry

Citation: "for her lyric poetry which, inspired by powerful emotions, has made her name a symbol of the idealistic aspirations of the entire Latin American world"

1946: Hermann Hesse (1877 – 1962), German-born Swiss poet, novelist, essayist, short story writer and painter; writing in German; awarded for novel and poetry

Citation: "for his inspired writings which, while growing in boldness and penetration, exemplify the classical humanitarian ideals and high qualities of style"

1947: André Gide, French novelist, essayist and playwright; writing in French; awarded for novel and essay

Citation: "for his comprehensive and artistically significant writings, in which human problems and conditions have been presented with a fearless love of truth and keen psychological insight"

1948: T. S. Eliot (1888 – 1965), American-born British poet, playwright, literary critic and editor; writing in English; awarded for poetry

Citation: "for his outstanding, pioneer contribution to present-day poetry"

1949: William Faulkner (1897 – 1962), American novelist, short story writer, playwright, poet and essayist; writing in English; awarded for novel and short story

Citation: "for his powerful and artistically unique contribution to the modern American novel"

1950: Bertrand Russell (1872 – 1970), British philosopher, logician, mathematician, historian, writer, social critic and political activist; writing in English; awarded for philosophy

Citation: "in recognition of his varied and significant writings in which he champions humanitarian ideals and freedom of thought"

1951: Pär Lagerkvist (1891 – 1974), Swedish poet, playwright, novelist, essayist and short story writer; writing in Swedish; awarded for poetry, novel, short story and drama

Citation: "for the artistic vigor and true independence of mind with which he endeavors in his poetry to find answers to the eternal questions confronting mankind"

1952: François Mauriac (1885 – 1970), French novelist, dramatist, critic, poet and journalist; writing in French; awarded for novel and short story

Citation: "for the deep spiritual insight and the artistic intensity with which he has in his novels penetrated the drama of human life"

1953: Winston Churchill (1874 – 1965), British politician, historian and biographer; writing in English; awarded for history, essay and memoirs

Citation: "for his mastery of historical and biographical description as well as for brilliant oratory in defending exalted human values"

1954: Ernest Hemingway (1899 – 1961), American novelist, short story writer and journalist; writing in English; awarded for novel, short story and screenplay

Citation: "for his mastery of the art of narrative, most recently demonstrated in *The Old Man and the Sea*, and for the influence that he has exerted on contemporary style"

1955: Halldór Laxness (1902 – 1998), Icelandic novelist, short story writer, playwright and poet; writing in

Icelandic; awarded for novel, short story, drama and poetry

Citation: "for his vivid epic power which has renewed the great narrative art of Iceland"

1956: Juan Ramón Jiménez (1881 – 1958), Spanish poet; writing in Spanish; awarded for poetry

Citation: "for his lyrical poetry, which in Spanish language constitutes an example of high spirit and artistical purity"

1957: Albert Camus (1913 – 1960), French novelist, short story writer, playwright, essayist, philosopher and journalist; writing in French; awarded for novel, short story, drama, philosophy and essay

Citation: "for his important literary production, which with clear-sighted earnestness illuminates the problems of the human conscience in our times"

1958: Boris Pasternak (1890 – 1960), Russian poet, novelist and literary translator; writing in Russian; awarded for novel, poetry, translation

Citation: "for his important achievement both in contemporary lyrical poetry and in the field of the great Russian epic tradition"

1959: Salvatore Quasimodo (1901 – 1968), Italian poet; writing in Italian; awarded for poetry

Citation: "for his lyrical poetry, which with classical fire expresses the tragic experience of life in our own times"

1960: Saint-John Perse (1887 – 1975), French poet-diplomat; writing in French; awarded for poetry

Citation: "for the soaring flight and the evocative imagery of his poetry which in a visionary fashion reflects the conditions of our time"

1961: Ivo Andrić(1892 – 1975), Yugoslav novelist, short story writer and diplomat; writing in Serbo-Croatian; awarded for novel and short story

Citation: "for the epic force with which he has traced themes and depicted human destinies drawn from the history of his country"

1962: John Steinbeck (1902 – 1968), American novelist and short story writer; writing in English; awarded for novel, short story and screenplay

Citation: "for his realistic and imaginative writings, combining as they do sympathetic humour and keen social perception"

1963: Giorgos Seferis (1900 – 1971), Greek poet-diplomat (born in Ottoman Empire); writing in Greek; awarded for poetry

Citation: "for his eminent lyrical writing, inspired by a deep feeling for the Hellenic world of culture"

1964: Jean-Paul Sartre (1905 – 1980), French philosopher, playwright, novelist, political activist, biographer and literary critic; writing in French; awarded for novel, philosophy, drama, literary criticism and screenplay

Citation: "for his work which, rich in ideas and filled with the spirit of freedom and the quest for truth, has exerted a far-reaching influence on our age"

1965: Mikhail Sholokhov (1905 – 1984), Soviet/Russian novelist; writing in Russian; awarded for novel

Citation: "for the artistic power and integrity with which, in his epic of the Don, he has given expression to a historic phase in the life of the Russian people"

1966: Shmuel Yosef Agnon (1888 – 1970), Israeli novelist; writing in Hebrew; awarded for novel and short story

Citation: "for his profoundly characteristic narrative art with motifs from the life of the Jewish people"

1966: Nelly Sachs (1891 – 1970), German-born Swedish poet and playwright; writing in German; awarded for poetry and drama

Citation: "for her outstanding lyrical and dramatic writing, which interprets Israel's destiny with touching strength"

1967: Miguel Ángel Asturias (1899 – 1974), Guatemalan poet-diplomat, novelist, playwright and journalist; writing in Spanish; awarded for novel and poetry

Citation: "for his vivid literary achievement, deep-rooted in the national traits and traditions of Indian peoples of Latin America"

1968: Yasunari Kawabata (1899 – 1972), Japanese novelist and short story writer; writing in Japanese; awarded for novel and short story

Citation: "for his narrative mastery, which with great sensibility expresses the essence of the Japanese mind"

1969: Samuel Beckett (1906 – 1989), Irish novelist, playwright, theatre director, poet and essayist; writing in English and French; awarded for novel, drama and poetry

Citation: "for his writing, which—in new forms for the novel and drama—in the destitution of modern man acquires its elevation"

1970: Aleksandr Solzhenitsyn (1918 – 2008), Soviet/Russian novelist and historian; writing in Russian; awarded for novel

Citation: "for the ethical force with which he has pursued the indispensable traditions of Russian literature"

1971: Pablo Neruda (1904 – 1973), Chilean poet-diplomat and politician; writing in Spanish; awarded for poetry

Citation: "for a poetry that with the action of an elemental force brings alive a continent's destiny and dreams"

1972: Heinrich Böll (1917 – 1985), German novelist and short story writer; writing in German; awarded for novel and short story

Citation: "for his writing which through its combination of a broad perspective on his time and a sensitive skill in characterization has contributed to a renewal of German literature"

1973: Patrick White (1912 – 1990), British Australian novelist, playwright, poet, short story writer and essayist; writing in English; awarded for novel, short story and drama

Citation: "for an epic and psychological narrative art which has introduced a new continent into literature"

1974: Eyvind Johnson (1900 – 1976), Swedish novelist; writing in Swedish; awarded for novel

Citation: "for a narrative art, farseeing in lands and ages, in the service of freedom"

1974: Harry Martinson (1904 – 1978), Swedish poet, novelist and playwright; writing in Swedish; awarded for poetry, novel and drama

Citation: "for writings that catch the dewdrop and reflect the cosmos"

1975: Eugenio Montale (1896 – 1981), Italian poet, prose writer, editor and translator; writing in Italian; awarded for poetry

Citation: "for his distinctive poetry which, with great artistic sensitivity, has interpreted human values under the sign of an outlook on life with no illusions"

1976: Saul Bellow (1915 – 2005), Canadian-born American novelist and short story writer; writing in English; awarded for novel and short story

Citation: "for the human understanding and subtle analysis of contemporary culture that are combined in his work"

1977: Vicente Aleixandre (1898 – 1984), Spanish poet; writing in Spanish; awarded for poetry

Citation: "for a creative poetic writing which illuminates man's condition in the cosmos and in present-day society, at the same time representing the great renewal of the traditions of Spanish poetry between the wars"

1978: Isaac Bashevis Singer (1902 – 1991), Polish-born Jewish-American novelist and short story writer; writing in Yiddish; awarded for novel, short story and memoirs

Citation: "for his impassioned narrative art which, with roots in a Polish-Jewish cultural tradition, brings universal human conditions to life"

1979: Odysseas Elytis (1911 – 1996), Greek poet; writing in Greek; awarded for poetry

Citation: "for his poetry, which, against the background of Greek tradition, depicts with sensuous strength and intellectual clear-sightedness modern man's struggle for freedom and creativeness"

1980: Czesław Miłosz (1911 – 2004), Polish poet, prose writer, translator and diplomat; writing in Polish; awarded for poetry and essay

Citation: "who with uncompromising clear-sightedness voices man's exposed condition in a world of severe conflicts"

1981: Elias Canetti (1905 – 1994), Bulgarian-born British novelist, playwright, memoirist, and non-fiction writer; writing in German; awarded for novel, drama, memoirs and essay

Citation: "for writings marked by a broad outlook, a wealth of ideas and artistic power"

1982: Gabriel García Márquez (1927 – 2014), Colombian novelist, short story writer, screenwriter and journalist; writing in Spanish; awarded for novel, short story and screenplay

Citation: "for his novels and short stories, in which the fantastic and the realistic are combined in a richly composed world of imagination, reflecting a continent's life and conflicts"

1983: William Golding (1911 – 1993), British novelist, playwright and poet; writing in English; awarded for novel, poetry and drama

Citation: "for his novels which, with the perspicuity of realistic narrative art and the diversity and universality of myth, illuminate the human condition in the world of today"

1984: Jaroslav Seifert (1901 – 1986), Czechoslovak poet and journalist; writing in Czech; awarded for poetry

Citation: "for his poetry which endowed with freshness, and rich inventiveness provides a liberating image of the indomitable spirit and versatility of man"

1985: Claude Simon (1913 – 2005), French novelist; writing in French; awarded for novel

Appendix I List of Nobel Laureates in Literature

Citation: "who in his novel combines the poet's and the painter's creativeness with a deepened awareness of time in the depiction of the human condition"

1986: Wole Soyinka (1934 –), Nigerian playwright, novelist and poet; writing in English; awarded for drama, novel and poetry

Citation: "who in a wide cultural perspective and with poetic overtones fashions the drama of existence"

1987: Joseph Brodsky (1940 – 1996), Russian-born American poet and essayist; writing in English and Russian; awarded for poetry

Citation: "for an all-embracing authorship, imbued with clarity of thought and poetic intensity"

1988: Naguib Mahfouz (1911 – 2006), Egyptian novelist; writing in Arabic; awarded for novel

Citation: "who, through works rich in nuance—now clear-sightedly realistic, now evocatively ambiguous—has formed an Arabian narrative art that applies to all mankind"

1989: Camilo José Cela (1916 – 2002), Spanish novelist, short story writer and essayist; writing in Spanish; awarded for novel and short story

Citation: "for a rich and intensive prose, which with restrained compassion forms a challenging vision of man's vulnerability"

1990: Octavio Paz (1914 – 1998), Mexican poet-diplomat and essayist; writing in Spanish; awarded for poetry and essay

Citation: "for impassioned writing with wide horizons, characterized by sensuous intelligence and humanistic integrity"

1991: Nadine Gordimer (1923 – 2014), South African novelist, short story writer and essayist; writing in English; awarded for novel, short story and essay

Citation: "who through her magnificent epic writing has—in the words of Alfred Nobel—been of very great benefit to humanity"

1992: Derek Walcott (1930 –), Saint Lucian poet and playwright; writing in English; awarded for poetry

Citation: "for a poetic oeuvre of great luminosity, sustained by a historical vision, the outcome of a multicultural commitment"

1993: Toni Morrison (1931 –), American novelist and editor; writing in English; awarded for novel

Citation: "who in novels characterized by visionary force and poetic import, gives life to an essential aspect of American reality"

1994: Kenzaburō Ōe (1935 –), Japanese novelist, short story writer and essayist; writing in Japanese; awarded for novel and short story

Citation: "who with poetic force creates an imagined world, where life and myth condense to form a disconcerting picture of the human predicament today"

1995: Seamus Heaney (1939 – 2013), Irish poet, playwright and translator; writing in English; awarded for poetry

Citation: "for works of lyrical beauty and ethical depth, which exalt everyday miracles and the living past"

1996: Wisława Szymborska (1923 – 2012), Polish poet, essayist and translator; writing in Polish; awarded for poetry

Citation: "for poetry that with ironic precision allows the historical and biological context to come to light in fragments of human reality"

1997: Dario Fo (1926 – 2016), Italian playwright, actor, director, composer; writing in Italian; awarded for drama

Citation: "who emulates the jesters of the Middle Ages in scourging authority and upholding the dignity of the downtrodden"

1998: José Saramago (1922 – 2010), Portuguese novelist, playwright and poet; writing in Portuguese; awarded for novel, drama and poetry

Citation: "who with parables sustained by imagination, compassion and irony continually enables us once again to apprehend an elusory reality"

1999: Günter Grass (1927 – 2015), German novelist, poet, playwright, sculptor and graphic designer; writing in German; awarded for novel, drama and poetry

Citation: "whose frolicsome black fables portray the forgotten face of history"

2000: Gao Xingjian (1940 –), Chinese-French novelist, playwright, critic, translator, screenwriter, director and painter; writing in Chinese; awarded for novel, drama and literary criticism

Citation: "for an oeuvre of universal validity, bitter insights and linguistic ingenuity, which has opened new paths for the Chinese novel and drama"

2001: V. S. Naipaul (1932 –), Trinidad-born British novelist, travel writer and essayist; writing in English; awarded for novel and essay

Citation: "for having united perceptive narrative and incorruptible scrutiny in works that compel us to see the presence of suppressed histories"

2002: Imre Kertész (1929 – 2016), Hungarian novelist; writing in Hungarian; awarded for novel

Citation: "for writing that upholds the fragile experience of the individual against the barbaric arbitrariness of history"

2003: J. M. Coetzee (1940 –), South African novelist, essayist, literary critic, linguist and translator; writing in English; awarded for novel, essay and translation

Citation: "who in innumerable guises portrays the surprising involvement of the outsider"

2004: Elfriede Jelinek (1946 –), Austrian playwright and novelist; writing in German; awarded for novel and drama

Citation: "for her musical flow of voices and counter-voices in novels and plays that with extraordinary linguistic zeal reveal the absurdity of society's clichés and their subjugating power"

2005: Harold Pinter (1930 – 2008), British playwright, screenwriter, actor, theatre director and poet; writing in English; awarded for drama

Citation: "who in his plays uncovers the precipice under everyday prattle and forces entry into oppression's closed rooms"

2006: Orhan Pamuk (1952 –), Turkish novelist, screenwriter and essayist; writing in Turkish; awarded for novel, screenplay and essay

Citation: "who in the quest for the melancholic soul of his native city has discovered new symbols for the clash and interlacing of cultures"

2007: Doris Lessing (1919 – 2013), British novelist, poet, playwright, librettist, biographer and short story writer; writing in English; awarded for novel, drama, poetry, short story and memoirs

Citation: "that epicist of the female experience, who with scepticism, fire and visionary power has subjected a divided civilization to scrutiny"

2008: J. M. G. Le Clézio (1940 –), French-Mauritian novelist, short story writer, essayist and translator; writing in French; awarded for novel, short story, essay and translation

Citation: "author of new departures, poetic adventure and sensual ecstasy, explorer of a humanity beyond and below the reigning civilization"

2009: Herta Müller (1953 –), Romanian-born German novelist, poet and essayist; writing in German; awarded for novel and poetry

Citation: "who, with the concentration of poetry and the frankness of prose, depicts the landscape of the dispossessed"

2010: Mario Vargas Llosa (1936 –), Peruvian and Spanish novelist, playwright, politician, essayist and journalist; writing in Spanish; awarded for novel, short story, essay and drama

Citation: "for his cartography of structures of power and his trenchant images of the individual's resistance, revolt, and defeat"

2011: Tomas Tranströmer (1931 – 2015), Swedish poet, psychologist and translator; writing in Swedish; awarded for poetry and translation

Citation: "because, through his condensed, translucent images, he gives us fresh access to reality"

2012: Mo Yan (1955 –), Chinese novelist and short story writer; writing in Chinese; awarded for novel and short story

Citation: "who with hallucinatory realism merges folk tales, history and the contemporary"

2013: Alice Munro (1931 –), Canadian short story writer; writing in English; awarded for short story

Citation: "master of the contemporary short story"

2014: Patrick Modiano (1945 –), French novelist; writing in French; awarded for novel

Citation: "for the art of memory with which he has evoked the most ungraspable human destinies and uncovered the life-world of the occupation"

2015: Svetlana Alexievich (1948 –), Belarusian investigative journalist and non-fiction prose writer; writing in Russian; awarded for history and essay

Citation: "for her polyphonic writings, a monument to suffering and courage in our time"

2016: Bob Dylan (1941 –), American songwriter, singer, artist and writer; writing in English; awarded for poetry and songwriting

Citation: "for having created new poetic expressions within the great American song tradition"

Appendix II   List of Poets Laureate of the UK

Court poets of Medieval England

12th century: Richard Canonicus employed by Richard I (king 1189 – 1199)

c. 1189 – 1207: Gulielmus Peregrinus (d. c. 1207) employed by Richard I

13th century: Master Henry employed by Henry III (king 1216 – 1272)

14th century: Andrew Baston in the reigns of Edward II (king 1307 – 1327) and Edward III (king 1327 – 1377)

c. 1374 – 1400: Geoffrey Chaucer (c. 1343 – 1400) in the reigns of Edward III and Richard II (king 1377 – 1399)

15th century: John Kay in the reign of Edward IV (king 1461 – 1483)

Poets Laureate of the Kingdom of England

c. 1485 – 1509: Bernard André (1450 – 1522), appointed by Henry VII (king 1485 – 1509)

c. 1513 – 1529: John Skelton (c. 1460 – 1529), appointed by Henry VIII (king 1509 – 1547)

c. 1590 – 1599: Edmund Spenser (c. 1552 – 1599), appointed by Elizabeth I (queen 1558 – 1603)

1599 – 1616/1619: Samuel Daniel (1562 – 1619) appointed by Elizabeth I

1616/1619 – 1637: Ben Jonson (1572 – 1637) appointed by James I (king 1603 – 1625)

1638 – 1668: William Davenant (also *d'Avenant*) (1606 – 1668) appointed by Charles I (king 1625 – 1649)

1668 – 1688/1689: John Dryden (1631 – 1700) appointed by Charles II (king 1660 – 1685)

1689 – 1692: Thomas Shadwell (c. 1642 – 1692) appointed by William III (king 1689 – 1702) and Mary II (queen 1689 – 1694)

1692 – 1715: Nahum Tate (1652 – 1715) appointed by William III and Mary II

Poets Laureate of the Kingdom of Great Britain

1715 – 1718: Nicholas Rowe (1674 – 1718) appointed by George I (king 1714 – 1727)

1718 – 1730: Laurence Eusden (1688 – 1730) appointed by George I

1730 – 1757: Colley Cibber (1671 – 1757) appointed by George II (king 1727 – 1760)

1757 – 1785: William Whitehead (1715 – 1785) appointed by George II

1785 – 1790: Thomas Warton (1728 – 1790) appointed by George III (king 1760 – 1820)

1790 – 1813: Henry James Pye (1745 – 1813) appointed by George III

Poets Laureate of the United Kingdom of Great Britain and Ireland

1813 – 1843: Robert Southey (1774 – 1843) appointed by George III

Appendix II List of Poets Laureate of the UK

1843 – 1850: William Wordsworth (1770 – 1850) appointed by Victoria (queen 1837 – 1901)

1850 – 1892: Alfred, Lord Tennyson (1809 – 1892) appointed by Victoria

1896 – 1913: Alfred Austin (1835 – 1913) appointed by Victoria

1913 – 1930: Robert Bridges (1844 – 1930) appointed by George V (king 1910 – 1936)

Poets Laureate of the United Kingdom of Great Britain and Northern Ireland

1930 – 1967: John Masefield (1878 – 1967) appointed by George V

1968 – 1972: Cecil Day-Lewis (1904 – 1972) appointed by Elizabeth II (queen 1952 –)

1972 – 1984: Sir John Betjeman (1906 – 1984) appointed by Elizabeth II

1984 – 1998: Ted Hughes (1930 – 1998) appointed by Elizabeth II

1999 – 2009: Andrew Motion (1952 –) appointed by Elizabeth II

2009 –   : Carol Ann Duffy (1955 –) appointed by Elizabeth II

Appendix III List of Recipients of the Golden PEN Award in English Literature

1993: Sybille Bedford (1911 – 2006), OBE, German-born English writer

1994: V. S. Pritchett (1900 – 1997), CBE, British writer & critic

1995: Stephen Spender (1909 – 1995), CBE, English poet, novelist & essayist

1996: William Cooper (1910 – 2002), English novelist

1997: Iris Murdoch (1919 – 1999), DBE, Irish-born British novelist & philosopher

1998: Muriel Spark (1918 – 2006) DBE, Scottish novelist

1999: Penelope Fitzgerald (1916 – 2000), Booker Prize winner, English novelist, poet, essayist & biographer

2000: Francis King (1923 – 2011) CBE, British novelist, poet & short story writer

2001: Harold Pinter (1930 – 2008) CBE, English playwright, screenwriter, director & actor

2002: Doris Lessing (1919 – 2013), British novelist, poet, playwright, librettist, biographer & short story writer

2003: Michael Frayn (1933 –), English playwright & novelist

2004: Nina Bawden (1925 – 2012), CBE, English novelist & children's writer

2005: Jan Morris (1926 –), CBE, Welsh historian, author & travel writer

2006: Michael Holroyd (1935 –), CBE, English biographer

2007: Josephine Pullein-Thompson (1924 – 2014), MBE, British writer

2008: J. G. Ballard (1930 – 2009), English novelist, short story writer & essayist

2009: John Berger (1926 – 2017), Booker Prize winner, English art critic, novelist, painter & poet

2010: Salman Rushdie (1947 –), British Indian novelist & essayist

2011: Margaret Drabble (1939 –), DBE, English novelist, biographer & critic

2012: Linton Kwesi Johnson (1952 –), UK-based dub poet

2013: Gillian Slovo (1952 –), South-African-born novelist, playwright & memoirist

2014: Eskinder Nega (1968 –), Ethiopian journalist & blogger

Appendix IV List of Winners of the Booker Prize for Fiction

1969: P. H. Newby (1918 – 1997), British novelist, awarded for *Something to Answer For* (novel)

1970: Bernice Rubens (1923 – 2004), British novelist & first woman to win the prize, awarded for *The Elected Member* (novel)

1970 (retrospective award): J. G. Farrell (1935 – 1979), British novelist, awarded for *Troubles* (novel)

1971: V. S. Naipaul (1932 –), Trinidad-born British novelist, travel writer & essayist, awarded for *In a Free State* (novel)

1972: John Berger (1926 – 2017) British art critic, novelist, painter & poet, awarded for *G.* (experimental novel)

1973: J. G. Farrell (1935 – 1979), British novelist, awarded for *The Siege of Krishnapur* (novel)

1974: Nadine Gordimer (1923 – 2014), South African novelist & playwright, awarded for *The Conservationist* (novel)

Stanley Middleton (1919 – 2009), British novelist, awarded for *Holiday* (novel)

1975: Ruth Prawer Jhabvala (1927 – 2013), German-born British & American novelist, short story writer &screenwriter, awarded for *Heat and Dust* (historical novel)

1976: David Storey (1933 –), British novelist, playwright & screenwriter, awarded for *Saville* (novel)

1977: Paul Scott (1920 – 1978), British novelist, playwright & poet, awarded for *Staying On* (novel)

1978: Iris Murdoch (1919 – 1999), Irish-born British novelist & philosopher, awarded for *The Sea, the Sea* (philosophical novel)

1979: Penelope Fitzgerald (1916 – 2000), British novelist, poet, essayist & biographer, awarded for *Offshore* (novel)

1980: William Golding (1911 – 1993), British novelist, playwright & poet, awarded for *Rites of Passage* (novel)

1981: Salman Rushdie (1947 –), British novelist & essayist, awarded for *Midnight's Children* (magic realism)

1982: Thomas Keneally (1935 –), Australian novelist, playwright & non-fiction writer, awarded for *Schindler's Ark* (biographical novel)

1983: J. M. Coetzee (1940 –), South African novelist, essayist, linguist & translator, awarded for *Life & Times of Michael K* (novel)

1984: Anita Brookner (1928 - 2016), British novelist, awarded for *Hotel du Lac* (novel)

1985: Keri Hulme (1947 -), New Zealand novelist, poet & playwright, awarded for *The Bone People* (mystery novel)

1986: Kingsley Amis (1922 - 1995), British novelist, poet, critic & teacher, awarded for *The Old Devils* (comic novel)

1987: Penelope Lively (1933 -), British fiction writer, awarded for *Moon Tiger* (novel)

1988: Peter Carey (1943 -), Australian novelist, awarded for *Oscar and Lucinda* (historical Novel)

1989: Kazuo Ishiguro (1954 -), British novelist, awarded for *The Remains of the Day* (historical Novel)

1990: A. S. Byatt (1936 -), British novelist & poet, awarded for *Possession* (historical Novel)

1991: Ben Okri (1959 -), Nigerian poet & novelist, awarded for *The Famished Road* (magic realism)

1992: Michael Ondaatje (1943 -), Sri Lankan-born Canadian novelist & poet, awarded for *The English Patient* (historiographic metafiction)

Barry Unsworth (1930 - 2012), British novelist, awarded for *Sacred Hunger* (historical novel)

1993: Roddy Doyle (1958 -), Irish novelist, dramatist, short story writer, screenwriter & teacher, awarded for *Paddy Clarke Ha Ha Ha* (novel)

1994: James Kelman (1946 -), British novelist, short story writer, playwright & essayist, awarded for *How Late It Was, How Late* (stream of consciousness)

1995: Pat Barker (1943 -), British novelist, awarded for *The Ghost Road* (war novel)

1996: Graham Swift (1949 -), British novelist, awarded for *Last Orders* (novel)

1997: Arundhati Roy (1961 -), Indian novelist & essayist, awarded for *The God of Small Things* (novel)

1998: Ian McEwan (1948 -), British novelist & screenwriter, awarded for *Amsterdam* (novel)

1999: J. M. Coetzee (1940 -), South African novelist, essayist, literary critic, linguist & translator, awarded for *Disgrace* (novel)

2000: Margaret Atwood (1939 -), Canadian poet, novelist, literary critic, essayist & environmental activist, awarded for *The Blind Assassin* (historical novel)

2001: Peter Carey (1943 -), Australia novelist, awarded for *True History of the Kelly Gang* (historical novel)

2002: Yann Martel (1963 -), Canadian novelist, awarded for *Life of Pi* (fantasy & adventure novel)

2003: DBC Pierre (1961 -), Australia novelist, awarded for *Vernon God Little* (black comedy)

2004: Alan Hollinghurst (1954 -), British novelist, poet, short story writer & translator, awarded for *The Line of Beauty* (historical novel)

2005: John Banville (1945 -), Irish novelist, playwright & screenwriter, awarded for *The Sea* (novel)

2006: Kiran Desai (1971 -), Indian novelist, awarded for *The Inheritance of Loss* (novel)

2007: Anne Enright (1962 -), Irish novelist, short story writer & essayist, awarded for *The Gathering* (novel)

2008: Aravind Adiga (1974 -), Indian-Australian writer & journalist, awarded for *The White Tiger* (novel)

2009: Hilary Mantel (1952 -), British novelist, short story writer, essayist & critic, awarded for *Wolf Hall*

Appendix IV List of Winners of the Booker Prize for Fiction

(historical novel)

2010: Howard Jacobson (1942 –), British novelist, columnist & broadcaster, awarded for *The Finkler Question* (comic novel)

2011: Julian Barnes (1946 –), British novelist, essayist & short story writer, awarded for *The Sense of an Ending* (novel)

2012: Hilary Mantel (1952 –), British novelist, short story writer, essayist & critic, awarded for *Bring Up the Bodies* (historical novel)

2013: Eleanor Catton (1985 –), Canadian-born New Zealand novelist, awarded for *The Luminaries* (historical novel)

2014: Richard Flanagan (1961 –), Australian novelist, awarded for *The Narrow Road to the Deep North* (historical novel)

2015: Marlon James (1970 –), Jamaican novelist, awarded for *A Brief History of Seven Killings* (novel)

2016: Paul Beatty (1962 –), American novelist & poet, awarded for *The Sellout* (novel)

Appendix V Periods in British History

1. Roman Britain (c. 43 – 410)

Britain, as the name of the island, came from the Britons, one of the Celtic tribes—the Celts were probably the first inhabitants of the British Isles in recorded history. The word "Britain" originally means "the land of the Britons," who came over in the 5th century BC and stayed for some five hundred years. In 55 BC, Celtic Britain was invaded by the Romans under Julius Caesar. A century or so later, in 43 AD, it became a province of the Roman Empire. Thus began the period of Roman Britain in British history.

Following the conquest of the Britons, a distinctive Romano-British culture emerged as the Romans introduced improved agriculture, urban planning, industrial production, and architecture. Meanwhile, during much of the later period of the Roman occupation, Britain was subject to barbarian invasions and often came under the control of Imperial usurpers and Imperial pretenders. At the beginning of the 5th century the Roman Empire declined, and its hold on Britain loosened. With the final Roman withdrawal from Britain around 410, there came the end of Roman Britain, which made it possible for the Germanic tribes to invade the larger part of Britain, later known as England.

2. Anglo-Saxon period (Old English period) (c. 500 – 1066)

The Anglo-Saxon period stretched from the invasion of Britain by such Germanic tribes as Angles, Saxons, and Jutes in the first half of the 5th century to the Norman Conquest in 1066 under the leadership of William the Conqueror (c. 1028 – 1087), the first Norman King of England, who reigned from 1066 until his death in 1087.

The Anglo-Saxon history thus traces the establishment of Anglo-Saxon kingdoms in the 5th and 6th centuries, their Christianization during the 7th century, the threat of Viking invasions and Danish settlers, the gradual unification of England under Wessex hegemony during the 9th and 10th centuries, and the Norman Conquest of England. Anglo-Saxon identity survived beyond the Norman Conquest, and came to be known as Englishry under the Norman rule and ultimately developed into the modern English people. Only after they had been converted to Christianity in the 7th century did the Anglo-Saxons, whose earlier literature had been oral, begin to develop a written literature.

3. Norman period (1066 – 1154)

The Norman period coincided with the rule of the House of Normandy, beginning with the Norman Conquest of England and lasting until the House of Plantagenet came to power in 1154. The Norman kings include William the Conqueror or William I, William II (c. 1056 – 1100, king 1087 – 1100), Henry I (c. 1068 – 1135, king 1100 – 1135) and Stephen (c. 1092/6 – 1154, king 1135 – 1154). The non-Latin literature of this period was written mainly in Anglo-Norman, the French dialect spoken by the invaders who had established themselves as the ruling class of England and who shared a literary culture with the French-speaking areas of mainland Europe.

4. Plantagenet period (1154 – 1485)

The Pantagenet period began with the accession of Henry II (1133 – 1189, king 1154 – 1189) and ended with the death of Richard III in 1485. The name Plantagenet is used by modern historians to identify four distinct royal houses—the Angevins (1154 – 1216), its cadet branch the House of Plantagenet (1216 – 1399), and the House of Lancaster (1399 – 1461) and the House of York (1461 – 1485), the Plantagenets' two cadet branches.

Under the Plantagenets, England was transformed, although this was only partly intentional. The Plantagenet kings were often forced to negotiate compromises such as Magna Carta (1215, Latin for "the Great Charter"). These constrained royal power in return for financial and military support. The king was no longer just the most powerful man in the nation, holding the prerogative of judgment, feudal tribute and warfare. He now had defined duties to the realm, underpinned by a sophisticated justice system. A distinct national identity was shaped by conflict with the French, Scots, Welsh and Irish, and the establishment of English as the primary language. In the 15th century, the Plantagenets were defeated in the Hundred Years' War and beset with social, political and economic problems. Popular revolts were commonplace, triggered by the denial of numerous freedoms. English nobles raised private armies, engaged in private feuds and openly defied Henry VI (1421 – 1471, king 1422 – 1461). The rivalry between the House of York and the House of Lancaster brought about the Wars of the Roses, a decades-long fight for the English succession, culminating in the Battle of Bosworth Field in 1485, when the reign of the Plantagenets and the English Middle Ages, which lasted from the end of the 5th century to the start of the Early Modern period in 1485, both met their end with the death of King Richard III. In 1485 Henry VII, a Lancastrian, became king of England; two years later, he married Elizabeth of York, thus ending the Wars of the Roses and giving rise to the Tudor Dynasty.

5. Tudor period (1485 – 1603)

The Tudor period of British history stretched from 1485 to 1603, including the Elizabethan era which ended with the death of Elizabeth I in 1603. The period coincided with the rule of the Tudor Dynasty in England whose first monarch was Henry VII. The Tudors worked to centralize English royal power, which allowed them to avoid some of the problems that had plagued the last Plantagenet rulers. The resulting stability allowed for the English Renaissance and the advent of early modern Britain. In terms of the entire 16th century, "England was economically healthier, more expansive, and more optimistic under the Tudors" than at any time in a thousand years, culminating with the Elizabethan era. (Guy, 1988: 32)

The **Elizabethan era/period** (1558 – 1603) was a brief period of largely internal peace between the English Reformation and the battles between the parliament and the monarchy that engulfed the 17th century. The term is also loosely used to refer to the late 16th and early 17th centuries, even after the death of Elizabeth. The era is highly viewed and usually depicted as the golden age in English history by historians. It was an age of exploration and expansion abroad, and was marked by a renaissance that inspired national pride through classical ideals, international expansion and naval triumph over the Spanish Armada. Witnessing a great flourishing of literature, especially in the fields of poetry and drama, the era is usually regarded as the height of the English Renaissance. The Protestant Reformation became more acceptable to the people, most certainly after the Spanish Armada was repulsed. The Protestant-Catholic divide was settled for a time by the Elizabethan Religious Settlement. England had a centralized, well-organized and effective government, though parliament was not yet strong enough to challenge royal absolutism. Its royal union with Scotland ended the history when England was a separate realm. Economically, the country began to benefit greatly from the new era of trans-Atlantic trade.

6. Stuart period (1603 – 1714)

The Stuart period of British history coincided with the rule of the House of Stuart, ending with the death of Queen Anne and the accession of George I (1660 – 1727) from the House of Hanover. It was plagued by internal and religious strife, and a large-scale civil war. The period is chiefly composed of the Jacobean age, the Caroline era, the Interregnum and the Restoration.

The **Jacobean age** (1603 – 1625) refers to the reign of James I (in Latin, "Jacobus") in English history, which followed the Elizabethan era and preceded the Caroline era. The age specifically denoted a style of architecture, visual arts, decorative arts, and literature that is predominant of that period. The English literary achievements in this period were chiefly represented by Francis Bacon's essays, John Donne's sermons, King James' translation of the *Bible*, William Shakespeare's greatest tragedies and tragicomedies, and *The Anatomy of Melancholy* (1621) by Robert Burton (1577 – 1640). The age also witnessed two signature changes of crucial significance. One was the practical if not formal unification of England and Scotland under one ruler, which was an important shift of order for both nations, and would shape their existence to the present day. The other was the foundation of the first British colonies on the North American continent, which laid the foundation for the future British settlement and the eventual formation of both Canada and the United States of America.

The **Caroline era** (1625 – 1649) refers to the era in English and Scottish history that coincided with the reign of Charles I, Carolus being Latin for Charles. The era followed the Jacobean era, the reign of Charles' father James I, and preceded the English Interregnum. It was dominated by the growing religious, political and social conflict between the King and his supporters, termed the Royalist party, and the Puritan opposition that evolved in response to particular aspects of Charles' rule. The Caroline period was one of an uneasy peace, growing darker as the civil conflict between King and Puritans worsened and developed into the English Civil War (1642 – 1651) toward the latter part of Charles' reign. However, this conflict between King and Parliament dominated society to such a degree that other developments seemed mere continuations of previous innovations. Some of those continuations, however, were of major significance for the future. English efforts at the colonization of North America continued throughout Charles' reign, with the foundation of new colonies in Maryland (1634), Connecticut (1635), and Rhode Island (1636) standing as important steps in the process. Development of previously-established colonies in Virginia, Massachusetts, and Newfoundland also continued.

In literature, and especially in drama, the Caroline period has often been regarded as a diminished continuation of the trends of the previous two reigns. Caroline theatre unquestionably saw a falling-off after the peak achievements of William Shakespeare and Ben Jonson, though some of their successors carried on to create interesting, even compelling theatre. In recent years the comedies of Richard Brome (c. 1590? – 1652) have gained in critical appreciation. In poetry, however, the Caroline period saw the flourishing of the Cavalier poets and the Metaphysical poets. If the Elizabethan era was the golden age of English drama, the Caroline age was nearly as rich in the realm of non-dramatic poetry, bringing as it did the beginnings of the career of John Milton, in addition to the poets of the movements already mentioned.

The **interregnum** (1649 – 1660) followed the Wars of the Three Kingdoms, an intertwined series of conflicts that took place in England, Ireland and Scotland between 1639 and 1651, the best-known of which was the English Civil War. It began with the execution of Charles I and ended with the arrival of his son Charles II in London on 29 May 1660 which marked the start of the Restoration. During the Interregnum England was under various forms of republican government, whose official name was the Commonwealth of England, a *de facto* political unit and military rule in the name of parliamentary supremacy. The Commonwealth was chiefly under the rule of Oliver Cromwell (1599 – 1658), who was in office from 1653 to 1658, and his son and successor Richard Cromwell (1626 – 1712), who was in office after his father's death till 1559. In the years between 1653 and 1659, although still legally known as a Commonwealth, the republic, united with the former Kingdom of Scotland, operated under different institutions (at times as a *de facto* monarchy) and is known by historians as the Protectorate. After the death of the Lord Protector Oliver Cromwell and the fall of his son Richard's regime, General George Monck (1608 – 1670), the military governor of Scotland, marched the English army in the south of Scotland and facilitated a Restoration of the monarchy in June 1660.

The **Restoration** (1660 – 1688/1714) of the English monarchy began in 1660 when the English, Scottish and Irish monarchies were all restored under Charles II after the Interregnum. The term *Restoration* is used to describe both the actual event by which the monarchy was restored, and the period of several years afterwards in which a new political settlement was established. It is very often used to cover the whole reign of Charles II and the brief reign of his younger brother James II. In certain contexts it may be used to cover the whole period of the later Stuart monarchs as far as the death of Queen Anne and the accession of the Hanoverian George I in 1714; for example Restoration comedy typically encompasses works written as late as 1710.

7. Georgian era/period (1714 – 1837)

The Georgian era of British history refers to the period in the reigns of the first four Hanoverian kings of Great Britain who were all named George: George I, George II, George III and George IV (1820 – 1830). The era stretched from 1714 to 1830, with the sub-period of the Regency (1811 – 1820) defined by the Regency of George IV as Prince of Wales during the illness of his father George III. The definition of the Georgian era is often extended to include the short reign of William IV (1830 – 1837), which ended with his death in 1837. The term "Georgian" is typically used in the contexts of social history and architecture.

The Georgian era was a time of immense social change in Britain. The Industrial Revolution started the process of intensifying class divisions and gave rise to the emergence of rival political parties like the Whigs and the Tories. In rural areas the Agricultural Revolution saw huge changes to the movement of people and the decline of small communities, the growth of the cities, the beginnings of an integrated transportation system, and a huge increase in emigration to Canada, the North American colonies (which became the United States during the period) and other parts of the British Empire. Some politicians and campaigners launched social reform, bringing about radical changes like the abolition of slavery, prison reform and social justice. In the Church of England the era witnessed an Evangelical revival and the rise of Non-conformists and various dissenting groups such as the Reformed Baptists.

The Georgian era was moreover a time of British expansion throughout the world. There was continual warfare, including the Seven Years' War, known in America as the French and Indian War (1756 – 1763), the American War of Independence (1775 – 1783), the French Revolutionary Wars (1792 – 1802), the Irish Rebellion of 1798 and the Napoleonic Wars (1803 – 1815). The British won all the wars except for the American Revolution, where the combined weight of the United States, France, Spain and the Netherlands overwhelmed Britain, which stood alone without allies. The loss of some of the American Colonies in the American War of Independence was regarded as a national disaster and was seen by some foreign observers as heralding the end of Britain as a great power. In Europe, the wars with France dragged on for nearly a quarter of a century, from 1793 to 1815. Victory over Napoleon at the Battle of Trafalgar (1805) and the Battle of Waterloo (1815) brought a sense of triumphalism and political reaction. The expansion of empire sowed the seeds of the worldwide British Empire of the Victorian and Edwardian eras which were to follow. However, with the ending of the wars with France, the United Kingdom entered a period of greater economic depression and political uncertainty, characterized by social discontent and unrest.

Georgian society and its preoccupations were well portrayed in the novels of such writers as Henry Fielding, Mary Shelley and Jane Austen, characterized by the architecture of Robert Adam (1728 – 1792), John Nash (1752 – 1835) and James Wyatt (1746 – 1813) and the emergence of the Gothic Revival style, which hearkened back to a supposed golden age of building design. The flowering of the arts was most vividly shown in the emergence of the Romantic poets, principally through Samuel Taylor Coleridge, William Wordsworth, Percy Bysshe Shelley, William Blake, John Keats, Lord Byron and Robert Burns. Their work ushered in a new era of poetry, characterized by vivid and colorful language, evocative of elevating ideas and themes.

8. Victorian era/period (1837 – 1901)

The Victorian era of British history refers to the period in the reign of Queen Victoria (1819 – 1901), the last Hanoverian monarch of the United Kingdom. It was a long period of peace, prosperity, refined sensibilities and national self-confidence for Britain. Some scholars date the beginning of the period in terms of sensibilities and political concerns to the passage of the Reform Act 1832. Within the fields of social history and literature, Victorianism refers to the study of late-Victorian attitudes and culture with a focus on the highly moralistic, straitlaced language and behavior of Victorian morality.

In politics, the House of Commons was headed by the two parties, the Whigs and the Conservatives during the early part of the era. From the late 1850s onwards, the Whigs became the Liberals. The unsolved problems relating to Irish Home Rule played a great part in the later era, particularly in view of Gladstone's determination to achieve a political settlement. Culturally there was a transition away from the rationalism of the Georgian period toward romanticism and mysticism with regard to religion, social values and arts. In international relations the era was a long period of peace, known as the *Pax Britannica* (1815 – 1914), and economic, colonial and industrial consolidation, temporarily disrupted by the Crimean War in 1854. The end of the period saw the Boer War (1899 – 1902). Domestically, the agenda was increasingly liberal with a number of shifts in the direction of gradual political reform, industrial reform and the widening of the voting franchise. In addition, whereas a large number of emigrants left the UK in the Victorian era, settling mostly in the United States, Canada, New Zealand and Australia, the UK's population rose rapidly in the late part of the era in all the nations—England, Scotland and Wales—except

Ireland, whose population decreased sharply.

9. Edwardian era/period (1901 – 1914)

The Edwardian era in Great Britain is the period covering the reign of King Edward VII and is sometimes extended beyond Edward's death to include the four years leading up to World War I.

The era was marked by significant shifts in politics as sections of society that had been largely excluded from wielding power in the past, such as common laborers and women, became increasingly politicized. There was a growing political awareness of the working class, leading to a rise in trade unions, the Labor movement and demands for better working conditions. Feminists of the era focused on educating and finding jobs for women, leaving aside the controversial issues of contraceptives and abortion, which in popular opinion were often related to promiscuity and prostitution.

The Edwardian era stands out as a time of peace and plenty. There were no severe depressions, and prosperity was widespread. Britain's growth rate, manufacturing output and GDP (but not GDP per capita) fell behind its rivals, the United States and Germany, but the nation still led the world in trade, finance and shipping, and had strong bases in manufacturing and mining. The industrial sector was slow to adjust to global changes, and there was a striking preference for leisure over entrepreneurship among the elite. However, major achievements should be underlined. London was the financial centre of the world—far more efficient and wide-ranging than New York, Paris or Berlin. Britain had built up a vast reserve of overseas credits in its formal Empire, as well as in its informal empire in Latin America and other nations. It had huge financial holdings in the United States, especially in railways. These assets proved vital in paying for supplies in the first years of the World War. The amenities, especially in urban life, were accumulating—prosperity was highly visible. The working classes were beginning to protest politically for a greater voice in government, but the level of industrial unrest on economic issues was not high until about 1908.

Despite its brief pre-eminence, the period is characterized by its own unique architectural style, fashion and lifestyle. In fiction, there emerged such famous writers as Arnold Bennett, Joseph Conrad, E. M. Forster, John Galsworthy, Rudyard Kipling, H. G. Wells, and others. A great number of novels and short stories were being published, and a significant distinction between "highbrow" literature and popular fiction emerged. Among the most famous works of literary criticism was *Shakespearean Tragedy* (1904) by A. C. Bradley (1851 – 1935). Mass audience newspapers became increasingly important.

Edward was the leader of the fashionable elite that set a style influenced by the art and fashions of Continental Europe—perhaps because of the King's fondness for travel. The Edwardian period is sometimes imagined as a romantic golden age of long summer afternoons and garden parties, basking in a sun that never sets on the British Empire. This perception was created in the 1920s and later by those who remembered the Edwardian age with nostalgia, looking back to their childhoods across the abyss of World War I. The Edwardian age was also seen as a mediocre period of pleasure between the great achievements of the preceding Victorian age and the catastrophe of the following war. Recent assessments emphasize the great differences between the wealthy and the poor during the Edwardian era and describe the age as heralding great changes in political and social life. Despite this, this type of perception has been challenged more recently by modern historians. The British historian Lawrence James (1943 –)

has argued that, during the early 20th century, the British felt increasingly threatened by rival powers such as Germany, Russia and the United States.

10. First World War period (1914 – 1918)

The United Kingdom of Great Britain and Ireland—then consisting of England, Scotland, Wales and the whole of Ireland—was one of the Allied Powers during the First World War, fighting against the Central Powers (the German Empire, the Austro-Hungarian Empire, the Ottoman Empire and the Kingdom of Bulgaria). The war marked the creation of the Royal Air Force (1918) and the raising of the largest all-volunteer army in British history. The UK's armed forces were reorganized and increased in size. The outbreak of the First World War worked as a socially unifying event. On the eve of the war, there was serious domestic unrest in the UK but much of the population rapidly rallied behind the government.

Fearing food shortages and labor shortfalls, the government passed legislation such as the Defence of the Realm Act 1914, to give it new powers. The war saw a move away from the idea of "business as usual" towards a state of total war—complete state intervention in public affairs. Newspapers played an important role in maintaining popular support for the war. Large quantities of propaganda were produced by the government under the guidance of journalists and newspaper owners. By adapting to the changing demographics of the workforce, war-related industries grew rapidly and production increased, as concessions were quickly made to trade unions. In that regard, the war is also credited by some with drawing women into mainstream employment for the first time. Debates continue about the impact the war had on women's emancipation, given that a large number of women were granted the vote for the first time in 1918. The experience of individual women during the war varied; much depended on locality, age, marital status and occupation.

The Empire reached its zenith at the conclusion of peace negotiations. However, the war heightened not only imperial loyalties but also individual national identities in the dominions (Canada, Newfoundland, Australia, New Zealand and South Africa) and India. Irish nationalists after 1916 moved from collaboration with London to demands for immediate independence.

11. Interwar period (1918 – 1939)

In the 20th-century history, the interwar period or interbellum was the period between the end of World War I marked by the Armistice with Germany that concluded World War I in 1918 and the following Paris Peace Conference in 1919, and the beginning of World War II marked by the invasion of Poland in September 1939.

In the British society, with the end of World War I, there emerged a lack of prewar technological developments and postwar competition, which damaged the economy and led to unemployment—the dominant issue of the British society during the interwar years. The Government deployed unemployment insurance schemes in 1920 to alleviate unemployment. Some have argued that an overly generous unemployment insurance system worsened the state of the economy; others have asserted that the Wall Street Crash in 1929, which heralded the global Great Depression, was responsible for the decline of the British economy after the war. Another noticeable factor of the decline of the UK economy is that Britain had run up a large national debt when the war ended as the Government had funded World War I largely through borrowing.

In the British government, the period saw frequent changes. In 1924, the first Labor Prime Minister was appointed in the absence of a clear majority for any one of the three major parties. In 1926, the Imperial Conference of the British Empire leaders in London issued the Balfour Declaration, which declared the United Kingdom and the Dominions to be "autonomous Communities within the British Empire, equal in status, in no way subordinate one to another in any aspect of their domestic or external affairs, though united by a common allegiance to the Crown, and freely associated as members of the British Commonwealth of Nations." (Marshall, 2001: 546) In the wake of a world financial crisis, the government was trying to achieve several different, contradictory objectives: trying to maintain Britain's economic position by maintaining the pound on the gold standard, balancing the budget, and providing assistance and relief to tackle unemployment. King George V encouraged the formation in 1931 of a National Government, a coalition of some or all major political parties, with the specific aim of balancing the Budget and restoring confidence. A small Cabinet of just ten ministers was formed to take emergency decisions, with ministerial posts divided as proportionally as possible between the three parties, but relatively few Labor members joined the government.

In the interwar period, political turmoil in Ireland continued as the Nationalists fought for independence. George V and his advisers were concerned about the rise of socialism and the growing labor movement, which they mistakenly associated with republicanism. The socialists no longer believed in their anti-monarchical slogans and were ready to come to terms with the monarchy if it took the first step. George adopted a more democratic, inclusive stance that crossed class lines and brought the monarchy closer to the public and the working class. He cultivated friendly relations with moderate Labor party politicians and trade union officials. Meanwhile, the 1931 Statute of Westminster formalized the King's position as "the symbol of the free association of the members of the British Commonwealth of Nations." The Statute established "that any alteration in the law touching the Succession to the Throne or the Royal Style and Titles" would require the assent of the Parliaments of the Dominions as well as the Parliament at Westminster, which could not legislate for the Dominions, except by consent.

12. Second World War (1939 – 1945)

The Second World War was a global war, the most widespread war in human history, beginning with the German invasion of Poland in September 1939 and ending with the Japanese surrender in August 1945. The war involved the vast majority of the world's nations and eventually formed two opposing military alliances: the Allies (chiefly composed of France, the US, the UK, the Soviet Union, China, Australia, Canada, Poland, and others) and the Axis (consisting of Germany, Italy and Japan). In a state of "total war," the major participants threw their entire economic, industrial and scientific capabilities behind the war effort, erasing the distinction between civilian and military resources.

When Germany invaded Poland, Britain declared war in tandem with France, supported by all of the Dominions except Ireland. For the first few months of war Britain saw comparatively little action apart from at sea, but the failure of the Norwegian campaign (1940) led to a massive outcry in Parliament. On 7 and 8 May 1940, a two-day debate took place in Parliament, known to history as the Norway Debate. The significant debate in the British House of Commons, initially a discussion of what had gone wrong in that field, soon turned into a general debate on the conduct of the war with fierce criticism expressed by all sides of the House. The widespread dissatisfaction with the Conservative-dominated National Government, led by Neville Chamberlain (1869 – 1940), eventually brought the life of the National Government to a close and led to the formation of a widely-based all-party coalition government headed by Winston Churchill (1874 – 1965), which was to govern Britain until the end of World War II in Europe.

After the German occupation of France in 1940, Britain and the empire stood alone against Germany until the entry of the Soviet Union to the war in 1941. Then Churchill successfully lobbied President Franklin D. Roosevelt (1882 – 1945) for military aid from the United States. In August 1941, Churchill and Roosevelt met and signed the Atlantic Charter, which included the statement that "the rights of all peoples to choose the form of government under which they live" should be respected. In December 1941, Japan launched, in quick succession, attacks on British Malaya, Hong Kong, and the United States naval base at Pearl Harbor. The US was thus involved in World War II. At first Churchill reacted to the entry of the United States into the war because Britain seemed assured of victory and the future of the empire appeared safe. However, that the British forces were rapidly defeated in the Far East irreversibly harmed its standing and prestige as an imperial power. Most damaging of all was the fall of Singapore (1942), the major British military base in South-East Asia and the keystone of British imperial interwar defence planning for South-East Asia as well as the South-West Pacific. Britain's colonies in South-East Asia were thus occupied by Imperial Japan. Despite the final victory of Britain and its allies, the damage to British prestige helped to accelerate the decline of the empire. Winston Churchill (2002: 518) called the ignominious fall of Singapore to the Japanese in 1959 in his book the "worst disaster" and "largest capitulation" in the British military history. The realization that Britain could not defend its entire empire pushed Australia and New Zealand, which now appeared threatened by Japanese forces, into closer ties with the United States. This resulted in the 1951 ANZUS Pact between Australia, New Zealand and the United States of America.

13. Postwar period (1945 –)

Postwar Britain covers the history of the United Kingdom since 1945. Though it emerged victorious from the Second World War, Britain was left essentially bankrupt, with insolvency only averted in 1946 after the installment loan from the United States, the last installment of which was repaid in 2006. Therefore one of the chief evaluation indicators for the party in power is its contribution to economic development and public welfare. The Conservative Party has been elected as the ruling party for the next seven decades, except for short intervals in which the government was under the Labor Party. In May 1945, following the defeat of Germany the coalition government broke up and Churchill formed a new administration, including Conservatives, Liberal Nationals and various non-party individuals who had been previously appointed to Ministerial posts. The government fought the 1945 general election as a National Government but failed. Back to power in 1951, the Conservatives accepted most of the postwar reforms (most notably, the National Health Service) of the Labor Party and presided over 13 years of economic stability. Prosperity returned in the 1950s and London remained a world centre of finance and culture. The period from 1952 onwards is sometimes known as the Second Elizabethan era. However, the nation was no longer a superpower after the financial cost of World War II. The Suez Crisis of 1956 very publicly exposed Britain's limitations to the world and confirmed Britain's decline on the world stage, demonstrating that henceforth it could no longer act without at least the acquiescence, if not the full support, of the United States. Its 1970 government, lasting only four years, oversaw the decimalization of British currency, the 1973 ascension of Britain to the European Economic Community, and the height of the Troubles in Northern Ireland. The 1979 general election brought the Conservative Party back to power and began its 18 years' government, first under the leadership of Margaret Thatcher (1925 – 2013) till 1990 and then under the leadership of John Major (1943 –). It was the victory in the Falklands War (1982) and the government's strong opposition to trade unions (which carried out a series of strikes and paralyzed the country) that helped lead the Conservative Party to another three terms in government. Thatcher initially pursued monetarist policies and went on to privatize many of Britain's Labor nationalized companies. The controversial Community Charge (poll tax), used to fund local government, attributed to Thatcher being ousted from her own party and replaced as Prime Minister by John Major in 1990. Major replaced the poll tax with the council tax and oversaw British involvement in the Gulf War (August 1990 – February 1991). Despite a recession, Major led the Conservatives to a surprise victory in 1992. The events of Black Wednesday in 1992, party disunity over the European Union and several scandals involving Conservative politicians led to the Labor Party under Tony Blair (1953 –) winning a landslide election victory in 1997. A global recession under the Labor Party in the late 2000s offered the Conservative Party another opportunity in the 2010 election. Headed by David Cameron (1966 –), the new government has pursued a series of public spending cuts to help reduce Britain's budget deficit.

In the postwar period, the Labor Party first came to power in 1945. It created a comprehensive welfare state, with the establishment of the National Health Service (1948), entitling free healthcare to all British citizens, and launched other reforms like the introduction of old-age pensions, free education at all levels, sickness benefits and unemployment benefits, most of which was covered by the newly introduced national insurance, paid by all workers. During this time, the Bank of England, railways, heavy industry, coal mining and public utilities were all nationalized. Britain was a founding member of the United Nations in 1945, with a veto in the Security Council. It collaborated closely with the United States during the Cold War after 1947, and in 1949 helped form NATO as a military alliance against the Soviet Union and became a founding member of the organization. The 1964 Labor government witnessed a series of social reforms again, including the decriminalization of homosexuality and abortion, the relaxing of divorce laws and the banning of capital punishment. Interrupted between 1970 and 1974, the Labor Party made a return to power but soon lost its majority in parliament due to a series of strikes carried out by trade unions over the winter of 1978/1979 (known as the Winter of Discontent). The 1997 government under Tony Blair had shifted its policies closer to the political center, under the new name "New Labor." The Bank of England was given independence over monetary policy; and Scotland and Wales were given a devolved Scottish Parliament and Welsh Assembly respectively. A devolved power sharing Northern Ireland Executive was established in 1998, believed by many to be the end of the Troubles. Blair led Britain into the controversial Iraq War in 2003, which contributed to his eventual resignation in 2007. Although the Labor Party succeeded in the following election, its leader Gordon Brown (1951 –) proved disappointing and ended his term of office in 2010.

Maintaining Britain's status as an empire was also difficult on ideological grounds in the postwar period as a rise in self-determinism after the War, particularly in colonies who had contributed a large number of troops to fight on Britain's behalf, made the British Empire increasingly harder to justify. Britain's imperial decline soon seemed inevitable and its focus increasingly turned towards promoting the Commonwealth (in the economic sphere) and the Atlantic Alliance (in the military sphere) during the period of political consensus.

In the postwar context, anti-colonial movements were on the rise in the colonies of European nations. British colonies such as India, Burma and Ceylon gained independence in the late 1940s. Ghana and Malaya were granted independence in 1957, and Nigeria in 1960. The "Wind of Change" speech, a historically significant address made by the British Prime Minister Harold Macmillan (1894 – 1986, in office 1957 – 1963) to the Parliament of South Africa on 3 February 1960 in Cape Town, ultimately meant that the days of the British Empire were numbered, and on the whole, Britain adopted a policy of peaceful disengagement from its colonies once stable, non-Communist governments were available to transfer power to. The two decades between 1945 and 1965 witnessed a sharp decrease in the population under the British rule outside the UK. Britain's remaining colonies in Africa were all granted independence by 1968, except for the self-governing Southern Rhodesia, which became independent in 1980. Whereas the Mediterranean colonies were granted independence from the UK in the 1960s, the Caribbean territories achieved independence one after another within the three decades after the departure in 1961 and 1962 of Jamaica and Trinidad from the West Indies Federation, established in 1958 in an attempt to unite the British Caribbean colonies under one government, but meeting with collapse after the loss of its two largest members. Britain's last colony on the American mainland, British Honduras, became a self-governing colony in 1964 and achieved full independence in 1981. British territories in the Pacific acquired independence in the 1970s. The handover ceremony of Hong Kong in 1997 from the UK to the PRC marked "the end of Empire" for many.

Britain retains sovereignty over fourteen territories outside the British Isles, which were renamed the British Overseas Territories in 2002. Some are uninhabited except for transient military or scientific personnel; the remainder are self-governing to varying degrees and are reliant on the UK for foreign relations and defence. The British government has stated its willingness to assist any Overseas Territory that wishes to proceed to independence, where that is an option. All the same, British sovereignty of several of the overseas territories is disputed by their geographical neighbors.

Decades, and, in some cases, centuries, of British rule and emigration have left their mark on the independent nations that arose from the British Empire. Most former British colonies and protectorates are among the 53 member states of the Commonwealth of Nations, a non-political, voluntary association of equal members. Sixteen Commonwealth realms, which are distinct and equal legal entities, voluntarily continue to share the British monarch, Queen Elizabeth II, as their head of state. Except in Africa where nearly all the former colonies have adopted the presidential system, the English parliamentary system has served as the template for the governments for many former colonies, and English common law for legal systems. The British Judicial Committee of the Privy Council still serves as the highest court of appeal for several former colonies in the Caribbean and Pacific. British Protestant missionaries who travelled around the globe often in advance of soldiers and civil servants spread the Anglican Communion to all continents. British colonial architecture in churches, railway stations and government buildings can be seen in many cities that were once part of the British Empire. Individual and team sports developed in Britain—particularly football, cricket, rugby, lawn tennis and golf—were also exported. The British choice of system of measurement, the imperial system, continues to be used in some countries in various ways. The convention of driving on the left hand side of the road has been retained in much of the former empire. The empire established the use of English in regions around the world. Today it is the primary language of up to 400 million people and is spoken by about one and a half billion as a first, second or foreign language. The spread of English from the latter half of the 20th century has been helped in part by the cultural and economic influence of the United States, which itself was originally formed from British colonies.

The British Empire was also responsible for large migrations of peoples. Millions left the British Isles, with the founding settler populations of the United States, Canada, Australia and New Zealand coming mainly from Britain and Ireland. Millions moved to and from British colonies, with large numbers of Indians emigrating to other parts of the empire, such as Malaysia and Fiji, and Chinese people to Malaysia, Singapore and the Caribbean. The demographics of Britain itself was changed after the Second World War owing to immigration to Britain from its former colonies. These migrations contributed to conflicts in formerly colonized areas. Tensions remain between immigrant settlers and indigenous inhabitants in these countries. Settlers in Ireland from Great Britain, for instance, have left their mark in the form of divided nationalist and unionist communities in Northern Ireland.

References

常耀信:《英国文学简史》,南开大学出版社 2006 年版。

陈嘉:《英国文学史》,商务印书馆 1982 年版。

郭群英:《英国文学新编》,外语教学与研究出版社 2001 年版。

侯维瑞:《英国文学通史》,上海外语教育出版社 1999 年版。

刘炳善:《英国文学简史(新增订本)》,河南人民出版社 2007 年版。

王佐良:《欧洲文化入门》,外语教学与研究出版社 1992 年版。

吴伟仁:《英国文学史及选读》,外语教学与研究出版社 1988 年版。

Abrams, M. H. *A Glossary of Literary Terms* (7th edition). Beijing: Foreign Language Teaching and Research Press, 2004.

Albert, Edward. *History of English Literature*. London: Oxford University Press, 1979.

Barfield, Owen. "Poetry in Walter de la Mare." *The Denver Quarterly* 8. 3 (1973): 69 – 81.

Bate, Walter Jackson. *Samuel Johnson*. New York: Harcourt Brace Jovanovich, 1977.

Braudy, Leo. "Penetration and Impenetrability in *Clarissa*," *New Approaches to Eighteenth-Century Literature: Selected Papers from the English Institute*. Ed. Philip Harth. New York: Columbia University Press, 1974.

Chandler, Alice. "Sir Walter Scott and the Medieval Revival." *Nineteenth-Century Fiction* 19. 4 (1965): 315 – 332.

Christiansen, Rupert, *Romantic Affinities: Portraits from an Age, 1780 – 1830*. Cardinal, 1989.

Churchill, Winston. *The Second World War* (abridged edition). London: Pimlico, 2002.

Damrosch, Leo. *Jean-Jacques Rousseau: Restless Genius*. Boston: Houghton Mifflin Company, 2005.

Drabble, Margaret. *The Oxford Companion to English Literature* (6th edition). London: Oxford University Press, 2000.

Drury, Kent. "Definitions." http://www.nku.edu/~rkdrury/422/satire_terms.html, 2016 – 02 – 26.

Dryden, John. *Religio Laici: Or, a Layman's Faith*. Michigan: Gale Ecco, Print Editions, 2010.

Eliot, T. S. "John Dryden." in *Selected Essays*. London: Faber and Faber, 1932.

Flood, Alison. "Swedish Academy Reopens Controversy Surrounding Steinbeck's Nobel Prize." *The Guardian*. 2013 – 01 – 03.

Flynn, Carol. *Samuel Richardson: A Man of Letters*. Princeton: Princeton University Press, 1982.

Green, Patricia. "The Golden Age of Satire: Alexander Pope and Jonathan Swift." http://www.uh.edu/honors/Programs-Minors/honors-and-the-schools/houston-teachers-institute/curriculum-units/pdfs/2008/comedy/

green-08-comedy. pdf, 2016 – 02 – 26.

Griffin, Dustin. *Patriotism and Poetry in Eighteenth-Century Britain*. Cambridge: Cambridge University Press, 2002.

Guy, John. *Tudor England*. London: Oxford University Press, 1988.

Halsband, Robert. *"The Rape of the Lock" and Its Illustrations, 1714 – 1896*. Oxford: Oxford University Press, 1980.

Hazlitt, William. *Characters of Shakespeare's Plays* (2nd edition). London: Taylor and Hessey, 1818.

Jones, Nigel. *Rupert Brooke: Life, Death & Myth*. London: Richard Cohen Books, 1999.

Jones, Vivien. *Introduction to Pride and Prejudice*. London: Penguin Classics, 2003.

Kinnaird, John. *William Hazlitt: Critic of Power*. New York: Columbia University Press, 1978.

Leader, Zachary. *The Life of Kingsley Amis*. London: Jonathan Cape, 2006.

Lezard, Nicholas. "Broken Hierarchies: Poems 1952 – 2012 by Geoffrey Hill—review." *The Guardian*. 2013 – 11 – 20.

Marshall, Sir Peter. "The Balfour Formula and the Evolution of the Commonwealth." *The Round Table* 90. 361 (2001): 541 – 53.

Montgomery, Henry Riddell. *Memoirs of the Life and Writings of Sir Richard Steele*. New York: Haskell House Publishers, 1865.

Moody, William Vaughan & Charles Morss Lovett. *A History of English Literature*. New York: Charles Scribner's Sons, 1918.

Moore, Seán. "Our Irish Copper-Farthen Dean: Swift's *Drapier's Letters*, the 'forging' of a modernist Anglo-Irish literature, and the Atlantic world of paper credit." *Atlantic Studies* 2. 1 (2005): 65 – 92.

Motion, Andrew. *Keats*. London: Faber, 1997.

Ousby, I. et al. *The Cambridge Guide to Literature in English*. Cambridge: Cambridge University Press, 1993.

Podzemny, Todd. "What Is Juvenalian Satire?" http://www.wisegeek.com/what-is-juvenalian-satire.htm, 2016 – 02 – 26.

Rankin, Alan. "What Is Horatian Satire?" http://www.wisegeek.com/what-is-horatian-satire.htm, 2016 – 02 – 26.

Richetti, John J. *The Life of Daniel Defoe*. Malden, MA: Blackwell Publishing, 2005.

Rogers, Pat. "Johnson, Samuel (1709 – 1784)." *Oxford Dictionary of National Biography*. Oxford: Oxford University Press, 2006.

Schmidt, Michael. *Poets on Poets*. Manchester: Carcanet Press, 1997.

Sidney, Philip. *A Defense of Poetry and Poems*. London: Cassell and Company, 1891.

Smith, David C. *H. G. Wells: Desperately Mortal: A Biography*. New Haven & London: Yale University Press, 1986.

Solomon, Harry M. *The Rape of the Text: Reading and Misreading Pope's "Essay on Man."* Tuscaloosa: The University of Alabama Press, 1993.

Strecher, Matthew c. "Magical Realism and the Search for Identity in the Fiction of Murakami Haruki." *Journal of*

Japanese Studies 25. 2 (1999): 263 – 298.

Thomas, Shamekia. "Satire in Literature: Definition, Types & Examples." http://study.com/academy/lesson/satire-in-literature-definition-types-examples.html, 2016 – 02 – 26.

Thompson, Ann & Neil Taylor, eds. *The Arden Shakespeare* (3d ser. Vol. 1). London: Arden, 2006.

Thrall, William & Addison Hibbard. *A Handbook to Literature*. New York: The Odyssey Press, 1960.

Voltaire. *Lettres Philosophiques*. New York: Courier Dover Publications, 2003.

Wardle, Ralph M. *Hazlitt*. Lincoln: University of Nebraska Press, 1971.

Watts, Isaac. "Miscellaneous Thoughts." *Works* lxxiii. iv (1810): 619.

Wilson, Edwin, ed. *Shaw on Shakespeare*. New York: Applause Theatre & Cinema Books, 1961.

Gulliver's Travels: Complete, Authoritative Text with Biographical and Historical Contexts. London: Palgrave Macmillan, 1995.

The Broadview Anthology of Literature: The Renaissance and the Early Seventeenth Century. Canada: Broadview Press, 2006.

http://en.wikipedia.org/wiki/Main_Page, 2013 – 10 – 14.

http://www.answers.com/topic/genre, 2012 – 01 – 08.

http://www.answers.com/topic/pamphlet, 2012 – 01 – 14.

http://www.literarydevices.com/satire/, 2016 – 02 – 26.

http://www.poetryfoundation.org/bio/george-herbert, 2015 – 04 – 12.

http://www.walterscott.lib.ed.ac.uk/works/novels/robroy.html, 2013 – 10 – 12.

http://www.walterscott.lib.ed.ac.uk/works/novels/ivanhoe.html, 2013 – 10 – 12.